THE
CHILDREN'S
ENCYCLOPEDIA
AND ATLAS

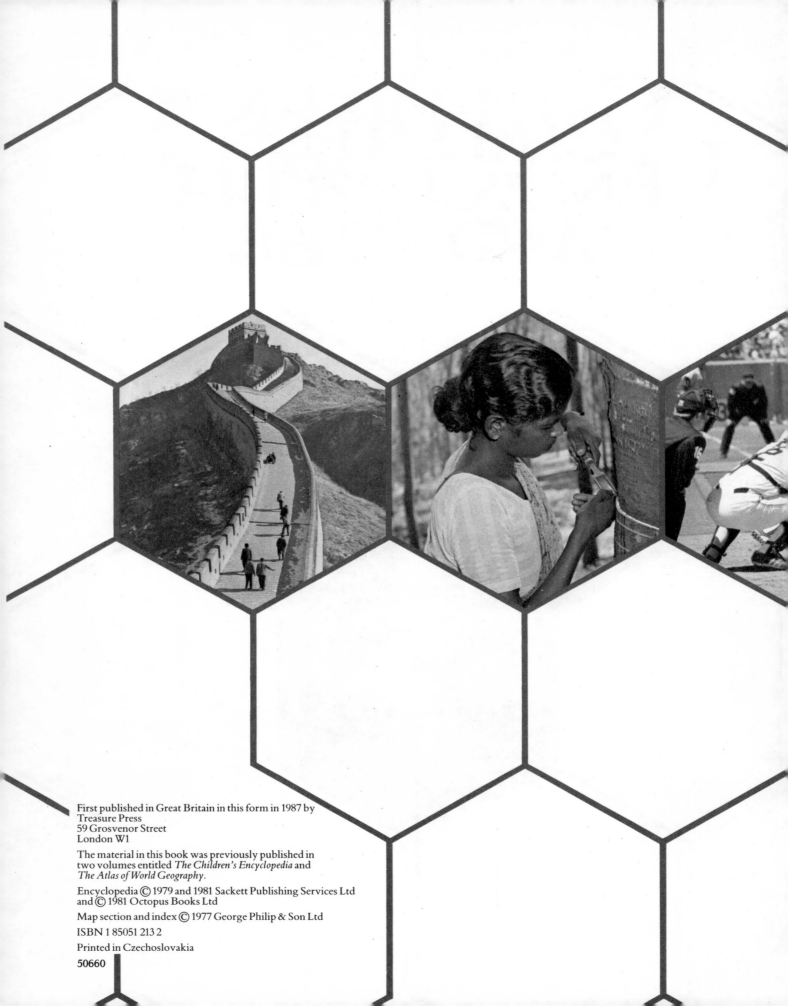

First published in Great Britain in this form in 1987 by
Treasure Press
59 Grosvenor Street
London W1

The material in this book was previously published in
two volumes entitled *The Children's Encyclopedia* and
The Atlas of World Geography.

Encyclopedia © 1979 and 1981 Sackett Publishing Services Ltd
and © 1981 Octopus Books Ltd

Map section and index © 1977 George Philip & Son Ltd

ISBN 1 85051 213 2

Printed in Czechoslovakia

50660

THE
CHILDREN'S ENCYCLOPEDIA AND ATLAS

TREASURE PRESS

Contents

The Encyclopedia

1 THE UNIVERSE

The universe stretches as far as the most powerful telescopes can see—and farther. It contains countless millions of galaxies, and each galaxy contains countless millions of stars. Our Sun is just one of these stars.

Studying the Heavens

People who study the heavens are called astronomers. They practise the science of astronomy. Astronomy is also a popular hobby. Thousands of amateur astronomers, young and old, enjoy gazing at the night skies with simple telescopes or through binoculars.

Early Astronomers

Astronomy is perhaps the oldest science of all. The Chaldeans and the Babylonians were skilled observers of the heavens

Below right: Some telescopes use curved mirrors to gather light rays. They are called reflectors. Others, called refractors, use lenses. The diagram shows how a refractor works. It has two sets of lenses held in a tube. The object lens collects the light. The eye-piece lens can be moved in and out for focusing.

Below and left: Astronomers pass starlight through a prism in an instrument called a spectroscope. The prism splits the starlight into a spectrum, or band of colour crossed by dark lines. These tell them many things, such as how hot the star is. Sirius, for example, is a hotter star than the Sun.

Words Used in Astronomy

eclipse The partial or complete 'hiding' of one heavenly body by another.

galaxy A large group of stars.

light-year A unit of distance used in astronomy. It is the distance travelled by light in one year—9.5 million million kilometres (5.9 million million miles).

moon A natural body that orbits a planet.

orbit The path of one heavenly body as it travels round another.

satellite Any body—natural or man-made—that orbits a heavenly body.

solar system A star and its satellites.

star A heavenly body that produces its own heat and light. Our Sun is a star.

universe Everything that exists. The universe appears to be expanding like a balloon being blown up.

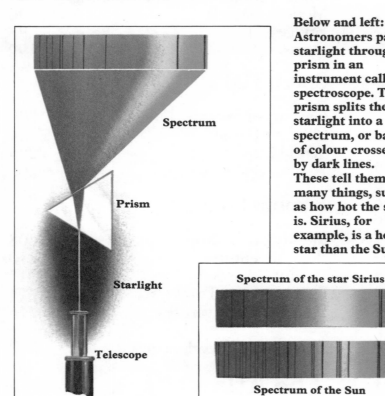

Spectrum

Prism

Starlight

Telescope

Spectrum of the star Sirius

Spectrum of the Sun

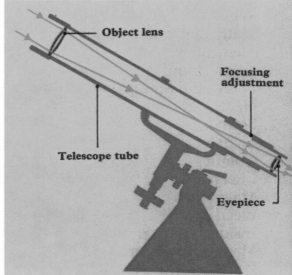

Object lens

Focusing adjustment

Telescope tube

Eyepiece

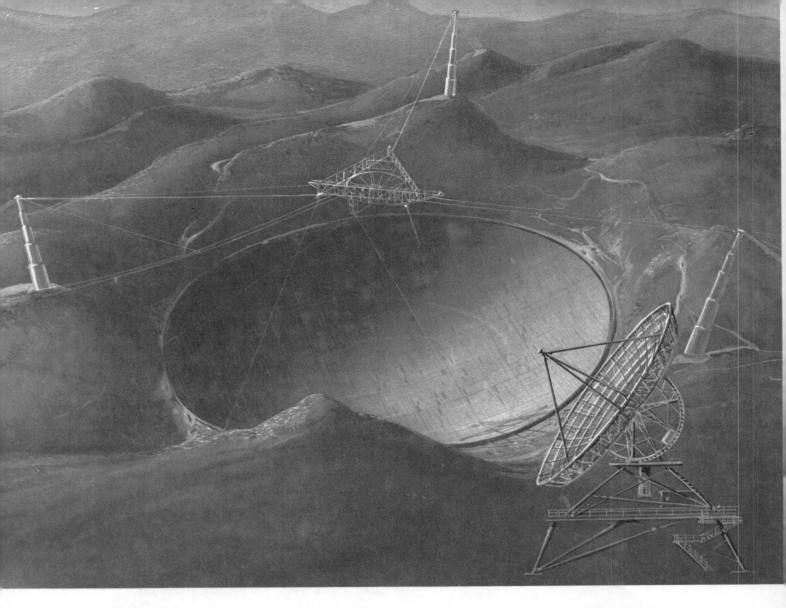

more than 5,000 years ago. Without the help of telescopes, they were able to make up a calendar from their observations.

The ancient Greeks mapped the stars over 2,000 years ago. Later, the Greek astronomer Ptolemy wrote the first books on the subject. He believed that the Earth was the centre of the universe, and all the other bodies revolved around it. This belief was widely held until the year 1543, when a Polish astronomer, Nicolas Copernicus, suggested that the Earth and the other planets revolved around the Sun.

The first simple telescopes were invented in the early 1600s. By studying the heavens through a telescope, the great Italian astronomer Galileo Galilei (1564-1642) was able to show that Copernicus had been correct. Later, other astronomers confirmed this.

Astronomy Today

Professional astronomers today work in observatories. These are large dome-topped buildings that house the giant telescopes used to observe the night sky. But astronomers seldom look through their telescopes. They use them as cameras to take pictures. By exposing film for long periods, they can spot some of the faintest stars.

Other modern 'tools' of the astronomer include the great dish-like radio telescopes which are used to study radio waves given out by stars. Since the start of the Space Age, astronomers have been able to send telescopes into space, where viewing conditions are ideal. They have also sent telescopes and cameras on spacecraft to the Moon and the planets to study these at close quarters and send back information.

Many stars give off radio waves as well as light. Astronomers study them with huge radio telescopes. The Arecibo telescope, above, in Puerto Rico, is built over a natural bowl in the mountains. Its dish, which is 305 metres (1,000 feet) across, collects radio waves from distant stars. The more common types use metal mesh dishes, as shown at the bottom right.

Stars and Galaxies

The stars you can see in the night sky are many billions of miles away. Even the Sun, which is a star, is 150 million kilometres (93 million miles) away. Some stars seem to be much brighter than others because they are nearer, and some are bright because they are very big.

Distances in space are so enormous that it is easier to measure them in light-years than in kilometres or miles. One light-year is the distance that light travels in one year, about 10 million million kilometres (6 million million miles). The nearest star to Earth, beyond the Sun, is more than 40 million million kilometres (25 million million miles) away. The light from this star takes 4·3 years to reach us, so you can say that it is 4·3 light-years away.

Our Sun is an average-sized star, about 1,400,000 kilometres (865,000 miles) across, but there are stars called giant stars that are several times bigger, and supergiant stars which are hundreds of millions of kilometres across. There are also stars called white dwarfs that are very much smaller than the Sun.

Stars seem to twinkle as you look at them, but this is because the Earth's atmosphere is bending the light. The stars normally shine very brightly, but some, called variable stars, periodically change in brightness. Stars called novae flare up and then fade in brightness and supernovae flare up so much that they blow themselves apart.

Pictures in the Sky

The bright stars in the sky seem to form patterns in groups. These groups of stars are called constellations. When the first astronomers noticed these groups, they imagined that they formed pictures in the sky. Constellations are named in Latin after the sort of picture that they form. For example, Ursa Major (the Great Bear), Leo (the Lion) and Orion (the hunter).

The stars that you can see in the constellations look close together, but they are sometimes light-years apart. They only seem

Below: On a clear night it is sometimes possible to see a faint band of light arcing across the sky. This is called the Milky Way and it represents a slice through our galaxy. It consists of millions of stars which you can see if you look through binoculars.

8

The constellations we can see depend on where we are on Earth. The best place to be is near the Equator where, over the year, we can see almost all the constellations.

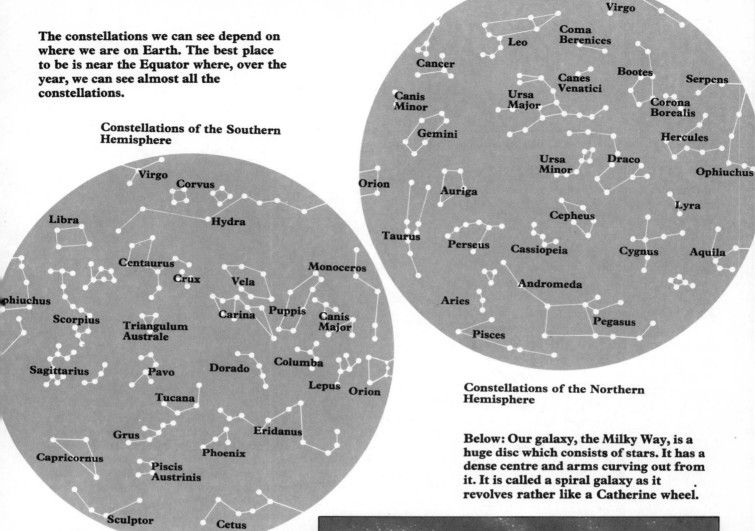

Constellations of the Southern Hemisphere

Virgo
Corvus
Libra
Hydra
Ophiuchus
Scorpius
Centaurus
Crux
Vela
Monoceros
Carina
Puppis
Canis Major
Triangulum Australe
Columba
Sagittarius
Pavo
Dorado
Lepus
Orion
Tucana
Grus
Eridanus
Capricornus
Phoenix
Piscis Austrinis
Sculptor
Cetus

Virgo
Leo
Coma Berenices
Cancer
Canes Venatici
Bootes
Serpens
Canis Minor
Ursa Major
Corona Borealis
Gemini
Hercules
Ursa Minor
Draco
Ophiuchus
Orion
Auriga
Lyra
Taurus
Cepheus
Perseus
Cassiopeia
Cygnus
Aquila
Andromeda
Aries
Pegasus
Pisces

Constellations of the Northern Hemisphere

Below: Our galaxy, the Milky Way, is a huge disc which consists of stars. It has a dense centre and arms curving out from it. It is called a spiral galaxy as it revolves rather like a Catherine wheel.

close together because they are behind one another as we look at them. Some stars travel through space alone, but most stars group together to form star clusters and galaxies. When two stars revolve around each other they are called a binary star system, and when there are more than two they are called a multiple star system. Sometimes stars group together in clusters of hundreds, known as open clusters, or even in clusters of many thousands which are known as globular clusters.

All the many constellations that we can see with the naked eye form a huge disc of stars that revolves in space. This is the Milky Way. The Milky Way is a galaxy, which is a huge group of millions of stars. Our galaxy is about 100,000 light-years from edge to edge and contains about 100,000 million stars. It is spiral shaped, with bands of stars curving out from the centre. Other galaxies are elliptical, or oval, and some are irregular in shape.

The Life-giving Sun

The Sun is a star, just like thousands of other stars you can see in the night sky. The reason it seems so much bigger and brighter than all the other stars is because it is so much nearer to us. But it is an average-sized star with a diameter of about 1,400,000 kilometres (865,000 miles).

The Sun was formed many thousands of millions of years ago. A cloud of gas and dust in space gradually began to spin until it became a huge disc. The centre of the disc was thicker than the edges and soon became a hot ball in the centre. This ball got hotter and smaller and detached itself from the disc to form the Sun. The planets of the solar system formed from the rest of the disc, and still revolve round their parent star, the Sun.

Like all stars, it will not shine forever. It will probably continue to shine for another 5,000 million years before it changes very much. After that time it will get bigger and bigger until it has become a giant red star many times its present size when it will scorch all life from Earth. Then it will begin to shrink again until it is very much smaller than it is now and will become first a white dwarf star, then end its life as a black dwarf.

A Nuclear Furnace

The Sun shines in the same way as all other stars. It is a huge ball of plasma that is white-hot on the surface. At the centre there is an enormous atomic reaction which 'burns' hydrogen. The process of nuclear reaction in the Sun is the same as in a hydrogen bomb. The very centre is the hottest part of the Sun where the temperature is several million degrees Centigrade. This nuclear reaction fuses atoms of hydrogen together to form atoms of helium and the energy produced in this natural nuclear reactor is given out as heat and light. At the surface of the Sun the temperature is very much less, about 6,000 degrees Centigrade, but is still extremely hot.

Scientists have studied the Sun's surface with special instruments and found that it is a huge sea of gas. Until recently it has been difficult to study the Sun because looking at it, especially through telescopes, damages

Above: Eclipses of the Sun were feared in ancient times. The Chinese believed that a dragon was trying to swallow the Sun. They would make a great noise to frighten it away, which, of course, always worked.

Bottom: The Moon is eclipsed when it moves into the shadow cast by the Earth, and the Sun, Earth and Moon are in a straight line. It takes the Moon up to two and a half hours to move through this shadow.

Below: An eclipse of the Sun occurs when the Moon comes between the Sun and the Earth. A total eclipse is when the Moon's disc covers the Sun's disc exactly. Day turns into night for about seven minutes.

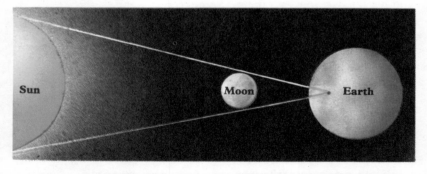

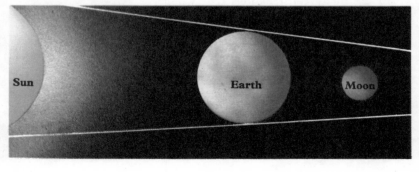

the eyes. Astronomers now use special equipment to tell them about the Sun. You should *never* look at the Sun, except through darkened glass.

Life-giving Energy

The energy that the Sun gives out is essential to life on Earth. It provides us with both heat and light. Plants need light to grow, and they are an essential part of our food chain. We eat plant food ourselves, but we also eat animals that live on plants. Some of the rays that the Sun sends out are very harmful to life, but these are filtered out by our atmosphere.

Changes in the Sun, or in the amount of energy reaching Earth, can affect conditions here. For example, scientists have observed dark sunspots which are cooler than the rest of the Sun's surface. Sunspots vary in size and sometimes they disappear altogether. Over a period of time, an absence of sunspots seems to make the weather on Earth generally colder. Some scientists believe this could have caused the great ice ages.

Eclipses of the Sun and Moon

Eclipses happen in our solar system when two planetary bodies are directly in line with the Sun. The planet farther away from the Sun is then in the shadow of the nearer body. An eclipse of the Sun happens when the Moon comes between the Earth and the Sun. In a partial eclipse, the Moon cuts out some of the light from the Sun, and in a total eclipse, the Moon appears to cover the Sun completely. Although the Moon is very much smaller than the Sun, because it is closer it almost exactly covers the Sun as we see it on Earth.

Another kind of eclipse is an eclipse of the Moon. This happens when the Earth comes between the Sun and the Moon. The Moon is then in the shadow of the Earth and is in darkness. An eclipse of the Moon can last for up to two and a half hours because the Earth's shadow is so large, but an eclipse of the Sun only lasts for a few minutes. When the Moon is eclipsed there is no light falling on its surface, but even in a total eclipse of the Sun, only a small part of the Earth's surface is in shadow.

A total eclipse of the Sun is a very strange event. Primitive people thought that it was some kind of sign from the gods, or even that the world was coming to an end. It is still a very peculiar sensation being at a total eclipse when, locally, day very quickly becomes night. Because the Sun played such a large part in ancient religions, many superstitions and myths have grown up about eclipses of the Sun.

Above: Huge flames shoot out from the surface of the Sun like fountains. These are called flares. Sometimes there are fountains of flaming gas thousands of kilometres high called prominences. In other places on the surface there are areas that are relatively cool. They look darker than the rest of the Sun and are called sunspots.

The Solar System

The solar system is the name given to our Sun and its planets. The word solar comes from the Latin name for the Sun, *sol*. The Sun is a star, and it is quite likely that many other stars have planets circling them, but so far no other system of planets has been discovered.

There are nine planets circling the Sun in huge oval paths called orbits. People of the ancient world observed the movements of the planets and thought they were wandering stars. They were frightened by the idea that stars could move about and gave them the names of powerful gods—Mercury, Venus, Mars, Jupiter, Saturn. They did not know that the Earth was one of these 'wandering stars'. The nearest planet to the Sun is Mercury, and it is probably the smallest planet in the solar system. It has a diameter of about 4,850 kilometres (3,015 miles) and is about the same size as Pluto, the planet farthest from the Sun. No one knows exactly how big Pluto is and it is thought by some scientists to be smaller than Mercury.

The second nearest planet to the Sun is Venus. It is only slightly smaller than the Earth. Venus is sometimes known as the 'evening star' although it is not a star at all. Stars shine because they are burning and produce their own light, but planets only reflect the Sun's rays. It is called the evening star because at certain times of the year it shines brightly in the sky just after sunset. Venus and Mercury are nearer to the Sun than the Earth and are very hot planets. It would be impossible for any life as we know it to survive on these planets because of the heat. Venus is also covered with thick clouds of carbon dioxide and sulphuric acid.

Our Sun is a very ordinary star. It is just one of millions in our galaxy. But it is more than a million times larger than the Earth. The planets move anti-clockwise around the Sun. It takes Mercury 88 days to orbit the Sun, Earth 365 days, and Pluto as long as 247 years.

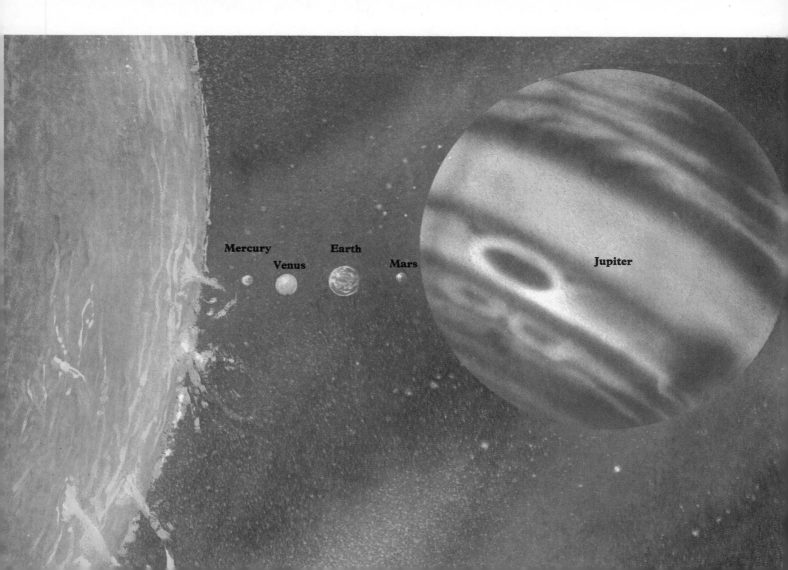

Mercury   Venus   Earth   Mars   Jupiter

The planet next distant from the Sun is our own planet, Earth, and next comes Mars. Mars is a little smaller than Venus and is often known as the red planet. The dust on its surface is red, and when it reflects light from the Sun, Mars appears to shine with a red light. When the Italian astronomer Schiaparelli observed Mars in 1877, he noticed straight lines across its surface which he called 'canals'. People thought that these canals had been made by animals or people who lived on Mars, but space probes have now indicated that there is probably no life on Mars. The surface of Mars is like a huge dusty desert covered with volcanoes and craters, and the atmosphere of carbon dioxide is very thin.

The Giant Planets
Jupiter, the fifth planet away from the Sun, is huge. It has a diameter of 142,600 kilometres (88,600 miles) and is more than a thousand times bigger than the Earth. When astronomers look at Jupiter through a telescope they can see that it has bands of different colours. There is a red spot on the planet. This may be a huge and violent storm that has been raging on the surface of the planet for centuries.

Saturn is almost as big as Jupiter. It is about 120,200 kilometres (74,700 miles) across and is the planet which has a set of rings around its equator. There are four rings, probably made of ice and dust, and they can be seen from the Earth at certain times, with the aid of a powerful telescope. When the angle of the rings means that they are edge-on to the Earth, it is very difficult to see them because they are so thin.

Beyond Saturn, Uranus and Neptune orbit the Sun. They are about the same size. Uranus is about 46,500 kilometres (28,900 miles) across and Neptune is about 48,000 kilometres (30,000 miles). Beyond them is the planet farthest from the Sun, Pluto. Not very much is known about these planets as they are so far away. Even when it is at its closest to the Earth, Pluto is about 5,000 million kilometres (3,000 million miles) away, well beyond the reach of space probes.

The idea that the planets revolved round the Sun, rather than around the Earth, was first suggested by the Greek philosopher Aristarchos in about 290 BC. But nobody would accept this idea until it was reintroduced by a Polish doctor called Nicolas Copernicus (below) in 1543.

Saturn

Uranus

Neptune

Pluto

The Moon

The Moon is Earth's nearest neighbour in space. It is close enough for us to see surface details. The bright regions are highlands covered with craters, and the dark regions are flat plains called 'maria'. The Apollo astronauts visited the Moon. They found that it is a lifeless wasteland covered with dust.

Several planets have smaller bodies circling them. These small planets are called satellites or moons. The Earth has only one satellite (which we call the Moon), and Mars and Neptune have two moons each. Uranus has five moons, and the two giant planets, Saturn and Jupiter, have several more. Saturn has ten, and Jupiter has 14.

The Earth's moon is only about 385,000 kilometres (240,000 miles) away. Because it is so close, scientists have discovered a great deal about it. Men have walked on the Moon and brought back samples of its rocks.

The Moon is very small compared with the Earth. Its diameter is about a quarter that of the Earth's, which means the Earth is about 50 times the size of the Moon. Because it is so small, it does not have a strong gravity. Things weigh far less on the Moon than they do here, and it is possible for a man to jump about six times as high as he can on Earth. The Moon's gravity, nevertheless, is strong enough to influence the tides on Earth.

Astronomers have examined the Moon's surface with telescopes for hundreds of years. They have now made maps of the surface and discovered mountain ranges and craters. They also found that many of the dark areas on the Moon are flat plains. Early astronomers thought that these plains were seas and called them 'maria' (the Latin for 'seas'), but we now know that there is no water on the Moon.

Before men invented rockets, it was

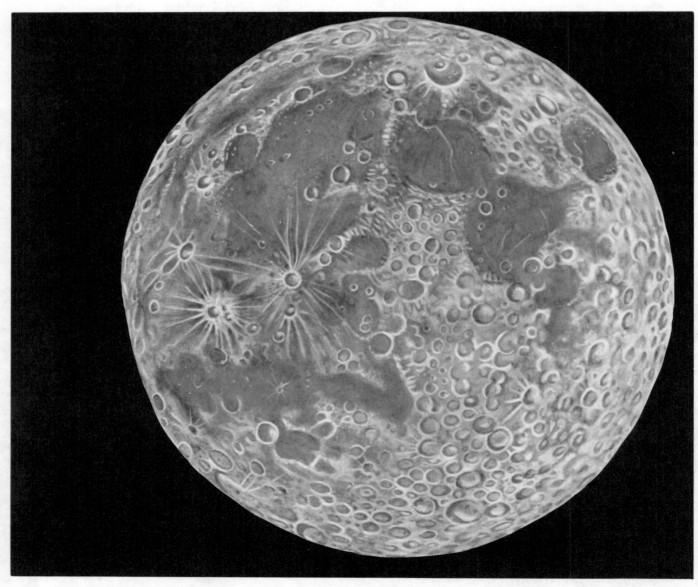

Moon Myths

The ancient Romans and Greeks thought that the stars and planets they could see were gods living in the sky. They gave these heavenly bodies the names of their gods and goddesses and the Moon was known as Diana, who was also goddess of the hunts.

Because of the colour of the Moon's surface and the dark patches on it, people used to think that it was made of green cheese! People also thought that the dark patches formed a kind of face which they called the Man in the Moon. We now know that these different colours are caused by the mountains, plains and circular craters on the Moon's surface.

Many people still believe that the Moon affects our lives here on Earth. Astrologers say that the different phases of the Moon are important when they are working out a person's horoscope.

The word 'lunatic' comes from the Latin word 'luna' which means 'moon'. People used to believe that anybody who was mad had been affected in some way by the Moon. Lunatics were supposed to be more mad at the time of the full moon.

Werewolves are also said to be affected by the Moon. In some areas people still think that some people change into wolves at the time of the full moon. Like vampires, werewolves only exist in horror films and books!

There are many superstitions connected with the Moon. It is said to be unlucky to look at a new moon through glass, but the full moon is the time to make wishes or choose a husband.

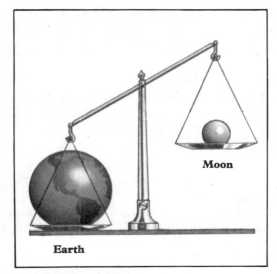

Earth

Moon

Left: The Moon is considerably smaller than the Earth. Its diameter is about a quarter of that of the Earth. If the Earth was hollow nearly 50 Moons could fit into it. But even though there is a big difference in size, the Moon and the Earth are still closer in size than the other planets and their satellites or moons.

Below and bottom right: The light of the Moon is not given out by the Moon itself. It is reflected from the Sun. As the Moon circles the Earth different parts of it are lit up by the Sun. It looks as if the Moon is changing shape. These different shapes are called the phases of the Moon. These two diagrams together show how the phases occur.

impossible to know what the other side of the Moon looked like. As the Moon circles the Earth, it rotates so that it keeps the same face towards us. Pictures taken from rockets circling the Moon have now shown us that the far side of the Moon has a much smoother surface than the one we can see.

The Moon reflects sunlight on to the Earth. It shines at certain times. Each month, the Moon appears to change shape as only part of it is lit up by the Sun. The full moon can be seen when the Sun shines directly on to the Moon, and the new moon when the Sun lights up the opposite side. There are several phases or stages of the Moon between the full moon and the new moon, when it has a semicircular or crescent shape.

Moon's phases

 1   2   3   4   5   6   7   8

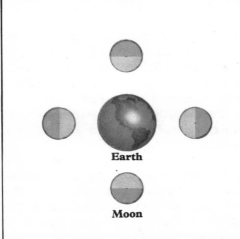

Earth

Moon

Left: Whenever there is a full moon you will always see the same face of the Moon. This does not mean that the Moon doesn't move, but that as it circles the Earth it spins on its own axis. It takes the same time to spin once on its axis as it does to circle once round the Earth. Rockets have enabled us to study the far side of the Moon for the first time.

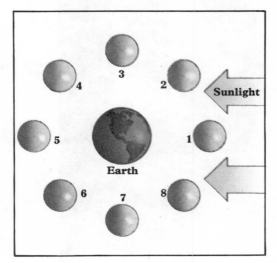

Sunlight

Earth

THE EARTH

2

Our planet, the Earth, is about 4,600 million years old. It was probably formed, along with the Sun and the planets in our solar system, from a massive cloud of gas and dust. It is the fifth largest planet in the solar system.

The Earth's Structure

How the Earth was Formed

Scientists do not know how the Earth was formed, and several theories have been put forward. The theory most generally accepted today is that the Sun and its planets were formed at about the same time from a huge cloud of gas and dust. The Sun was probably the centre of this cloud. As the dust swirled around the centre it flattened out, like a huge wheel, and a number of eddies or whirlpools formed in it. In time, the Sun became smaller and very hot and separated from the disc. Each of the eddies drew more dust and gas into it, and gradually they contracted to form the Earth and the other planets.

It is thought that as the mass of dust and gas shrank in upon itself it produced great heat—the heat we know is present today under the Earth's surface. The heat led to a number of chemical reactions, which in due course produced the water of which the oceans are made, and the mixture of nitrogen, oxygen and other gases which forms the Earth's atmosphere.

Earth's partner, the Moon, was formed at the same time as the Sun. One theory is that the Moon was originally another, smaller planet which was 'captured' by the Earth's gravitational pull.

The Earth's Cross-section

If you could cut a wedge out of the Earth you would find a very dense, heavy inner core. As the Earth was forming, heavy materials, such as iron and nickel, formed this solid core. Around this is the outer core. Scientists believe that the materials in this layer are hot and liquid. The diameter of the whole core is about 6,920 kilometres (4,300 miles). The next layer is the mantle, about 2,900 kilometres (1,800 miles) thick and around this is the outermost layer or crust. The crust varies between 8 and 32 kilometres (5 and 20 miles) in thickness and is formed from lighter materials, mostly granite and basalt. The mantle beneath it consists of heavier rocks. You would not be able to see exactly where one layer ends and another begins, because they all blend into each other.

Unlike prehistoric man, we now know that the world is not flat. But it is not completely round either. The constant rotation of the Earth pulls out the Equator. So the diameter of the Earth at the Equator is greater than the diameter from pole to pole.

The Earth is not a true sphere. The diameter at the Equator is 12,756 km (7,926 miles), while from pole to pole it is 12,713 km (7,899 miles). The Earth's mass is 5,976 million million million tonnes (5,882 million million million tons).

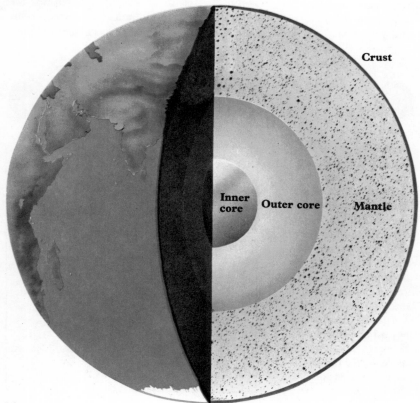

Crust

Inner core   Outer core   Mantle

Dictionary

abyss The deepest part of the ocean.

atmosphere The layer of gases that surrounds the Earth. It consists mainly of nitrogen and oxygen and smaller amounts of other gases and water vapour.

continent A large land mass and the islands around its coast.

continental drift The gradual movements of the continents to their present positions from those that they occupied in the distant past.

continental plate A large area of the Earth's crust that lies under oceans and land areas of the surface.

continental shelf The part of a continent that is under the sea.

continental slope The steep slope which goes from the continental shelf to the abyss. The continental slope is the true edge of the continent.

core The centre of the Earth. The inner core is solid and is surrounded by an outer core of liquid rock.

crust The outer shell of the Earth.

delta The area formed at the mouth of a river by the deposit of sediment.

equinox The days on which the Earth's position in relation to the Sun allows equal hours of daylight and darkness.

erosion The way that the land is worn away by wind and water.

fault A crack between two continental plates which forms an unstable line in the Earth's crust, along which earthquakes and volcanoes may occur.

glacier A slow-moving 'river' of ice.

igneous rocks Rocks made of solidified magma.

lava Molten rock that comes to the Earth's surface.

magma The liquid rock under the Earth's surface.

mantle The layer of the Earth between the core and the crust.

metamorphic rocks Rocks that have changed because of the effects of heat, pressure, and chemical action.

Pangaea The name given to the land mass formed when all the continents were joined together 200 million years ago.

sedimentary rocks Rocks formed from fragments of older rocks, which were suspended in water and settled down to the bottom of the sea in layers that have become compressed.

solstice The days on which the Earth is tilted at such an angle to the Sun to allow the most or the fewest hours of daylight.

water cycle The circulation of water from the sea to the clouds, on to the land as rain and back to the sea in rivers.

water table The level below which the land is saturated with water. It may vary according to the amount of rainfall.

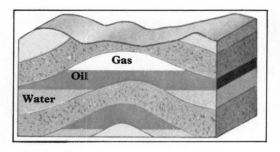

Left: Natural gas and oil are often found in layers of porous rock in an upfold or anti-cline. The porous rocks are trapped between layers of solid rock.

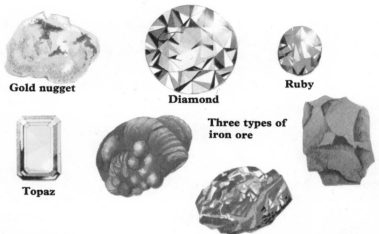

Gold nugget

Diamond

Ruby

Three types of iron ore

Topaz

Natural Resources

The Earth's crust is full of valuable substances that we use in everyday life. These include many minerals, and the fuels coal, oil and natural gas. These are called fossil fuels because they were formed from the remains of prehistoric forest trees and smaller plants. To get these substances we either dig them up (mine them) or extract them from the crust. Solid materials such as coal are mined and gold and precious stones are also found by mining deep into the Earth. Oil and natural gas are often trapped between layers of rocks. We drill through the rock to release the oil or gas.

Many of the Earth's most important minerals and fuels are becoming scarce. As natural resources dwindle, the difficulty and expense of mining them increase and scientists seek alternative materials.

Above: The Earth's crust contains many metals. Gold is a rare metal—that is why it is so expensive. There are also precious stones like diamonds which are cut to make jewellery.

Below: This diagram shows how long we can expect the resources of various fuels and metals that we currently know about to last at our present rate of consumption.

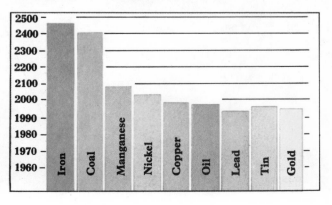

Surface Features

Interesting Facts

The largest continent, Asia, has an area of 44,426,000 square kilometres (17,153,000 square miles).

Greenland is the largest island in the world. It covers 2,175,590 square kilometres (840,000 square miles).

The Himalayas, a range of mountains to the north of India, contain the ten highest mountains in the world. The highest mountain is Mount Everest, whose peak is 8,848 metres (29,029 feet) above sea level. The second highest mountain is Godwin Austen (sometimes called K2).

The Dead Sea is 392 metres (1,286 feet) below sea level. It is in western Asia.

The largest desert in the world is the Sahara.

Europe is the only continent which does not contain a desert.

The Earth's surface features can be divided into three parts. Although we think of the Earth as a solid object, the atmosphere, or air, and the hydrosphere, the water areas, are as much a part of the Earth as the land. The land areas are sometimes called the lithosphere.

The surface of the Earth's crust is very irregular and varies a great deal in height. It consists of two thin layers: the continental or outer layer and the subcontinental or inner layer. The continents, or large land masses, are constantly moving very slowly

Right: Kilimanjaro is the highest mountain in Africa. Despite being very close to the Equator it always has snow at its summit.

Below: Volcanoes erupt when molten magma forces its way to the vent. Magma sometimes solidifies underground forming batholiths.

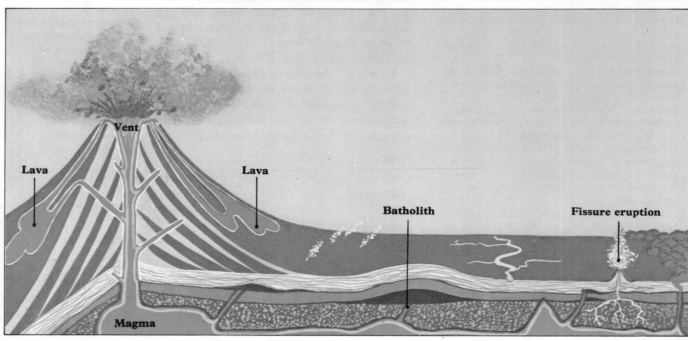

Lava   Vent   Lava   Batholith   Fissure eruption

Magma

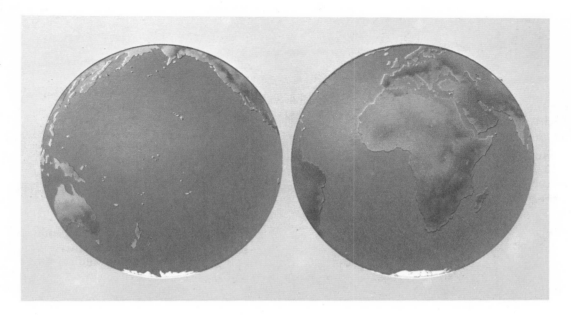

Left: These two views of the Earth show how oceans cover more than seven-tenths of the Earth's surface. These water areas are called the hydrosphere.

and this movement is called continental drift. The true edges of the continents are not the coasts you can see. Beneath the water is a sloping shelf and then a steep slope down to the depths of the ocean, called the abyss.

The continents of the world sit on large blocks of the Earth's crust which are called plates. These plates drift away from and towards each other. The areas near the edges of the plates are very unstable. This means that volcanoes and earthquakes can happen there. Volcanoes form when the magma or molten rock inside the Earth forces its way to the Earth's surface. It then appears as either ash or lava. Lava is the name used to describe the liquid rock that pours out of some volcanoes. When volcanoes erupt on land, they can, in time, form high mountains. In the ocean, a volcanic eruption can create islands. The Hawaiian Islands were formed in this way.

Earthquakes happen when continental plates move suddenly. This causes an earthquake along the fault or crack.

Below: This oasis in the south of Morocco has a good supply of water. Rainfall in desert areas is unreliable. It often falls in fierce storms and disappears rapidly.

The Continents

Africa The second largest continent. It contains the longest river in the world, the River Nile.

Antarctica Antarctica is a continent. The Arctic is a frozen ocean.

Asia Asia is the largest of the continents.

Australia Australia is the smallest continent.

Europe Europe's eastern edge is joined on to Asia. Together they form the Eurasian plate.

North America Reaching from the Arctic ice to the tropics, the terrain of North America contains forest and mountains, deserts, plains and jungles.

South America Scientists believe that North and South America were once connected to Europe and Africa until continental drift separated them. Now these two continents separate the two largest oceans, the Atlantic and Pacific.

Rocks

The Earth beneath our feet is moving, slowly but surely, all the time. Apart from continental drift, the rocks in the Earth's crust are changing all the time too.

Rocks are made of different kinds of minerals and are formed in three main ways. First there are igneous (or firelike) rocks formed from magma. Magma is hot, molten rock from the Earth's interior which solidifies as it cools, forming igneous rocks. Lava from volcanoes is magma that is still hot and flowing.

Sedimentary (or settled) rocks are formed from worn fragments of other rocks. Tiny particles, or sediments, are collected by water as it travels through rock and soil to the sea. Layers of this sediment gradually build up on the sea bed to form rocks, such as sandstone and shale. Sedimentary rocks are the most common rocks found on the surface of the Earth.

Lastly, as the Earth's crust moves, some rocks are changed by heat, pressure or chemical action. They become new kinds of rock called metamorphic (or changed) rocks. not the coasts you can see. Beneath the In this way, the sedimentary rock known as shale becomes another, metamorphic rock, called slate; and limestone is turned into marble.

Some Important Minerals

Asbestos A heat-resistant mineral. It is often used to make fireproof materials.

Calcite The mineral that makes up the chalk and limestone you can see in cliffs.

China Clay (kaolin) Used for making pottery and fine paper.

Diamond A form of carbon. Diamond is the hardest substance known.

Fluorspar (fluorite) Some kinds of fluorspar can glow in the dark. It is used in the steel industry.

Graphite The 'lead' of pencils is made of graphite. Like diamond, it is another form of carbon.

Gypsum 'Chalk' used on blackboards and 'Plaster of Paris' are made of gypsum.

Haematite An ore of iron. It is a deep blood-red colour.

Halite This is used in the home as salt for cooking and in industry to make soda and chlorine.

Quartz The mineral that makes up sand and gravel. It is used in making electrical instruments.

Talc The softest mineral. It is sometimes called soapstone. Talcum powder is made from talc.

Below: In the top 16 km (10 miles) of the Earth's crust 95 per cent of the rocks are either igneous or metamorphic. Only 5 per cent are sedimentary, although they are the most common on the surface. Basalt and granite are igneous rocks. Heat and pressure turn shale and limestone (sedimentary rocks) into slate and marble (metamorphic rocks). Coal is a sedimentary rocks but many other rocks of this type consist of fragments of sand, silt and pebbles, called sandstones and conglomerates.

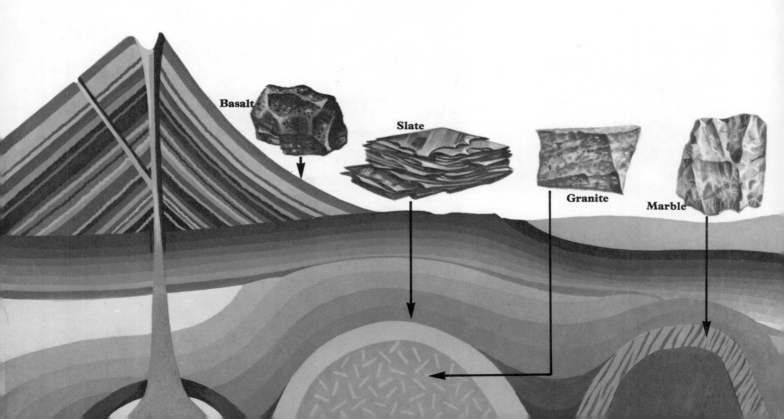

Basalt
Slate
Granite
Marble

Sedimentary rocks and lava flow are usually laid down in horizontal layers. But there are such tremendous forces at work within the Earth's crust that the rocks are pushed into great folds. When the rocks are folded into an arched shape it is called an anticline, and when they form a basin it is a syncline.

Rocks on the Earth's crust are subjected to great strain and occasionally they fracture. When the two rock masses move in relation to each other the fracture is called a fault. The rock layers on either side of the fault no longer match. The most famous fault is the San Andreas fault in California in the United States.

The Changing Face of the Earth

Erosion, the wearing away of the land, is happening all the time and is one of the main forces that changes the appearance of the Earth. Water is one of the main causes of rock erosion. If you watch waves pounding on a beach, or a river roaring down from a mountain, you can understand how rocks can be worn away after millions of years. Frozen water, in the form of glaciers, or great ice rivers, has also carved through rock, and wind, too, can gradually erode rock faces. The desert winds drive sand along, and this wears away the surface of rocks like sandpaper.

How Mountains are Formed

Some mountains begin as volcanoes with steep cones of ash and layers of hardened lava. Japan's Mt. Fuji is a volcanic mountain. Other mountains are made by the movements in the Earth's crust. When the moving plates push sideways against each other, flat layers of rocks are squeezed into folds. These are called fold mountains. Block mountains are blocks of land that have been pushed up between faults, or cracks, in the Earth's crust. Lastly, pressure inside the Earth sometimes pushes up blister-like mounds, called dome mountains. A mountain range can include two or more types of mountains. The Alps, for example are fold mountains that have also known some volcanic activity in the past.

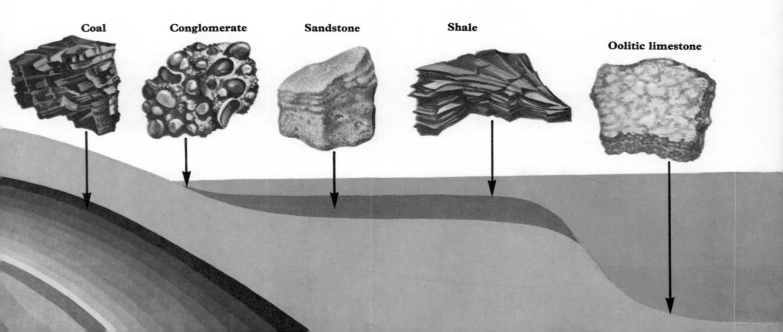

Coal   Conglomerate   Sandstone   Shale   Oolitic limestone

Seas, Lakes, Rivers

It is surprising how little of the Earth's surface is covered by land. In fact, 70.8 per cent of the Earth is covered by water.

The sea is moving all the time. The wind blows currents of water round the Earth and they constantly mix the oceans' waters. Much of the sea rises and falls twice daily and we call these movements *tides*. They are caused by the pull of gravity from the Moon and Sun.

The Sun also makes water circulate constantly from sea to land. It heats and evaporates sea water into vapour, which rises to form clouds. These clouds of vapour are now fresh water because salt from the sea does not evaporate. When the clouds become cool, this vapour turns into drops of water, which fall as rain. As rainwater falls over land, it seeps down through the soil and rocks until every tiny space and crack in the rocks is saturated or filled with water. Above this level of saturation is the 'water table'. Often the water table is underground but where it meets the land surface, lakes and swamps form.

Below: Rivers flow through three stages. In its old age a river flows slowly across flat plains in wide meanders. It slowly changes course and eventually meanders may be by-passed by the river. The portion that is cut off is called an ox-bow lake.

Interesting Facts

The second tallest mountain in the world is under the Pacific Ocean. It is between New Zealand and Samoa and its peak is 365 metres (1,197 feet) below sea level.

The longest river is the Nile in Africa. It is 6,700 kilometres (4,160 miles) long. The Amazon River in South America is the second longest and is 6,300 kilometres (3,900 miles) long.

The Caspian Sea is not really a sea, but is the world's largest lake. It has an area of about 423,400 square kilometres (163,500 square miles). The second largest lake is Lake Superior.

The Dead Sea, which lies between Israel and Jordan, is a lake that is so salty that people can float in it very easily.

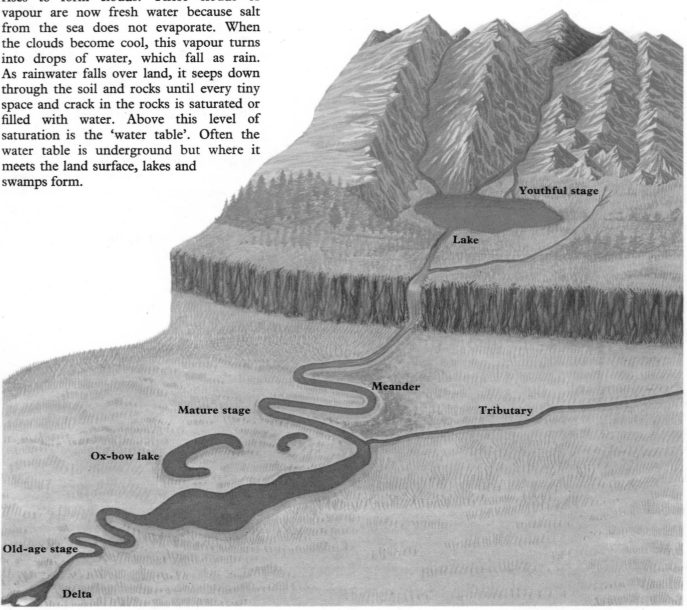

Youthful stage

Lake

Meander

Tributary

Mature stage

Ox-bow lake

Old-age stage

Delta

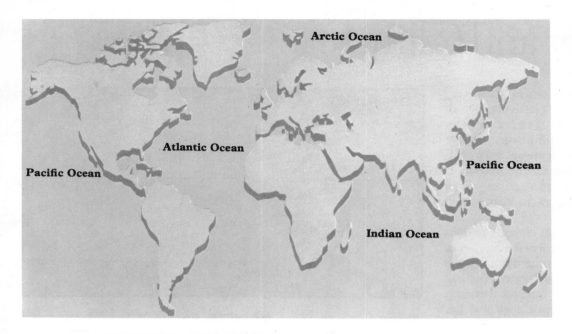

Left: This map shows the position of the world's great oceans. They cover an extraordinary amount of the Earth's surface—nearly 71%. The Pacific is by far the largest ocean. The Arctic is mostly frozen over.

Oceans

Arctic Ocean Most of the Arctic Ocean is frozen over.

Atlantic Ocean There is a huge chain of mountains under the surface of the Atlantic Ocean.

Indian Ocean The Indian Ocean is almost as large as the Atlantic.

Pacific Ocean The Pacific is the largest of the oceans. It covers more than 165 million square kilometres (63½ million square miles) and reaches a depth of 11,000 metres (36,000 feet).

Left: Rivers are of great use to people as a means of transporting goods from the centre of a country to its sea ports. Large cities grow up on the banks of rivers, like Paris on the River Seine in France.

The Life of a River

Rivers form in quite different ways. Some flow from inland lakes or melting glaciers. (A glacier is a slow-moving river of ice.) But others grow from small mountain springs. When a river starts its life as a spring in the mountains it is small and very fast-moving. This stage in a river's life is called the 'youthful' stage. As the youthful river makes its way to the sea several things can happen to it. Sometimes it flows into a lake and reappears at the other end.

Sometimes small rivers and streams flow into a river. The smaller rivers are called tributaries. They add more water to the main river and this is why rivers get wider and deeper as they flow away from the mountains.

After the youthful stage, as the river gets older, it usually gets slower. This is because it is flowing down a gentler slope than before. This stage is known as the mature stage.

Very often, after the river has flowed down from the hills, it has to cross a large flat plain to the sea. It is now in its 'old age'. Rivers in the last part of their lives flow slowly in huge curves and bends called meanders. Meandering is a common feature of old rivers. It means that the river 'wanders about'.

Once the river reaches the sea, it spreads out into a delta, a 'V' shaped area where the river deposits the solid particles it has been carrying as a sediment. It then flows slowly into the sea.

The water cycle is then repeated, with the Sun evaporating water from the sea and returning it to land in the form of vapour which becomes rain.

23

Weather and Climate

Different regions of the world have very different weather. At the North and South Poles, for example, the weather is very different from that at the Equator. Because the weather at the poles is always very cold, we say it is a cold climate. The climate of an area is the average weather, or the sort of weather you would expect in that region most of the time.

There are many different climatic regions in the world, but there are five main types of climate. The polar climates are found in the icy regions of the Arctic and Antarctic, and the area either side of the Equator (between the Tropics of Cancer and Capricorn) has tropical rainy climates with no cool seasons. Between these two areas are cold forest climates, temperate climates and desert climates.

The reason that it is generally cooler farther away from the Equator is because of the shape of the Earth. When the Sun shines on to the equatorial regions its rays do not have to pass through so much air as

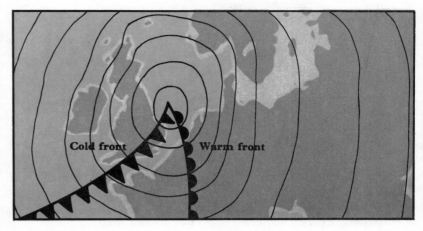

Above: A meteorologist's map has lines, or isobars, joining all areas of the same atmospheric pressure. Warm fronts and cold fronts are usually associated with rain.

Below: The five main climatic types—polar climates (white), cold forest climates (yellow), temperate (green), desert (brown) and tropical rainy climates (red).

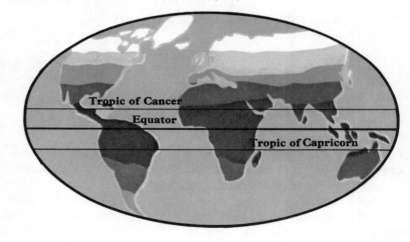

The Beaufort Scale

Beaufort Number	(km/h)	Wind
0	below 1·6	Calm
(Smoke rises straight up)		
1	1·6—4·8	Light air
(Movement of smoke shows wind direction)		
2	6·4—11·2	Light breeze
(Enough to rustle the leaves in the trees)		
3	12·8—19·2	Gentle breeze
(Enough to hold out a small flag)		
4	20·8—28·8	Moderate breeze
(Small branches move)		
5	30·4—38·4	Fresh breeze
(Small trees sway in the wind)		
6	40—49·6	Strong breeze
(Telegraph wires whistle)		
7	51·2—60·8	Moderate gale
(Large trees sway in the wind)		
8	62·4—73·6	Fresh gale
(Twigs and leaves blow off trees)		
9	75·2—86·4	Strong gale
(Can damage roofs of houses)		
10	88—100·8	Whole gale
(Trees blow over and houses are damaged)		
11	102·4—120	Storm
(Causes great damage to buildings)		
12	Above 120	Hurricane
(Only found in tropical storms)		

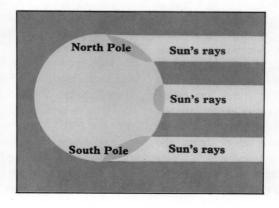

Left: The spherical shape of the Earth explains why temperatures are hotter at the Equator. The rays of the Sun are concentrated in a much smaller area near the Equator. Near the poles the rays are spread over a wider area.

they do at the two poles.

Climate is also strongly affected by the sea. Areas in the middle of large continents are often very dry, but along the coast there is more rainfall. This is because rain and snow come from the sea in the process called the water cycle. The clouds of water blow on to the land, then cool and fall as rain or snow. This happens more frequently in coastal areas near the sea as the clouds cool before they have the chance to reach areas far inland.

So that we can forecast weather accurately, it is necessary to measure the different elements of the weather. Scientists called meteorologists measure the force of the wind with anemometers and its direction with wind vanes. They use a scale to measure the speed strength of the wind. This is called the Beaufort Scale after the British naval officer who developed it in 1805.

Meteorologists also use rain gauges and sunshine recorders, and thermometers to measure air temperature. It is also important to measure the pressure of the air and this can be done by using an instrument called a barometer.

Nowadays, meteorologists have satellites out in space which send back pictures of the clouds over the Earth's surface. These pictures also tell them a lot about the wind and rain in different places and about the movement of weather from one area to another all over the world. Meteorologists keep a record of the day-to-day weather and this shows them the sort of weather that we can expect at different times of the year and helps to predict future weather.

The photographs below illustrate the two extremes of climate on the Earth. Polar climates are very cold all the year round and only small hardy plants like mosses or lichens can survive, where there is no snow. In tropical rainy climates the temperature is hot all the year round and the very high rainfall produces dense forests of vegetation.

The Changing Year

Although to us the Earth seems to be quite still, it is moving all the time. It is moving in three different ways. First, it is spinning like a top. It is also going round and round the Sun, with all the other planets of the solar system, and the whole solar system is moving through space too.

The spinning motion of the Earth, which is called its rotation, causes night and day. It takes about 24 hours for the Earth to rotate once. The side of the Earth which is facing the Sun is in daylight, while the other half is in darkness. The Earth spins round two points, the North and South Poles. The imaginary line between the poles is called the Earth's axis. The axis tilts a little bit away from the Earth's path around the Sun, and this tilt is what causes the seasons.

The Earth revolves around the Sun once every 365 days. So once each year our planet is back at the same point in its orbit around the Sun. Because the Earth's axis is tilted, the Sun's rays shine at a different angle to the Earth's surface at different times of the year, creating the different seasons of the year.

On about 21 December, the North Pole is tilted as far away from the Sun as it can be and the Northern Hemisphere (the northern half of the world) is in winter. The South Pole, however, is tilted towards the Sun, and the Southern Hemisphere is in summer. This is why the seasons are reversed in the two Hemispheres. On about 21 June, the situation is exactly the opposite. The Earth's axis is tilted the other way and the Northern Hemisphere has summer, while in the South it is winter. These two

Imaginary Lines on the Earth

North and South Poles The poles are the points round which the Earth rotates.

Equator The Equator is the line that runs round the middle of the Earth, halfway between the poles. It divides the Earth into the Northern and Southern Hemispheres. At the equinoxes, 21 March and 23 September, the Sun is directly overhead at the Equator.

Lines of Latitude The lines of latitude are parallel to the Equator. They are measured in degrees north and south of the Equator. This refers to the angle that is formed by imaginary lines from the line of latitude and the Equator to the centre of the Earth.

Lines of Longitude The lines of longitude are at right angles to the Equator and lines of latitude. They are lines that run across the surface of the Earth from pole to pole and are measured in degrees east or west of Greenwich, in England. This means the angle formed by imaginary lines from the line of longitude and the line that runs through Greenwich to the centre of the Earth.

Axis The Earth's axis is a line through the middle of the Earth between the North and South Poles. The Earth rotates round this axis a very 24 hours.

Tropics of Cancer and Capricorn The lines of latitude 23°28′N and 23°28′S. On 21 June the sun is above the Tropic of Cancer (north of the Equator) and on 21 December it is above the Tropic of Capricorn (south of the Equator). These dates are the solstices.

Arctic and Antarctic Circles The areas inside these two circles have either continuous night or continuous day at the solstices. In summer they always face the Sun and in winter they always face away from it. On the Arctic and Antarctic Circles this continuous day or night lasts only a few days, but at the poles it lasts several months.

This diagram shows how the Earth's axis is tilted in relation to its path around the Sun. The results of this are the regular changes of climate which we call the seasons. Places that are closer to the Sun are warmer than those that are farther away. This means that the Southern Hemisphere has summer when it is winter in the Northern Hemisphere.

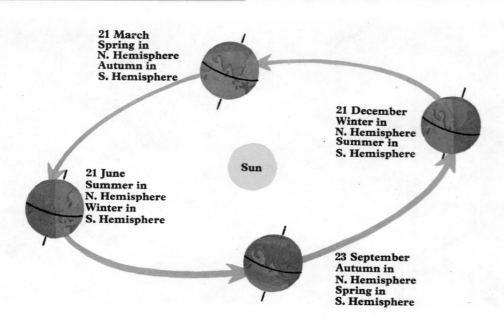

21 March
Spring in
N. Hemisphere
Autumn in
S. Hemisphere

21 December
Winter in
N. Hemisphere
Summer in
S. Hemisphere

21 June
Summer in
N. Hemisphere
Winter in
S. Hemisphere

Sun

23 September
Autumn in
N. Hemisphere
Spring in
S. Hemisphere

dates are the solstices. At the summer solstice it is the longest day of the year, and the winter solstice is the shortest day.

On 21 March and 23 September the days and nights are the same length. These are called the equinoxes. The vernal equinox is the beginning of spring and the autumnal equinox the beginning of autumn.

When the Northern Hemisphere is tilted towards the Sun and is in summer, the weather is generally warmer than in the winter. At the Equator the tilt has little effect, and the weather is hot all the time. In the polar regions, however, the axial tilt has a very strange effect. In mid-winter, the Earth tilts so much that there is no daylight at all. In mid-summer, the polar regions have no night. These areas inside the Arctic and Antarctic circles are sometimes called the 'lands of the midnight sun'.

In the temperate zones between the tropics and the polar circles, the seasons have always had special meaning for farmers who plant their crops to take advantage of the warm, growing seasons in spring and summer. From ancient times, people have celebrated the passing of the seasons at the solstices and equinoxes.

Above: These pictures were taken in England. They show the effect of the tilting of the Earth's axis. When the Northern Hemisphere is tilted towards the Sun it is warm and plants grow. It is summer. When the Northern Hemisphere is tilted away from the Sun it is much colder.

3 PLANT WORLD

Without the plants no life would exist on Earth. Animals rely on plants for their food, or eat other animals that feed on plants. Only the plants themselves can make their own food—by the process called photosynthesis.

The Plant Kingdom

The countryside is mostly green in colour, due to the presence of plants. There are familiar plants, such as grasses, flowers and trees. But there is also an enormous number of other kinds of plants, some of which are so small that they can only be seen through a microscope.

Scientists divide the plant kingdom into a number of groups. The simplest plants are the fungi (see page 30), including moulds, toadstools and mushrooms. They are not green and have no leaves.

The tiniest green plants belong to a group called the algae. There are single-celled algae, some of which can move about by using whip-like organs called flagella. There are also larger, many-celled algae. Some of these have their cells in long threads or filaments. Others are made up of larger masses of cells. The largest algae of all are the seaweeds, such as the wracks and kelps.

Most algae live and reproduce in water, but liverworts and mosses live on land. Liverworts are small plants that live in wet places. Nearly all liverworts have flat plant bodies. Mosses have stems and leaves and they generally grow in mats or cushions on moist soil.

Liverworts and mosses have to remain moist; most of them cannot tolerate living in dry places. But, more importantly, they need moisture for reproduction. They produce male sex cells which have to swim to the female sex cells.

Ferns do not dry out so easily and can therefore live in dry places, although most kinds of fern, including large tree ferns, are found in steamy tropical forests. They also produce swimming cells during reproduction, but these are not produced by the adult plants. Instead, adult plants produce

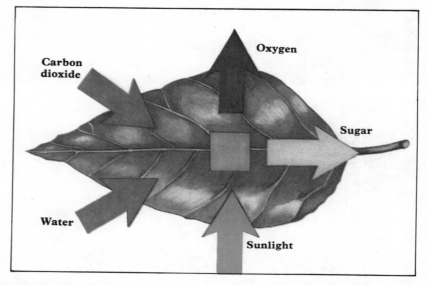

Above: The process of photosynthesis—how plants make food.

Right: All plants fall into the six main groups shown here.

Prehistoric Plants

From fossil evidence we know that very simple algae existed on Earth 3,100 millions years ago. But we know little of how the higher groups of plants evolved. About 420 million years ago there was a group of marsh plants, known as psilophytes, that produced spores at the tips of their leafless, branching stems. These plants appear to have become extinct by about 340 million years ago. But between 400 and 250 million years ago many land plants appeared. There were vast, steamy swamp forests. After these forest plants died, they eventually formed coal and many fossils have been preserved in the coal. There were ferns and tree-sized clubmosses, such as *Lepidodendron*, and quillworts, such as *Calamites*. There were also tall, conifer-like plants, known as the Cordaitales, which in fact were the ancestors of modern conifers and their relatives. Another group, the pteridosperms, looked like ferns but produced seeds. These seed ferns were the ancestors of modern flowering plants. About 150 million years ago several interesting groups of plants were flourishing. Among these were the cycads, of which only a few remain, and the ginkgos, of which there is only one survivor—the Maidenhair Tree. The cycads and the Maidenhair Tree, like the conifers, belong to the plant group known as gymnosperms. Gymnosperms produce naked seeds which are not enclosed in fruits.

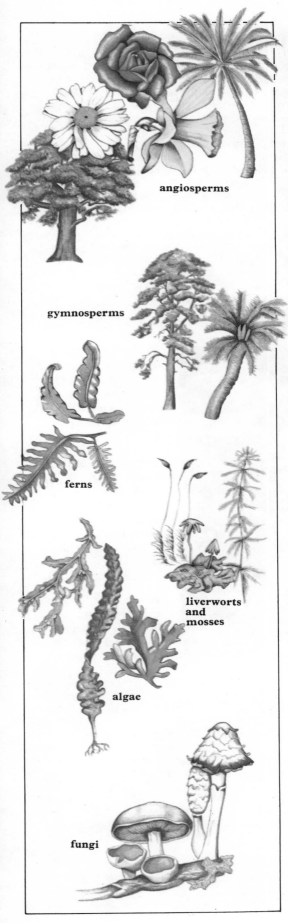

angiosperms

gymnosperms

ferns

liverworts and mosses

algae

fungi

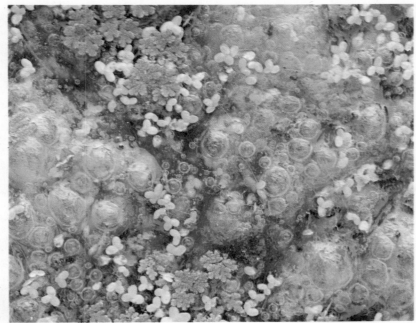

spores, which develop into tiny heart-shaped plants containing the sex organs.

Conifers (see page 32) and flowering plants (see page 34) have succeeded in doing away with the need for water during reproduction. The male sex cells are carried in grains of pollen and these plants produce tough seeds that can withstand dry conditions.

Photosynthesis

Plants make their food by taking carbon dioxide from the air and using it, together with water, to produce sugar and oxygen. This is done with the aid of sunlight and chlorophyll, the green pigment in the leaves of plants. Chlorophyll absorbs the light energy from the Sun and converts it into chemical energy, which enables the water to react with the carbon dioxide. The sugar that is produced is either used to provide energy for other plant processes or it is stored as starch.

Above: Spirogyra is an alga made up of long threads, one cell thick. It is seen here with the red-tinged water-fern, Azolla.

Below: Mosses can survive almost anywhere provided there is moisture. There are about 14,000 species in the world. They rarely grow more than a few centimetres high.

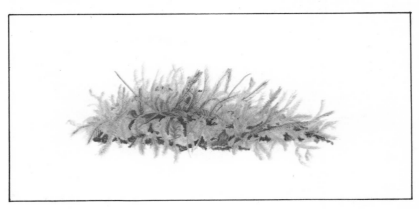

Fungi

The fungi are an unusual group of plants. Some people do not regard them as plants at all, but place them in a separate kingdom. However, fungi are usually regarded as specialized plants that do not contain chlorophyll.

Without chlorophyll fungi cannot make their own food, and so have to obtain food from other sources. Fungi which live on decaying plants and animal material are called *saprophytes*. They produce enzymes which break down the chemicals of the material they are living on into a form that the fungi can absorb. This function plays a very important role in sustaining life because plants and animals depend on constant recycling of the elements carbon, oxygen and nitrogen through the decay of organic matter. Fungi that feed in this way include the pin moulds and yeasts.

Other fungi are *parasites*; that is, they live on the tissues of living plants or animals, without being useful in return. Fungal parasites often cause disease. Powdery mildews, rusts, smuts and the ergot of rye are all plant parasites. Ringworm and athlete's foot in humans are also caused by fungal infections. Dutch elm disease and potato blight are serious diseases which result in the destruction of infected plants.

The plant body of a fungus consists of a mass of tiny threads or hyphae, known as the mycelium. Simple fungi reproduce both asexually and sexually. When a pin mould reproduces asexually it puts up special hyphae with tiny round spore-containers at the tips, hence the name 'pin

Useful Fungi

In addition to edible fungi, such as the field mushroom, horse mushroom, chanterelle, cèpe and fairy ring champignon, there is a number of useful fungi. Among the most useful are the yeasts. These are unusual fungi because they consist of single cells instead of threads. There are several different kinds of yeast. Some are used in baking and in brewing.

Baker's yeast has been used for making bread and cakes since the time of the ancient Egyptians. The yeast is left in warm dough for some time before cooking. It ferments some of the dough, producing carbon dioxide and alcohol. Bubbles of carbon dioxide gas cause the dough to rise. When the dough is cooked, the yeast is killed and the alcohol evaporates. Brewer's yeast is used to produce beers, wines and spirits. In this case the alcohol remains as part of the final product.

Fungi are also used in scientific research, medicine and the production of food. A species of red bread mould, *Neurospora*, was used to study laws of heredity. The antibiotic drug penicillin comes from the fungus *Penicillium notatum*, and two other species, *Penicillium roquefortii* and *Penicillium camembertii*, are used in the making of Roquefort and Camembert cheeses. A related fungus, *Aspergillus niger*, is used in the production of soy sauce.

Left: The fruiting body of the Earth Star fungus releases its spores through a small raised opening at its top.

Below: The antibiotic drug, penicillin, comes from the fungus *Penicillium notatum*. It was discovered in 1928 by Alexander Fleming.

Below left: Mould that forms on bread is a fungus. The black dots are the fruiting bodies.

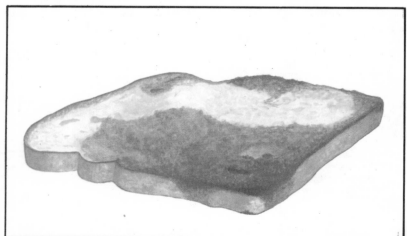

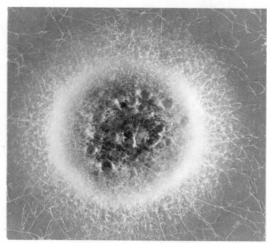

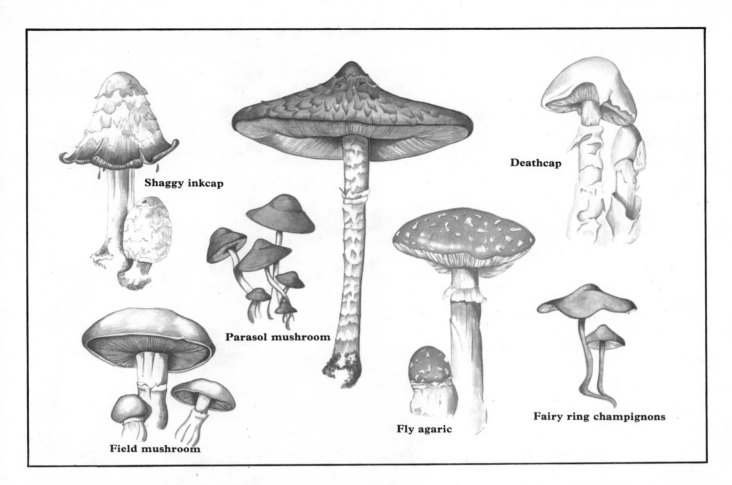

Shaggy inkcap

Parasol mushroom

Deathcap

Fly agaric

Fairy ring champignons

Field mushroom

mould'. When the pin mould reproduces sexually, two hyphae come together to produce a tough spore called a zygospore. This germinates to produce a new mycelium.

As a result of sexual reproduction fungi produce vast numbers of spores to be scattered by the wind. These spores are produced in fruiting bodies, of which there are a number of types. Some are too small to see with the naked eye, but a cup-fungus produces spores inside a large cup-shaped fruiting body. A morel produces spores on the head of its sponge-like fruiting body.

Mushrooms and Toadstools

The most familiar fruiting bodies are the mushrooms and toadstools. The well-known 'fairy ring' is evidence of a large, circular fungus colony growing just below the surface of the ground. At intervals, the hyphae on the ends of the mycelium develop into mushrooms above ground.

A toadstool consists of a stalk and a flattish cap. The spores are usually produced on gills on the underneath of the cap, but in some cases there are pores or spines instead of gills. Bracket fungi, attached to trees, have similar caps, but no stalks.

As in other groups of fungi there are both parasites and saprophytes among the toadstools. The honey fungus, which can severely damage fruit trees, is an example of a parasite. However, most toadstool fungi are saprophytes. Some can be found in woods, often near particular kinds of tree. Others are more commonly found in fields.

In addition to the well-known and delicious field mushroom, there is a number of edible toadstools. However, many are inedible and some are poisonous. Great care must be taken to identify any toadstool correctly before eating it.

Conifers

Conifers are cone-bearing trees and shrubs that belong to a group of plants known as the gymnosperms. This name literally means 'naked seed' and refers to the fact that the seeds of gymnosperms are not enclosed and protected in fruits, like those of flowering plants (see page 34). The seeds of conifers lie exposed to the air on the scales of their cones.

Many conifer trees themselves are shaped like cones or pyramids. Conifers include pines, spruces, firs, redwoods, cedars and cypresses. Most conifers are found in the northern hemisphere. There is a broad band of coniferous forest that stretches round the world just below the Arctic Circle. Some conifers are found in warmer northern areas, such as the Mediterranean and North Africa, but very few are found in the southern hemisphere.

Most conifers are evergreens. This does not mean that their leaves never fall off. In fact each leaf of a conifer lives for about three or four years. Dead leaves are continuously dropping off and being replaced with new ones. But the conifer always has a large number of living leaves. Two kinds of conifer, larches and the Swamp Cypress,

Largest and Oldest Trees

Among the conifers are the largest and oldest trees in the world. The coast redwoods that grow on the coastal plains of California, USA, are the world's tallest trees. Many of them live for about 1,800 years and grow to a height of 60-80 metres (196-262 feet).

The world's most massive trees are the giant redwoods. Also called Giant Sequoias, California Big Trees or Wellingtonias, they grow to a height of 75-80 metres (245-262 feet) with a girth of about 23 metres (75 feet) near the base.

The oldest trees in the world are the Bristlecone pines. These short, rather twisted, mountain trees live for over 4,000 years. The oldest living specimen is named 'Methuselah' and is over 4,600 years old. It is in California.

Right: A giant redwood tree in the Sequoia National Park in California. Visitors are dwarfed by the trees.

Left: A branch of the Chile pine tree, also known as the monkey puzzle tree because it is so difficult to climb.

Below: A selection of cones. The largest cone is that of the sugar pine.

Bottom: Conifers covered by snow in the Black Forest.

Cedar

Scots pine

Douglas fir

Larch

are deciduous; that is they lose all their leaves in autumn.

The leaves of conifers are like long needles and are tough and leathery. This helps to reduce the amount of water lost through the leaves and so conifers can survive in drier and colder places than broad-leaved trees.

Conifers can also live on poorer soils than broad-leaved trees. This, and the fact that they grow quickly, makes them popular trees to grow for their timber. Conifers are called softwoods because their wood is softer and easier to work than the wood of most broad-leaved trees. Conifer wood is much in demand for making paper, chipboard and plywood, as well as for telegraph poles, fence posts and some furniture. Conifers supply around 75 per cent of all timber used for commercial purposes.

A conifer also contains resin, the purpose of which is to protect wounds in the tree from attack by fungi and insects. It consists of a wax-like material called rosin dissolved in a fluid known as turpentine. Resin is used to make paints and varnishes.

Because these trees are so valuable, experts have developed ways of ensuring that the conifer forests will not be depleted. This science is called forest management and it involves planting new trees and cutting old ones when they have reached a certain stage of development.

Flowering Plants

The most successful and advanced group of plants are the angiosperms, or flowering plants. They are successful because of their efficient method of reproduction. The flowers give rise to fruits that contain seeds. The seeds have their own food supply and a protective coat. They can survive away from the parent flower for many months until conditions are right for them to germinate. This group of plants has colonized almost every part of the world's land surface and there is a vast range of different types. As well as the more familiar flowers of the hedgerows and gardens, such very different plants as trees, grasses and cacti are all flowering plants.

Herbaceous plants are those which do not form woody tissues, but have green stems. Some live for only one or two years (annuals and biennials), but others, known as perennials, may live for many years, dying down in the autumn and producing new shoots in the spring. Shrubs are low-growing, woody plants. They are perennials that do not have a single, large trunk, but branch repeatedly from a point near the ground. Trees are tall, woody plants with large trunks. Most trees that live in temperate climates are deciduous; that is, they lose their leaves in autumn.

Flowering Plant Reproduction

In a flowering plant, the flower is very important because it contains the reproductive organs. The male organs are called *stamens*, and the female organs are called *carpels*. Pollen from the stamens of the flower is transferred to the *stigma* (part of the carpel) so that seeds may develop. When this happens in the same flower it is called *self-pollination*. But most plants transfer the pollen to the stigma of another flower of the same species. This is called *cross-pollination*, and usually results in stronger and healthier plants.

Some flowers, such as those of grasses, are small and green. These are wind-

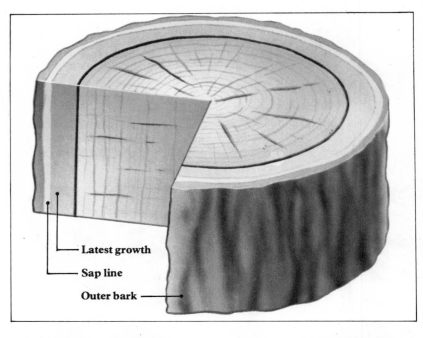

Latest growth

Sap line

Outer bark

Above: A cross-section of a tree trunk with its pattern of growth shown by the rings in the wood.

Below: The hairs and pollen sacs of the honeybee make it a very efficient distributor of pollen.

Plant Adaptations

Many flowering plants are specially adapted to life in places where conditions are harsh or otherwise unusual. Water plants, for example, have to survive the battering they receive from currents or waves. River plants, therefore, tend to have long narrow leaves and very supple stems.

Desert plants are among the most spectacular of flowering plants. Cacti are plants that use their stems as water storage organs. Their leaves are often reduced to spines, which may deter animals in search of a juicy meal. Pebble plants use their leaves as storage organs. Plants that store water in this way are called succulents.

A few plants that live in poor soil conditions have become carnivores, which means that they derive their food from insects. The Venus fly-trap and the bladderwort have ingenious insect traps. Sundews have sticky leaves that attract insects, then hold them fast, like adhesive tape.

Some plants live on other plants. Dodder and mistletoe, for example, are parasites that draw their nutrients from the plant on which they are living. Epiphytes grow on other plants but are not parasitic. They make their own food and take in water through aerial roots.

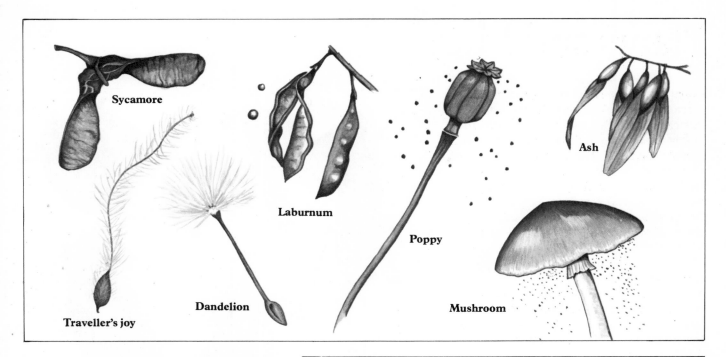

Sycamore

Laburnum

Poppy

Ash

Traveller's joy

Dandelion

Mushroom

pollinated flowers. The stamens produce vast amounts of light pollen that is blown to other flowers. In order to prevent self-pollination, the male and female parts of some wind-pollinated flowers ripen at different times. Other plants may have separate male and female flowers or even separate male and female plants.

Flowers that are pollinated by insects are generally brightly coloured to attract the insects. In addition they produce nectar, and the insects fly from plant to plant carrying pollen with them.

Seed Dispersal

After pollination, seeds develop, usually within a fruit. To avoid overcrowding, the seeds are dispersed as far from the parent plant as possible. Some single-seeded fruits have parachutes or wings, so that they are carried by the wind. Other fruits open explosively, scattering their seeds over several metres. Fruits with hooks may get caught in the fur of animals and juicy fruits are eaten by animals. When the seeds have passed through their stomachs they are deposited elsewhere unharmed.

Right: The main parts of a flower, which all grow from the stem, are shown in this diagram. The ovary (containing ovules), style, stigma and stamens are all concerned with reproduction and seed formation. The petals attract insects who transfer pollen from one flower to another. The sepals protect the inner parts of the flowers.

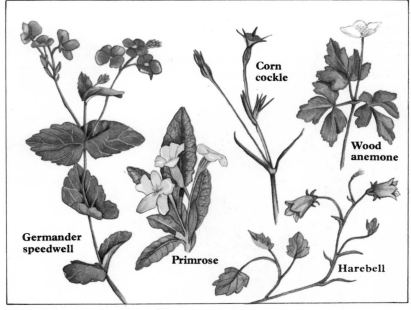

Corn cockle

Wood anemone

Germander speedwell

Primrose

Harebell

Top: Seeds are usually dispersed by four methods: wind, animals, water and explosion of the fruit.

Above: The variety of form and colours of flowering plants is enormous. The plants shown here are native to the woods, meadows and hedgerows of northern temperate regions.

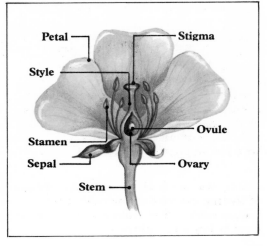

Petal

Stigma

Style

Stamen

Ovule

Sepal

Ovary

Stem

Plants and Man

Plants have very many uses for man. They provide us with food and shelter, with fuel and chemicals. But most importantly they supply the oxygen in the air that people and animals breathe. During the process of photosynthesis (see page 28) plants take in the carbon dioxide that people and animals breathe out, and give out oxygen, so that the amounts of carbon dioxide and oxygen in the air are always constant. This is a vital function.

Plants as Food

All the parts of a plant are represented in our food. We eat roots (turnips and radishes), stems (potatoes, which are modified underground stems, and asparagus), leaves (spinach and watercress), flowers (cauliflower and broccoli), fruits (plums, oranges, runner beans and tomatoes) and seeds (cereals and broadbeans) for examples. The oils that cook and flavour our food come from corn, olives and sunflowers.

Plants also provide us with many different

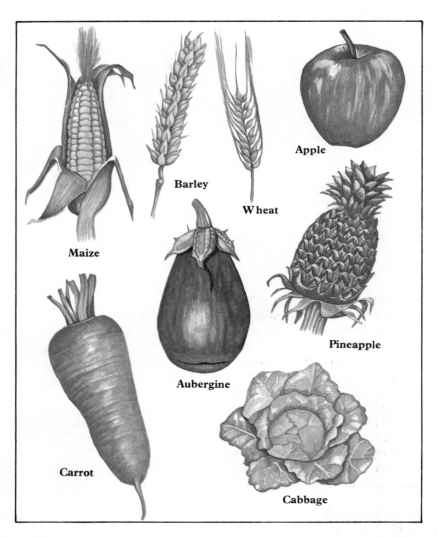

Above right: Plants are very important to humans. They provide us with nearly all the food we eat. Even when we eat meat the animals have usually been fed on plant products.

Above: Rubber is obtained by the process of slitting the bark of the rubber tree. Liquid rubber flows into a small cup fixed below and solidifies.

Endangered Plants

The world's rarest plants include the rose purple Alpine coltsfoot, the adder's tongue spearwort and the lady's slipper orchid. Man's activities around the world have caused many plants to become rare or extinct. The reasons for this vary. In some cases man has destroyed the habitats of plants in order to provide more farming or building land. This is going on today in the tropical forests of Borneo, the Philippines and the Amazon basin. Many plants that we do not even know of are probably being wiped out. In other cases man has introduced plants that take over the habitats of the native plants and make them die out. Man has also introduced grazing animals, such as goats. Grazing has prevented many plants from successfully reproducing and overgrazing has led to the formation of barren deserts.

We should all be more concerned about this. Plants are very necessary for supplying the air with its vital oxygen. Many people believe that the removal of vast areas of tropical rain forest will cause undesirable changes in the climate of the world. Also, many of the plants that are becoming extinct may have undiscovered uses as food or drugs.

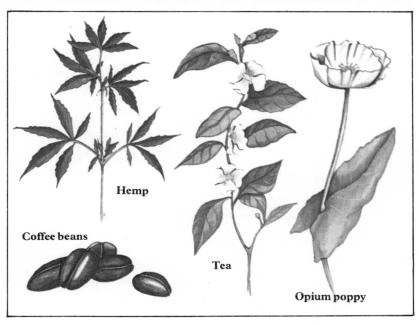

Hemp

Coffee beans

Tea

Opium poppy

drinks. Coffee and cocoa are made from the seeds of small trees, and tea is made from the leaves of small bushes. Oranges and lemons are squeezed to give us juice, and apples are pressed to make cider. Wine is made from grapes, and many other alcoholic drinks come from cereals and roots.

Plants for Materials

Trees are valuable for their wood, or timber, of which there are two main types. Softwoods come from conifers. Hardwoods are broad-leaved trees, such as oak, beech, ash and walnut. The hardest woods include mahogany, teak, ebony and rosewood.

Softwoods are mostly used to make paper. The wood is pulped by using chemicals or a machine, and squeezed between rollers to emerge as a thin, flat sheet of paper. Different treatments during the manufacturing process produce different kinds of paper, such as fine writing paper, brown wrapping paper, newspaper, cardboard or blotting paper.

Hardwoods are used in a variety of ways. A considerable amount of timber is used for building houses. Some woods, such as mahogany and teak, are prized for making furniture.

Trees also provide other useful materials. Cork is the bark of the cork oak. Rubber is made from the milky white latex that oozes from a cut made in the bark of a rubber tree. Wax from the leaves of the carnauba palm is used in making polishes, crayons, carbon paper and cosmetics.

We also use the fibres of several plants. Cotton fibres come from the seed pods of the cotton plant. Fibres from the stems of flax are used to make linen. Hemp fibres are used to make rope and sisal fibres are leaf fibres used to make string.

Today plants are not the important source of fuel they once were, but wood and peat are still burned for domestic heating and for industrial purposes. And it was prehistoric vegetation which formed the basis for the coal and oil that fuel modern life.

Some plants contain useful drugs. The foxglove contains poisonous digitalis, which is used, in small quantities, in the treatment of heart disease. Opium, from the unripe seed capules of the opium poppy, is used to make pain-killing medicines such as codeine and morphine.

Top left: Orchids are among the exotic flowers which are becoming extinct through over-picking.

Top: Sisal fibres come from the large spiky leaves of the sisal agave. The leaves are crushed by machines to free the fibres.

Above: Many plants contain drugs. Tea and coffee contain the drug caffeine and the pain-killer opium comes from the poppy.

ANIMAL WORLD

Life on earth began more than 600 million years ago and today there are well over a million different kinds of animals. They live everywhere, except in the frozen wastes of Antarctica. Some are enormous, others so tiny you need a microscope to see them.

The Animal Kingdom

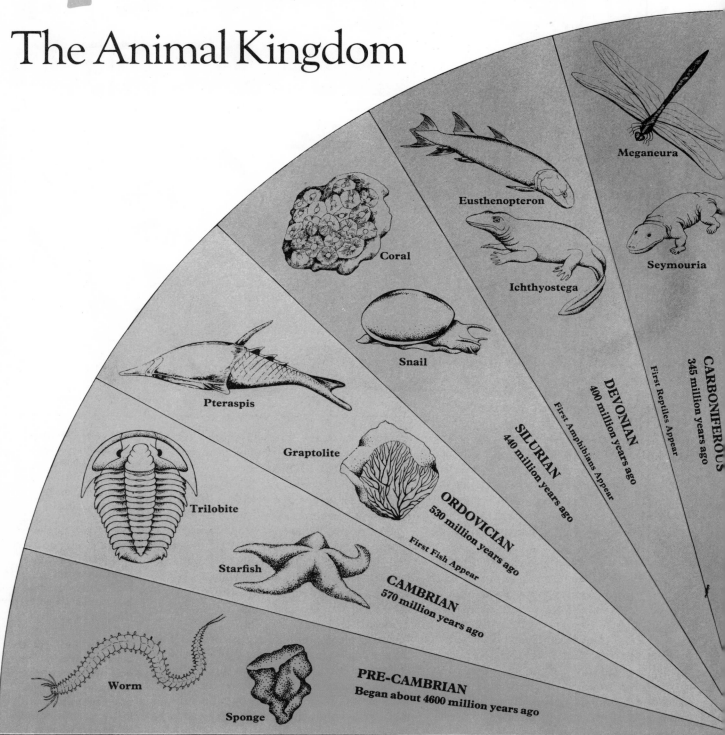

Meganeura

Eusthenopteron

Coral

Ichthyostega

Seymouria

Snail

Pteraspis

CARBONIFEROUS
345 million years ago

First Reptiles Appear

DEVONIAN
400 million years ago

First Amphibians Appear

Graptolite

SILURIAN
440 million years ago

Trilobite

ORDOVICIAN
530 million years ago

First Fish Appear

Starfish

CAMBRIAN
570 million years ago

Worm

PRE-CAMBRIAN
Began about 4600 million years ago

Sponge

Below: A chart showing the development of the animal kingdom from the first traces of life in the Pre-Cambrian period to the appearance of Man.

There are today two main groups of animals: those which have backbones, which are known as vertebrates, and those which have no backbones, and are called invertebrates. The vast majority of creatures in the world belong to the invertebrate group, but it is the vertebrates that are usually of more interest to us. This is because vertebrates include human beings and all the animals with which we are familiar, for example cats, dogs, horses and birds.

The basic differences between animals and plants, which are also living things, are: most animals can move freely about, while plants cannot; green plants can make their own food from oxygen in the air, chemicals in the soil, and water, using sunlight as energy, while animals have to eat plants or other animals as food. Animals that eat plants are called herbivores, and those which eat flesh are carnivores.

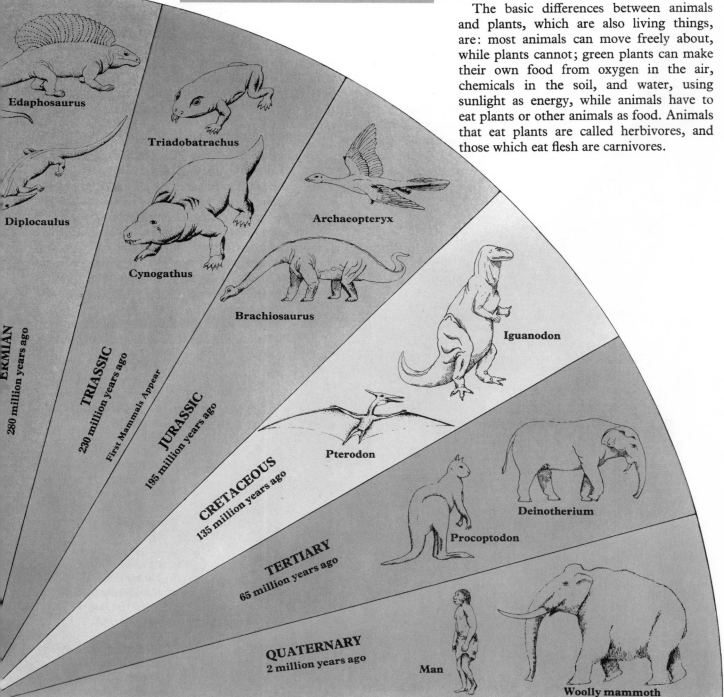

Edaphosaurus

Diplocaulus

Triadobatrachus

Cynogathus

Archaeopteryx

Brachiosaurus

Iguanodon

Pterodon

Deinotherium

Procoptodon

Man

Woolly mammoth

PERMIAN
280 million years ago

TRIASSIC
230 million years ago
First Mammals Appear

JURASSIC
195 million years ago

CRETACEOUS
135 million years ago

TERTIARY
65 million years ago

QUATERNARY
2 million years ago

39

Prehistoric Animals

When we use the word 'prehistoric' we mean anything that existed before history was written down—that is, about 5,000 years ago. Although we have no pictures or written records of what prehistoric animals looked like, we can find out in many ways: from fossils—bones preserved in rock—cave paintings, or mammoths preserved whole as frozen specimens (in Siberia, for example).

The first animals appeared over 600 million years ago, and were tiny water creatures that slowly developed more complex bodies and lifestyles. The earliest animals with backbones were types of fishes. One of the earliest kinds of fish we know of, because of its fossilized remains, is the *Dinichthys*.

Gradually, over millions of years, some fish began to emerge from the water and develop the ability to live on land and breed in water. These new animals were the amphibians. Some of the amphibians evolved into land animals called reptiles.

The biggest reptiles, the dinosaurs, were the rulers of the world about 225 million years ago. Dinosaurs were, like all reptiles, cold-blooded. That means that they depended on the sun for warmth to heat their bodies. The first dinosaur was probably *Ornithosuchus*, a kangaroo-shaped reptile that hopped on its hing legs. Like all carnivores (flesh-eaters) it lived on herbivorous (plant-eating) animals.

Carnivorous Dinosaurs

Some herbivores' size made them slow and clumsy, so they could easily be caught by the swift carnivores. Although four-legged, some of the carnivorous dinosaurs walked on their hind legs in an erect position, which meant they could move more quickly to catch their prey. The largest of these was the *Tyrannosaurus*. 'Rex' is often added to its name because it means 'king', and it certainly seemed to be the king of the dinosaurs.

Many other reptiles that lived in prehistoric times are now extinct (which means

Dinosaurs were the most common animals on Earth for about 150 million years. Some of the larger dinosaurs were as tall as a three-storey building whilst others were only the size of hens. Regardless of their size, all of the dinosaurs were reptiles that evolved from the same amphibious ancestors. The word 'dinosaur' means 'terrible lizard' although many of them were not terrible at all.

A Dinosaur Dictionary

Apatosaurus A giant sauropod which lived in the swamp lands. It was about 25 metres (80 feet) long. It was also called the *Brontosaurus*.

Brachiosaurus Another sauropod. It was the biggest land animal ever—14 metres (45 feet) tall and weighed up to 100 tonnes.

Carnosaur A kind of dinosaur that ate meat. It walked on its hind legs.

Ceratopsian A horned animal, one of the ornithischian dinosaurs.

Compsognathus One of the smaller dinosaurs.

Dinosaur The name given to reptiles that lived between 225 million and 65 million years ago.

Diplodocus The longest dinosaur.

Hypsilophodon ('high ridge tooth'). Probably the fastest dinosaur.

Iguanodon ('iguana tooth'). An ornithopod that stood on its hind legs.

Ornithischian ('bird-hipped dinosaur'). One of the two biggest groups of dinosaurs. They include ankylosaurs, ceratopsians, ornithopods and stegosaurs. The other main group was the saurischians.

Ornithosuchus One of the first flesheating dinosaurs.

Pterosaur ('flying lizards'). These were the first backboned animals to fly.

Saurischian The 'lizard-hipped' dinosaurs, one of the two main groups of dinosaurs. The include sauropods (planteaters) and theropods (meat-eaters). The other main group was ornithischians.

Sauropod ('reptile feet'). One of the groups of saurischians.

Stegosaurus ('roof lizard'). A dinosaur which had two rows of armour-like plates sticking out along its back.

Theropod ('beast feet'). One of the groups of saurischians.

Triceratops ('three-horned face'). A ceratopsian dinosaur with three horns on its face—one on its nose and two above its eyes.

Tyrannosaurus ('tyrant lizard'). The fiercest and largest carnivorous dinosaur.

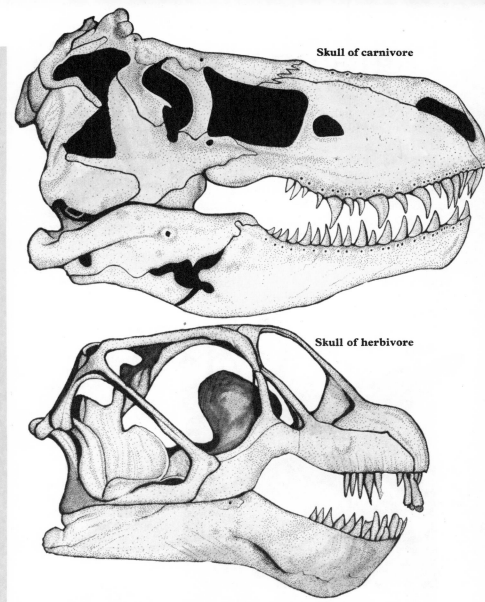

Skull of carnivore

Skull of herbivore

that they no longer exist). They include the flying reptiles, called pterosaurs. The ancestors of the pterosaurs were probably reptiles that lived in trees, and gradually developed webs of skin attached to the forelimbs. Some of the pterosaurs were small, the size of modern thrushes, and others were huge. One of the biggest was the *Pteranodon*, which had a wingspan of eight metres (25 feet). Another pterosaur with a wingspan of more than 16 metres (50 feet) has recently been discovered.

Some reptiles spent their lives in the sea. Ichthyosaurs evolved fish-like bodies, similar to those of whales, and, like the whales, they had to surface to breathe air. As they evolved they stopped laying eggs and gave birth to live young. Nothosaurs were more like lizards, and laid their eggs on land, although they were basically true marine animals that lived on fish.

Carnivorous dinosaurs, those that ate meat, had well-developed jaws to tear flesh from their prey and chew it. They were either very speedy and could catch their prey easily or else they were strong with vicious claws. Herbivorous dinosaurs, which ate plants, usually had teeth adapted to grinding food. The jaw of some herbivorous dinosaurs was projected in a horny beak.

Prehistoric Animals (2)

The time in which the dinosaurs existed is known by scientists as the Mesozoic Era. It is divided into three periods: the Triassic Period, the Jurassic Period and the Cretaceous Period. Although some people think the dinosaurs died out very quickly, they ruled the world for much of the Mesozoic Era. Man has only existed for about 40,000 years so far, and the dinosaurs lived for over 150 million years!

During this time, the dinosaurs were not the only members of the animal kingdom. There were many different insects that had developed a long time before the first

Below left: The *Triconodon*, a primitive carnivorous mammal with a hairy coat that evolved at the end of the Triassic Period. It was barely larger than the egg of a dinosaur but its relatives were able to survive where the dinosaurs could not.

Below: The *Dimetrodon* belonged to a strange-looking group of carnivores called the pelycosaurs. They carried a large 'sail' of skin over bony projections on their backs which absorbed heat from the sun to help maintain body heat for these cold-blooded reptiles.

reptiles. The early insects did not have wings but by the time that dinosaurs appeared, flying insects such as flies and bees had evolved.

During the Mesozoic Era, other kinds of animals began to evolve. About 150 million years ago, the first bird appeared. It was called *Archaeopteryx*, and was probably descended from small dinosaurs such as *Compsognathus*. The early birds did not fly very well, but by the end of the age of the dinosaurs they had developed into the kinds of birds that we could recognize today.

Mammals Evolve

Another kind of animal that developed at the same time was the first mammal. Mammals first appeared in the Triassic Period, about 200 million years ago. They were very small, furry animals and were only active at night when the dinosaurs were sleeping. Until the dinosaurs became extinct (died out), mammals were not very important animals, but after the dinosaurs they ruled the world.

The dinosaurs became extinct about 65 million years ago. There are many ideas about why this happened, but the most likely one is that their end was caused by a great change in the Earth's climate. About that time, the Earth became a lot colder, and so there was not enough heat to warm their huge bodies. They would have become

sluggish with the cold and too weak to eat. So the dinosaurs probably died of cold and starvation. The small mammals survived because they could hide from the cold in small burrows, and because they could manufacture their own heat from the food they ate.

Animals that lived in the water avoided the cold to some extent. In this way, some reptiles such as snakes, lizards and crocodiles have survived to the present day when their enormous, land-living relatives, the dinosaurs, died out.

Dinosaur Records

The biggest dinosaur was the *Brachiosaurus*. It was the largest land animal ever. It weighed up to 100 tonnes and stood about 14 metres (45 feet) tall. Fossils of the *Brachiosaurus* have been found in Africa and North America.

The longest dinosaur was the *Diplodocus*. It lived in swampland and measured up to 30 metres (100 feet) long.

The smallest dinosaur was the *Compsognathus*. It was only about 300 millimetres (12 inches) long, and looked rather like a bird without wings or feathers.

The first dinosaur was probably *Ornithosuchus*. It lived almost 300 million years ago, and was the ancestor of the carnosaurs (flesh-eating dinosaurs).

Pterosaurs, flying lizards, were the first vertebrates to fly. Some were only about 150 millimetres (6 inches) long.

The *Pteranodon* was one of the largest flying animals ever. Its wingspan was about 8 metres (25 feet).

The fiercest dinosaur was probably *Tyrannosaurus*. It had enormous teeth and sharp claws which it used to catch and kill its food.

Above: During the Earth's history thousands of creatures have flourished for periods of time and died out. The bird known as the dodo became extinct in 1861.

Left: A fossil and illustration of the earliest bird known to man called *Archaeopteryx*, which appeared in the Jurassic Period. It was about the size of a pigeon and evolved from reptilian ancestors. It had sharp teeth and a bony tail, much like that of a lizard. Clawed toes on its wings helped the bird to climb trees.

43

Fishes

The first true fishes evolved about 400 million years ago and they were jawless. Later, some fish developed thick, scaled fins and vicious teeth which many fish today still have. They all had well-developed fins.

At this time, a big division into two groups occurred. These two main groups still exist today. The fish in one group lost nearly all their bony skeletons, although they still had a backbone. They developed bodies made of cartilage, a softer, lighter and more elastic substance. Modern relatives of this group are sharks and rays. Sharks swim by snake-like movements of of their bodies and by thrashing their powerful tails. Two side fins act like airplane wings to stop the shark diving down. A shark must swim non-stop or it will sink. Rays and skates live on or near the sea bed. Their bodies are specially flattened to suit this lifestyle.

The second group of fish kept their bony skeletons and are now the largest group. Perch, salmon, herring and flatfish, like plaice and sole, are all bony fishes.

Above: A perch is a common type of bony fish that is very popular with anglers. It lives in lakes, ponds and slow-moving rivers. In spring and summer it can be seen in shallow water.

Left: The shark is also a fish. Like the perch it has a backbone and fins, but it does not have a gill cover and its tail is not symmetrical. Its body is made of cartilage. The large blue shark is ferocious—it even eats small specimens of its own species.

Far left: Sticklebacks are among the few fishes that make nests. The throat of the male goes red during courtship.
Left: Female tilapia hatch their eggs in their mouths.

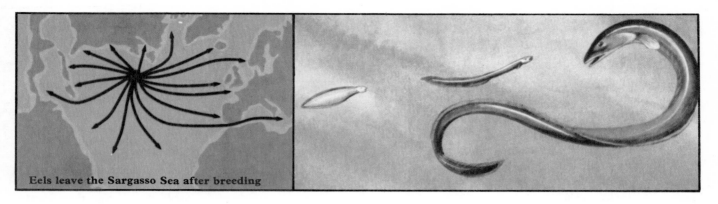

Eels leave the Sargasso Sea after breeding

How a Fish Breathes

All fish breathe through gills, tissues under covers at each side of the head. The fish takes in water when the gill covers are closed. Then the water flows out over the gills. Oxygen from the water passes into the blood in the gills and at the same time the water rids the body of waste carbon dioxide.

Bony fish have an extra way of breathing. Many of their ancestors lived in warm, shallow lakes where it was difficult to get enough oxygen. They began to rise to the surface to take gulps of fresh air. This air goes down into a pouch called a swim bladder. The air helps the fish to float without having to beat its tail all the time.

Some amazing fish can spend a long time out of water. Lungfish breathe air so they can survive when rivers dry up. They burrow deep into a muddy river bed and surround themselves with slime. Some fish can even walk or balance on their fins on land. Climbing perch and mudskippers can do this.

Fish spawn (lay eggs). Some species leave the eggs to develop by themselves, so they have to lay thousands for enough to survive. Many other animals, including Man, like to eat fish eggs. Certain fish, such as the salmon, swim long distances to lay their eggs where they themselves were spawned.

Above: Eels swim thousands of kilometres from the rivers of Europe and the eastern USA to spawn in the Atlantic near the Sargasso Sea. The young larvae then swim back. It takes them about three years.

Left: Fish are a valuable source of protein for human beings. They are found in greatest numbers in the shallow waters of the continental shelves. They are caught by trawlers dragging huge trawl nets behind them.

Left: Bony fish come in many different shapes, sizes and colours. These bright blue and yellow fishes live among the coral reefs in the Indian Ocean. Bright colours help fish to identify others of the same type and also those that are dangerous to them.

Amphibians and Reptiles

Amphibians evolved from fish-like animals. They spend part of their lives on land but they have to return to the water to breed. Only three of the eleven major groups that existed in prehistoric times still remain. They are frogs and toads; newts and salamanders; and caecilians. They all lay eggs. Frogs lay them in large masses to form spawn. Tree frogs lay their eggs in foam nests. The male rhinoderma, for example, a tiny South American frog, seems to eat its eggs, which the female has laid on damp ground. In fact, he takes them into his vocal sac inside his body. The young then develop and jump out of their father's mouth as little frogs.

Toads also produce spawn, but unlike frog spawn it is produced in long strings. The eggs are embedded in threads of jelly that may be up to 4·5 metres (15 feet) long. Toads can live in drier places than frogs. They have very rough brownish skin and usually walk about rather than jump.

Watching the development of baby frogs

Left: It takes a frog or toad about six weeks to develop from an egg to an adult. As a tadpole it looks rather like a fish with gills and tail, but first hind legs and then front legs appear and replace the tail. The adult can then hop on to land.

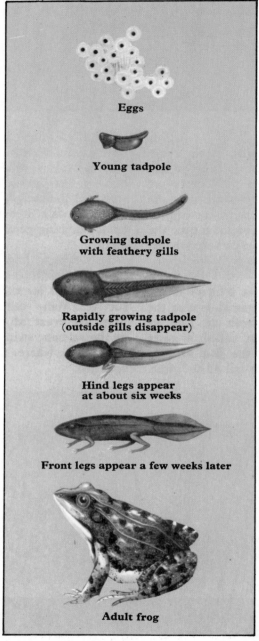

Eggs

Young tadpole

Growing tadpole with feathery gills

Rapidly growing tadpole (outside gills disappear)

Hind legs appear at about six weeks

Front legs appear a few weeks later

Adult frog

Above: The male midwife toad wraps strings of eggs around his hind legs and carries them there for about three weeks while the tadpoles grow inside the eggs. He then places them in water to finish their development and hatch.

Below: Newts and salamanders are amphibians. The crested newt grows up to 15 cm (six inches) long. The axolotl breathes through the feathery gills on the sides of its head. The mud-puppy gets its name from the barking sound it makes.

Crested newt

Axolotl

Mud-puppy

Chameleons

Lizards have striking colour patterns, and many kinds are able to change colour. Chameleons have become known as masters of disguise as they stalk their prey. Their scaly skin has the unusual ability to change colour to blend into the environment. This lizard can assume the look of a rock or a piece of tree bark as the occasion requires. Like all lizards, the chameleon's eyes are set so that they can move independently of each other. They also have very long tongues for catching food. The chameleon gives birth to living young which are able to care for themselves.

is quite interesting. When the frog's eggs first hatch, the young are called tadpoles and they look very much like small fish. Tadpoles breathe through gills like fish and live only in the water. Legs begin to grow when the tadpoles are about six weeks old and soon replace their tails. They then begin to come on land and breathe with lungs.

Newts and salamanders still have their tails as adults. Caecilians are legless, worm-like, burrowing creatures.

Reptiles

Reptiles were the first true land animals. Although turtles live in water, they have to breed on land. Reptiles are cold-blooded animals. Only four groups survive today from the 16 groups of prehistoric times. These are lizards and snakes; turtles, tortoises and terrapins; crocodiles and alligators; and the New Zealand tuatara. The tuatara is a large lizard-like creature with a row of spines along its body.

There are about 3,000 species of lizard. Geckos, agamids, iguanas and monitors are some of the most common. Monitors can be as big and powerful as crocodiles. Some lizards can actually grow up to 3·75 metres (12 feet) long. Some have long bodies and are legless, and so look like snakes. The difference between these lizards and snakes is that lizards have movable eyelids and

Left: The cobra is one of the most dangerous snakes alive. It kills by injecting venom into its victim through fangs. It eats rodents, frogs and toads.

Below: Crocodiles are now the sole survivors of the group of reptiles that included the dinosaurs.

Left: Turtles live in water but always return to the land to breed. They lay their eggs in holes which they dig in the sand.

Left: Lizards are among the most common reptiles. They live in many types of habitat including trees, swamps and rivers.

fixed jaws, while snakes do not.

Snakes' jaws are joined together by an elastic ligament, so they can open very wide to swallow food whole. Snakes have forked tongues and kill by poisoning, i.e., biting and injecting poison into their victims. Boas and pythons are constrictors. They coil themselves around animals and crush them to death.

Tortoises, terrapins and turtles have large, horny shells on their backs and bellies. The limbs of sea-dwelling turtles have evolved into flippers.

Mammals

What do the horse, whale and Man have in common? Believe it or not, we all belong to the same group of animals: mammals. Mammals are the largest group of animals and have two main characteristics. They all have hair or fur, and suckle (feed) their young on milk. This milk comes from the mother's mammary (milk-producing) glands.

There is a huge variety of mammals, including bats (the only flying mammals), dogs, cats, horses, elephants and the giant blue whale. But we can divide them into three main groups: egg-laying mammals, marsupials (pouched mammals) and placental mammals.

The strange-looking duck-billed platypus from Australia lays eggs. Most other mammals give birth to their young. This usually means that the egg stays inside the female's body until it is fertilized by a male. It then grows inside the mother. Young marsupials only stay there for a short time and then develop fully in the mother's pouch. The eggs of reptiles and birds are also fertilized internally by male sperm.

Placental Mammals

Most mammals are placentals. The young stay inside their mother's body (in her womb, also called a uterus) for a longer time, until they are more developed. They can do this because of the placenta, a structure attached to the wall of the uterus. Food and oxygen pass through this placenta from the mother's blood. The food goes along the umbilical cord to the unborn young (the foetus). After birth the cord is broken, which leaves us with a stump where it once was: our navels.

The young of different mammals grow inside their mother for different lengths of time. The period of waiting for the young

Marsupials

Some mammals have a pouch for their young to develop in, and are called marsupials. The vast majority live in Australia and New Guinea and some live in South America. Kangaroos are the best-known. A baby kangaroo is only a few centimetres long when it is born. This little worm-like creature crawls into its mother's pouch and attaches itself to her teat. It stays there for two months, feeding and growing. By the third month it can wander about. Other well-known marsupials are the koala and the opossum.

Above: Koalas, also known as native bears, are marsupials found only in Australia. They eat only the leaves of the eucalyptus tree.

Far left: The duck-billed platypus, an egg-laying mammal which forages for food with its duck-like bill. The word 'platypus' means web-footed.

Left: There are about 2,000 varieties of bats—the only mammals that can fly. They are nocturnal—appearing at twilight and sleeping by day.

to be born is called pregnancy or gestation. For example, the gestation period for shrews is only 13 to 20 days, but for Man it is nine-months and for elephants 20 to 22 months. Mammals also look after their young for some time after they are born. They suckle and often carry them too, and so develop strong family groups. This way of producing young protects them for a longer time, so they are strong by the time they have to fend for themselves. That is one of the reasons why mammals survive so well all over the world.

Insect-eating Mammals

Many of the smaller mammals such as moles, hedgehogs and shrews, are insect-eaters. They have sharp teeth, and eat molluscs, worms and sometimes reptiles, as well as insects. Moles have specialized feelers to help them move around in their underground burrows. The flying lemur, in spite of its name, is more a glider than a true flyer. The only true flying mammal is the bat, which has wings made of skin stretched between its legs and supported by very long fingers.

Many bats are nocturnal (active at night) so have a very advanced sense of hearing. They find their way in the dark by using a kind of sonar (sound detection) system. Although they eat insects, there are also fruit-eating and blood-sucking bats.

Rodents are gnawing mammals which include mice, rats and squirrels. They feed mainly on fruit, seeds and nuts. The beaver is an interesting member of the rodent family. Like many rodents, it has highly developed front teeth. Its broad, flat tail and webbed hind feet are adapted to life in the streams and rivers where the beaver builds its dams and 'lodges'.

Left: Elephants are the survivors of a once mighty group which lived all over the world with the exception of Australia. They are now the largest and most powerful living land mammals. To maintain their weight and strength, they need a quarter of a tonne of food per day.

Left: The hedgehog belongs to the order of insect-eating mammals. It cannot move quickly and when under attack from its enemies, it will roll itself into a ball, using its spines for protection. New-born hedgehogs are blind and are covered with white spines which harden in three weeks.

Left: Squirrels are medium-sized rodents with long bushy tails, short rounded ears and sharp, hooked claws which they need for climbing. The tail is most important as it corrects the balance of the squirrel as it flies from tree to tree or along ledges and branches.

Mammals (2)

Many large mammals are carnivorous, which means that they eat flesh. There are two main groups with various sub-groups in each. Firstly, there are cats, dogs, weasels and bears. They are all strong, athletic hunters with very powerful limbs. Cats have retractable claws. This means that they can draw their sharp claws into their paws when they are not hunting, and this keeps them sharp for when they want to attack. Carnivores have specially long canine teeth that form fangs for tearing meat. Wild dogs, such as wolves and hyenas, often hunt in packs (groups). Man often uses tame dogs to help him hunt, too.

The second group of carnivores are sea animals. They are seals, sea-lions and walruses and they feed on fish, shellfish and sometimes even on penguins.

Whales are among the most interesting of the marine (sea) mammals. They are found in all seas of the world, and they never leave the water. They have long, tapering bodies and grow to vast sizes although many of them feed on tiny creatures called plankton. Some whales can survive

Man

Modern Man, *Homo sapiens*, now dominates the world. Ten thousand years ago there were only about 10 million of us, but today there are over 4,000 million people alive on Earth.

Fossils (bones preserved in rocks) show us that our early ancestors were ape-men. When the naturalist Charles Darwin first suggested this in 1859, in his book *The Origin of Species*, people were shocked. People hated to think of themselves as animals. Many believed that the Bible story of Adam and Eve was the real beginning of Man.

So why did human beings come to rule the world? Five million years ago ape-men began to leave the forests and colonize (make their homes) on the plains. They began to stand upright (which helped them to see longer distances) so we call them Upright Man. They became great hunters, they invented tools and, most important, learned to speak and communicate. Many people believe that communication is the real reason why we now rule the world. Through talking and writing we can learn from the experience of others, and in turn we can pass on our learning to others.

Top: The whale is the largest known mammal. It breathes air but cannot survive on dry land. It provides many items useful to man but is in danger of extinction.

Above: Leopards are ferocious mammals which can strike faster than any other cat. They will prey on any animal, including man.

Right: The horse is a domesticated mammal which has been bred and trained by man, usually for transportation, for thousands of years. It has strength and speed as well as a high degree of intelligence.

under water for as long as an hour and can dive to depths of 1.1 km (4,000 feet). Marine mammals look rather like huge fish, but they give birth to their live young and then suckle them. Porpoises and dolphins are close relatives of the whales. The hearing of dolphins is very acute, and they use echoes to locate their prey.

The Primate Group

Primates are the order (group) to which Man belongs. They have large, complicated brains and supple, movable hands. Primates include monkeys, which have long limbs and grasping hands and feet, and so can move quickly through the trees. They also have long tails for balance. But apes are our nearest relatives. They are the gibbons and orang-utans of Asia, and gorillas and chimpanzees of Africa. Apes have no tails, walk more or less upright and have highly-developed brains. Their arms are longer than their legs. Chimpanzees are great imitators and can often be taught tricks, because they are so intelligent. They have good memories, too, and are capable of solving quite complex problems.

Above left: An orang-utan in a zoo. Out of captivity it lives almost entirely in the trees and rarely comes down to the ground. Its arms are so long that they almost reach the ground when the animal stands up.

Left: There are only two species of camel—the Arabian, or dromedary, which has one hump and is used for riding, and the Bactrian camel which has two humps and is used for carrying goods. Camels also provide meat, milk and hair for weaving cloth.

Birds

It is easy to identify the type of animal known as a bird. Birds are the only animals that have feathers and beaks. There are almost 8,000 species of bird living today, all of them warm-blooded, two-legged animals with backbones. Birds evolved from reptiles as the scales on their feet and legs show.

Feathers

Feathers are composed of the same substance as reptilian scales (and mammalian hair). There are two kinds of feathers. Down is soft and fluffy and acts like a woolly undervest to keep birds warm. Over the down, and especially on the wings, there are quill feathers. These are much harder and stronger than down feathers and have a stiff stem.

Feathers are often very beautiful colours, and some birds have many different coloured feathers arranged in special patterns. Parrots, birds of paradise and kingfishers are particularly colourful. Very often the male bird of a species has a colourful plumage in order to attract the female who, in contrast, may be a dull colour.

Beaks

Beaks are all shapes and sizes. Birds use their beaks, or bills, for many different purposes. Most wading birds need long, slim beaks to reach deep into mud and water for their food.

The ostrich, which lives in the grasslands of Africa, is the largest living bird. Ostriches grow up to 2.45 metres (8 feet) tall. The hummingbird is the smallest bird. It is only 6 cm (2.5 inches) in length including its long beak.

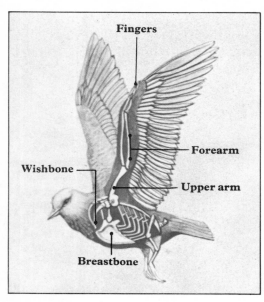

Fingers

Forearm

Wishbone

Upper arm

Breastbone

Left: The skeleton of a bird is like that of a human being, but the bones are of different proportions. The ribs are very similar to our ribs, but the breastbone is much larger because it must act as an anchor for the powerful flight muscles. A bird's knee is close to its body and most birds have four toes on each foot. The arm bones carry the wing feathers.

Cleaning Time

Feathers, like hairs on humans, do not grow evenly all over a bird's body. If you look at a plucked chicken ready for the oven you can see that the feathers grow on less than two-thirds of the skin area. To keep the feathers even, birds must rearrange them regularly. This is called preening and for the bird it serves the same purpose as brushing your hair or straightening your clothes.

Birds also have to groom and clean themselves regularly to get rid of pests and keep their feathers in good condition so that they can fly efficiently. Many birds bathe in water or roll in dust and then preen themselves. In preening the bird transfers oil from a gland at the base of its tail to its feathers to keep them waterproof. If you have a basin of water in your garden you may see birds bathing, but we do not see birds preening themselves very often. They prefer to do this alone, out of sight, in case an enemy should take them off their guard.

Extinct Birds

Many species (kinds) of birds have become extinct and some have been killed off by Man. Among them was the dodo, a flightless bird which was about the size of a turkey, which lived on the island of Mauritius. Sailors visiting the island used to kill the birds for food, and rats which came to the island on the ships ate the eggs. The last dodo died about 1681.

There were only comparatively few dodos, but the passenger pigeon of North America lived in incredibly huge flocks. There were literally thousands of millions of them in the early 1800s. But hunters shot them for food, and sadly the last passenger pigeon died in a zoo in 1914.

The moa was a huge flightless bird that lived peacefully in New Zealand. It reached a height of almost 4 metres (13 feet). But it did not long survive the coming of Man, who hunted it for food.

Right: During the breeding season birds come together to produce young. Many birds live on their own at other times of the year and the male has to persuade a female to be his mate. The peacock does this by displaying his fine tail feathers.

Hummingbirds have long, tubular beaks specially developed for drinking nectar from deep inside flowers. The pelican has a large beak with an expanding pouch which it uses to store the fish it catches.

Birds of prey, like eagles and hawks, have strong, hooked beaks which they use to tear the meat off their prey. Another bird with a strong, hard beak is the parrot. This bird can crack nuts easily in its powerful mouth. The woodpecker's beak is specially adapted for drilling into trees to find insects.

Feet and Legs

Birds also have specially adapted feet and legs which suit their ways of life. Perching birds need only short legs and strong feet to grasp the branches of trees, but other birds need more specialized limbs. The group of birds known as waders have very long legs so that they can stand in water. Storks, herons and flamingoes are a good example of this group. The eagles, hawks and other birds of prey have strong, sharp claws or talons to catch hold of their food. Other birds have webbed feet to help them swim and dive. Swans and ducks are members of this group.

Right: Toucans live in the rain forests of Central and South America. They use their large beaks to grasp the tree fruits they live on. Although the beak looks heavy it is very light.

Herons stand motionless in shallow water for long periods of time waiting to catch their prey.

How Birds Live

Birds fly by using their wings. All birds have wings, but not all of them are able to fly. The ostrich, which is the largest bird in the world, never leaves the ground. Nor do emus, kiwis, cassowaries, or penguins.

The turkey and the chicken sometimes make 'flights' that are really only big jumps. Other birds, particularly some sea birds, spend most of their time in the air. And many birds can fly with amazing speed and accuracy. The swift, one of the fastest flyers, can race at full speed through a hole scarcely as big as itself, and is said to fly at speeds of over 96 kilometres (60 miles).

How Birds Fly
A bird can fly for the same reason that an airplane can. The air pressure on the upper surface of its wings is less than the pressure on the lower surface. The reason for this is that the upper surface is *convex* (curved outwards) and the lower is *concave* (curved inwards). As the bird flies forward, the air passing across the upper surface has to travel farther than the air passing across the lower. This creates a force that lifts the bird into the air and keeps it there.

But the lifting force exists only while the bird is moving forward. To move forward, the bird glides on an air current or else flaps its wings up and down. On the downstroke, the feathers are pressed together so that no air can pass through them. The wing pushes the air down and back, and the bird moves forward. On the upstroke, the feathers part and let the air through. Then the wing comes down again and moves the bird forward.

Bird Territories
Nearly all birds have a territory—an area that they look on as their own. They attack other birds entering their territories, but only birds they consider a danger. Usually, a strange bird is felt to be a danger or a threat if it is searching for exactly the same kind of food, or is likely to interfere with life in some other way.

The size of a bird's territory depends on the way it lives. It may cover several square kilometres, or else it could simply be the ground that can be touched from the nest.

Social Birds and Lone Birds
Some birds prefer to live on their own. Usually, the reason is that there is not enough suitable food in their area to feed more than one of them.

Below: As a bird moves its wings downwards, the feathers press tightly together. The wings push the air down and back, and the bird moves forward. As the wings move up again, the feathers part and let the air through.

Downstroke

Primary feathers used for forward movement

Covert feathers give the wings a smooth surface

Secondary feathers help to give lift

Tail feathers used for steering and slowing down

Upstroke

A golden eagle soars through the air above its territory. Its sharp eyes search the ground for the small animals that it eats. Hunting birds generally live alone, and form pairs only to breed. But many birds, including goldfinches, live in busy, noisy flocks.

Goldfinches

Left: Before a bird can land on the ground or on a perch, it has to slow down. To do so, it spreads its wings and tail to catch the wind and act as a type of parachute.

However, even lone birds come together in the breeding season. Many birds form pairs to mate and rear their young. When the young leave the nest they resume their solitary life. Some birds, such as swans and storks, mate for life.

Other birds live in flocks all the year round. A flock is a group of birds that live, travel and feed together. Many species of birds form flocks for at least part of the year. They seem to need each other's company. When food becomes scarce in the place where they are living, the whole flock moves somewhere else. Other social birds come together only at night, in order to roost in a safe and favourite spot. Such birds are a familiar sight in city centres. Thousands of them meet together at dusk. Then they settle down for the night on sheltered window ledges or on trees in a city square.

Nesting

Birds choose many different places to lay their eggs and bring up their young. Eggs need to be kept warm to hatch, so most birds construct some sort of nest. The materials they use and the locations they choose can vary widely.

Some nests are built in convenient places like the fork of a branch or a rocky ledge. These nests can look untidy but are quite strong and comfortable. Some eagles use the same nest (eyrie) year after year.

Swallows and martins make their nests out of mud and clay, so they have to construct them in a sheltered place away from the rain. The tailor bird sews leaves together to make its nest. Others weave their nests from grass.

Hollows in the ground and small burrows are also used as nests. Flightless birds, such as the ostrich, dig holes in the ground to hatch and protect their young, and the kingfisher cuts a tunnel into the river bank.

Parrots, doves and some owls do not bother to build a nest at all. They try to find one ready-made to take over. And the cuckoo simply lays its egg in another bird's nest and leaves it there for the other bird to rear.

Left: A nest is usually made with several different types of material. Coarse twigs or leaves make up the outer layer. There are finer plant fibres inside and many perching birds line their nest with feathers and down. Most birds' nests are made by the female of the species, and she guards the eggs until they hatch.

Right: Woodpeckers use their powerful bill to make a hollow in a tree for their nest. It only takes the great spotted woodpecker ten days to hatch its eggs.

Below: Adélie penguins breed on the coast of the Antarctic in large colonies. They lay their egg on a nest made of stones. Emperor penguins do not make a nest. They sit their egg on their feet and cover it with a fold of skin. The parents take turns to keep it warm.

Below: The mallee fowl of Australia buries its eggs in a mound of rotting plants and warm sand. The heat in the mound hatches the eggs.

Migration

Many birds do not stay in the same country all year round. They lay their eggs and raise their young in the temperate parts of the world, where in summer insect food is plentiful and the climate is not too hot. They fly to warmer lands in the winter when food becomes scarce.

Birds which breed in the northern hemisphere fly south in winter. Some go only a few hundred kilometres to where the climate is warmer. Others go right across the Equator. For similar reasons, birds in the south fly north.

Migrating birds may fly enormous distances, sometimes more than 10,000 kilometres (6,000 miles). The Arctic tern makes the longest journey of all. Each year it flies from the Arctic region right down to the Antarctic and back.

Choosing a Route

Birds that normally live on land like to migrate over land. In this way they can stop and rest on their journey. Seabirds are happier over the oceans.

Migratory birds have a very good sense of direction and often return to the same local area each year. Nobody really knows how they find their way on these long journeys. Even young birds migrating for the first time without adults do not get lost. Like sailors, they may be able to navigate by the Sun and stars.

Many birds migrate in huge flocks. They gather together in the summer or autumn and all take off together. Some ducks and geese also migrate. They fly in smaller groups, usually either in a line or in a V-shaped formation.

Birds that Cannot Fly

There are several species of birds which have wings but cannot fly. Some, such as the African ostrich and the Australian emu, have adapted to a life on the ground, and are fast, powerful runners. The cassowary, another large flightless bird, lives in the forests of Australia and New Guinea, and the kiwi, a smaller flightless bird, is found in New Zealand. Other flightless birds, the penguins, are strong swimmers and their wings are more like flippers.

Top: Waxwings roam out of their own area in flocks during the winter to find berries.
Above: Swallows avoid flying far over the Mediterranean as they migrate south. They fly overland and cross at the Strait of Gibraltar or the Bosporus.
Right: Wheatears migrate from Greenland to Europe for the winter.

Insects and Spiders

Insects are a large group of animals which include flies, beetles, butterflies, bees and ants.

An insect does not have bones, but it has a hard outer shell rather like a suit of armour. These shells are built in sections with joints to let the insect bend its body freely. All adult insects have six legs and a body divided into three parts, the head, thorax and abdomen. The middle part, the thorax, often has wings attached to it, and many adult insects can fly. Insects usually have one pair of wings but some, such as dragonflies, have two pairs. Sometimes these wings are wide and brightly coloured like those of butterflies, or they can be very thin and delicate, like those of lacewings. The rear end of an insect's body, the abdomen, is often divided into sections so that the insect can bend it.

Insects have very strange eyes. They are made up of many tiny lenses. Each eye is in fact a collection of many eyes—sometimes up to 30,000.

Like many other animals, insects lay eggs.

But these eggs do not usually hatch into the familiar insects. What come out of the eggs of most insects is a little worm-like animal called a larva. The larva of a butterfly is called a caterpillar. It grows bigger and fatter all the time until it forms a casing round itself. At this stage the young butterfly is known as a pupa or chrysalis. Inside the casing, the insect is changing its shape completely and when it is ready it will burst out as a fully grown butterfly.

Some other insects, such as grasshoppers and dragonflies, produce not a larva but a nymph—which looks like a miniature, wingless version of its parents, until it becomes adult.

Social Insects

Many insects live together in large groups or colonies. Ants, termites, bees and wasps are good examples of these social insects. They build large nests rather like insect 'towns'. The insects in these colonies have many jobs to do. Some are builders, some collect food, some defend the colony and others just breed more insects. These social insects all work together to look after each

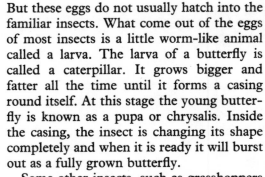

Above: The main difference between a spider and an insect is the number of legs that each has. A spider has eight, while an insect has six. The spider's body has two main parts but the insect's body has three, and the hind part of the insect's body is made up of sections to allow it to bend, and the spider's is not. The make-up of their eyes is also different, and unlike many insects, spiders do not have wings.

Some spiders hunt their prey but others use a trap made of silk. The silk is woven from an organ at the end of the body, called a spinneret. The spiral of silk is sticky and no insect that blunders in can escape. The spider hides nearby and darts out to bite its victim and wrap it in silk.

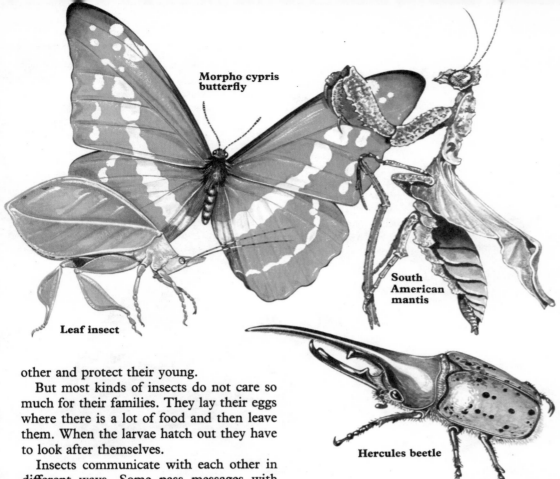

Morpho cypris butterfly

South American mantis

Leaf insect

Left: Insects live, by the million, all over the world. The dazzling morpho butterflies live in the trees of Central and South America. The praying mantis eats insects and even small lizards and frogs. It looks as if it is praying, but is waiting to pounce. Beetles form the largest single group in the animal kingdom. There are 278,000 different kinds already known. They are easily recognized by their shell-like front wings, called elytra. Their mouthparts are well developed for chewing. Leaf insects are a good example of an insect protecting itself by looking like something else.

other and protect their young.

But most kinds of insects do not care so much for their families. They lay their eggs where there is a lot of food and then leave them. When the larvae hatch out they have to look after themselves.

Insects communicate with each other in different ways. Some pass messages with scent or by chirping, some by rubbing their legs on their wings. If you watch a procession of ants marching toward an anthill, you will see that they communicate by touching their feelers.

Hercules beetle

Eight-legged Animals

Spiders are not insects. They have eight legs, not six, and their bodies are divided into two parts not three. If you look at a spider's eyes you can see that they are not in sections like the large eyes of an insect. Spiders use silken nets and webs to catch insects and other small animals for their food. The spider makes its beautiful web out of thread which it spins from its own body.

There are many different kinds of spiders. Some of them are really tiny, but others, such as bird-eating spiders, are as big as a man's hand. Many spiders have a poisonous bite which they use to kill their victims but only a few large spiders can hurt humans.

Spiders belong to a much larger group of eight-legged animals called arachnids. The spiders' relatives among the arachnids include mites and scorpions. A scorpion has a long tail with a poisonous sting in it. Scorpions live only in warm countries.

Interesting Facts

Bees pass messages to each other by 'dancing'. Different 'dances' tell other bees where they can find food.

In a colony of ants, termites or bees only one insect, the queen, lays eggs.

The dragonfly catches its food in mid-air.

Some insects, such as wasps, are not good to eat, and birds learn to avoid them. Such insects have what is called 'warning coloration', usually yellow and black. A number of other insects that are perfectly edible have developed similar colouring, so birds avoid them, too. This is known as mimicry.

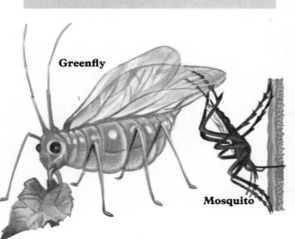

Greenfly

Mosquito

Left: Insects feed on both plants and animals and their mouthparts vary depending on the way they feed. Mosquitoes have a piercing mouth which sucks blood from animals. Aphids, such as greenflies, feed on plants and are a pest to gardeners.

Animals as Pets

All sorts of animals share homes with us as pets. Many people keep dogs and cats, but there are many more unusual pets. Pets are often kept as companions but there are other reasons for keeping them. For example, an aquarium full of tropical fish is a very pleasant sight and canaries and budgerigars are both beautiful and tuneful. Some insects and reptiles make fascinating pets.

Some animals are happy living with people, but it would be very cruel to keep wild animals in cages and boxes. Large or fierce animals do not make good pets, although some people keep snakes or even young lions in their homes.

If you go to any dog show you will see that there are hundreds of different kinds of

Below: Budgerigars make ideal pets. They are happy in captivity and are easily looked after. Breeders have cross-bred them to produce many colours for show purposes.

The Golden Hamster

Did you know that the golden hamster, so popular as a pet, was a rare animal at one time? Naturalists first saw a specimen in 1839—and then nobody saw another for nearly a hundred years. In 1930 a zoologist in Syria found a female with 12 young. Nearly all the golden hamsters kept as pets today are descended from this one family. The name 'hamster' comes from a German word meaning 'hoarder', because hamsters hoard any food they cannot eat. They are clean animals that hibernate in the winter.

dog. Big dogs such as German shepherds (alsatians) need a lot of food and exercise. Many people prefer to keep medium-sized dogs, such as terriers, because they do not need so much room and some people like very small dogs such as the chihuahua. Dogs are very intelligent animals and can be easily trained.

Cats are also common pets. There are many different types of cats, but all are part of the same family as lions and tigers. They do not need as much attention as dogs because they are very independent animals. They are also very curious and often go out exploring on their own.

If you live in a small house or an apart-

Right: The hamster is a rodent which is often kept as a pet. It has short legs, a bobbed tail and large cheek pouches for holding food. The name comes from a German word meaning 'hoarder'. Any food a hamster does not eat he will hoard. All pet golden hamsters are descended from one female and her litter of 12 babies.

Homes for Pets

Wild animals usually make their own homes if they need one, but pets often need some sort of house to live in. An outdoor kennel is a good home for a large dog and pet birds are best kept in a cage large enough for them to move around freely. Small pets such as mice, rats and hamsters can be kept in small cages but larger animals such as rabbits and guinea pigs should have a bigger cage or a hutch.

Many people have fish as pets. If they are coldwater fish, they can live in an aquarium or a fish pond in the garden. Tropical fish need a lot more looking after and will die unless they are in a warm tank with an air pump. Stick insects can be kept in a jar with fine net tied over the top. Ants can also be kept in a glass container where you can see them working in their tunnels.

Most pets also like something to do. It would be a very boring life for a budgerigar in its cage without a ladder and a bell or a mirror. Hamsters and mice love exercising on a treadwheel. Another thing that is essential in a cage or hutch is a supply of fresh food and water that is changed daily. Fish, too, need more than just a home. A fish tank should have a floor of gravel and a few stones. It is also a good idea to have some plants growing in the water, to help the fish breathe properly.

ment without a garden, it makes more sense to keep a small pet. Mice, rats and hamsters make good pets. They can be kept in cages and are cheap to keep. Small lizards and salamanders can also be kept at home, but only if you can provide the special environments they require.

There are several types of bird that make good pets. Canaries, budgerigars, parrots and finches are all very pretty and some of them sing sweetly. Mynah birds are not so colourful but they can learn to talk.

Rabbits and guinea pigs often live in hutches in the garden. Tortoises can be kept in the garden as long as they are safely fenced in. Many people keep goldfish and keeping tropical fish in a heated aquarium can soon become a fascinating hobby.

Above: Cats do not need a great deal of attention apart from food and drink. There are more than 30 pure breeds of cats divided into two main groups: short-haired (including orientals and tabbies) and long-haired (Persian and Angora).

Left: A cocker spaniel. Dogs have been 'man's best friend' for many thousands of years. They were first used in the role of hunting companion and for guarding homes and families. They can now be trained to act as guide dogs for blind people.

5 HISTORY OF MAN

BC

10,000–2500	Middle and New Stone Ages (use of stone tools).
8000	The first farmers.
3200	Bronze Age (use of bronze tools by Sumerians).
1500	Iron Age (use of iron tools by Hittites).

Timechart

	EUROPE		AFRICA AND THE MIDDLE EAST
BC			
		About 4000	Civilization of Sumer.
		1184	End of Trojan War.
753	Traditional founding of Rome.	814	Carthage founded by the Phoenicians.
510	Rome becomes a republic.		
356	Birth of Alexander the Great.	30	Egypt becomes part of the Roman Empire.
58–51	Julius Caesar conquers Gaul (France).		
44	Julius Caesar murdered in Rome.		
27	Augustus becomes first Roman Emperor.		
AD			
43	Roman invasion of Britain.	293	Roman Empire divided into 'Western' (European) and 'Eastern' (Byzantine).
313	Roman Empire becomes Christian.		
476	End of the Roman Empire in Europe.		
711	Muslims invade Spain.	630–660	Muslims conquer the Middle East.
1095	Pope Urban II calls for a Crusade.		
1096	Start of the First Crusade.		
1099	Crusaders capture Jerusalem.		
1215	King John signs Magna Carta.	1230	Sondiata becomes King of Mali.
1303	Last Crusaders defeated in the Holy Land.		
1347–51	The Black Death (bubonic plague) in Europe.		
1439	Johann Gutenberg develops printing press.	1453	Ottoman Turks capture Constantinople. End of Byzantine Empire.
1450 (approx.)	Start of the Renaissance.		
1517	Martin Luther begins Reformation.		
1517	Ferdinand Magellan starts first voyage round the world (completed 1522).		
1649	King Charles I of England executed. England becomes a republic.		
1660	Restoration of the monarchy in England. Charles II becomes king.		
1700–25	Peter the Great modernizes Russia.		
1733	Start of the Industrial Revolution.		
1769	Birth of Napoleon Bonaparte.		
1789	Start of the French Revolution.		
1804	Napoleon becomes Emperor of France.	1869	Opening of the Suez Canal.
1815	Napoleon defeated at Waterloo.		
1830	First public railway (British).	1899–1902	Boer War between South African Boers and Britain.
1848	Revolutions in Europe.		
1861	Unification of Italy.		
1870	German states come under the rule of Prussia.		
1914–18	First World War.	1957	Ghana gains independence. First African British colony to do so.
1933	Adolf Hitler and Nazis come to power in Germany.		
1939–45	Second World War.		
1945	Start of the 'Cold War'.		

The history behind the development of Man and civilization is both dramatic and fascinating. In this chapter we describe life from the time of the cavemen through all the great advances made in the fields of science, technology, the arts, philosophy, religion and revolutions to the age in which we live.

THE AMERICAS		ASIA		AUSTRALASIA/PACIFIC	
1300	Olmec civilization founded in Mexico.	1500	Advanced civilization in China.		
		1000	First Hindu states established in India.		
		207	Great Wall of China completed.		
900	Toltec civilization founded in Mexico.				
1000	Incas founded Cuzco, in Peru.				
1325	Aztecs founded Tenochtitlan in Valley of Mexico.	1206	Genghis Khan becomes Mongol leader.		
		1211	Mongols invade China.		
		1250	Mongol Empire at its greatest extent.		
1438	Inca Empire founded.	1497-98	Vasco da Gama sails to India.		
1492	Christopher Columbus arrives in America.				
1519-40	Spanish conquest of Mexico and Peru.	1526	Moghul Empire established in northern India.		
1607	English colony founded in Virginia.			1642	Abel Tasman discovers New Zealand.
1776	American Declaration of Independence.			1770	Captain James Cook discovers eastern Australia.
1783	End of American War of Independence.				
1809-25	Wars of Independence in South America and Mexico.	1857-58	Indian Mutiny. British Government rule India.		
1860-65	American Civil War.				
1903	Wright Brothers fly first aircraft.	1947	India and Pakistan gain independence.	1911	South Pole reached for the first time by Roald Amundsen.
1945	United Nations set up.	1949	China taken over by Communists.		
1969	First men on the Moon.				

Early Man and the First Civilizations

The first human beings on Earth were hunters. They followed herds of animals and killed them. The flesh provided food and the skins gave clothing. The hunters had no homes. At night, they slept in shelters made from brushwood, or in caves.

In some places, though, the hunting was so good that families could live in caves for long periods of time. While the men went hunting, the women, children and older people scraped skins, gathered firewood, or made tools from pieces of flint (stone) and animal bone. The age in which these people lived has been called the Stone Age.

Growing their Food

In about 7000 BC, people discovered how to grow grain. They became farmers. They also kept small herds of goats and sheep.

The best place to live was near a large river, where the land was fertile and could be easily irrigated. Because farmers could grow plenty of food, large numbers of people could live there. So, the first towns and the first civilizations began to grow up. One of the first was at Sumer, between the Rivers Tigris and Euphrates in Mesopotamia. Some 5,500 years ago, the Sumerians were constructing canals, using ploughs in their fields and building beautiful palaces

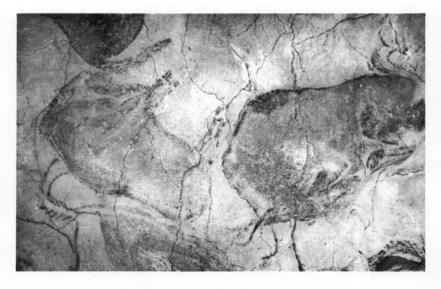

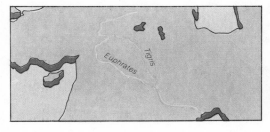

and, some time later, temple towers called ziggurats. Some Sumerians became very rich. They wore splendid embroidered robes and jewels. They even used perfumes. The Sumerians wrote in cuneiform (wedge-shaped) letters. They scratched their writing onto baked clay tablets with hard reeds.

Civilizations along the Hwang Ho River in China began about 4,000 years ago. The Chinese grew millet, barley and rice along the Hwang Ho. They kept herds of

Above: Art began with the cave paintings of the early hunters over 3,000 years ago, when they painted over shadows on cave walls. This painting was found in Altamira, Spain.

Above left: The map shows the importance of the Tigris and Euphrates rivers to the existence of Sumer. The Sumerians had the first civilization based on trade.

Cave Paintings at Lascaux

One day in 1940, a boy wandered into a cave at Lascaux in south-western France and made a tremendous discovery. There, on the walls of the cave, were some very ancient pictures of animals.

Archaeologists and scientists became very excited when they learned of these pictures. It was not surprising, because the pictures were about 20,000 years old. They were painted on the walls of the cave by the people called Cro-Magnon who lived in Europe during the Stone Age. The Cro-Magnon artists painted their pictures with charcoal and coloured earth mixed with oil. This was their paint. Their paintbrushes were sticks, feathers—or their fingers!

Some scientists believe the Lascaux cave pictures were meant to give hunters good luck when they went after the animals shown in the paintings. After 1940, more pictures were found on cave walls in France, and also in Spain.

Left: An early Chinese bronze vessel belonging to the Shang period (14th-12th century BC). The vessel shows a tiger protecting a man.

Above: Indus Valley sculpture from the 3rd century BC.

Above: Sumerian ziggurats were thought to be the dwelling places of the gods.

Left: The all-powerful pharaohs supervised the building of their pyramids.

cattle. They learned how to make silk from the cocoon (cover) of silkworms.

The civilization in the Indus Valley of India arose 4,500 years ago. Its centres were Mohenjo-Daro and Harappa. The Indus Valley peoples grew wheat and barley, and lived in houses made from bricks. Like the Sumerians, they wrote in the form of pictures.

The Ancient Egyptians, too, used picture-writing. Their hieroglyphics (pictures) have been found by archaeologists on the great tombs which were built for the pharaohs of Egypt. Civilization began in Egypt over 4,000 years ago. Here, as in Sumer, rich people lived in great luxury. Poorer people in Ancient Egypt had to work very hard. Egyptian farmers used to irrigate, or water, their fields with water from the River Nile. They used machines like the 'shaduf', which was a bucket on a pole. You can still see Egyptians lifting water from the Nile with a 'shaduf', and pouring it on the land to water it, just as their ancestors did.

Ancient Greece

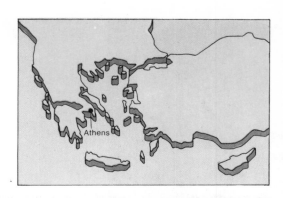

About 4,000 years ago, wandering tribes from central Europe made their homes in the country we now call Greece. These first Greeks were farmers. They lived in villages with wooden houses. They used horses and carts for transport and grew wheat in their fields.

Later, about 2,600 years ago, the Greeks produced brilliant poets, artists, scientists, builders, craftsmen and philosophers. They also developed the idea of democracy, a form of government in which all citizens have the right to choose their rulers. This idea began in Athens. Athens was one of the city states formed in Greece after about 850 BC. There were other city states in Thebes, Argos, Corinth and Sparta.

Sparta was the chief rival of Athens. It was a military state, which meant that its most important activity was war. The Spartans thought only weak people liked comfort, good food, art, music, poetry or philosophy as the Athenians did. Spartan boys and girls were trained in special schools to make them tough and strong.

Life in Athens was quite different. There, houses had comfortable furniture, and floors made of beautiful mosaics. Craftsmen

Right: A map of Ancient Greece.

Below: The temple of Athena at Delphi, built about AD 300.

Below right: The philosopher Socrates (469-399 BC). He believed that there should be discussion about all aspects of life because wisdom came from knowledge and badness came from ignorance.

The Greek Gods

The Greeks believed their gods lived in a palace above the clouds on Mount Olympus. Zeus and Hera, father and mother of the gods, sat on beautiful thrones in the palace. Zeus' throne was made of black marble and gold. Its seven steps were in the seven colours of the rainbow. Hera's throne was made of shining crystal, decorated with golden cuckoos. In front of Zeus and Hera sat five gods and five goddesses. One of these gods was Poseidon, god of the sea, rivers and horses. Demeter was the corn goddess. The Romans called her 'Ceres'. From this name, we get our word 'cereal'. Although the gods lived on Mount Olympus, they often disguised themselves as humans and visited the Earth.

Left: The gown which was worn by most Greek men and women was called the *chiton*. It was worn at either knee- or ankle-length and was usually made of wool.

Right: Throwing the discus was one of the most popular sports in Ancient Greece. It was always included in the Olympic Games, which were held in Greece for over 1,000 years.

Right: A Hoplite, a heavily-armed Greek soldier who, with his comrades, fought in close formation. Hoplites replaced the role of chariots and cavalry.

made mosaics by forming a sort of patterned 'carpet' from small coloured stones. The Athenians loved to play music on lyres or flutes, and they admired beauty in sculpture and architecture. They also liked to see plays performed in theatres and discussed the ideas of great philosophers.

Like other Greeks, Athenians were fond of sport. The Olympic Games were begun in Greece in 776 BC.

If the Spartans, or anyone else, thought Athenians were weak because they lived comfortable lives, they were wrong. The Athenians were brave, skilful fighters. They won many wars against their enemies, including Sparta and Persia. The Athenian navy also won great victories. In 480 BC Athenian ships helped to defeat the Persian fleet at the battle of Salamis. This was a splendid triumph, because the Greek fleet was much smaller than the Persian fleet.

Greek merchants were also brave, adventurous people. They sailed to places all round the Mediterranean Sea and often set up colonies there.

Unfortunately, there were many quarrels among the Greek city states and later, this made it possible for powerful enemies to conquer them. First, King Philip of Macedonia made himself ruler of all Greece in 338 BC. Then, in 130 BC, the Romans overcame the Greeks and Greece became part of the Roman Empire.

The ideas of the Greeks survived, though. Today, many countries have democratic governments, just like the Athenians. Also, many of our ideas about science, philosophy, art, architecture, music and theatre come from those of the Greeks.

The Roman Empire

In the 8th century BC, two small villages stood on the Palatine Hill above the River Tiber in Italy. The villagers were farmers. They lived in thatch-roofed huts made of wood and wickerwork and covered in clay.

It seems amazing that these villages could grow into one of the mightiest powers Europe has ever known. But that is what happened. From these villages there grew the city of Rome. From the city of Rome, there grew the Roman Empire.

Rome Becomes a Republic

At first, the Romans were ruled, not by emperors, but by kings. The trouble was, some of these kings were cruel tyrants. The Romans decided to get rid of them. In 510 BC, they threw out the Etruscan king, Tarquinius, and made Rome into a republic. The republic was governed by two consuls and a powerful senate, made up of aristocrats or patricians. The poorer people, called plebeians, were represented by elected tribunes. The Romans, both patrician and plebeian, hated kings. The famous dictator and general Julius Caesar was murdered in 44 BC because some people thought he wanted to make himself king in Rome.

Right: A map of the Roman Empire.

Above: Augustus became the first emperor of Rome in 29 BC.

Right: Two consuls were elected every year to govern the Roman Empire.

Below: The remains of the Forum in Rome. Meetings were held there.

Caesar was the greatest and most powerful of all the Roman generals who led the Roman Army. Rome's army was by far the best organized and most disciplined of its time. Their victories built up an empire which finally stretched from the north of England east to the deserts of Arabia.

A Fine Existence

Life inside the empire could be very comfortable. Rich Romans lived in splendid mansions warmed by hypocausts. This was an early central heating system whereby heat from fires in the basement was spread through pipes into the hollow walls of the rooms. At great banquets held in these mansions, people lay on couches and ate enormous meals of meat, fish, cheese, vegetables and fruit. While they ate and drank, they were entertained by dancers, musicians and poets. There were also many

people in Rome whose lives were very hard. The poor lived in blocks of flats called *insulae* (islands). Insulae were usually badly built and often fell down, killing many people. Others died in fires which burned down the insulae or from the diseases caused by dirt and lack of hygiene in their homes.

The life led by slaves was even harder. Some became gladiators and fought in the arena to entertain huge crowds. When a gladiator fell or was injured, the crowd could decide whether or not his opponent should kill him. People also watched wild animals fighting in the arena, and enjoyed the very dangerous chariot races held in the Circus. The charioteers were usually slaves, like the gladiators.

Romulus and Remus

The Romans believed that their city was founded, in 753 BC, by the twins Romulus and Remus. According to Roman legend, the twins were thrown into the River Tiber by a great-uncle who was jealous of them. They floated down the river and came ashore near the place where Rome now stands. There, they were fed by a she-wolf and eventually rescued by a shepherd.

When they were building the city of Rome, Remus made fun of the city wall which Romulus was building. For this, Romulus killed him. Later, Romulus became the first king of Rome. When he died, Romulus was believed to have become a war god called Quirinus.

Top: Gladiators were usually slaves who fought with weapons to entertain the Roman crowds. The most famous gladiator was Spartacus, who led the other slaves into revolt. He, however, was killed, as were about 6,000 of his followers.

Above: Roman shopkeepers selling their goods in the market place.

The Empire Crumbles

Far away from Rome, out on the borders of the empire, the Roman Army stood guard against wild barbarian invaders. As long as the Army was strong, the inhabitants of the empire could lead their lives in peace and travel the magnificent Roman roads in safety. However, in the 5th century AD, the Roman Army was finding it more and more difficult to keep back the barbarians. Rome itself was attacked, by the Visigoths (AD 410) and the Vandals (AD 455). Later, more and more barbarians flooded into the empire. At last, in AD 476 a barbarian called Odoacer made himself king of Italy. So, after 750 years, the Roman Empire came to an end in Europe.

Civilizations of Asia and Africa

About 1,200 years ago, the civilization of China was the richest and most advanced in the world. Its capital, Chang-an, was the world's largest city—more than one million people lived there. There was a rich trade in furs, jade, skins, carpets, jewels, spices and other luxuries. Very good roads were built, and in the harbours of Chinese sea ports, there were hundreds of sailing ships. These ships carried Chinese porcelain, silk and tea to other countries. Long before printing was known in Europe, the Chinese were printing books from wood blocks. They also invented gunpowder, which was used for firework displays. Like the Japanese, who copied their civilization, the Chinese loved to make ornamental gardens, with bushes, trees and pools that looked like living paintings. Chinese herbal medicine, surgery, astronomy and mathematics were also the most highly developed in the world.

Life in India

The Indians were Hindus, and they were very interested in philosophy, science, medicine and art. By about the 5th century AD, Indian mathematicians had worked out a system of numbers, and the sciences of algebra and trigonometry. Indian writers produced many wonderful books. At this time, too, the Indians developed yoga. This

The Mongols

In the year 1212, Temujin, later known as Ghenghis Khan, came to believe that he was meant to conquer the world. At the time, this sounded ridiculous. For Ghenghis was the leader of the poor, wandering Mongol tribes. However, the Mongols were splendid warriors and great fighters. The empire they conquered became the largest land empire ever known. By about 1250, it extended from eastern Europe, down into India and right across China.

Later Ghenghis' grandson, Kublai Khan, became Emperor of China. Babur, one of Ghengis' descendants, founded the Moghul (Mongol) Empire in northern India in 1526.

Above: Buddhist temples were often highly decorative.

Right: A silk-screen painting of Chinese ladies about AD 800.

was a form of meditation (thinking) and it is still practised today.

The influence of Hindu India spread to other parts of Asia, such as Malaysia, Indonesia, Kampuchea and Sri Lanka. Hindu ideas also spread throughout India and remained strong there even after India was invaded by the Muslims in about AD 700.

Above left: An earthenware statue, splashed with coloured glazes, of a tomb guardian. This dates from the Chinese T'ang Dynasty which lasted from AD 618-906.

Above: Genghis Khan (1162-1227) was the military leader of a group of people called the Mongols. His ambition was to rule the world and in 1212 his armies began to sweep through China, Asia and Persia.

Left: The kingdom of Benin produced some beautiful examples of bronze sculpture. This bronze head represents a peak in African art.

The Muslims originally came from Arabia. There, in AD 622, the prophet Muhammad founded the new religion of Islam. In less than 100 years, the Muslims, followers of Islam, had spread their religion from Spain in the west to India in the east. Islam also spread into Africa. There, the Muslim kings of the central African empire of Mali were so rich and learned that their fame was known in Europe.

One of the richest was Mansa Musa who became king of Mali in 1307. Mansa used to sit on a throne of ebony decorated with elephant tusks. All his weapons of war were made of solid gold. Timbuktu, capital of Mali, was known as a great centre of Muslim learning and trade.

There were other great trading civilizations in Africa. The Kingdom of Ghana (not the Ghana of today), founded in about AD 300, was known as the Land of Gold because of its rich trade in that metal. Axum, on the east coast of Africa, had a very valuable trade in ivory. On the east African coast, too, Muslim cities like Malindi had ships in their harbours which were loaded with silk, ivory and gold.

Later, in west Africa, there arose the kingdom of Benin. This was a great centre of art and culture, deep inside the forests. The bronze sculptures produced by Benin artists after the 15th century AD were such that Europeans thought they were as beautiful and inspiring as the work of Renaissance artists.

Civilizations of America

The first inhabitants of the Americas came from Asia. About 20,000 years ago, they began crossing a land bridge now covered by the Bering Strait. Gradually, they spread all over North and South America. These were the people Christopher Columbus called 'Indians' when he arrived in America in 1492 because he thought that he had reached India. Most of them lived by hunting wild animals, fishing or gathering plants for food. Some had become farmers. Others had set up villages and towns after 1500 BC and had powerful chieftains as their rulers.

At about the same time, Indian civilizations began to grow up in Central and South America. The earliest was founded in about 1300 BC by the Olmecs who lived around the Gulf of Mexico.

The three Indian civilizations about which we know most arose much later. The first was the civilization of the very learned, very skilful Mayas, who lived in southern Mexico and Guatemala. By about AD 300, they were writing hieroglyphics (picture signs) and setting down their history on large stone slabs. Mayan astronomers studied the stars and knew how to calculate the length of a year. Mayan sculptors made beautiful statues and carvings, and architects built splendid pyramid temples. Then, in the 9th century AD, the Mayan civilization collapsed. The reason may have been some disease, or a war. No one yet knows for sure.

Five hundred years later, the Aztec civilization was developing in the Valley of Mexico. The Aztecs' capital city, Tenochtitlan, was an amazing place. The Spaniards who went there in 1519 found it was larger than any European city of the time. Begun in 1325, Tenochtitlan was built on Lake Texcoco. It had 60,000 houses, 350,000

Rooms of Gold and Silver

In 1532, when Pizarro arrived in Tahuantinsuyu, he made the Sapa Inca Atahualpa his prisoner. Knowing the Spaniards were greedy for gold, Atahualpa offered a magnificent ransom for his freedom: a room full of gold and two rooms of silver. The Inca people brought gold and silver statues, ornaments and other subjects from all over Tahuantinsuyu. They even took gold and silver from the walls of temples. The rooms were filled, as Atahualpa promised. But the Spaniards feared he would lead his people against them, and they put him to death.

inhabitants and was joined to the shores of the lake by three huge causeways. Each causeway was wide enough to allow ten horsemen to ride along it side by side. The Aztec ruler, Montezuma, lived in a palace which had 300 rooms and 20 entrances. The economy was based on agriculture. Aztec farmers planted chinampas, or 'floating gardens' on the lake. They also grew maize, fruit and other crops.

Top left: The map shows the empire of the Incas, which, over a period of 2,500 years, extended 4,000 km north to south over what is today Ecuador, Peru, Bolivia, Chile and north-west Argentina.

Above: Between AD 300 and 850 the Mayas built many beautiful cities, palaces and shrines. This temple is a typical example of their buildings. It is pyramid-shaped with steep staircases leading to the top.

Above: The historic meeting in 1519 between Hernando Cortes, the Spanish explorer, and Montezuma the emperor of the Aztecs.

Left: This turquoise and mosaic skull mask, found in Mexico, represents the art of the Aztecs.

Below: The lost city of the Incas, Machu Picchu, was discovered high in the Andes in 1911.

Meanwhile, in the Andes Mountains of South America, a great empire called Tahuantinsuyu (Peru) had been conquered by rulers called Sapa Incas (Supreme Lords). The empire stretched 4,000 km (2,500 miles) through the Andes mountains and encompassed almost six million people. The Incas built a system of roads to link all parts of the empire with the capital at Cuzco. Swift runners carried messages from one end of the empire to another. Like the Aztecs, the Incas worshipped the Sun, but they did not make human sacrifices as the Aztecs did. They treated conquered tribes well, and the Inca state was a 'welfare state'. Everyone had enough food, clothing and a home to live in, and everyone knew exactly his duties to society which he was obliged to carry out.

Both the Incas and the Aztecs were conquered by the same people, the Spaniards, and it happened in the same way. Both peoples believed that a white-skinned god would come across the Great Water (the Atlantic Ocean) to reclaim their lands. When the white-skinned Spaniards arrived in Mexico (1519), their leader Hernando Cortes, was mistaken for this god. In 1532, the Incas made the same mistake about the Spanish leader Francisco Pizarro. These mistakes helped the Spaniards conquer both Mexico and Peru which they afterwards ruled for 300 years.

The Middle Ages

Some historians have looked on the 1,000 years from the end of the Roman Empire to the Renaissance (see pages 76-7) as a sort of 'in between' time. This is why these thousand years have been called the Middle Ages, or medieval times.

The Romans had given Europe an organized government. When this was gone, barbarians ran wild all over western Europe. Visigoths, Vandals and other tribal nations created havoc in France and Spain. In England, the inhabitants were attacked by the Anglo-Saxons from Germany, and after the 8th century AD, by the Vikings from Scandinavia. These attackers burned villages and farms, robbed and killed the inhabitants or carried them off as slaves. They raided

Christian monasteries and murdered the monks.

People lived in village communities under the protection of a lord of the manor. This became known as the feudal system. Peasants became subjects or vassals of great noblemen. The peasants worked on the estates of their lords, who were their military commanders when fighting broke out. The nobles, in their turn, were vassals of kings or dukes. In return for the king's protection and his gifts of land, the noblemen provided him with troops in time of war.

Of course, all vassals had to be absolutely loyal and obedient to their 'liege lords'. If a vassal broke his oath or fealty (fidelity), or betrayed his lord or harmed him in any way, this was a terrible crime. Anyone who did

The Crusades

In the year 1095, Pope Urban II called on all Christian knights in Europe to go to the Holy Land of Palestine and fight against Christ's enemies, the Muslims. These wars were called the Crusades.

The First Crusade was a great success. The Crusaders took Jerusalem (1099) and set up the Kingdom of Jerusalem. People in Europe danced in joy when they heard the news. Soon, 'taking the Cross' (going on crusade) became the finest thing Christians could do.

During the next 200 years, thousands of Crusaders went to the Holy Land on a total of eight Crusades. But not all went to fight for the sake of Christ. Some went because they loved war, others because they wanted to win riches and lands.

Top: In 1348, the Black Death reached Europe from China. It was caused by a virus carried by fleas which lived on rats. It killed up to a third of the population of Europe.

Above: Part of the Bayeux tapestry, which represents the Norman conquest of England in 1066. It is one of the best records we have of feudal life.

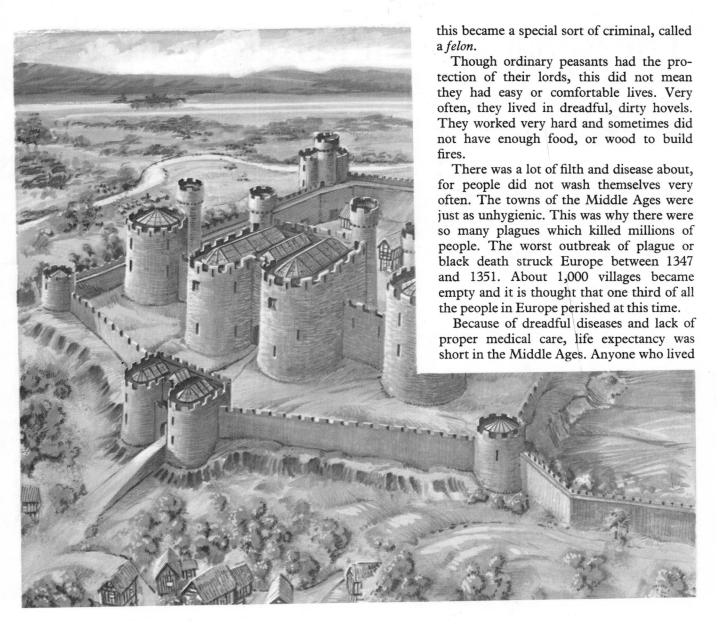

this became a special sort of criminal, called a *felon*.

Though ordinary peasants had the protection of their lords, this did not mean they had easy or comfortable lives. Very often, they lived in dreadful, dirty hovels. They worked very hard and sometimes did not have enough food, or wood to build fires.

There was a lot of filth and disease about, for people did not wash themselves very often. The towns of the Middle Ages were just as unhygienic. This was why there were so many plagues which killed millions of people. The worst outbreak of plague or black death struck Europe between 1347 and 1351. About 1,000 villages became empty and it is thought that one third of all the people in Europe perished at this time.

Because of dreadful diseases and lack of proper medical care, life expectancy was short in the Middle Ages. Anyone who lived

Above: Each medieval town or city had a castle which served as a means of defence.

Left: King John signed the Magna Carta in 1215. It considerably lessened his power over the English barons.

to the age of 40 was thought to be old. In the face of invasion, war and disease, the Roman Catholic Church served as a guardian of intellectual life in Europe. In the monasteries and later, in a few universities, the study of philosophy, history and Latin survived. Art was preserved in richly illustrated scripts called illuminated manuscripts, in church decoration, and in the building of the great cathedrals. The Church became a strong unifying force in a period when society was torn in many directions.

75

The Renaissance and Reformation

Because life was so dangerous and uncertain in the Middle Ages (pages 74-5), most people had no time for learning, art or poetry. Few people could even read or write. All they thought about was how to survive and avoid death or slavery at the hands of their enemies. However, learning, education and the arts did not die out altogether. People became interested in these subjects again after about 1450, when Europe was a much more peaceful place. About that time, there began, in Italy, a 'Renaissance' or rebirth of interest in the civilizations of Ancient Greece and Rome. The Renaissance did not end there, however. There were new facts to be learned about science, astronomy, art and also about the world.

Discovering the World

Previously, European ships had only sailed around the coasts of Europe and in the Mediterranean Sea. Now, great voyages of exploration were made across the oceans. In 1492, Columbus reached America. Between 1519 and 1522, Ferdinand Magellan's ship made the first voyage round the world. This proved that the world was round. Before, most people thought it was flat.

Above: Johann Gutenberg (1397-1468) invented printing with movable type.

Left: Leonardo da Vinci (1452-1519) left behind many notebooks full of his thoughts and anatomical drawings.

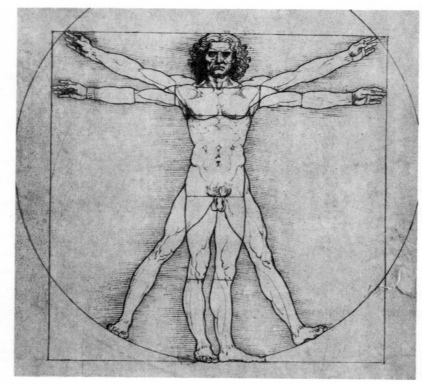

In the Middle Ages, people thought the Earth was the centre of the Universe and that the Sun and other planets revolved around it. Renaissance astronomers proved this was not true. Instead, the Polish astronomer, Copernicus, found the Earth and the planets went round the Sun, and others used improved instruments to back up his findings.

Renaissance artists painted pictures that were quite different from those painted before. Until then, paintings had looked rather unreal. The people shown in them seemed rather 'flat'. In Renaissance paintings, people looked more as they did in real life. The artists and also sculptors who made statues were following Greek and Roman ideas of how people should look.

Painting the Sistine Chapel

Michelangelo, the great sculptor, produced many beautiful works of art. One of his greatest works, was the painting on the ceiling of the Sistine Chapel in Rome. This consisted of 145 separate pictures. They showed scenes from the Bible and took Michelangelo four years to complete (1508-1512). Two of the most famous scenes are the Creation of Adam and the Fall of Man, when Adam and Eve were forced out of the Garden of Eden.

Michelangelo worked while standing or lying on scaffolding (a tower made of wooden poles and planks). For hours on end, he painted his pictures looking upwards at the ceiling to see what he was doing. His arms and neck ached terribly, and paint dripped into his eyes and beard. Today, this painting can still be seen in the Sistine Chapel.

Above: Galileo Galilei (1564-1642) was an Italian astronomer and scientist who conducted many experiments.

Left: Martin Luther (1483-1546) pinned up his protests against the authority of the Church in 1517.

Below: A map showing the extent of the Reformation in Europe. John Calvin (1509-1564) founded the Calvinist Churches.

The Spread of Ideas

The printing press developed in about 1439 by the German, Johann Gutenberg, helped to spread these new ideas. Ideas spread by means of printed books made people question and criticize everything about them. In particular, they began to question religion and how it was taught by the Church.

This led to the serious split in the Christian Church known as the Reformation. In 1517, a monk called Martin Luther protested about some of the practices of the Church. The people who agreed with Luther became known as 'Protestants'. There were now two Churches instead of one: the Catholic Church, which remained loyal to the Pope in Rome, and the Protestant Church, made up of people who did not want the Pope to rule over them. Luther's ideas and his new Church soon spread to Sweden and to Denmark.

The Reformation came to England under King Henry VIII. When Henry asked the Pope for permission to divorce his wife, Catherine of Aragon, the Pope refused him. The King was angry and declared that the Pope did not have supreme power. Henry replaced the Pope as head of the Church of England and divorced Catherine. In 1534, Henry dissolved all the monasteries in England and seized Church lands.

At about the same time, John Calvin was leading the Reformation in Switzerland. His teachings were taken up in Scotland and, in 1560, the Church of Scotland was established under Calvinist principles.

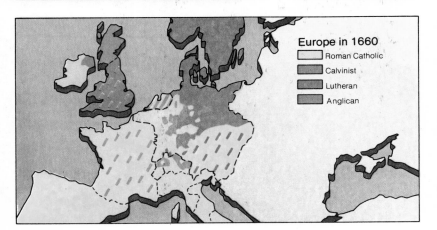

Europe in 1660
- Roman Catholic
- Calvinist
- Lutheran
- Anglican

The Industrial Revolution

The word 'revolution' means a turning round, or a complete change in the way things are done. A very important change of this kind took place between 1733 and about 1840. It was called the Industrial Revolution. During this time, machines began to do much of the work which people formerly did by hand. A large number of people had no alternative but to work on these machines in factories, instead of working as craftsmen and craftswomen in their own homes.

This first happened in northern England, with the spinning and weaving of cloth. For centuries, they had been done by hand. Then, in 1733, John Kay invented a machine which could throw a weaving shuttle from side to side on a loom ten times more quickly than weavers could do it by hand. This machine was called the Flying Shuttle and it put many weavers out of work.

James Hargreaves' Spinning Jenny (1764-69) could do the work of eight hand spinners. Richard Arkwright's Water Frame (1769) was a machine driven by water which twisted thread to make a harder, stronger

Above: In 1812, riots broke out by unemployed workers against the use of machines.

Below: The Water Frame was invented in 1769 by Richard Arkwright.

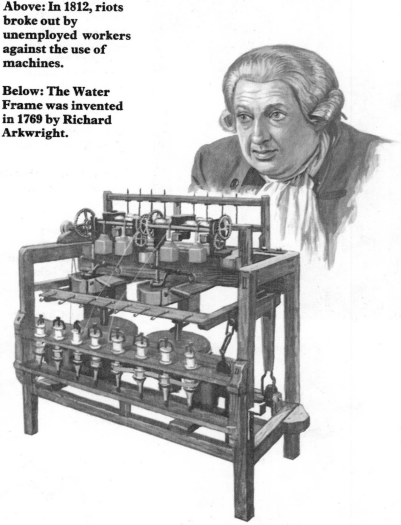

Canals and Railways

By greatly increasing production, the Industrial Revolution created a need for improved methods of moving goods. At the same time, the new technology also provided methods of solving problems of transport.

Manufacturers found that it was both cheaper and safer to ship goods on water than on land. They began to build canals across the countryside. The first canal in Britain was finished in 1776 and carried coal from collieries in Bridgewater to Manchester, where it fuelled the growing cotton industry.

The first railways were developed when engineers discovered that Watt's steam engine could be used to make a self-propelled engine that would pull a carriage on a rail. A Cornishman, Robert Trevithick, built the first steam-powered locomotive in 1804.

Some other famous early locomotives were William Hedley's *Puffing Billy*, built in 1813, and George and Robert Stephenson's *Rocket*, built for a competition sponsored by the Liverpool and Manchester Railway in 1829. The *Rocket* made history when it ran at 30 miles per hour, winning its designers a prize of £500.

Left: Lord Shaftesbury (1801-1885) promoted new laws which benefited workers in factories and mines.
Below: Iron foundries and coal mines provided machines and power for the new factories.
Bottom: Young children worked long hours in factories and mines under harsh conditions.

yarn than could be made by hand. The Water Frame could be operated by children and manufacturers began to hire even very young children to run the machines.

Most important of all was the steam engine developed by James Watt in 1764-5. At first, most large machines of the Industrial Revolution were driven by water power. But machines powered by steam engines could work better, longer and more reliably. They created a large demand for coal as a fuel. This led to an increase in deep coal mining rather than open-cast mines. It also led to an increase in the iron industry as machines made of wood were no longer strong enough to withstand the power of the steam engines.

The new factories also required large quantities of raw material and, for a time, the demand for raw cotton helped to perpetuate the slave trade. Traders from Liverpool would take black slaves from Africa to America where their labour was used to produce cotton. In exchange, the traders would receive raw cotton for English cotton mills.

Before long, machinery was being used in other industries, like pottery making and machines were introduced into factories in other European countries.

Appalling Conditions

Conditions of work in the factories were terrible. At first, machinery was not fenced in, and many workers were killed or badly injured when they fell against them. Children were made to work so long and hard that they often fell sleeping into the machines. The air was stifling and thick with dust and in some rooms the workers were soaked to the skin with steam, which led to rheumatism and consumption.

Men, women and children worked 13 or 14 hours a day for very low wages. They had to live in dirty and overcrowded hovels because they could not afford anything else. They were often ill because they worked so hard in such unhealthy conditions and because they never had enough to eat. If they could not work they had to find someone to take their place, or pay a fine.

It was a long time before laws were passed in Britain to improve this dreadful situation. After 1842, there were laws which prohibited women and children from working such long hours, but bad conditions in factories and mines persisted well into the 20th century.

79

Great Revolutions

One night in 1773, a group of Americans crept on board three ships in Boston harbour. They grappled the ship's cargo of tea and threw it into the water. This was later called 'The Boston Tea Party'. Their protest against a tax on tea was one of the first defiant acts of American colonists against their British rulers.

Following the Boston Tea Party, the Parliament in London passed other laws that the colonists found intolerable. Many colonists felt that their rights as free people were not being respected by the King and Parliament. They wanted to have a say in decisions about the taxes they paid, the way they carried on trade, and how they would be governed. In July 1776, the colonists voted to declare their independence from Britain.

The ideas set forth in this Declaration of Independence were democratic ideas, similar to those of the ancient Athenians. Naturally, the British and other governments did not like these ideas because they had a lot to lose. At that time, European countries were rather like the personal possessions of the king or the 'ruling class' of nobles. They owned all the land and most

Above: In protest against the British attempt to control their taxes, Bostonians boarded an East India Company ship and threw the cargo of tea into the harbour.

Left: On 14th July 1789, the French people stormed the Bastille prison in Paris, releasing prisoners, killing the governor and burning the building. This marked the beginning of the French Revolution.

The Long March

Between October 1934 and October 1935, the Chinese communist leader Mao Tse-tung made an amazing escape from his great enemy and rival, Chiang Kai-shek, the general of the government forces. Mao set out with 100,000 men on a journey of 9,656 kilometres (6,000 miles) right across the vast land of China. The journey took 368 days. During that time, Mao and his army crossed 18 ranges of mountains and 24 rivers. Mao and his army fought 15 big battles with their enemies. Only 5,000 of Mao's men survived to reach safety in a town near the Great Wall of China. This meant that 19 out of every 20 communists who set out with Mao had died on the way. Those who survived the Long March are very highly regarded in China today.

of the wealth, and governed exactly as they wished.

The governing class did not want to share their power with the people. The people, however, took their power from them, by force in revolutions. In America, the colonists fought a long war against the British. In 1781, they gained their independence and formed the country known today as the United States of America.

In France, ordinary people paid very heavy taxes while nobles, churchmen and the king lived in luxury. The French thought this was unjust. Revolution broke out in 1789. The king, Louis XVI, was overthrown and executed. So was his queen, Marie Antoinette, and thousands of nobles.

After this, there were many revolutions in which people rose up against bad rulers or foreign masters. In 1804, the slaves in the Caribbean colony of Haiti threw out their French masters. By 1830, the Spanish colonies in South America had driven out the Spaniards. The French again rebelled against their kings in 1830 and 1848. The year 1848, in fact, saw revolutions all over Europe, in Italy, Austria, Hungary and Germany.

These European revolutions were defeated, sometimes very cruelly. However, the rulers who did this could not kill the wish of ordinary people to be governed in a democratic way. What is more, even greater and more violent revolutions were about to happen. These were the 'Communist' revolutions inspired by the ideas of Karl Marx (1818-83). Karl Marx believed that countries belonged to the people who lived

in them, and that the rightful rulers were not kings or nobles, but ordinary workers.

The first successful Communist revolution took place in Russia in 1917. The Tsar (king) Nicholas II believed he had been chosen by God to rule Russia. However, ordinary peasants and workers lived in dreadful poverty. Led by the Communists, the Russians overthrew Nicholas. Later, he and his family were murdered. Russia has had a Communist government ever since.

In China, too, people were desperately poor and very harshly governed. Here, in 1949, the Communists led by Mao Tse-tung achieved a Communist revolution.

Above: The last Tsar of Russia, Nicholas II and his wife Alexandra. His rule was overthrown by the Bolsheviks and he and his family were executed.

Below: Mao Tse-tung (1893-1976). His influence left its mark on many aspects of Chinese political, social and cultural life.

The World Wars

Stretcher bearers, carrying wounded soldiers to safety, often had to struggle knee-high through the mud of the battlefield. The opposing armies on the Western Front sheltered in trenches—deep ditches—dug in the muddy ground.

High above the battlefield, pilots from the warring countries fought each other in their flimsy airplanes. Those who shot down several enemy planes became famous as 'aces'.

The two worst wars in history were both fought in the 1900s. World War I lasted from 1914 to 1918, and World War II from 1939 to 1945. In each, tens of millions of people were killed, and millions more were injured or left homeless.

WORLD WAR I

World War I was caused by rivalry between certain large countries. The *Central Powers*, on one side, included Germany, Austria-Hungary and Turkey. The *Allies*, on the other side, included Britain and France. The Allies won.

Russia was one of the Allies until the Russian Revolution of 1917. In 1917, too, the USA joined the Allies.

Terrible battles were fought on the Western Front in France and Belgium. Often, thousands of men died just to gain a few metres of ground.

Events of World War I

Aug. 1914 Germany won the Battle of Tannenberg against the Russians.
Apr. 1915 Poison gas first used in war.
May 1916 Battle of Jutland. British and German High Seas fleets clash.
Dec. 1916 Allies won the Battle of Verdun, in France.
Sep. 1916 British used first tanks.
Feb. 1917 German submarines started to attack all ships friendly to Allies.
Aug. 1917 Germans halted Russian attack.
Nov. 1917 Allied tank attack at Cambrai.
Mar. 1918 Last German offensive.
Aug. 1918 Allies attacked on Western Front.
Nov. 3, 1918 Austria made peace.
Nov. 11, 1918 Germany made peace.

WORLD WAR II

In World War I, great armies fought each other for months at a time without moving more than a few kilometres. But World War II was a war of movement. Powerful forces of fast-moving tanks and guns fought their way deep into enemy territory. Parachute troops dropped from the air behind enemy lines. And huge fleets of airplanes bombed enemy cities.

More than 50 countries took part in the war. Most were among the *Allies*, who included Britain, the Commonwealth countries, France, Russia and the USA. Opposing them were the *Axis* countries, including Germany, Italy and Japan.

At the beginning of the war, German armies quickly seized much of Europe. In 1941, they invaded Russia. In the same year, Japan attacked the USA without warning. The Japanese, too, had success at first, and took over many colonial countries of Asia.

Later in the war, the Russians began to push the Germans back. Allied armies invaded western Europe, and defeated the

Winston Churchill was British prime minister for most of the war. Even when the allies were losing every battle, he believed in victory.

Dictators in conference. Adolf Hitler (left) led Germany into a war of conquest that ended in defeat. Benito Mussolini (centre) gave him Italy's help. With the dictators is the skilful German General von Kluge.

Axis forces there. In May 1945, Germany surrendered. And the war with Japan ended shortly afterwards when the Americans dropped atomic bombs on two Japanese cities.

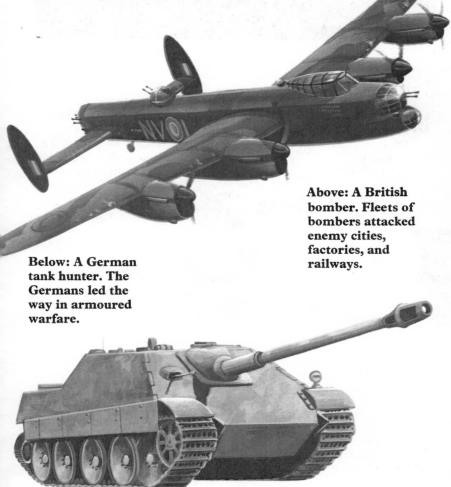

Above: A British bomber. Fleets of bombers attacked enemy cities, factories, and railways.

Below: A German tank hunter. The Germans led the way in armoured warfare.

Events of World War II

Sep. 1, 1939 Germany invaded Poland.
Sep. 3, 1939 France and Britain declared war on Germany.
June 22, 1940 France surrendered.
June 22, 1941 Axis invaded Russia.
Dec. 7, 1941 Japan attacked American naval base at Pearl Harbor.
Oct. 1942 British offensive against Axis troops at El Alamein.
Feb. 1943 Germans at Stalingrad surrendered to Russians.
Sep. 3, 1943 Allies landed in Italy.
Mar. 1944 Japanese reached the Indian border.
June 6, 1944 D-day. Allies invaded Normandy, and began their drive towards Germany.
Oct. 1944 American naval victory over Japanese in Battle for Leyte Gulf.
Jan. 1945 Russians captured Warsaw.
May 7, 1945 Germany surrendered.
Aug. 1945 Americans dropped atomic bombs.
Sep. 1945 Japan surrendered.

The World Today

For much of history, the lives people led were almost the same as those led by their parents and grandparents. This situation is not the same for people who live in the world today. This is because scientific progress has been very fast in the last two or three decades.

More Gadgets

Twenty years ago, for example, most people did not have central heating, television, transistor radios, tape recorders, washing machines, dishwashers and refrigerators. Today many homes have some or all of these objects. Not so very long ago, most people in Europe did not find it easy to travel to other continents. It is now possible to fly to the other side of the world in a day.

Jet aircraft and machines in the home are only some of the machines which have changed people's lives in the last few years. In offices, for example, there are now electric typewriters, photocopying machines and electronic calculators.

Above: Nuclear power plants are being built all over the world to replace coal and oil as a source of power. The first of these plants was built in Britain in 1936.

Left: A United Nations Observer team. These people help to keep the peace between countries who are in dispute with each other.

Living in the Future

Today, some planners think that in the future, people will live in cities built on the sea. These cities, they believe, might solve the problem of overcrowding in cities today.

The Sea City which these planners have designed is built inside a heated lagoon. Around the city, there is a high wall to keep out the cold winds from the sea and to stop storms from disturbing the calm waters of the lagoon. The inhabitants of Sea City will live in large floating blocks of flats. Covered moving pathways run from the flats to the shops. People can travel around the lagoon in electrically-powered boats.

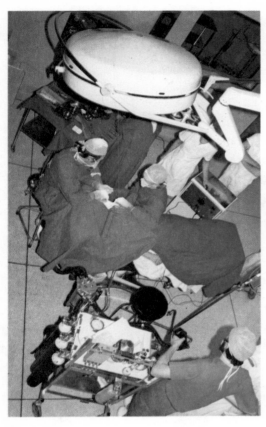

Left: The work of the medical profession has been greatly helped by the development of more life-saving machines.

Below: Jumbo jets are a fine example of the high degree of technology which has been developed by the aircraft industry within the last few decades.

Bottom: *Telstar* was the first active communications satellite to be launched by the United States in 1962.

Today we think it is quite normal for astronauts to travel to the Moon, or to see television programmes that come from the other side of the world. Thirty years ago, these things seemed practically impossible. It was also impossible to think that rockets could be sent from Earth to carry spacecraft to other planets like Venus, Mars, Jupiter and Saturn. Today, men have lived for over six months in space stations, thousands of kilometres above the Earth's surface. And there are other artificial satellites far out in Space which circle the Earth and send back information about the weather and military installations.

Medical Progress

Medicine, too, has made great advances in the last few years. It was only after 1945 that doctors were able to make regular use of antibiotics to cure infections. There are also new drugs and medicines to help reduce pain, and doctors can now cure many diseases which once killed or crippled thousands of people. New surgical techniques allow doctors to replace joints in the

body with artificial ones and to transplant organs such as the kidneys and even the human heart.

Of course, these advances have not benefited everyone. In parts of South America, Asia and Africa, life is still poor and backward. Fortunately, though, international organizations like the United Nations can send doctors, scientists, teachers and engineers to help poorer countries. With this help, poorer countries can improve the health, farming methods, industry and education of their citizens.

85

Flags of the World

43 Canada

42 USA

41 Mexico

40 Venezuela

39 Peru

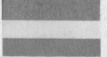
38 Brazil

37 Bolivia

36 Chile

35 Argentina

34 Angola

33 Zaire

32 Nigeria

31 Mauritania

30 Morocco

29 Algeria

28 Libya

NORTH AMERICA

SOUTH AMERICA

ATLANTIC OCEAN

PACIFIC OCEAN

EU

AFR

1

3

2

9

8

10

12

30

29

31

32

43

42

41

40

39

38

37

36

35

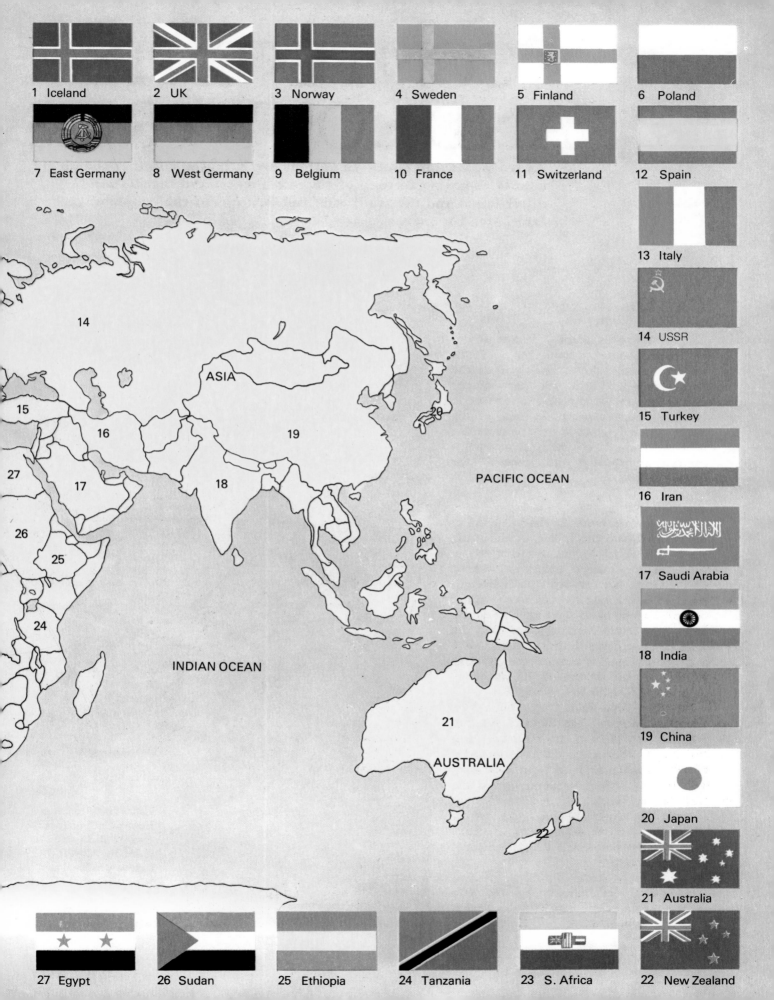

1 Iceland
2 UK
3 Norway
4 Sweden
5 Finland
6 Poland
7 East Germany
8 West Germany
9 Belgium
10 France
11 Switzerland
12 Spain
13 Italy
14 USSR
15 Turkey
16 Iran
17 Saudi Arabia
18 India
19 China
20 Japan
21 Australia
22 New Zealand
23 S. Africa
24 Tanzania
25 Ethiopia
26 Sudan
27 Egypt

ASIA

PACIFIC OCEAN

INDIAN OCEAN

AUSTRALIA

CONTINENTS AND COUNTRIES

As transport and communications are bringing continents and countries nearer to each other, our interest and fascination in other lands and the traditions and customs of the people of those lands steadily increases.

Asia

Asia is the world's largest continent. It also has more people than any other continent. Its area equals almost one-third of the Earth's total land area, and nearly 60 per cent of the total world population live there. In Asia's huge expanse lie some of the world's driest deserts and some of its wettest regions. The world's highest mountains contrast majestically with some of the deepest depressions.

The Land

Asia's shores are washed by the Arctic Ocean in the north and the Indian Ocean in the south. The Ural Mountains separate the continent from Europe in the west, and the Pacific Ocean lies between Asia and North America in the east. In the south-west it borders Europe along the Caspian Sea, the Black Sea, and the Mediterranean. Only the Suez Canal separates Asia from Africa. And in the north-east, the gap between Asia and North America narrows to 72 kilometres (45 miles) across the Bering Strait.

Northern Asia is a vast, cold, often featureless region that includes Russian Siberia. Several huge rivers drain these lowlands. In the middle of the continent the Himalayan mountain range forms a towering triangular mass that is sometimes called 'the roof of the world'. It includes Mount Everest, the world's highest peak, which soars up to 8,848 metres (29,028 feet). Mongolia, parts of western China, and Tibet meet in this central region.

To the south of the Himalayas the land forms a series of ancient plateaux. The teeming nations of Bangladesh, India, Pakistan, Bhutan, and Afghanistan are found

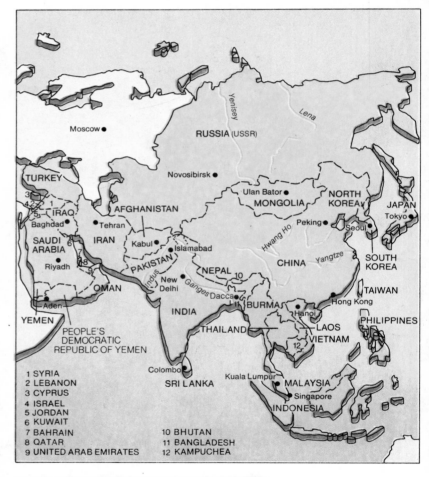

1 SYRIA
2 LEBANON
3 CYPRUS
4 ISRAEL
5 JORDAN
6 KUWAIT
7 BAHRAIN
8 QATAR
9 UNITED ARAB EMIRATES

10 BHUTAN
11 BANGLADESH
12 KAMPUCHEA

Left: The Dead Sea lies on the borders of Jordan and Israel. It is 395 m (1,296 ft) below sea-level and is so salty that swimmers can float easily on its surface without sinking.

there. To the south-west the land dries out into a region known as the Middle East, where Asia nudges Europe. Turkey, Iran, and the Arabian Peninsula form part of the area.

South East Asia is that part of the continent located to the east of India and south of China. It is a region largely made up of forested islands and peninsulas, and includes Malaysia, Vietnam, Indonesia, Thailand, and the Philippines.

In the extreme east, a region known as the Far East, is a mountainous area, parts of which are regularly disturbed by earthquakes. Korea, China, and Japan are found there, and their combined populations add up to more than half the people of Asia.

Rivers, Lakes and Deserts

Some of the world's greatest rivers water the huge plains of Asia. In India the Ganges and Brahmaputra flow into the Bay of Bengal, and the Indus empties into the Arabian Sea. The Hwang Ho and the Yangtse rise in Tibet and flow through China. The Ob, Lena, and Yenisei, which wind across northern Russia, are frozen over parts of their courses during six months of the year. In the warmer parts of Asia, river valleys and deltas (flat areas at the mouths of rivers) are the chief population centres.

Most of the Middle East is hot desert and is thinly-populated except near the few rivers and around oases (waterholes). There are also bleak, cold deserts in the interior of Asia, notably the vast Gobi desert of China and Mongolia.

Top: Mount Everest, 8,848 m (29,028 ft) high, soars above the Khumbu glacier in Nepal.

Above: Tropical rain forest in Indonesia. Indonesia consists of about 3,000 mostly mountainous islands.

Left: The River Ganges at Varanasi, in India. Many Hindus gather here to bathe in the waters of this holy river.

Asia (2)

Asia has more people than all the other continents put together and nearly 60 out of every 100 people in the world live there. Its population increases by about 100,000 every day.

Asia has people from all the chief racial groups—Mongoloid, Caucasoid and Negroid. They speak hundreds of different languages and belong to many different religions of which Buddhism and Hinduism have the most followers. Some live in remote

Tibet

This Chinese province is the highest country in the world. The plateau of Tibet is more than 4,876·8 metres (16,000 feet) above sea-level and many summits are 6,096 metres (20,000 feet) in height. Few people can live there as it is so high and so cold and most of those who do live in the south of the country and can earn a living from their livestock which produce leather, skins, wool, butter, milk, eggs, meat and cheese. Many men studied there to become Buddhist monks or *lamas* before the Chinese took over in 1958.

desert areas. Others live in the most crowded cities of the world. One of the main problems in Asia is how to grow enough food for the population. Millions of Asians live at subsistence level—they have barely enough food to eat. Not all Asian countries are poor. Japan, for example, is one of the richest countries in the world.

The Taj Mahal at Agra in India is often called 'the world's most beautiful building'. It was built in the 1600s by the Emperor Shah Jahan as a tomb for his wife.

Chinese children enjoy a meal at school. Rice and wheat are the most important foods for hundreds of millions of Asians.

Far left: Asians in many countries find work in the rice paddies—small fields surrounded by low mud walls. Many Asians, however, are now receiving a good education and are leaving the land for work in the cities.

Left: Tokyo, the capital of Japan, is one of the world's largest and most crowded cities. Most of the streets have no names, but each block of buildings is numbered.

Important Dates in the History of Asia

3000s BC The Sumerians developed the first city civilization in Mesopotamia in south-western Asia.

2500s BC Cities were built in the Indus Valley in the Indian Peninsula.

1500s BC Beginning of the Shang dynasty in China, probably the first dynasty.

1500s BC The Aryans from northern Asia settled in the Indus Valley.

1200s BC The Israelites left Egypt.

500s BC The Buddha was born in India, and Confucius was born in China.

336-323 BC Empire of Alexander the Great.

300s BC The building of the Great Wall of China began.

about 6 BC Jesus Christ born in Palestine.

AD 570 Muhammad born in Arabia

618 Beginning of the T'ang dynasty in China.

1206 Genghis Khan led the Mongols in the conquest of China and Central Asia

1264 Kublai Khan began his rule of the Mongol Empire.

1526 Babar created the Mogul Empire in India.

1500s European traders and adventurers began to visit Asia.

1757 The British East India Company began its rule in Bengal.

1774 Warren Hastings was appointed the first British governor-general of India.

1857-58 The Indian Mutiny

1876 Queen Victoria was declared Empress of India

1911 End of the Chinese Empire.

1939-45 World War II. The Japanese invaded many countries, but later suffered defeat.

1940s-1960s Many Asian countries became independent of colonial rule.

Asia (3)

Natural Resources

Much of Asia's soil is useless for growing food. As a result, farming land is precious all over the continent. Rice, which is the main food for most Asians, is often grown in flooded paddy fields that are terraced all the way down steep hillsides, to take advantage of every cultivable scrap of land.

In the drier parts of Asia other field crops are grown. These include cereals, such as maize, wheat, millet, and soybeans; and items for selling abroad, such as tobacco, tea, rubber, dates, jute, olives, and cotton.

Asian forests provide some of the world's most valuable timber. This includes pine and teak.

Animals are used mainly for work and transportation. Among such animals are reindeer (in the north), yaks, horses, donkeys, camels, buffalo, and elephants. Cattle, sheep, and goats are raised mainly for meat.

A Wealth of Minerals

Asia is particularly rich in minerals. Most of the world's oil—its most valuable fuel in the late 1970s—comes from south-western Asia. About three-quarters of the world's tin comes from South East Asia, and China sells large quantities of tungsten and tin overseas. Turkey and the Philippines supply chromite, and manganese and mica come from India and China.

Top: Tea grown in Asia is exported all over the world. These Sri Lankan women are picking the leaves by hand.

Above: Silk is an important Asian product. It is made from the cocoon of a moth which lives on mulberry leaves.

Left: China is becoming a great manufacturing nation. This factory in Shanghai produces optical lenses.

Above: Rubber trees are native to South America but are now cultivated in South East Asia. The liquid rubber, or latex, oozes from cuts made in the bark of the trees.

Below: Rice fields in the Philippines. The young plants are grown in flooded fields, or paddies. Rice is grown widely in Asia and for many Asians it is their staple diet.

Asia's Industries

Virtually all Asia's heavy industry is located in Asian Russia, Japan, China, and Israel. Most of the other nations rely on such rural industries as handicrafts, fishing, and tourism for their income. The four major nations, especially Japan, which leads the world in many industries, produce automobiles, electric and electronic equipment, weapons, ships, precision tools, textiles, machinery, and iron and steel.

The Outlook

Many Asian nations are making desperate efforts to increase their factories and compete more closely in world markets with Japan and the Western nations. At the end of the 1970s, for example, China largely dropped its policy of self-imposed isolation started by Chairman Mao Tse-tung and openly invited Western experts to help with their industrial know-how. Other parts of Asia, such as Taiwan and Hong Kong, expanded their factories and produced a flood of cheap electronic products and watches. One major problem is that, in many nations, the population is increasing quickly. For example, India's population is rising by 2.1 per cent per year so that, every year, India must provide for an extra 12 million people. This makes it hard to raise the people's living standards.

Europe

Europe extends from the North Atlantic Ocean in the west to the Ural Mountains and the Caspian Sea in the Soviet Union. Hence, it is essentially a large peninsula (a piece of land almost totally surrounded by the sea) attached to Asia. There are dozens of smaller peninsulas. Along the Mediterranean coast the Italian Peninsula is one of the largest. Immediately to the east of this is the Balkan Peninsula, made up of Yugoslavia, Romania, Albania, Greece and European Turkey. Farther east, the Crimean Peninsula juts into the Black Sea.

In the south-western corner of the continent, separating the Mediterranean Sea from the Atlantic Ocean lies the Iberian Peninsula, made up of Spain and Portugal. The small peninsula of Denmark, in the north-west of the continent, is separated from the much larger Scandinavian Peninsula to the north by the Skagerrak and Kattegat straits. Norway, Sweden, and part of Finland make up the Scandinavian Peninsula. In the far north, the Kola Peninsula separates the White Sea from the Barents Sea.

With so many peninsulas, as well as hundreds of bays, inlets, harbours, and gulfs, Europe's coastline covers about 80,500 kilometres (50,000 miles). This is more than three times longer than Africa's coastline, although Africa is three times as big as Europe.

Some important islands lie off the mainland. The largest of these are the British Isles. Others include the Balearic Islands, Corsica, Sardinia, Sicily, and Crete.

Left: A view of Prague, the picturesque capital city of Czechoslovakia. It lies on the Moldau river.

Above: Mont Blanc is the highest mountain peak in Europe at 4,810 m (15,781 ft). It is on the French/Italian border.

Rivers and Lakes

Europe is criss-crossed by several large and important rivers. Many of these are linked to other waterways by means of canals and have become busy highways for the transportation of goods and passengers.

The longest river is the Volga, which flows north to south through the Soviet Union and empties into the Caspian Sea. Other major Russian rivers are the Don, the Dnieper, and the Dniester. Europe's second longest river is the Danube, which rises in Germany's Black Forest and flows into the Black Sea. One of the most important rivers, historically and commercially, is the Rhine. It rises in Switzerland and flows through West Germany and the Netherlands before emptying into the North Sea.

Although Europe's lakes are small compared with those of some other continents, they are among the most beautiful in the world. Millions of tourists are attracted to the lakes of Switzerland and Italy. The saltwater Caspian Sea is sometimes regarded as a lake; it is the largest inland body of water in the world.

Mountain Ranges

In the past, Europeans tended to be separated into many groups by the several high mountain ranges that stretch across the continent. But the people were never completely isolated because there were always passes through the mountains, and many of these are still in use today.

The major mountain system in southern Europe is the Alps. These mountains range from south-eastern France, through northern Italy, southern Germany, and Switzerland. Two major arms of the Alps are the Apennines, which form a great barrier down the middle of Italy; and the Carpathians, which ring the Hungarian plain. The Caucasus, which run from the Black Sea to the Caspian Sea, claim the highest peak in Europe—Mount Elbrus at 5,634 metres (18,481 feet).

Above right: Corsica, an island in the Mediterranean Sea which belongs to France. Most of Corsica consists of low mountains and rugged hills reaching down to the sea.

Right: Norway is a country of great splendour with pine-topped mountain ranges and narrow deep-sided fiords like the Sogne Fiord seen here.

Europe (2)

The People

Europe holds about 650 million people, which means that it has more people than any other continent except Asia. It is also more crowded than any of the other continents. One reason why Europe has always been so important and why so many people live there is that the continent stands at the crossroads of eastern and western nations, and northern and southern nations. The earliest civilizations grew up along the coasts of the Mediterranean and that sea for centuries was a highway for trade and colonizers, and for the exchange of new ideas.

Another reason is Europe's climate, which is generally mild, with enough rain to water the fertile soil all the year round. The warm waters of the Gulf Stream flow round Europe's western and southern coasts and keep the harbours there ice-free. The winds also help because they usually blow from the west, sweeping warm air across the continent.

Europe has many large and famous cities. London, Paris, Rome, Madrid, Dublin and other historic places attract visitors all the year round to enjoy their sights and sounds. Southern cities, such as Barcelona and Naples, where the climate is generally warm and sunny, encourage customers to sit outdoors on the sidewalk at cafe tables. More northerly centres, such as London and Oslo, are colder and wetter. They have more indoor entertainment.

Above: Artists working in the open air in the Place du Tertre, Montmartre. This quarter of Paris has long been famous as an artistic centre.

Below: Moscow lies in Europe. These visitors to Lenin's tomb are waiting outside the Kremlin, a citadel which houses the government.

The peoples of Europe can be conveniently grouped according to the languages they speak. One major group is made up of so-called Germanic peoples. These include the Germans, English, Dutch, Swedes, Norwegians, Danes, and Icelanders. The Latin peoples originally spoke Latin and are descended from the inhabitants of the Roman Empire. They are made up of Italians, Romanians, French, Portuguese, and Spanish. Russians, Bulgarians, Serbo-Croats, Poles, and Czechs belong to the Slavic group. Many of the people who live in Brittany in France, and in Wales, Scotland, and Ireland are Celts. Another group is made up of Turks, Estonians, Lapps, Finns, and Hungarians. The Albanians, Armenians, Greeks, and Basques each form separate groups of their own. More than one language is spoken in several countries. Language differences may lead to conflict if the people who speak minority languages feel that their local culture is threatened.

Left: Amsterdam, the capital of the Netherlands, was built on a system of canals. Visitors may tour the city in glass-sided motorboats like these.

Below left: The coastline of Norway is deeply indented by fiords. Many Norwegians still make their living by fishing.

Below: Venice, in northern Italy, was built on a group of islands linked by canals and bridges. It has many fine churches and palaces.

Ways of Life

Although they all live on the same continent, Europeans vary widely in their ways of life. There are many reasons for this — politics, religion, history, language and education being the main ones.

Such differences have caused many wars in the past. In the last 30 years, West European peoples have drawn closer together because of such things as increased travel and the setting up of common markets.

Europe (3)

Natural Resources

Some of the world's richest farmland is in Europe and, as a result, more than half the land is used for farming. But methods are extremely varied. In Western Europe and European Russia, farmers use the latest methods and the most up-to-date machinery. But in many southern and eastern regions primitive ploughing and hand labour is common.

Europeans produce most of their own food. This includes wheat, potatoes, barley, rye, oats, sugar beet, beans, corn, fibre flax, tobacco, olives, peas, dates, figs, grapes, and citrus fruits. Denmark, Great Britain and the Netherlands have huge dairy herds of cattle. Pigs, sheep, goats, poultry, and beef cattle are also raised in various parts of Europe for meat.

European fishermen sail the world in search of big catches. Iceland, Great Britain, Norway, the Soviet Union, and Spain are among the world's leading fishing nations.

Industrial Muscle

Industry usually means the making of things, as well as digging for minerals hidden deep in the ground, and the building of anything from offices and houses to ships and cars.

Raw materials in plenty are needed for healthy industry, and these are found in

Right: An oil production platform operating in the North Sea. During the 1970s several companies successfully drilled for oil and natural gas in these waters.

Above right: Cattle grazing on pastureland in Ireland. The mild, rainy climate of Ireland is well-suited to dairy farming.

Right: Europe is well-known for the variety and high quality of its wines. Grapes (the main ingredient of wine) are grown in sunny fields or on slopes. After harvesting, the grapes are pressed to extract their juice which is then fermented.

The European Economic Community

After World War II, when much of Europe lay divided and shattered, it became obvious to clear-thinking politicians that the only way European nations could compete against super-powers such as the United States, the Soviet Union, and Japan, was to form some kind of union for trade and commerce. In 1957 six nations (Belgium, France, Italy, Luxembourg, the Netherlands, and West Germany) formed what they called the European Economic Community (EEC), which later popularly became known as the European Common Market. In 1973 they were joined by Great Britain, Denmark, and Ireland.

various parts of Europe. Coal is one of the most important items, and three-fifths of the world's coal comes from Europe. The richest coalfields lie in East and West Germany, Great Britain, Czechoslovakia, Poland, and the Soviet Union. Half the world's iron ore is found in Europe, and a quarter of its *bauxite* (the ore from which aluminium is made). Sweden, France, and the Soviet Union lead in the production of iron ore, while bauxite is found mainly in Hungary, Yugoslavia, the Soviet Union, France, and Greece. Iron ore is used in industry to manufacture steel. The Soviet Union, Sweden, France and Spain are leading producers of iron ore.

Heavy industry is located mainly in East and West Germany, Great Britain, France, Poland, and the Soviet Union. This includes iron and steel production, machinery, and the building of cars and ships. Light industry is found in nations such as Switzerland, the Netherlands, and Belgium, where the people make clothing and process food. Traditional craftsmen, such as watch and clockmakers, are still found in the Black Forest region of Germany and in Switzerland.

In addition to coal, Europe relies on a number of other sources for power. In common with most of the rest of the world, Europeans understand that oil and natural gas reserves will run out before long. As a result, they are turning to nuclear energy, hydroelectricity (electric power obtained from falling water) and solar energy. Hydroelectricity is important in nations such as Norway and Switzerland, which have plenty of rivers flowing down steep slopes.

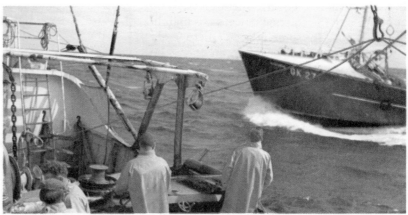

Top: Tourists resting on the steps of the Propylaea, the gateway to the Acropolis in Athens. Athens was an important city of ancient Greece and reached the height of its power in the 5th century BC. Today it is the capital city of Greece.

Above: Fishing is an important European industry. Factory ships are able to freeze or can their catches while still at sea. The north Atlantic has rich fishing grounds but now there are fears that some areas are being overfished.

Below: Harvest-time in Hungary. Like those of other nations with Communist governments, Hungary's farms are organized on a collective system. Individual farmers do not own their own land but work on state-run farms.

Africa

Africa is the second largest continent. It was once called the 'dark continent', because it was largely unexplored and thought to be covered with dense forests. Actually, forests cover less than a fifth of Africa. The rest of the land is more or less equally divided between desert and grassland.

Today, this huge region is going through a period of great change. By 1900, nearly all of Africa was under the rule of European powers. Even in 1950, only four African countries—Egypt, Ethiopia, Liberia and South Africa—were independent. But many Africans were inspired by the conviction that they should govern themselves. The opposition to the colonial powers was mainly political but, in some places, there were long, costly wars. One after another, the colonies won nationhood. Today, Europeans retain control only in southern Africa. Africa's chief problems are now economic, because many Africans are desperately poor.

The Land

The equator crosses the middle of Africa. Much of the northern half is covered by the Sahara Desert, the world's greatest desert. To the north of the Sahara, along the Mediterranean coast, lie the Arab countries of Morocco, Algeria, Tunisia, Libya, and Egypt. To the south of the Sahara are the Negro countries. The Sahara is made up mostly of shifting sand dunes and barren rocks. Oases here and there, and a fertile strip along the River Nile are the only places where farmers can raise crops. Two other, smaller, deserts are the Kalahari Desert and the Namib Desert, both in south-western Africa.

There are mountains in the north-west of the continent (the Atlas Mountains) and high plateaux in the east and south. The Drakensberg Range, with some peaks rising to more than 3,400 metres (11,000 feet), covers a large area of the south-eastern part of the continent. Africa's highest peak is Kilimanjaro, an extinct volcano in Tanzania that is 5,895 metres (19,340 feet) high.

Right: The Sahara, in northern Africa, is the largest desert in the world. It covers an area of 8,600,000 sq km (3,320,000 sq miles).

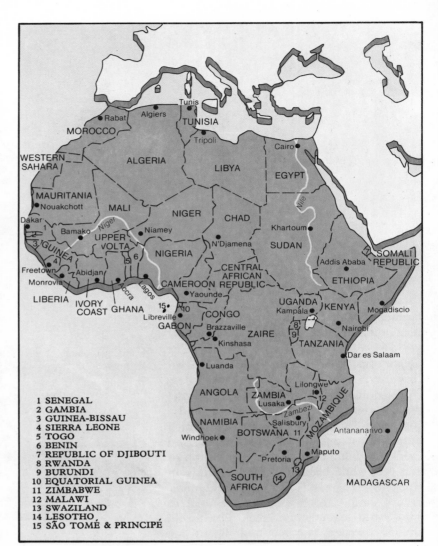

1 SENEGAL
2 GAMBIA
3 GUINEA-BISSAU
4 SIERRA LEONE
5 TOGO
6 BENIN
7 REPUBLIC OF DJIBOUTI
8 RWANDA
9 BURUNDI
10 EQUATORIAL GUINEA
11 ZIMBABWE
12 MALAWI
13 SWAZILAND
14 LESOTHO
15 SÃO TOMÉ & PRINCIPÉ

Left: Victoria Falls, one of the world's greatest waterfalls. It lies on the Zambezi river and divides Zimbabwe from Zambia.

Below: The River Nile is seen here flowing past Cairo, the capital of Egypt. The Nile is the world's longest river. It is regulated by several dams, the most important of which is the Aswan dam, which controls Egypt's irrigation.

Tropical rain forests cover much of the Zaire River basin and the coastal regions of West Africa. There are also forested areas in south-central Africa, the highlands of Ethiopia, in parts of South Africa, and on some of the mountain slopes of north-western Africa. Between the rain forests and the deserts, there are vast regions of savanna, or tropical grassland. In areas where there is abundant rainfall, the savanna is characterized by frequent clumps of trees and tall, luxuriant grass. But, towards the deserts, trees become less and less common and the grass is shorter. Finally, there is a zone of dry scrub between the savanna and the deserts. The savanna, especially in eastern Africa, is the home of some of the world's greatest populations of wild animals. However, hunting and the destruction of many animal habitats have threatened many species with extinction.

One other outstanding feature of the continent is the Great Rift Valley. This is a series of valleys that link up and cut through much of East Africa. The Rift Valley stretches from Syria in Asia to Mozambique in south-eastern Africa. It was formed when blocks of land sank down between roughly parallel sets of faults (cracks) in the Earth's surface. Cracking also occurred on the valley floor. Molten rocks welled up through the cracks. This has widened the Rift Valley by about 10 kilometres (1.6 miles) in the last 20 million years.

The Rivers of Africa

The Nile, the world's longest river, rises in east-central Africa and flows northwards for 6,741 kilometres (4,187 miles) through the deserts of northern Sudan and Egypt before emptying into the Mediterranean Sea. Its source is Lake Victoria, Africa's largest lake and the world's second largest freshwater lake.

Other great rivers are the Niger and Zaire. The Niger rises quite close to the coast of Guinea in West Africa, but it flows northwards and eastwards before turning south into Nigeria, where it empties into the Gulf of Guinea. It is 4,000 kilometres (2,485 miles) long. The Zaire River was formerly called the Congo River, when the country through which it flows was named the Belgian Congo. When the country was renamed Zaire, the river's name was also changed. The Zaire River is 4,370 kilometres (2,715 miles) long.

Two important rivers, the Limpopo and Zambezi, empty into the Indian Ocean in south-eastern Africa. The Zambezi is interrupted by the continent's greatest waterfall, the Victoria Falls.

Africa (2)

The People

Although more than 400 million people live in Africa, their land is so large that in many parts there are no people at all. About 70 out of every 100 Africans are Negroes, who live south of the Sahara. Most of the remainder are Arabs and Europeans, who live on the Mediterranean coasts of North Africa. Some Europeans also live in South Africa and in Zimbabwe (Rhodesia).

Eight out of ten Africans live in the countryside and most of them are farmers. Those who live on the plains of eastern and southern Africa are herdsmen, looking after cattle. But more and more young Africans are moving into the cities, where they work at whatever jobs they can find.

In southern Africa the richer white people can afford to employ black people in business, industry, government, or domestic service. In South Africa, the official policy of *apartheid* (which means 'apartness' in Afrikaans) keeps whites and non-whites apart. In practice it has meant that non-whites have had to make do with inferior housing, schooling, jobs, justice, rights, and recreation. This has led to deeply bitter feelings among the majority of non-whites.

A few Africans are still wanderers and hunters. These include the pygmies, who live in the rain forests of the upper Zaire River basin. They are noted for their small size, few of them growing to more than 1.5 metres (4 feet 10 inches) tall. Other primitive hunters are the Bushmen of the Kalahari Desert. They are yellowish brown in colour and live in small bands, hunting small desert animals and eating roots where they can find them. The Hottentots are related to the Bushmen and live in desert regions of south-western Africa.

Education varies from country to country. In some places six or seven people out of ten can read and write; in others there may be only one out of ten who can do so. Most

Top: Church Square in Pretoria, South Africa. The modern office block contrasts sharply with the older European-style buildings.

Above: African people in ceremonial dress at a tribal gathering.

Left: Supplies are delivered to a remote part of Ethiopia in north-east Africa.

Left: The Tuareg are a nomadic people of northern Africa. They travel across the Sahara with their herds, stopping only to make temporary camps. Their long robes protect them from the fierce heat of the sun and the cold desert nights. Tuareg men also wear long blue veils.

nations try to send all of their children to school, but some are too poor to provide free education for everybody.

Africa has more than 1,000 languages and dialects. In some areas, people must learn a common language so that they can communicate with each other. For example, in East Africa, most people speak Swahili. A European language is also often used as the common and official language. South Africa's official languages are English and Afrikaans, a tongue derived from Dutch. Arabic is the main language in North Africa.

Africans who live outside the cities live mostly in villages with houses made of sun-dried mud bricks. Many have dirt floors and thatched roofs. Some African men have more than one wife, and a household may be made up of brothers all living together with their wives and children, as well as their parents and grandparents.

Herders who live in or near the Sahara and keep camels, cattle, and goats live mainly on milk, butter, and cheese. Many African farming people eat a thick porridge made from grain, fresh or dried root crops, meat when it can be had, all cooked in a variety of sauces, and bananas. Women do most of the heavy farm work, planting, weeding, and harvesting the crops.

Above right: A herd of impala, accompanied by a family of giraffes, visit a waterhole in the African bush. Much of Africa's wildlife is declining in numbers but some countries have set up special safari parks with game wardens to protect the animals.

Right: A group of Moroccan musicians playing traditional instruments in the ancient city of Marrakesh.

Africa (3)

The Natural Wealth of Africa

Although many African tribes still use primitive farming methods, more scientific methods are gradually taking over. Much land is useless for farming but other parts have been cleared and turned into profitable industries.

Western Africa supplies about 70 per cent of the world's cacao, from which cocoa and chocolate are made. About three-quarters of the world's palm oil and palm kernels, for use in cosmetics and soap, come from Africa. Other important farm exports include coffee, bananas, olives, cotton fibre and cotton seed, tea, tobacco, rubber, and pyrethrum (used in insecticides). Africa also exports a huge amount of peanuts, and farms in eastern Africa supply about two-thirds of the world's sisal, which is used in making rope.

Manufacturing and Mining

Apart from growing food, the natural wealth of the continent is unevenly divided. Some nations have hardly any natural wealth in the way of minerals or raw materials.

Most of the continent's factories are in South Africa. Other nations that have important and growing manufacturing

The Future of Africa

Some countries, such as Ivory Coast, have made steady progress since independence. Others have benefited from the discovery of valuable minerals. For instance, Nigeria's economy has expanded greatly because of its oil production. The progress of many nations, however, has been marred by instability, with the armed forces seizing power from elected governments. Recently there have been hopeful signs. For example, in 1979, the people of Central African Republic, Equatorial Guinea and Uganda removed their military dictators, while the military leaders of Ghana and Nigeria held elections and restored civilian rule in their nations. Africa's main problem, however, remains. How can living standards be raised in this poor continent?

Top: A copper refinery in Zambia, a land-locked country in south-central Africa. Zambia has rich deposits of copper which it exports to the industrial nations of the world.

Left: Washing gravel to extract diamond deposits at an African diamond mine. Africa is the world's main supplier of these precious gems.

Above: The mighty Kariba dam spans the Zambezi river on the borders of Zambia and Zimbabwe. The 128 m (420 ft) high dam provides hydroelectric power for both countries. Behind the dam lies Lake Kariba, one of the largest reservoirs in the world.

Top:East African fishermen prepare for the day's catch in their Arab dhows (sailing boats).

Below: Herdsmen driving their camels at an oasis in southern Tunisia.

industries are Zaire, Kenya, Algeria, Morocco, Tunisia, Egypt, and Zimbabwe (Rhodesia).

The mining picture is quite different. In some places, Africa is a treasure house of minerals. Nearly all the world's diamonds come from African mines and much gold comes from South Africa.

South Africa is also extremely well-endowed with other minerals apart from gold. It is a leading producer of gem-quality diamonds, copper, chrome ore, asbestos, iron ore, uranium and other metals.

Except for South Africa, the leading producers of diamonds are Zaire (mainly industrial diamonds), Botswana, Ghana, Namibia and Sierra Leone. Africa's other copper producers are Zambia and Zaire. Chrome ore and asbestos are also mined in Zimbabwe, while the other main iron ore producers are Liberia and Mauritania. South Africa and Niger are the two leading producers of uranium. Bauxite (aluminium ore) is mined in quantity in Guinea.

In the late 1970s, the leading oil producers in Africa were Nigeria, Libya, Algeria, Egypt, Gabon, Angola, Tunisia, Congo and Zaire.

Transport

Because of Africa's great size, there are problems of transport. Of Africa's total railways, which amount to about 72,000 kilometres (45,000 miles) of track, nearly four-fifths is in only 11 countries.

Railways are costly to build and roads are the main form of transport in most of Africa, although, even today, many roads have earth surfaces and turn to mud in the rainy season. For non-bulky, high value goods, air transport is ideal and Africa's air services have expanded greatly in recent years.

North America

North America is the world's third largest continent, after Asia and Africa. It includes Canada and the United States, Mexico, the countries of Central America, and the islands of the West Indies.

The Land

The three great landform regions are made up of a huge chain of mountains running down the west of the continent, and known as the *Cordillera;* a smaller, older mountain system covering mainly the eastern region of the United States and part of Canada; and the Great Central Plain, which lies between the two mountain systems.

The Cordillera (a Spanish word meaning 'chain of mountains') is made up of the Rocky Mountains and the Sierra Madre. The Rockies stretch from northern Alaska to the south-western United States. The Sierra Madre is a southern continuation that runs through Mexico.

The Appalachians stretch from the Gulf of St Lawrence in Canada southwards to central Alabama. Quite different from the rugged Rockies, they have been worn smooth over the centuries, and few peaks rise more than 1,800 metres (6,000 feet).

The Great Central Plain stretches from the Arctic to the Gulf of Mexico. In the north the land is frozen or swampy, and

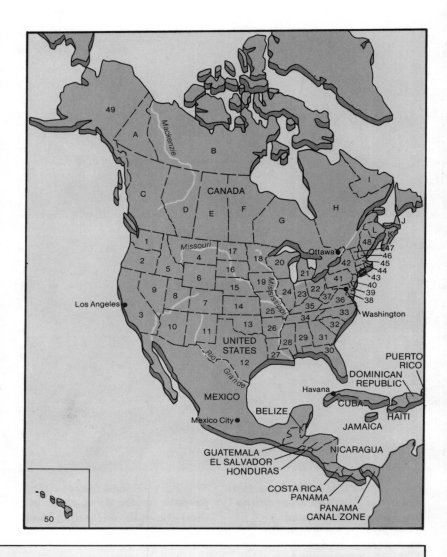

The United States of America

Pacific Coast States
1. Washington
2. Oregon
3. California

Rocky Mountain States
4. Montana
5. Idaho
6. Wyoming
7. Colorado
8. Utah
9. Nevada

South-western States
10. Arizona
11. New Mexico
12. Texas
13. Oklahoma

Mid-western States
14. Kansas
15. Nebraska
16. South Dakota
17. North Dakota
18. Minnesota
19. Iowa
20. Wisconsin
21. Michigan
22. Ohio
23. Indiana
24. Illinois
25. Missouri

Southern States
26. Arkansas
27. Louisiana
28. Mississippi
29. Alabama
30. Florida
31. Georgia
32. South Carolina
33. North Carolina
34. Tennessee
35. Kentucky
36. Virginia
37. West Virginia
38. Maryland
39. Delaware

Mid-Atlantic States
40. New Jersey
41. Pennsylvania
42. New York

New England
43. Connecticut
44. Rhode Island
45. Massachusetts
46. New Hampshire
47. Vermont
48. Maine
49. Alaska
50. Hawaii

The Provinces and Territories of Canada

A. Yukon Territory
B. Northwest Territories
C. British Columbia
D. Alberta
E. Saskatchewan
F. Manitoba
G. Ontario
H. Quebec
I. Newfoundland
J. Prince Edward Island
K. Nova Scotia
L. New Brunswick

quite useless. Farther south it becomes more temperate and is famed for the huge lakes that lie on the borders of Canada and the United States. South of where the Mississippi and Missouri rivers join, the plains are grassy and well watered in the east, drier in the west. On the coasts of the Gulf of Mexico there is a low, flat, hot plain that winds all the way from Texas to Mexico.

Rivers and Lakes

North America is a well-watered continent. Two of its most famous rivers are the Mississippi and the Missouri, which water the Great Central Plain. Other great rivers are the St Lawrence, which flows into the Atlantic; the Colorado, which flows into the Gulf of California; and the Rio Grande, which forms part of the border between the United States and Mexico.

North America is noted for its numerous beautiful lakes. Among these are Lake Superior, the largest of the Great Lakes that straddle the border between Canada and the United States, with an area of nearly 82,900 square kilometres (32,000 square miles); Great Salt Lake, in Utah; and Lake Nicaragua, which is the largest lake in Central America. Other natural wonders include the Niagara Falls, between Lake Erie and Lake Ontario, Florida's Everglades, the active volcanoes of Central America and the spectacular Grand Canyon in north-western Arizona. California's bleak Death Valley contains the lowest place on land in North America. It reaches 86 metres (282 feet) below sea-level.

Top: An airplane flies past the breathtaking scenery of the Grand Canyon in Arizona, USA.

Above: Thousands of people flock to see Niagara Falls on the borders of Canada and the USA.

Right: The coastline of the independent republic of Haiti lying in the Caribbean Sea. The island has a mountainous terrain.

North America (2)

The People

Most of the people who live in North America originally came from Britain, France, Spain, and Africa. The first inhabitants were the American Indians and the Eskimos, both of whom are thought to have travelled from Asia many thousands of years ago.

The British settled mainly in Canada and the northern United States. The French became established in the Quebec and Montreal regions of Canada and in some southern parts of the United States. The Spaniards colonized most of the southern United States, Mexico, Central America and the larger islands of the West Indies. Negroes from Africa were carried in slave ships to the southern United States and the West Indies and later, when they were freed, set up their own communities in these areas. In the late 1800s and early 1900s millions of people (Poles, Greeks, Italians, Dutch, Swedes, and others) fled from Europe to the United States in the hope of starting a new and better life there. Later, they were joined by large numbers of Chinese and Japanese.

Languages

Most of the people of North America speak English. But in and around Quebec, in Canada, most of the people speak French, and many of them would like to be free from the rest of English-speaking Canada. In Mexico, Central America, and some islands of the West Indies such as Cuba, Puerto Rico, and the Dominican Republic, the people speak Spanish. In the other islands of the West Indies language varies according to the nationality of their last conquerors: it may be English, French, or Dutch.

Life of the People

Because North America is so vast, its climate and landscapes vary considerably. The people, too, come from widely separated areas of the world and bring their own customs with them. As a result, there is no single North American way of life. But as in most countries, there is a steady drift of workers from the countryside to the cities, where they hope to make more money for easier work.

Above: A cowboy rides a bull at a rodeo in Cheyenne, Wyoming, in the American West. These popular displays of the cowboy's skill also include bareback bronco-riding and steer wrestling.

Top: The Statue of Liberty overlooks the skyscrapers of Manhattan Island in the heart of New York City. The first Europeans to settle there were the Dutch, in 1625.

Many North Americans, especially in the United States and Canada, travel long distances to work in their cars and, as a result, there is little public transportation compared with, for instance, the cities of Europe.

Food Favourites

Food for most North Americans is plentiful. The continent produces more food than its people can eat. In Canada and the United States, turkey, chicken, steaks, hamburgers, hot dogs, corn on the cob and apple pie are strong favourites. In the Spanish-speaking nations they prefer hot chili dishes and pancakes made of maize-meal, such as *tortillas*, which they eat, instead of bread, with spicy meat and vegetable dishes. *Enchiladas* are tortillas which are stuffed with meat and cheese and baked in a spicy sauce. Many people in the West Indies are poor and live mainly on fish, fruit and beans. But the wealthier people have distinctive dishes which include ingredients and employ methods which originated in far-away Europe, Asia and Africa.

North Americans are lucky in having plenty of wide open spaces for leisure and play, and most people make full use of these. They can swim and sail from thousands of beaches. There are mountains for climbing and skiing down, forests to hunt in, and rivers and lakes for fishing. Farther south the people favour spectator sports of a more gory kind, such as bullfighting and cock-fighting.

Top: A palm-fringed beach on the island of Tobago in the West Indies.

Above: The futuristic architecture of the City Hall at Toronto, Canada. Toronto is the capital of Ontario province.

Right: Chicago, on the shores of Lake Michigan, is the chief city of the American mid-West. It markets farm products and manufactures machinery.

North America (3)

Natural Wealth

The soil provides some of North America's greatest wealth. The United States and Canada have been called the granary of the world. They produce corn, wheat, soybeans, hay, flax, and vegetables in such abundance that not only have they enough for their own peoples but have plenty to export to the rest of the world as well. The main farming regions are located on the vast plains in the interior and in the coastal areas. Some cotton, rice, and fruits are also grown—the latter especially in Florida and California.

The rolling prairies and the foothills of the Rockies support huge herds of cattle both for dairy products and for meat.

Farther south, food production is spread unevenly because much of the land, in the shape of mountains, deserts, and forests, is unusable. Mexico raises livestock such as goats, chickens, and cattle, and also grows enough maize for the needs of the people. The Central American republics have long been noted for their coffee. They also produce bananas by the million, and are rich in sugar-cane, rice, and tobacco.

The West Indian islands rely mainly on sugar-cane, citrus fruits such as grapefruit, lemons, limes, and oranges for export, and tourism for their income. Their sunny weather, uncrowded beaches, and beautiful scenery attract holidaymakers from all parts of the world.

In addition to its wealth of food most of North America is very rich in minerals and sources of power. The United States is a major producer of iron ore, zinc, lead, molybdenum and copper. Iron ore, zinc, and copper are also found in large quantities in Canada which is the world's largest producer of nickel. Mexico has large deposits of nickel, silver and lead.

Power for the Factories

Until the 1970s North America had more or less all the power it needed to carry on its enormous factory output. The energy came from coal, oil, natural gas, and electricity. Great bodies of moving water, such as those found at Niagara and in some fast-flowing rivers, provide power that can be harnessed to make electricity. Water is also important

Top: The vast prairies of Kansas, USA, are a major area for wheat production. Much of the grain is exported.

Above: A steel foundry in Pittsburgh, USA. This important industrial centre also has coal mines and oil refineries.

Left: Golden cobs of maize (Indian corn) are harvested by machine. Maize is native to the American continent.

because it provides a cheap method of transportation. That is why most of North America's heavy industry is centred on the Great Lakes region. Cars, machinery, weapons, tools, clothing, instruments of various kinds, are all made there. But there are also factories of every kind scattered throughout the continent. As a result, everything that can be made by man is made somewhere in North America.

The Rich and the Poor

The United States and Canada are by far the greatest manufacturing nations of the continent. The gross national product (GNP) per person is a way of measuring the wealth of a country. This is worked out by adding up the total value of all goods and services produced in a country in one year, and then dividing it by the population. The GNP per person in the United States in 1976 was US$7,900. Canada was not far behind, with US$7,500. To the south, however, the GNPs of the countries of Central America and the West Indies are much lower. For instance, Mexico's GNP per person was less than one-seventh of that of the United States. However, Mexico is becoming richer as it expands its industries and oil production. Most nations in Central America and the West Indies had GNPs per person in 1976 of less than US$1,000, and some GNPs were less than US$500. Poverty has led to unrest in many places.

American Inventions

1793 Cotton gin	1877 Phonograph
1819 Patent leather	1878 Cash register
1834 Reaping machine	1884 Linotype
1840 Electric telegraph	1889 First fully automatic
1852 Safety elevator	machine gun
1854 First practical sewing	1903 First successful airplane
machine	1911 Motor car electric self-
1857 Steam plough	starter
1868 Typewriter	1947 Polaroid Land camera
1868 Air brake	1947 Transistor
1876 Telephone	

Above: Sugar-cane is harvested by hand in Barbados, a fertile island of the West Indies. Sugar-cane is the world's major source of sugar.

Left: A paper factory in Minnesota, USA. The extensive forests of North America provide wood in abundance for paper-making.

South America

South America is the fourth largest of the world's continents. Although it is twice as large as the United States, it has only about the same number of people. This means that there are huge areas that are completely uninhabited, and some parts that are still unexplored today.

The Land

South America is shaped roughly like an upside down triangle, with its broad base facing the south of North America and the Caribbean, and its point aiming straight at the South Pole. The continent is surrounded by sea, except for a narrow bridge of land in the north-west corner that links it to Panama and Central America.

The equator cuts across South America near the continent's widest point, and more than three-quarters of the land lies in the tropics. The long chain of the Andes Mountains runs down the whole of the western coast and towers above the Pacific Ocean. Lower, and older mountains form the north-eastern highlands. About three-fifths of the land is made up of the central plains. In the north these take the form of dense, hot rain forests, especially around the Amazon River. Further south they give way to scrubland and semi-desert—the *Chaco*—and still further south to the lush grasslands of Argentina and Uruguay called the *pampas*.

Climate varies a good deal with altitude. The higher you go, the colder it gets. In the Amazon basin the weather is generally very hot and muggy. The tops of the Andes, on the other hand, are always covered with snow, even at the equator.

Natural Resources

South America is rich in minerals. Copper is found in Chile, and Bolivia mines large quantities of tin. Venezuela produces nearly all of the continent's oil, and Brazil has very large deposits of diamonds and iron ore. Colombia produces more emeralds than any other country in the world; and Guyana and Surinam are rich in bauxite, an ore from which aluminium is made.

Right: The vast expanse of the Amazon rain forest. Plans are being formed to clear large areas for industrial use.

and French in French Guiana. The only countries where non-Romance languages are officially used are Guyana, where English is spoken, and Surinam, where Dutch is used. The people of South America are descended from three main groups: American Indians, Europeans and Africans. People of mixed origin are called *mestizos*. The American Indians were the earliest inhabitants. One group, the Incas, built up a great civilization in the Andes. This civilization was destroyed in the early 1500s by Spanish soldiers. Spain and Portugal colonized most of the continent and, in some areas, they imported African slaves to work on their plantations.

Most South Americans work on the land and are poor. But every year, the cities attract more and more people from the countryside. The cities are growing so fast that new arrivals have nowhere to go except into expanding slum areas around the cities. There is a great contrast between the many poor and the few rich people. However, the people still show their natural gaiety in carnivals, when everybody dresses up and dances and sings in the streets, eating and drinking for days on end.

Most South American governments today are developing new industries, which means more jobs for the people. They are also building more houses and opening up the interior of the continent with new highways. But there is still a long way to go before large-scale starvation and disease are wiped out in many parts of South America.

Huge herds of cattle and sheep graze on the rich pasturelands of the pampas. As a result, the people of Argentina are able to sell wool, hides, and beef to much of the world overseas. Brazil and Colombia are famous for the coffee grown there. The vast forests that cover the northern part of the continent provide valuable timber for many different uses.

But travel and transportation is still difficult in South America and much of it has to be done by air. This means that most of the continent's natural riches still remain to be made use of.

The People

More than 200 million people live in South America. They are mostly Latin Americans —that is, they speak Romance languages derived from Latin, namely, Spanish in most of the continent, Portuguese in Brazil

Top: Rio de Janeiro, at the foot of the Sugar Loaf Mountain. Rio is one of the most highly developed cities in Brazil.

Above: Coffee beans are dried and graded in the sunshine on this plantation in Colombia.

Right: The brightly-dressed citizens of La Paz, capital city of Bolivia, sell their wares on market day.

Australasia

Australia

Australia is both the smallest inhabited continent and the largest island in the world. It is the only continent inhabited by a single nation.

The Land

Australia is geologically older than any other continent. It is made up mostly of broad, rolling plains eroded from ancient mountains and hills. The land can be divided into three vast natural regions that run across Australia from north to south.

The eastern edge is made up of a range of mountains that runs for about 3,200 kilometres (2,000 miles) along the eastern coast. This range is called the Eastern Highlands, or sometimes the Great Dividing Range.

Westwards of the mountains is the dry Central Lowland. This region makes up about a third of the continent and is covered mostly with grasslands and scrub. Thousands of cattle and sheep are grazed there.

In the west are the deserts of the Western Plateau, an enormous region that covers nearly half of Australia.

The Nation and the People

Australia is a commonwealth (a group of states that are linked politically). There are six states. The five mainland states are Queensland, New South Wales, Victoria, South Australia, and Western Australia. The sixth is the island state of Tasmania.

Australians are generally easy-going, sporting, outdoor types of persons. Their wealth once came from wool and meat. Farming remains important, but mining and manufacturing are the most valuable industries. Most Australians live in cities. More than half live in either Sydney, Melbourne, Brisbane or Adelaide.

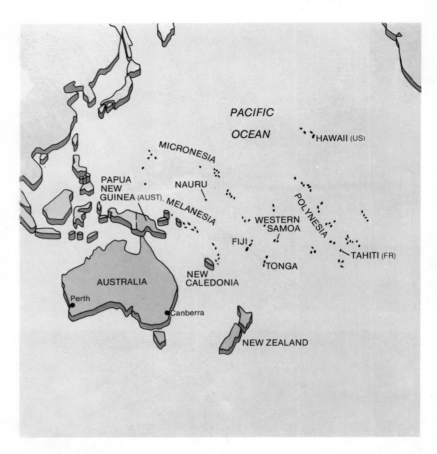

Above: Australasia is a collective name for Australia, New Zealand, New Guinea and the islands of the South Pacific.

Below: A view of Sydney harbour, Australia, with its famous bridge.

Fiji is a group of islands in the Pacific. Once part of the British Empire, it is now independent. The members of this cult (left) are taking part in a fire-walking ceremony.

Centre left: Sheep grazing in South Island, New Zealand. In the background are the peaks of the Southern Alps. Sheep farming is an important part of New Zealand's economy.

New Zealand
New Zealand is an independent nation made up of two main islands located in the Pacific Ocean to the south-east of Australia. The two islands are called North Island and South Island and they are separated by a stretch of water called Cook Strait. Although New Zealand is a little larger than Great Britain in area, only about 3 million people live there.

The Land
North Island has a varied landscape. The sub-tropical climate of the far north gives way to lakes, volcanoes and hot springs further south. Most of the region is dairy country, but citrus orchards and vineyards abound.

The mountainous South Island is dominated by the Southern Alps, a high chain of mountains that runs down the western part of the island. The huge flat region known as the Canterbury Plains is an outstanding feature of New Zealand. There sheep, cattle, and pigs in their millions are raised.

The People
In the 1800s and early 1900s many people from Britain went to seek a new life in New Zealand. There they found a warlike people with light brown skins, called Maoris. After a lot of fighting, white New Zealanders and Maoris today live in peace and cooperation.

Most of New Zealand's wealth comes from farming. The country has about 56 million sheep, 10 million cattle and half a million pigs. Wool, meat and dairy products are sold abroad. Arable farming is less important than pastoral farming.

The island continent of Australia was isolated from the rest of the world for millions of years. Lack of competition from more highly-evolved mammals enabled Australia's marsupials, such as the kangaroo (below), to flourish. Young marsupials are born at an under-developed stage and are then nursed in their mother's pouch.

Polar Regions

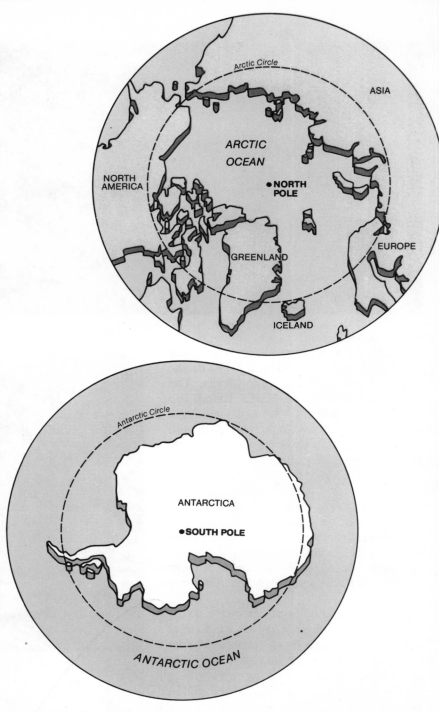

The Arctic

The Arctic is not a continent in its own right. It is mainly made up of the Arctic Ocean. Within this region there are thousands of islands, including Greenland. There are also the northern parts of the continents of Europe, Asia, and North America.

Although the Arctic is very cold, most of it is free of snow and ice during the short summer. At that time the days are so long that there is almost no night there. The reverse is true in the long winter when darkness covers the land for most of the time.

Plant life is low-growing, scattered, and short-lived. It is made up mainly of mosses, lichens, sedges, grasses, and low shrubs. The most common animals are reindeer. There are also many fur-bearing animals such as sables, foxes, martens, bears, and ermine, which are often shot or trapped. In the air, ducks, ptarmigan, puffins, petrels, gulls, and terns are common; while in the sea whales and seals abound.

There are probably rich mineral and fuel deposits in the Arctic but because the subsoil is permanently frozen, they are difficult to extract.

People living in the Arctic have adapted to the cold, harsh conditions. They wear thick clothing made from animals' skins, and eat plenty of fat taken from the land animals and fish which they hunt and kill. The best-known and most widespread of these peoples are the Eskimos. They are found in Greenland, through northern Canada and its offshore islands, to Alaska and north-eastern Asia.

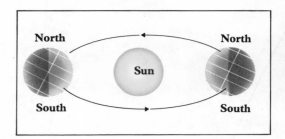

When the Northern Hemisphere is tilted towards the Sun, the Arctic has almost continuous daylight, and the Antarctic has almost continuous night.

Explorers and Exploration

Arctic

1909 Robert Peary Led first expedition to reach the North Pole.

1926 Umberto Nobile With Roald Amundsen he flew over the North Pole in an airship.

1926 Richard Byrd With Floyd Bennett, he flew over the North Pole in an airplane.

Antarctic

1911 Roald Amundsen First man to reach the South Pole.

1929 Richard Byrd Flew over the South Pole.

1957-58 Sir Vivian Fuchs Led the Trans-Antarctic Expedition which made the first overland crossing of Antarctica.

The Antarctic

Unlike the Arctic, the Antarctic consists of a large, uninhabited continent called Antarctica. This region is the coldest and bleakest place on earth. Gale force winds howl over a landscape that is ruggedly mountainous and covered with a mass of ice and snow. Freezing seas surround the land and huge icebergs, many kilometres across, regularly break off and float out into the waters.

Nobody lives there permanently, and parts of Antarctica are still unexplored. The seas around the continent are sometimes called the Antarctic Ocean, but they are really portions of the Indian, Pacific, and Atlantic Ocean that meet at the foot of the world.

Plant life in the Antarctic is almost non-existent, and land animals are confined to a few tiny insects and similar creatures. Penguins are the best known birds in the region, and there are also several flying birds, such as fulmars, skuas, and petrels. Thousands of whales and seals swim in Antarctic waters.

Ever since the Norwegian explorer Roald Amundsen reached the South Pole in 1911, Antarctica has been a centre of interest for scientific exploration. Today there are a number of manned scientific stations located in various parts of the continent. Several countries also claim portions of Antarctica as part of their national territory. Nations with such claims include Great Britain, Argentina, Chile, France, Australia, New Zealand and Norway. Antarctica is thought to contain considerable mineral wealth which might, one day, be exploited.

Above: Reindeer, or caribou, live in herds and feed on lichen in winter.

Left: Seals have layers of fat under their skin to protect them from the intense cold.

Below left: Penguins spend much of their time in the sea but raise their young on land.

Below right: Eskimos traditionally wore clothes of fur and animal skins.

7 EXPLORATION AND DISCOVERY

Men have wanted to explore the world about them since the Stone Age. They had to explore to find food to eat and enjoyed the challenge of going into new territory. The challenge of exploration and the thrill of discovery are just as strong today.

FAMOUS EXPLORERS

The Seas

Eric the Red	(Norse)	Sailed to Greenland in about 980.
Leif Ericson	(Norse)	Probably the first European to sail to America in about 1000.
Bartolomeu Diaz	(Portuguese)	First European to sail round the Cape of Good Hope in 1487.
Christopher Columbus	(Italian)	Made several voyages to the West Indies between 1492 and 1504.
John Cabot	(Italian)	Sailed across the Atlantic to Canada in 1497.
Amerigo Vespucci	(Italian)	Travelled to the West Indies and South America between 1497 and 1503.
Vasco da Gama	(Portuguese)	First European to sail to India in 1498.
Pedro Alvares Cabral	(Portuguese)	Discovered the Brazilian coast in 1500.
Ferdinand Magellan	(Portuguese)	Sailed round the world in 1521.
Sir Martin Frobisher	(English)	Looked for the Northwest Passage in the 1570s.
Sir Francis Drake	(English)	First Englishman to sail round the world in the 1570s.
Abel Tasman	(Dutch)	Discovered Tasmania and New Zealand in 1642.
Vitus Bering	(Danish)	Explored the Bering Straits and the coasts of Asia and Alaska in the 1720s.
James Cook	(English)	Made several journeys especially to the South Pacific in the 1760s and 1770s.

Africa

Mungo Park	(Scottish)	Explored the River Niger in 1796 and 1805.
David Livingstone	(Scottish)	Discovered the Victoria Falls and explored the River Zambezi from 1852 to 1856.
Sir Richard Burton	(English)	Explored Africa and Arabia in the 1850s. Discovered Lake Tanganyika.
John Hanning Speke	(English)	Discovered Lake Victoria in 1858.
Sir Henry Stanley	(Welsh)	Explored the Nile and Congo Rivers in the 1870s and 1880s.

Asia

Marco Polo	(Italian)	Explored China, India, Ceylon and Persia in the late 13th century.
Sven Anders Hedin	(Swedish)	Explored Asia between 1885 and 1933.
Roy Chapman Andrews	(American)	Explored the Gobi Desert and Tibet between 1910 and 1930.

The Americas

Vasco Nunez de Balboa	(Spanish)	Crossed Panama and discovered Pacific Ocean in 1513.
Hernando Cortes	(Spanish)	Conquered Mexico in 1521.
Francisco Pizarro	(Spanish)	Explored Peru in the 1530s.
Francisco de Orellano	(Spanish)	Explored the Amazon in 1541.
Sir Alexander Mackenzie	(Scottish)	Explored Canada and discovered the Mackenzie River.

Polar Explorers

William Baffin	(English)	Discovered Baffin Bay in 1616.
Sir Ernest Shackleton	(Irish)	Explored Antarctica from 1908 to 1916.
Robert Peary	(American)	First man to reach the North Pole in 1909.
Roald Amundsen	(Norwegian)	First man to reach the South Pole in 1911.
Robert Falcon Scott	(English)	Reached the South Pole shortly after Amundsen.
Sir Vivian Fuchs	(English)	First man to cross Antarctica in 1958.

Left: The Norsemen were among the first explorers. Eric the Red discovered Greenland in 982. He gave it an attractive name to encourage other settlers. His son, Leif Ericson, was probably the first European to land in North America. He landed in a place he named Vinland, which may have been Newfoundland. He called it Vinland because he found grapes growing there.

Early Explorers

The first explorer we know of was an Egyptian called Hennu. He lived about 4,000 years ago and sailed from Egypt to a land he called the Land of Punt, which was probably on the Red Sea coast of Somaliland.

The Egyptians were not really a seafaring nation, but the Minoans, who lived on the island of Crete, explored most of the Mediterranean in their tiny boats without any kind of navigation instruments. Crete was captured by Achaean Greeks in about 1400 BC and another nation, the Phoenicians, succeeded the Minoans as the sea traders of the Mediterranean. They made much bigger and better boats which could travel further and faster. They sailed through the Strait of Gibraltar about 600 BC and explored the Atlantic coast of Europe as far north as England. The next great exploring nation was Carthage in North Africa. The Carthaginians explored south of the Mediterranean as far as Cape Verde.

Across the Hellespont

Before about 300 BC the Ancient Greek civilization was at its height and explorers like Alexander the Great and Pytheas made great journeys of discovery. Alexander the Great crossed the Hellespont (now the

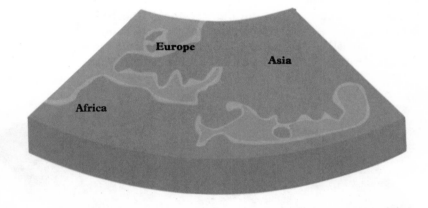

Dardanelles) into Asia and marched through Phrygia and Afghanistan to India. He went as far as the Indian Ocean before returning home. At about the same time, Pytheas was exploring Europe.

In the Middle Ages very little exploration was done until the Vikings made their great voyages from Norway across the northern seas to the Faroe Islands and then to Iceland, Greenland and eventually America. These voyages took place between about AD 800 and 1000.

One explorer of Asia was Marco Polo, who came from Venice. He set out in 1271 and travelled as far as China. Marco Polo was received in the court of the Chinese Emperor, Kublai Khan, and remained in China for 20 years. When he returned to Venice, he wrote an account of his experiences. It was his discovery of the size and riches of Asia that led to people wanting to find new routes to Asia.

Above: Europeans of ancient times had very little knowledge of the world as we know it now. Their experience was limited to the lands around the Mediterranean. A Greek named Ptolemy summarized this knowledge in his book *Geography* written in the second century AD. Ptolemy underestimated the size of the Earth, but his book remained a standard work for 1,400 years.

The Great Age of Exploration

During the Middle Ages, very few voyages of exploration were made from the more advanced European countries. Then, during the 1450s, the Great Age of Exploration began.

There are several reasons why this Great Age started when it did. In 1453 the Turks closed the main route to the East, which meant that European traders had to find a new way to get the silks and spices they wanted. Another reason was that Christian countries wanted to convert other countries to their religion. But the main reason may have been that people felt the urge to explore just as they had done years before.

Henry the Navigator

Perhaps the most important man at the beginning of the Great Age was not an explorer at all. The King of Portugal's brother, Prince Henry, opened a school of navigation in 1416. He also studied ship designs and helped to develop a new ship called the caravel, which was good for long ocean voyages.

Because of Henry the Navigator, Portugal became a nation of explorers. Many Portuguese had explored Africa looking for a sea-route to the East and Bartolomeu Diaz went round the Cape of Good Hope into the Indian Ocean. An Italian called Christopher Columbus went to Portugal and announced that he wanted to sail west to India, the other way round the world. The Portuguese would give him no assistance so Columbus persuaded the Spanish rulers to help him. He sailed across the Atlantic in 1492 and reached some islands he thought were off the coast of Asia. They were in fact the Bahama Islands off America, but Columbus called them the Indies. They are now called the West Indies.

Trade with Asia

One of the reasons that Marco Polo made his journey to China was to see if it was possible to trade directly with Asian countries. Before he went there, Europeans bought all their silk and spices from the Arab merchants who had bought them from China and India. Marco Polo discovered that it was easier and cheaper to deal with Asia direct.

The caravel was an ocean-going ship developed for use in exploration by the Portuguese and the Spaniards. The ships were small but they had room for good supplies of water and food. They had two main types of sail. A square sail was used for moving fast when there was a strong wind behind the ship. Triangular sails, called lateens, were used when the wind was very light, or from the side.

Exploration East and West

The Portuguese still believed the best way to the East was round Africa. In 1497 Vasco da Gama succeeded in reaching India round the Cape of Good Hope. The route to the East was open.

Columbus's discovery had led other nations to travel west from Europe. John Cabot set out from England in 1497 to explore the coast of the country we now call Canada. Many people still thought that this land was Asia, but a few realized that it could be a new continent.

Other explorers followed Columbus from Spain, also. The explorations of Balboa, Cortes and Pizarro firmly established Spain's claim in the land people were beginning to call the New World. There the Spaniards found gold to rival the riches of Asia. Yet the desire to find a western route to the East remained strong.

The Portuguese were not particularly interested in exploring the new continent. They still wanted to reach the spice islands. A Portuguese explorer called Ferdinand Magellan asked Spain to support him in his latest venture. He planned to sail round the new continent of America and on to Asia. He set out with five ships in 1519 and by the end of 1520 he had reached the southern-most tip of South America. Beyond that he discovered a huge sea which he called the Pacific Ocean. After a terrible voyage across this ocean, his expedition reached the spice islands, but Magellan had been killed on the journey. Only one of the five ships returned by the route around Africa. It was the first ship to sail completely round the world.

Now that a south-west passage had been found to Asia, explorers began to search for a north-west passage. Although nobody found this until 1906, the search brought great discoveries in the huge continent of North America. All the European countries joined in the exploration and eventually wars were fought about who owned different parts of North America. The Spanish, French and English all claimed part of the land, and it was not until after the Declaration of Independence in 1776 that their fighting stopped.

The Southern Continent

By this time, navigators had fairly accurate maps of most of the world but there were still a few gaps. For thousands of years, people had thought that there was another continent in the south. In 1776 James Cook set out to explore the Pacific Ocean. He found many small islands and sailed around New Zealand, and also discovered that there was a southern island continent, now called Australia.

In the 19th century explorers turned to the unknown continent of Africa. The most famous of them was David Livingstone, who spent nearly 25 years as a missionary crossing unknown parts of the continent.

By 1900, nearly all the continents of the world had been explored, but there were still some areas about which men knew very little. These included the polar regions.

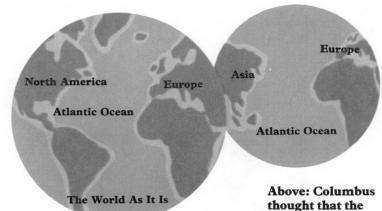

North America
Atlantic Ocean
Europe
Asia
Europe
Atlantic Ocean

The World As It Is

Above: Columbus thought that the Earth was much smaller than it is. When he reached the other side of the Atlantic Ocean he thought he had reached Asia.

Below: Sailors in the 1400s feared long sea journeys. They thought that they might be attacked by vast sea serpents, or might fall off the edge of the Earth.

Polar Exploration

The Arctic region is a very cold area and many men died trying to sail through the Arctic Ocean to find the Northwest Passage. The mistake they made was to try to cross the Arctic during the summer, when the sun never sets there. In the summer the Arctic ice melts a little and breaks up into huge ice floes or islands. It is extremely difficult to navigate ships safely between these ice floes, and only a few explorers, such as Roald Amundsen, succeeded in sailing through these dangerous waters.

Explorers finally decided it would be easier to explore this region during winter when the Arctic ocean is completely frozen and can be crossed on foot with dog sleds. The weather is very much worse at this time of the year and the Arctic is in continual night. In 1909, however, Robert E. Peary braved these conditions and reached the North Pole.

A Race to the South

The South Pole did not have the same problems as the North Pole as it is, in fact, land. It is still a difficult place to reach, however, because it is so terribly cold. Robert Falcon Scott explored part of the continent in 1902 with the British Navy and was later to reach the South Pole itself. In 1908 Sir Ernest Shackleton crossed far inland to within 200 kilometres of the Pole, but it was first reached by Roald Amundsen in 1911 (see picture, left). His team beat a team of Englishmen, led by Scott, to the Pole by a month. After suffering from scurvy, frostbite and other hardships in blizzards and in the intense cold, Scott and his companions died on the return journey. His diary was found later and tells us of his disappointment at being beaten so narrowly by Amundsen. The first complete crossing of Antartica took place in 1957-8.

The conditions and weather of the polar regions are now studied by scientists in research stations there.

Right: Polar exploration has been made very much easier by the invention of vehicles that can cross snow and ice. Sno-cats have caterpillar tracks. They are very much better than teams of dogs and sleds.

122

Exploration Today

Below right: Much research now goes into the designing of equipment for expeditions. For instance, model boats are tested in a tank with a strong current of water in it. This reduces the risk of accidents.

Below: Satellites now play an important part in the search for knowledge about our planet. Space exploration began in 1957 with Sputnik I. Today many satellites send back information on weather, land use, and so on.

Now that even the polar regions have been discovered and explored, you may think that there is very little left to explore. This is certainly not true. There are still many parts of the world where no man has set foot, and we still know very little about the huge areas that are under the oceans. Exploration has also begun of the vast unknown space of our universe.

New inventions have changed the way

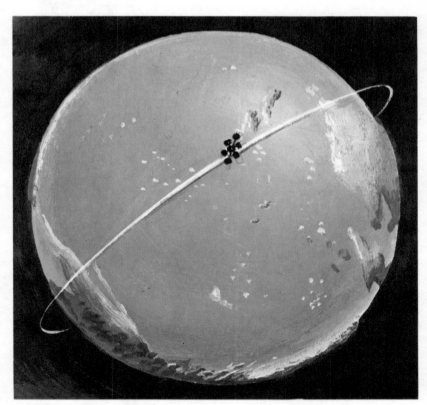

that explorers work, and people can discover much more about lands and seas than before. Explorers in the 19th century sometimes travelled by balloon on their voyages of discovery, and the invention of the airplane meant that explorers could visit even more places quickly and observe them from above. One of the first explorers to make use of the airplane was Amundsen, and he was followed by Commander Richard Byrd. Byrd flew over the North Pole in 1926 and then in 1929 over the South Pole. Nowadays, airplanes are used on many explorations and the aerial photographs that can be taken are very useful to map-makers.

Other means of transport have helped men to explore new regions of the world. Hovercraft have now been used to explore parts of the River Amazon, because they can travel equally well over open water, marsh, and flat country. Cars are also being adapted for this type of exploration.

Oceanic Exploration

More than two-thirds of the Earth's surface is covered by sea, and it is now being explored very thoroughly. The early submarines were not very good for exploring the oceans as they could not go very deep and had to surface frequently for air. But today there are nuclear-powered submarines that can make long journeys deep under the ocean's surface. As early as 1958, a nuclear submarine went under the Arctic ice-cap to the North Pole and surfaced on the other side. Scientists also use small submarines connected to ships on the surface. These often use bathyscaphes, to study the bottom of the oceans and the animals that live there. Scientists have developed new techniques in underwater photography and they can use drills to take samples of the ocean floor. They are particularly interested in finding oil and other valuable minerals under the oceans.

Exploration is now continuing outside our world. Space explorers are travelling out of the Earth's atmosphere and have already explored parts of the Moon's surface. Mars, Venus, Mercury and Jupiter and its moons are also being observed. This space exploration helps scientists to explore the Earth. Satellites out in space can send back pictures of the Earth's surface which give new information about unknown lands, and enable map-makers to make even more accurate maps. Satellite pictures also provide information about the weather.

8 SPACE TRAVEL

Man has dreamed for hundreds of years of travelling in space. That dream has recently come true. The challenge of unexplored places has led us to make the first space flights. Scientists have learned much about the universe, and will discover much more.

Getting into Space

The first problem that has to be overcome before we can send anything into space is the pull of gravity. Gravity is the force that pulls objects towards the Earth (or any other body in space). Everything that is dropped near the Earth's surface falls to the ground and accelerates or gets faster on its way down. To beat this force of gravity, objects must travel away from the Earth very fast. When you throw a stone into the air this defeats gravity for a short time before the stone starts to fall back to the ground. But rockets can now travel fast enough to escape the pull of the Earth's gravity.

To do this, they have to travel at more than 40,000 kilometres (25,000 miles) per hour. This is an enormous speed which even our fastest jet planes cannot reach. Scientists had to invent new kinds of engines to propel rockets into space. The most powerful rocket engines are powered with liquid fuels, such as hydrogen and a substance similar to kerosene, but there are some that work on solid fuels. Ordinary jet engines would be useless in space because they need air to work properly. So rockets carry a supply of oxygen as well as fuel to propel the rocket. The propellants, as the oxygen and fuel are called, are burnt in a combustion chamber at the base of the rocket. A jet of hot gases shoots out from this chamber and pushes the rocket forward. Liquid fuel engines have several advantages over solid fuel ones. They are easier to control and can be restarted.

Because space rockets have to carry so much fuel to push them out of the Earth's gravity, they are very big. The smallest are about 40 metres (130 feet) high and some are more than 100 metres (330 feet) high.

Rockets as Weapons
The rocket was first invented in China over a thousand years ago. It was just like the firework rocket of today but was used as a weapon. These rockets were powered with the solid fuel, gunpowder, and it was not until 1926 that a liquid-fuelled rocket was made. These rockets were not powerful enough to travel very far, and certainly not to get into space.

The Space Age really began in 1957 when the Russians launched the first artificial satellite into space. The rocket that took it into space was developed from the V2 rockets used by the Germans in the 1940s. Very soon after the first satellite, another was launched with a dog on board. The success of the early space flights with animals showed that it was possible to put a man into space without harming him.

Man in Space
On 12 April 1961 the first man was launched into space. His name was Yuri Gagarin. This was the first of many manned space flights and the beginning of an exciting period of exploration.

The largest rocket yet built was the massive Saturn V that successfully launched the Apollo spacecraft on their voyages to the Moon. It was 111 metres (365 feet) tall and it was the most powerful rocket ever launched.

Space is a very difficult place for human beings to survive in. Outside the protection of the rocket they would die immediately because there is no air, and because of the extreme heat and cold. But astronauts do have to leave their spacecraft now and again to do repairs on the exterior, to check cameras or even to walk on the Moon. So when they do this they have to wear protective spacesuits. Spacesuits have several layers which protect astronauts from radiation and temperature. They are also pressurized and supplied with oxygen, to give astronauts the same atmospheric conditions they have on Earth.

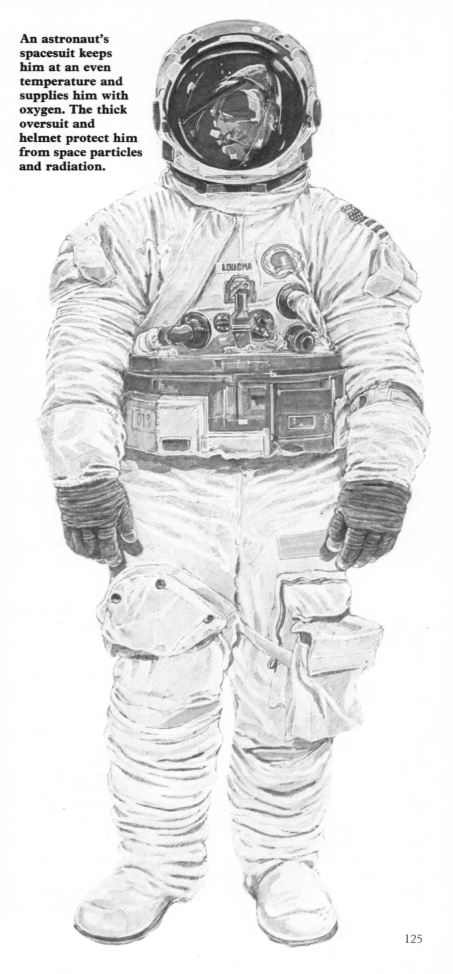

An astronaut's spacesuit keeps him at an even temperature and supplies him with oxygen. The thick oversuit and helmet protect him from space particles and radiation.

A First Dictionary of Space Travel

aerial (antenna)   A metal wire or rod used to send or receive radio signals.

booster   The first stage of a rocket, which usually falls away after launching.

capsule   The cabin which the early astronauts travelled in.

cosmonaut   The name given to Russian astronauts.

docking   When two spacecraft meet and join together in space.

escape velocity   The speed needed to escape the Earth's gravity.

heat shield   A covering on a spacecraft which will protect it from heat during re-entry.

launch pad   The area from which a rocket is launched.

lift-off   The end of a countdown when the rocket leaves the launch pad.

module   A section of a spacecraft.

orbit   The path a satellite takes around the Earth, or any object takes around any other in space.

probe   An unmanned spacecraft sent into space to obtain information.

re-entry   The time when a spacecraft is coming back into the Earth's atmosphere.

satellite   Any small body that circles a planet.

splashdown   When a returning spacecraft lands in the sea.

Satellites and Spacecraft

A satellite resembles a man-made moon that orbits around the Earth. Satellites can stay in orbit and overcome the Earth's gravity by travelling very fast, at more than 28,000 kilometres (17,500 miles) per hour. If a satellite were to slow down to below this speed it would be pulled back to Earth.

To launch a satellite into space, rockets are used. A multistage or step rocket is the best way to do this. Step rockets are made in sections which are arranged one on top of the other. When the bottom stage has used up its fuel, it drops away and the next stage takes over. In this way the spacecraft gets faster and lighter as it travels into space.

Use of Satellites

Artificial satellites are of many different shapes and sizes and are sent into orbit for several different reasons. They usually have solar cells to use the energy from the Sun for their instruments and to keep them on the correct course. The first artificial satellite was the Russian *Sputnik 1* which was launched in 1957. Twenty years later, more than 4,000 satellites had been sent into space and were still orbiting the Earth. All satellites orbit at different heights above the Earth. The closer ones eventually fall back into the Earth's atmosphere.

A common use for satellites is to improve international communications. Communications satellites can pick up signals from a point on the Earth and relay them to the other side of the world by amplifying them and then beaming them down to a ground station. This means that radio, telephone and television signals can now be sent round the world.

Some satellites carry cameras which take pictures of the Earth's surface to help meteorologists forecast the weather and map-makers to make accurate maps. Other satellites carry cameras and telescopes which are pointed out into space so that astronomers can get more information about distant stars and planets. These satellites can see into space more clearly than we can from Earth because they are outside the Earth's atmosphere, which distorts images of the stars. Satellites are also used for military reconnaissance.

Satellites do not have to be streamlined to travel through space because there is no air in space. They can be any shape that suits the job for which they are designed. But they all have the same basic units performing different functions. There is an instrument unit, a power unit, and communication and control units.

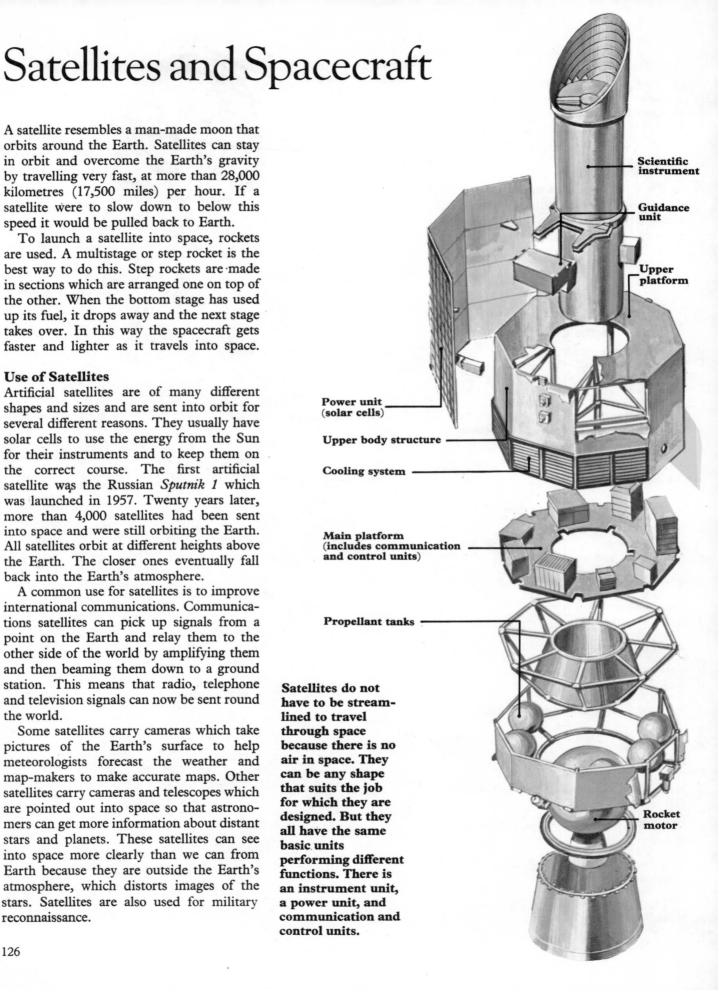

Scientific instrument

Guidance unit

Upper platform

Power unit (solar cells)

Upper body structure

Cooling system

Main platform (includes communication and control units)

Propellant tanks

Rocket motor

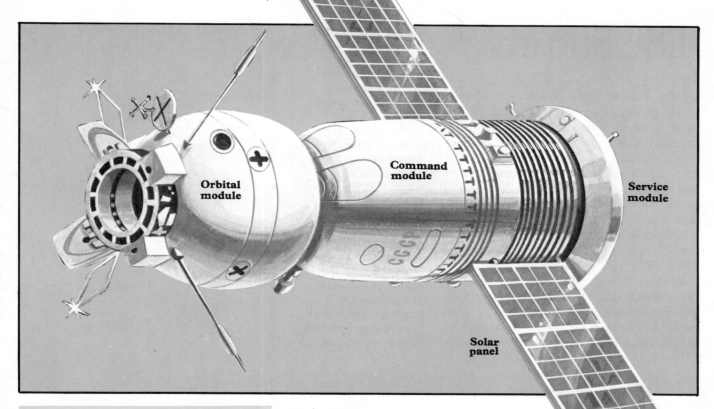

Orbital
module

Command
module

Service
module

Solar
panel

Satellites

Ariel A series of satellites designed in Britain for scientific research. They were launched from the United States of America.

Cosmos Scientific satellites launched from Russia.

ERTS Earth Resources Technology Satellite (see Landsat).

Explorer American scientific satellites. The first American satellite was an Explorer.

Intelsat Communications satellites. They relay telephone and television signals over the oceans.

Landsat Satellites that observe the Earth from above. They used to be called ERTS (see above).

Meteor Russian weather satellites.

Molniya Russian communications satellites.

Nimbus American weather satellites.

Sputnik 1 The world's first artificial satellite. Sputnik 2 contained the first live space traveller—Laika, a dog.

Telstar The first communications satellite to carry a live transatlantic television broadcast.

Manned Satellites

Manned satellites are built like unmanned satellites in modules or sections. One of these modules contains the crew, and it is this module that returns to Earth. There are also large satellites which stay out in space to be used as space stations. The US Skylab and the Russian Salyut are examples of these.

Manned satellites do not stay in orbit for long as there is not enough room for the crew to live comfortably. Space stations, however, contain a living area with continually circulated air, toilet facilities and places for the men to sleep and work. They also provide means for the astronauts to exercise to keep fit. Man can stay in space for several months.

Above: Soyuz is Russia's chief manned spacecraft. It is used to take cosmonauts to and from their space station, Salyut. The orbital module is used for working in space. The cosmonauts sit in the command module for take-off.

Left: Communications satellites operate by picking up a radio beam from a ground station, amplifying it, and beaming it back to another station. Many are in orbit 35,900 km (22,300 miles) from Earth. At this height they orbit at the same rate as the Earth turns and so appear to be stationary.

The Future

In the future, space travel will change just as rapidly as it already has done. Multi-stage rockets may soon become old-fashioned and be replaced by new types of rocket. Scientists will spend long periods of time orbiting the Earth in space stations and astronauts will travel much farther into space than they can today, to discover new facts about the universe.

Scientists have already developed new kinds of spacecraft which will be used in the 1980s. The space shuttle will replace the multistage rocket. The main advantage of the shuttle is that it can be used many times, but a multistage rocket can only be used once. The shuttle is in three sections. The orbiter looks like a modern jet plane and is

Right: It is hard to imagine how big space is. If you imagine that you are in a rocket you will get some idea of the size from this diagram. It would take 2½ days to reach the Moon, 3 weeks to reach the Sun and thousands of years to reach Proxima Centauri, our nearest star after the Sun.
It would take the rocket thousands of millions of years to reach the next nearest galaxy to our solar system.

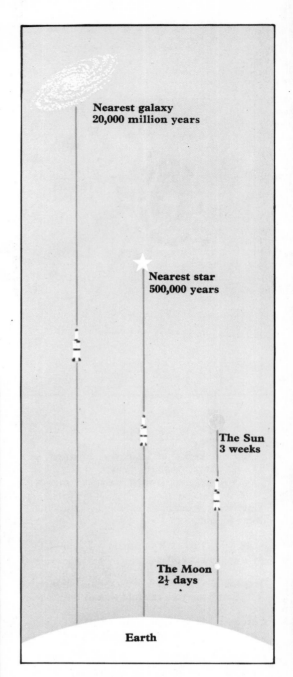

Nearest galaxy
20,000 million years

Nearest star
500,000 years

The Sun
3 weeks

The Moon
2½ days

Earth

Man on the Moon

On 21 July 1969 at 2.56 a.m. GMT Neil Armstrong became the first man to step on to the Moon. He was joined by Edwin Aldrin.

The spacecraft used to get the astronauts to the Moon was the Apollo spacecraft, which was perched high on top of the huge Saturn V rocket. This rocket launched the spacecraft into space where it orbited the Earth before blasting off towards the Moon. The spacecraft then moved into an orbit around the Moon and one of the three modules, the lunar module, separated and descended to the Moon's surface.

After a rest, the astronauts left the lunar module for the first walk on the Moon. In their protective spacesuits, they explored the Moon's surface for nearly three hours and collected samples of the rocks and dust. They left automatic instruments to send back information. After the Moon-walk, the lunar module docked with the main spacecraft and returned to Earth, leaving behind the plaque below.

HERE MEN FROM THE PLANET EARTH
FIRST SET FOOT UPON THE MOON
JULY 1969, A. D.
WE CAME IN PEACE FOR ALL MANKIND

NEIL A. ARMSTRONG
ASTRONAUT

MICHAEL COLLINS
ASTRONAUT

EDWIN E. ALDRIN, JR.
ASTRONAUT

RICHARD NIXON
PRESIDENT, UNITED STATES OF AMERICA

the section which carries the crew and equipment. This is attached to the main fuel tank which contains the propellants that power the spacecraft. There are also two booster rockets which are used for launching.

When a shuttle is launched, the booster rockets fall away and parachute back to Earth, and the orbiter continues out into orbit until the fuel tank is empty. This then drops away and the orbiter continues its mission. Once it has completed the mission, the orbiter returns to Earth and is flown like a glider after re-entry into the Earth's atmosphere.

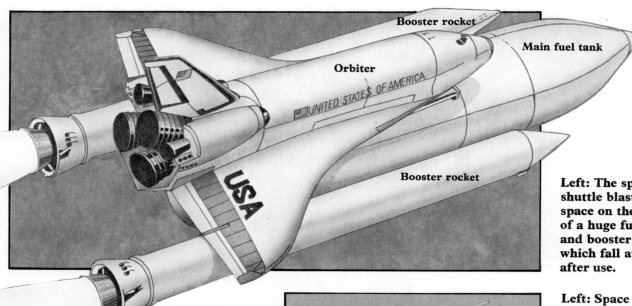

Booster rocket

Main fuel tank

Orbiter

UNITED STATES OF AMERICA

USA

Booster rocket

Left: The space shuttle blasts into space on the back of a huge fuel tank and booster rockets which fall away after use.

Left: Space stations of the future will be constructed on Earth and ferried into orbit by space shuttles one section at a time. In orbit the sections will be joined together by teams of skilled space engineers.

The orbiter can do many things in space. One of its advantages is that it can bring back satellites that need repair and then take them back to their orbit. It will also be used for placing new satellites in orbit.

Spacelab

Its most important cargo will be a space laboratory called Spacelab which is being designed by the European Space Agency. The laboratory, which will have room for four scientists, will be launched in the shuttle's payload bay. When the shuttle is in orbit, the doors of the bay will be opened and Spacelab will have a direct view of the sky for astronomical and Earth observations. It will orbit in the shuttle's bay for up to a month and then be brought down to Earth. It will be re-used about 50 times. The shuttle will also take out parts of new space stations. This means that space stations can be much bigger than before when the whole station had to be launched at the same time.

Now that men have been in space and landed on the Moon, they want to travel even farther into space, to new planets and stars. But there are great problems with travelling so far away from Earth. One of the main problems is the hostile conditions on most other planets' surfaces. There is no air for men to breathe, and the other planets in our solar system are either too hot or too cold, depending on their distance from the Sun, for people to survive.

Another problem which is even more difficult to overcome is the vast distances between Earth and even its nearest neighbours. It took the Viking probes to Mars ten months to get there, and using rockets travelling at the speeds they do today it would take many years to reach even the nearest star. Scientists are working on new ideas for powering rockets with intense beams of light, but even if they could travel at thousands of kilometres per second it would take a very long time to reach the solar system's nearest neighbours in space.

In spite of the problems of space travel, highly reputable physicists and space scientists foresee great advances before the end of this century. Their predictions include a permanent base on the Moon, manned, orbiting space stations supplied by rockets taking off from airports on Earth, the colonization of space, and use of space technology in developing solar energy as a source of heat and electricity.

9 WORLD RELIGIONS

All the earliest-known peoples worshipped gods or spirits and (except in recent times) no tribe or nation has ever existed without religion. Many once-great religions have died out, including those of the ancient Egyptians, Greeks, Romans and Vikings.

Religions from the Middle East

Judaism, the religion of the Jews, began in the Middle East before 1200 BC. The Jews were probably the first people to believe in one, all-powerful God to whom they could speak but not see. Traditionally, Abraham founded Judaism, and the Jews awaited the coming of a *Messiah* (anointed of the Lord) who would lead them through difficult times. Their great leader, Moses, led them out of slavery in Egypt to the 'promised land' of Palestine.

Christianity developed from the teachings of Jesus, a Jew born in Palestine nearly 2,000 years ago. Many people thought Jesus was the promised Messiah and called him *Christos*—a Greek word meaning 'anointed one'. This became *Christ*, and his followers became known as *Christians*. Christians believed that God 'redeemed' their sins because Jesus had taken the punishment upon himself when he was crucified before ascending to heaven as the Son of God. Christianity later became the religion of almost all Europeans.

Islam began in AD 622 when an Arabian merchant, Muhammad, fled from the city of Mecca to Medina. Many Muslim (Is-

lamic) beliefs are similar to those of Jews or Christians. Muslims believe in one God (Allah). The 'revelations' of Allah to Muhammad are recorded in Islam's holiest book, the *Koran*. Muslims pray direct to Allah, facing towards Mecca, at least five times a day wherever they are, but preferably in mosques. They have no priests.

Religions from India

Hinduism is the religion of most Indians. It has hundreds of gods and goddesses, many of whom can be seen as idols in Hindu

Above: A Roman Catholic priest celebrating Mass. Since the Vatican II Council meeting called by Pope John XXIII in 1962, changes have taken place in many aspects of Roman Catholic religious practice and belief.

EIGHT GREAT RELIGIONS

RELIGION	MAIN AREAS	WHEN IT BEGAN	FOUNDER
HINDUISM	India	Before 2000 BC	Unknown
JUDAISM	USA, Israel, USSR	Before 1200 BC	Abraham
SHINTO	Japan	By 600 BC	Unknown
TAOISM	China	By 500 BC	Lao-tzu
BUDDHISM	Far East and South East Asia	About 500 BC	Siddhartha Gautama
CHRISTIANITY	Europe, North and South America	After AD 4	Jesus Christ
ISLAM	From West Africa to Indonesia	AD 622	Muhammad
SIKHISM	Punjab (India)	About AD 1500	Guru Nanak

Above: The Hall of Annual Prayer, situated in the compound of the Temple of Heaven in Peking. Built in 1420 and later reconstructed, it was here that the emperor of China offered sacrifices to the god of heaven.

Above right: An Orthodox Jewish family celebrates the festival of *Pesach* (Passover) which commemorates the exodus of the Jews from Egypt in Biblical times. The festival lasts for eight days. The first two evenings are called *Seders*.

Right: When in AD 630 Muhammad led the Medinan army and captured Mecca, he chose this city to be the centre of Islam and the Ka'abah to be the holy shrine. Thousands of Muslims flock here every day to pray at this symbolic site.

temples. But many Hindus say that all these deities are only aspects of one Supreme Being.

Buddhism began in around 500 BC when Siddhartha Gautama, an Indian prince, later called the Buddha, sought a 'middle way' that rejected both the harsh life and poverty of Hindu holy men and the luxury of the wealthy. True Buddhism has no gods, but Buddhists worship images of the Buddha.

Sikhism, begun by Guru Nanak in Punjab, India, over 500 years ago, incorporated aspects of Islam and Hinduism in an attempt to end hatred between followers

of the two rival religions. Sikhs believe in one God.

Religions from the Far East

Taoism, said to have been taught in China by Lao-tzu, encouraged men to work in harmony with nature, rather than to strive to change things. Another important Chinese religion was Confucianism, founded in the 6th century BC by the philosopher Confucius (K'ung Fu-tzu).

Shinto, a religion of Japan, is a form of spirit worship. Like Chinese religions it places great importance upon the honouring of ancestors.

10 SCIENCE

When we learn about science, we find out about nature, about the Universe, our world and living things. A good scientist understands how things happen and may make discoveries that help people, or our environment.

What is Science?

Science is a search for knowledge. Scientists watch things, take measurements and work out explanations for the answers. If the explanations are correct a scientist will be able to say how something is going to work. In this way, scientists make discoveries. For example, Sir Isaac Newton watched how the planets move around the Sun, and wondered why they move in this way. He worked out that a force called gravity keeps them moving in their paths around the Sun. With this knowledge, astronomers later searched for and discovered two additional planets, Neptune and Pluto.

Scientific Method
Many scientists carry out experiments to see if their explanations are correct. First, they make observations of something that interests them. Then they form a theory to explain their observations. They test the theory with experiments. If the experiments support the theory, the theory then becomes a law of science. However, new evidence may later cause a law to be modified. A new law will then be formulated.

Kinds of Science
There are several different kinds of science. Biology is the principal life science. Biologists study all forms of life: microbes, plants, animals and human beings. The study of plants is called botany, and the study of animals, zoology.

Physical sciences involve the study of non-living things. Chemists study gases, fuels, new plastics and drugs. Physicists study atoms and states of matter. They also study energy and electronics. Discoveries in the physical sciences are important in engineering, which puts the knowledge to use.

Above: Scientists are always trying to solve problems and setting themselves more and more difficult tasks. Research on any topic often takes many years of careful experimentation and analysis before any practical application can be found for new products. New drugs, in particular, have to be tested and approved before they are marketed to ascertain that they will cause no harmful side-effects.

Other sciences include geology, which is the study of rocks and minerals and how the land is formed. Geologists also study the history of the Earth from fossils and other evidence in the rocks. The atmosphere and weather are studied in meteorology. Oceanography is the scientific study of the oceans. In astronomy, everything in space is studied —the Sun, Moon, comets, meteors, planets, stars and galaxies.

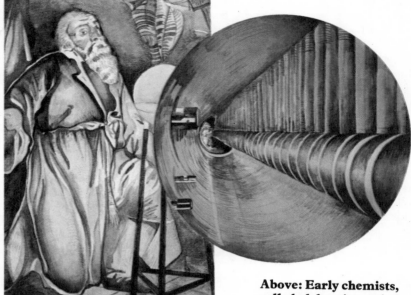

First Dictionary of Science

friction The retarding force that tries to stop one object from sliding over another.

gas A liquid turns into a gas when it boils. A gas always expands until it fills its container.

gravity The force of attraction exerted by any object. The force exerted by a small object is weak, but the force exerted by large bodies, such as the Earth, Moon or Sun, is very powerful.

liquid A solid melts to form a liquid, such as water.

magnetism The result of electrical forces between moving, electrically charged particles.

mass The amount of matter in a body. Mass differs from weight because the mass of a body is the same wherever it may be, while the weight depends on the pull of gravity.

matter Everything having any mass consists of matter.

molecule A group of atoms linked together.

solid A liquid becomes a solid when it freezes. For example, water becomes a solid when it freezes into ice.

theory An attempt to explain an observed result. If a theory is supported by experiments, it will become a law of science.

vacuum Space that is completely empty of matter.

weight The force exerted by gravity on a body. For example, on the Moon an astronaut weighs only one-sixth of his weight on Earth. This is because the force of gravity on the Moon is only one-sixth of that on Earth. But the mass of the astronaut remains exactly the same.

Above: Early chemists, called alchemists, tried unsuccessfully to turn base metals into gold. Radioactive elements such as uranium can now be changed into other elements. Huge machines called linear accelerators are used to split elements. Using this method, gold can be made from mercury.

Left: Sir Isaac Newton studied the movement of the planets. In 1687 he published his theory on the law of gravity, stating that gravitational force kept the planets moving in their paths around the Sun. He made many discoveries and invented the reflecting telescope.

Below: A laser beam is reflected off the Moon to accurately measure the distance from Earth. It is also used in surgery and holography.

Mathematics and Measurement

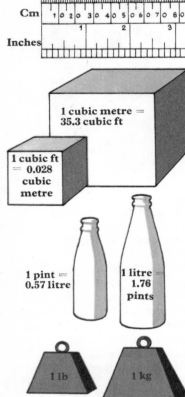

Cm

Inches

1 cubic metre = 35.3 cubic ft

1 cubic ft = 0.028 cubic metre

1 pint = 0.57 litre

1 litre 1.76 pints

1 lb

1 kg

°F   °C

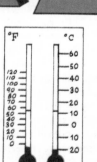

1 cubit

7 palms

4 digits 1 palm

1 foot

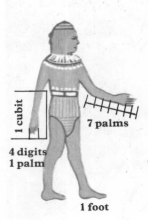

We all need to have some knowledge of mathematics and measurement. When we buy anything, we need to use simple mathematics to work out how much to pay. When we make something, we need to use measurements to make it the right size or shape.

Scientists of all kinds find mathematics essential. When a scientist discovers a new law, he often presents it as a mathematical formula. He also has to be able to make accurate measurements.

The SI System

To measure correctly, we need systems of units. Scientists and engineers use the SI system of units. They use metres to measure length and kilograms to measure weight. There are smaller and larger multiples of these. For example, there are 100 centimetres in a metre and 1,000 metres in a kilometre. SI stands for *Systeme International d'Unités* (International System of Units). It is based on the metric system of measurement which dates from the 1790s.

Below left: The ancient Egyptians based their units of measurement on the length of various parts of the body.
Below: The metre is based on a wavelength of light given off by the gas krypton. Length can be measured by using an instrument called a krypton interferometer.

The imperial system of measurement is still used in Britain and some other English-speaking countries. Some imperial units are shown on the left. Another unit used in these countries is the degree Fahrenheit (°F) for measuring temperature.

Weights and Measures

Length

millimetre (mm)
10 mm   = 1 centimetre (cm)
100 cm = 1 metre (m)
1000 m = 1 kilometre (km)

Area

square millimetre (mm²)
100 mm² = 1 square centimetre (cm²)
10,000 cm² = 1 square metre (m²)
10,000 m² = 1 hectare (ha)
100 ha = 1 square kilometre (km²)

Volume

cubic millimetre (mm³)
1000 mm³ = 1 cubic centimetre (cm³ or cc)
1000 cm³ = 1 cubic decimetre (dm³)
1000 dm³ = 1 cubic metre (m³)

Capacity

millilitre (ml)
1000 ml = 1 litre (l)
(1 ml is approximately equal to 1 cm³; and 1 litre is approximately equal to 1 dm³)

Weight

milligram (mg)
1000 mg = 1 gram (g)
1000 g = 1 kilogram (kg)
1000 kg = 1 tonne or metric ton

Time

second (s)
60 s   = 1 minute (min)
60 min = 1 hour (h)
24 h   = 1 day (d)
(7 days equal 1 week; and 365 days are approximately equal to 1 year)

Angle

second (″)
60″ = 1 minute (′)
60′ = 1 degree (°)
90° = 1 right angle or quadrant
4 quadrants = 1 circle = 360°

Useful Formulae

It is easy to calculate the area or volume of a simple shape with the aid of a formula for the area or volume. In these formulae, the letters stand for the lengths of the various dimensions of the shapes. For example, if the sides of a square are 6 centimetres (cm) long, then its area will be 36 cm² (6^2 or 6 x 6). π (pi) is equal to 3.14159 or approximately 22/7.

Circumference
Circle of radius r	$2\pi r$

Area
Circle of radius r	πr^2
Surface of sphere of radius r	$4\pi r^2$
Triangle of base b and height h	$\frac{1}{2}bh$
Square of side a	a^2
Rectangle of sides a and b	ab

Volume
Sphere of radius r	$4/3\,\pi r^3$
Cylinder of radius r and height h	$h\pi r^2$
Cone of radius r and height h	$\frac{1}{3}h\pi r^2$
Cube of side a	a^3

Decimal Multiples

Units smaller and larger than the SI units have prefixes that indicate their size. For example, kilo means 1,000 times bigger, so 1 kilometre is equal to 1000 metres.

Prefix	Symbol	Multiplication Factor
mega	M	1,000,000
kilo	k	1,000
hecto	h	100
deca	da	10
deci	d	0.1
centi	c	0.01
milli	m	0.001
micro	μ	0.000001

SI Units
Basic Units

Length	metre (m)
Mass or weight	kilogram (kg)
Time	second (s)
Electric current	ampere (A)
Temperature	kelvin (K)
Amount of substance	mole (mol)
Luminous intensity of light	candela (cd)

Derived Units

All the units below can also be expressed by combinations of some of the basic units. However, for simplicity, they are given their own special names.

Frequency	hertz (Hz)
Force	newton (N)
Pressure, stress	pascal (Pa)
Energy, work, quantity of heat	joule (J)
Power	watt (W)
Electric charge, quantity of electricity	coulomb (C)
Electric potential, potential difference, emf	volt (V)
Electrical resistance	ohm (Ω)
Electrical conductance	siemens (S)

Right: Whether you are making a scientific experiment or baking a cake, it is important to understand weights and measures. The ingredients for a cake must be weighted accurately and the cake must be baked at the right temperature.

Below: Modern inventions such as electronic calculators can be a great help in mathematics.

Left: Many everyday instruments give us measurements automatically. The speedometer measures speed (the distance travelled in a given time). The barometer measures pressure (the weight of air acting on a given area of the Earth's surface).

Elements

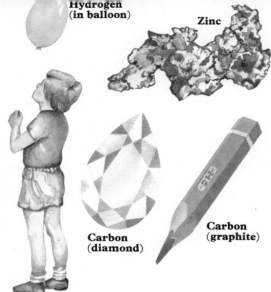

Hydrogen
(in balloon)

Zinc

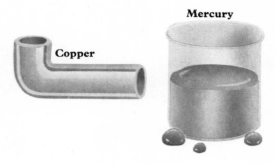

Mercury

Copper

Carbon
(diamond)

Carbon
(graphite)

Left: Most
elements are
metals. Metals
include copper and
zinc (solids), and
mercury, a liquid
element.
Hydrogen is a gas,
and carbon is a solid
with more than one
crystalline form.

The Elements

Elements are the simplest substances, from which everything is made. They are themselves made up of atoms. An atom of one element has different chemical *properties*, or characteristics, from an atom of another element. There are 92 elements which occur naturally on the Earth. A few have been created by scientists. Two elements, bromine and mercury, exist normally as liquids. Eleven, including hydrogen and helium, are normally gases. The rest are solids, mostly metals, such as aluminium and copper. They have widely differing properties. Some are hard, some soft, some are strong, others brittle.

Studying the Elements

It was not until the 1800s that scientists really began to understand the nature of chemical substances. But several of the chemical elements, such as iron and

sulphur, were known in prehistoric times. The ancient peoples did not know these were elements, though. In the Middle Ages, scientists called alchemists tried to make gold from other substances—without success.

The 'father' of modern chemistry was an English scientist, Robert Boyle, who lived in the 1600s. He was the first to say what an element was. More and more elements were discovered in the 1700s and 1800s.

Below: Most
metals look glossy
and are good
conductors of heat
and electricity.
They can be mixed
to form alloys.
Brass, for
example, is an
alloy of copper
and zinc.

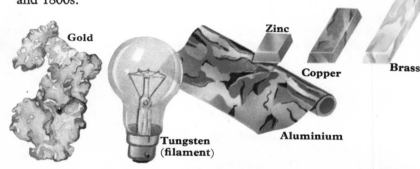

Gold

Zinc

Copper

Brass

Tungsten
(filament)

Aluminium

Words used in Chemistry

chemical change A change in a substance due to an alteration in the arrangement of its atoms and also physical changes, for example, crystalline structure and melting.

compound A substance that consists of two or more elements combined chemically. Water (H_2O), for example, contains hydrogen (H) and oxygen (O).

mixture Two or more substances mixed together, but not combined chemically as in a compound.

oxide A substance in which oxygen (O) is combined with another element.

**Above: Separating
iron filings from
sulphur.**

react To undergo a chemical change, as when one element combines with another.

reaction The action on each other of two or more substances, resulting in chemical changes.

reagent A chemical substance used to produce a reaction.

refine To purify.

solution The result when one substance dissolves in another, usually a solid dissolving in a liquid.

solvent A liquid in which other substances can be dissolved.

The Periodic Table of elements arranges them in groups according to their properties. For example, the 'light metals' are in yellow on the left, the 'heavy metals' in light brown in the centre, the non-metals in light red to the right, and the rare gases in red on the far right.

H 1																	He 2
Li 3	Be 4											B 5	C 6	N 7	O 8	F 9	Ne 10
Na 11	Mg 12											Al 13	Si 14	P 15	S 16	Cl 17	Ar 18
K 19	Ca 20	Sc 21	Ti 22	V 23	Cr 24	Mn 25	Fe 26	Co 27	Ni 28	Cu 29	Zn 30	Ga 31	Ge 32	As 33	Se 34	Br 35	Kr 36
Rb 37	Sr 38	Y 39	Zr 40	Nb 41	Mo 42	Tc 43	Ru 44	Rh 45	Pd 46	Ag 47	Cd 48	In 49	Sn 50	Sb 51	Te 52	I 53	Xe 54
Cs 55	Ba 56	La 57	Hf 72	Ta 73	W 74	Re 75	Os 76	Ir 77	Pt 78	Au 79	Hg 80	Tl 81	Pb 82	Bi 83	Po 84	At 85	Rn 86
Fr 87	Ra 88	Ac 89															

Names: Hydrogen (H, 1); Helium (He, 2); Lithium (Li, 3); Beryllium (Be, 4); Boron (B, 5); Carbon (C, 6); Nitrogen (N, 7); Oxygen (O, 8); Fluorine (F, 9); Neon (Ne, 10); Sodium (Na, 11); Magnesium (Mg, 12); Aluminium (Al, 13); Silicon (Si, 14); Phosphorus (P, 15); Sulphur (S, 16); Chlorine (Cl, 17); Argon (Ar, 18); Potassium (K, 19); Calcium (Ca, 20); Scandium (Sc, 21); Titanium (Ti, 22); Vanadium (V, 23); Chromium (Cr, 24); Manganese (Mn, 25); Iron (Fe, 26); Cobalt (Co, 27); Nickel (Ni, 28); Copper (Cu, 29); Zinc (Zn, 30); Gallium (Ga, 31); Germanium (Ge, 32); Arsenic (As, 33); Selenium (Se, 34); Bromine (Br, 35); Krypton (Kr, 36); Rubidium (Rb, 37); Strontium (Sr, 38); Yttrium (Y, 39); Zirconium (Zr, 40); Niobium (Nb, 41); Molybdenum (Mo, 42); Technetium (Tc, 43); Ruthenium (Ru, 44); Rhodium (Rh, 45); Palladium (Pd, 46); Silver (Ag, 47); Cadmium (Cd, 48); Indium (In, 49); Tin (Sn, 50); Antimony (Sb, 51); Tellurium (Te, 52); Iodine (I, 53); Xenon (Xe, 54); Caesium (Cs, 55); Barium (Ba, 56); Lanthanum (La, 57); Hafnium (Hf, 72); Tantalum (Ta, 73); Tungsten (W, 74); Rhenium (Re, 75); Osmium (Os, 76); Iridium (Ir, 77); Platinum (Pt, 78); Gold (Au, 79); Mercury (Hg, 80); Thallium (Tl, 81); Lead (Pb, 82); Bismuth (Bi, 83); Polonium (Po, 84); Astatine (At, 85); Radon (Rn, 86); Francium (Fr, 87); Radium (Ra, 88); Actinium (Ac, 89).

Rare earth group

Ce 58	Pr 59	Nd 60	Pm 61	Sm 62	Eu 63	Gd 64	Tb 65	Dy 66	Ho 67	Er 68	Tm 69	Yb 70	Lu 71

Cerium (Ce, 58); Praseodymium (Pr, 59); Neodymium (Nd, 60); Promethium (Pm, 61); Samarium (Sm, 62); Europium (Eu, 63); Gadolinium (Gd, 64); Terbium (Tb, 65); Dysprosium (Dy, 66); Holmium (Ho, 67); Erbium (Er, 68); Thulium (Tm, 69); Ytterbium (Yb, 70); Lutetium (Lu, 71).

Actinide group

Th 90	Pa 91	U 92	Np 93	Pu 94	Am 95	Cm 96	Bk 97	Cf 98	Es 99	Fm 100	Md 101	No 102	Lr 103

Thorium (Th, 90); Protactinium (Pa, 91); Uranium (U, 92); Neptunium (Np, 93); Plutonium (Pu, 94); Americium (Am, 95); Curium (Cm, 96); Berkelium (Bk, 97); Californium (Cf, 98); Einsteinium (Es, 99); Fermium (Fm, 100); Mendelevium (Md, 101); Nobelium (No, 102); Lawrencium (Lr, 103).

In the mid-1850s, scientists noticed a connection between the relative weights of the elements and their chemical properties. The atomic weights (now called 'relative atomic masses') could at that time be calculated in relation to each other. The Russian chemist Dmitri Mendeleyev built up a Periodic Table of elements. The modern Table groups the elements in order of their atomic number and according to their properties (see the section *Inside the Atom*).

Chemical Symbols

Each element is represented by a symbol consisting of a capital letter by itself or of a capital letter and a small letter. For example, H stands for hydrogen and He for helium. Some of the symbols come from the Latin names of elements. The symbol Pb for lead, for example, comes from the Latin *plumbum*.

Chemical symbols are used in writing chemical equations. An example of an equation is:

$$H_2 + Cl_2 \rightarrow 2HCl$$

This represents the simple reaction between the gases hydrogen (H) and chlorine (Cl), which combine to form hydrochloric acid (HCl), a liquid.

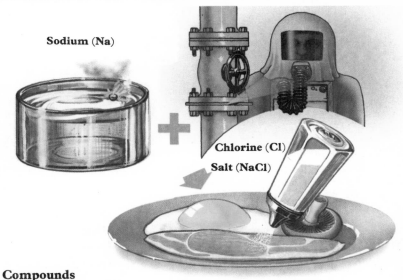

Sodium (Na)

Chlorine (Cl)

Salt (NaCl)

Compounds formed when elements combine are very different from those elements. Sodium (Na) and chlorine (Cl), for example, are unpleasant and highly active alone. Yet they combine to form common salt (NaCl), a harmless substance.

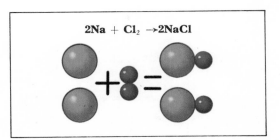

$$2Na + Cl_2 \rightarrow 2NaCl$$

Solids, Liquids and Gases

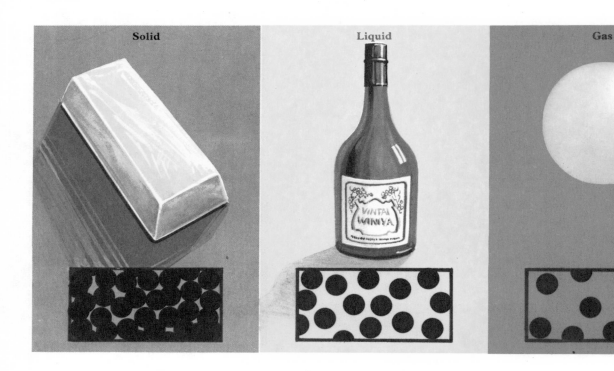

Solid

Liquid

Gas

Above: Matter exists in three states—solid, liquid or gas. It consists of small particles, called atoms, which are held together by 'cohesive forces'. In the solid state the particles are tightly bound like bricks in a wall. A solid has a definite shape. As the temperature rises, the atoms begin to vibrate and the cohesive forces weaken. The particles are loosely attached and can slide over each other. A liquid does not have a shape but adopts the shape of its container. At higher temperatures the energy within the atoms is **much greater than the force binding the atoms. The particles are not attached and fly about at random. A gas has no shape but is limited by its container.**

Solids, liquids and gases are the three common states of matter. Most substances are in one of these three states. If it is made cold enough, every substance will become solid. Many substances, such as rocks, are solid at the normal temperature at which we live. Substances that are liquid at normal temperature have to be cooled to make them freeze. Water must be cooled to 0°C (32°F) to change into ice, which is solid water. However, most substances that are gases at normal temperature have to be cooled to a much lower temperature than this to make

them condense into a liquid. Then they have to be cooled even more to make them freeze into a solid. Oxygen, which we breathe in the air, becomes a liquid at —183°C (—297°F) and a solid at —219°C (—362°F).

Everything will become a gas if made hot enough. Water boils at 100°C (212°F) and becomes steam. Some metals, such as solder, melt at temperatures not much higher than this, but iron does not melt until it reaches 1539°C (2802°F); it boils at 2800°C (5072°F).

Pressure also influences the change of

Below: Although a submarine is made of metal which is heavier than water, the air in the ballast tanks allows it to surface. The tanks are filled with water to make the sub sink and when the water is blown out it re-surfaces.

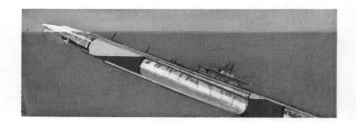

their state. A liquid under high pressure has to be heated more than a liquid at low pressure to make it boil. But if the pressure is reduced, the molecules can escape more readily; at 3,000 metres (10,000 feet), water boils at only 90°C (194°F), so it is difficult to cook a boiled egg! Pressure also affects melting and freezing. No matter how much helium is cooled, it will not solidify unless it is compressed as well.

Atoms and Molecules

Why are some substances normally solid, some liquid and others gaseous? It depends on the forces exerted between the atoms and molecules in the substance. In most substances the atoms are held together in groups called molecules. Even the largest molecules are so small they can only just be seen in the most powerful microscopes. This page is about half a million atoms thick.

In a solid, the atoms and molecules all

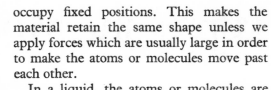

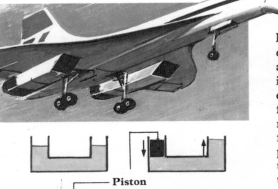

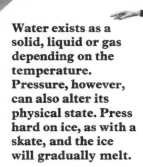

Above: Many digital watches use liquid crystal in the display panel. Liquid crystal has characteristics of a crystal and a liquid and many others that are unique.

Water exists as a solid, liquid or gas depending on the temperature. Pressure, however, can also alter its physical state. Press hard on ice, as with a skate, and the ice will gradually melt.

—Piston

Left: Hydraulics deals with the use of a liquid, because of its ability to be compressed and to flow, to perform mechanical work. If a fluid in a pipe is pushed by a piston, the force exerted on the fluid can be made to do work. Aircraft undercarriages use this system.

occupy fixed positions. This makes the material retain the same shape unless we apply forces which are usually large in order to make the atoms or molecules move past each other.

In a liquid, the atoms or molecules are free to move about, so that the liquid can easily change its shape. It always flows to the bottom of any container. The atoms and molecules stay close together but can slide past each other. Thus, when a ship is pushed through the sea, the molecules of seawater slide out of the way and, after being churned about in the ship's wake, they will return gradually to rest. In doing so they become warmed, as the energy is being supplied by the motion of the ship.

As in a liquid, atoms or molecules in a gas can move in all directions. Unlike a liquid, they can move away from each other wherever they can. Because they are free to move, gases tend to expand indefinitely. Hence, in practice, a small amount of gas will completely fill any container.

Density and Floating

The density of a substance is the relation between its mass, or weight, and its volume. For example, expanded polystyrene foam has an extremely low density and even large pieces seem to weigh hardly anything. But if you hold a comparatively small piece of the metal lead in your hand, it will feel very heavy. This is because lead has a high density, like most metals and rocks. In fact, lead is over 11 times as heavy as an equal volume of water.

Any solid placed in a liquid of higher density will float. Ships made of metal float because they contain empty spaces, which make the boat as a whole less dense than the water.

Forces and Motion

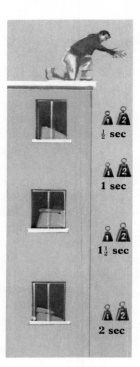

A force is basically a push, a pull or a twist. A force is needed to start a mass moving, to change its speed, to make it change direction, or to bring it to rest.

We use our muscles to produce force. We move ourselves and objects by exerting force with our arms and legs. We also produce force with engines to drive our machines. However, force is not needed to keep objects moving unless there is some resistance. When you throw a ball into the air, you use the muscles in your arm to move your hand and push the ball into the air. The ball is then slowed down by the resistance of the air, and pulled downwards by the Earth's gravitational attraction. If there were no atmosphere and no gravity, the ball would go on at the same speed and in the same direction for ever.

Friction

Almost everything that moves on Earth is resisted by some form of friction, because no surface is absolutely smooth. Hence, friction is the force that slows down a book as it slides across a table. And if you place a brick on a plank, you will soon find how far you will have to tilt the plank before the brick will slide down it.

When a bicycle or car is moving at a constant speed, the force pushing it forward is equal to the friction acting to slow it. Some of the friction is inside the engine (or inside our bodies as we pedal along). Some is in the moving parts of the vehicle. Some is due to the rolling resistance of the tyres, and some to our resistance.

Away from the Earth, out in space, there is no air to cause friction and to slow down a spacecraft. A satellite moving around the Earth, therefore, continues to move in its orbit without stopping. Similarly the Moon always moves around the Earth and the Earth moves around the Sun.

Above left: Racing cyclists use muscle power to move their cycles at high speeds. In doing this they overcome air resistance. Even fast riders try to follow in the 'slipstream' created by the leaders. This reserves power for the final dash to the finish.

Above: Until Galileo proved otherwise, people believed that heavier objects fell faster. Earth's gravity pulls at a constant 9.8m (32 ft) per second per second, but air resistance slows the speed of some falling objects.

Left: Newton's third law of motion states that for every action there is a reaction. When a car hits another the first stops, throwing the driver forwards, and the other accelerates, throwing the driver backwards. Snooker uses this law.

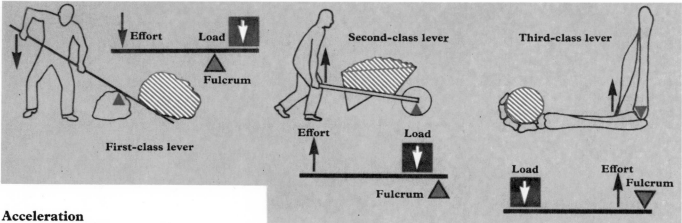

Effort   Load

Fulcrum

First-class lever

Second-class lever

Effort   Load

Fulcrum

Third-class lever

Load   Effort
Fulcrum

Acceleration

If the force pushing a moving object is greater than the total retarding force, the speed increases. If you pedal harder on your bicycle, it accelerates until the increasing friction and air resistance once more balances the force with which you are pedalling. Then the acceleration stops and the bicycle travels at a steady, higher speed.

When you stop pedalling, the forces are again unbalanced and you slow down. If you put on the brakes, you increase the friction. You therefore slow down much more rapidly.

Gravity

Scientists do not fully understand gravity. It is a force that makes objects attract each other. It is quite separate from magnetism, because it is possessed by everything, and depends on mass (the weight of an object). Two people attract each other, but we do not notice this because the force is so small.

What we do notice is the very powerful attraction of the Earth. This is why things fall to the ground. Gravity extends out into space. It is gravity that keeps a satellite circling around the Earth, and the Earth in orbit around the Sun.

Inertia

Imagine a very heavy weight hung from a strong wire. Even though there is little friction, we would have to push hard to start it swinging. Once it was swinging, it would need a large force to stop it. This is because of inertia, which makes every mass resist a change in its motion. The heavier the object, the greater the force you will need to accelerate it to a particular speed, or to make it stop. A force is required to overcome inertia. This explains why, in a moving car which stops suddenly, a passenger will continue to move forward unless stopped by a safety belt.

On the Moon, where there is no air resistance, everything falls at the same rate. On Earth, gravity accelerates everything at a rate of 9.8 metres (32 feet) per second per second. People once thought that heavy objects fell faster than light ones. This was disproved by the scientist Galileo (1564-1642), who is supposed to have dropped two weights of different sizes off the top of the Leaning Tower of Pisa. The weights hit the ground at the same time. Light feathers and pieces of paper fall more slowly only because of air resistance.

Above: A machine is a device which enables energy to be used more efficiently. A lever allows effort applied at one place to create movement at another. The three types of lever shown differ according to the position of the effort applied, load and fulcrum (or point on which the lever turns).

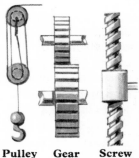

Pulley   Gear   Screw

Above: There are several other devices which simplify work. A pulley enables a heavy weight to be lifted with a small amount of effort. A gear is used to transmit motion or to change speed or direction. A screw can be used to raise and support heavy weights.

In the event of a crash, a car safety belt prevents the driver from being thrown by the force of inertia.

Above: Cranes are powerful lifting machines which combine the principles of the lever and pulley. Cranes are versatile because they can pivot to move loads horizontally as well as vertically. Many cranes can be moved to different sites.

Heat

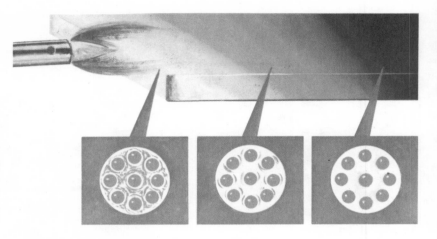

Heat makes us warm. We get heat from the Sun, from fires and radiators. The food we eat produces energy inside our bodies, some of which appears as heat. The more heat anything receives, the hotter it becomes. If anything loses heat, it gets colder. We measure how hot or cold things are by taking their temperature with a thermometer. Temperature is usually measured in degrees Celsius (°C).

A cold substance, for example ice, still has heat, but much less than a hot object. Heat is a form of energy. It makes the atoms or molecules in an object vibrate. The more heat there is in an object, the faster its atoms and molecules vibrate. As an object cools, its atoms and molecules slow down. At a temperature called absolute zero, the atoms and molecules stop moving. This temperature is —273°C (—459°F). It can never quite be reached because nothing can lose all its heat.

Heat travels from a hotter object to a colder object in three ways. Heat spreads through solids by conduction. Very bad conductors insulate heat, one example is glass-wool put on a hotwater tank. In liquids or gases, the heated matter rises causing convection currents. For example, the Sun may heat the ground intensely so that the warm air near the ground rises in a strong current. This air finally cools, spreads out and then sinks again. Heat also travels through empty space by radiation in the form of infra-red rays.

First Dictionary of Heat

boiling point The temperature at which a liquid changes into vapour. The boiling point of water is 100°C.

Celsius The standard scale of temperature. It was named after a Swedish astronomer, Anders Celsius (1701-1744).

Centrigrade An old name for Celsius.

degree Units of the temperature scale. Temperature is usually measured in degrees Celsius (°C).

Fahrenheit A scale of temperature in which the freezing point of water is 32°F, and the boiling point is 212°F. To convert Celsius to Fahrenheit, multiply by 9/5 and add 32. The scale was invented by a German physicist, Daniel Fahrenheit (1686-1736).

freezing point The temperature at which a liquid freezes to a solid. The freezing point of water is 0°C.

heat insulator A substance that does not conduct heat well. Good insulators include a vacuum, air, glass, wool and asbestos.

melting point The temperature at which a solid melts to a liquid.

temperature The temperature of an object shows how hot or cold it is. Temperature is measured in degrees.

thermometer An instrument that measures temperature. In a mercury or alcohol thermometer, the liquid in a small container expands and contracts up and down a thin, graduated tube.

thermostat A device that keeps a heater or heating unit, such as a central heating system, at a steady temperature.

Above: Heat has an influence on the movement of atoms. The atoms and molecules in a hot flame vibrate quickly, whereas, farther away where it is cooler, they vibrate at a much slower rate. At a temperature of 0° Kelvin (—273°C/ —459°F), atomic and molecular movement would stop, but this is an impossible temperature, so atoms and molecules are always moving.

Left: A solar house has insulated roof panels with glass covers. Inside are copper tubes filled with water. These are heated by the Sun, even on cloudy days. The hot water from these panels goes into the heating system of the house to warm the rooms. The Sun's heat is free, and solar houses save fuels such as coal, gas or oil, that are becoming scarce.

Sound

We hear sounds because our Earth has an atmosphere (it is silent on the Moon!). Any disturbance to the air causes waves to expand out from that point, like ripples from a stone dropped in a pond. As the waves pass our ears we hear the sounds.

Sound waves consist of air molecules vibrating to and fro. We cannot feel most sound waves because the pressures are not strong enough. But they make our eardrums vibrate, and this causes us to hear the sound.

Sound waves move through air, at a speed of about 330 metres (1,082 feet) per second (a little faster on a hot day, slower in winter). This is much slower than light. We would see an explosion 1 kilometre (0.62 miles) away in 1/300,000 second, but we would not hear it until more than three seconds had elapsed.

Sound also travels through liquids such as water, and solids such as glass and stone. This happens because these materials, like air, can transmit vibrations. This is why you can hear sounds coming through walls and windows. But sound does not travel through empty space. The astronauts on the Moon had to speak to one another by radio because there is no air on the Moon to carry sound waves.

When a sound wave hits a hard surface, it bounces off it. If you are far enough away from a wall or cliff, you can hear your voice return to you as an echo. The echo is caused by your sound waves bouncing off the wall or cliff. In a large building, a church for example, you may be able to hear many echoes as sound bounces to and fro off the walls. Concert halls are designed to avoid echoes.

The speed at which a sound wave vibrates makes it sound higher or lower. A deep

sound, such as a drum, vibrates slower than a shrill sound, such as a flute. Some sounds vibrate so fast that they are too high for us to hear. These sounds are called ultrasonic, and they have many uses in today's world. This is because ultrasonic waves can be focused, much like a beam of light from a searchlight. Ultrasonic devices are used to locate and measure objects underwater, to separate different signals on the same lines in telephone systems, and so on.

Below: An echo is caused by physical conditions, where sound waves from a noise reverberate off surrounding surfaces, and bounce back to make an echo. Echoes are common in hilly areas.

Above: By sending down sound vibrations from special equipment and calculating the length of time it takes for the echo to bounce back, the warship can accurately gauge how far the submarine has submerged.

Below: Crossing the sound barrier (from left to right). As a plane travels, pressure waves that travel at the speed of sound are created. As it accelerates, the plane catches up with the waves and a shock wave builds up. As the plane crosses the sound barrier a sonic boom can be heard on the ground.

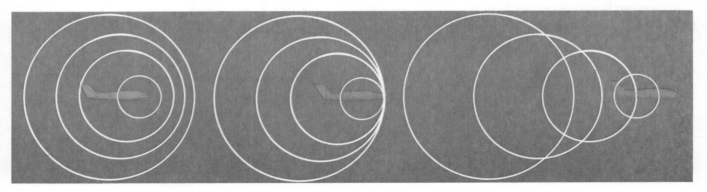

Light

We see objects because light rays coming from them enter our eyes. Most objects do not generate their own light. Only bright objects, such as the Sun or a lamp, are sources of light. They illuminate other objects by sending out light rays which are reflected by the surfaces of the objects into our eyes.

Light is like a succession of waves and also like a stream of particles. Light rays travel in straight lines and move at the tremendous speed of 300,000 kilometres a second. Nothing, in fact, can move faster than light.

Objects produce light if they are made very hot. The Sun shines because it is very hot. The filament of a light bulb glows when

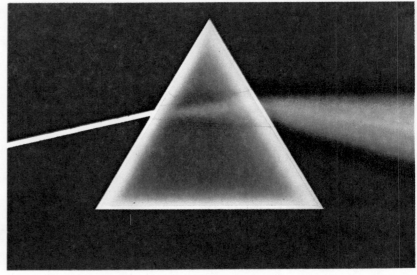

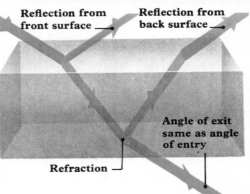

Reflection from front surface

Reflection from back surface

Refraction

Angle of exit same as angle of entry

Above: Light enters a glass prism and is split up into the colours of the spectrum, showing how light is composed of colours. Left: Light rays bend and distort as they pass through different mediums like glass or water. This is how lenses work.

Below: The brightness of a light bulb is measured in units called candelas. A domestic light bulb has a brightness of about 35 candelas.

First Dictionary of Light

focus The place near a lens or curved mirror where a sharp image of a distant object forms.

image A picture of a real object produced by a lens or mirror.

lens Pieces of transparent material, notably glass, shaped to bend light rays to form an image. Convex lenses bend outwards and concave lenses bend inwards.

mirror A shiny surface that reflects light rays to give an image. Flat mirrors give images the same size as the object they reflect. Convex mirrors bend outwards and make things look smaller. Concave mirrors bend inwards and can make things look larger. A parabolic concave mirror can send out light from a point source at its focus into a parallel beam, as in car headlights.

prism A triangular block of glass that splits up white light to form a spectrum.

retina The part of the back of the eye that is sensitive to light.

spectrum Each wavelength of visible light corresponds to a colour. The longest waves look red and the shortest violet. The spectrum is all the colour spread out according to wavelength. Sunlight passed through a prism can throw a spectrum on white paper. Sunlight refracted through raindrops makes the rainbow.

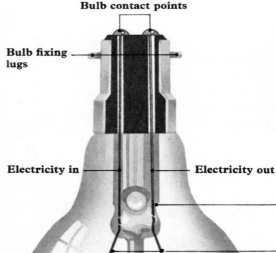

Bulb contact points

Bulb fixing lugs

Electricity in

Electricity out

Glass mount

Wires carrying electric current

Glass bulb

Support wires

Filament

it is heated by electricity. Some substances emit light without getting hot. Strip lights and television sets contain luminous substances that light up when fed with electricity.

The surfaces of most objects are not smooth, and so they scatter light in all directions. If the surface is flat and smooth, each ray of light is reflected in one direction. We call such surfaces mirrors. When you stand in front of a mirror, light rays from your face strike the mirror and are reflected back into your eyes.

Light travels through empty space, and also through transparent substances such as air, water and glass. Whenever it enters a new substance, its speed changes slightly. This makes the light rays bend if they enter the surface of the new substance at an angle. This bending is called *refraction* of light.

Refraction causes strange images to form. A stick when plunged into water appears bent where it enters the water, and things seen underwater look nearer than they are. Lenses like those in a magnifying glass or spectacles refract light rays to form images. A magnifying glass concentrates all the rays at one point, called the focus. If the light from the Sun is focused into a small bright point on dry paper, the paper will soon char and burst into flames. Other lenses can project a beam through a film or slide on to a screen.

Right: A magnifying glass is a lens with convex surfaces. The lens is fatter in the centre than at the edges. Light rays take longer to pass through the thick part, and this bends them more, so that when they focus the objects being magnified appear larger than they really are. The diagram shows how the object (O) appears as an enlarged image (I).

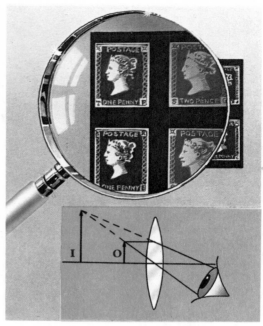

Below left and below: A magnifying glass can be used to concentrate the Sun's rays (see diagram). If the hot rays are focused on to a piece of paper the paper will smoulder and burn. Do not try to do this yourself because you may easily start a fire.

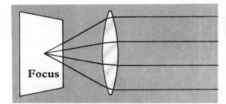

Focus

Light rays are sometimes bent, or refracted, near the Earth's surface so that they create kinds of optical illusions. For example, on a hot day, the shimmer over a road looks like a pool of water. Even more striking are mirages of cool pools of water seen by thirsty travellers in hot, sandy deserts. Sometimes the effect of a mirage is to make distant objects appear to be nearby. Sometimes objects appear to be upside down. For example, at sea, the dense layers of air near the water focus rays from a distant object, such as a ship, into an upside-down image in the sky. Because mirages are caused by light rays passing through layers of air of differing density, they can be photographed as well as seen.

Above: Light travels very fast—at a speed of about 300,000 km (186,000 miles) per second. It takes $8\frac{1}{2}$ minutes for light to travel from the Sun to the Earth. Special instruments measure very accurately the speed of light. They use lasers and microwave aerials (shown here).

Colour

A transparent prism splits up white light into a spectrum of colours. Raindrops act in a similar way, breaking up sunlight into a rainbow. This happens because sunlight and white light consist of a mixture of colours. As light passes through the prism or raindrops, it is bent or refracted. However, the different wavelengths are bent by different amounts, so the colours in the light are spread out.

White and almost all colours can be made by mixing light of other colours. Black is seen when no light is reflected. A colour television set makes colours by mixing light of three colours: blue, green and red. If you look closely at the screen, you will see that the whole picture is made up of dots or lines of these three colours. They merge to form a colour picture. Green and red light make yellow light, and all three colours, green, red and blue, make white light. Lights over the stage in a theatre are used to make colours in much the same way.

Most of the colours we see do not come

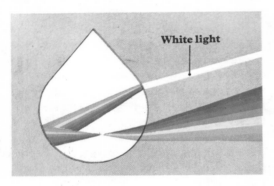

White light

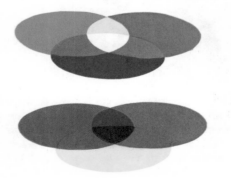

Above: A red pencil appears to the eye as red because the surface of the pencil absorbs all the colours of the spectrum except red. Red is reflected, making the pencil appear red coloured. A black object absorbs all the light, and a white object reflects all the light.

Left and centre left: A rainbow is formed when light is refracted and reflected. The light enters the raindrops which act as thousands of tiny prisms reflecting the light back in the colours.

from original sources of light, but from surfaces that reflect or scatter the light falling on them. Hence a colour television picture is quite different from a colour illustration in a book or a colour photograph, because the light entering the eyes from a colour television is produced by the picture itself. On the other hand, a coloured illustration does not produce light. It is illuminated by the Sun or by artificial light. The light that enters our eyes is, therefore, light that has been reflected from the surface of the illustration or some other object. Each surface absorbs some colours and reflects others. For instance, a blue surface absorbs most colour except blue. The blue light is reflected into our eyes and we see the surface as blue. White cinema screens reflect all colours.

Below left and above: The primary colours in light are red, blue and green. The primary colours in paint pigments are special shades of red, blue and yellow. From these primary colours all shades can be made. In the case of light, a combination of the primary colours produces white.

146

Energy

Energy is the capacity to do work. It is found inside atoms. Some of this is turned into another form of energy, heat, when the atoms combine chemically in what we call burning. Far more heat is generated in nuclear fission.

Heat, light and radio waves can transmit energy through space. Potential energy is found in a compressed spring, or a rock that could fall from a high cliff. If it fell it would gather speed, gaining kinetic energy. When it hit the ground the energy would be transformed into noise and heat.

We are always using energy. As we digest food, we use its chemical energy to produce body heat and power our muscles. The Sun's light makes daylight and its heat rays give enough warmth for life to exist on Earth. We use the chemical energy in petrol to drive cars, and we use electrical energy to power machines and light our houses. Light rays and radio waves bring us information as we read or look at television. We use the kinetic energy of a hammer to drive in a nail.

Most energy is produced by changing one kind into another. In a power station, we burn coal to raise steam, to drive a generator and make electricity. Burning the coal changes chemical energy in the coal

into heat. This heat is turned into kinetic energy as the steam turns the generator, and the generator turns the kinetic energy into electricity.

Some kinds of energy can be created. Energy is made in a nuclear reactor and inside the Sun and other stars. This is done by using up matter.

Above: An offshore drilling rig. In the search for further sources of fuel, new drilling techniques have been employed to enable valuable gas and oil to be extracted from beneath the sea bed. Special pipes carry the oil or gas inland.

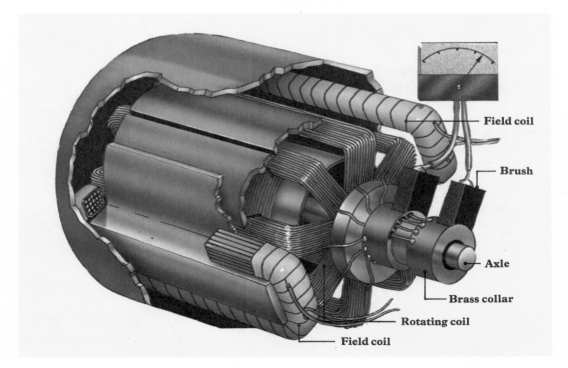

Field coil

Brush

Axle

Brass collar

Rotating coil

Field coil

Left: An electric generator works on the principle of magnetism. A magnetic field is created in a field coil of wire. Several field coils are arranged around moving coils, so that large electric currents are produced. The generator is turned by a water or steam turbine.

Magnetism

A magnet will pick up steel pins at close range and hold them. Its force is stronger than the force of gravity. You can feel this force by putting two magnets together. In one position, they cling together and you will have to pull hard to part them. In the other position, they will twist away from each other.

If you hang a bar magnet on a thread it will turn until one end faces north and the other faces south. The end that points north is called the north pole, and the south-seeking end is the south pole.

When two bar magnets are brought together, they pull themselves together if the north pole of one faces the south pole of the other. If the two north poles face each other,

Left: A magnet can separate iron filings from a mixture of iron and other non-metallic mixes. When a magnet picks up a pin, the pin is temporarily turned into a magnet and picks up more pins. The molecules in the unmagnetized pin point in all directions until they are lined up by the magnet. The magnetic field is strongest at the poles (the ends).

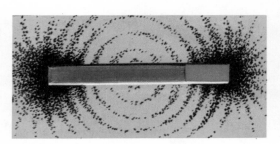

Left and far left: The magnetic field surrounding a magnet becomes visible if a sheet of paper is laid over the magnet and iron filings are sprinkled over the paper.

the magnets will repel one another. This is a law of magnetism: like poles repel each other, and unlike poles attract each other.

The force exerted by a magnet falls away as the square of the distance: twice the distance means only one-quarter of the force. Thus, though the effect of a magnet can in theory be felt at any distance, in fact it is felt only within a limited space. We call this space the field of the magnet.

The Earth is a huge magnet, with its poles quite near the Earth's North and South Poles. The Earth's magnetic field extends all over the world, so that every magnet in the world is acted upon by the Earth's magnetic field. Therefore, every magnet that can do so aligns itself with the Earth's field.

A compass needle is a small magnet balanced on a pivot so that it can turn. It responds to the Earth's magnetic field so that it always points to the magnetic poles. These poles do not lie exactly at the North and South geographic poles, so a compass needle does not indicate true north exactly. In fact, the magnetic poles are always

slowly moving. However, their location from one year to the next is well-known, and it is easy to allow for this movement and work out where true north is from a compass. Around the Earth is a magnetic field which may be upset during magnetic storms, when radio communications are interrupted and compass needles swing round. These storms may be caused by a solar wind, which consists of a stream of charged particles emanating from the Sun. The Earth's magnetism is probably caused by movements in the liquid inner core of the Earth.

You can think of the field surrounding every magnet as consisting of many in-

Below: Unlike poles attract and like poles repel one another. The dog's head and the bone both contain magnets and the dog will only accept the bone at one end.

148

visible lines of magnetic force linking its poles. The lines of force bulge outwards between the poles. You can see where the lines of force extend in a magnet. Place a piece of paper over a bar magnet and sprinkle some iron filings on the paper. Now tap the paper. The filings act as tiny magnets and move to follow the lines of force. They make a pattern of lines between the poles of the magnet. This pattern is an outline of the magnetic field.

Below: The tape in a tape recorder is coated with a paste containing iron or chromium oxide crystals, which act as hundreds of tiny magnets. They form a magnetic pattern when a recording is made. This pattern is picked up by the playback head and changed back into sound again.

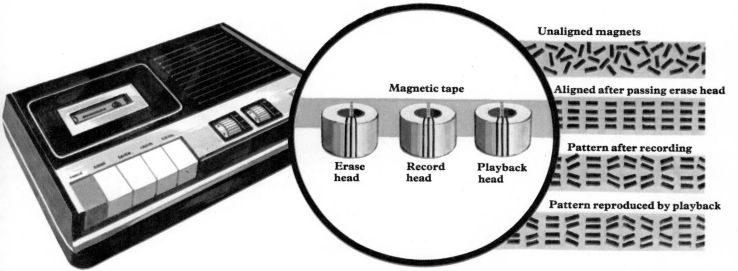

Unaligned magnets

Magnetic tape

Aligned after passing erase head

Erase head   Record head   Playback head

Pattern after recording

Pattern reproduced by playback

It is easy to make iron and steel objects magnetic. When a magnet picks up a pin, its magnetic field turns the pin into a small magnet. However, the pin loses most of its magnetism when it is separated from the magnet. A permanent magnet can be made by continually stroking an iron bar with one pole of a magnet in the same direction. Most magnets are made by placing them in the strong magnetic field inside a coil of wire carrying a current.

Not all materials are magnetic. Iron, nickel and cobalt are among the most magnetic materials. Other metals and materials are only slightly magnetic and cannot be used for magnets. If you cut a bar magnet into pieces, every piece will be found to have its own N and S poles! Thus we can see that a magnet is made of a large number of extremely small magnetic parts. When we magnetize iron we do so by making all the parts rotate to point in the same direction.

Right: The Earth's magnetic lines of force all point along magnetic north and south. These magnetic poles are different from the geographic poles. Magnetic north is 74N 100W and magnetic south is 67S 142W.

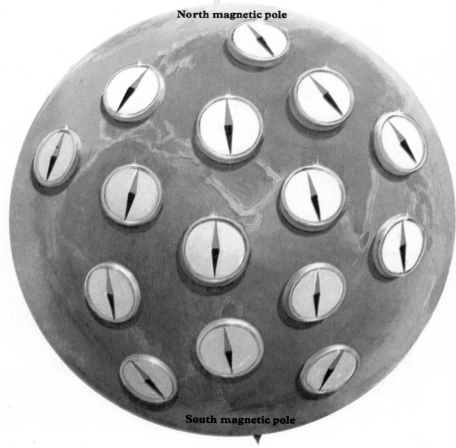

North magnetic pole

South magnetic pole

Electricity

Electricity is a form of invisible energy which is very important to us. In nature, we can see the effect of electricity in a flash of lightning. But electricity can be generated, stored in a battery or carried along a cable. Because it is ready for use whenever we need it, it has been called 'man's most useful servant'. It is also cheap and clean.

There are two kinds of electricity. Current flows along a wire. It consists of a stream of electrons. This is the kind that powers our homes. The other kind is static electricity. Clouds may build up charges of static electricity. When the charge becomes too great, lightning flashes between the cloud and the ground.

You can produce static electricity by rubbing an insulator (something that will not conduct current), such as a plastic comb.

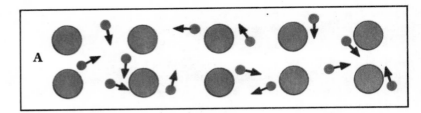

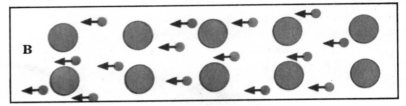

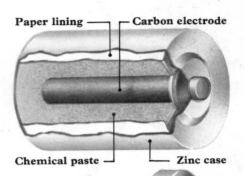

Paper lining — Carbon electrode
Chemical paste — Zinc case

Above: In most materials the electrons (red) move about the nucleus (blue) of atoms in a random motion (A). Electrons have a negative charge while the nucleus is made up of protons (which have a positive charge) and neutrons (no charge). When a current flows (B) through the material, the electrons flow in an orderly manner away from the negative pole towards the positive pole. Some materials, such as copper and aluminium, are good conductors.

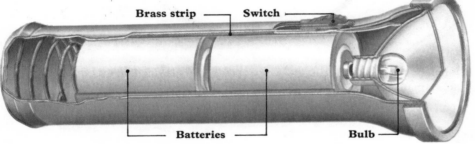

Brass strip — Switch
Batteries — Bulb

Left: A dry cell or battery produces a direct current (DC), i.e. it flows in one direction—from the negatively charged zinc outer case to the positively charged inner carbon rod when a connection is made. Current flows in a torch when the circuit is completed. This is done by moving the switch to join the two brass strips.

First Dictionary of Electricity

accumulator A battery that can store electricity. Unlike a dry battery, it can be recharged.

ampere (amp) The unit of electric current.

conductor Any substance through which electricity can flow. Most metals are good conductors.

dry cell A battery containing dry chemicals.

electrical resistance Every substance resists the flow of electricity to some degree. Conductors have a very low resistance and insulators a very high resistance. Resistance is measured in *ohms*.

fuse A piece of wire that protects electrical machines and wiring from dangerously high currents. The fuse heats up and melts before the machines or wiring are damaged.

insulator Any substance that resists the flow of electric current. Many plastics are good insulators, and are therefore used to cover electric cables and wires.

volt The unit of 'electro-motive force'; we can think of this as being equivalent to pressure in a water pipe. To contain a high voltage we need good insulation.

watt The unit of power (not necessarily electric power). Power is the rate at which something does work. One bar of an electric fire has a power of 1000 watts (1 kilowatt).

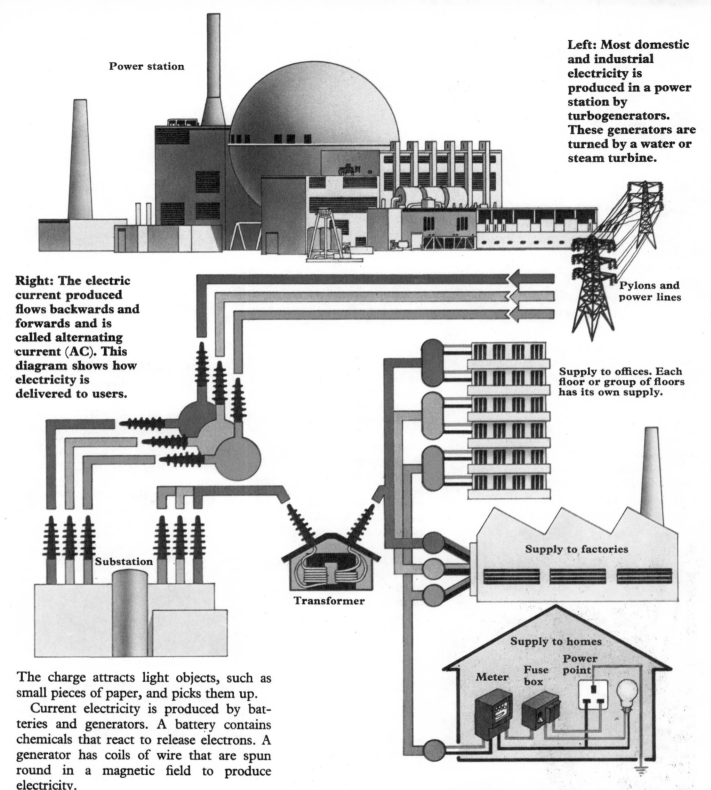

Power station

Left: Most domestic and industrial electricity is produced in a power station by turbogenerators. These generators are turned by a water or steam turbine.

Pylons and power lines

Right: The electric current produced flows backwards and forwards and is called alternating current (AC). This diagram shows how electricity is delivered to users.

Supply to offices. Each floor or group of floors has its own supply.

Substation

Supply to factories

Transformer

Supply to homes

Meter Fuse box Power point

The charge attracts light objects, such as small pieces of paper, and picks them up.

Current electricity is produced by batteries and generators. A battery contains chemicals that react to release electrons. A generator has coils of wire that are spun round in a magnetic field to produce electricity.

Many machines run on electricity. Electricity can easily be turned into heat and light. Electric motors use the magnetic effects of an electric current to produce power. Current electricity always flows round a closed circuit, from a battery or other source of current, through the heater, lamp or other device and then back to the source.

Above: Electricity from the power station flows through cables to local substations. There the voltage is regulated and reduced. It is then further transformed for use in homes, offices and factories.
Smaller cables carry electricity into homes. The meter records the amount used and the fuse box controls the current flowing.

Inside the Atom

Except for a very few things, such as light and electricity, everything is made of tiny particles called atoms. An atom is about one hundred-millionth of a centimetre across. Atoms, however, are not the smallest particles. They are made up of even smaller particles. Yet it is these minute particles in the atom that create the power of the Sun, of nuclear power stations and nuclear weapons.

An atom is mostly empty space. At the centre is a group of particles called the nucleus. Around the nucleus move even smaller particles called electrons. We are not even sure if they *are* particles—often they seem to fill a completely hollow shell surrounding the nucleus. Some atoms have several electron shells, which appear to form one inside the other.

Groups of Atoms

There are 92 naturally recurring types of atom. The simplest is that of hydrogen, with a nucleus containing one positively charged proton surrounded by one negatively charged electron. All other atoms are more complex and each type of atom forms

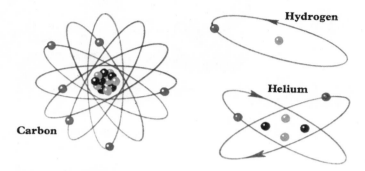

Carbon, Hydrogen, Helium

Above: Atoms consist of protons (red), neutrons (black) and electrons (green). The nucleus of the atom consists of protons and neutrons with electrons circling around it. Atoms have the same number of protons and electrons and it is the number of these that determines the type of element. Hydrogen has one of each, helium two of each and carbon six of each.

Left: Radioactivity is harmful to human beings. Radioactive isotopes, therefore, have to be handled with mechanical arms like these. The operator is protected by a special glass which prevents rays from passing through and usually protective clothing is also used. Rays are also used by doctors but under controlled conditions.

First Dictionary of the Atom

atom The smallest particle of an element with the properties of the element. Atoms are made up of electrons and nuclei. Atoms of different elements have different nuclei and different numbers of electrons.

electron A tiny particle in the atom that moves around the nucleus. It has a negative electric charge.

isotopes Different forms of the same element, with different numbers of neutrons in the nucleus.

neutron A particle in the nucleus with no electric charge.

nuclear power Energy obtained by breaking nuclei apart. The energy is in the form of heat and radiation.

nucleus A group of particles at the centre of an atom. Nuclei consist of protons and neutrons. The nuclei in the atoms of a particular element always contain the same number of protons, but the number of neutrons varies.

proton A particle in the nucleus with a positive electric charge.

radiation Some radiation, such as heat and light, is harmless. The rays sent out by radioactive substances can be dangerous.

radioactivity Anything that produces nuclear radiation is radioactive. Some elements found in nature, such as uranium, are radioactive.

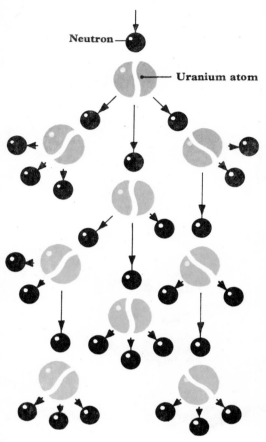

Neutron

Uranium atom

a substance called an element. Some elements are gases, such as oxygen and hydrogen. Some are solids such as sulphur. Some are metals, like iron. Elements combine to make compounds. Water is a compound of hydrogen and oxygen. Elements may occur in more than one form, because the atoms are arranged differently. For example, carbon occurs as soft graphite and hard diamond.

The number of protons is always equal to the number of electrons. This number is called the atomic number and is different for each element. The nucleus can also contain particles which have no electric charge, called neutrons.

Nuclear Energy

The particles in the nucleus are held together by strong forces. If a nucleus is broken into two smaller nuclei (the plural of nucleus), much energy may be released. This process is called fission. It is used to make energy from the elements uranium and plutonium in nuclear power stations.

Nuclear fusion occurs if small nuclei are joined to make a larger nucleus. This process produces huge amounts of energy in the Sun and in hydrogen bombs.

Above: Rutherford's theory said that electrons orbited a solid nucleus.

Above: When uranium atoms are bombarded with neutrons they split and a nuclear chain reaction is set off. The atoms break up, forming other atoms with less concentrated nuclei and release a lot of heat energy and radiation. This is known as fission. The atom bomb is an uncontrolled chain reaction. Fusion is the opposite reaction when atoms combine to form different, heavier elements.

Left: Nuclear power stations are used to produce electricity. In these stations the chain reaction is controlled in a nuclear reactor.

Man the Inventor

We are surrounded by inventions. We take such things as cars, airplanes, computers, fridges and vacuum cleaners for granted. But at one time none of these things existed. They all had to be invented.

The Need for Invention

Man invents to make his life and work easier. Early man invented tools and weapons for such purposes as hunting, skinning and cutting up his prey. When men became farmers, they needed different tools to cultivate the land. They also needed transport to carry their goods. Thus the two most important early inventions were probably the plough and the wheel.

A variety of needs provides the impetus for invention. For example, the need to defeat enemies in war has, over the years, produced a wide range of hand weapons, cannons, guns and bombs, including the atom bomb. The need for communication has stimulated many of our other inventions, such as printing, telegraph and faster means of transport.

Some Important Inventions

DATE	INVENTION	INVENTOR	COUNTRY
4000 BC	Plough	—	Sumeria
3500 BC	Wheel	—	Sumeria
250 BC	Screw water pump	Archimedes	Greece
AD 100	Paper	—	China
AD 800	Gunpowder	—	China
1608	Refracting telescope	Hans Lipershey	Holland
1698	Steam pump	Thomas Savery	Britain
1804	Steam locomotive	Richard Trevithick	Britain
1821	Electric motor	Michael Faraday	Britain
1837	Telegraph	William Cooke	Britain
		Charles Wheatstone	Britain
		Samuel Morse	USA
1867	Dynamite	Alfred Nobel	Sweden
1876	Telephone	Alexander Graham Bell	USA
1877	Electric light	Thomas Alva Edison	USA
1885	Petrol engine	Karl Benz	Germany
		Gottlieb Daimler	Germany
1893	Diesel engine	Rudolf Diesel	Germany
1895	Radio	Guglielmo Marconi	Italy
1895	X-ray machine	Wilhelm Roentgen	Germany
1937	Jet engine	Frank Whittle	Britain
1944	Digital computer	Howard Aiken	USA
1946	Electronic computer	J. Presper Eckert	USA
		John Mauchly	USA
1948	Transistor	William Shockley	USA
		John Bardeen	USA
		W. H. Brattain	USA

Top: Many new inventions are patented. A patent gives the inventor the exclusive right to make, use or sell a new product, commodity, process or any kind of improvement.

Above: The Spinning Jenny, the first hand-powered multiple spinning machine, was one of the products of the Industrial Revolution. With this machine it became possible to spin many threads of wool, cotton or flax together rather than singly. It was invented by James Hargreaves in 1767. He named it after his daughter, Jenny.

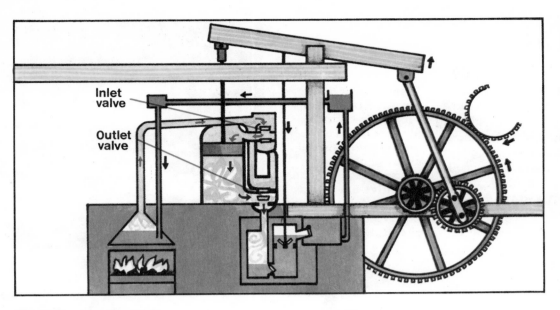

Left: James Watt's (1736-1819) steam engine. Originally a maker of mathematical instruments, Watt became interested in the use of steam as power after helping to mend a model of an early steam engine which had been built by Thomas Newcomen (1663-1729). Watt also invented the famous 'sun and planet' engine and a speed regulator for engines.

The Effects of Invention

Inventions have had a tremendous effect on the way people live. For example, in the 1700s in England there was an increasing demand for cotton cloth. This led to the invention of several machines that could spin cotton yarn quicker than it could be spun by hand. The owners of the cotton industry built factories to house these machines, and the peasants who had previously spun the cotton in their homes had to go and work in the factories instead. The factories were usually built in towns and so more and more people left the land and went to live in the cities. This process, which was also speeded up by the invention of the steam engine, was called the Industrial Revolution, and it led to very many more inventions. For example, one consequence of the Industrial Revolution was a more rapid increase in population. Inventors therefore sought ways of raising food production. In the 1800s, inventors produced the reaper, the seed drill, better ploughs and combine harvesters driven by steam engines.

Invention is a continuous process. Many inventions lead to others. For example, the invention of the petrol engine gave us the motor car and the airplane. The desire for faster speeds in the air led to the invention of the jet engine. The discovery of electricity led to the electric motor, which in turn has given us many everyday electrical appliances from electric lights to electric toothbrushes. Just as the inventions of the 1700s revolutionized life, so too has the supply of electricity. The modern world would be very different without telephones, television, radio or X-ray machines.

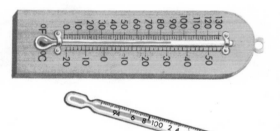

Left: The invention of the thermometer, the instrument we use to measure temperature, was attributed to Galileo in 1595. His experiments often led to discoveries in the field of medicine.

Left: A laser beam bores a hole through metal. The laser was invented in 1960 by an American, Theodore Maiman. His product has been used in the fields of technology, industry and medicine. The word laser means 'light amplification by stimulated emission of radiation'. There are many different types, including ruby and gas lasers.

The most important recent inventions have been in the field of electronics and computers. It is now possible to make computers small enough to be used for very many different things. On more and more occasions it will no longer be necessary to have a person working. A computer will do the job instead, and again our way of life will be changed.

Photography

Photography is a method of making a picture using a camera and a plate or film coated with light-sensitive chemicals. The earliest form of camera was called a pinhole camera, or *camera obscura*. Light from an object passes through the pinhole and an image is formed on the screen at the back of the camera. A modern camera works in the same way. However, instead of a pinhole a lens is used. This allows more light to pass through to the film.

Early Photographers

The first known photograph was taken by Joseph Niepce, a Frenchman, in 1826. It was very blurred, but it was the first time anyone had succeeded in preserving the

Right: Joseph Niepce was the first man to succeed in taking a photograph. The results were blurred as the equipment he used was primitive but he was the true 'father' of modern photography.

Words Used in Photography

aperture The opening that controls the amount of light passing through the lens. On some cameras apertures are indicated by symbols for bright sun, hazy sun and cloud. On other cameras apertures are shown by f-numbers, such as f.16, f.8, f.5.6 and f.4 (f.16 is the smallest of these apertures). Generally, small apertures are used in bright light and wider apertures are used in poorer light.

automatic camera A camera in which the aperture and/or shutter speed are controlled by a light meter.

developer A chemical that changes the exposed silver salts in a film into dark grains of metallic silver, producing a negative.

film A length of cellulose acetate wound on to a spool, either with a paper backing or inside a cassette. The surface of the film is coated with a layer of emulsion containing silver salts. When these are exposed to light they change chemically; different amounts of light cause different amounts of change.

shutter speed The length of time for which the shutter opens to allow light to the film. Some cameras have only one or two shutter speeds; others have several, ranging from 1 second or more to 1/1000 second or less. In normal conditions a shutter speed of about 1/60 second is used. However, for fast moving subjects faster speeds may be necessary.

image produced on the screen. In 1835 Louis Daguerre began producing clearer images on metal plates (*daguerreotypes*). In 1841 an Englishman called W. H. Fox-Talbot devised a method of making paper negatives from which several duplicate positives could be produced.

Above: Louis Daguerre was the first to use metal plates in the photographic process. This gave a much clearer image.

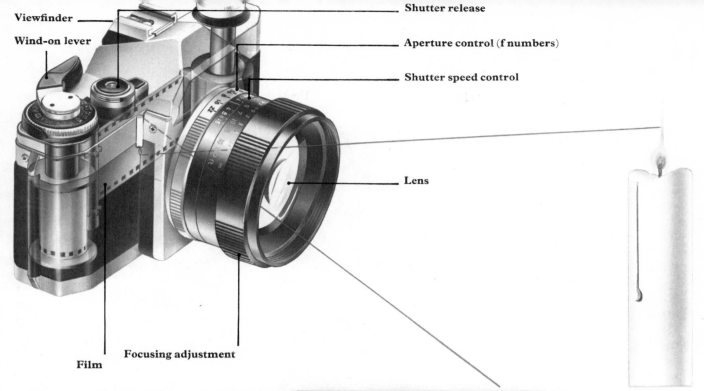

Viewfinder

Wind-on lever

Shutter release

Aperture control (f numbers)

Shutter speed control

Lens

Focusing adjustment

Film

By the 1860s there were many photographers using cumbersome cameras and glass plates. But in 1889 the Eastman Company in the USA produced the first celluloid film, for use in their small, simple Kodak box camera. With this camera anyone could take photographs and photography became the popular hobby it is today.

How to Use Your Camera

Your camera is basically a light-proof box with a lens at the front and a film contained in the back. The lens produces an upside down image on the film.

First, you must decide how much light you can allow to enter the camera to produce an accurate reproduction of the scene you wish to photograph. This is called the exposure, and it requires setting the shutter speed and the aperture if your camera has these controls. For example, to photograph a stationary subject on a bright day you might use a shutter speed of 1/60 second and an aperture of f.16. This combination will change as light conditions change.

Next, you must focus the camera. Just set the focusing adjustment (generally marked in both feet and metres) to the distance between the camera and the subject.

Finally, look through the viewfinder and check that the scene is exactly what you want to photograph. Make sure that you are holding the camera upright and steady and press the shutter.

36 → 36A

Above: A modern camera. This image of the candle is transmitted by light rays through the lines, which react with the celluloid film to make a negative image.

Above left: A negative photograph. During the developing process the image becomes positive when it is printed on special paper and treated with chemicals.

Left: The image on the film can be increased to many times its size by using a photographic enlarger. The photograph can lose sharpness and clarity if it is enlarged too much.

Radio and Television

Electricity was discovered during the 1700s. As scientists began to learn more about its properties, James Maxwell, a Scottish physicist, predicted that it would one day be used to send messages through the air.

In 1887 he was proved right. Heinrich Hertz, a German physicist, succeeded in sending a signal over a very short distance. By 1901 the Italian Guglielmo Marconi was sending messages from Cornwall to Newfoundland.

What are Radio Waves?

Radio waves belong to a group called electromagnetic waves. They are given this name because of their electrical and magnetic properties. Other types of electromagnetic waves include radar waves, infra-

Radar

In 1904 a German inventor called Christian Hulsmeyer had the idea of using radio waves to detect distant objects.

Guglielmo Marconi suggested the idea again in 1922. By 1932 the Americans. Germans and Japanese were all doing research, but the British led the field. By 1939 Britain was the only country with radar-equipped planes. Radar means *r*adio *d*etection *a*nd *r*anging.

Radar uses pulses of radio waves. A rotating scanner emits a constant stream of pulses. When these strike an object they are reflected back to the scanner and the information is transferred electronically to a screen on which the object appears as a bright area or dot.

red rays, light rays, ultraviolet rays and X-rays. The only difference between them is their wavelength. Light rays are a band of waves to which our eyes are sensitive. This band is called the visible spectrum. Ultraviolet rays and X-rays have shorter wavelengths. Infra-red rays and radar have longer wavelengths. Radio waves have the longest wavelengths of all.

Broadcasting

The first radio messages were sent in Morse Code. This system of dots and dashes is sent as bursts of radio waves.

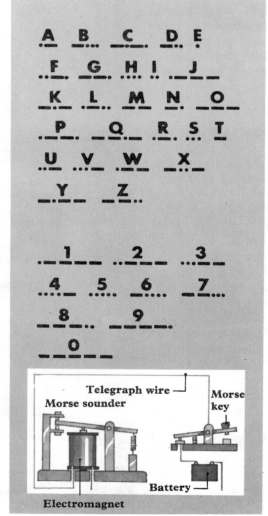

Above: Guglielmo Marconi (1874-1937) with his radio transmitter and receiver. He produced the first practical wireless telegraph when he was 21 and set about developing this. The Italian government showed no interest in his invention, so he went to Great Britain where, in 1899, he sent the first wireless telegraph across the English Channel. In 1901 he sent the first radio signals across the Atlantic.

Left: Morse Code is a method of telegraphy—a means of sending messages by electricity. It was invented by Samuel Morse (1791-1872).

Below: A colour television receiver. Electron beams pass through a mask to a phosphor dot screen. When the dots are struck by electrons they light up with colour—either red, blue or green.

Above: A television studio during the shooting of a play. Note the quantity of cameras needed to film the action from several angles and the strong lighting for the maximum effect.

By 1918, however, scientists had discovered how to use radio waves to carry speech. Today radio waves are also used to carry television signals.

Sending Pictures

Modern television uses the electronic system devised by the Russian-American Vladimir Zworykin in the 1920s. In a television camera a beam of electrons scans the image of the scene in a series of lines. The information is then converted into a radio signal.

In a television set the signal is used to control another electron beam, which scans the screen. This is coated with a material that glows when it is struck by an electron. In this way the light and dark areas of the original scene are reconstructed on the screen. The process is much the same for colour television. Three basic colours—red, green and blue—are transmitted as one signal, with other signals indicating how they should be mixed.

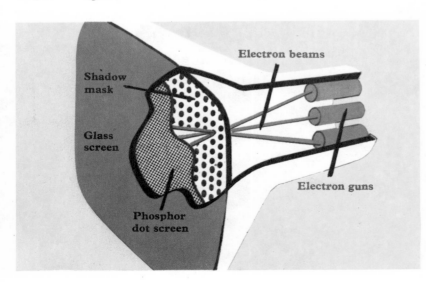

Electron beams

Shadow mask

Glass screen

Phosphor dot screen

Electron guns

Computers

When early man settled down and acquired possessions, he began to develop methods of counting. At first he used his fingers, which is why most civilizations developed systems that involved the numbers one to ten. Numbers have fascinated mathematicians ever since. But in everyday life people needed to be able to do calculations quickly. They therefore developed machines to help them.

Calculating Machines

The first type of calculator was the abacus. This uses beads on wires strung across a wooden frame. Each of the beads on a wire has the same value. The beads on the next wire are all worth ten times as much. The abacus can be used to add, subtract, multiply and divide.

The first calculating machine was invented by the French mathematician Blaise Pascal in 1642. Instead of beads his machine had cogs, each with ten teeth. In 1671 Gottfried Leibniz, a German mathematician, devised an improved mechanical calculator. In the 19th century, Charles Babbage, an English mathematician, invented a small calculator. Then, in 1832, he devised a machine that used most of the

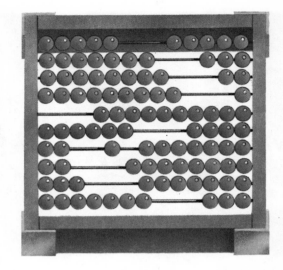

Left: The abacus is the simplest form of calculating machine. It was invented by the Arabs many centuries ago and is still used in many parts of the world today for solving mathematical problems.

Centre left: Today most shops and supermarkets use electric cash registers to add up shoppers' bills and to calculate how much change should be given. Each item is recorded so that at the end of the day, the shopkeeper can quickly see how much money he has taken.

Below: United States space missions are controlled from this room in Houston, Texas. Every modern computer facility is in use to ensure the success and safety of each mission.

Numeral Integrator and Calculator. ENIAC used electronic devices called valves. However, in modern computers these have been replaced by much smaller and more reliable devices known as transistors.

The first electronic computers were large. However, modern technology has enabled engineers to miniaturize complicated circuits, including transistors, so that they fit on to tiny slivers of silicon, known as silicon chips. As a result even very complicated computers can be relatively small. At present, pocket calculators are the smallest form of computer.

A computer has to be told what to do. Therefore, information in the form of a program is fed into the input unit. The information is stored in the memory, or core

The Language of Computers

Computers use a code language known as the binary code. Any number can be expressed by different combinations of just two digits, 1 and 0. This system can be used to show the presence (1) or absence (0) of certain selected numbers. In practice these numbers are 1, 2, 4, 8, 16, 32, 64, 128 and so on. Some examples are shown below:

128	64	32	16	8	4	2	1		
	1	0	0	0	0	0	0	=	64
1	1	0	0	0	1	0	0	=	196
	1	1	0	0	0	0	1	=	97
			1	0	0	1	1	=	19
				1	1	1	1	=	15

Information in binary code may be fed into a computer in the form of punched cards or tape. A punched hole indicates 1 and no hole indicates 0. Or the presence or absence of electrical impulses on magnetic tape can be used to represent 1 or 0.

Above: Programs are fed into the computer on tapes or cards. Information is translated into 'computer language' by punch-card operators who use a keyboard machine. The information required from the computer is printed on paper or shown on a Visual Display Unit (VDU for short).

features of modern computers. But it was very complicated and he failed to interest people in it. It was not until 1944 that the first successful mechanical computer was developed by the American, Howard Aiken. Aiken's calculator contained counter wheels, electric motors to turn them, electromagnets and other parts. There were 750,000 parts in all.

Electronic Computers

In 1946 Aiken's computer was outdated by a new type of computer. In America J. Presper Eckert and John Mauchly built ENIAC, which stands for Electronic

store. Then the data—the information that is to be used in the calculation—is fed in. The control unit then directs the central processor to carry out the calculation. Because there are no mechanical parts, this process takes only seconds. Finally, the results are produced by the output unit. They may be displayed on a screen or printed out on paper.

The speed of computers has increased and their size has been reduced as smaller and smaller components have been used. The speed of a computer is now set not by the time taken to do calculations, but the speed at which the computer prints out results.

11 TRANSPORT

Transport is the means by which people and freight are moved from one place to another. As we will see, the uses to which transport is put have changed throughout history as a result of changes in the methods of transportation.

The Urge to Travel

Prehistoric people were always on the move, in search of food and shelter. The earliest method of moving heavy loads was to drag them on two branches tied together. Sledges and skis gradually replaced the branches. Later, animals were used to drag these, or to carry loads on their backs, the most important being the horse. The invention of the wheel enabled heavier weights to be pulled more easily.

As different groups of people developed special skills and discovered the different things that grew or were found in various parts of the world, they began to trade. One tribe would, for example, exchange woollen

Right: Sir Francis Drake's ship, the *Golden Hind,* made two world voyages.

Below: Stephenson's *Rocket,* built in 1829, was one of the first steam locomotives.

Transport Dates

In ancient times most transport was used for goods, or freight. The dates are not exact, but are estimated from the oldest known examples.

8000 BC   Loads dragged on branches.

5000 BC   Sledges and skis.

4000 BC   Boats with built-up sides and sails.

3500 BC   Invention of the wheel.

3000 BC   Animals used to pull or carry loads. Horses, dogs, oxen, reindeer, elephants, camels and other animals are still used for this purpose.

1500 BC   Road network established in China, probably in the Hsia Dynasty.

Left: Hot-air balloons were invented long before passenger aircraft. The first hot-air balloon was built in the 1780s.

Below: The search for economy in air travel has led to the invention of jumbo jets. They are the largest heavier-than-air craft.

cloth for another's metal tools. For thousands of years trade was the single most important use of transport and, as new methods were found, trade routes were established across the oceans and continents of the world.

With the Industrial Revolution, improved transport was required to move raw materials to factories and finished products to markets at home and abroad. It was at this time—about 200 years ago—that passenger transport began to become available to large numbers of people. Previously, people would only travel long distances for special reasons. Merchants, scholars, diplomats, official messengers, explorers and so on would undertake long journeys, but most people stayed in, or close to, the place where they were born. Now it became

Below left: The Free State Interchange in Miami, Florida, showing a complex network of roads. As road traffic increases, elevated roads and highways are built to help solve the problem of traffic jams.

possible for people to move their homes more easily than ever before. Many people moved from the country to the cities, and many others moved across oceans seeking greater opportunities.

The development of railways in the 19th century both enabled more and more people to travel and reduced the time taken for journeys of hundreds of miles from days to hours. The railway was followed by the motor car in the early 20th century. Finally, passenger-carrying aircraft have made it possible to travel thousands of miles in a few hours.

The effect of this has been to change our way of life. Most people now travel at least a few miles to work or school. This has produced a new growth of public transport, with buses, trains, ships and aircraft provided by the community for anyone to use on journeys of all distances.

Many people now travel for pleasure. They may take holidays at special resorts in their own countries. Or they may go abroad to enjoy better weather, and to experience other ways of life.

Modern Milestones

Although new inventions have made it easier to transport goods, their main effect has been on passenger transport.

1681 The first steam-driven vehicle is built in Peking, China.

1783 The first steamship, *Pyroscaphe*, is launched in France.

1886 The first petrol-driven car is built in Germany.

1919 The first passenger aircraft services start in Europe.

Road Transport

Probably the single most important invention in the history of transport was the wheel. We do not know when the first wheel was made, but wheeled vehicles are described in the earliest known writings, which are dated around 3100 BC.

The first use of the wheel was on carts pulled by animals or by hand. These replaced the earlier sledges on which loads were simply dragged. And as the use of wheeled vehicles spread, roads began to be made for them.

The earliest roads were simple ruts in the ground made to guide cart wheels. But in China by 1500 BC a whole network of paved roads had appeared. The roads were graded according to their size, the biggest being wide enough for three carts to travel side by side. During the next 1,000 years the Chinese also developed the first traffic

Roman Roads

The Romans began to build roads for reasons of trade, but then began to build them out into the areas which they had conquered so that the Roman armies could keep them under control. By the beginning of the 2nd century BC, so many roads radiated from the capital of the empire that it was said, 'All roads lead to Rome'.

The remarkable thing about Roman roads was their straightness, regardless of obstacles. The roads were made up of several layers, beginning with a layer of brown clay to act as mortar. Then came large flat stones, covered with broken-up stones and then sand or gravel to make a smooth surface. When suitable material wasn't available, large paving slabs of stone were used.

Above: The wheel probably developed (about 3100 BC) from sledges or rollers which were used to transport heavy goods.

Below: Early steam vehicles were powered by stationary steam engines that had been adapted for use in carriages.

Bottom: Gottlieb Daimler's petrol car of 1886 was one of the first petrol-engined vehicles.

regulations. These were needed to control the increasing amount of traffic on the roads. Today, many countries have special police forces just to control the traffic.

In Europe the greatest early road-builders were the Romans. Between 300 BC and AD 200 the Romans built roads throughout western Europe and northern Africa for their armies to march quickly from place to place. The next great road-builders were the Incas in South America. Like the Romans, the Incas built roads to connect all parts of their empire to the capital. Their roads, however, were used only by foot soldiers and messengers because the Incas did not know about the wheel or the horse.

Until the end of the 19th century, many new types of road vehicles were produced. But they all depended on horses or other animals to pull them. The steam engine was later used to power some road vehicles, and, until quite recently, steam-driven traction engines were used as tractors and road

Above: The first Model T Ford was built in the United States in 1908. It made popular motoring possible.

rollers. But steam engines were very heavy, and found their best use on the railways.

Then, at the end of the 19th century, the internal combustion engine was invented. This burnt diesel oil and petrol, and was more powerful for its size than any other previous type of engine. It proved to be the ideal way to power road vehicles.

The first motor cars began to be mass-produced in the United States in 1908. Since then, cars have become the most common type of road vehicle. They allow people to go anywhere where there is a road. And because of the enormous number of cars, buses and lorries a whole new road system has had to be developed. There are wide fast roads for long journeys, and smaller roads in towns connecting each street and house.

Below: The Harley Davidson motorbike has been developed with fast, long-distance travel in mind.

Below: A Rolls-Royce Phantom II (1939). They were built for reliability, speed and comfort.

Los Angeles

Los Angeles, in California, is one of the world's biggest cities. In order to connect the different districts, a system of roads known as freeways has been built. The inhabitants of Los Angeles own an average of almost two cars each, and the car dominates life there. There are drive-in shops, banks and even churches so that people do not need to leave their cars. Unfortunately, this causes a great deal of pollution from exhaust fumes, and the city is often covered by smog.

Crossing the Seas

The first method people found of crossing water was probably to float on logs and to paddle with their hands. The next step was to hollow out the logs so that they would float better and loads could be carried inside them.

The dugout canoe was given built-up sides of planks, so that bigger loads could be carried. But for bigger vessels, carrying large loads across open seas, the most common form was a boat built up from a keel. Stem and stern posts at each end were joined by planks curved outwards in the middle. This meant that the typical boat was wide in the middle, tapering to a point at each end.

By 1000 BC the people of Crete and Carthage, in the Mediterranean, had begun to make long sea voyages. Usually warships were driven by large numbers of oars arranged in rows, one above the other. But the oarsmen left little room for cargo, and merchant ships were usually propelled by a sail. The next important development was the lateen sail, which could be positioned to take account of the wind's direction. By AD 1000 the triangular lateen sail was used on most European and Asian ships but in China a different form of ship had developed. This is called a junk, and has a flat bottom with square bow and stern.

Above: An ancient Greek ship called a *trireme*. It had about 170 oarsmen.

Above: The *Mayflower*, the ship used by the Pilgrim Fathers in 1620 when they set off from Plymouth, England for Massachusetts in North America.

Types of Ships

Ferries carry people across water too wide for a bridge.

Paddle steamers are river boats driven by flat boards turning on a big wheel.

Clippers were the fastest sailing ships, carrying perishable goods such as tea.

Packet boats are small ships carrying letters, a few passengers and light cargoes.

Oil tankers are the biggest cargo vessels. Some carry up to half a million tonnes of oil.

Passenger liners carry people long distances in great luxury.

Tugs are small, powerful boats which tow the bigger ships into harbour.

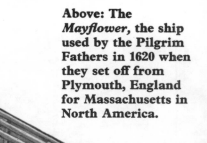

The Eskimo kayak is made from animal skins over a wooden frame.

Another Chinese invention was the stern rudder for steering. This was not used on European ships until AD 1200, more than 1,000 years after it was first used by the Chinese. The stern rudder greatly improved steering, and allowed ships to become much larger. As they grew in size, they were given more masts, each carrying a number of sails controlled by complicated arrangements of ropes and pulleys, known as rigging.

Improvements in navigation and the great voyages of discovery led to the opening of long-distance trade routes, with goods transported across the oceans. A great advance in worldwide trade came with the opening of the Suez Canal in 1869. This waterway joined the Mediterranean and the Indian Ocean and provided the shortest route from Europe to the Orient and the east coast of Africa. Its opening was followed, in 1914, by the Panama Canal which joined the Atlantic and Pacific

Top: The hovercraft, invented by Christopher Cockerell in 1955, glides over the surface of water supported by a cushion of air. It can also operate on land.

Above: Cunard's *Queen Elizabeth II,* one of the great transatlantic passenger liners, cruises at about 30 knots (56 km/h, or 35 mph).

Canals

One of the main advantages of water transport is that much heavier loads can be carried than is possible on land or by air. Rivers, therefore, became important routes. In more recent times the industrial nations have built networks of level waterways, called canals. Flat-bottomed boats called barges operate on canals. These are used to carry raw materials from the ports to the factories, and then to carry the finished goods from the factories to the customers. Canals have also opened new shipping routes and allow sea-going ships to reach inland ports. The biggest ships, however, must use special deep-water harbours.

Oceans. No longer was it necessary to make the long, dangerous journey around Cape Horn at the tip of South America.

By the beginning of the twentieth century, steam and oil-powered engines were being used to drive screw propellers, while metal construction allowed ships to become much bigger. Old sailing ships would simply anchor in a shallow bay or alongside a simple jetty, to load and unload their cargo, so that ports grew up around natural harbours or river mouths. For the largest modern ships, however, special docks have had to be built. These are designed for handling the large cargoes of oil tankers or container ships.

Railways

Railways existed long before the invention of the locomotive. People had known since the 1500s that carts run more easily along rails than on the rough ground. But these railway carts could move only as fast as men or horses could pull them.

The invention of the steam locomotive changed everything. Steam trains could travel much faster than any earlier vehicles. And they could carry very heavy loads. They helped the growth of industry. And they made it possible for people to build cities in places where hardly anyone had lived before—for example, in the western part of the United States.

The first steam railway to carry passengers on regular services opened in England in 1830. It was the London and Manchester Railway. But steam railways spread quickly. By the 1870s, many cities in Europe, North and South America, Australia, Asia and Africa had rail connections. Everywhere the 'iron horse' was taking over.

Steam, Electric, Diesel

Over the years, engineers developed faster and more powerful steam locomotives. But these were dirty, difficult to start, and had other faults. In the late 1800s, the first electric locomotives were built. They were extremely efficient, but they had to collect electric power from a third rail or an overhead cable. Later, locomotives driven by diesel engines were made. They were powerful, but ran less smoothly than electric locomotives. A further development has been the diesel-electric loco-

The first passenger coaches on the steam railways were modelled on the horse-drawn stage coaches that were still being used on the roads. They were uncomfortable, cold, and badly lit. Freight wagons, too, were based on horse-drawn vehicles.

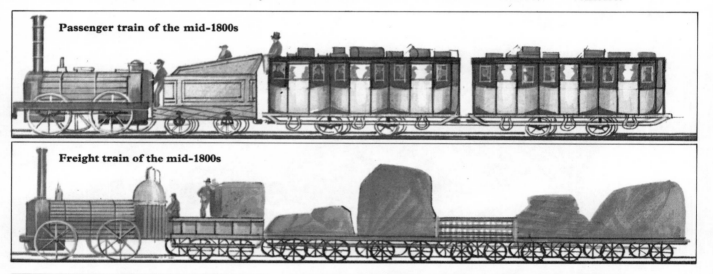

Passenger train of the mid-1800s

Freight train of the mid-1800s

City Railways

In industrial countries, special rail networks have been built in and around large cities. Each day, these are used by thousands of *commuters*—people who live in city suburbs but travel into the cities to work.

The trains on these networks are designed for short, fast journeys. Often, they carry more people than long-distance trains. Some of them are double-deck.

Within cities, railways are usually built underground, and run through tunnels. Modern underground systems are always electric, to avoid dirt and fumes in the tunnels.

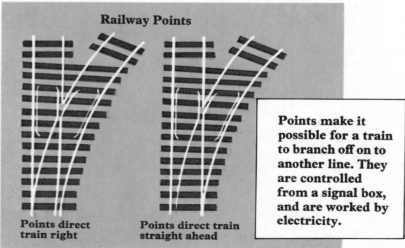

Railway Points

Points direct train right

Points direct train straight ahead

Points make it possible for a train to branch off on to another line. They are controlled from a signal box, and are worked by electricity.

motive. In this vehicle, a diesel engine drives a generator that provides power for the smooth electric motors that turn the wheels. Today, engineers are experimenting with various other forms of power.

Railway Words

bogie The carrier on which the wheels of a locomotive or carriage are mounted.

communication cord A cord that passengers can pull to stop a train in emergency.

cutting A valley cut through a small hill to keep a railway track level.

footplate The part of a steam locomotive in which the driver and fireman work.

freight train A train that carries goods.

gauge The distance between the rails of a railway track.

level crossing The place where a railway crosses a road on the level.

locomotive An engine that moves under its own power. Locomotives are used for pulling trains.

monorail A railway line with only a single track.

siding A line off the main track used for temporary accommodation of trains.

Top: New railways were not always welcomed. As they pushed farther west in the USA, the American Indians objected to the invasion of their lands.

Centre: A powerful diesel-electric freight locomotive of the Union Pacific Railway in the USA.

Left: A high-speed experimental train of the French Railways. It is known as the TGV, and has turbine engines.

Travel by Air

Although the first airplane did not fly until 1903, flying soon became the fastest method of transport. Today it is easily the most popular way of travelling long distances.

The first airplanes were not big or powerful enough to carry more than a pilot and perhaps a co-pilot, but during the First World War (1914–18) larger aircraft with up to four engines were developed to carry bombs. After the war some of these were converted to carry a few passengers. In 1919 the first regular passenger services were started between several cities in Europe.

Air transport was even then too expensive for most cargoes, but mail began to be carried by air at an early stage. This was partly because letters are small and light, and partly because businessmen, particularly, were prepared to pay more for their mail to be delivered by the fastest method. Especially in the United States, where

Above: The Canadair CL-215 is known as a flying boat. It takes off and lands on water.

Right: The Handley Page HP 42 was built in 1930. It flew mainly on the European routes.

Above: After World War II, commercial aircraft using various types of jet engines were soon in production. The Boeing 747 was built in 1968/69 and was the first of the jumbo jets. It is able to carry more than 400 passengers in lounges on two storeys.

Helicopters

While ordinary aircraft rely on air passing over curved wings to lift them into the air, helicopters are lifted by very narrow wings, or rotors, spinning round above them. This means they can take off straight up into the air instead of having to race along a runway to gain enough speed. They can, therefore, be used in very small spaces, such as in the middle of cities. Their use has increased considerably since 1945—they were first used in the Korean and Vietnam wars to carry troops and wounded soldiers. The largest helicopters can lift enormous loads and are used nowadays for many tasks including crop spraying, forest-fire fighting and traffic control. Helicopters have proven especially useful in rescue work after floods and earthquakes.

Air Speed Records

	Km/h	mph
1909 Wright biplane	54.77	34.04
1909 Curtiss biplane	69.75	43.35
1910 Blériot monoplane	109.73	68.18
1923 Curtiss R-2 C-1	429.96	267.16
1928 Macchi M-52 bis	512.69	318.57
1931 Supermarine S.6B	654.90	406.94
1939 Messerschmidt		
Me 209 V-1	754.97	469.12
1947 Lockheed P-80R	1,003.60	623.61
1958 Lockheed F-104A		
Starfighter	2,259.18	1,403.80
1961 McDonnell F4H-1F		
Phantom 2	2,585.43	1,606.51
1965 Lockheed YF-12A	3,331.51	2,070.10
1976 Lockheed SR-71A	3,529.56	2,193.17

The versatile helicopter is used by police, fire and rescue services all over the world. It is also used by farmers to spray their crops. Below: The layout of an airport. Every day thousands of passengers pass through its doors and hundreds of airlines use its runaways. There is a large staff to run the airport.

Flying Boats

The flying boat, which lands on and takes off from water, was first used for long-distance flights during the 1920s. One of the most notable was the Dornier DoX super flying boat of 1929 which could carry 170 people. It was 40 metres (131 feet 5 inches) long and had a span of 48 metres (157 feet 6 inches). They did not need special runways and in the early days of air travel were much safer for long journeys over the sea. But the airfields built all over the world during the Second World War meant that ordinary airplanes could go almost anywhere and so the main advantage of the flying boat disappeared.

letters could take over a week to cross the country by train, airmail services were the first regular transport flights.

The early passenger aircraft could carry only a dozen or so passengers, and only enough fuel for short journeys. For long distances, such as from Europe to the United States, airships, filled with very light gas and able to float through the air, began to be used in the 1930s. Unfortunately, the most common gas then used to fill airships, hydrogen, explodes very easily. A number of airships crashed and this type of transport was abandoned. More recently, new airships using the safe gas helium, have been built and airships may be used again to carry passengers and freight.

By the end of the Second World War in 1945, much larger airplanes had been produced. At the same time, military airfields had been built all over the world, and long-distance routes had been established. After the war, therefore, many military aircraft were bought by commercial airlines. The introduction of the jet engine, which provides much greater power than propellers, allowed even bigger and faster aircraft to be built. Today's wide-bodied airplanes can carry as many as 350 passengers.

Modern air transport passenger services are divided into two types. Scheduled services are regular flights, leaving for the same destination at the same time each day. Charter flights, on the other hand, are aircraft hired for one particular journey by a group of people. Air transport has allowed more people to travel abroad than ever before.

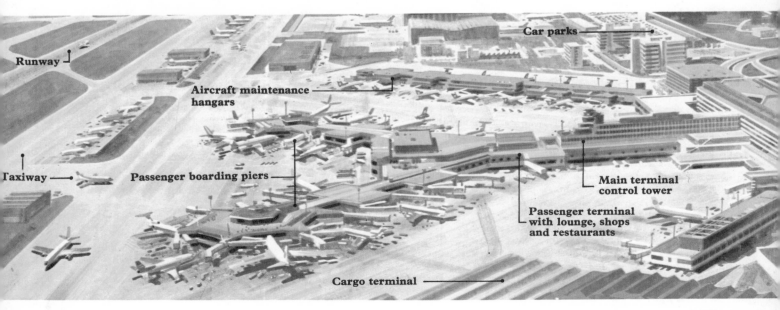

Car parks

Runway

Aircraft maintenance hangars

Taxiway

Passenger boarding piers

Main terminal control tower

Passenger terminal with lounge, shops and restaurants

Cargo terminal

12 THE BODY

The human body is one of nature's miracles. Consisting of millions of cells, it is more complex, better made, and more efficient than any machine invented by Man. It needs care and attention to keep it in good working order.

Anatomy and Physiology

The skeleton acts as the body's scaffolding or framework. Covered entirely with skin, the skeleton supports the body, gives it shape, and protects the vital organs inside the body such as the brain and heart. The spine, which consists of 26 interlocking bones or *vertebrae*, is the skeleton's central structure.

There are 206 bones in a normal adult skeleton. Bone consists mainly of minerals such as calcium and phosphorus which are essential for health and growth. The outer layer of bone is hard and rigid, but inside the bone there is a soft, fatty substance called *marrow*.

Where one bone meets another there is a joint. This can be movable or immovable. Movable joints include hinge joints such as knee and finger joints, and ball-and-socket joints like the hip joints. *Cartilage*, a tough elastic tissue, pads the joints. *Ligaments*, cords of stringy tissue, hold them together.

Muscles are the fleshy tissue of the body. There are about 650 muscles in the body and they consist of spindle-shaped bundles of fibres controlled by nerves. Together

Blood Groups

There are four main blood groups—A, B, AB, and O. The letters refer to the presence, or absence, of types of protein in the blood. These are known as A and B. Each person has blood which belongs to one of these four groups. Group A people have substance A in their blood; group B people have substance B. People in group AB have both and people in group O have neither. It is essential to know a person's blood group for a blood transfusion. The blood groups of the people giving and receiving blood must match each other.

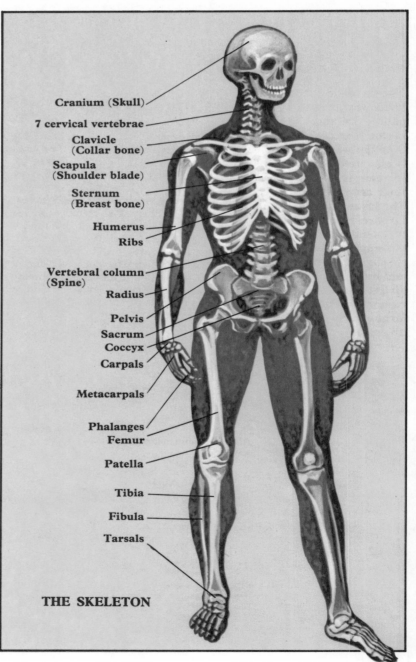

Cranium (Skull)
7 cervical vertebrae
Clavicle (Collar bone)
Scapula (Shoulder blade)
Sternum (Breast bone)
Humerus
Ribs
Vertebral column (Spine)
Radius
Pelvis
Sacrum
Coccyx
Carpals
Metacarpals
Phalanges
Femur
Patella
Tibia
Fibula
Tarsals

THE SKELETON

172

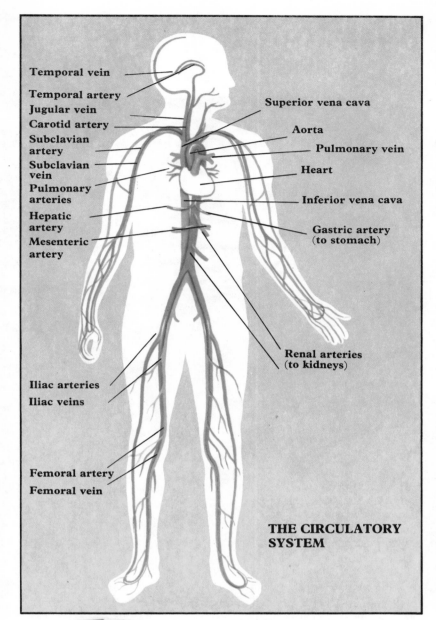

Temporal vein
Temporal artery
Jugular vein
Carotid artery
Subclavian artery
Subclavian vein
Pulmonary arteries
Hepatic artery
Mesenteric artery

Superior vena cava
Aorta
Pulmonary vein
Heart
Inferior vena cava
Gastric artery (to stomach)
Renal arteries (to kidneys)

Iliac arteries
Iliac veins

Femoral artery
Femoral vein

THE CIRCULATORY SYSTEM

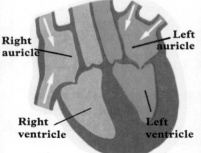

Right auricle
Left auricle
Right ventricle
Left ventricle

Right: Cells are the basic unit of life. The human body is composed of about 100 million million cells. They differ in type but each has the same basic structure.

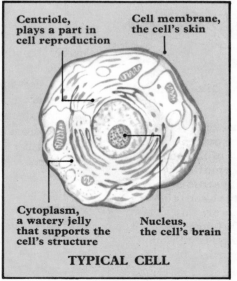

Centriole, plays a part in cell reproduction
Cell membrane, the cell's skin
Cytoplasm, a watery jelly that supports the cell's structure
Nucleus, the cell's brain

TYPICAL CELL

with the skeleton, muscles help the body to move. There are two kinds of muscles—voluntary and involuntary. *Voluntary* muscles are those that can be moved at will. They are attached to the bones by cords of tissue called *tendons*. When we move an arm, the brain sends a signal to the arm muscles. These contract or get shorter and pull on the bones of the forearm so that the arm moves up. When the muscles relax, the arm drops down. *Involuntary* muscles are those over which we have no conscious control. They are always at work and are found in the arteries, intestines, stomach, veins and many other organs. The lung and heart muscles are examples of involuntary muscles at work.

The heart and the lungs work together to supply the body with the oxygen that every cell needs to live. The heart (far left) consists of four chambers: two upper auricles and two lower ventricles. Large veins bring blood to the right side of the heart. From there it is pumped to the lungs.

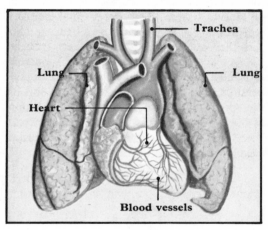

Trachea
Lung
Lung
Heart
Blood vessels

When we breathe in, oxygen passes into the lungs (above) through the trachea or windpipe. The lungs fill with air which enters a network of tubes ending in tiny air sacs or alveoli. Oxygen passes through these into the bloodstream and at the same time carbon dioxide moves from the blood into the lungs. When we breathe out, carbon dioxide is expelled.

The blood, now filled with oxygen, returns to the left side of the heart. It is then pumped out to the rest of the body by the arteries. Tiny blood vessels called capillaries link arteries and veins. The blood also carries food to the body's cells and takes away waste materials. In addition, specialized blood cells help to rid the body of harmful germs.

173

Anatomy and Physiology (2)

The brain is the body's control centre. It is sometimes compared to a computer but it is very much more complicated than any computer ever invented. The brain receives nerve impulses from sense organs in all parts of the body. In turn it sends signals to muscles and glands to take whatever action is necessary. In this way the brain controls all bodily functions and activities. It also controls our emotions, stores memory, and is where the thinking process occurs.

The brain consists of several parts. Each one is connected but each has its own specific job. The *cerebrum* is the top and largest part of the brain. It looks rather like a large walnut and is made up of two identical parts. Its surface is a mass of folds consisting of *grey matter*. Below is a mass of *white matter* consisting of bundles of nerve fibres. The cerebrum controls sensations such as seeing and hearing and activities such as movement and speech. Below is the *cerebellum*. This controls muscular movement and helps to maintain balance. The *medulla*, which lies on top of the spinal column, controls those functions of the body over which we have no control. The heart, lungs, stomach—all internal organs—are regulated through a system of

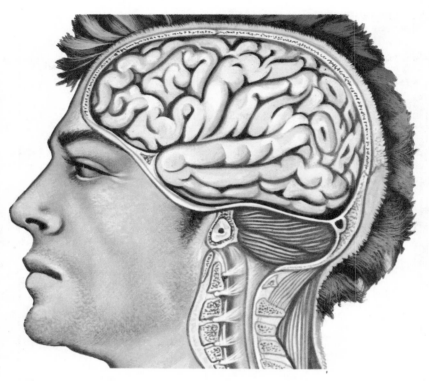

Above: The brain's soft mass is protected by the skull. The brain is made up of some 30,000 million nerve cells.

If we touch something hot a *reflex action* occurs. Nerve impulses travel as far as the spinal cord then back again.

A network of nerves (left) covers every part of the body. Information comes from sense organs. In the hand (above) there are more than 1,000 touch receptors on each fingertip.

nerves bundled together in groups called *ganglia*.

The nervous system co-ordinates all the body's activities. It consists of the brain, the spinal cord, and all the nerves that radiate from them. The nervous system works rather like a telephone network with the nerves acting like telephone wires. *Sensory* nerves react to various stimuli such as heat, cold, light or pressure. They send messages or impulses from the sense organs to the brain. The brain, like a switchboard, then sends instructions via the *motor* nerves to the muscles and glands to take the necessary action.

Dictionary

axons Nerve fibres that send impulses.

blind spot Point where optic nerve leaves the eye. It is not light sensitive.

central nervous system Consists of the brain and the spinal cord.

cortex The outer layer of the cerebrum.

dendrites Nerve fibres that receive impulses.

motor nerves Nerves that send instructions from the brain to muscles and glands.

neuron A nerve cell with fibres that connect with other nerve cells or organs.

olfactory nerves Nerves that deal with smell.

synapse The gap between nerve fibres over which nerve impulses must 'jump'.

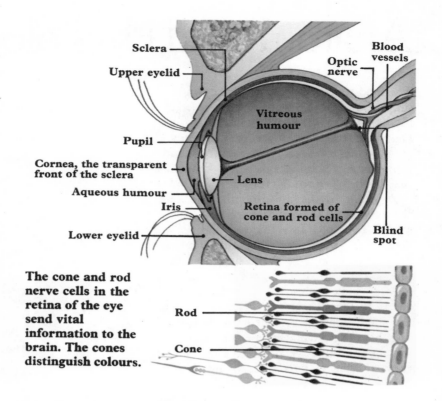

The cone and rod nerve cells in the retina of the eye send vital information to the brain. The cones distinguish colours.

Below: Sound vibrations reach the middle ear. The inner ear turns them into nerve impulses that travel to the brain.

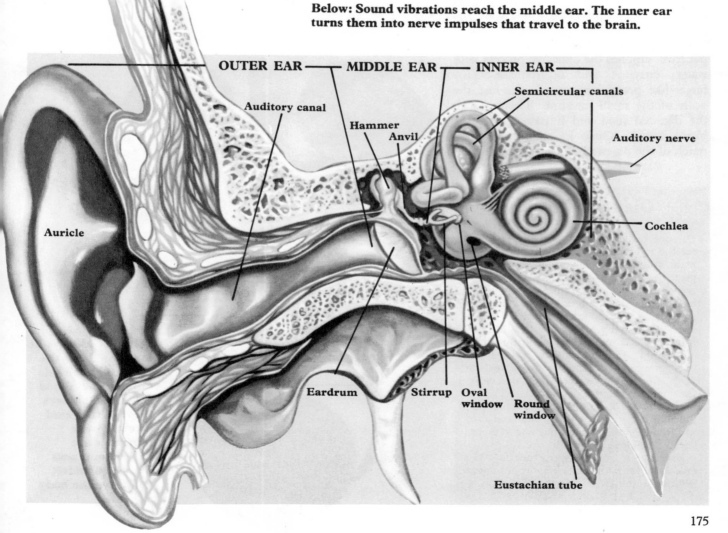

Anatomy and Physiology (3)

The food we eat must be broken down into simple substances that can be absorbed by the blood. This process is called digestion. Digestion takes place in the alimentary canal, a long tube that runs from the mouth to the anus. Chemical substances known as *enzymes* break down the food.

Digestion begins in the mouth. The teeth chew food into small pieces and mix it with saliva. The food is swallowed and passes down the oesophagus into the stomach. Muscular movements of the stomach churn the food and mix it with gastric juices.

After some hours the now liquid food enters the small intestine. The top part of the small intestine is called the *duodenum*. It is here that several important substances join in the digestive process. First among these substances is *bile* which digests fats. Bile is produced in the liver and stored in the gall bladder. A system of ducts allows the right amount of bile to pass from the gall bladder into the duodenum where it mixes with juices from the pancreas. The pancreas supplies the digestive process with water, enzymes and bicarbonate. Tiny finger-like projections called *villi* line the walls of the small intestine. These absorb the digested food and it passes into tiny blood vessels. Once in the bloodstream much of the digested food goes to the liver

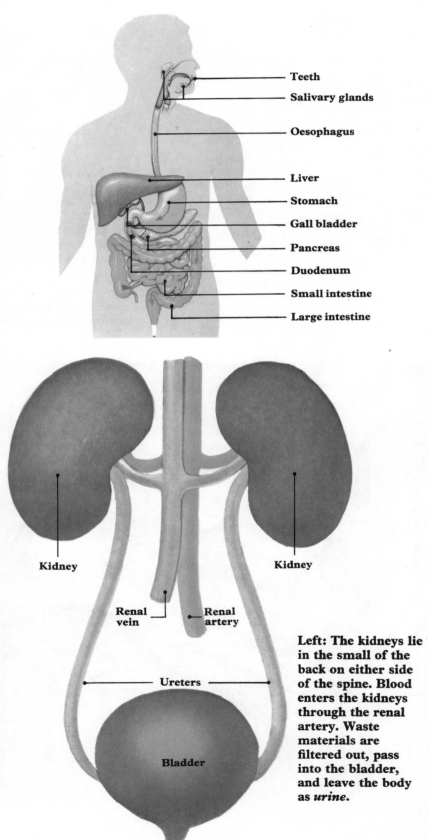

Teeth
Salivary glands
Oesophagus
Liver
Stomach
Gall bladder
Pancreas
Duodenum
Small intestine
Large intestine

Kidney

Kidney

Renal vein

Renal artery

Ureters

Bladder

Left: The kidneys lie in the small of the back on either side of the spine. Blood enters the kidneys through the renal artery. Waste materials are filtered out, pass into the bladder, and leave the body as *urine*.

Diet and Health

For our bodies to work properly we must eat the right kinds of food. There are five main groups of food—carbohydrates, fats, proteins, minerals and vitamins. Fats and carbohydrates are the chief energy-giving foods. They include bread, butter, potatoes and sugar. Proteins are essential for health and growth and are found in cheese, eggs, fish, milk and meat. Only small quantities of vitamins and minerals are needed but they are vital. Vitamin sources include fresh fruit and vegetables, meat and milk. Calcium, for healthy bones and teeth, and iron are two of the most important minerals. Calcium is found in cheese, milk and fish, and iron in meats such as liver and in green, leafy vegetables like spinach.

Exercise is necessary to develop the muscles of the body, including the heart, and sufficient rest is also required.

where it is stored until needed. Undigested, or waste, food goes to the large intestine. It leaves the body through the anus as *faeces*.

Human Reproduction

Human life continues through the process of sexual reproduction. This involves the fertilization of a female egg cell by a male sperm cell.

Fertilization takes place inside a woman's body. The female egg cells or *ova* are stored inside the ovaries. Once a month an egg ripens and leaves the ovaries. During intercourse male sperm cells pass through a man's penis into a woman's vagina. If a sperm meets a ripened egg, fertilization occurs. One single cell is formed and attaches itself to the lining of the woman's uterus. There, during a period of nine months, it develops into a new human being. The fertilized egg divides first into two cells which in turn also divide, and so on. By this process the thousands of cells that form a human body are produced. In its earliest stages the bundle of cells is known as an *embryo;* after eight weeks the developing

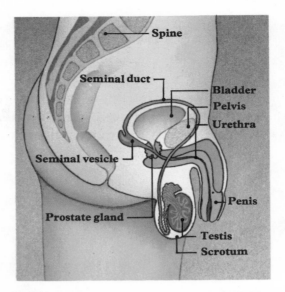

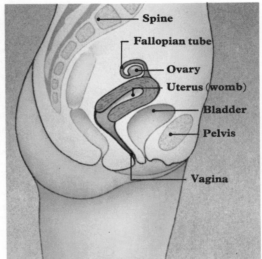

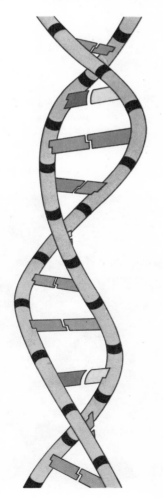

baby is called a *foetus.* The baby inherits characteristics from both parents.

The Chain of Life

Every human being starts life as one single cell. This divides time and time again to form thousands of other cells. Near its centre each cell contains a *nucleus,* the most important part of a cell. The nucleus contains minute thread-like *chromosomes.* Each cell in a woman's body contains 23 identical pairs of chromosomes including a pair known as X chromosomes; the cells in a man's body contain 22 pairs plus one X and one Y chromosome.

Chromosomes themselves contain long twisted strands of molecules known as DNA (deoxyribonucleic acid). Often called 'the chain of life', DNA contains all the *genetic* information needed to create a new individual. Among other things DNA determines a person's sex and body shape.

13 THE ARTS

'The arts' mean different things to so many people. This chapter traces the history and development of the arts and the contributions made to them by many cultures and individuals from nations all over the world.

What is Art?

Left: *Richmond Hill* by the English painter Joseph Mallord William Turner (1775-1851). He is renowned for his dramatic use of light and colour.

Below: By the end of the 12th century, the art of creating stained-glass windows had been perfected. One of the finest examples is this rose window of the Sainte Chapelle in Paris.

The word 'art' has two different meanings. It can mean drawing, painting and sculpture. When people say that they are interested in art, they usually mean that they enjoy painting and drawing or looking at paintings and drawings. But when we talk about 'the arts' we mean much more than this. 'The arts' include not only drawing, painting and sculpture, whose origins stretch back to ancient times but also music, literature, drama, dancing and more modern forms of art, such as photography, cinema and television.

Artists and Performers

An artist can be a painter, but a composer or author can also be called an artist because he works in one of the arts. Some of the arts, such as music, drama, cinema and television,

need performers. They are often called the 'performing arts' and the performers (musicians and actors) can also be called artists.

Arts and Crafts

All the arts are concerned with creating things, but not everything that is made is a work of art. Some things are made to be used rather than just admired. For example, a man could make a wooden bowl and carve designs on the outside for decoration. He has made a bowl for people to eat out of, although it may be beautiful. Another wood-carver could carve a model of an animal, for example, which can only be used as an ornament. The wooden bowl is an example of a craft, as it is mainly a useful object, and the model animal is an example of an art. An artist makes beautiful things for people to admire but a craftsman makes things that can be used. Very often a craftsman makes something that is very beautiful, and is often considered a work of art, but this is not the main reason for making it. Some examples of craftsmen are potters, furniture makers, watchmakers and instrument makers.

Why do Artists Want to Create?

Artists write, paint and compose for many different reasons. The main reason is to communicate their ideas to other people. For example, when a painter sees a beautiful sunset, he may want other people to share the feelings he has about it. So, he might paint a picture of that sunset. Because the painting will not look exactly like the real sunset, the artist also tells us in his painting a little bit about what he feels about it. In

Right: The ancient Egyptians were skilled artists and craftsmen. This solid gold mask covered the head of King Tutankhamun's mummy.

Below: The Phillip Jones Brass Ensemble. Music is probably the oldest known art form for expressing people's thoughts and feelings.

Below: Ballroom dancing is one of the most popular forms of dance, especially in Great Britain.

the same way, writers can describe things in ways that let us know exactly what they think about them. Artists do not only describe things to us, but can also convey their ideas to us. A writer can, for example, tell us what he thinks life will be like in a hundred years' time, or even what he thinks is wrong with the world today. Poets are especially skilled in conveying feelings through their art, for the essence of poetry is the expression of emotions. In the dramatic arts, not only the playwright but also the actors want to communicate their thoughts and ideas through a play. Music, too, is a medium which can communicate a lot to us. In ancient times it was thought of as the gift of the gods. We all respond to music at some level—some pieces of music sound happy and gay, others sad and mournful. The composer of the music is telling us a little about how he felt when he was writing the music or is perhaps describing an experience he has had.

179

Drawing and Painting

Today, the easiest way to make a picture of something is to take a photograph, but before the camera was invented artists had to draw and paint pictures. Drawing is usually done with a pen or pencil on paper and makes a picture out of lines. Artists can indicate colour and shadow by shading.

Some pictures that look like drawings have not been made with a pen or pencil. They are engravings. They are made by cutting the picture on a flat block of wood or metal and then inking over the top of it. When the block is pressed on to paper it prints the picture in reverse. Another way of making line pictures is etching. It is like engraving but wax and acid are used to etch the picture on to a metal plate. With both etching and engraving, it is possible to make many prints.

Above: An Egyptian painting found on a tomb in Thebes. The Ancient Egyptians painted people in profile

Left: *Great Piece of Turf* by Albrecht Durer (1471-1528). Although a competent painter, he was famed for his woodcuts, engravings and drawings.

Painting

The first paints were made from natural substances, for example, soot and powdered earth. Later, artists painted on to the plaster of walls with colours mixed with egg white and vinegar. Artists then found that if colours were mixed with linseed oil they lasted much better and held their brightness longer. Another kind of paint is water colour. Water colour paints are used on paper, and oil paints on canvas.

Cave men decorated the walls of their caves with pictures of animals. The ancient Egyptians also covered their walls with pictures, as did the Romans and Greeks.

In the Middle Ages, most pictures were of religious subjects. After the Renaissance, or rebirth of art in Europe, artists began to paint other subjects, like scenes from history and portraits of people. Some artists painted scenes in the countryside, which we call landscapes, or pictures of flowers or objects, which we call still-life pictures.

After the invention of the camera, artists

Some Famous Artists

Leonardo da Vinci (1452-1519) Italian. One of the greatest artists of the Renaissance period. He was also an architect, engineer, musician and anatomist.

Albrecht Dürer (1471-1528) German. Dürer was a painter and engraver and invented the art of etching.

Michelangelo Buonarroti (1475-1564) Italian. Another great artist of the Italian Renaissance. He painted the ceiling of the Sistine Chapel in Rome.

Titian (1477-1576) Italian. A great oil painter famous for the rich colours in his pictures.

Rembrandt van Rijn (1606-1669) Dutch. Perhaps the most famous Dutch painter. He painted many portraits.

Pierre Renoir (1841-1919) French. Painted in a soft sensitive style that made him one of the leaders of the Impressionist school.

Paul Gauguin (1848-1903) French. He lived in Tahiti for a while and painted many Tahitian scenes in vivid colours.

Pablo Picasso (1881-1973) Spanish. One of the most famous 20th century artists. He led many modern movements, one of which was Cubism, where objects were transformed into geometric shapes.

Salvador Dali (1904-   ) Spanish. Dali's pictures are called 'surreal' because they appear realistic, but have a strange dream-like quality.

no longer had to draw or paint realistic pictures because they could just take a photograph. Many decided to paint things in a different way. The first artists to break with traditional painting were called Impressionists because their works gave only a quick, general impression of a scene, instead of a very realistic view. Many years before this, Arab artists had made pictures using geometrical shapes and patterns. Now modern artists also started to make patterns and shapes rather than pictures of things. We call this abstract art. Artists began to look at things in a new way and to communicate their vision in imaginative, new styles.

Above left: The *Mona Lisa* was the most famous portrait painted by Leonardo da Vinci.

Above: *Luncheon of Boating Party, Bougival* by the great Impressionist, Pierre Renoir.

Below: *Whaam!* by Roy Lichtenstein, an example of modern 'pop' art.

Sculpture

There are many ways of making sculptures. They can be modelled, using a soft material like clay, carved in stone or wood, or cast in a mould.

The first sculptures were pots and bowls made in clay, but very soon people began making clay models of their gods and sacred animals, and sculpture changed from being a craft into an art.

Carving of wood and stone soon became a popular method of sculpture. It is more difficult than modelling as pieces cannot be added and special tools are needed. In ancient Greece and Rome, sculpture in marble was very popular, but nowadays all kinds of materials are used.

To make a sculpture out of metal the sculptor first makes a mould out of clay and then pours in molten metal. This method uses a lot of metal, but the 'lost wax' method uses less. The sculptor makes a shape in clay, and then covers it with wax. After this he covers the wax with another layer of clay and heats the whole thing. As the wax melts and runs away, there is a gap left between the two layers of clay. When metal is then poured into this gap, it forms the shape that the wax had. When the metal is hard the clay can be taken off leaving a hollow metal sculpture.

The lost wax method of casting metal

Above: Portrait of Michelangelo, the famous Italian Renaissance sculptor.

Above right: Michelangelo's most moving sculpture, 'the Pieta', in Rome.

Right: Sir Henry Moore simplified human forms in this family group.

182

Some Famous Sculptors

Michelangelo Buonarroti (1475-1564) Italian. Specialized in marble sculptures of the human body, such as his 'David', his great statue of Moses, his pietas, and also figures for tombs.

Bernini, Gianlorenzo (1598-1680) Italian. Used interesting mixtures of materials, such as marble, bronze and glass. Fine examples of this are his 'Ecstasy of Saint Theresa' and his works in St. Peter's Cathedral, Rome.

Houdon, Jean-Antoine (1741-1823) French. Best-known for his portraits, such as statues of Molière and Washington. Also well-known is his 'Anatomical Man'.

Rodin, Auguste (1840-1917) French. Well-known for his figures 'Bronze Age', 'The Kiss', 'The Burghers of Calais', 'The Thinker' and his 'Gate of Hell', a huge bronze door.

Epstein, Sir Jacob (1880-1959) b. New York. Many of his sculptures are in public places, such as his 'Rima' in Hyde Park, London and a bronze group for Coventry Cathedral.

Calder, Alexander (1898-1976) American. An engineer and sculptor who invented mobiles.

Moore, Sir Henry (1898-   ) English. Mainly famous for abstract sculptures, such as 'The North Wind'.

Left: From earliest times, men have made figures of wood to represent their ancestors or gods. This African figure has a hornbill on his head.

sculpture was used very skilfully in Africa. In the kingdom of Benin (c.1100 to the early 1700s), in what is modern Nigeria, many fine bronze sculptures were produced. Benin artists created striking heads of family members to be used in ancestor worship. They also produced delightful pieces for decoration.

Subjects for Sculpture

The most common subject for sculpture is the human figure. There are statues of famous people in most towns and the best can be seen in art galleries all over the world. But statues are not the only form of sculpture. Some are like half statues attached to a background. These are often carved on stone walls and are called reliefs. If the sculpture is of somebody's head (or head and shoulders) we call it a bust. The ancient Greeks and Romans carved many beautiful statues and busts of their emperors and gods. Later, sculptors copied their graceful style, which we call the 'classical' style.

Recently, artists have made sculptures that are not so realistic. They have simplified, or complicated, and distorted the shapes of what they are carving, to make it more expressive. Other sculptors do not try to make realistic shapes at all. They are more interested in making unusual shapes out of wood, stone and metal, rather than models of people and animals.

Artists are now finding new ways of making sculptures. Instead of cutting or moulding materials, some sculptors stick things together or build sculptures out of many different parts. Using string, wire, pieces of wood, metal, and plastic, they can make very interesting shapes.

Perhaps the most interesting new idea is moving sculptures. Alexander Calder invented a kind of sculpture which he called a 'mobile'. In a mobile, pieces of wood, cardboard or plastic hang from pieces of wire and string. They are very carefully balanced and the slightest breeze makes them move.

Left: Chinese gilt dancing figures. They represent Bodhisattvas, or Buddhists who delay reaching nirvana in order to teach others.

Music

Music is the art of arranging sounds. The origin of music is lost in time, but we can imagine that it was a primitive form of communication or a part of man's earliest religious ceremonies. We do know, however, that music has always had the power to affect people's emotions. A stirring march, a lively dance, a song to share with friends or make a job go quickly—these were some uses of music in ancient civilizations, just as they are for us today.

Musical Instruments

The first musical instruments were probably invented by accident. When someone found that hitting a clay pot on the bottom produced an interesting sound, the first drum was born. Today, instruments that are struck—drums, cymbals or xylophones—are called percussion instruments.

Primitive man may also have discovered stringed instruments. Perhaps he heard the 'twang' of his bowstring. To play a harp or a guitar, you pluck the strings just like you pluck a bowstring. Later, somebody found

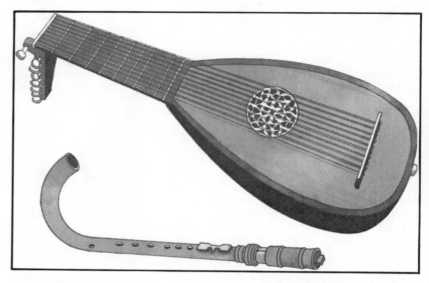

Above: The lute (top) is one of the earliest stringed instruments. It was very popular until the 17th century. The crumhorn (bottom) is a reed-cap instrument, popular in the Middle Ages.

Below: The Vienna Philharmonic Orchestra is one of the greatest symphony orchestras of today. It is just as happy playing Brahms as Stockhausen, and is famous for performing Strauss waltzes and marches.

Some Famous Composers

Claudio Monteverdi (1567-1643) Italian. Wrote some of the first operas and a great deal of church music.

Johann Sebastian Bach (1685-1750) German. Wrote many pieces for orchestra, choirs, organ and harpsichord.

George Frederick Handel (1685-1759) German. The composer of the 'Messiah' and 'Water Music'.

Wolfgang Amadeus Mozart (1756-1791) Austrian. Began composing as a child. Wrote many operas, symphonies, and concertos.

Ludwig van Beethoven (1770-1827) German. Famous composer of symphonies. Started to go deaf at about the age of 30.

Johannes Brahms (1833-1897) German. Wrote symphonies and works for piano.

Johann Strauss (1825-1899) Austrian. Wrote the 'Blue Danube' waltz.

Peter Ilich Tchaikovsky (1840-1893) Russian. Wrote symphonies, operas and ballets, including the 'Nutcracker Suite'.

Edward Elgar (1857-1934) English. Wrote the 'Pomp and Circumstance' marches and the 'Enigma Variations'.

Benjamin Britten (1913-1976) English. Famous for his operas and music for young people, e.g. 'The Young Person's Guide to the Orchestra'.

Karlheinz Stockhausen (1928-   ) German. A modern composer who writes experimental music.

that the strings made a nice long sound when they were scraped rather than plucked. He had invented the musical bow, which violinists use today. The harpsichord and piano are also stringed instruments. Inside them is a mechanism that plucks or hits the strings when the keys are pushed down.

Another kind of musical instrument is the wind instrument. There are many different sorts, but they are all blown into to produce sounds. Reed instruments (oboe, clarinet, bassoon, and saxophone), whose notes are made by air vibrating a reed inside them, and flutes, are known as woodwind instruments because they used to be made entirely of wood. The brass horns of the orchestra are really only tubes made of brass. The most common are the trumpet, tuba, French horn and trombone.

Today, there are many kinds of electronic instruments such as synthesizers, and many ways to amplify instruments that would be very quiet on their own, for example, the electric guitar used in pop groups.

Above left: The greatest composer of his time, Ludwig van Beethoven. Many of his most famous pieces were composed after he had become deaf.

Above: Pop groups of the 1960s and 1970s revolutionized the musical scene. Amplified electric guitars and light shows added to the excitement of pop.

Below: A group of West Indians make their own music using empty metal oil drums, which are tuned and used as instruments. These groups are called steel bands.

Dancing

People dance for many reasons. Folk dancing and tribal dancing usually celebrate some special event. For example, African tribes often dance to celebrate the birth of a baby or a wedding, and even today in Europe people celebrate the beginning of summer by dancing round the maypole, or the success of the harvest with a barn dance. This kind of folk and country dancing is done for fun and for everyone to join in. People do not usually want to just watch this kind of dancing.

In the 17th century, these folk dances became quite popular with people other than the peasants who normally did them. The kings, queens and noblemen also wanted a kind of dance they could join in. They invented versions of the peasant dances that were stately and not so lively.

Right: This picture from a medieval manuscript shows early court dancing.

Below: Dame Margot Fonteyn and Nureyev in the ballet *Romeo and Juliet*.

Above: The Pirin Dance, danced standing on drums, comes from the mountains of south-west Bulgaria. Folk dancing is always done in the national costume of the dancers.

Right: The dancers of South-east Asia are very graceful and supple. Their dances tell stories and every movement of their arms, hands and eyes means something specific. This dancer comes from the island of Bali.

Above right: The Flamenco is danced in southern Spain to the sound of the classical guitar and the clack of castanets. It is a colourful and vivacious dance.

These dances included the minuet, allemande, gigue and gavotte. Then, in the 19th century, everyone wanted to dance in ballrooms like the nobility and the new dance, the waltz, became very popular.

Today, ballroom dancing is still popular. People not only like to dance the tango, waltz and cha-cha, but also enjoy watching other people dance. New dances are always being invented, and with jazz and pop music there are many dances for the ballroom and discotheque.

Most of this ballroom and disco dancing is not done in front of an audience. There is a kind of dancing, though, that is usually performed for an audience. It is called ballet. Ballet is a way of telling a story by

Choreography

Choreography is the art of writing dances. A choreographer must work out all the movements that he wants the dancers to make and then go through them with the dancers.

Folk dances have nearly always been passed from one dancer to another without being written down. The person who is learning the dance watches it and then copies. This system has not always been accurate enough, so dancers and choreographers invented ways of writing down the movements. At first they used little pictures like 'pin men' which were drawn under the music. Later a new system was invented which used dots to represent the hands, feet and head of the dancer on lines. This system looks rather like music. Choreography can be used for all kinds of dancing, from ballroom dancing to ballet.

In classical ballet, some of the best choreographers came from the traditional Russian companies. The ballets written in the early 1900s by Michel Fokine and by the famous dancer, Nijinsky, are still performed frequently. Some of the greatest living choreographers are Sir Frederick Ashton of Great Britain and the Americans George Balanchine and Martha Graham.

moving to a piece of music. In this way it is very much like opera or drama, but without the words. Classical ballet developed from the court dances of the 17th century. There is a large number of standard movements. Modern ballet is much freer in style, but it still tries to tell a story and express the feelings of the dancer through his or her movements with the music.

Dancing often plays a part in other dramatic forms such as operas and musicals, and variety shows often include scenes with a group of dancers dancing to a popular tune.

Literature

Literature is the written art. People write things down for several reasons. Text books and newspapers are examples of writing done to pass on information. Another example of this kind of writing is this encyclopedia. But this is not usually called art, as it is written to be useful rather than to entertain. Most literature is the art of telling a story, or describing thoughts and feelings.

Literature comes in two main forms, prose and poetry. Poetry is often written in verses with a regular rhythm and sometimes with rhymes at the end of lines. Prose is different from poetry as it does not use rhymes at all. Whether they write to inform or to entertain, prose writers do not write in verses. They divide their writing into sentences and paragraphs instead.

Story-telling is an art that began long before Man had discovered how to write. Most stories were first passed on by word of mouth. Literature began when a method of writing down these stories was discovered. Most of these stories are fiction. In fiction the people, or characters, in the story are imaginary, although the story may be based on real-life events. Sometimes an author (a writer of prose) writes a story about the future. We call this science fiction, 'sci-fi', or simply SF.

There are many different forms of fiction, but the two most common types are short stories and novels. A short story is exactly what it sounds like, a single story told in a short way. A novel usually has several stories told at the same time. These plots (stories) are connected together in the novel by the characters in them. Sometimes the plots get very complicated and the novels have many different characters all connected in some way.

Not all prose literature is pure fiction.

Right: One of the greatest French writers was Victor Hugo (1802-1885). He wrote drama and prose but his best works were thought to be his poems. Other French poets of the time were Alfred de Musset and Charles Baudelaire.

Below: Charles Dickens surrounded by the characters from some of his stories. He was probably the greatest English author of his time (1812-1870). His works tell of some of the dreadful social conditions of his age.

Left: *Alice in Wonderland* is one of the most famous books ever written for children, although it has been enjoyed by people of all ages. The author is Lewis Carroll (1832-1898), whose real name was Charles Dodgson.

Some authors write historical novels which tell the reader a little bit about a period of history. These novels contain a certain amount of fact as well as fiction. For example, an author could write a novel set in the time of the First World War and describe events that really happened, but at the same time include in his novel characters that he has made up. An author can also write novels set in his own time which are partly fact and partly fiction.

Some literature can be completely true. This type of prose is called nonfiction. If an author writes the life story of a famous person, we call this a biography. When people write about their own lives, these stories are called autobiographies. Both are examples of nonfiction writing. Other examples are histories, scientific articles and books that teach new skills.

Poetry

Poetry can also tell a story. The poet Homer, who lived nearly 3,000 years ago, wrote long stories such as the 'Iliad' and the 'Odyssey' in verse. This kind of poetry which tells a story is known as an epic poem. There are as many different kinds of poetry as there are types of prose. Most do not tell a story, but express ideas or feelings.

The different kinds of poetry can be recognized by the number of lines in each verse, or by noticing which lines rhyme. The most important feature of poetry, though, is its rhythm and different forms of poem have different rhythms. For example, the sonnet, which is a form of poem used by many poets, has a completely different rhythm and rhyme scheme from the humorous limerick.

Below: A common theme in science fiction stories is that of the space ship that transports people backwards and forwards in time. One of the first science fiction writers was H. G. Wells. Others include C. S. Lewis and John Wyndham.

The Theatre

The art of acting in a theatre and writing plays for the theatre is known as drama. Most dramatic events take the form of actors acting out a story by a writer, called a playwright or dramatist.

Because this is usually done on a stage in a theatre, drama is also called theatre. The stories acted in the theatre are called plays. Drama is very much like literature, but is not written only to be read from books. In a way it is a kind of literature brought to life. Poetry too can be brought to life in the form of a play. The early plays were often written in verse, and Shakespeare's plays are in a form called blank verse. Blank verse is a kind of poetry where the lines have a regular rhythm, but there are not usually rhymes at the end of the lines. Most modern plays, though, are written in prose, which makes them more natural and realistic.

Some drama is not written down, but is made up by the actors as they go along. This is called improvisation. Another form of drama is mime. In mime, the actors do not say anything, but tell the story by their movements and facial expressions. In mime make-up and costume is important to show the kind of character that the actor is playing.

Early Drama

The first recorded play was performed by the ancient Egyptians around 2700 BC. The beginning of drama as we know it, however, was in ancient Greece, where it was origi-

nally part of a religious ceremony. The Greek plays were performed in semi-circular theatres built around an altar to the god Dionysus. These outdoor theatres could often hold over 20,000 people who came to see tragic and comic plays. The church in the Middle Ages also used drama as part of its worship, and the Bible stories used in the Christian Mass were later acted outside the church. These mystery and miracle plays became very popular and groups of actors went from town to town with a mobile stage to put these plays on.

Soon, actors and playwrights found new subjects for their plays. Towards the end of the 15th century, the Italians developed the

Above: The ancient Greek theatre at Ephesus. Western drama is said to have its beginnings in Greek theatre.

Below left: Mime (acting without speech) has been perfected by Marcel Marceau.

Below: David Garrick, (1717-1779) was an English actor, dramatist and theatre manager.

commedia dell'arte in which the actors made up their lines as they went along. A hundred years later, in England, William Shakespeare (1564-1616) was writing many plays on historical subjects. Nowadays, plays have as many different subjects as novels do and there are dramatists in many countries writing all kinds of plays.

Often there is some music in plays which we call incidental music. It helps to add atmosphere to the play. When a dramatist asks the actors to sing some songs as well as speak, we call the play a musical. If the actors do not speak at all, but sing all their lines and there is an orchestra playing with them, it is called opera.

Drama can also be found in places other than the theatre. At the end of the last century, cinematography was invented. Today there is a great deal of drama written

for the cinema and it has become a popular art form. At first, the films were silent and the cinema was rather like mime on film. But when the 'talkies' were invented this gave dramatists a much more realistic atmosphere to work with.

Almost the exact opposite of mime and silent films is drama for the radio. Radio plays became popular soon after the invention of the radio in the 1920s. Dramatists had to change their style of writing to write radio plays as the audience could not see the movements or the expressions of the actors. The writers of radio plays have to make their stories clear by the words and sounds in their plays. They are still popular today, even though we have television, because people feel that they can use their imagination more when they listen to them.

Television, too, has changed drama. It has brought plays out of the theatre and cinema and into our homes. We can now see productions of all kinds of plays, from Shakespeare to detective stories, without leaving our homes.

Above: William Shakespeare (1564-1616), probably the world's greatest playwright.

Left: A Japanese kabuki play. These plays are full of colour, life and movement.

Below: Behind the scenes of a typical modern, Western theatre.

14

MAN THE BUILDER

From the time that Man moved out of his cave he has been a builder. First it was to provide a roof over his family. Then temples to glorify his gods, and castles to give protection against his enemies. Now, we have the marvels of modern architecture.

Housing

Houses provide a home and a place to keep belongings, but they also protect people from the weather. In hot climates, houses are built to be cool; in cold climates they keep off the rain and keep out the cold. Houses can be built of many different materials and there are almost as many different kinds of houses as people.

The First Houses

In early days houses protected people from wild beasts and enemy tribes. Caves were used because the entrance could be guarded and because, if you go deep enough, the temperature is always mild. Early men also built houses on stilts on lakes, where beasts could not reach them.

In the past, many people earned their living by working in their home. Farmers lived in the same building as the animals who gave them milk, eggs or meat. In Dutch towns, Venice and Hong Kong there are houseboats or houses by canals because people worked or traded on the water.

In most cities, people had their shops or offices on the ground floor of their houses, their living rooms on the first floor, and their bedrooms on the top. This system is as old as the Ancient Romans, and continues today, although now many more people leave their home each day to work elsewhere.

Ruling from Home

Rich and powerful men, whose job it was to rule, also worked from their houses. They needed strong buildings of stone in which the people they ruled and protected could take shelter when enemies attacked. These

Above: Prehistoric cavemen did not build houses. They simply selected a suitable cave, probably near a good hunting ground, and moved in with their few belongings.

Below: In many parts of the world people still lead a wandering life. Their homes must be easy to erect and dismantle like these Bedouin tents in the Negev Desert of Israel.

were castles. Poor people usually lived in hovels which could easily be knocked down or set on fire.

From Castle to Palace

After the Middle Ages, when law and order was established, rulers turned their castles into palaces. Palaces are unfortified houses where kings and princes ruled and had offices for their court—the people who served them. Many palaces and grand houses survive in Europe. An early and beautiful palace was built by the Duke of Urbino in Italy, and the great French king Louis XIV built a number of palaces, of which Versailles, near Paris, is the largest—the size of a small city.

Even today, heads of government live in special houses. The British Prime Minister rules from a house, No. 10 Downing Street in London, and the President of the United States lives and works in the White House in Washington, D.C. Most people, however, have houses just to sleep and relax in.

Building Terms

beam Horizontal support for floor or wall resting on at least two columns.

brickwork A wall made of equal-sized blocks of hard baked clay. Bricks are laid in a pattern to make the wall strong.

column Vertical support used for holding up a roof or floor.

girder A beam, often made of iron or steel, used to support the framework of a building or a bridge.

masonry Natural stone blocks cut to a shape and fitted together to form walls.

mortar A mixture of sand, cement and water used to bind bricks together.

timber frame Heavy timber beams and columns make up a skeleton of a house and the outside walls are built on to it using bricks.

Ancient Monuments and Buildings

The first buildings men constructed were probably houses, but from very earliest times people made other kinds of buildings, too.

Some monuments, like Stonehenge in England and similar groups of stones in Malta, Africa and China are difficult to understand. Why did people drag huge stones over miles of ground to arrange them in complicated circles? Was it to make a place to gather for a religious ceremony? Was it to build a temple for worship of the sun? What was its importance to its builders? The usual theory today is that Stonehenge was a primitive clock and calendar.

In order to have Stonehenge built, the priests must have been able to command hundreds of people. In the same way, the Pharaohs of Egypt must have needed thousands of people to build the pyramids for them. The pyramids were built as tombs for the Pharaohs. A Pharaoh would put into his tomb everything he thought he would want in his life after death. The pyramid had to be strong and thief-proof, for he believed that if his goods were stolen his spirit would suffer.

Another reason why people built huge structures was the need for protection. The Romans built two walls in the north of England, Hadrian's Wall and the Antonine Wall, many miles long, to protect them from Scottish invaders. The Great Wall of China was also used for defence.

Above: The ruins of Stonehenge near Salisbury in southern England. It is the best-preserved structure which remains from the New Stone Age.

Below: The Great Wall of China, built as a monument to Shih Huang-ti, the founder of the Ch'in Dynasty. It took many years to build.

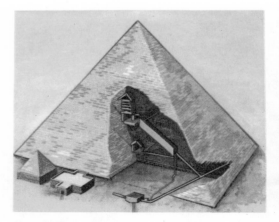

Above: The Great Pyramid, showing the entrance to the inner chambers. The pyramids were built by the ancient Egyptians as tombs for their pharaohs.

The Pyramids

There are 70 pyramids in Egypt, some of which are made of stone blocks and others of large clay bricks.

The largest—the Pyramid of Cheops—was 147 metres (482 feet) tall, and 230 metres (756 feet) along the sides.

Many of the stone blocks were cut from local stone which splits fairly easily in good straight faces. If the quarry for the stone was too far away the blocks would be transported by river in special boats and then rolled on logs by slaves because the wheel had not been invented. Ramps built up the side of the pyramid were used to haul the stones to the top. The ramps were afterwards removed.

The Beginning of Architecture

The Greeks and Romans also had buildings of stone—temples for worship, stadiums for contests, theatres, gymnasiums and palaces. They discovered that to make a building beautiful the balance between the different parts that make up the building, or its proportions, must be just right.

Until recently, many Europeans and Americans took their idea of what made a building beautiful from the Romans and Greeks. There are other languages or 'styles' of building, but it was the Greeks who first mastered the art of 'architecture' rather than just building. The Parthenon in Athens is a perfect example of this. The architects of the Parthenon knew exactly how to balance the height and circumference of the columns to achieve a pleasing design. The shape of the columns also contributes to the light effect that was achieved, even in solid stone.

Many buildings built before the 20th century have columns and domes and many other 'classical' parts, in imitation of the great buildings of the past.

The largest church in the world, St Peter's in Rome, was built in the 15th and 16th centuries to rival the great architecture of the Romans. The architects of St Peter's had studied the Roman Colosseum, which had been built to hold thousands of people. In stone, St Peter's speaks the same language—it is made up of carefully proportioned and beautifully carved columns. Even modern buildings, which are not built in the 'classical' way, need good proportions if they are not to be ugly.

Top: The Colosseum was the largest and most famous amphitheatre to be built by the Romans. Beast hunts and battles between gladiators were held there regularly.

Above: The Parthenon, the temple of Athena on the Acropolis of Athens. Its beautiful proportions have been an inspiration to many architects since it was built in the 5th century BC.

Modern Marvels

Using iron and concrete, modern engineers have made bridges, towers, dams and other buildings of an enormous height and size. But nobody would want tall structures like the Eiffel tower, or the huge blocks of flats or offices that are now in every city, without lifts. Lifts (or elevators) made today's enormous buildings possible. In 1852 an American called Elisha Otis invented the safety lift—not just a lift with a motor to haul people up and let them down, but a lift with a patent safety device to prevent the lift falling if the cable holding it broke.

Before the 18th century, if people wanted a large building, they had to build it in wood and stone. During the Industrial Revolution, however, they learnt how to make iron girders, which are stronger than wooden beams, and so they could make larger buildings.

In the 20th century people discovered that by putting steel girders inside concrete ('reinforced concrete') they had something even stronger than stone. Large modern buildings are built of steel and concrete—they are really huge steel and concrete skeletons clothed with walls. Architects often disguise the bulk of the building's construction by using glass to cover the exterior of skyscrapers.

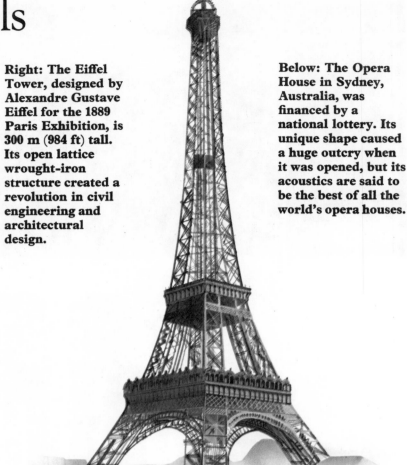

Right: The Eiffel Tower, designed by Alexandre Gustave Eiffel for the 1889 Paris Exhibition, is 300 m (984 ft) tall. Its open lattice wrought-iron structure created a revolution in civil engineering and architectural design.

Below: The Opera House in Sydney, Australia, was financed by a national lottery. Its unique shape caused a huge outcry when it was opened, but its acoustics are said to be the best of all the world's opera houses.

Tallest Structures

The tallest structures in the world are radio masts. They are made of steel with cables called 'guy ropes' to keep them up. The tallest, the Warszawa mast, is in Poland. It is 645 metres (2,110 feet) tall.

The second tallest group of structures is broadcasting towers. The tallest is the Canadian National in Toronto. It is 553 metres (1,815 feet) tall, and it was built in one continuous operation. The main part of the tower is built of concrete and this was poured day after day into a special mould which climbed up the tower as the core grew taller. This special method is called slipforming and when the weather permitted the special moulding apparatus was climbing at a top speed of 6 metres (20 feet) a day.

The tallest office building is the Sears Tower in Chicago. It is 442 metres (1,975 feet) high.

Britain's tallest structure is the Post Office tower—189 metres (613 feet) tall.

Top: The Olympic Stadium built for the 1972 Games used modern materials to create a splendid venue for the athletic events.

Above: The two towers of the World Trade Centre in New York dominate the skyline of lower Manhattan.

Left: The tallest tower in the world is the CN Tower in Toronto, Canada. It is 553 m (1,815 ft) high.

High Rise

Even with a lift to go up in, most people prefer to live close to the ground, so that they can come in and go out without a journey. The reason why blocks of flats and offices are built so tall is that there is so little space on the ground in the centre of cities. If you spread out Manhattan, the centre of New York, into ordinary buildings of three or four floors, it would make the city at least five times wider—and this is impossible, since Manhattan is an island.

When buildings were made of stone, there was a limited number of shapes they could take. With reinforced concrete, architects can design buildings in almost any shape they like. The Sydney Opera House is a good example of the new trend in modern architecture.

Bridges

Bridges are platforms crossing empty spaces, and they need to be supported. Through history engineers have found better means of supporting their platforms and of making them longer.

The simplest sort of bridge is a log bridge. The Romans supported their bridges on arches. They built bridges several miles long with hundreds of arches to carry water from the mountains to the cities—these bridges are called aqueducts.

Another way to cross space is to support the platform on a kind of scaffolding. Both wooden and iron bridges have been built with various kinds of scaffolding. The ancestor of the huge modern bridges was the first bridge built of metal girders, at Coalbrookdale in Shropshire in 1779. There are two main types of scaffolding bridges: those with scaffolding underneath which supports the platform by pushing and those with scaffolding above (suspension bridges) which supports it by pulling.

Left: The first bridges were probably built by early man to overcome the problem of getting from one side of a river to the other. They simply placed a tree trunk over the water so that an end rested on each bank.

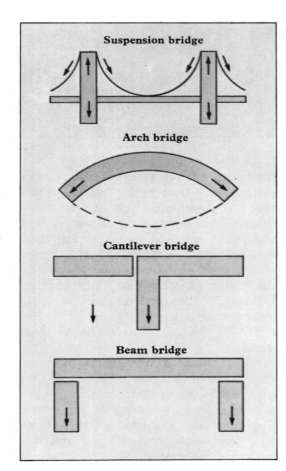

Suspension bridge

Arch bridge

Cantilever bridge

Beam bridge

Above: Tower Bridge, across London's River Thames, is a famous example of a *bascule* bridge—it moves up and down rather like a drawbridge.

Below: Suspension bridges, such as the George Washington bridge in New York, are very graceful structures which can easily span a gap of 1000 metres.

Dams

The first reason why men built dams was to control the watering of their crops. The ancient Egyptians built small dams to control the way the Nile River flowed into their fields, and Asian farmers do the same today in their paddy fields.

Later, dams were built to control rivers, to prevent them flooding or to keep them deep enough for boats to travel on. These dams, called locks, had gates which opened to let the boats go by, and openings called sluices which let the water through the gate when the level of water behind it was high enough.

Then people found that water passing through a sluice could turn a wheel and produce power. Before electricity was invented, watermills provided power all over Europe and Asia.

Water is still used today to provide power, and this is the chief reason why dams are built. 'Hydroelectric' dams build up a store of water which escapes through sluices and turns dynamos that produce electricity. The largest hydroelectric dams can provide electricity for domestic and industrial use over a wide region. Scientists are now experimenting with ways of damming the waves of the sea to make power.

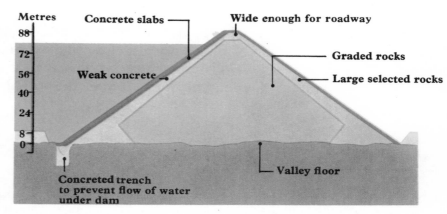

Metres
88
72
56
40
24
8
0

Concrete slabs — Wide enough for roadway

Weak concrete — Graded rocks — Large selected rocks

Concreted trench to prevent flow of water under dam — Valley floor

The Largest Dam in the World

The tallest dam in the world is the giant Nurek embankment dam in Russia. It stands 317 metres (1,040 feet) high and is 730 metres (2,400 feet) long.

But the largest dam in the world, if you go by the amount of material taken to form the embankment, is the Tarbela Dam in Pakistan. This dam rises to a height of 143 metres (470 feet) and stretches 3 kilometres (nearly 2 miles) in length.

The biggest reservoir in the world is in Russia. It holds enough water to cover the state of Texas 300 millimetres (1 foot) deep in water.

Above: A cross-section of a rock-fill dam showing the various materials used in its construction. The choice of site depends upon the purpose of the dam.

Below: The Kariba dam, on the Zimbabwe/Zambian border, is 128 m (420 ft) high and 618 m (2025 ft) long. A road runs along the top of the dam.

15 SPORTS

Games and sports are exciting and colourful features in the lives of many people. Sporting events and personalities have created traditions which have played a strong part in the social history of many nations all over the world.

Glossary of Sports

Archery A sport in which competitors use bows and arrows. The main variations of archery are target shooting, flight, field and cross-bow. In target shooting, archers are awarded points for shooting a given number of arrows at a target made up of five circles, within one another.

Baseball Outdoor bat-and-ball game played by two teams of nine players each, on a diamond-shaped pitch. Teams take it in turn to bat and field. Each team tries to score more runs than the other. A player scores a run when he circles all the bases round the pitch without being put out.

Basketball Indoor or outdoor ball game played on a marked court between two teams of five players each. The object is to hold on to the ball by bouncing it and passing it by hand to team mates, and finally throw it into the other team's basket and thus score a goal. *Baskets* are small bottomless nets, one of which hangs three metres (ten feet) above the ground at each end of the court.

Above: A young archer aims for the innermost circle.

Below: Baseball in San Francisco —Giants v Dodgers.

Above: Bicycle road racing
is run on public roads.

Above: Fishing is one of the
world's most popular sports.

Below: The Oakland Raiders,
an American football team.

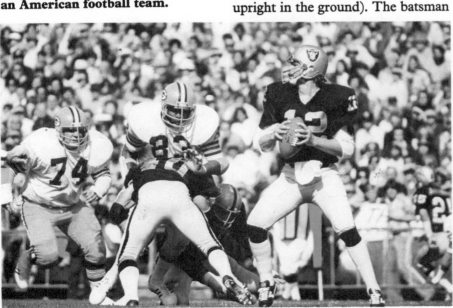

Billiards games Indoor ball games played on a long table covered with green felt with six pockets around the edges. Players drive coloured plastic balls against other balls and into the pockets with a long stick called a *cue*.

Boxing Ancient sport in which two fighters in a roped square and wearing special boxing gloves, punch each other on the face and on the body above the waist. A fighter wins by scoring most points for good punching or by knocking the other man down for more than ten seconds (*a knock-out*).

Cricket Outdoor bat-and-ball game played on grass between two 11-man teams. The bowler bowls a ball at the *wicket* (three wooden sticks stuck upright in the ground). The batsman defends the wicket and tries to hit the ball with a bat and score runs.

Cycling Bicycle racing between individual people or teams.
Track races are run on oval tracks that slope inward at a steep angle at each end.
Road races are run on public roads, and may be 80 kilometres (50 miles) or more long.

Fishing The catching of various kinds of fish for sport, using rods, lines, hooks, and bait; also called *angling*. Freshwater fishing is carried out in inland waters such as rivers and lakes; sea fishing is done in the sea, either from land or from boats.

Football Outdoor ball game in which two teams of eleven players each try to carry, throw or kick an egg-shaped ball across the other team's goal-line. Played almost wholly in the United States, it is often called *American Football*.

Golf Outdoor club-and-ball game in which the player knocks a small white ball over a long grass course into a small hole. He uses sticks with bent or shaped heads and tries to hit the ball as few times as possible. A golf course has nine or 18 holes.

Gymnastics Indoor sport of strength, grace and speed, using special equipment. Set exercises for men are floor exercises, vault, pommel-horse, parallel bars, horizontal bars, and rings. Women do floor exercises, vault, beam and asymmetrical bars.

Hockey Stick-and-ball game of two main kinds: *ice hockey* and *field hockey*. Ice hockey is played on an ice rink by two six-man teams wearing skates. They try to drive a hard wooden disc, called a *puck*, with long wooden sticks along the ice and into a goal cage at each end of the rink. Field hockey is played by two teams of eleven players each on a grass pitch. They use curved sticks to try and hit a small ball into one of the goals at each end of the pitch.

201

Glossary of Sports (2)

Above: HRH Princess Anne on her event horse, Goodwill.

Below: Unarmed combat is practised for self-defence.

Horse-riding events Competitions to test the speed, strength and ability of horse and rider. They include *dressage* (a series of special movements) and *show jumping*. The *three-day* event includes a cross-country test.

Japanese martial arts Forms of competitive sport based on self-defence and unarmed combat.

Judo developed from a form of self-defence called *jujitsu*. An opponent could be crippled or killed using only bare hands and feet. Judo means 'the gentle way'. A judo fighter yields to his opponent's attack until the right moment to counter-attack. He then tries to unbalance his opponent, throw him, and pin him to the floor.

Karate is another form of unarmed combat in which the hands, feet, elbows and knees are all used to strike an opponent. Karate means 'empty hand'. Blows are aimed at the softest parts of the body, such as the throat and stomach. In sport, contestants stop short of actually hitting each other or, at most, just touch each other lightly.

Kendo is the Japanese art of sword fighting. The word means 'sword way'. Contestants wear protective clothing or armour and usually fight with bamboo sticks. Real swords are sometimes used by experts. The object is to land two scoring blows on the opponent's target area.

Rugby football Outdoor game played with an egg-shaped ball by two teams. The ball is passed backwards, or kicked, or carried until a player can kick it over the other team's goal crossbar or touch it down behind the goal line, for points. Amateur teams play *Rugby Union* (15 players), professionals play *Rugby League* (13 players).

Soccer Football game played with a round ball between two teams of eleven players. Players try to kick or head the ball through the other team's goal. When in play, the ball may be handled only by the goalkeepers, in their own area. Also called *football* or *assocation football*.

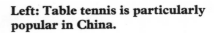

Left: Table tennis is particularly popular in China.

shot-put, discus, and hammer. Also called *athletics*.

Water sports Sports that can be divided into two main groups: swimming and diving, and boating.

Pool swimming includes races over 100, 200, 400, and 1,500 metres, using either free-style or some other predetermined stroke such as butterfly, breast stroke, or back stroke; or a mixture of strokes.

Water polo is a team water sport with seven strong swimmers in each team. The object is to throw or head a large inflated ball into the opponents' goal.

Diving takes place in pools. High diving is from platforms at 5, 7.5 and 10 metres above the water. Springboard diving is from springboards fixed at heights of 1 and 3 metres.

Boating covers rowing, canoeing, sailing and powerboat racing. Rowing is divided into *sculling* and *sweep-oar* racing. In sculling, each oarsman uses two oars. Such boats include single sculls, double sculls and quadruple sculls. In sweep-oar racing each member of the crew handles one much bigger and heavier oar. Such crafts hold two, four, or eight men. Eights, and sometimes fours, hold an extra man—the *coxswain* or *cox*—who steers the boat.

Canoeing is a sport in which one or more people sit in a small craft facing forwards, and paddle through the water. The craft may be a *canoe*, which is pointed at both ends and is propelled with a single-bladed paddle; or a *kayak*, in which the paddler uses a double-bladed paddle.

Sailing or yachting can be carried out in many different types of sailing boats. Boats in the same class compete against each other.

Squash Indoor game played by two or four players in a special four-walled court. Players hit a small, hard ball with long-handled rackets so that it bounces off walls and floor.

Table tennis Speedy indoor game for two or four players, played on a long table. Players face each other and, with a rubber-covered paddle, hit a small plastic ball so that it passes over a net stretched midway across the table. The ball must bounce once each time before being hit.

Tennis Game for two or four players played with rackets and a ball on a specially marked indoor or outdoor court. Players hit the ball to and fro over a net across the middle of the court. Each player tries to hit the ball so that the opponent cannot hit it back over the net within the court. Also called *lawn tennis*.

Track and field General name for running, jumping and throwing competitions. *Track* events are races over various distances, usually from 100 to 10,000 metres. *Field* events include long jump, high jump, pole vault and triple jump; and throwing competitions such as the javelin,

Above left: **Sir Francis Chichester, lone yachtsman.**

Left: **Undersea diving is a fascinating sport.**

Wrestling Form of unarmed combat using arms and legs to grasp and throw, and usually hold, an opponent on the floor. *Sumo* wrestling takes place mainly in Japan; *free-style* and *Graeco-Roman* are practised in many parts of the world.

Olympic Games

The Olympic Games are the greatest celebrations of sport in the world. They are held every four years. Nearly all the nations of the world take part. Thousands of athletes gather to compete in all kinds of sports, from athletics and swimming to archery and weightlifting.

Team sports include soccer and hockey outdoors and basketball and volleyball indoors. Combat sports include fencing, boxing, and wrestling. There are also water sports, such as sailing and rowing. Horse-riding, gymnastics and cycling are other major Olympic sports.

A separate festival is held in the same year for winter sports. These include skating, skiing, tobogganing, bobsledding and ice hockey.

The Olympics are for amateurs—that is, the competitors do not get paid. The winners receive gold medals, the seconds silver, and the thirds bronze. It is considered a great honour by many sportsmen and women to compete in the Games.

Far left: Baron Pierre de Coubertin, the Frenchman who pioneered the modern Olympics. He modelled them on the ancient Greek Olympics.

Below: Speed skating, one of the winter sports, which are held as a separate games at a different venue.

Bottom: Nadia Comaneci, the young Romanian gymnast who won 3 gold medals in the 1976 Olympics at the age of 14.

Olympic Games		Winter Olympics
1896	Athens, Greece	*The first separate Winter Olympics were held in 1924. But previous to that, figure skating and ice hockey had been included in the main Games.*
1900	Paris, France	
1904	St. Louis, USA	
1908	London, England	
1912	Stockholm, Sweden	
1920	Antwerp, Belgium	
1924	Paris, France	Chamonix, France
1928	Amsterdam, Holland	St. Moritz, Switzerland
1932	Los Angeles, USA	Lake Placid, USA
1936	Berlin, Germany	Garmisch-Partenkirchen, Germany
1948	London, England	St. Moritz, Switzerland
1952	Helsinki, Finland	Oslo, Norway
1956	Melbourne, Australia	Cortina, Italy
1960	Rome, Italy	Squaw Valley, USA
1964	Tokyo, Japan	Innsbruck, Austria
1968	Mexico City, Mexico	Grenoble, France
1972	Munich, W. Germany	Sapporo, Japan
1976	Montreal, Canada	Innsbruck, Austria
1980	Moscow, USSR	Lake Placid, USA

World Cup

The World Cup rivals the Olympics as the greatest event in international sport. All the world's soccer-playing nations compete in groups over a period of nearly two years. The winners of these groups go forward to the finals, which are held every four years. Most of the finalists are from Europe and South America.

The sixteen teams that reach the finals are divided into four groups, in which the four teams play each other. The top two teams in each group then go forward to two semi-final groups of four. The winners of these meet in the final, which is watched on television by hundreds of millions of viewers in all parts of the world.

Brazil have been the most successful team in the World Cup. When they won it in 1970 for the third time, they kept the famous Jules Rimet Trophy, named after the Frenchman who was president of FIFA, Soccer's international governing body, from 1920 to 1954. The new trophy is the FIFA World Cup, presented by FIFA. Uruguay, Italy and West Germany have each won the World Cup twice. England and Argentina have won it once each.

World Cup Finals

Year	Where held	Winners		Runners-up	
1930	Montevideo, Uruguay	Uruguay	4	Argentina	2
1934	Rome, Italy	Italy	2	Czechoslovakia	1
1938	Paris, France	Italy	4	Hungary	2
1950	*Rio de Janeiro, Brazil	Uruguay	2	Brazil	1
1954	Berne, Switzerland	West Germany	3	Hungary	2
1958	Stockholm, Sweden	Brazil	5	Sweden	2
1962	Santiago, Chile	Brazil	3	Czechoslovakia	1
1966	Wembley, England	England	4	West Germany	2
1970	Mexico City, Mexico	Brazil	4	Italy	1
1974	Munich, West Germany	West Germany	2	Netherlands	1
1978	Buenos Aires, Argentina	Argentina	3	Netherlands	1

*Deciding match of final group.

Top: The colourful scene at the opening ceremony of the 1970 World Cup, at the Aztec Stadium in Mexico City.

Left: Tostão of Brazil in action during the 1970 World Cup. With Jairzinho and the great Pelé, he was one of the exciting stars who helped Brazil to win the trophy for the third time.

Famous Sporting Figures

Muhammad Ali stands scowling in triumph over Sonny Liston after knocking him down in the first round of their second fight in 1964. Liston did not get up, and Ali was still champion.

ALI, Muhammad

American boxer, world heavyweight champion. As Cassius Clay, he first won the title in 1964, from the ferocious Sonny Liston. He forfeited the title for refusing, for religious reasons, to join the armed forces, but regained it in 1974 from George Foreman. Remarkably quick for a heavyweight, he also became known for his fast talking. After losing to Leon Spink in 1978, he won the return fight the same year to take the championship for a record third time.

BANNISTER, Sir Roger

British athlete, the first man to run a mile in under 4 minutes. His time of 3 minutes 59.4 seconds at Oxford in 1954 was a great milestone in athletics.

BEAMON, Bob

American athlete, Olympic long jump champion in 1968. His leap of 8.90 metres (29 feet $2\frac{1}{2}$ inches) in Mexico City beat the world record by 55 centimetres (1 foot $9\frac{1}{2}$ inches).

BORG, Bjorn

Swedish tennis player, Wimbledon champion for the third consecutive time in 1978. Only 22 at the time, he was the first man to accomplish this feat for over 40 years.

BRADMAN, Sir Donald

Australian cricketer, widely regarded as the finest batsman of all time. He captained Australia in 5 Test series and averaged 99.94 runs per innings in his 52 Test matches from 1928 to 1948.

EVERT-LLOYD, Chris

American tennis player, the outstanding

Right: Chris Evert-Lloyd, outstanding tennis star of the 1970s.

Centre: Roger Bannister breaks the tape in his historic mile.

Bottom: Babe Ruth, the man who brought the crowds to baseball.

figure in the women's game from the mid-1970s. She first won the Wimbledon singles titles in 1974, at the age of 19.

FRASER, Dawn
Australian swimmer, the first woman to break 60 seconds for the 100 metres freestyle. She won her third successive Olympic gold medal at this event in the 1964 Games.

LAVER, Rod
Australian tennis player, the only man to win the 'Grand Slam' twice. This involves winning the world's four major traditional titles (Wimbledon, US, Australian, and French) in one year. He did it as an amateur in 1962 and then as a professional in 1969.

MEADS, Colin
New Zealand ruby union lock-forward. He won 55 international caps, and captained the All Blacks.

MOORE, Bobby
English soccer player, and captain of the side that won the World Cup in 1966. A wing-half at first and then a central defender, he won 108 international caps.

NICKLAUS, Jack
American golfer, one of the biggest hitters in the game, consistently the world's leading golfer since the late 1960s, he set numerous records in the major tournaments.

PELÉ
Brazilian soccer player, the star of the 1958 and 1970 World Cups. He scored over 1,200 goals for Brazil and his club Santos. He helped to make soccer popular in the United States when he played for the New York Cosmos in 1977 before retiring. His name was Edson Arantes do Nascimento.

PLAYER, Gary
South African golfer, the first non-American to win the world's four major titles (including the British and US Open Championships). He was a consistent big tournament winner from the mid-1960s.

RUTH, 'Babe'
American baseball player. He set numerous batting records with the New York Yankees, including 60 home runs in a season (1927) and 714 in his career. His big hitting brought huge crowds flocking to watch baseball in the 1920s.

SOBERS, Sir Gary
West Indian cricketer, from Barbados. The outstanding all-rounder in the game, he scored a world record 8,032 runs in 93 Tests, including a record 365 not out against Pakistan in 1958. He also took 235 Test wickets. He once hit 6 sixes in an over when playing against Glamorgan (1968).

SPITZ, Mark
American swimmer, winner of a record 7 gold medals at the 1972 Olympic Games. Four were for individual events (freestyle and butterfly) and all were won in new world record times.

SURTEES, John
The only man to win the world championship in both motorcyling and motor racing. An Englishman, he won all his titles with Italian machines—MV Agusta motorcycles (late 1930s) and Ferrari cars (1964).

VIREN, Lasse
Finnish athlete, the leading middle-distance runner of the 1970s. He won the 5,000 and 10,000 metres Olympic titles at the 1972 and the 1976 Games in Munich and Montreal.

16 FAMOUS LIVES

There are a great many people who have made history through various actions and achievements. Whether through a spirit of adventure, curiosity or a deeply-felt cause, these people played an important part in shaping our world.

Mighty Conquerors

ALEXANDER THE GREAT (356-323 BC) was one of the greatest generals of all time. At 20 he was crowned king of Macedonia, a mountainous region in south-east Europe.

In 334 BC he invaded Persia with an army of 35,000 men and little money. But he won a quick victory and stormed on into Asia Minor. A year later, when King Darius of Persia had raised another large army to fight him, Alexander defeated the Persians again with his newly-formed *phalanx* (a solid square of soldiers with long spears).

He freed Egypt from the Persians and built the great city of Alexandria there, naming it after himself. He conquered the whole of Asia Minor, and marched eastwards to Afghanistan and India. Eventually his men refused to go any further, and he had to turn back. He died of a mosquito bite at the age of 32.

HANNIBAL (247-183 BC) was the greatest general of Carthage, an ancient North African city. When the Romans declared war on Carthage in 218 BC, Hannibal decided to invade Italy from Spain.

It was a bold and risky adventure, and was quite unexpected by the Romans. Hannibal led 60,000 men, 6,000 horses, and 37 elephants across the Pyrenees and the Alps.

In 216 BC he defeated a large army at Cannae in southern Italy. It was the worst defeat ever suffered by a Roman army, but because of poor support from Carthage Hannibal never did capture Rome. He spent his last years helping other rulers to fight the Romans in Syria and what is now Turkey. When he was faced with capture by his old enemies the Romans, Hannibal ended his life by swallowing poison.

Above: Alexander defeating the Persians at Issus.

Below: Hannibal and his elephants in the Alps.

CAESAR, JULIUS (*c.* 100-44 BC) was a Roman soldier and statesman, and one of the great rulers of his time. He became one of the rulers of Rome in 60 BC together with Marcus Licinius Crassus and Gnaeus Pompey.

In order to gain more power, Caesar invaded Gaul (France) and Britain. But Pompey became alarmed and jealous at Caesar's success and popularity and in 49 BC ordered him to give up his army. Caesar refused and launched a civil war. Pompey fled and Caesar conquered Italy in less than 50 days.

He was made absolute ruler for life, but some Romans feared that he would crown himself king. They plotted to prevent this and stabbed him to death.

Above: Caesar was a proud and ambitious man.

ATTILA (*c.* 406-453) was king of the Huns, a mongoloid tribe centred in what is now Hungary. The rulers of the eastern Roman Empire paid him a lot of money each year to keep him from invading their land. But if dues were late thousands of fierce warriors on horseback would attack. He was referred to as 'the scourge of God'.

He attacked Germany and Gaul (France) but in 451 the Romans managed to force him back over the Rhine. In 452 he invaded Italy but his army was hungry and sick and he had to return to his homeland. He died on his wedding night and shortly afterwards his kingdom was split up.

Above: Attila was much feared by the Romans.

NAPOLEON I (**Bonaparte**) (1769-1821) was born in Corsica. He became a soldier and was soon promoted to major and then brigadier general.

In 1796 he was sent to Italy to drive out the Austrians. He succeeded brilliantly and returned to Paris a hero.

In 1804 Napoleon was made emperor. He defeated the Austrian and Russian armies at Austerlitz, but was beaten by the British under Lord Nelson in a sea battle at Trafalgar in 1805.

He invaded Russia in 1812 and fought his way to Moscow, but he had to retreat when the Russian winter set in.

In 1814 he gave up his throne and was exiled to Elba. He escaped and raised an army but was beaten by Wellington at Waterloo. He died in exile on St. Helena.

HITLER, ADOLF (1889-1945) was born in Austria and during his early years he was very poor. He built up a hatred of all Jewish people because he blamed them for his wretched state. During the First World War he fought bravely in the German army and after the war he became leader of the 'Nationalist Socialist Workers' (Nazi) Party.

Within a few years he became master of all Germany. He carried out cruel acts against the Jews and other groups of people, and re-armed the German forces. He believed that the Germans were a master race and he invaded neighbouring lands to gain more territory for the German nation. His invasion of Poland in 1939 sparked off the Second World War. After nearly six years of fighting Germany was defeated in 1945. In the last days of the war Hitler was thought to have shot himself.

Right: Hitler salutes his armies in 1941.

Below: Napoleon at the battle of Austerlitz.

Bold Adventurers

RALEIGH, SIR WALTER (*c.* 1552-1618) was an adventurous English soldier, and a favourite of Queen Elizabeth I.

Raleigh explored parts of North America from North Carolina to Florida and tried more than once to establish an English colony there, but failed. He called the whole region Virginia, after Queen Elizabeth, who was known as the Virgin Queen.

Raleigh helped to introduce the potato and tobacco into Ireland from America. He helped to defeat the Spanish Armada in 1588. But he lost the Queen's favour when he married one of her maids-of-honour.

Elizabeth died in 1603, and the new king, James I, did not like or trust Raleigh. He eventually had Raleigh beheaded for disobeying orders.

LAWRENCE, THOMAS EDWARD (1888-1935) was a British soldier, secret agent, and author who so greatly helped the Arab cause in the First World War that he became known as Lawrence of Arabia.

When war broke out in 1914 Lawrence was sent to Egypt and found himself helping the Arabs free themselves from Turkish rule. Promoted to the rank of colonel, and

Above: Sir Walter Raleigh.

Below: Lawrence of Arabia.

often dressed and disguised as an Arab himself, he led many daring and successful raids across the desert against the Turks.

But after the war Lawrence was not able to do much for his Arab friends. Disappointed, he left his government job and joined the Royal Air Force. In 1926 he published a book, *Seven Pillars of Wisdom*, which recounts his experiences in fighting for the Arab cause. He was killed some years later while riding a powerful motorcycle.

EARHART, AMELIA (1897-1937?) was an American airwoman. She was the first woman passenger to cross the Atlantic Ocean by air and the first woman to fly it alone.

Miss Earhart set up a number of other records, including the first flight made by a woman from Honolulu to the United States mainland, and the first flight by a woman across the United States in both directions.

Her colourful career was suddenly cut short when she vanished mysteriously in 1937 near Howland Island in the Pacific, during an attempt to fly around the world. No trace of her or her airplane was ever found.

STANLEY, SIR HENRY MORTON

(1841-1904) was a British journalist and explorer who will always be remembered for his journey to find the Scottish explorer and missionary **DR DAVID LIVING-STONE** (1813-73).

Livingstone was sent out to Bechuanaland in Africa (now Botswana) by the London Missionary Society in 1841. He wanted to convert people to Christianity, and he hoped to end the slave trade by replacing it with legitimate commerce. He also wanted to explore the largely unknown continent of Africa. He discovered Victoria Falls in 1855 and explored the eastern Zambezi River from 1858 to 1864 and in 1866 set off on an unsuccessful journey to find where the Nile River began.

Nobody heard from him for some years. Because of fears for his safety, Henry Morton Stanley, a British journalist working for the New York *Herald*, was sent out to look for him. After many exciting adventures he found him in the town of Ujiji on the shores of Lake Tanganyika. On seeing this gaunt white man in the jungle, Stanley,

ever polite, is reported to have said: 'Dr Livingstone, I presume!' Livingstone refused to go back to the coast with Stanley, and died a year later at Lake Bangweulu. The local people had loved this old doctor for his courage and healing touch, and they mourned his death.

On hearing of Livingstone's death, Stanley returned to Africa to continue his friend's work. He led a number of daring expeditions, made important discoveries, and established the Congo Free State for Belgium, after the British had showed no interest in the region.

Top: Amelia Earhart, American airwoman.

Middle: Stanley went in search of Livingstone.

Above: Livingstone went to Africa as a missionary.

Right: Hillary and Tenzing on top of the world.

HILLARY, SIR EDMUND PERCIVAL

(1919-   ) and **TENZING NORGAY** (*c.* 1914-   ) were the first mountaineers to reach the top of Mount Everest, the world's highest mountain. Hillary, a New Zealander, had already climbed part of the way up Mount Everest in 1951 and 1952. In 1953 he reached the top with Tenzing Norgay, the Sherpa guide to the expedition. Queen Elizabeth II later knighted Hillary for this feat.

Hillary wrote the story of this wonderful climb in a book called *High Adventure* (1955). In 1957 and 1958 he set up base camps for Sir Vivian Fuchs' famous expedition across Antarctica from McMurdo Sound to the South Pole.

In 1960 he led an expedition that climbed the Himalayan peak, Mount Makalu I (8,480 metres, 27,824 feet). This was in order to test man's ability to live at great heights without using oxygen. The expedition also looked for a creature called the Abominable Snowman. Hillary described this climb in a book called *High in the Thin Cold Air* (1962).

Valiant Crusaders

BOOTH, WILLIAM (1829-1912) was the founder of the Salvation Army. As a Methodist minister he became unhappy with his work and in 1861 he left the church and devoted the rest of his life to working among the poor.

In 1865 he and his wife started holding open-air meetings in the poorest parts of London. They formed their followers into a mission band, and in 1878 named it the Salvation Army. It was a semi-military organization formed to declare war on the devil and all his works. Booth was tireless in organizing meetings and encouraging effort and self-denial among the workers. His courage and sincerity gained him respect throughout the world and turned the Salvation Army into the vast and honoured movement it is today.

JOAN OF ARC (1412-31) was a French heroine. When still very young she said she saw visions which she believed were messages from heaven telling her to lead the French armies. At the time, much of northern France was held by England. Joan believed it was her mission to free her country from the English.

At 17 she persuaded King Charles VII of France to let her command the French soldiers against the English at Orleans, which was under siege, or blockaded. By the clever use of her armies and her own bravery she defeated the enemy and lifted the siege of the city. She went on to free Reims and saw the coronation there of Charles VII as king of all France. Joan defeated the English wherever she met them. But she failed to take Paris. Badly wounded, she was captured by the Burgundians who sold her to their English allies.

The English accused her of being a witch and of being disobedient to the Church. They sentenced her to death, and on 30 May 1431 she was cruelly burnt to death tied to a stake in the city of Rouen.

Because of Joan's victories, however, the French gained a dominant position over the English armies and by 1453 had turned them out of France. In 1456 Joan was found innocent and in 1920 the Roman Catholic Church declared her a saint.

Above: William Booth (1829-1912), founder and first general of the Christian Mission, later renamed the Salvation Army.

Below: Joan of Arc (1412-1431) who, after performing many valiant deeds for her country, was burned as a witch.

SAINT PAUL (*c*. AD 3- *c*. 68) was the most important of the early Christian leaders. His story is told in the Bible.

Paul was at first called Saul, and he was a well-educated, very religious Jew. He had never met Jesus, but he hated all Christians and whenever he found them he had them thrown into prison.

One day, on his way from Jerusalem to Damascus to arrest more Christians, Saul was suddenly surrounded by a dazzling bright light and fell to the ground, blinded.

He claimed he heard Jesus saying: 'Saul, Saul, why do you persecute me?' Saul immediately saw the wrong he had been doing, humbly changed his name to Paul, and soon recovered his sight.

The rest of his life was spent preaching Christianity in much of Asia Minor. He had many hair-raising adventures. He was stoned, flogged, and shipwrecked, but his faith in God never failed. He was finally imprisoned in Rome and executed.

YOUNG, BRIGHAM (1801-77) was the second president of the Church of Jesus Christ of Latter-Day Saints, better known as the Mormons.

Joseph Smith, the founder of the church, was shot and killed by unbelievers in Illinois in 1844. To avoid further trouble, Brigham Young led the little band of Mormons on a long trek to the Great Salt Lake valley in Utah.

The desert all round was barren and the settlers were faced with many problems, but under Young's leadership they made the desert bud and blossom. Young i credited with leading 100,000 persons to the mountain valleys.

Revolutionary Thinkers

BUDDHA (*c.* 563–483 BC) was the title given to Siddhartha Gautama, the Indian who founded the Buddhist religion.

When he was a young man he left home to look for an answer to life's problems. He finally found the answer, or enlightenment, while sitting under a bodhi tree in Gaya. He realized that *nirvana*, a state of absolute peace and happiness, could bring release from the pressures of life. This state could only be reached by giving up all desires for worldly things.

ARISTOTLE (384–322 BC) was a Greek thinker, educator, and scientist. His ideas have had more influence on the thinking of the western world than those of almost any other person. He was a pupil of the philosopher Plato for 20 years and these two men are regarded as the most important of the ancient Greek thinkers. Aristotle was the tutor of Alexander the Great.

In 334 BC Aristotle founded a school in Athens called the Lyceum. He wrote and taught deeply on many subjects, including science, religion, astronomy, logic and politics. Aristotle's philosophy is characterized by its emphasis on reason and practicality. But the people of Athens accused him of not worshipping their gods properly and he left Athens to avoid a sentence of death.

Above: Buddha, the Enlightened One.

Right: Aristotle, a great scholar.

Below: Darwin, and HMS *Beagle*.

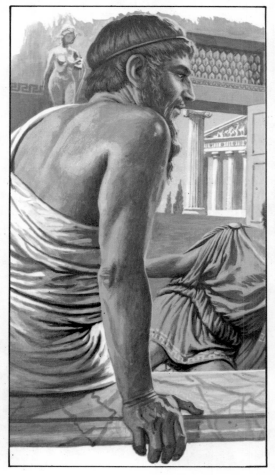

DARWIN, CHARLES (1809-82) was an English scientist who worked out the *theory of evolution by natural selection*. In *The Origin of Species*, Darwin showed that living things evolve, or develop, because some individuals are produced with characteristics that make them better able to adapt to their environment. These plants and animals are more likely to survive to pass on their special characteristics than those that are not so well adapted.

Darwin worked out his ideas after a long expedition in HMS *Beagle* to South America and the Galapagos Islands in the eastern Pacific Ocean.

Top: Karl Marx lived and studied in England for many years.

Above: Gandhi walked barefoot around India preaching peace and love.

Left: Martin Luther King spoke out against the injustices to black people.

MARX, KARL (1818-83) was a notable German thinker. His ideas were published in three long books called *Das Kapital*.

Marx believed that there was a constant struggle between what he called the ruling, and the working classes. He preached that *capitalism*, or free enterprise, was doomed, and that *socialism*, which means that land, money, and other means of production should be owned and controlled by the workers, was bound to take its place through revolution.

Today Marx is regarded as the founder of the Communist movement.

GANDHI, MOHANDAS KARAM-CHAND (1869-1948) was one of India's greatest men. He lived for many years in South Africa where he led strikes and protests against the unjust treatment by whites of non-whites. Back in India he used totally non-violent methods—fasting, marches, non-payment of taxes—to assist in freeing his country from the rule of the British. He believed in the brotherhood of all men and tried to unite India's Muslims and Hindus, its rich and its poor.

KING, MARTIN LUTHER, Jr (1929-68) was an American Negro who led the fight for fair treatment for his fellow Negroes. King first gained national attention in 1955 when he organized a boycott of segregated buses in Montgomery, Alabama. Like Gandhi, he used non-violent methods. He made an inspired speech during a massive demonstration in Washington. This was a turning point: soon laws were passed to give Negroes equal rights with whites. He received the Nobel peace prize for his efforts. Like Gandhi, King was killed by someone who opposed his ideas.

215

Pioneers and Inventors

The Archimedean screw

The principle of specific gravity

Gold　　Silver

The area
of a
sphere

The principle of buoyancy

ARCHIMEDES (*c.* 287-212 BC) was a Greek mathematician and inventor who discovered a scientific law by proving that the King of Syracuse had been cheated. The king wanted to know if his crown was made of pure gold or not. Archimedes solved the problem while sitting in his bath and watching some of the water spill out. He was so excited that he rushed into the street, dripping wet and naked, shouting 'Eureka' (which means 'I have found it' in Greek).

Archimedes realized that all he had to do was to plunge the crown into a bucketful of water and measure the overflow. He then did the same with an equal weight of gold. The amounts of spilled water were not the same, so Archimedes sadly told the king that the gold in his crown must have been mixed with some other metal.

Archimedes had discovered the scientific rule of specific gravity. He also discovered the principle of buoyancy. He found that an object becomes lighter when it is submerged in water. The weight it loses is equal to the weight of the water it displaces.

One of his most useful inventions was the Archimedean screw. This is a long spiral screw that is turned by a handle and raises water from a lower to a higher level.

Archimedes was killed by the Romans when they captured Syracuse in 212 BC.

EDISON, THOMAS ALVA (1847-1931) was a famous American inventor, whose inventions have had a dramatic effect on modern life.

As a boy he sold newspapers at railroad stations and learnt how to use the telegraph machines for sending messages. During several years in Boston as a telegraphist, he invented many electrical gadgets.

People began to pay for his inventions and his fame spread. In 1876 he moved to Menlo Park, New Jersey, and the world came to know him as 'the Wizard of Menlo Park'. A year later he invented the phonograph or record player.

His most famous and useful invention was the electric light bulb in 1879. Altogether he filed more than 1,100 inventions under his name.

WRIGHT BROTHERS, Wilbur (1867-1912) and Orville (1871-1948) were the inventors and builders of the first truly successful airplane.

They developed their interest in the science of flying at the end of the 1800s. In those days flying meant balloons, kites and gliders. The Wright Brothers concluded that one could make a flying machine by attaching an engine and a propeller to a glider.

In their bicycle shop they began to develop their first gliders between 1900 and 1902. Each autumn they built and flew the gliders at Kitty Hawk, North Carolina, where the sand dunes and wind conditions made an ideal test ground. After successfully

Top: Archimedes'
discoveries. The
Archimedean
screw was used
to irrigate land.
Middle left: The
law of specific
gravity. Because
silver is lighter
than gold, 1 kg of
silver displaces
more water than
1 kg of gold.
Middle right: The
area of a sphere
equals four times
the area of the
half circle when the
sphere is halved.

flying these, they planned their first powered airplane. By the fall of 1903 it was ready. It cost less than $1,000 to build, had wings that were 12 metres (40½ feet) long, and weighed 340 kilos (750 lbs) with pilot. The plane was powered by a lightweight gasoline engine specially built for it by the brothers.

They tossed a coin to see who should pilot it first, and Orville won. He flew 37 metres (120 feet) and stayed in the air for 12 seconds. The brothers had made history.

FLEMING, SIR ALEXANDER (1881-1955) was a British scientist who discovered the germ-killing power of penicillin.

In 1928, he was preparing some common germs for an experiment when he noticed a mould growing in the middle of them. It had accidently fallen into the germs from another plate. A mould is a tiny, simple plant of the fungus family that is related to mushrooms, rusts and mildews. Fleming could see that all around this mould the

Above: Thomas Edison's best-known invention was the electric light bulb.

Left: The Wright brothers made the first engine-powered flight.

Below: Sir Alexander Fleming discovered the power of penicillin.

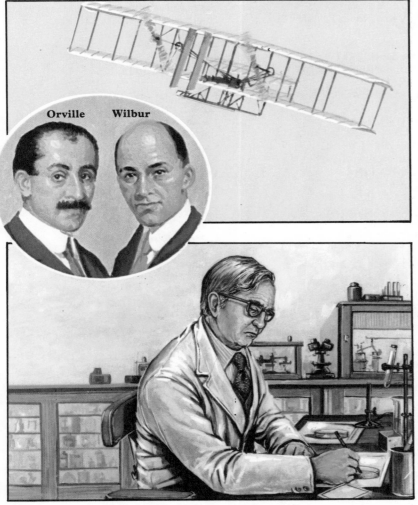

Orville   Wilbur

germs were unable to grow.

Fleming realized what this could mean. He decided on a simple experiment. He grew the same mould on broth. Then he took some test tubes that contained disease germs and put some of the prepared broth into the test tubes. As he had suspected would happen, the living germs were destroyed.

Fleming called the broth penicillin, but later that name was applied only to the chemical substance in the broth.

Penicillin was eventually purified for practical use as a medicine in 1940 by two other scientists, Howard W. Florey of Australia and Ernst Chain of Great Britain. All three shared the 1945 Nobel prize for medicine for their work.

The discovery of penicillin started a new age of medicine. It is used in the treatment of many common illnesses such as pneumonia, and has led to the making of many more equally useful drugs.

Index to the Encyclopedia

ACKNOWLEDGEMENTS

The Publishers would like to thank the following individuals and organizations for their kind permission to reproduce the photographs in this book.

All-Sport 197 above, 200 below, 201 below, 202, 203; Heather Angel/Biofotos 29, 30, 34, 37, 111 above; Anglo Chinese Educational Institute 90 below, 91 left; Associated Press 207 centre; Australian News & Information Service 48; Clive Bardon 179; Norman Barrett 200 above; B.B.C. 159; B.P. Photographic Library 98 above; Paul Brierley 132; Peter Clayton 71 below; Colorpix 92 centre, 93, 96 below, 101 above, 105 centre and below, 199; Colorsport 204 below, 205 below, 207 above; Cooper-Bridgeman Library 71 above, 78 above, 180 below, 181 right, 182 above, 183, 190 below right; G. & P. Corrigan 92 below; Council of Christians and Jews 130, 131 above; Decca 184; Douglas Dickins 187, 190 above; A. M. Ehrlich 64 above, 103 below, 156, 158, 167, 186 above, 188, 189; E. T. Archive 79 below; Geoslides 104 below; Giraudon 181 left; Robert Harding 70; M. Holford 64 below, 65, 74, 180 above; Hong Kong Tourist Office 193 below; Alan Hutchison Library 84 left, 89 centre, 102 below, 103 above, 104 above, 105 above, 112, 113 above and centre; Illustrated London News 81; Japan Information Centre 91 right; Japan National Tourist Organisation 204 centre; H. R. Lewis 73 below; Mansell Collection 76; MEPhA 131 below; Henry Moore Foundation 182 below; National Portrait Gallery 78-79; New Zealand House 115 centre; The Patent Office 154; Popperfoto 82, 83, 90 above; Publicare 204 above; Salvation Army 212; Satour 102 above and centre, 103 centre; Solar Films 99 centre; Tate Gallery 181 below; UKAEA 84 right; U.P.I. 205 above, 207 below; U.S. Travel Service 32, 107 above, 108 below; John Watney 85; Werner Forman Archive 73 above; Reg Wilson 186 below, 190 below left; ZEFA 18, 19, 23, 25, 27, 33, 45, 51, 66, 68, 72, 88, 89 above and below, 94, 95, 96 above, 97, 98 centre and below, 99 above and below, 100, 101 below, 107 centre and below, 108 above, 109, 110, 111 below, 113 below, 114, 115 above, 117, 155, 163, 178 below, 192, 193 above and centre, 194, 195, 196, 197 centre and below, 198.

GENERAL REFERENCE

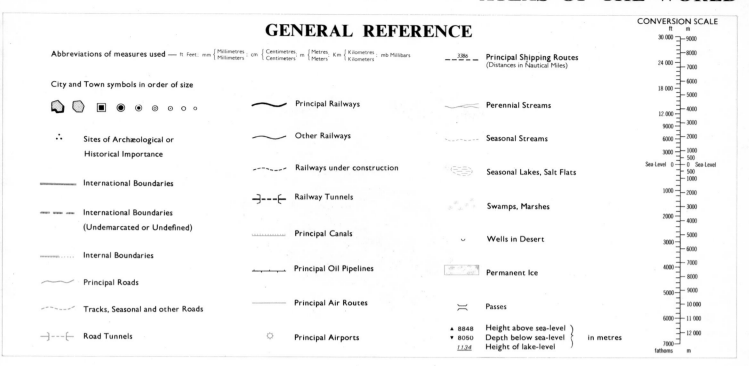

Abbreviations of measures used — ft Feet; mm Millimetres/Millimeters; cm Centimetres/Centimeters; m Metres/Meters; Km Kilometres/Kilometers; mb Millibars

City and Town symbols in order of size

Sites of Archæological or Historical Importance

International Boundaries

International Boundaries (Undemarcated or Undefined)

Internal Boundaries

Principal Roads

Tracks, Seasonal and other Roads

Road Tunnels

Principal Railways

Other Railways

Railways under construction

Railway Tunnels

Principal Canals

Principal Oil Pipelines

Principal Air Routes

Principal Airports

Principal Shipping Routes (Distances in Nautical Miles)

Perennial Streams

Seasonal Streams

Seasonal Lakes, Salt Flats

Swamps, Marshes

Wells in Desert

Permanent Ice

Passes

▲ 8848 Height above sea-level
▼ 8050 Depth below sea-level ⎫ in metres
_1134_ Height of lake-level ⎭

CONVERSION SCALE

THE WORLD: Physical

1:150 000 000

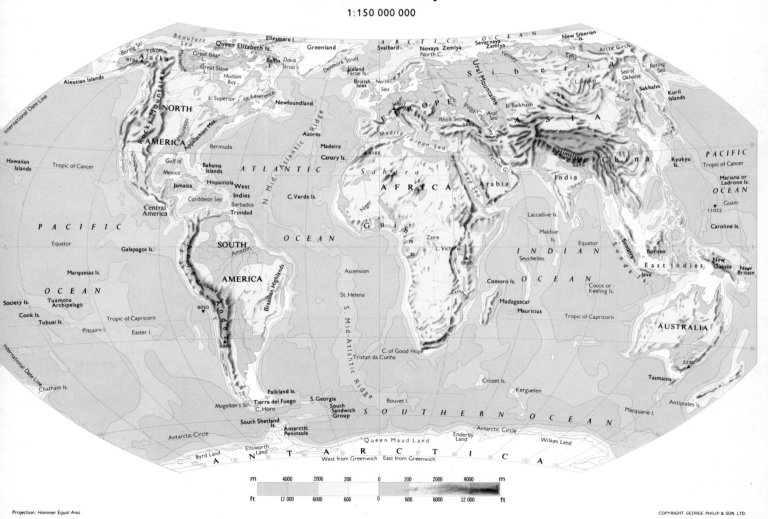

Projection: Hammer Equal Area

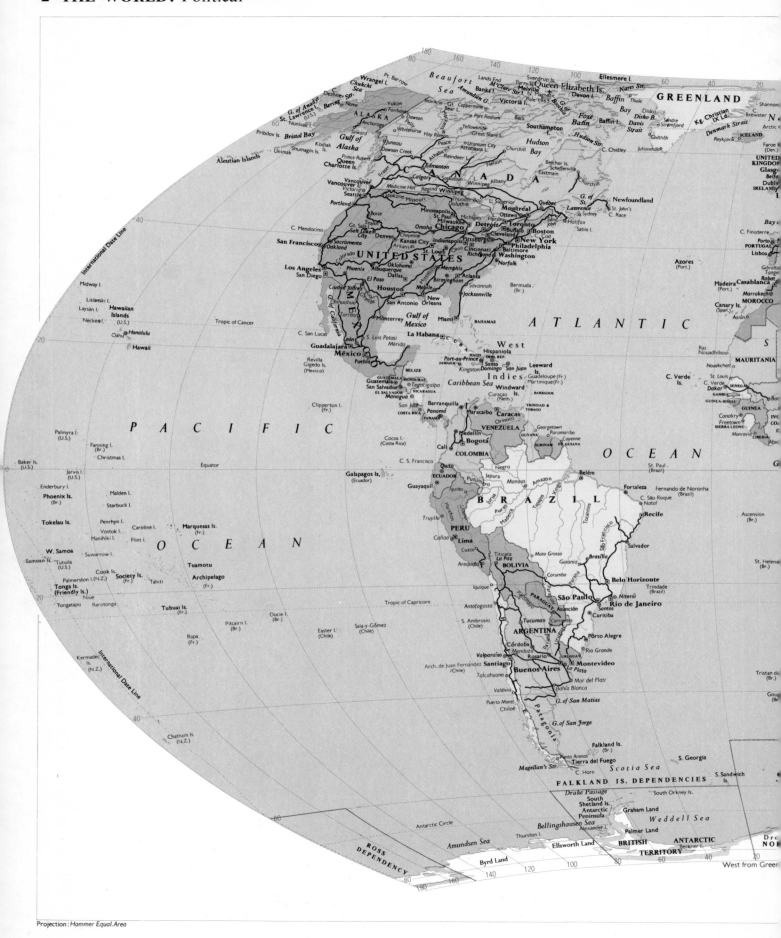

Projection : Hammer Equal.Area

4 POLAR REGIONS

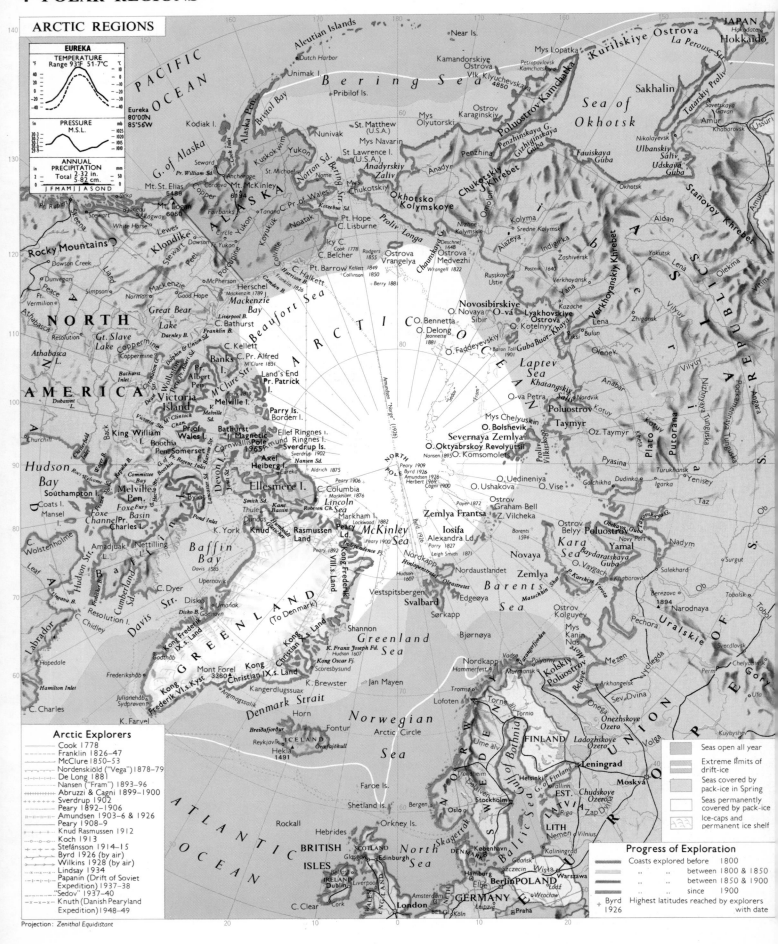

ARCTIC REGIONS

EUREKA

TEMPERATURE
Range 93°F 51.7°C

Eureka
80°00'N
85°56'W

PRESSURE
M.S.L.

ANNUAL
PRECIPITATION
Total 2.32 in.
5.82 cm.

Arctic Explorers

Cook 1778
Franklin 1826–47
McClure 1850–53
Nordenskiöld ("Vega") 1878–79
De Long 1881
Nansen ("Fram") 1893–96
Abruzzi & Cagni 1899–1900
Sverdrup 1902
Peary 1892–1906
Amundsen 1903–6 & 1926
Peary 1908–9
Knud Rasmussen 1912
Koch 1913
Stefánsson 1914–15
Byrd 1926 (by air)
Wilkins 1928 (by air)
Lindsay 1934
Papanin (Drift of Soviet Expedition) 1937–38
"Sedov" 1937–40
Knuth (Danish Pearyland Expedition) 1948–49

Projection: Zenithal Equidistant

	Seas open all year
	Extreme limits of drift-ice
	Seas covered by pack-ice in Spring
	Seas permanently covered by pack-ice
	Ice-caps and permanent ice shelf

Progress of Exploration

Coasts explored before 1800
" " between 1800 & 1850
" " between 1850 & 1900
" " since 1900
+ Byrd 1926 Highest latitudes reached by explorers with date

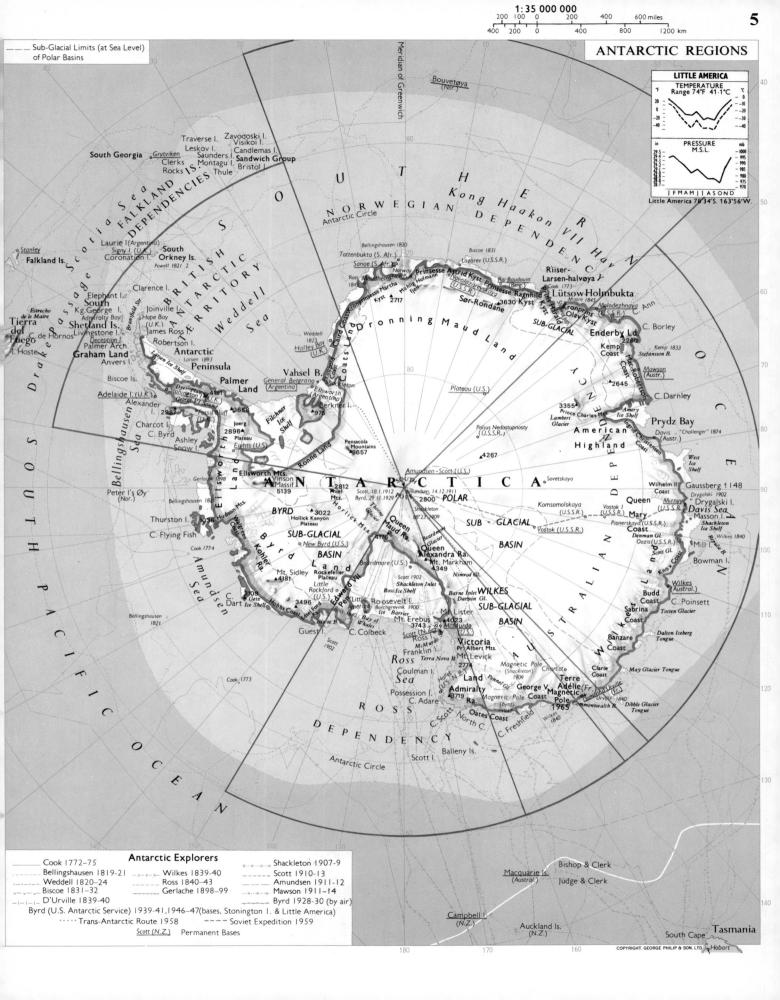

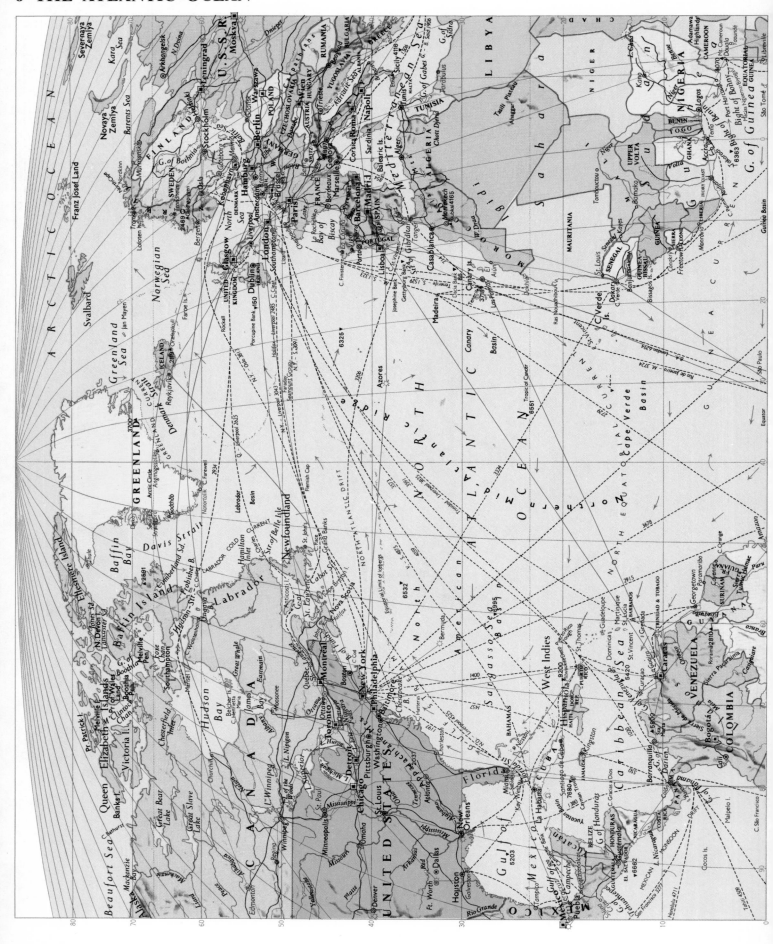

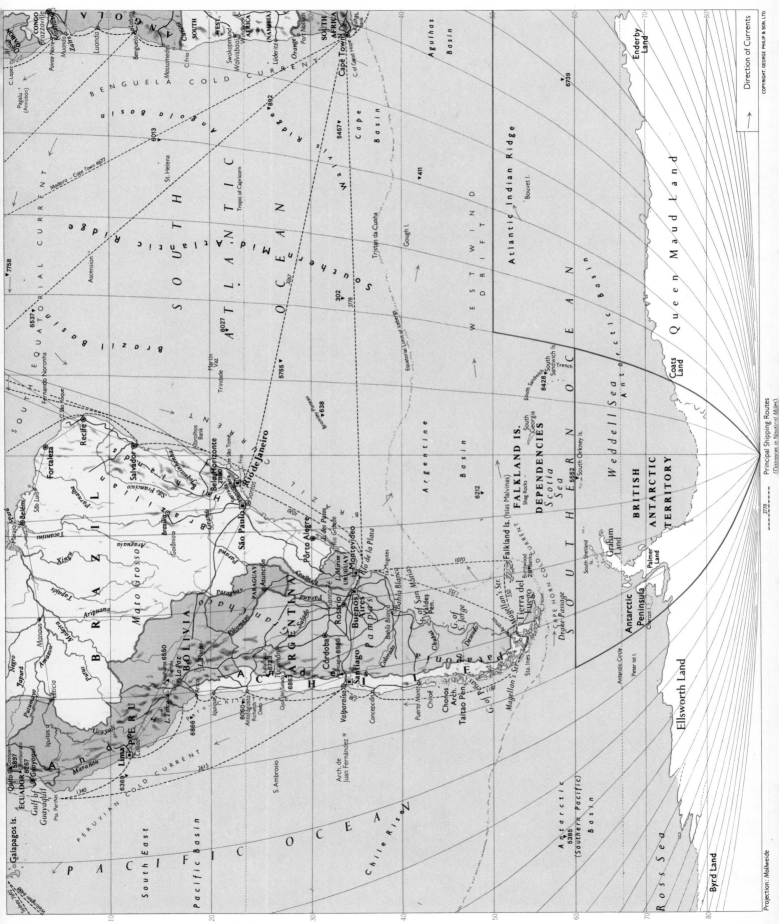

Direction of Currents

COPYRIGHT. GEORGE PHILIP & SON. LTD.

Principal Shipping Routes
(Distances in Nautical Miles)

Projection : Mollweide

EUROPEAN ORGANIZATIONS
1 : 40 000 000

E.E.C. Members

E.F.T.A. Member

All E.F.T.A. and associated states have
Free Trade Agreements with the E.E.C.

States with Association
Agreement with E.E.C.

Associate Member of E.F.T.A.

States with Trading Agreement
with E.E.C.

Warsaw Pact Countries

The E.E.C. has Trading Agreements with
certain countries in the Mediterranean,
Pacific and Latin American areas.

NORWEGIAN SEA

Iceland
Reykjavik
Hekla 1491
Öræfajökull 2119
3734

Arctic Circle

Faroe Is.

Rockall

St. Kilda
Hebrides
Shetland Is.
Orkney Is.
Lindesnes

British Isles

NORTH SEA

Ben Nevis 1343
Edinburgh

Belfast
Ireland
Irish Sea
Dublin
Great Britain
Snowdon 1085
Jutla

C. Clear
St. George's Channel
Cardiff
Thames
London
Amsterdam
Frisian Is.
Weser

Lands End
Scilly Is.
English Channel
Channel Is.
Str. of Dover
Netherlands

Brussel

ATLANTIC

OCEAN

Brittany
Paris
Seine
Ardennes
Eifel
Westerwald
Meuse
Hunsrück
Taunus

Flores

Pico
Terceira
Azores
São Miguel

Bay of Biscay
4861
Gironde
Loire

Vosges
Black Forest
Saône
Zürich
Jura

C. Finisterre

Cantabrian Mts.

Massif Central
Mt. Dore 1886
Garonne
Mt. Blanc 4807
Rhône
Cévennes
A

Old Castile
Iberian
Douro
Madrid

Pyrenees
Maladetta 3404
G. of Lion
Ebro
Riv
Ligurian Sea

Lisboa
C. da Roca
Tagus
Peninsula
New Castile
Guadiana
Sierra Morena

Corsica

Sardinia
Str. of Bonifac

C. St. Vincent

Guadalquivir
Andalusia
Mulhacén 3478
Sa. Nevada

Balearic Is.

MEDITER

Str. of Gibraltar
C. Trafalgar
Gibraltar

6293

Madeira

Casablanca
E. Rif

Alger
Tunis

Palma
Canary Is.
Tenerife

Toubkal 4165
Great Atlas
Maritime Atlas
Plateau of the Shotts
Saharan Atlas

Gulf of Gabes

Gran Canaria
Fuerteventura

Tropic of Cancer

Sahara

Projection: Bonne.
West from Greenwich

m   4000 0 2000 1000 400 200
ft   12 000 6000 3000 1200 600

2000   4000 m
600   6000   12 000 ft

1:17 500 000

Nordkapp   Nordkinn

Lofoten

L. Inari

Torne älv

Kebnekaise
2123

Lappland

Kanin
Peninsula

Pechora

L. Narodnaya
1894

Ural Mountains

West
Siberian

Ob

Irtysh

Tundra

Kola
Peninsula

White
Sea

Mezen

N. Dvina

Telpos Iz.
1617

Plain

Scandinavia

Indalsälven

Umeälv

Finland

Onega

L. Onega

Svir

Plain

Plain

Kama

Tobol

Snøhetta
2469

Oslo

Stockholm

Vänern

Mälaren

Åland Is.

Helsinki

Gulf of Bothnia

Lake
Ladoga

Neva Leningrad

Gulf of Finland

L.
Chudskoye

Valdai
Hills

Central Russian Uplands

Rybinsk
Res.

Gorkiy

Volga

Oka

Volga

Volga Heights

Obshchi Syrt

Ural

Kirgiz

Steppe

Vättern

Gotland

BALTIC SEA

Dvina

Dnieper

Vistula

Neman

Moskva

Skaw

Katte
-gat

København

North

Berlin

Oder

European

Warszawa

Pripet
Marshes

Pripet

Kiyevo

Dnieper

Ukraine

Tsimlyansk
Res.

Volga

Ust Urt
plateau

Karagiye Depression
-132

Caspian

Elbe

Mts.
Prahao

Ore

Sudetes

Bohemian Forest

Moravia
Hts.

Danube

Tatra
2655

Carpathians

Dniester

Bug

Prut

Don

Kara
Bogaz

Inn

Wien

Bakony Forest

Budapest

Plain of
Hungary

Drava

Mureș

Tisza

Sava

Transylvanian Alps

Odessa

Dnieper

Sea of
Azov

Crimea

Mouths
of the
Danube

Kuban

Terek

Caucasus

Elbrus

Transcaucasia

Kura

Araks

Baku

Caspian Sea

Sea

Dinaric Alps

Dalmatia

Adriatic

Beograd

Wallachia

Bucureşti

Morava

Danube

2211

Black   Sea

5633

Pontine Mts.

Ararat
5165

L. Van

L. Urmia

Elburz Mts.

Tehran

Apennines

Gran Sasso
2914

Sofiya

Balkans

Rhodope

Balkan
Peninsula

Pindus

Str. of
Otranto

Istanbul

Bosporus

Sea of
Marmara

Ankara

Kızıl

Anatolia

Kurdistan

Strait of Messina

Etna 3263

Sicily

Calabria

Ionian

Sea

Ionian Is.

Morea

Dardanelles

Aegean

Sea

L.Tuz

Erciyas
3770

Taurus Mts.

Mesopotamia

Tigris

Halab

Euphrates

Baghdad

Malta

Pelleria

5121

C. Matapan

Rhodes

Crete

Cyprus

Bayrut

Syrian

Desert

Persian
Gulf

Tripoli

SEA

Gulf of Sidra

Nile Delta

Tel Aviv-
Yafo

Dead
Sea
-395

Levant

C. Spartivento

Strait of Messina

AN

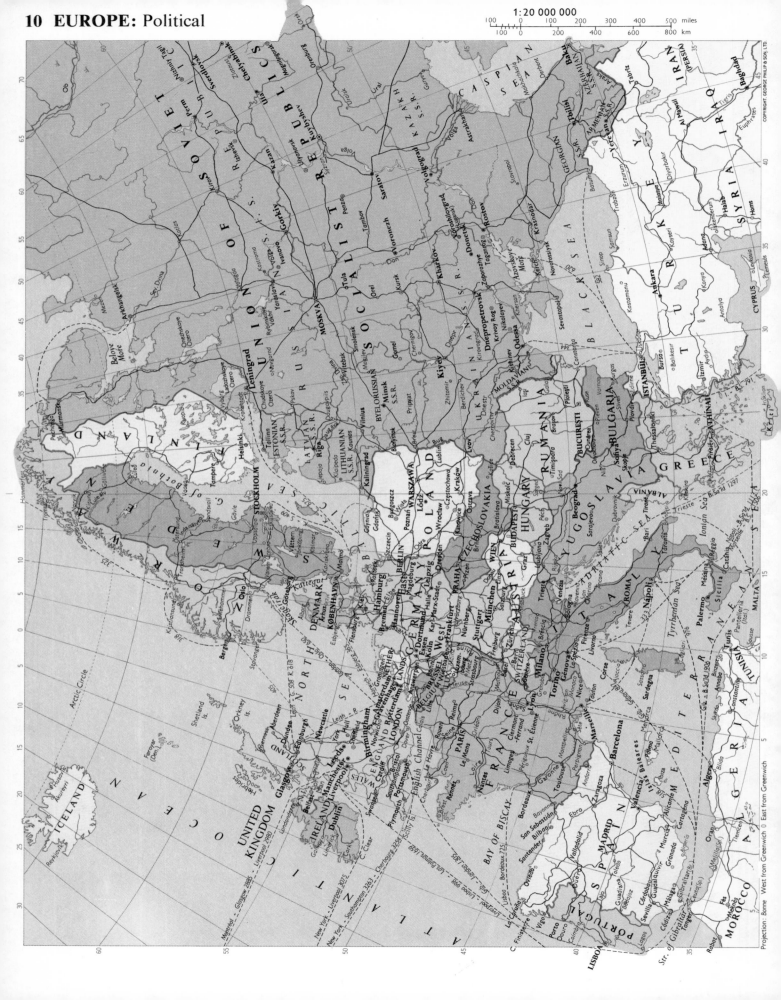

1 : 20 000 000

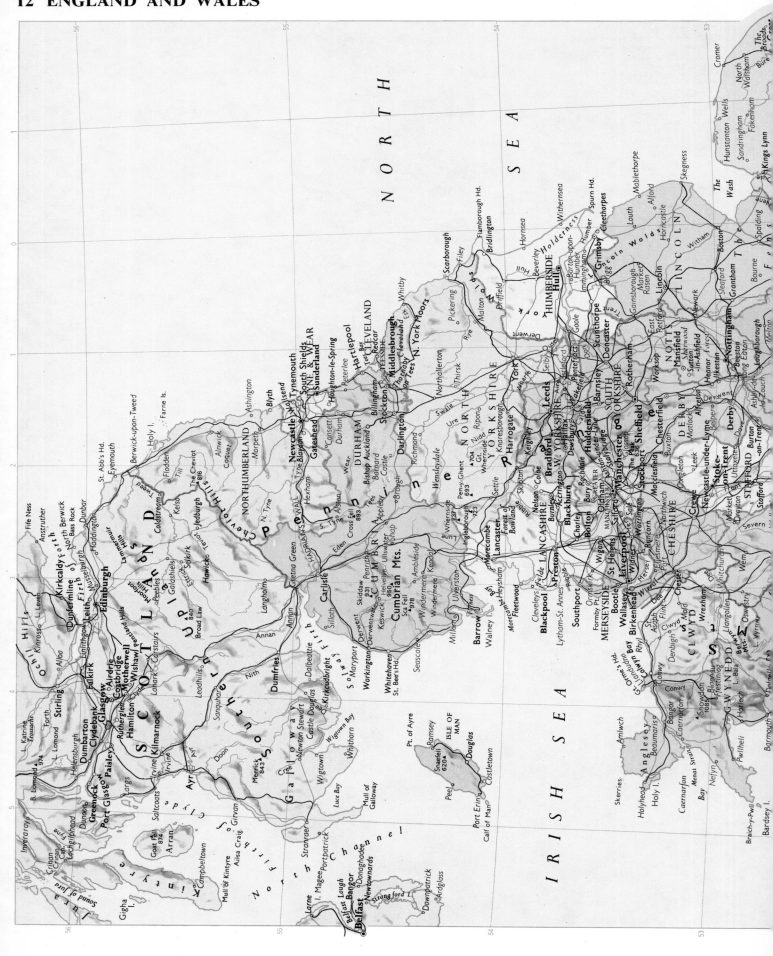

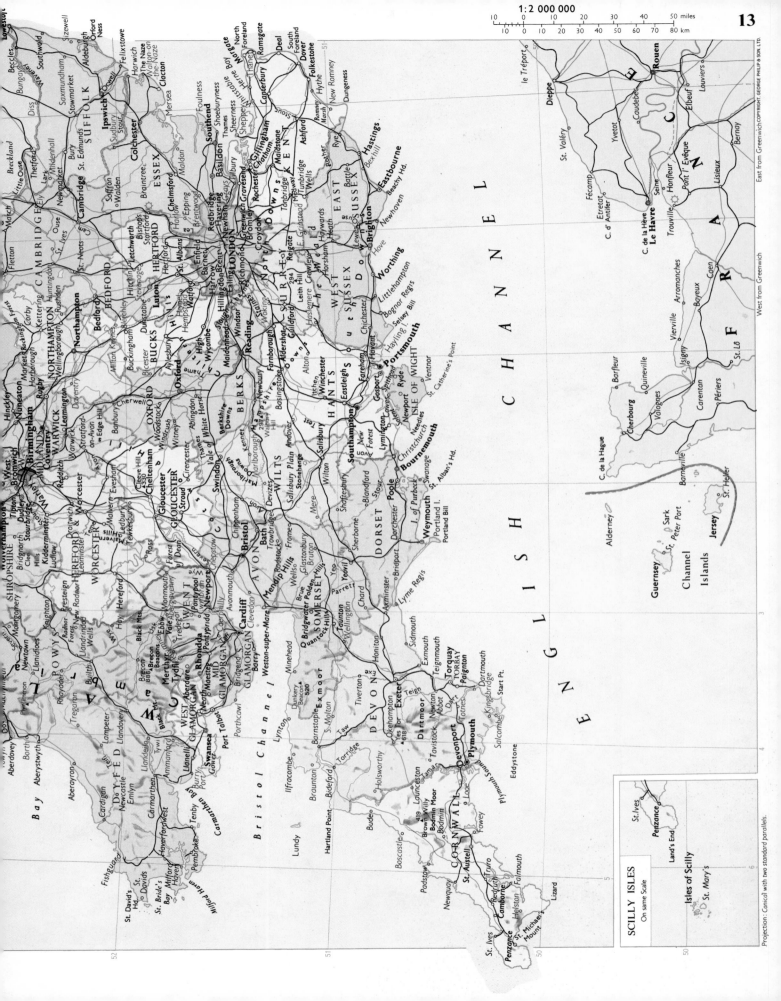

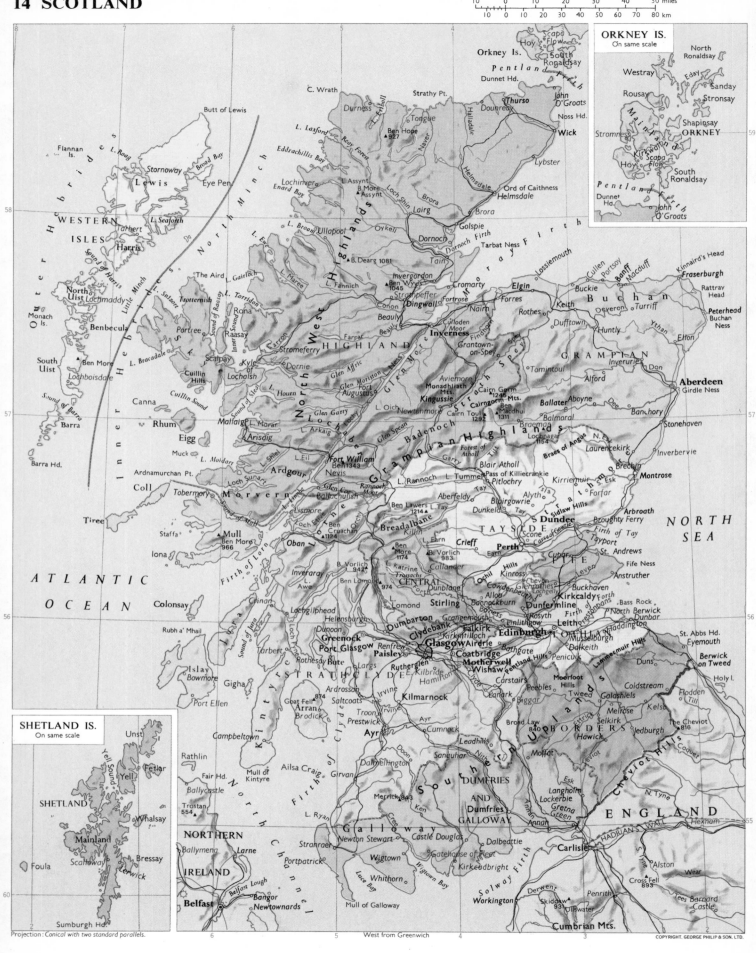

14 SCOTLAND

1:2 000 000

Projection : Conical with two standard parallels.

West from Greenwich

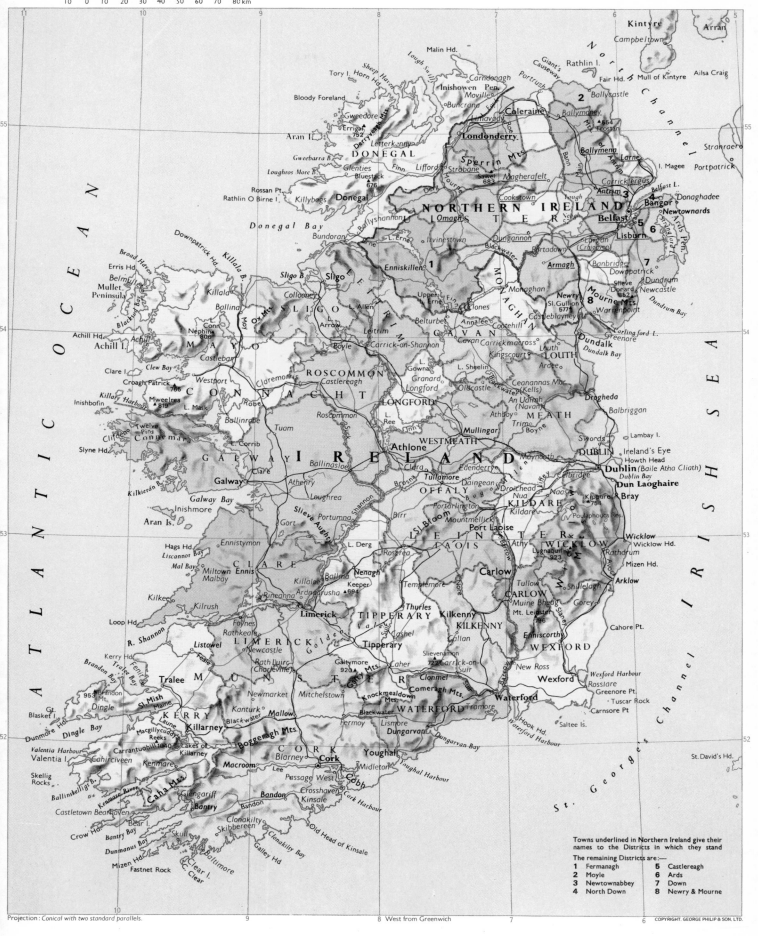

1:2 000 000

Projection: Conical with two standard parallels.

Towns underlined in Northern Ireland give their
names to the Districts in which they stand

The remaining Districts are:—

1	Fermanagh	5	Castlereagh
2	Moyle	6	Ards
3	Newtownabbey	7	Down
4	North Down	8	Newry & Mourne

COPYRIGHT. GEORGE PHILIP & SON. LTD.

1 : 2 500 000

10 0 10 20 30 40 50 miles
10 0 10 20 30 40 50 60 70 80 km

NORTH SEA

ENGLAND

North Walsham · Caister · Great Yarmouth · Lowestoft · Beccles · Bungay · Southwold · Aldeburgh · Orford Ness

Dover · Calais · Wissant · Gris Nez · Boulogne-sur-Mer · Le Touquet-Paris-Plage · Berck · Étaples

NETHERLANDS

WADDENEILANDEN · Terschelling · Ameland · Schiermonnikoog · Rottum · Borkum

Vlieland · Texel · Den Helder · Leeuwarden · Franeker · Harlingen · Bolsward · Sneek · FRIESLAND · Heerenveen

Den Burg · Schagen · Medemblik · Enkhuizen · Hoorn · IJsselmeer · Lemmer · Urk · DRENTHE

Alkmaar · Bergen · Beverwijk · IJmuiden · Haarlem · Zandvoort · Heemstede · AMSTERDAM · Zaandam · Edam · Marken

Groningen · Winschoten · Delfzijl · Assen · Emmen · Hoogeveen · Meppel · Zwolle · OVERIJSSEL · Almelo · Hengelo · Enschede

's-GRAVENHAGE (The Hague) · Scheveningen · Leiden · Katwijk-aan-Zee · Noordwijk · Delft · UTRECHT · Hilversum · Amersfoort · Apeldoorn · Deventer · Zutphen

Hoek van Holland · ROTTERDAM · Vlaardingen · Schiedam · Dordrecht · Gouda · GELDERLAND · Arnhem · Nijmegen · Winterswijk

Vlissingen (Flushing) · Middelburg · Walcheren · Goes · Bergen-op-Zoom · Roosendaal · Breda · Tilburg · Eindhoven · Helmond · Venlo · Roermond

GERMANY

Emden · Oldenburg · Bremerhaven · Wilhelmshaven · Nordenham · Ostfriesland · OSTFRIESISCHE INSELN · Norderney · Juist · Wangerooge · Spiekeroog · Langeoog

Osnabrück · Münster · RHEIN · Dortmund · Bochum · ESSEN · DUISBURG · Oberhausen · Mülheim · Gelsenkirchen · Recklinghausen · Hamm

DÜSSELDORF · Mönchengladbach · Neuss · Krefeld · Solingen · Wuppertal · Remscheid · Hagen · WESTFALEN

KÖLN (Cologne) · Leverkusen · Bergisch-Gladbach · Aachen · Bonn · Bad Godesberg · Siegburg · RHEINLAND · Koblenz · Wiesbaden · Mainz · Bingen · SAARLAND · Saarbrücken · Kaiserslautern · Trier · Neunkirchen · Homburg

BELGIUM

Oostende (Ostend) · Brugge (Bruges) · Knokke · Zeebrugge · Blankenberge · Antwerpen · Gent (Gand) · BRUSSEL (Bruxelles) · Mechelen · Leuven · Tienen · BRABANT · HAINAUT · Mons · Charleroi · Namur · Liège · Verviers · Hasselt · Genk · Maastricht · Tongeren

Roeselare · Kortrijk · Menen · Tournai · Mouscron · Leuze · Ath · Nivelles · Waterloo · Wavre · Gembloux · Dinant · Huy · Andenne · Spa · Malmedy

LUXEMBOURG

Luxembourg · Esch · Differdange · Clervaux · Diekirch · Ettelbruck · Wiltz · Echternach

FRANCE

Dunkerque · Gravelines · St. Omer · Hazebrouck · Cassel · Lille · Roubaix · Tourcoing · Armentières · Béthune · Lens · Douai · Valenciennes · Cambrai · Maubeuge · Avesnes

Abbeville · St. Valery · Amiens · Albert · Péronne · St. Quentin · La Fère · Laon · Soissons · Compiègne · Reims · Épernay · Châlons-sur-Marne · Vitry-le-François · St. Dizier

Beauvais · Clermont · Creil · Chantilly · Senlis · Meaux · PARIS · Versailles · St. Denis · Corbeil · Melun · Provins · Champagne · ARDENNES

Charleville-Mézières · Sedan · Bouillon · Montmédy · Longwy · Thionville · Metz · Montigny-les-Metz · Nancy · Toul · Verdun · Bar-le-Duc · Commercy · St. Mihiel

Strasbourg · Saarguemines · Sarre-Union · Saverne · BAS-RHIN

Projection: Conical with two standard parallels

East from Greenwich

1:5 000 000

20 10 0   20   40   60   80   100 Statute Miles
40   20   0   40   80   120   160 Km

FRENCH DEPARTMENTS

A.	01	Ain
Ai.	02	Aisne
Al.	03	Allier
A.H.P.	04	Alpes-de-Haute-Provence
H.A.	05	Hautes-Alpes
A.M.	06	Alpes-Maritimes
Ard.	07	Ardèche
Ard.	08	Ardennes
Ar.	09	Ariège
Aub.	10	Aube
Aud.	11	Aude
Av.	12	Aveyron
B.R.	13	Bouches-du-Rhône
C.	14	Calvados
Ca.	15	Cantal
Ch.	16	Charente
Ch.M.	17	Charente-Maritime
Che.	18	Cher
Co.	19	Corrèze
C.O.	20	Corse a) Haute-Corse b) Corse du Sud
C.O.	21	Côte-d'Or
C.N.	22	Côtes-du-Nord
Cr.	23	Creuse
D.	24	Dordogne
Do.	25	Doubs
Dr.	26	Drôme
E.	27	Eure
E.L.	28	Eure-et-Loir
F.	29	Finistère (Nord et Sud)
G.	30	Gard
H.G.	31	Haute-Garonne
Ge.	32	Gers
Gi.	33	Gironde
H.	34	Hérault
I.V.	35	Ille-et-Vilaine
I.	36	Indre
I.L.	37	Indre-et-Loire
Is.	38	Isère
J.	39	Jura
L.	40	Landes
L.C.	41	Loir-et-Cher
Lo.	42	Loire
H.L.	43	Haute-Loire
L.A.	44	Loire-Atlantique
Loi.	45	Loiret
Lot	46	Lot
L.G.	47	Lot-et-Garonne
Loz.	48	Lozère
M.	49	Maine-et-Loire
Ma.	50	Manche
M.	51	Marne
H.M.	52	Haut-Marne
May.	53	Mayenne
M.M.	54	Meurthe-et-Moselle
Meu.	55	Meuse
Mo.	56	Morbihan
Mos.	57	Moselle
Ni.	58	Nièvre
No.	59	Nord
O.	60	Oise
Or.	61	Orne
P.C.	62	Pas-de-Calais
P.D.	63	Puy-de-Dôme
P.A.	64	Pyrénées Atlantiques
H.P.	65	Hautes Pyrénées
P.O.	66	Pyrénées (Orientales)
B.R.	67	Bas Rhin
H.R.	68	Haut Rhin
Rh.	69	Rhône
H.S.	70	Haute Saône
S.L.	71	Saône-et-Loire
Sa.	72	Sarthe
Sa.	73	Savoie
H.Sa.	74	Haute-Savoie
P.	75	Paris
S.Me.	76	Seine-Maritime
S.M.	77	Seine-et-Marne
Yv.	78	Yvelines
D.S.	79	Deux-Sèvres
So.	80	Somme
T.	81	Tarn
T.G.	82	Tarn-et-Garonne
V.	83	Var
Va.	84	Vaucluse
Ve.	85	Vendée
Vi.	86	Vienne
H.V.	87	Haute Vienne
V.	88	Vosges
Y.	89	Yonne
B.	90	Belfort
Es.	91	Essonne
H.Se.	92	Hauts-de-Seine
S.S.D.	93	Seine-St. Denis
V.M.	94	Val-de-Marne
V.O.	95	Val-d'Oise

CORSICA On same scale — Corse

Projection: Conical with two standard parallels

East from Greenwich / West from Greenwich

MEDITERRANEAN SEA

ENGLISH CHANNEL

BAY OF BISCAY

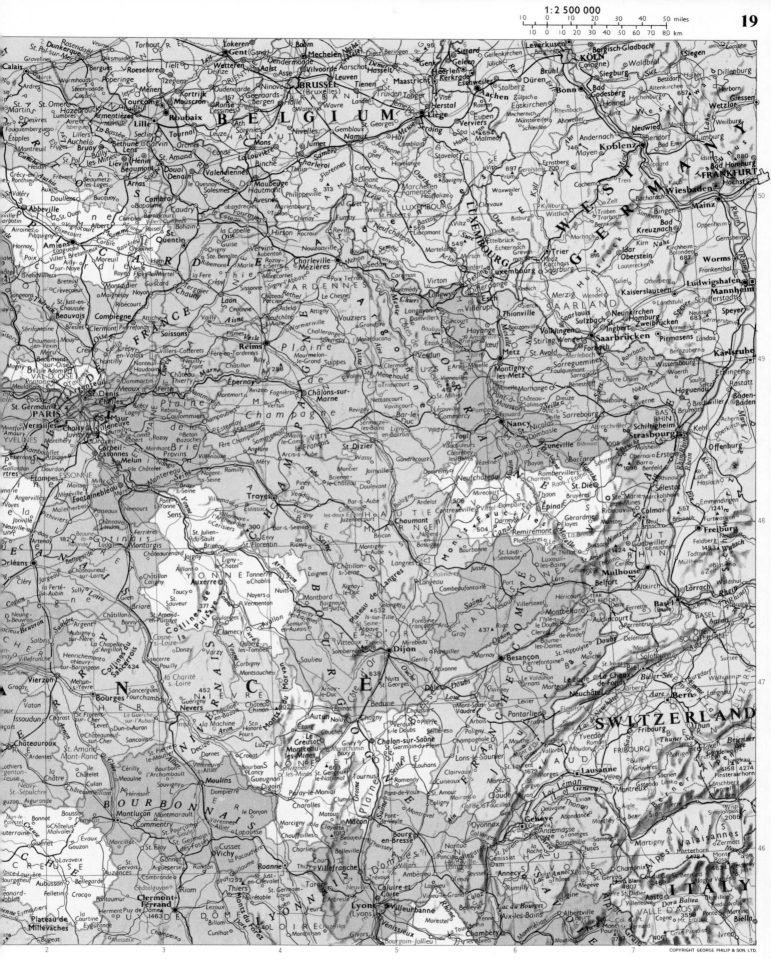

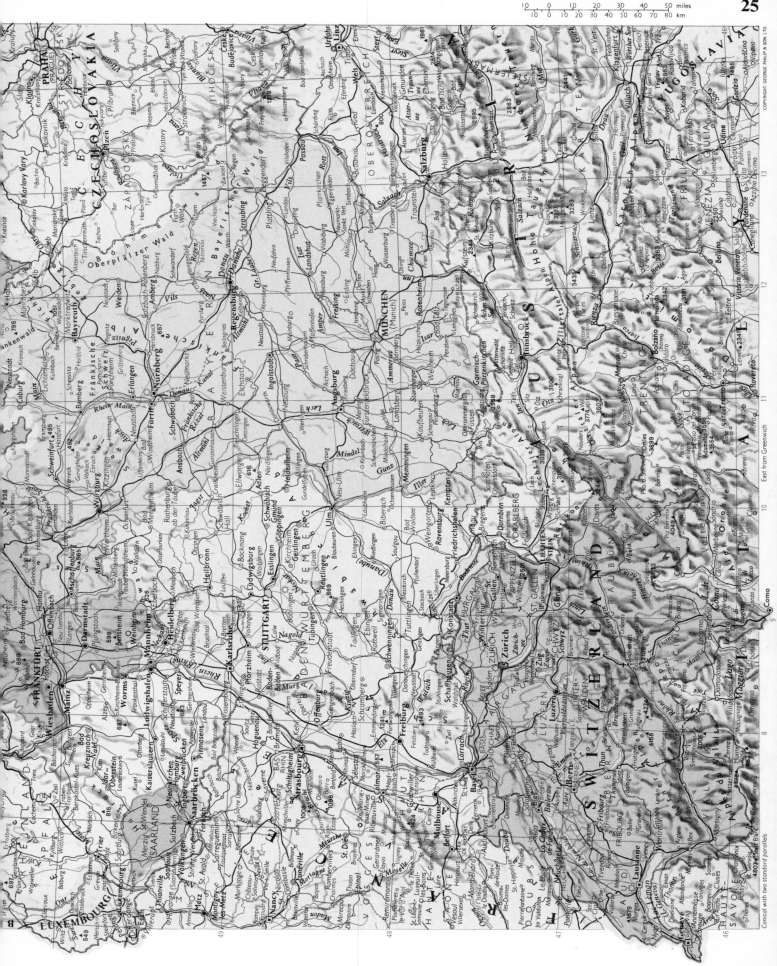

10   0   10   20   30   40   50 miles
10   0   10   20   30   40   50   60   70   80 km

East from Greenwich

Conical with two standard parallels

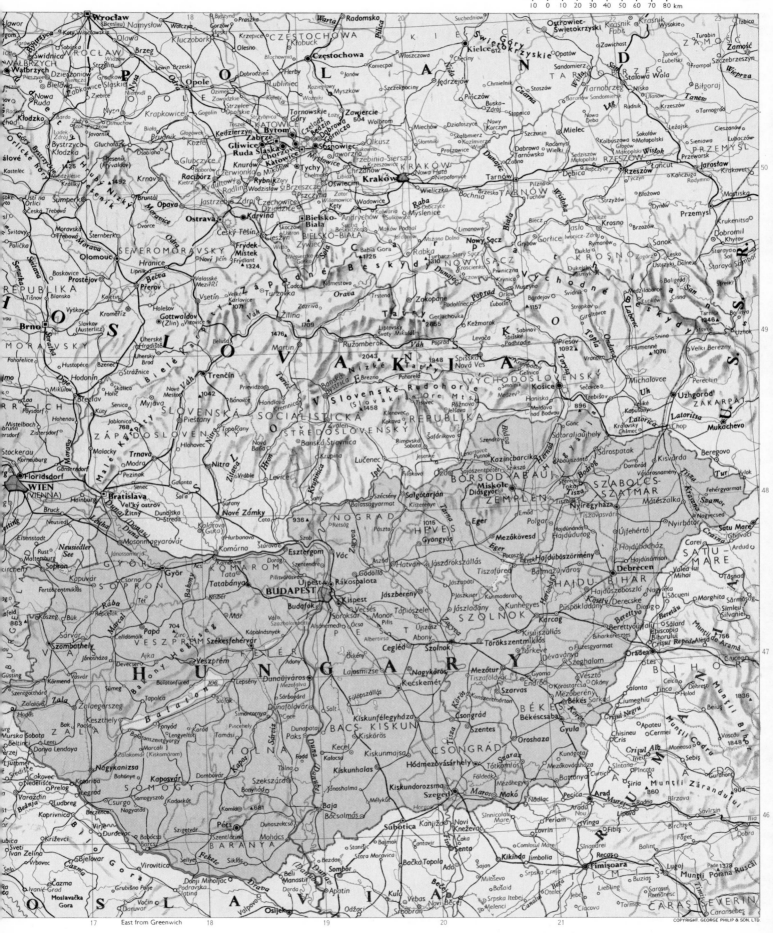

1:2 500 000

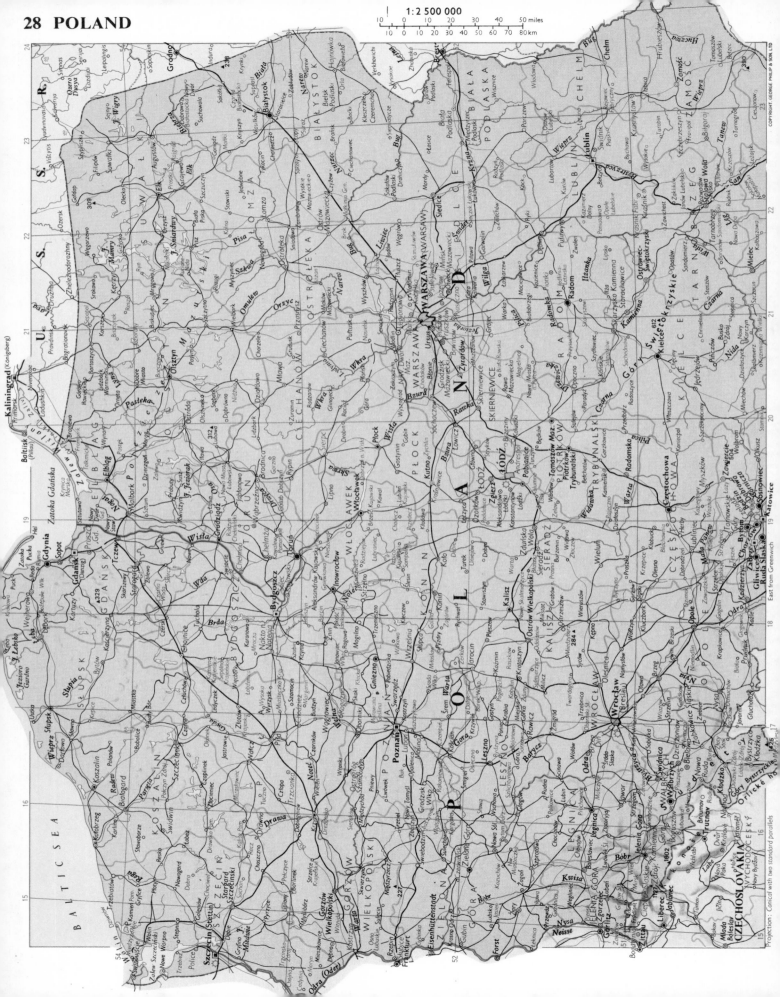

1:2 500 000

Projection: Conical with two standard parallels

COPYRIGHT GEORGE PHILIP & SON LTD

East from Greenwich

1:5,000,000

50   0   50   100 miles
50   0   50   100   150 km

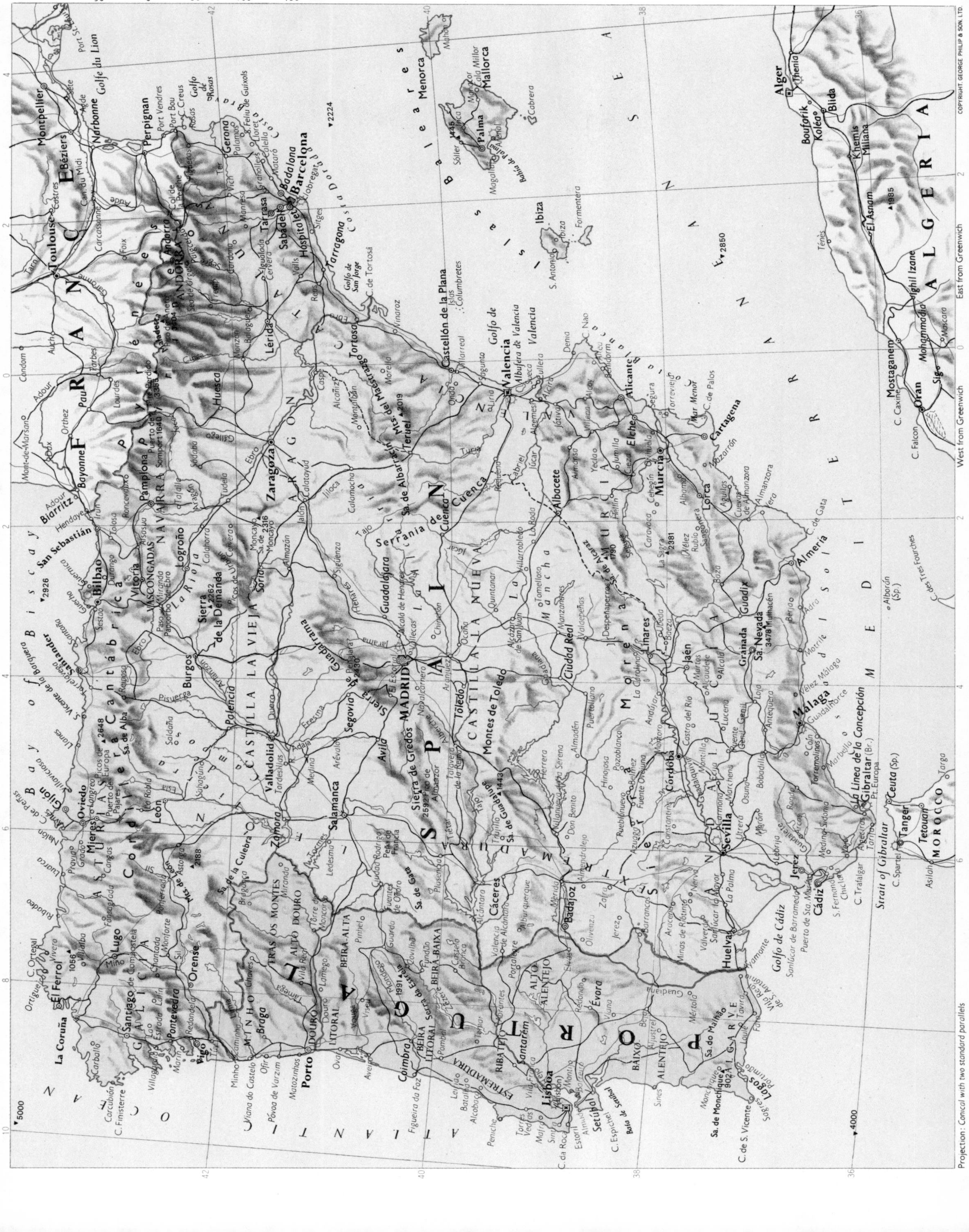

COPYRIGHT GEORGE PHILIP & SON LTD.

Projection: Conical with two standard parallels

East from Greenwich

West from Greenwich

FRANCE

Montpellier
Béziers
Narbonne
Golfe du Lion
Toulouse
Carcassonne
Perpignan
Port Vendres
Golfe de Rosas

PYRÉNÉES
ANDORRA
Pamplona
NAVARRA
Huesca
Lérida
ARAGON
Zaragoza
Gerona
Barcelona
Badalona
Sabadell
Tarrasa
Hospitalet
Tarragona
Costa Brava

Bayonne
Biarritz
Hendaye
San Sebastián
Bilbao
VASCONGADAS
Vitoria
Logroño
LA RIOJA
Sierra de la Demanda
Soria

Bay of Biscay
Santander
Gijón
Oviedo
ASTURIAS
Cordillera Cantábrica
GALICIA
La Coruña
El Ferrol
Santiago de Compostela
Lugo
Orense
Pontevedra
Vigo

Burgos
Valladolid
Palencia
León
Zamora
Salamanca
CASTILLA LA VIEJA
Sierra de Gredos
Ávila
Segovia
Guadalajara
MADRID
Toledo
CASTILLA LA NUEVA
Cuenca
Serranía de Cuenca
Teruel

SPAIN

Valencia
Golfo de Valencia
Castellón de la Plana
Albacete
MURCIA
Murcia
Cartagena
Lorca
Alicante
Elche

ANDALUCÍA
SIERRA MORENA
Córdoba
Jaén
Linares
Granada
Sierra Nevada
Almería
Málaga
Sevilla
Cádiz
Huelva
Jerez
Gibraltar (Br.)
La Línea de la Concepción
Ceuta (Sp.)
Strait of Gibraltar
Golfo de Cádiz

EXTREMADURA
Cáceres
Badajoz
Mérida

PORTUGAL
Porto
DOURO
MINHO
Braga
TRAS OS MONTES
BEIRA ALTA
BEIRA BAIXA
BEIRA LITORAL
Coimbra
ESTREMADURA
RIBATEJO
Santarém
Lisboa
Setúbal
ALTO ALENTEJO
BAIXO ALENTEJO
Évora
ALGARVE
Lagos
C. de S. Vicente

MOROCCO
Tánger
Tetouan
ALGERIA
Alger
Oran
Mostaganem

BALEARES
Mallorca
Palma
Menorca
Ibiza
Formentera

MEDITERRANEAN SEA

ATLANTIC OCEAN

1 : 2 500 000

10   0   10   20   30   40   50 miles
10   0   10 20 30 40 50 60 70 80 km

MEDITERRANEAN

SEA

MOROCCO

Projection : Conical with two standard parallels

West from Greenwich

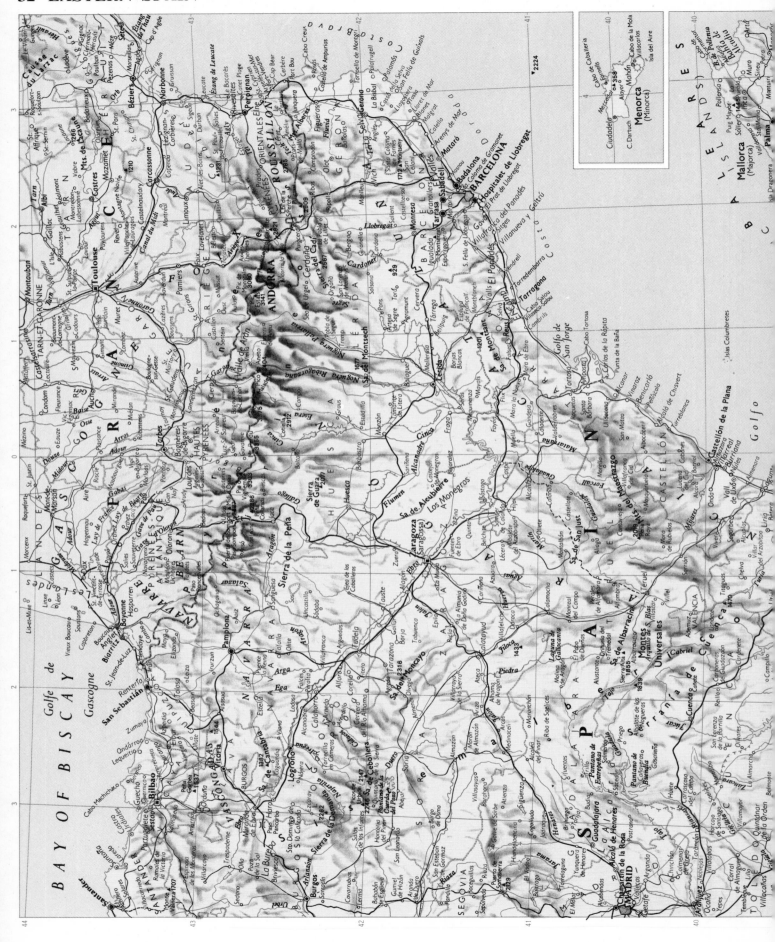

1:2 500 000

Projection: Conical with two standard parallels

1 : 2 500 000

10   0   10   20   30   40   50 miles
10   0   10   20   30   40   50   60   70   80 km

HUNGARY

YUGOSLAVIA

BOSNA

HERCEGOVINA

DALMACIJA

Golfo di
Venézia

A D R I A T I C   S E A

Innsbruck · Graz · Klagenfurt · Maribor · Zagreb · Ljubljana · Trieste · Venézia (Venice) · Pádova · Ferrara · Bologna · Ravenna · Rímini · SAN MARINO · Ancona · Pescara · Firenze (Florence) · Perúgia · L'Aquila · ROMA (ROME) · Vatican City

Rijeka (Fiume) · Pula · Zadar · Split · Dinara Planina

MARCHE · UMBRIA · LAZIO · ABRUZZI · MOLISE · TOSCANA

East from Greenwich

1:2 500 000

10   20   30   40   50 miles
10 0 10 20 30 40 50 60 70 80 km

A D R I A T I C

S E A

I O N I A N

S E A

M E D I T E R R A N E A N   S E A

Channel

COPYRIGHT, GEORGE PHILIP & SON LTD

1:2 500 000

miles
km

BALTIC SEA

POLAND

Gotland
Visby

KALMAR LÄN
Kalmar
Öland
Oskarshamn
Västervik
Nybro

JÖNKÖPINGS LÄN
Jönköping
Huskvarna
Nässjö
Tranås

KRONOBERGS LÄN
Växjö
Ljungby
Älmhult

BLEKINGE LÄN
Karlskrona
Ronneby
Karlshamn

Bornholm
Rønne

ÖSTERGÖTLAND
Norrköping
Linköping
Motala
Mjölby
Finspång

Nyköping
Oxelösund

SKARABORG
Skövde
Lidköping
Falköping
Mariestad

ÄLVSBORG
Borås
Alingsås
Vänersborg
Trollhättan

GÖTEBORGS OCH BOHUS LÄN
Göteborg
Kungälv
Uddevalla
Mölndal

HALLAND
Halmstad
Varberg
Falkenberg
Laholm

KRISTIANSTADS LÄN
Kristianstad
Hässleholm
Ängelholm

MALMÖHUS LÄN
Malmö
Helsingborg
Lund
Landskrona
Trelleborg
Ystad
Eslöv

Kattegat

Skagen
Frederikshavn
Hjørring

NORDJYLLANDS AMT
Ålborg
Nørresundby
Limfjorden

VIBORG AMT
Viborg
Skive
Thisted

RINGKØBING AMT
Ringkøbing
Herning
Holstebro
Esbjerg

ÅRHUS AMT
Århus
Randers
Silkeborg
Horsens
Grenå
Djursland

VEJLE AMT
Vejle
Kolding
Fredericia

RIBE AMT
Ribe
Varde

SØNDERJYLLANDS AMT
Haderslev
Åbenrå
Sønderborg

FYNS AMT
Odense
Svendborg
Nyborg
Middelfart
Fåborg

SJÆLLAND
VESTSJÆLLANDS AMT
Slagelse
Kalundborg
Holbæk
Næstved
Roskilde
KØBENHAVN (COPENHAGEN)
Frederikssund
Hillerød
Helsingør

STORSTRØMS AMT
Vordingborg
Nykøbing
FALSTER
LOLLAND
Maribo
Nakskov
Rødby

Kiel
Flensburg
Schleswig
Rendsburg
Husum
Tønder

W. GERMANY
E. GERMANY
Rügen
Rostock
Stralsund

Słupsk
Łeba
Ustka

Skagerrak
Norwegian Sea
Arendal
Risør
Tvedestrand

Projection: Conical with two standard parallels
East from Greenwich

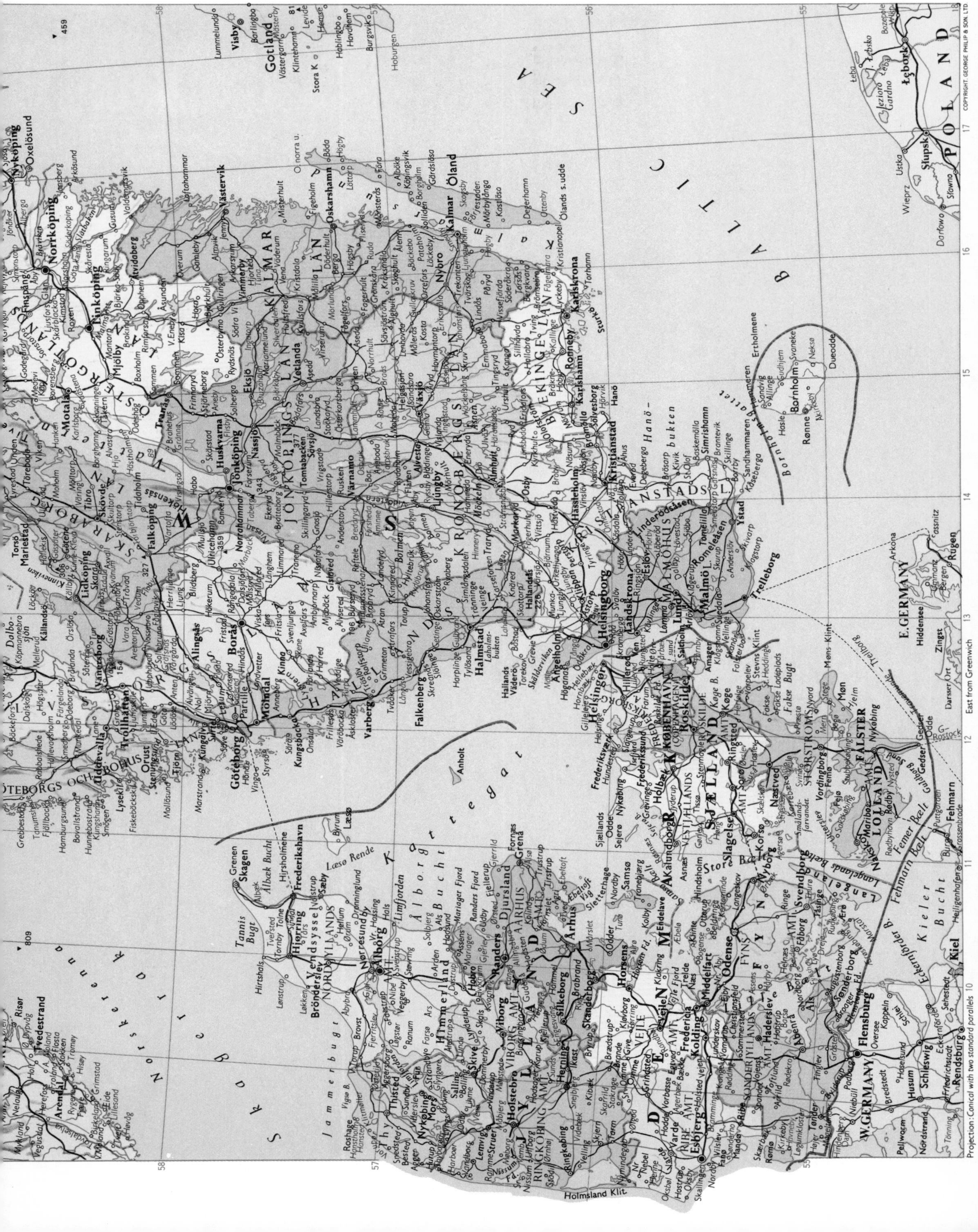

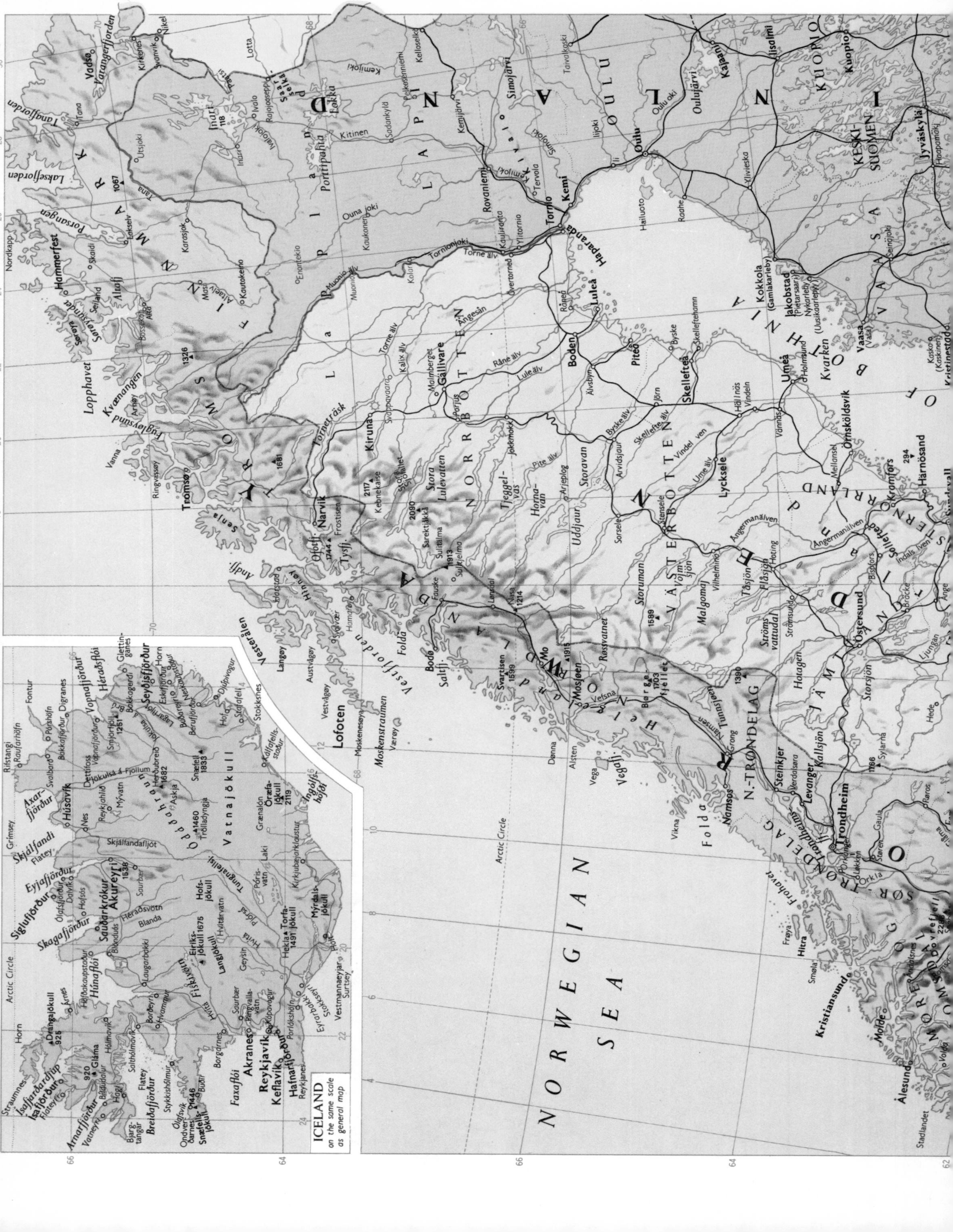

NORWEGIAN SEA

ICELAND
on the same scale
as general map

West from 18 Greenwich

Arctic Circle

Lofoten

Vesterålen

LAPLAND

FINMARK

TROMS

NORDLAND

NORRBOTTEN

VÄSTERBOTTEN

ÅNGERMANLAND

JÄMTLAND

VÄSTERNORRLAND

N.-TRÖNDELAG

SÖR-TRÖNDELAG

MÖRE

HELGELAND

OULU

VAASA

KESKI-SUOMEN

VASTRA

Reykjavik · Keflavik · Hafnarfjörður · Akranes · Akureyri

Vatnajökull

Hammerfest · Nordkapp · Vadsö · Kirkenes

Tromsö · Narvik · Bodö · Mosjöen · Namsos · Steinkjer · Trondheim · Kristiansund · Ålesund

Oulu · Kemi · Torniö · Haparanda · Luleå · Boden · Piteå · Skellefteå · Umeå · Örnsköldsvik · Härnösand · Kramfors

Kiruna · Gällivare · Jokkmokk · Arvidsjaur · Storuman · Lycksele · Vilhelmina · Östersund · Hede

Rovaniemi · Jyväskylä · Kuopio · Iisalmi

RUSSIAN SOVIET FEDERATED SOCIALIST REPUBLIC

MOSKVA (Moscow)

LENINGRAD

Murmansk

Arkhangelsk (Archangel)

KARELIAN A.S.S.R.

KOMI A.S.S.R.

Kolskiy Poluostrov

Timanskiy Kryazh

Bolshezemelskaya Tundra

U r a l s k i y e   G o r y

Severnyye Uvaly

SVERDLOVSK
Pervouralsk

Perm
Solikamsk
Berezniki
Kizel

Nizhniy Tagil

Ufa
BASHKIR A.S.S.R.
Sterlitamak
Magnitogorsk

Orenburg
Orsk
Novotroitsk

UDMURT A.S.S.R.
Izhevsk
Glazov
Votkinsk
Sarapul

TATAR A.S.S.R.
Kazan
Zelenodolsk
Chistopol
Bugulma

MARI A.S.S.R.
Yoshkar Ola

CHUVASH A.S.S.R.
Cheboksary

GORKIY (Gorki)
Dzerzhinsk
Arzamas
Murom

MORDOVIAN A.S.S.R.
Saransk

Kuybyshev
Novokuybyshevsk
Togliatti
Syzran

Penza

Kirov

Syktyvkar

Ukhta
Pechora

Vorkuta

Narjan-Mar

Kotlas
Velikiy Ustyug

Vologda
Cherepovets
Kostroma
Ivanovo
Yaroslavl
Rybinsk (Andropov)

Kalinin
Rzhev

Smolensk
Vitebsk

BYELORUSSIAN S.S.R. (WHITE RUSSIA)
Minsk
Mogilev
Bobruysk
Gomel
Baranovichi
Pinsk

LATVIAN S.S.R.
Riga
Daugavpils
Liepaja

LITHUANIAN S.S.R.
Vilnius
Kaunas
Siauliai
Klaipeda (Memel)

ESTONIAN S.S.R.
Tallinn
Pärnu
Tartu

Kaliningrad (Königsberg)

FINLAND
Helsinki
Tampere
Turku
Oulu
Kuopio
Kemi

N O R W A Y

S W E D E N
Stockholm
Luleå
Umeå

Gulf of Bothnia

Gulf of Finland

Ladozhskoye Ozero

Onezhskoye Ozero

Beloye More (White Sea)

Dvinskaya Guba

Onezhskaya Guba

Kandalakshskiy Zaliv

Cheshskaya Guba

P-ov Kanin

Ostrov Morzhovets

Kolguyev

Novgorod
Pskov
Velikiye Luki

Ryazan
Tula
Kaluga
Bryansk
Orel
Lipetsk
Tambov
Michurinsk
Yelets

Serpukhov
Podolsk
Kolomna
Orekhovo-Zuyevo
Vladimir
Suzdal

Volga

Kama

Pechora

Severnaya Dvina

Petrozavodsk

POLAND
WARSZAWA (Warsaw)
Białystok
Brest
Lublin
Grodno

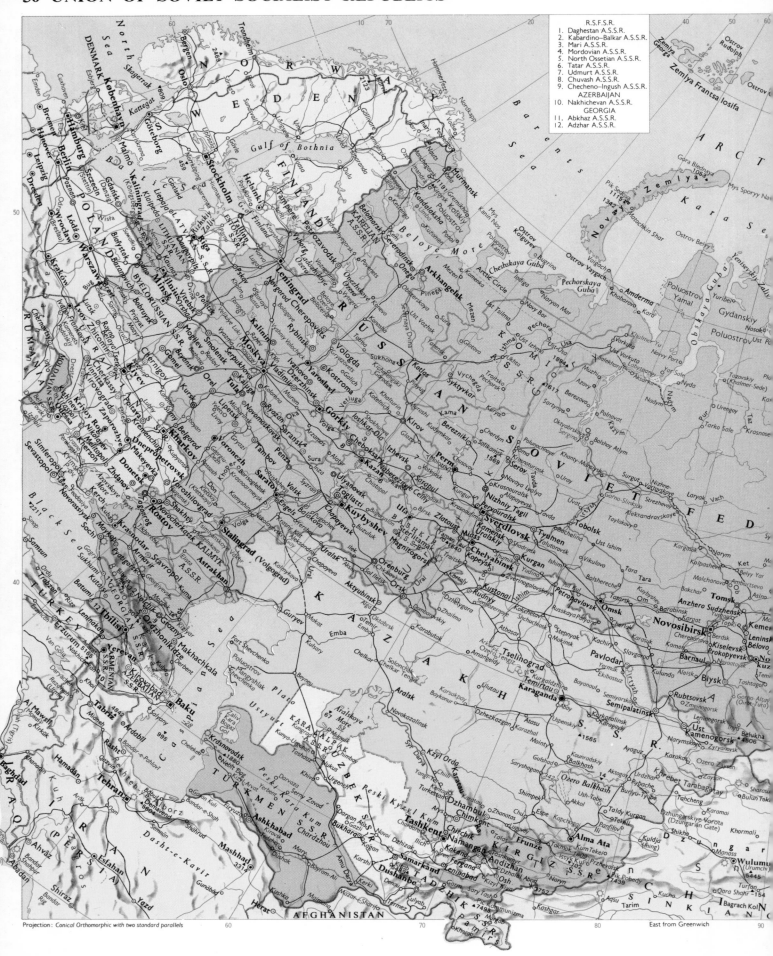

R.S.F.S.R.
1. Daghestan A.S.S.R.
2. Kabardino-Balkar A.S.S.R.
3. Mari A.S.S.R.
4. Mordovian A.S.S.R.
5. North Ossetian A.S.S.R.
6. Tatar A.S.S.R.
7. Udmurt A.S.S.R.
8. Chuvash A.S.S.R.
9. Checheno-Ingush A.S.S.R.
AZERBAIJAN
10. Nakhichevan A.S.S.R.
GEORGIA
11. Abkhaz A.S.S.R.
12. Adzhar A.S.S.R.

Projection: Conical Orthomorphic with two standard parallels

East from Greenwich

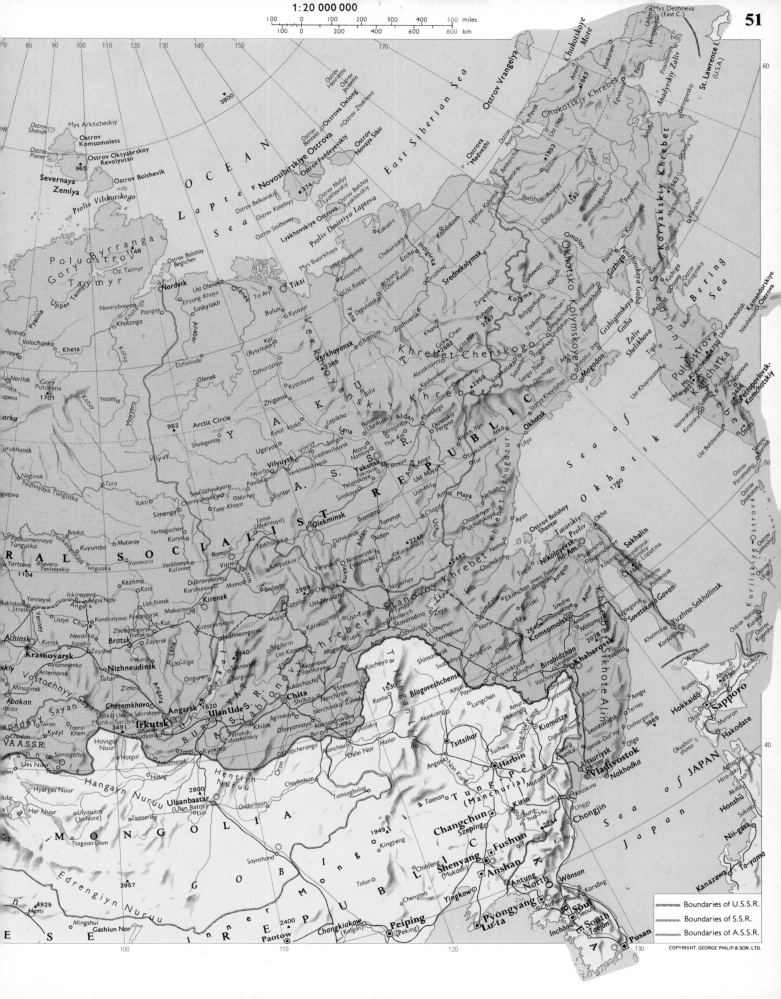

1:20 000 000

100   0   100   200   300   400   500 miles
100   0   200   400   600   800 km

COPYRIGHT. GEORGE PHILIP & SON. LTD.

Boundaries of U.S.S.R.
Boundaries of S.S.R.
Boundaries of A.S.S.R.

1:50 000 000

250   0   250   500   750   1000 miles

250   0   500   1000   1500   km

COPYRIGHT GEORGE PHILIP & SON, LTD.

Projection: Bonne

Oceans and Seas

PACIFIC OCEAN

ARCTIC OCEAN

INDIAN OCEAN

Bering Sea
Sea of Okhotsk
Sea of Japan
Yellow Sea
East China Sea
South China Sea
Philippine Sea
Sulu Sea
Celebes Sea
Banda Sea
Java Sea
Arafura Sea
Molucca Sea
Bay of Bengal
Arabian Sea
Red Sea
Persian Gulf
G. of Oman
G. of Aden
G. of Siam
G. of Tonkin
Laptev Sea
Kara Sea
Barents Sea
White Sea
Baltic Sea
North Sea
Black Sea
Caspian Sea
Aral Sea
Mediterranean Sea
Adriatic Sea
Dead Sea
Lake Tricono

Physical features and places

Aleutian Is.   7532
Kamchatka Peninsula
Sredinny Ra.
Koryak Vol.   4750
Gydan Ra. (Kolyma)
Wrangel I.
New Siberian Is.
Severnaya Zemlya
Novaya Zemlya
Svalbard
Greenland
Iceland
British Isles
North Cape
Kolguyev
Kola Pen.
Finland
Scandinavia
North European Plain
Russian Central Uplands
Carpathians
Anatolia
Taurus Mts.
Cyprus
Suez Canal
Sinai Pen.
Nile
Libyan Desert
Syrian Desert
Mesopotamia
Tigris
Euphrates
Arabia
Rub' al Khali
Ras Asir (C. Guardafui)
Socotra
Somali Peninsula
Amirantes
Seychelles
Chagos Arch.
Maldive Is.
Laccadive Is.
Ceylon
C. Comorin
Western Ghats
Eastern Ghats
Deccan
Godavari
Krishna
Gulf of Mannar
Polk Strait
Nicobar Is.
Andaman Is.
Narmada
Ganga
Yamuna
India
Thar Desert
Indus
Sutlej
Himalaya
Everest   8848
Tsangpo
Brahmaputra
Plateau of Tibet
Kunlun Shan
Karakoram Ra.   8611
Pamirs
Hindu Kush
Komunizm Pk.   7495
Tien Shan
Pobeda
Turfan Basin
Takla Makan
Tarim
Tarim Basin
Lop Nor
Altai   4506
Belukha   4506
Plateau of Mongolia
Koko Nor
Sayan Mts.
Selenge
Angara
Great Khingan Mts.
Plateau of China
Great Plain of China
Si-kiang
Yangtze
Hwang-ho
Manchurian Plain
Korea
Formosa
Hainan
Luzon
Mindanao   2954
Cape Johnson   10 497
Palawan
Kinabalu   4101
Borneo
Celebes
Halmahera
Ceram
Timor
Flores
Bali
Sumatra
Sunda Is.
Java
Malay Peninsula
Str. of Malacca
Sunda Str.
Makasar Strait
Irrawaddy
Salween
Mekong
Menam
Hong (Red)
New Guinea
Caroline Is.   1022
Pelew Is.
Bonin Is.   10 834
Kurili Is.   7632
Sakhalin
La Pérouse Str.
Hokkaido
Honshu
Shikoku   3798
Kyushu
Korea Str.
Ryukyu Is.
Sikhote Alin Ra.
Amur
Stanovoy Ra.
Yablonovy Ra.
Lena
Aldan
Vilyui
Central Siberian Plateau
Lower Tunguska
Angara
Yenisei
Ob
Irtysh
Tobol
West Siberian Plain
Ural Mountains   1640
Narodnaya   1894
Ural
Volga
Don
Dnepr
N. Dvina
Danube
Vistula
Oder
Elbe
Rhine
Steppe
Turanian Plain
Syr Darya
Amu Darya
Chu
Ili
L. Balkhash
Plateau of Iran
Zagros Mts.
Elburz Mts.
Demavend   5604
Great Salt Desert
Caucasus
Elbruz   5633
Ararat   5165
Helmand
Hamun
Suleiman Range
Bosporus

Verkhoyansk Range
Indigirka
Kolyma
C. Dezhnev (E.C.)
Chelyuskin
Taimyr Peninsula
Khatanga
Olenek

Bering Str.

Tropic of Cancer
Arctic Circle
Equator
East from Greenwich

m   6000   4000   2000   1000   600   200   0
ft   18 000   12 000   6000   3000   1200   600   0   600   2000 6000   4000 12 000   6000 18 000   9000 24 000   ft

1 : 50 000 000

250   0   250   500   750   1000 miles

250   0   500   1000   1500 km

COPYRIGHT GEORGE PHILIP & SON LTD.

Projection: Bonne

East from Greenwich

Major labels (selection):

ARCTIC OCEAN · PACIFIC OCEAN · INDIAN OCEAN

U. S. S. R. · MONGOLIA · INNER MONGOLIA · MANCHURIA

CHINESE REPUBLIC · CHINA · SINKIANG UIGUR · TIBET

KASHMIR · NEPAL · BHUTAN · BANGLADESH · INDIA · PAKISTAN

AFGHANISTAN · IRAN (PERSIA) · IRAQ · TURKEY · SYRIA

SAUDI ARABIA · OMAN · YEMEN · SOUTH YEMEN · KUWAIT

QATAR · BAHRAIN · UNITED ARAB EMIRATES · JORDAN · ISRAEL · LEBANON

BURMA · THAILAND (SIAM) · LAOS · VIETNAM · CAMBODIA

MALAYSIA · MALAYA · INDONESIA · PHILIPPINES · BRUNEI

SRI LANKA (CEYLON) · JAPAN · KOREA

EGYPT · LIBYA · SUDAN · ETHIOPIA · SOMALI REP. · KENYA

UGANDA · TANZANIA · ZAIRE · ZAMBIA · MALAWI · RWANDA · BURUNDI

EUROPE · UNITED KINGDOM · ICELAND

Tropic of Cancer · Equator · Arctic Circle

Cities: London · Paris · Roma · Berlin · Warszawa · Wien · Beograd · Athínai · Istanbul · Ankara · Moskva · Leningrad · Murmansk · Arkhangelsk · Sverdlovsk · Chelyabinsk · Omsk · Novosibirsk · Tomsk · Krasnoyarsk · Irkutsk · Chita · Khabarovsk · Vladivostok · Tashkent · Samarkand · Alma Ata · Tehran · Esfahān · Shiraz · Baghdad · Basrah · Al · Kuwait · Riyadh · Al Madinah · Makkah (Mecca) · Aden · Muscat · Karachi · Kabul · Kandahar · Lahore · Delhi · Kanpur · Lucknow · Varanasi · Allahabad · Calcutta · Bombay · Hyderabad · Madras · Pondicherry · Colombo · Ahmadabad · Rangoon · Mandalay · Bangkok · Hanoi · Ho Chi Minh City · Kuala Lumpur · Singapore · Jakarta · Manila · Hong Kong · Macau · Canton · Foochow · Shanghai · Nanking · Wuhan · Peiping · Tientsin · Harbin · Changchun · Shenyang · Chungking · Chengtu · Lanchow · Sian · Kunming · Lhasa · Ulaanbaatar · Tokyo · Yokohama · Kyoto · Osaka · Nagasaki · Sapporo

1:1 000 000

1949–1967 Armistice lines between Israel and the Arab States.

LEBANON

SYRIA

MEDITERRANEAN SEA

Nahariyya
Akko (Acre)
HAIFA
Qiryat Yam
Qiryat Bialik
Qiryat Ata
Tirat Karmel
'ATLIT
Nazareth
Hagalil (Galilee)
Qiryat Shemona
BIRKET RAM
Quneitra
TEL HAZOR
Zefat
KEFAR NAHUM (CAPERNAUM)
Yam Kinneret (Sea of Galilee)
Tiberias −209
Irbid
Ar-Ramthā
Dar'ā

Netanya
Hadera
QESARI (CAESAREA)
Or 'Aqiva
Afula
TEL MEGIDDO
Emeq Yizre'el
Jenin
Shomron (Samaria)
Tülkarm
SAMARIA
Nablus
SHECHEM
JACOB'S WELL

Herzliyya
Ramat HaSharon
TEL AVIV YAFO (Jaffa)
Ramat Gan
Bat Yam
Holon
Petah Tiqwa
Or Yehuda
JORDAN
SHILO
As Salt
'AMMAN
Az-Zarqa'

Rishon Le Zion
Nes Ziyyona
Ramla
Rehovot
Lod (Lydda)
TEL GEZER
Ashdod
Rām Allāh
El Arihā (Jericho)
JERUSALEM (Yerushalayim, Al Quds)
Eizariya (Bethany)
QUMRAN

Ashqelon
Qiryat Gat
BET GUVRIN
TEL LAKHISH
Bayt Lahm (Bethlehem)
BURAK SULAYMAN (SOLOMON'S POOLS)
Hebron

Gaza
Gaza Strip
Khān Yūnis
Be'er Sheva'
MESADA

EGYPT

Inset (Continuation Southwards 1:2 500 000):
ISRAEL
JORDAN
EGYPT
Gaza Strip
Gaza
Hebron
Be'er Sheva'
Dimona
SHIVTA
Mizpe Ramon
Makhtesh Ramon
Har Ramon 1035
PETRA
1727
Elat
Al 'Aqaba

Projection: Conical with two standard parallels

East from Greenwich

COPYRIGHT. GEORGE PHILIP & SON. LTD.

Continuation Southwards 1:2 500 000

1:15 000 000

100   0   100   200   300   400 miles
100 0 100 200 300 400 500 600 km

SYRIA
LEBANON
Bayrūt
Dimashq (Damascus)
Haifa
ISRAEL
Tel Aviv-Yafo
Jerusalem
Gaza
Amman
JORDAN
El 'Arîsh
El Qantara
Ismâ'îlîya
El Suweis (Suez)
Gebel el Tih
Under Israeli Occupation
Es Sina
Khalîg es Suweis
2637
2578
Tabûk
Ma'ân
Turayf
Kaf
Bahr el Miyet -395
1128
TRANS-ARABIAN OIL PIPELINE ('TAPLINE')
Badanah
Rafhâ'
Dûmat al Jandal (Al Jawf)
Qal'at al Akhdar
An Nafûd
Hafar al Bâtin
Al Wari'ah
Safaniya
KUWAIT
Al Kuwayt (Kuwait)
Bandar-e Büshehr
PERSIAN GULF

IRAQ
Rutba
Hit
Al Jazirah
Nahr al Furat (Euphrates)
Baghdad
Karbalâ
Al Hillah
Kut Dujail
An Nâsiriyah
Al 'Amârah
Al Qurna
Hawr al Hammar
Al Basrah
Abadan
Al Fao
Umm Qasr
Bubiyan
Failaka
Mesopotamia

IRAN (PERSIA)
Borujerd
Dezfül
Karun
Masjed Soleyman
Ahvâz
Bandar Shahpur
Khorramshahr
Bandar Dilam
Shohriza
Esfahân
Yazd
Dasht-e Lüt
Shahriza
Shiraz
Kazerun
Deyyer
Tâheri
Jahrom
Neyrîz
Kharg
Kuh-e Hazar 4419
Bâft
Kermán
Bam
Zabol
Bandar 'Abbâs
Minab
Khâmir
Band-e Nakhila
Gâbrik
Bampur
Gulf of Oman

AFGHANISTAN

SAUDI-ARABIA
Ha'il
Tabah
Az Zilfi
Buraidah
'Unaizon
Al Majma'ah
Shaqra'
Ar Riyâd (Riyadh)
Sulaimiya
Hilla
Harad
Al Hufuf
Al Uqayr
Al Hariq
Mubarraz
Ad Dammam
Dhahran
BAHRAIN
QATAR
Doha
Musay'id
UNITED ARAB EMIRATES (TRUCIAL STATES)
Abū Zabi
Abu Dhabi
Dubayy
Sharjah
Al Khābūrah
Sühar
Al Buraimi
Miskin
Wudham
Masqat (Muscat)
Matrah
Sür
3019
2151
OMAN
Umm az Zamul
Yibal
Al Ubailah
Qasr Hamam
2057
102

EGYPT
Aswân
El Shallâl
Sadd el Aâli 1st Cataract
Buheiret en Naser (Lake Nasser)
Kôm Ombo
Isna
Qena
Qûs
El Uqsur (Luxor)
Bûr Safâga
Quseir
Ras Banâs
Bir Shalatein
2nd Cataract
Wadi Halfa
Haldib
Bîr Ungat
Es Sahrâ esh Sharqîya

SUDAN
Abri
Delgo
3rd Cataract
El Kab
Argo
Abu Dis
Dongola
Kareima
Merowe
4th Cataract
5th Cataract
Korti
Atbara
Ed Dâmer
Berber
Adarama
Es Sahrâ en Nûbîya (Nubian Desert)
Abu Hamed
6th Cataract
Shendî
Omdurmân
El Khartûm-Bahrî
El Khartûm (Khartoum)
Kassala
Khashm el Girba
Gedaref
El Geteina
Wâd Medanî
El Kamlin
Gallabat
Er Raseires
Sennar
Singa
Metema
Kôsti
Mafaza
Umm Ruwaba
El Dueim
Rashad
Renk
Gelhak
Kaka
Melut
Kôdok
Malakal
Nil el Abyad (White Nile)
A'ÂLA EN NIL
Fangak
Tungaru
Nasir
Abwong
Sobat
Duk Fadiat
Kongor
Pibor P.
Bôr
Nil Nile
Tirol
Tâli P.
Yei
Kaju Kaji
Nimule
3187
EL ISTWÂ'YA
Jûba
Mongalla
Torit
Kapoeta
Lokitaung
Todenyang

KORDOFAN
ZILLAEZRAQ

ETHIOPIA
Keren
Asmerâ (Asmarà)
Adwa
Aksum
Adigrat
Mekele
Ras Dashen 4620
Debre Tabor
Gonder
Dabat
L. Tana
Sekota
Debre Markos
Dembecha
Talo
Mota 4154
Dese (Dessye)
Alibo
Nekemte
Gimbi
Dembi Dolo
Gore
Addis Abeba (Addis Ababa)
Awash
3381
Harer
Dire Dawa
Gidole
Jima
L. Ziway
Asela
L. Shala
4307
Goba
Ginir
Sodo
Omo
L. Abaya
Chencha
Hula
L. Shamo
Burji
Arba Minch
Negele
Yabelo
Arero
Chew Bahr (L. Stefanie)
El Niybo
Moyale
Dolo
Mega
Buna

YEMEN
Maydi
3200
Khamir
3600 Sana
Mukeiras
Hodeida
2469
Zabid
Ta'izz
1122
Al Mukha
Mocha
Perim
Bab al Mandab
Madinat al Shaab (Aden)
Al 'Adan

SOUTH YEMEN
Ash Shudhayf
Ṣa'dah
Al Matamma
Marib
Jau al Milah
Shibam
Al Hauta
Dhula
Nisab
Ataq
Haura
Lodar
Ahwar
Shuqra
Zinjibar
5143
Mukalla
Ras al Kalb
Saihut
Ghail
Laila
Najran

HADRAMAWT
ZUFÂR
Shisur 1678
Marbat
Salâlah
Ghubbat al Qamar
Ar Rab al Khâli
Al 'Ayn al Mugshin
Al Juwara
Al Jazir
Al Khalaf

SOMALI REP.
Borama
Hargeisa
Zeila
Bulhar
Berbera
Karin
Erigavo
2406
Las Khoreh
Bosaso (Bender Cassim)
Candala
Alula
Ras Asir (C. Guardafui)
Bereda
Bargal
Handa
Ras Hafun
Scusciuban Hafun
Gardo
Bender Beila
Eil
5824
Burao
Ainabo
Las Anod
Garoe
Domo
Badweyn
Dusa Mareb
Galcaio
Ghelinsor
Obbia
Bohotleh
Sasabeneh
Warandab
Welwel
Geladi
Werder
Gerlogubi
Scillave
Imi
Kebri Dehar
Wabi Shebele
Ferfer
Sinadogo
El Dere
Oddur
Belet Uen
Bur Acaba
Lugh Ganana
Iscia Baidoa
Bardera
Mahaddei Uen
Giohar
Adale
Afgoi
Wareiek
Mogadiscio (Mogadishu)
Merca
Brava

KENYA
Gulu
Masindi
4321
Kitale
Eldoret
Mbale
L. Kyoga
Lira
Moroto
Lodwar
South Horr
North Horr
L. Turkana
Marsabit
Wajir
Habaswein
Buna
El Wak
Haradera
Dif
Afmadu

ZAÏRE
UGANDA

RED SEA
Jiddah
Makkah (Mecca) 2565
Al Lith
At Ta'if
Turaba
Dhurm
Ad Dam
Tamra
Tropic of Cancer
Dafina
Mastura
Rabigh Qasr
Yanbu'al Bahr
Al Madinah 1814
Hadiya
Umm Lajj
W. Hamdh
2216
Al Wajh
Madâ'in Sâlih
Taimâ
Mada in Salih
Usfan
Khurm
Khurma
Al Qunfidha
Hali
Abha
Dhahran
3200
Qizan
Abu Arish
Abu Saud
Jazâ'ir Farasân
Dahlak Kebir
Mitsiwa
Zula
Mersa Fatma
Edd
Aseb
Kamaran
Loheia
Hanish
Bur Sûdân (Port Sudan) 2635
Suakin
Sinkat
Tokar
Trinkitat
Ras Kasar
Aqiq
Karora 2780
Nakfa
Akordat
Barentu
Haiya
Musmar
Derudub
Adarama

ASIR
NEJD
Jabal Tuwaiq
1143
Ar Rab al Khâli

Gulf of Aden
Tadjoura
DJIBOUTI
Djibouti
Obock
Bab al Mandab

INDIAN OCEAN
'Abd al Kûri
Hadibu 1503
Socotra (South Yemen)
El Gal
Darror

Projection: Sanson-Flamsteed's Sinusoidal   East from Greenwich   COPYRIGHT GEORGE PHILIP & SON LTD

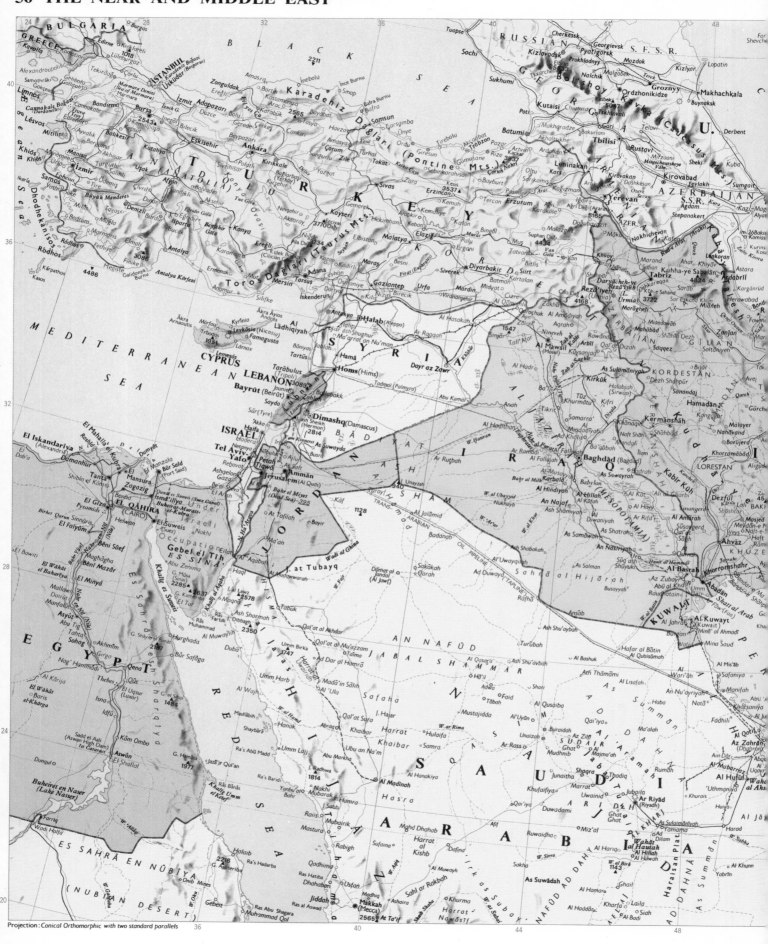

Projection : Conical Orthomorphic with two standard parallels

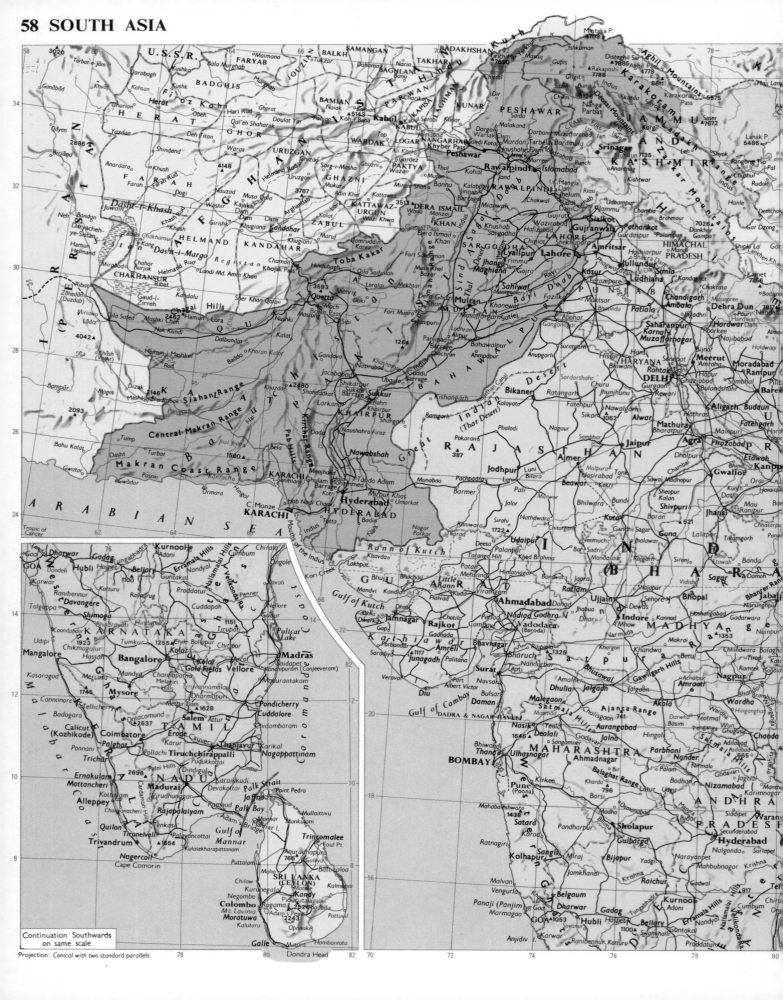

Continuation Southwards
on same scale

Projection: Conical with two standard parallels

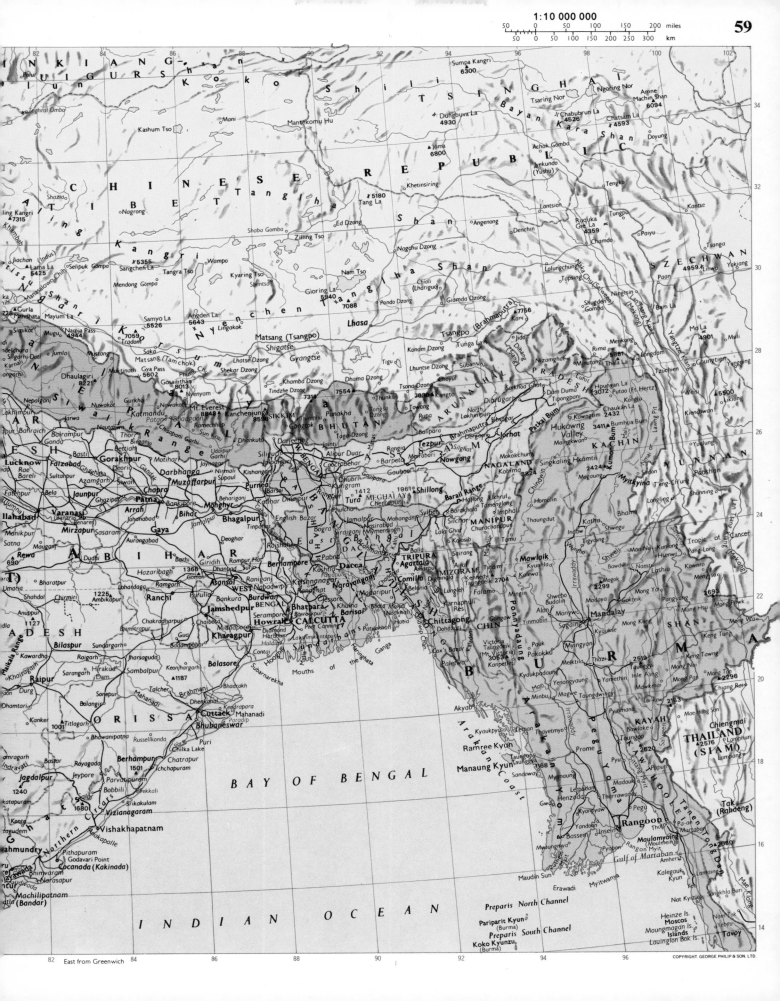

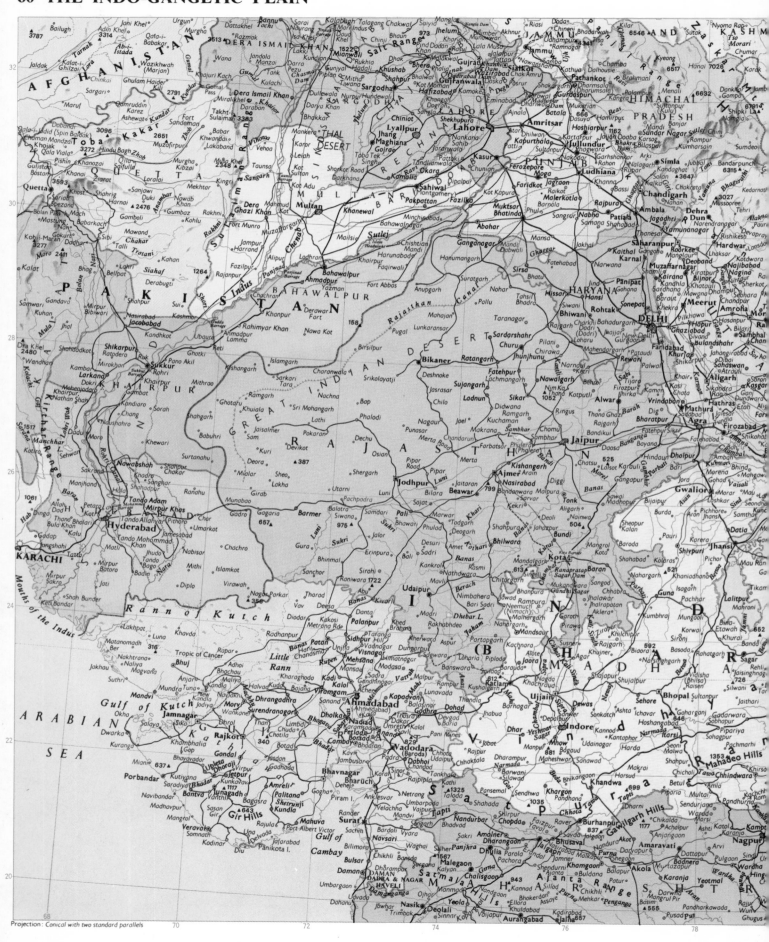

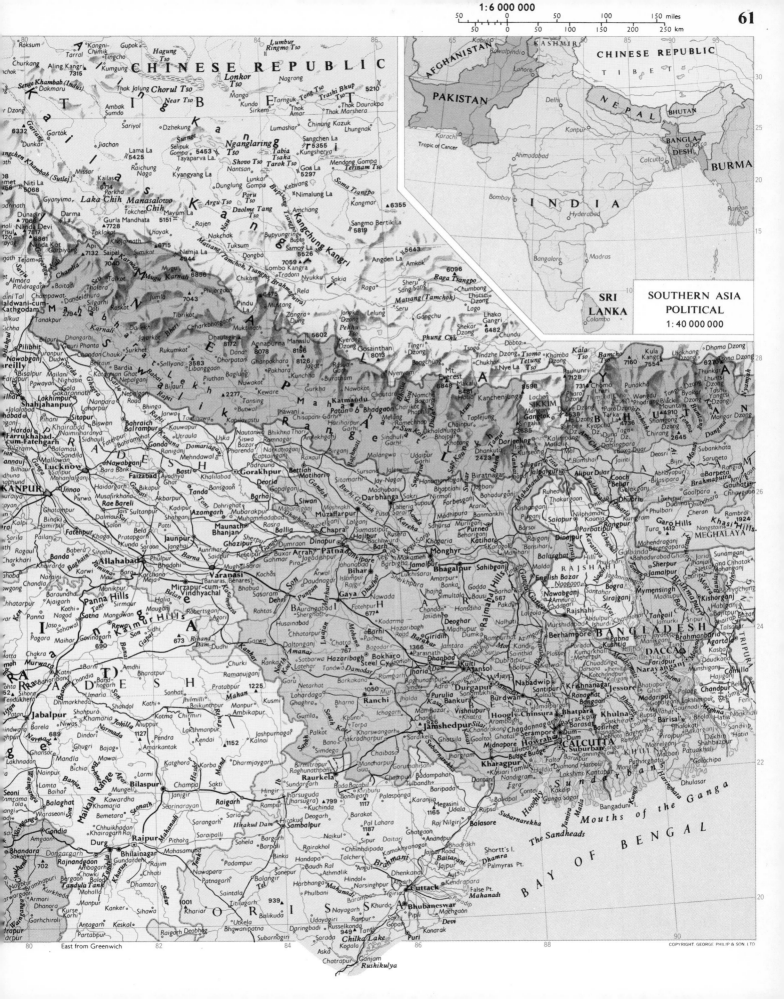

1:6 000 000

50   0   50   100   150 miles
50   0   50 100 150 200 250 km

MAHARASHTRA

Ajanta Range

Balaghat Range

Satmala Hills

BOMBAY
Pune (Poona)
Nasik
Deolali
Aurangabad
Ahmadnagar
Jalna
Nander
Nizamabad
Karanja
Yeotmal

MADHYA PRADESH

ANDHRA PRADESH

HYDERABAD
Secunderabad
Warangal
Nalgonda
Gulbarga
Bijapur
Raichur
Kurnool
Nandyal
Kamam
Rajahmundry
Eluru (Ellore)
Vijayawada (Bezawada)
Guntur
Tenali
Machilipatnam (Bandar)
Ongole
Nellore
Kakinada (Cocanada)
Vishakhapatnam
Waltair
Vizianagaram

KARNATAKA

Belgaum
Hubli-Dharwar
Gadag
Bellary
Davangere
Chitradurga
Shimoga
Chikmagalur
Hassan
BANGALORE
Mysore
Kolar Gold Fields
Tumkur
Chik Ballapur

GOA
Panaji (Panjim)
Marmagao
Margao

Mangalore
Udipi
Cannanore
Tellicherry
Calicut (Kozhikode)

ARABIAN SEA

BAY OF BENGAL

Coromandel Coast

TAMIL NADU

MADRAS
Vellore
Arcot
Kanchipuram (Conjeeveram)
Chingleput
Pondicherry
Cuddalore
Salem
Erode
Coimbatore
Tiruchchirappalli
Thanjavur
Nagappattinam (Negapatam)
Madurai
Tuticorin
Tirunelveli
Nagercoil
C. Comorin

Cochin
Ernakulam
Alleppey
Quilon
Trivandrum

Nilgiri Hills
Anaimalai Hills

Gulf of Mannar (Mannar)

Palk Strait
Palk Bay

Adam's Bridge

Pearl Banks

SRI LANKA (CEYLON)

SRI LANKA
On same scale

Palk Strait
Jaffna
Point Pedro
Elephant Pass
Mannar
Trincomalee
Anuradhapura
Puttalam
Negombo
COLOMBO
Dehiwala
Moratuwa
Kandy
Ratnapura
Galle
Matara
Batticaloa
Little Basses
Great Basses
Dondra Head

1:10 000 000

50   0   50   100   150   200 miles
50   0   100   200   300 km

Major labels

INDIA
BANGLADESH
CHIN
BURMA
CHINA
Mandalay
SHAN
KAYAH
THAILAND (SIAM)
Rangoon
LAOS
VIETNAM
Hanoi
Haiphong
Gulf of Tongking
Hainan
Luang Prabang
Vientiane
ANNAM
Hué
Da Nang (Tourane)
Krung Thep (Bangkok)
Thonburi
CAMBODIA
Angkor
Tonlé Sap
Phnom Penh
Ho Chi Minh City (Phanh Bho Ho Chi Minh)
Gulf of Siam
ANDAMAN SEA
North Andaman
Middle Andaman
South Andaman
Little Andaman
Andaman Islands (India)
Preparis North Channel
Preparis South Channel
Koko Kyunzu (Burma)
Coco Channel
Moscos Islands
Maungmagan Is.
Myeik Kyunzu (Mergui) Archipelago
Mergui
Tavoy
Kho Khot Kra (Isthmus of Kra)
Chumphon
SOUTH CHINA SEA
George Town
Pulau Pinang
Butterworth
Ipoh
WESTERN MALAYSIA
MALAYA
Kuala Lumpur
Kelang
Seremban
Melaka
Johor Baharu
SINGAPORE
SUMATERA INDONESIA
Kepulauan Natuna Besar
Kepulauan Anambas
Kepulauan Natuna Selatan

Inset

THAILAND (SIAM)
PERLIS
KEDAH
Alor Setar
PINANG
George Town
Butterworth
Bukit Mertajam
PERAK
Taiping
Ipoh
KELANTAN
Kota Baharu
TERENGGANU
Kuala Terengganu
MALAYA
Kuala Lumpur
SELANGOR
Kelang
NEGERI SEMBILAN
Seremban
MELAKA
Melaka
JOHOR
Johor Baharu
PAHANG
Kuantan
SUMATERA INDONESIA
SINGAPORE
Straits of Singapore

MALAYA AND SINGAPORE

1:6 000 000

50   0   50 miles
50   0   50 km

Projection: Conical with two standard parallels

East from Greenwich

COPYRIGHT. GEORGE PHILIP & SON. LTD

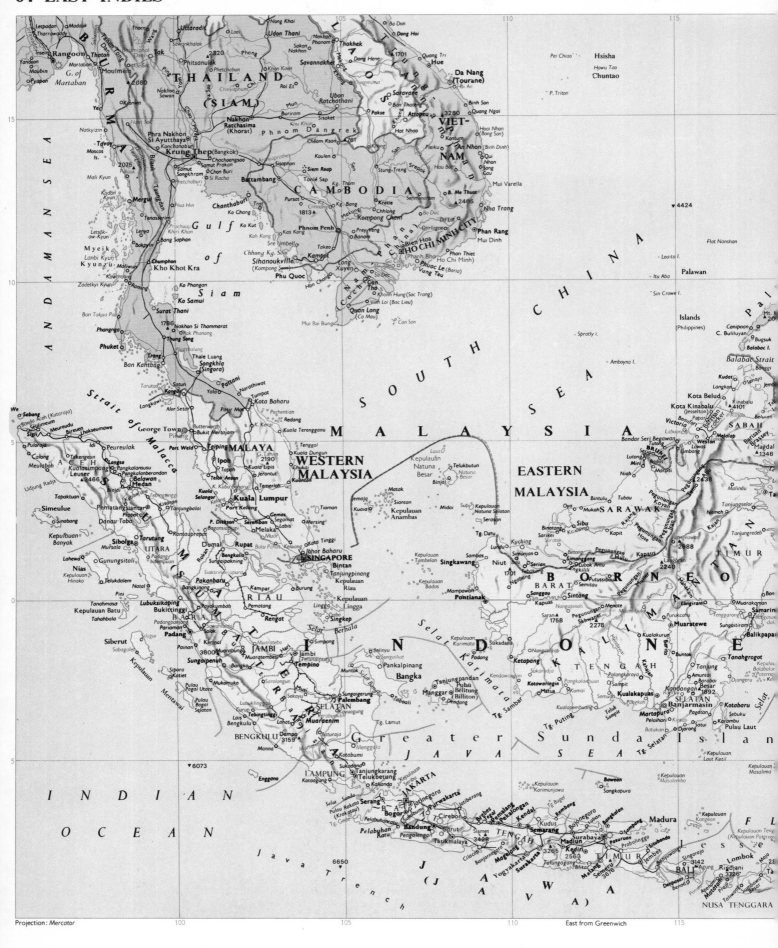

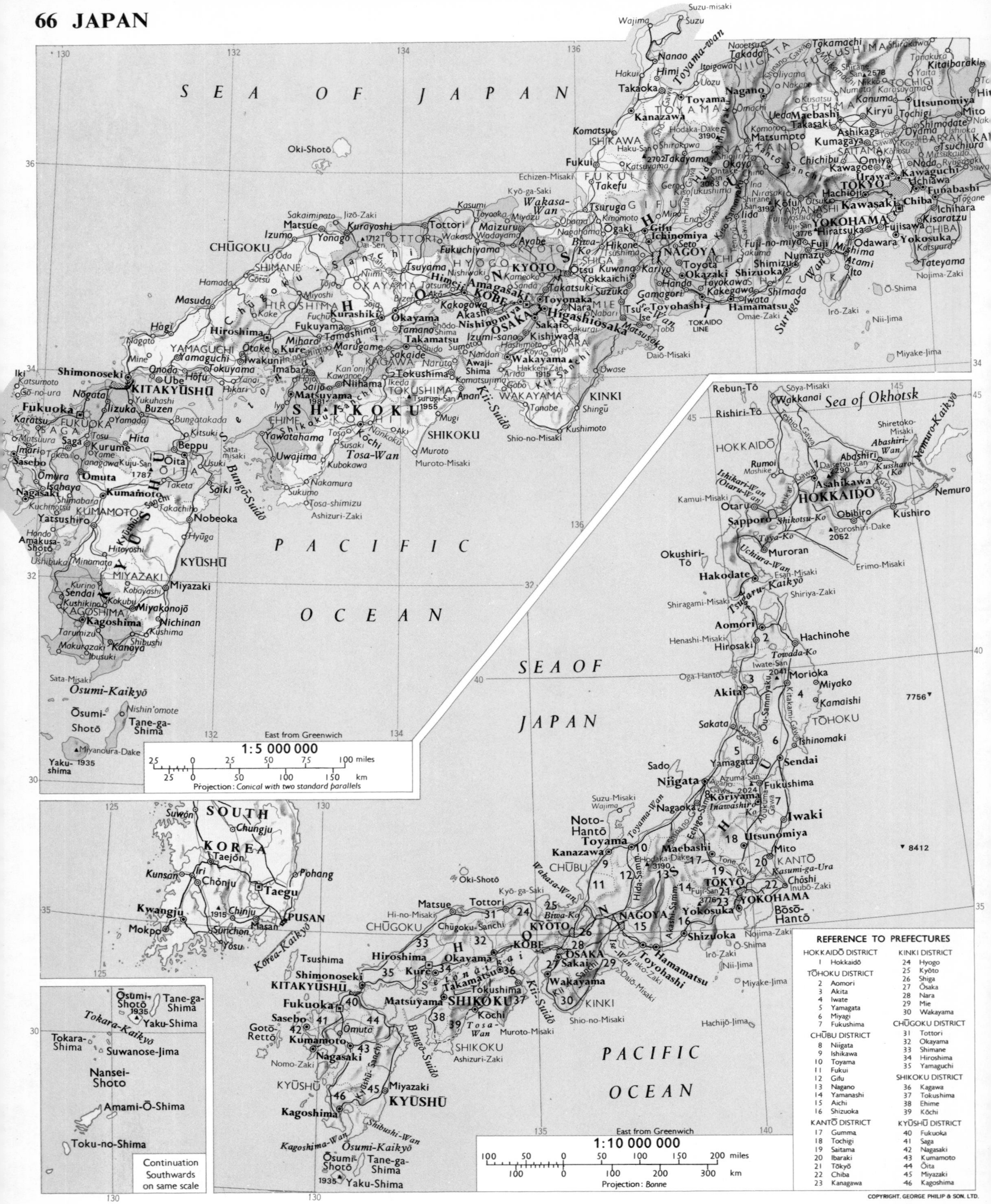

SEA OF JAPAN

PACIFIC OCEAN

SEA OF JAPAN

Sea of Okhotsk

1:5 000 000

25 0 25 50 75 100 miles
25 0 50 100 150 km
Projection: Conical with two standard parallels

East from Greenwich

SOUTH KOREA

Nansei-Shoto

Tokara-Kaikyo
Tokara-Shima
Suwanose-Jima
Amami-Ō-Shima
Toku-no-Shima

Ōsumi-Shoto 1935
Tane-ga-Shima
Yaku-Shima

Continuation Southwards on same scale

1:10 000 000

100 50 0 50 100 150 200 miles
100 0 100 200 300 km
Projection: Bonne

East from Greenwich

HOKKAIDŌ

TŌHOKU

CHŪBU

KANTŌ

KINKI

CHŪGOKU

SHIKOKU

KYŪSHŪ

PACIFIC OCEAN

REFERENCE TO PREFECTURES	
HOKKAIDŌ DISTRICT	**KINKI DISTRICT**
1 Hokkaidō	24 Hyogo
TŌHOKU DISTRICT	25 Kyōto
2 Aomori	26 Shiga
3 Akita	27 Ōsaka
4 Iwate	28 Nara
5 Yamagata	29 Mie
6 Miyagi	30 Wakayama
7 Fukushima	**CHŪGOKU DISTRICT**
CHŪBU DISTRICT	31 Tottori
8 Niigata	32 Okayama
9 Ishikawa	33 Shimane
10 Toyama	34 Hiroshima
11 Fukui	35 Yamaguchi
12 Gifu	**SHIKOKU DISTRICT**
13 Nagano	36 Kagawa
14 Yamanashi	37 Tokushima
15 Aichi	38 Ehime
16 Shizuoka	39 Kōchi
KANTŌ DISTRICT	**KYŪSHŪ DISTRICT**
17 Gumma	40 Fukuoka
18 Tochigi	41 Saga
19 Saitama	42 Nagasaki
20 Ibaraki	43 Kumamoto
21 Tōkyō	44 Ōita
22 Chiba	45 Miyazaki
23 Kanagawa	46 Kagoshima

1:20 000 000

Projection: Bonne

East from Greenwich

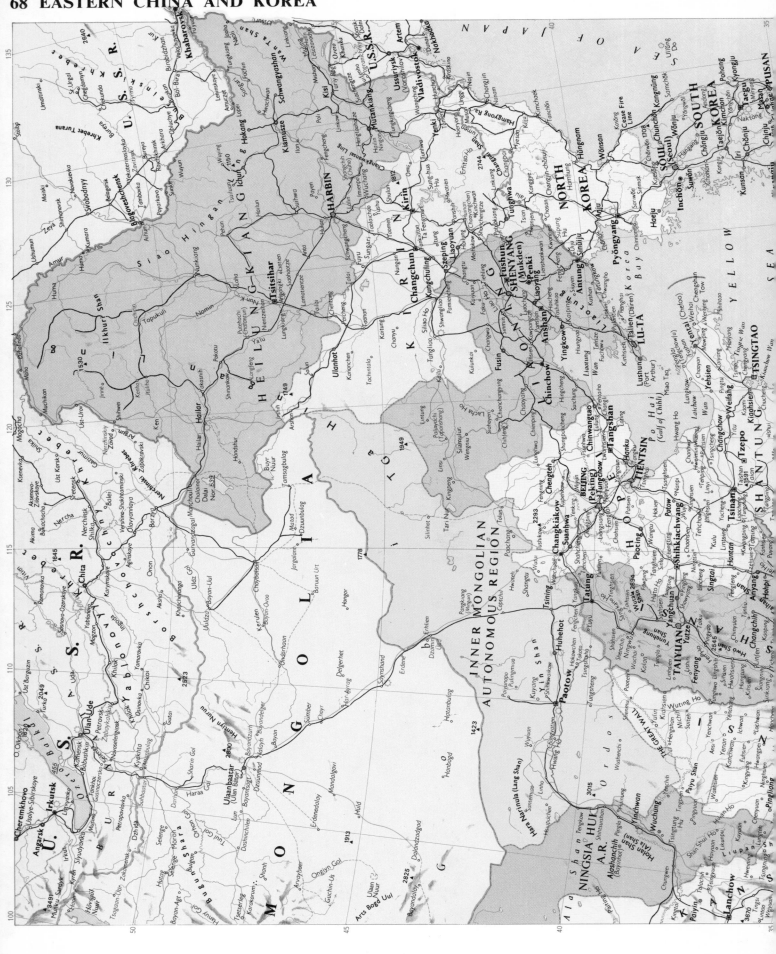

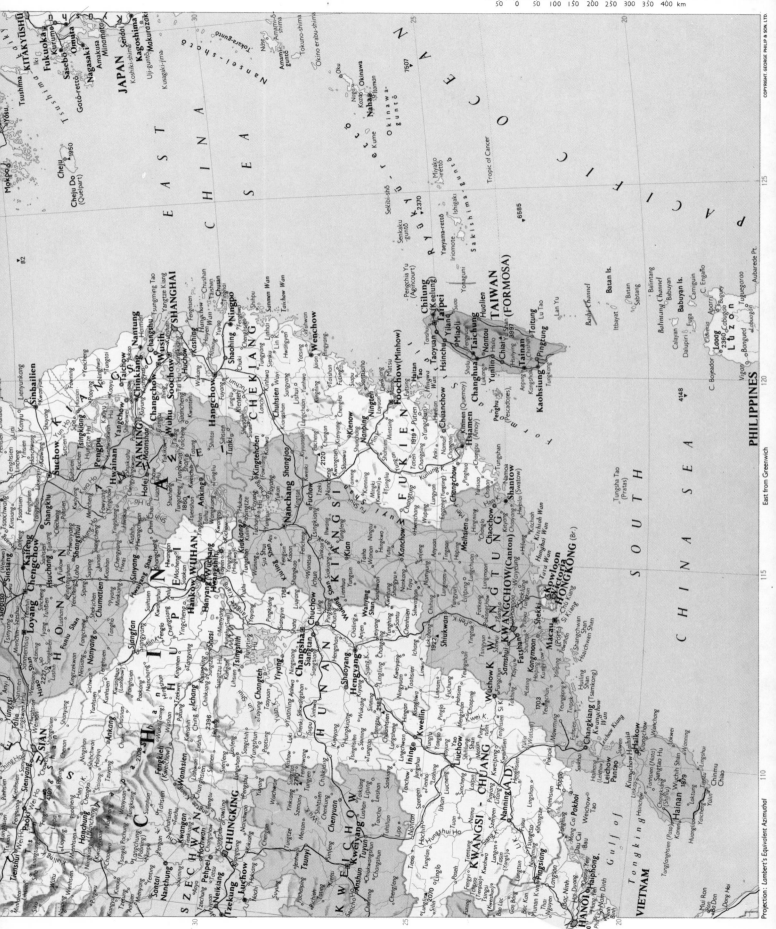

1:10 000 000

50   0   50   100 150 200 250 miles

50 0 50 100 150 200 250 300 350 400 km

COPYRIGHT GEORGE PHILIP & SON, LTD.

Projection: Lambert's Equivalent Azimuthal

East from Greenwich

1:40 000 000

200   0   200   400   600   800   1000 miles

200   0   200   400   600   800 1000 1200 1400 1600 km

ATLANTIC OCEAN

British Isles

Bay of Biscay

Mt. Blanc 4807

Alps

Pyrenees

Dinaric Alps

Apennines

Adriatic Sea

Carpathians

Black Sea

Elburus 5633

Caucasus

Caspian Sea

Aral Sea

Iberian Peninsula

Corsica

Sardinia

Anatolia

6578

Madeira

Str. of Gibraltar

Middle Atlas

High Atlas

High Plateaus

Saharan Atlas

Mediterranean Sea

C. Bon   Sicily

Malta

5121

Crete

Cyprus

Mesopotamia

Tigris

Euphrates

Syrian Desert

Levant

Canary Is.

Tenerife 3718

Anti Atlas

Toubkal 4165

Dra

Barbary

Tripolitania

G. of Gabes

Chott Djerid

G. of Sidra

Cyrenaica

Siwa

Arabian Desert

Sinai 2285

Red Sea

Hejaz

Arabia

Tropic of Cancer

Persian G.

Bahrain

C. Blanc

Igidi

Sahara

El Juf

Tasili Plateau

Fezzan

Libyan Desert

Egypt

Nile

1st Cat.

El Kharga

Kufra

Rub' al Khali

Adrar

Hoggar

Air

Tibesti

3415

Bilma

Nubian Desert

2nd Cat.

3rd Cat.

4th Cat.

5th Cat.

Nubia

Attara

6th Cat.

Ras Dashan 4620

L. Tana

Perim I.

Str. of Bab el Mandeb

Gulf of Aden

Ras Asir

Socotra

Senegal

C. Vert

Senegambia

Gambia

Fouta Djalon

Niger (Joliba)

Volta

Benue

Niger

L. Chad

Chari

Wadai

Darfur

Kordofan

White Nile

Blue Nile

Ethiopian Highlands

Somali Peninsula

Shabelle

Sudan

Grain Coast

C. Palmas Ivory Coast

Gold Coast

Slave Coast

Bight of Benin

Macias Nguema Biyoga

6363

Adamawa Highlands

Cameroon Peak 4070

Bahr el Ghazal

Dar Banda

Bahr el Jebel

Guinea

Gulf of Guinea

Principe

São Tomé

Pagalu

C. Lopez

Ogoue

Uele

Turkana

Congo

Zaire

L. Mobutu Sese Seko

Chutes Boyoma

Ruwenzori 5109

Idi

Amin Dada

L. Kivu

Elgon 4321

Kenya 5199

Tana

INDIAN OCEAN

Equator

Ascension

ATLANTIC OCEAN

St. Helena

Congo

Pool Malebo

Kasai

Sankuru

Lualaba

L. Victoria

Kilimanjaro 5895

Basin

Kasai

Cuanza

Cuilo

Luvua

L. Tanganyika

Pemba

Zanzibar

Aldabra Is.

C. Delgado

Comoro Is.

Bié Plateau

Mweru

Katanga

L. Bangweulu

Luapula

Rungwe 2961

L. Nyasa

Malawi

Ruvuma

Mozambique Channel

Madagascar 2643

C. Fria

Cunene

Cuando

Cubango

Zambezi

Zambezi

Mlanje 3000

Maur

Réunion

Walvis Bay

Namib Desert

Victoria Falls

Matopo

Tropic of Capricorn

Kalahari

Delagoa Bay

Orange

High Veld

Vaal

3482

Drakensberg

Limpopo

Compass B. 2505

Nieuveldberge

Gt. Karoo

Swartberg

Orange

C. of Good Hope

C. Agulhas

Agulhas Bank

Algoa Bay

m 4000 3000 2000 1500 1000 400 200 0 200

ft 12 000 9000 6000 4500 3000 1200 600

1000 2000 4000 6000 m

600 3000 6000 12 000 18 000 ft

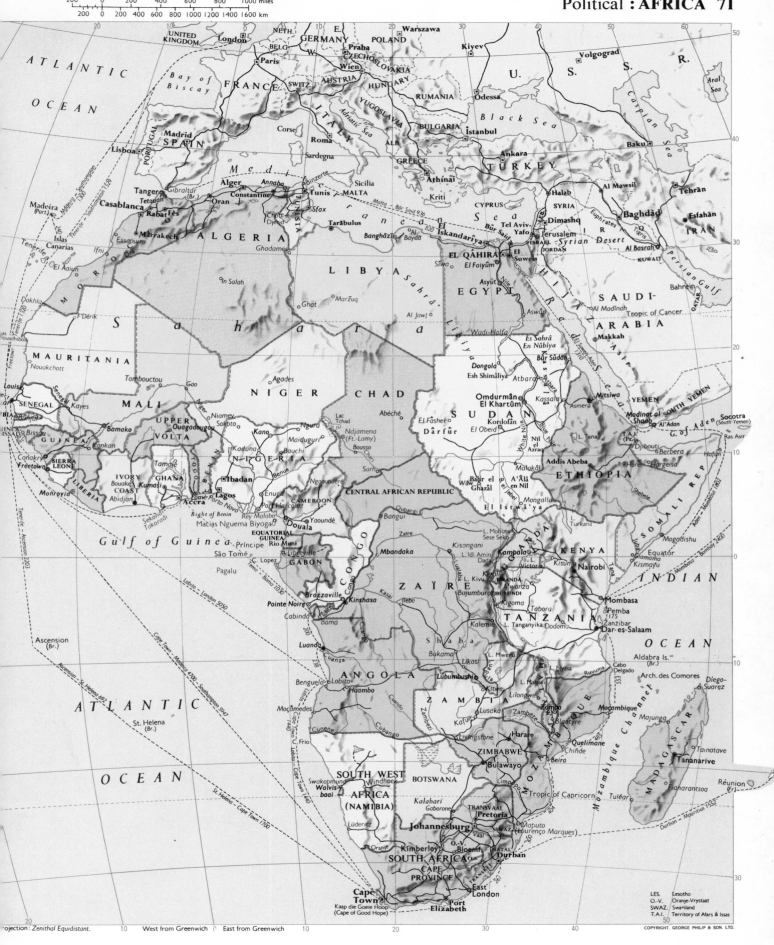

1:40 000 000

200   0   200   400   600   800   1000 miles
200   0   200 400 600 800 1000 1200 1400 1600 km

ATLANTIC

OCEAN

UNITED
KINGDOM   London

NETH.   GERMANY   POLAND   Warszawa
BELG.   E.   Kiyev
Bay of   Praha   Volgograd
Biscay   FRANCE   W.   CZECHOSLOVAKIA
Paris   AUSTRIA   HUNGARY
SWITZ.   YUGOSLAVIA   RUMANIA
Madrid   ITALY   Odessa   U.   S.   S.   R.
SPAIN   Corse   BULGARIA   İstanbul   Black Sea   Aral
Lisboa   Roma   GREECE   Baku   Sea
PORTUGAL   Sardegna   ALB.   TURKEY   Ankara   Caspian
Athínai   Sea
Tanger   Gibraltar   Alger   Annaba   Tunis   MALTA   Kriti   CYPRUS   SYRIA   Al Mawsil   Tehrān
Casablanca   Tetouan   (Br.)   Oran   Constantine   Binzerte   Sfax   Halab
Rabat   Fès   TUNISIA   Tarābulus   Dimashq   Baghdād   Esfahān
Essaouira   Chott   Tel Aviv-   Syrian   IRAN
Marrakech   el Djerid   Banghāzī   El   Yafo   Desert   Al Basrah
Madeira   Ghadames   Iskandariya   ISRAEL   JORDAN   KUWAIT
(Port.)   Ifni   EL QÂHIRA   El Suweis
Islas   Siwa   El Faiyûm   Persian Gulf   Bahrein
Canarias   El Aaiun   Asyût   SAUDI-   QATAR
Dakhla   MOROCCO   LIBYA   Sahrâ'   Libiya   EGYPT   Aswān   Tropic of Cancer   ARABIA
F'Dérik   Ghat   Marzûq   Al Madinah
MAURITANIA   In Salah   Al Jawf   Wadi-Halfa   Es Sahrâ   Makkah   HIJAZ
Nouakchott   En Nûbiya   Bûr Sûdân
Tombouctou   Dongola   Atbara
Gao   Agades   SUDAN   Esh Shimâliya   Kassala   Mitsiwa   YEMEN
SENEGAL   Niamey   NIGER   CHAD   El Fâsher   El Khartûm   Asmera   Madinat al   SOUTH YEMEN
Louis   Sokoto   Dârfûr   Kordofan   Omdurmân   Shaab   Al 'Adan   Socotra
MALI   Kano   Nguru   El Obeid   White Nile   L. Tana   Djibouti   (South Yemen)
SENEGAL   Bamako   UPPER   Kaduna   Maiduguri   Abéché   Nil el   ETHIOPIA   Berbera   Ras Asir
Kayes   Ouagadougou   Ndjamena   Azraq   Addis Abeba   Hargeisa
GUINEA   VOLTA   Bauchi   (Ft.-Lamy)   A'Âla   Harer
Bissau   Kankan   Bousso   en Nîl   SOMALI REP.
SIERRA   Tamale   NIGERIA   Benue   Sarh   Wâw   Bahr el   Mongalla
LEONE   Freetown   IVORY   GHANA   Ibadan   Enugu   Ngaoundéré   CENTRAL AFRICAN REPUBLIC   Ghazâl
Monrovia   COAST   Kumasi   Lagos   Port Harcourt   CAMEROON   Bangui   EL Istwâ'ya   Mogadishu
LIBERIA   Bouake   Accra   Porto Novo   Douala   Yaoundé   Ubangi   Zaire   L. Turkana
Abidjan   Tomé   Bight of Benin   Yaoundé   Qubangi   UGANDA   KENYA   Equator
Sekondi-   Macias Nguema Biyogo   Kisangani   L. Mobutu   Kisumu   INDIAN
Takoradi   EQUATORIAL   Rio Muni   Mbandaka   Sese Seko   Kampala   Nairobi
Gulf of Guinea   GUINEA   Libreville   L. Idi Amin   L.   Mombasa
Príncipe   Dada   Victoria   Kismayu
São Tomé   GABON   Lualaba   Kigali   RWANDA   Pemba
Pagalu   C. Lopez   Tremo   CONGO   ZAÏRE   L. Kivu   Mwanza   Zanzibar
Brazzaville   Kisangani   BURUNDI   Dar-es-Salaam
Pointe Noire   Kinshasa   Kasai   Bujumbura   Kigoma   Tabora   TANZANIA
Cabinda   Boma   Ilebo   L. Tanganyika   Dodoma   OCEAN
Luanda   Kalemie   L. Mweru   Aldabra Is.
ATLANTIC   Cuanza   Shaba   Bukama   Likasi   (Br.)
Ascension   Lubumbashi   L. Nyasa   Cabo   Arch. des Comores   Diego-
(Br.)   ANGOLA   L. Malawi   Delgado   Suarez
St. Helena   Benguela   Lobito   Kitwe   Lilongwe   Moçambique   Majunga
(Br.)   Huambo   ZAMBIA   Zambezi   Zomba   MADAGASCAR
Moçâmedes   Lusaka   Blantyre   Quelimane   Réunion
OCEAN   Cunene   Kafue   Livingstone   Harare   Chinde   Fianarantsoa   (Fr.)
Cubango   Zambezi   Beira
SOUTH WEST   Swakopmund   Windhoek   BOTSWANA   ZIMBABWE   Bulawayo   MOZAMBIQUE   Tuléar   Tananarive
Walvis   AFRICA   Kalahari   Tropic of Capricorn
baai   (NAMIBIA)   Gaborone   Limpopo   Maputo
Lüderitz   TRANSVAAL   Pretoria   (Lourenço Marques)
Johannesburg   SWAZ.
Oranje   Vaal   NATAL
Kimberley   O.V.   Durban
SOUTH AFRICA   Bloemf.   LES.
Cape Town   CAPE   East
PROVINCE   London
Kaap die Goeie Hoop   Port
(Cape of Good Hope)   Elizabeth

LES.   Lesotho
O.-V.   Oranje-Vrystaat
SWAZ.   Swaziland
T.A.I.   Territory of Afars & Issas

Projection: Zenithal Equidistant.   West from Greenwich   East from Greenwich   COPYRIGHT. GEORGE PHILIP & SON. LTD.

NORTH ATLANTIC

OCEAN

6578

Cabo de São Vicente

SPAIN ● Málaga ● Almería

Cádiz

Str. of Gibraltar
Gibraltar (Br.)
Tanger
Ceuta (Sp.)
Tetouan
Sidi bel Abbès
Oran
Mostaganem
Alger (Algiers)
Skikda
Annaba

Ksar-el-Kebir
Melilla
Al Hoceima
Ghazaouet
Tlemcen
Blida
Médéa
Constantine
Sétif
Batna

Kenitra (Port-Lyautey)
Salé
Rabat
Fès
Taza
Oujda
Jerada
Saïda
El Aricha
El Bayadh
Hodna
Biskra

Meknès
Khenifra
El Aricha
Méchéria
Laghouat
El Oued

Casablanca
El Jadida
Berrechid
Settat
Khouribga
Beni Mellal
Ksar es Souk
Aïn Beni
Figuig
Béchar
Hassi R'Mel
Ouargla
Chott El Djerid
Gafsa
Nefta

C. Cantin
Safi
Marrakech
Anti Atlas
Haut Atlas
Bou Arfa
Ghardaïa
Hassi Messaoud

C. Rhir
Agadir
4165
Taroudant
Ouarzazate
Abadla
El Goléa
Ft. Miribel
Ft. Lallemand
Hassi el Gassi
Ghudāmes

Sidi Ifni
Tiznit
Dra
Tinjoub
Igli
Beni Abbès
Adrar
In Salah
Ohanet

MADEIRA (Port.)
Funchal
Pto. Santo

Islas Canarias (Sp.)
Lanzarote
Fuerteventura
Arrecife
La Palma
Tenerife
Sta. Cruz
Gomera
Gran Canaria
Las Palmas
Hierro
El Aiún
Smara
Bu Craa

ALGERIA
Plateau du Tademaït
Chech
Erg

Boujdour
C. Bojador
Ain Ben Tili
Chegga
Ouallene
Bj.-in-Eker
Idelès
Djanet
Illizi

Dakhla
Pta. Durnford
Tamsagout
Terhazza
Taoudenni
Arak
Sardales
Tarat

C. Barbas
F'Dérik
Zouérate
Char
Chounn
Tanezrouft
Poste Maurice Cortier (Bidon 5)
Tahat 3018
Tamanrasset
Admer

Nouadhibou (Port Étienne)
Cite de Cansada
Atar
Ouadane
Oujeft
Chinguetti
Adrar des Iforas
Tessalit
Ahaggar

MAURITANIE
El Djouf
Araouane
Etelia
Kidal
Aïr (Azbine)
Monts Tamgak
1900

C. Timris
Akjoujt
Rachid
Tidjikdja
Tichit
Arhrijit
Bou Djebeha
Iférouane
Agadez
Aouderas

Nouakchott
Boutilimit
Moudjéria
Yagba
Oualata
Tombouctou
Bamba
Kerchoual
I-n-Gall

St. Louis
Louga
Pador
Bogué
Kaédi
Kiffa
Tichit
Néma
Timbédra
Gourma-Rharous
Gao
Ménaka

Rosso
Dagana
Matam
Nioro
Nara
Goundam
Diré
Ansongo

C. Vert
Dakar
SENEGAL
Thiès
Dahra
Tiel
Bakel
Sokolo
Mourdiah
Douentza
Hombori
Tahoua
Tamaské
Gangara
Tanout
Boultum
Kellé

GAMBIA
Banjul (Bathurst)
Georgetown
Tambacounda
Bafoulabé
Kayes
Didiéni
Ségou
Djenné
Mopti
Bandiagara
Djibo
Dori
Téra
Filingué
Niamey
Madaoua
Birni Nkonni
Zinder
Matameye
Nguru

GUINEA-BISSAU
Bissau
Bolama
Arquipélago dos Bijagós
Bafatá
Gaoual
Koundara
Labé
Fouta Djalon
Kankan
Bamako
Koutiala
San
Tougan
Ouahigouya
Dori
Dosso
Say
Sokoto
Gusau
Katsina
Kano
Hadejia
Azare

GUINEA
Conakry
Forécariah
Kindia
Mamou
Dabola
Kouroussa
Siguiri
Bougouni
Sikasso
Bobo-Dioulasso
BURKINA FASO (Upper Volta)
Ouagadougou
Fada N'Gourma
Kandi
Birnin-Kebbi
Gummi
Funtua
Zaria
Kaduna

SIERRA LEONE
Freetown
Waterloo
Makeni
Magburaka
Kabala
Kissidougou
Beyla
Odienné
Korhogo
Bouna
Wa
Tamale
Parakou
Kontagora
Minna
Abuja

Bo
Kenema
Nzérékoré
Man
IVORY COAST
Bouaké
Bondoukou
Bouna
Salaga
GHANA
Tamale
TOGO
BENIN
Ilorin
Oshogbo
Ogbomosho
Oyo
Iwo

LIBERIA
Monrovia
Buchanan
Greenville
Tabou
Sassandra
Gagnoa
Daloa
Dimbokro
Kumasi
Lake Volta
Ho
Lomé
Cotonou
Porto-Novo
Lagos
Ibadan
Abeokuta
Ife
Benin City
Onitsha
Enugu

Abidjan
Grand Bassam
Axim
Sekondi-Takoradi
Cape Coast
Winneba
Accra
Bight of Benin
Port Harcourt
Aba
Calabar
CAMEROON
Douala
Yaoundé
Victoria
Rey Malabo
Macias Nguema Biyoga

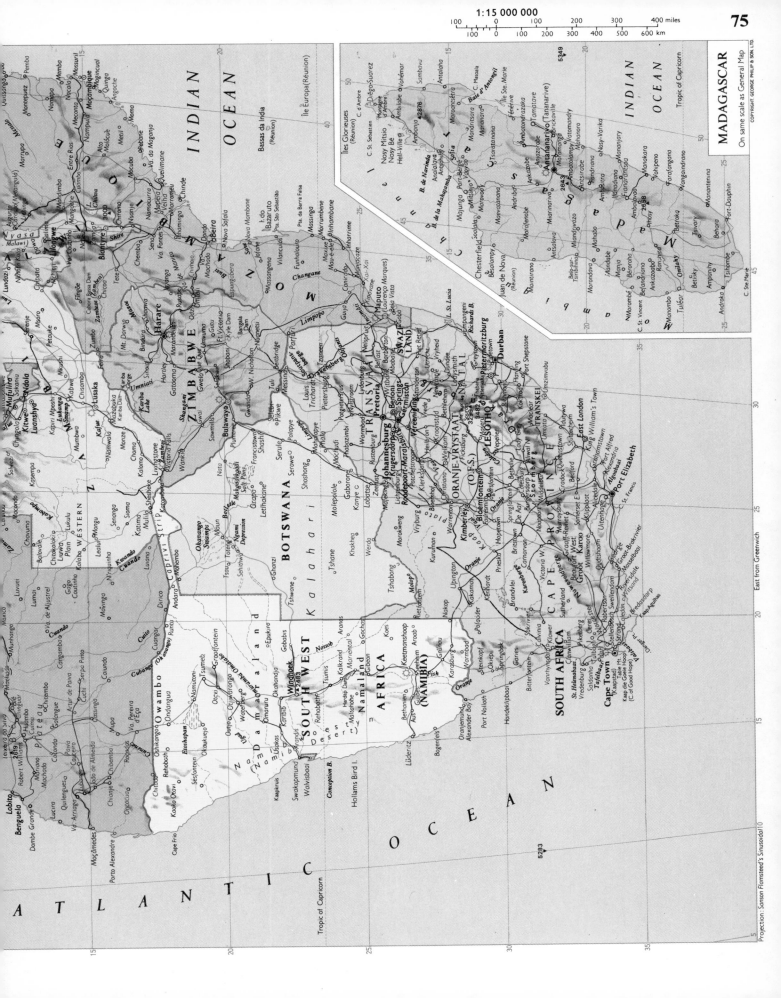

MADAGASCAR
On same scale as General Map

COPYRIGHT GEORGE PHILIP & SON LTD.

1:15 000 000

100   0   100   200   300   400 miles
100   0   100   200   300   400   500   600 km

INDIAN OCEAN

ATLANTIC OCEAN

Projection: Sanson Flamsteed's Sinusoidal

East from Greenwich

Tropic of Capricorn

East from Greenwich

```
---5615--- Principal Shipping Routes
            (Distances in Nautical Miles)
```

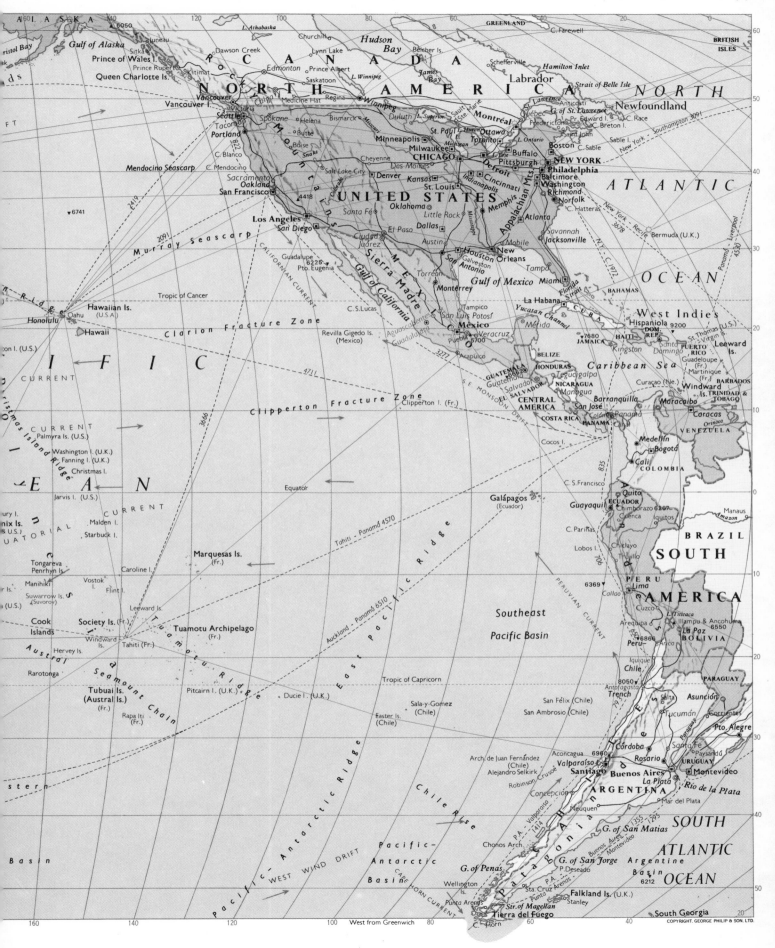

TIMOR SEA

INDIAN OCEAN

Ashmore Reef
Cartier I.
Scott Reef
Rowley Shoals
Koolan & Cockatoo Is.
Lacepede Is.

C. Londonderry
C. Talbot
Vantittart B.
C. Bougainville
Admiralty G.
York. Sd.
Brunswick B.
King Sd.
C. Levêque
Yampi Sound
C. Baskerville
Carnot B.
C. Boileau
C. Latouche Treville
C. Bossut
Derby
Broome
La Grange

Cambridge G.
Jos. Bonaparte Gulf
Wyndham
Mt. Hann 776
Glenroy
Meda
Hall's Creek
Fitzroy
Fitzroy Crossing

Croker
Cobourg Pen.
Goalburn
Junction B.
Elcho
Crocodile Is.
Castlereagh B.
Buckingham
Arnh

Bathurst I.
Melville I.
Van Diemen Gulf
Clarence Str.
P. Darwin
Darwin
Pt. Blaze
Anson B.
C. Ford
Batchelor
Rum Jungle
Frances Creek
Pine Creek
Katherine
Daly
Roper
Mataranka
Victoria
Wave Hill
Victoria River Downs
Newcastle Waters
L. Woods
Powell Creek
Renner Springs T.O.
Tanami Desert
Gordon Downs

NORTHE
TERRITO

Dampier Archipelago
Hampton Harb.
Monte Bello Is.
Barrow I.
N.W. Cape
Exmouth G.
Learmonth
Pt. Cloates
Deepdale
Onslow
Exmouth
C. Farquhar
C. Cuvier
Geographe Chan.
Bernier
Dorre I.
Naturaliste Chan.
Dirk Hartog
S. Passage
Steep Pt.
Shark

P. Hedland
Finucane I.
Cape Lambert
Dampier
Roebourne
Pilbara
Preston
Mt. Enid
Hamersley Ra.
Mt. Bruce 1227
Mt. Meharry
Ophthalmia Ra.
Mount Tom Price
Parraburdoo
Mount Whaleback
Ashburton
Barlee Ra.
Mt. Augustus 1105
McLeod
Lyons
North West
Carnarvon
Gascoyne
Wooramel
Basin
Denham
Sanford
Murchison
Meekatharra
Nannine
Cue
L. Austin
Sandstone
Wiluna
Mt. Magnet
Yalgoo
Tallering Peak 453
Mullewa
L. Monger
L. Barlee

Mount Goldsworthy
De Grey
Nimingarra
Marble Bar
Shaw
Yule
Throssell Ra.
Nullagine
Mt. Nicholas
Newman
Robertson Ra.
Peak Hill
Robinson Ra.
L. Carnegie
Eighty Mile Beach
Canning Basin
Great Sandy Desert
L. Dora
L. Blanche
L. Disappointment
Gibson Desert
L. Buchanan
L. Wells 661
L. Yeo
Rawlinson Ra.

WESTERN

AUSTRALIA

Gregory Lake
Hordern Hills
The Granites
Mt. Singleton 844
Mt. Freeling 998
Reynolds Ra.
Mt. Liebig 1510
Mt. Ziel 1524
L. Macdonald
L. Mackay
Barrow Creek T.O.
Sandov
Murchison Ra.
Hatch
Davenport Ra.
Mt. Laughlen 1169
Macdonnell Ras.
Alice Springs
James Ra.
Hugh
Finke
Palmer
Blackstone Ra.
Barrow Ra.
Musgrave Ranges 1440
Mt. Woodroffe
Everard Ras.
L. Amadeus
Mt. Olga 1069
Ayers Rock 867
Hamilton
Alberga
Oodnadatta
Charlot Waters
Warrin

Great Victoria Desert

L. Maurice
Coober Pedy
Stuart
Tarcoola

SOUTH AUS

Leonora
Malcolm
L. Carey
L. Raeside
Menzies
L. Ballard
L. Minigwal
L. Rason
Laverton

Geraldton
Dongara
Northampton
Houtman Abrolhos
P. Gregory
Champion B.
Jurien B.
Wedge I.
L. Moore
Mingenew
Coastal
Plains
Basin
Bencubbin
Bonnie Rock
Bullfinch
Merredin
Kellerberrin
Northam
Swan
Perth
Fremantle
Kwinana
York
Beverley
Brookton
Narrogin
Pinjarra
Bunbury
Collie
Wagin
Nyabing
Gnowangerup
Katanning
Geographe B.
Busselton
C. Naturaliste
Augusta
C. Leeuwin
Bridgetown
Manjimup
Pemberton
Flinders B.
Pt. d'Entrecasteaux
Pt. Nuyts
Denham
Stirling Ra.
Mt. Barker
Albany
Tor B.
King George Sound
Doubtful B.
Pt. Hood
C. Knob
Esperance
Hopetoun
Ravensthorpe
Newdegate
L. Grace
The Johnston Lakes
Southern Cross
Coolgardie
Kalgoorlie
Boulder
Kanowna
Norseman
L. Lefroy
L. Cowan
L. Dundas
Zanthus
Esperance B.
C. Le Grand
C. Arid
Archipelago of the Recherche
C. Pasley
Rocky Pt.
Pt. Culver
Pt. Dover
Premier Downs
Rawlinna
Forrest
Deakin
Eucla Basin
Nullarbor Plain
Hampton Tableland
Eyre
Maralinga
Ooldea
L. Harris
L. Everard
Penong
Ceduna
C. Adieu
Fowlers B.
Nuyts Archipelago
C. Radstock
Streaky B.
Anxious B.
Investigator Group
L. Gair
Nukey
Ga
Head of Bight
Great Australian Bight
Coffin B. Penin.
Whidbey Is.
Port Lincoln
C. Catastrophe
Thist
Ey
Pen

Great Northern

Eastern

Coolgardie Great

Boundaries of the artesian basins

10 / 15 / 20 / 25 / 30 / 35
115 / 120 / 125 / 130 / 135

Bass Strait
TASMANIA
Hobart
Launceston
CORAL SEA
Great Barrier Reef
Cape York Peninsula
Gulf of Carpentaria
Great Dividing Range
QUEENSLAND
GREAT AUSTRALIAN
NORTHERN TERRITORY
Barkly Tableland
Arnhem Land
Simpson Desert
Cairns
Townsville
Mackay
Rockhampton
Gladstone
Mount Isa
Alice Springs
Charters Towers
Hughenden
Winton
Cloncurry
Groote Eylandt
Wellesley Is.
Tropic of Capricorn
Macdonnell Ranges

TIMOR SEA
INDONESIA
INDIAN OCEAN
NORTHERN TERRITORY
Tanami Desert
Great Sandy Desert
Gibson Desert
Tropic of Capricorn
Darwin
Port Darwin
Melville I.
Bathurst I.
Van Diemen Gulf
Cobourg Pen.
Timor
Roti
Sawa
Semau
Sumba
Sumbawa
Raidjoea
Danu
Joseph Bonaparte Gulf
Cambridge Gulf
Bonaparte Archipelago
King Leopold Ranges
Durack Range
Hamersley Range
Eighty Mile Beach
Wyndham
Kununurra
Katherine
Daly Waters
Halls Creek
Fitzroy Crossing
Derby
King Sound
Broome
Roebuck B.
Port Hedland
Dampier
Dampier Archipelago
Exmouth
Exmouth Gulf
North West C.
Tom Price
Mt. Newman
Goldsworthy
Marble Bar
Lake Mackay
Lake Disappointment
Macdonnell Ranges
Rowley Shoals
Scott Reef
Seringapatam Reef
Ashmore Reef
Cartier I.
Hibernia Reef
Browse I.
Adele I.
Lynher Reef
Mermaid Reef
Clerke Reef
Imperieuse Reef

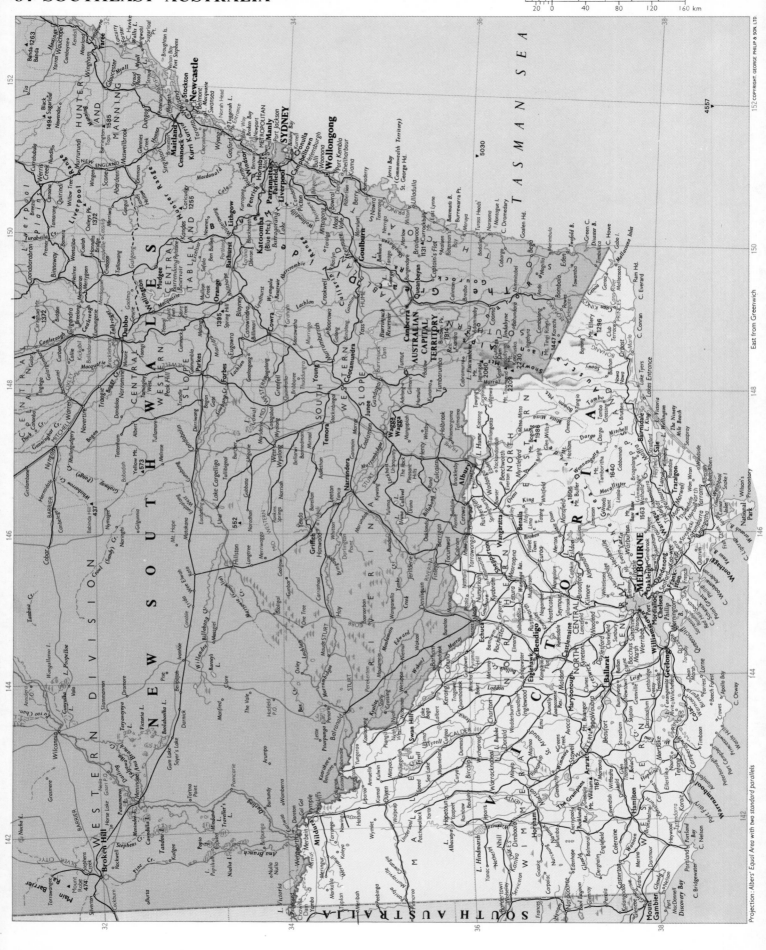

Projection: Albers' Equal Area with two standard parallels

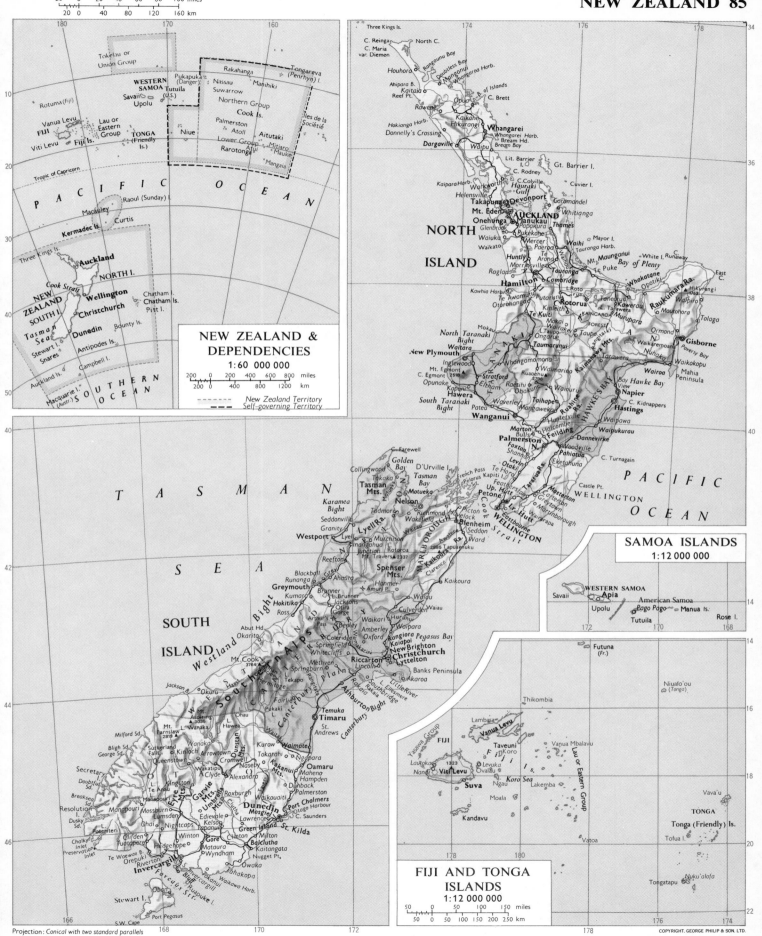

1:6 000 000

20 0 20 40 60 80 100 miles
20 0 40 80 120 160 km

NEW ZEALAND & DEPENDENCIES
1:60 000 000

200 0 200 400 600 800 miles
200 0 400 800 1200 km

— — — — New Zealand Territory
– – – – Self-governing Territory

SAMOA ISLANDS
1:12 000 000

WESTERN SAMOA
Savaii **Apia**
Upolu
American Samoa
Pago Pago **Manua Is.**
Tutuila
Rose I.

FIJI AND TONGA ISLANDS
1:12 000 000

50 0 50 100 150 miles
50 0 50 100 150 200 250 km

NORTH ISLAND

SOUTH ISLAND

TASMAN SEA

PACIFIC OCEAN

SOUTHERN OCEAN

FIJI

TONGA
Tonga (Friendly) Is.

Projection: Conical with two standard parallels

COPYRIGHT. GEORGE PHILIP & SON. LTD.

1:30 000 000

100 0 100 200 300 400 500 600 700 miles

100 0 200 400 600 800 1000 km

Puerto Rico
Milwaukee Deep 9200
Bahama Islands
Hispaniola
Tropic of Cancer
Florida
Florida Strait
C. Sable
La Habana
Cuba
Jamaica
Greater Antilles
Lesser Antilles
Caribbean Sea
Port-au-Prince
Trough
Bartlett
7680
Cayman
C. Catoche
Yucatán Strait
Yucatán Basin
Gulf of Honduras
Colombian Basin
Colombia Basin
Venezuelan Basin
G. of Venezuela
Maracaibo
Sierra de Mérida
Cordillera Oriental
Cordillera Central
Bogotá
Cordillera Occidental
Quito
Cotopaxi 5897
Chimborazo 6262
Orinoco
Napo
Ucayali
Marañón
Japurá
Purus
Juruá
Bolivian Plateau
La Paz 6550
Illimani
Titicaca
Andes
Peru Trench
Chile
Limão
Chincha Is.
Pta Parinas
Pta Aguja
Lobos Is.
C. de San Francisco
G. de Guayaquil
Tropic of Capricorn
Galapagos

New Orleans
Gulf of Mexico
Houston
Mississippi Delta
México
Rio Grande del Norte
Monterrey
Eastern Sierra Madre
Mexican Plateau
Western Sierra Madre
Puebla 5452
Orizaba
Balsas
Guadalajara
C. Corrientes
C. San Lucas
Gulf of California
California
Revilla Gigedo Is.
Clarion Fracture Zone
Guatemala
Isthmus of Tehuantepec
Gulf of Campeche
Yucatán Peninsula
Tapanatepec
Guatemala Trench 6662
3837
3700
Panama Canal
G. of Panama
G. of Darién
C. Gracias á Dios
Coco
L. Nicaragua

OCEAN
PACIFIC

1:70 000 000

ARCTIC OCEAN
GREENLAND (Denmark)
Denmark Str.
Davis Strait
Baffin Bay
Baffin Island
Ellesmere I.
Queen Elizabeth Islands
Parry Is.
Banks I.
Victoria I.
M. Clure Str.
Beaufort Sea
Barrow
Arctic Circle
ALASKA (U.S.)
Yukon
Anchorage
Juneau
Pr. Rupert
Queen Charlotte Is.
Victoria
Vancouver
Seattle Spokane
Portland
Oakland
San Francisco
Los Angeles
Revilla Gigedo (Mex.)
Baja California
CANADA
Hudson Bay
Hudson Strait
Labrador
Churchill
Gt. Bear L.
Gt. Slave L.
Mackenzie
Athabasca L.
Edmonton
Calgary
Lethbridge
Medicine Hat
Regina
Winnipeg
Saskatoon
Fraser
Montreal
Quebec
Ottawa
Toronto
Buffalo
Detroit
Pittsburgh
Cincinnati
Chicago
Milwaukee
Minneapolis
St. Paul
Omaha
Kansas City
St. Louis
Memphis
Atlanta
Washington
Baltimore
Philadelphia
New York
Boston
UNITED STATES
Denver
Salt Lake City
Snake
Platte
Missouri
Red
Dallas
Houston
Galveston
New Orleans
Mississippi
El Paso
MEXICO
Monterrey
Tampico
Veracruz
México
Guadalajara
Acapulco
Gulf of Mexico
Yucatán Strait
CUBA
Habana
Mérida
BELIZE
GUATEMALA
HONDURAS
EL SALVADOR
NICARAGUA
COSTA RICA
PANAMA
CENTRAL AMERICA
JAMAICA
Kingston
HAITI
DOM. REP.
Puerto Rico (U.S.)
BAHAMAS
Miami
Hatteras
Bermuda (Br.)
Caribbean Sea
Maracaibo
Caracas
VENEZUELA
COLOMBIA
SOUTH AMERICA
GUADELOUPE
MARTINIQUE
BARBADOS
TRINIDAD
ATLANTIC OCEAN
Tropic of Cancer
ICELAND
Liverpool
Newfoundland
Nova Scotia
Halifax
Timmins
Liverpool 1972
2611
1380
Valparaiso 5138
Yokohama 4700
Aleutians (U.S.)
Bering Sea
Bering Str.
PACIFIC OCEAN
Projection: Bonne

ft m
12 000 4000
9000 3000
6000 2000
4500 1500
3000 1000
1200 400
600 200
0 0
600 200
1200 400
3000 1000
4500 1500
6000 2000
9000 3000
12 000 4000
18 000 6000
24 000 8000

West from 90 Greenwich

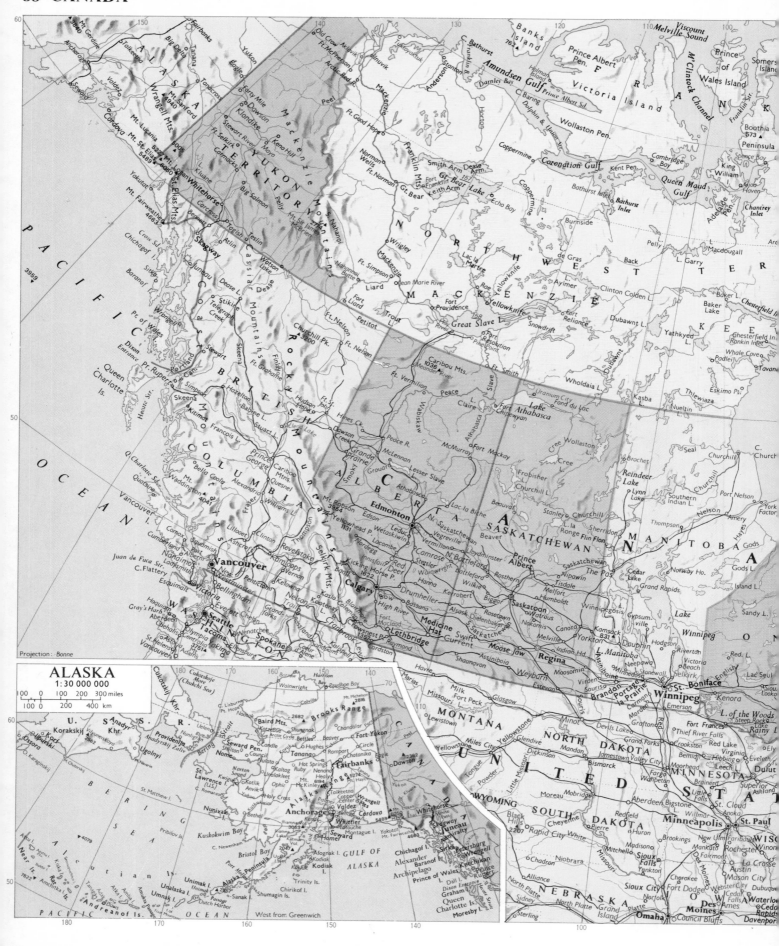

ALASKA
1:30 000 000
100 0 100 200 300 miles
100 0 200 400 km

Projection: Bonne

West from Greenwich

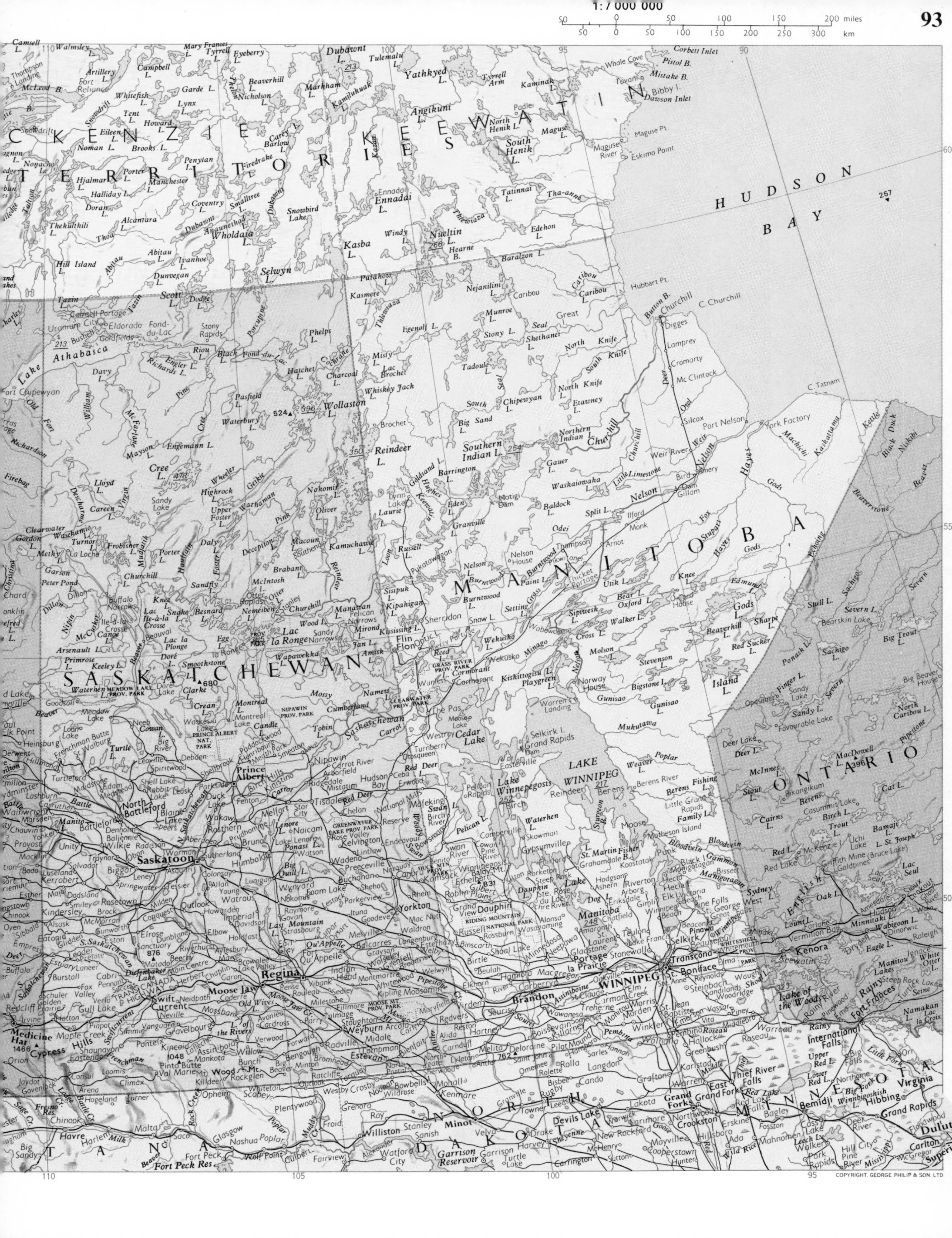

1:7 000 000

50   0   50   100   150   200 miles
50   0   50   100   150   200   250   300 km

KENZIE
TERRITORIES KEEWATIN

HUDSON
BAY

SASKATCHEWAN

MANITOBA

ONTARIO

Lake
Athabasca

Cree
L.

Reindeer
L.

Lac
la Ronge

Lake
Winnipegosis

LAKE
WINNIPEG

Cedar
Lake

Saskatoon

Prince
Albert

Regina

Moose Jaw

Swift
Current

Medicine
Hat

Brandon

WINNIPEG

Portage
la Prairie

Selkirk

Kenora

Churchill

MONTANA

NORTH DAKOTA

MINNESOTA

Duluth

Superior

110   105   100   95

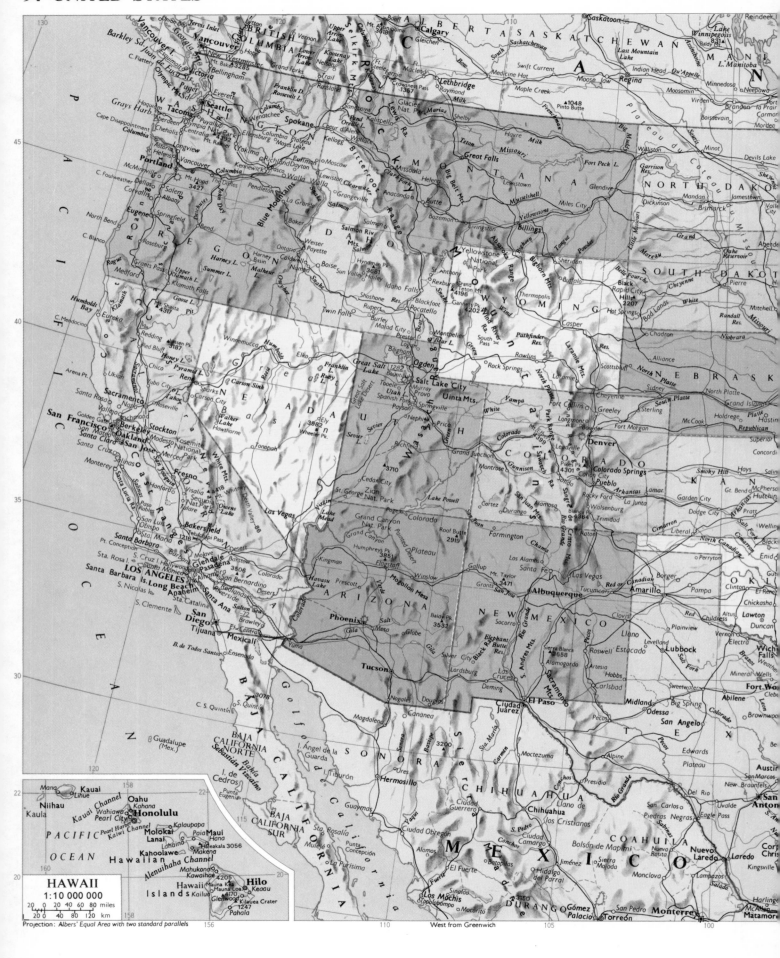

HAWAII
1:10 000 000

20 0 20 40 60 80 miles
20 0 40 80 120 km

Projection: Albers' Equal Area with two standard parallels

West from Greenwich

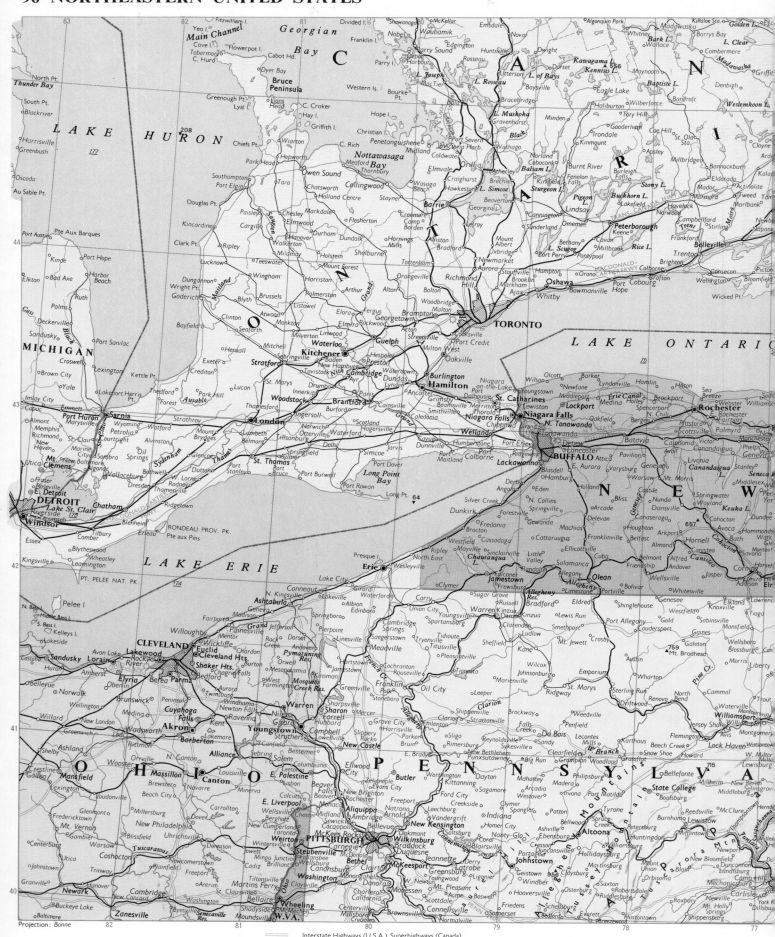

Projection: Bonne

══════ Interstate Highways (U.S.A.), Superhighways (Canada)
═ ═ ═ ═ Interstate Highways and Superhighways under Construction

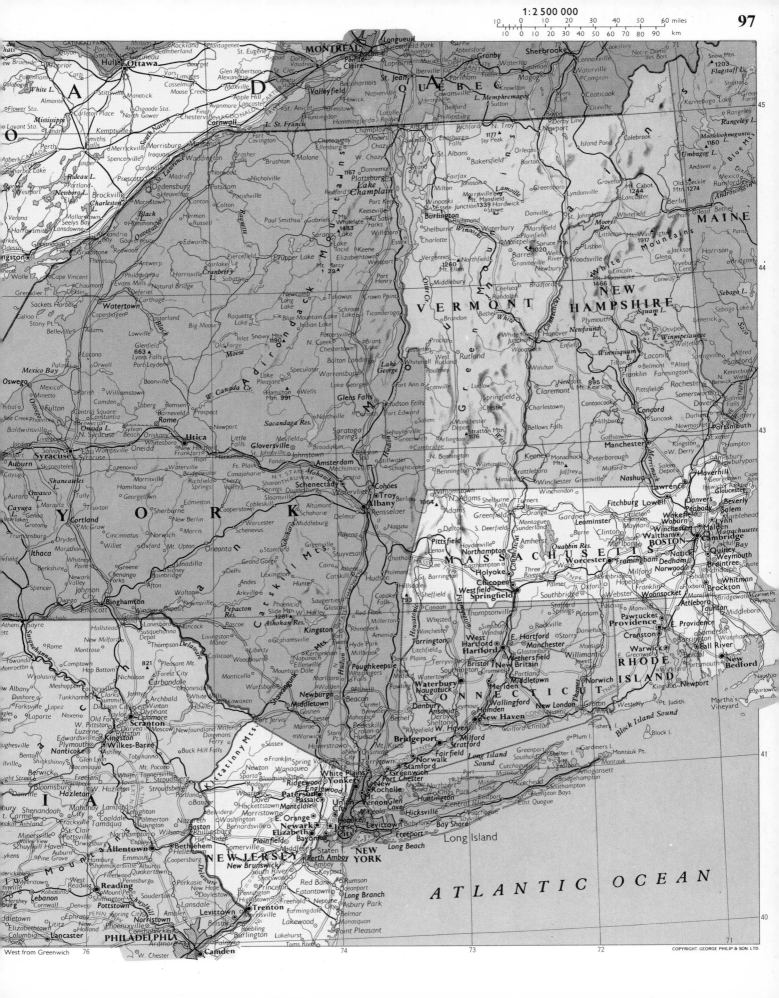

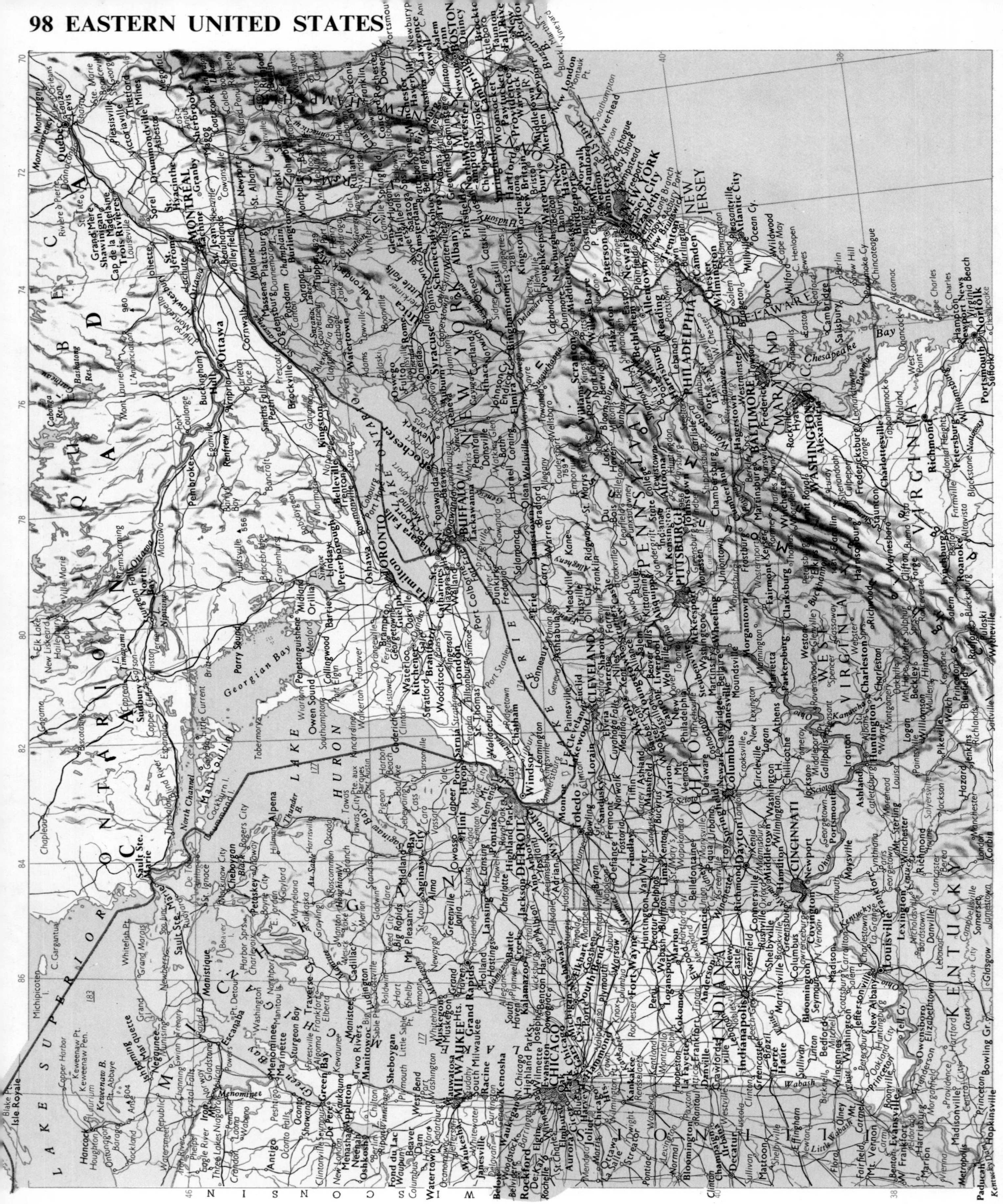
LAKE SUPERIOR
LAKE HURON
Georgian Bay
LAKE ERIE
LAKE ONTARIO
ONTARIO
QUEBEC
MICHIGAN
WISCONSIN
ILLINOIS
INDIANA
OHIO
KENTUCKY
WEST VIRGINIA
VIRGINIA
PENNSYLVANIA
NEW YORK
NEW JERSEY
DELAWARE
MARYLAND
Chesapeake Bay
MONTREAL
OTTAWA
TORONTO
DETROIT
CHICAGO
MILWAUKEE
CLEVELAND
PITTSBURGH
BUFFALO
PHILADELPHIA
BALTIMORE
WASHINGTON D.C.
CINCINNATI
NEW YORK
BOSTON

1:6 000 000

50   0   50   100 miles
50   0   50   100   150 km

COPYRIGHT GEORGE PHILIP & SON LTD.

Continuation
Eastwards
On same scale

MAINE

NEW HAMPSHIRE

ATLANTIC OCEAN

BAHAMAS

Great Abaco I.
Little Abaco I.
Hope Town
Gt. Guana Cay
Grand Cays
Grand
Bahama I.
Settlement
Freeport

NORTH CAROLINA

SOUTH CAROLINA

GEORGIA

FLORIDA

TENNESSEE

ALABAMA

MISSISSIPPI

GULF OF MEXICO

EVERGLADES NAT. PARK

Miami
Miami Beach
Ft. Lauderdale
Hollywood
West Palm Beach
Pompano
Boynton Beach
Delray Beach
Palm Beach
Ft. Pierce
Vero Beach

St. Augustine
Jacksonville
Daytona Beach
Orlando
Tampa
St. Petersburg
Clearwater
Sarasota

Savannah
Charleston

Wilmington
Raleigh

Atlanta
Columbus
Montgomery
Birmingham
Mobile
Pensacola
Tallahassee

West from Greenwich

Projection: Alber's Equal Area with two standard parallels

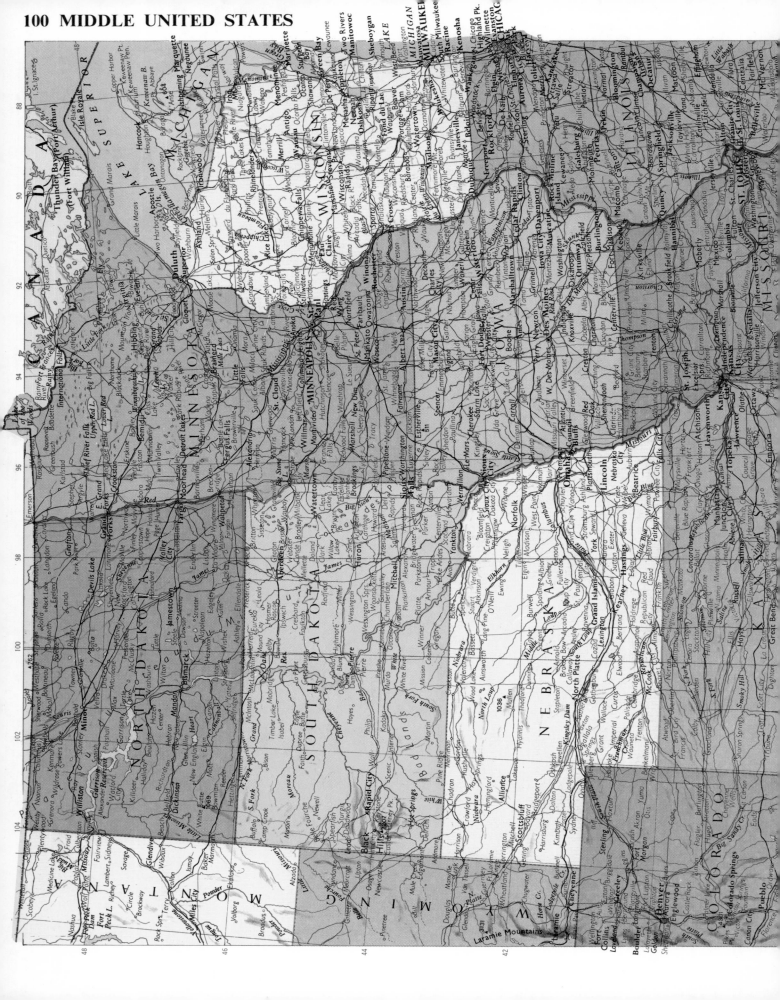

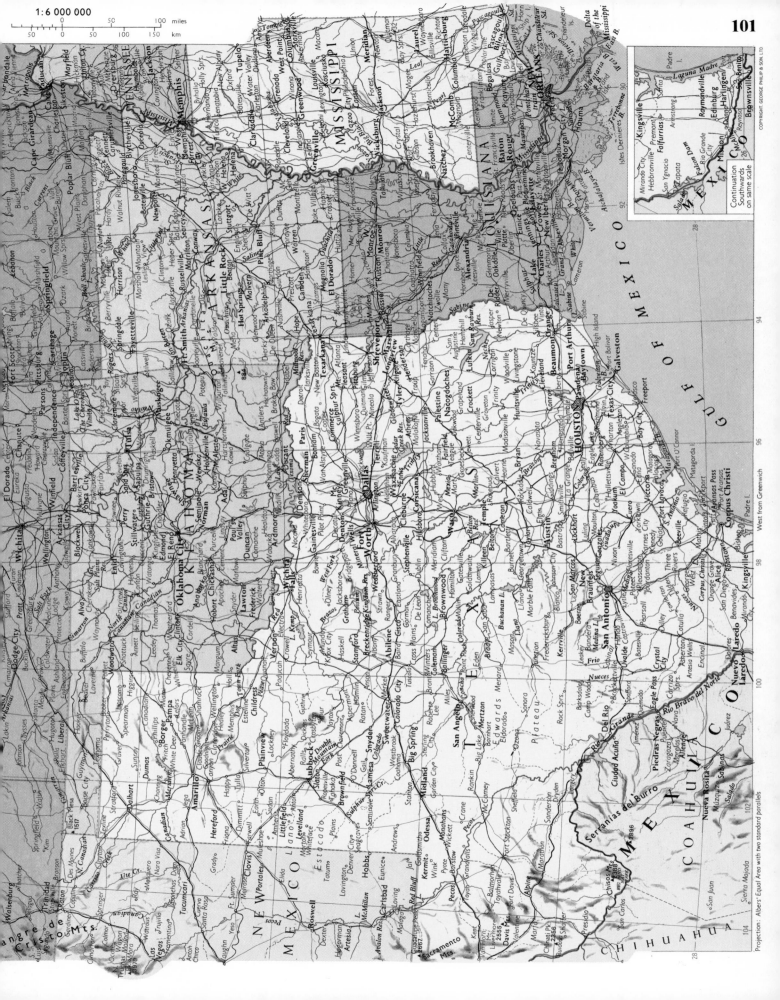

1:6 000 000

50 · 0 · 50 · 100 miles
50 · 0 · 50 · 100 · 150 km

SASKATCHEWAN

ALBERTA

BRITISH COLUMBIA

MONTANA

WYOMING

IDAHO

WASHINGTON

OREGON

NEVADA

UTAH

CALIFORNIA

Bighorn Mountains

Medicine Bow Range

Park Range

Great Falls

Helena

Butte

Billings

Bozeman

Missoula

Kalispell

Lewis Range

Cabinet Mountains

Sapphire Mts.

Clearwater Mountains

Salmon River Mountains

Bitterroot Range

Lemhi Range

Wind River Range

Uinta Mountains

GREAT SALT LAKE

Great Salt Lake Desert

Salt Lake City

Ogden

Pocatello

Idaho Falls

Blackfoot

Spokane

Coeur d'Alene

Lewiston

Pullman

Walla Walla

Pendleton

Wallowa Mts.

Blue Mountains

Boise

Nampa

Caldwell

Seattle

Tacoma

Olympia

Everett

Bellingham

Olympic Mts.

Mt. Rainier 4392

Mt. Adams 3751

Yakima

Wenatchee

Columbia

Columbia River

Snake River

Portland

Vancouver

Salem

Albany

Corvallis

Eugene

Medford

Klamath Falls

Bend

Three Sisters 3158

Mt. Hood 3427

Cascade Range

Harney Basin

Malheur L.

Owyhee

Humboldt

Shoshone Mountains

Independence Mts.

Ruby Mts.

Elko

Winnemucca

Reno

Sparks

Carson City

Lake Tahoe

Sacramento

Redding

Mt. Shasta 4317

Lassen Peak 3185

Klamath Mts.

Coast Ranges

Sierra Nevada

Great Divide Basin

South Pass

Rock Springs

Green River

Flaming Gorge Res.

Casper

Sheridan

Buffalo

Rawlins

Laramie

Fort Peck Reservoir

Fort Peck Dam

Missouri

Yellowstone

Bighorn

YELLOWSTONE NAT. PARK

GRAND TETON NAT. PARK

1:12 000 000

REFERENCE TO NUMBERS

1 Distrito Federal   5 México
2 Aguascalientes   6 Morelos
3 Guanajuato   7 Querétaro
4 Hidalgo   8 Tlaxcala

PANAMA CANAL
1:1 000 000

Projection: Bi-polar oblique Conical Orthomorphic

COPYRIGHT GEORGE PHILIP & SON, LTD.

West from Greenwich

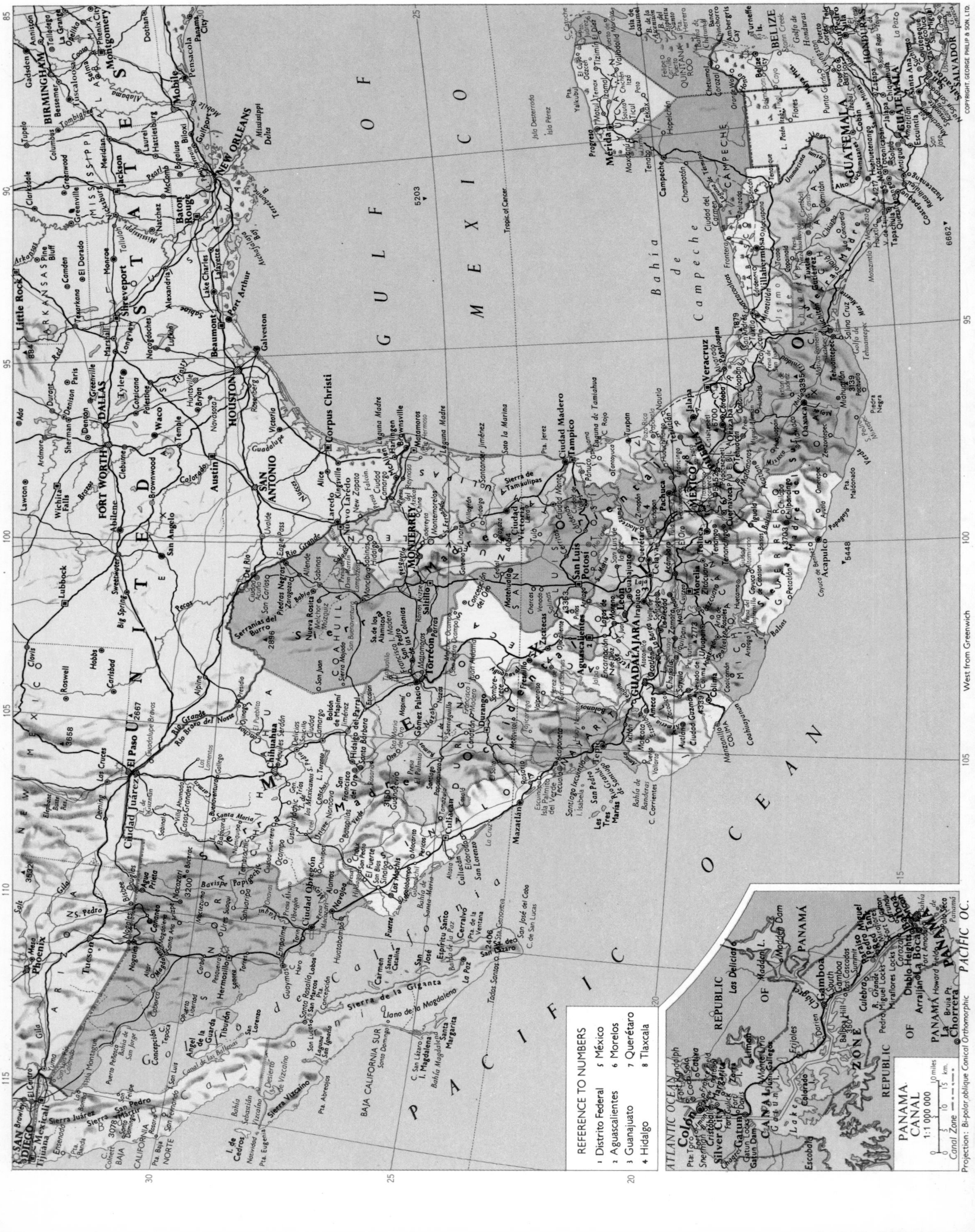

1 : 12 000 000.

100 ___ 100 ___ 200 miles
100 ___ 0 ___ 100 ___ 200 ___ 300 km

WINDWARD ISLANDS
1 : 8 000 000
0 25 50 miles
0 20 40 60 80 km

TRINIDAD & TOBAGO
1 : 8 000 000

JAMAICA
1 : 8 000 000

LEEWARD ISLANDS
1 : 8 000 000

BERMUDA
1 : 1 000 000
0 5 miles
0 8 km

GULF OF MEXICO

BAHAMAS

GREAT BAHAMA BANK

FLORIDA

MIAMI

La Habana

C U B A

Santiago de Cuba

Camagüey

JAMAICA

Kingston

Montego Bay

Cayman Islands

HAITI

Port-au-Prince

DOMINICAN REP.

Santo Domingo

HISPANIOLA

PUERTO RICO

Turks Islands

Caicos Islands

ATLANTIC OCEAN

LEEWARD ISLANDS

WINDWARD ISLANDS

LESSER ANTILLES

GREATER ANTILLES

CARIBBEAN SEA

BARBADOS

Bridgetown

TRINIDAD & TOBAGO

Port of Spain

GRENADA

St. Vincent

St. Lucia

MARTINIQUE

Fort-de-France

DOMINICA

GUADELOUPE

Antigua

Montserrat

St. Christopher

Anguilla

Barbuda

V E N E Z U E L A

CARACAS

Maracaibo

Barquisimeto

Valencia

Maturín

Ciudad Bolívar

Orinoco

C O L O M B I A

BARRANQUILLA

Cartagena

Bucaramanga

P A N A M A

Panamá

CANAL ZONE

Colón

COSTA RICA

San José

NICARAGUA

Managua

HONDURAS

Tegucigalpa

MEXICO

Isla de Cozumel

PACIFIC OCEAN

Projection: Bi-polar oblique Conical Orthomorphic

West from Greenwich

COPYRIGHT. GEORGE PHILIP & SON, LTD.

1:30 000 000

100 0 100 200 300 400 500 miles
100 0 200 400 600 800 km

Panama Canal
Sa. Nevada de Santa Marta
Barranquilla ▲5800
Maracaibo
G. of Darién
Margarita
Caracas
Tobago I.
Trinidad
5994 ▼

ATLANTIC OCEAN

Medellín
Cali
Cordillera Occidental
Cordillera Central
Cordillera Oriental
Magdalena
Bogotá
Cord. de Mérida
L. Maracaibo
Orinoco
Llanos
Meta
Guaviare
Georgetown
Guiana Highlands
2810 Roraima
Sierra Pacaraima
C. Orange
Serra de Tumucumaque
Essequibo
Courantyne

C. de San Francisco
Quito
Cotopaxi 5897
Chimborazo 6267
Guayaquil
G. of Guayaquil
Pta. Pariñas
Pta. Aguja
Lobos Is.
Caquetá
Putumayo
Napo
Marañón
Ucayali
Japurá
Negro
Branco
Amazon
Manaus
Equator
Pará
Marajó I.
Belém
Fortaleza
São Roque

A n d e s

S e l v a s

Juruá
Purus
Madeira
Roosevelt
Aripuaná
Tapajós
Xingu
Araguaia
Tocantins

Huascarán 6768
Madre de Dios
Guaporé
Plateau of Mato Grosso
São Francisco
Parnaíba
Plateau of Borborema
Recife
C. Branco

Lima
Chincha Is.
L. Titicaca
Bolivian Plateau
Ancohuma & Illampu 6550
La Paz
L. Poopó
Mamoré
Guaporé
Brasília
Brazilian Highlands
Salvador

P A C I F I C   O C E A N

Chile
Peru
Trench

Tropic of Capricorn
S. Félix
S. Ambrosio
8050
Atacama Desert
Ojos del Salado 6863
Tucumán
Salado
Salinas Grandes
Pilcomayo
Paraguay
Gran Chaco
Asunción
Paraná
Iguaçu Falls
Uruguay
São Paulo
Belo Horizonte
Serra da Mantiqueira
2890 Pico da Bandeira
C. Frio
Rio de Janeiro
Abrolhos Bank

Arch. de Juan Fernández
Córdoba
Sierra de Córdoba
L. Mar Chiquita
Rosario
Entre Ríos
Paraná
Pôrto Alegre
Lagoa dos Patos
Serra do Mar

Aconcagua 6960
Uspallata Pass
Valparaíso
Santiago
Buenos Aires
La Plata
Montevideo
Río de la Plata
Pta. Mogotes

P a m p a s

Colorado
Negro
Bahía Blanca

Chile Rise
Chiloé I.
Chubut
G. of San Matías
Valdés Peninsula
Argentine Basin

SOUTH ATLANTIC OCEAN

Chonos Archipelago
Taitao Peninsula
4058 S. Valentín
G. of Peñas
G. of San Jorge

P a t a g o n i a

6212

Wellington I.
Madre de Dios I.
Magellan's Strait
Santa Inés I.
Tierra del Fuego
Cockburn Chan.
Beagle Chan.
C. Horn

West Falkland
Magellan's Strait
Falkland Islands
East Falkland
Staten I.

West from Greenwich
COPYRIGHT. GEORGE PHILIP & SON. LTD.

m 6000 4000 3000 2000 1000 400 200 0 200 2000 4000 6000 8000 m
ft 18 000 12 000 9000 6000 3000 1200 600 0 600 6000 12 000 18 000 24 000 ft

1:30 000 000

100   0   100   200   300   400   500 miles
100   0   200   400   600   800 km

NORTH ATLANTIC OCEAN

COSTA RICA
San José
CANAL ZONE (U.S.)
PANAMA
Golfo de Panamá
Golfo de Darién

Barranquilla
Cartagena
Maracaibo
Cabimas
Ciénaga
Monteria
Cúcuta
San Cristóbal
Bucaramanga
Medellín
Manizales
Pereira
Ibagué
Buenaventura
Bogotá
Cali
Popayán
Pasto

COLOMBIA

Punto Fijo
Isla de Margarita
Valencia
Caracas
Cumaná
Port of Spain
Tobago
TRINIDAD AND TOBAGO
Trinidad
Maturin
Barquisimeto
Mérida
San Fernando
Orinoco
Ciudad Guayana
Ciudad Bolívar

VENEZUELA

Pto. Ayacucho
Orinoco

Georgetown
New Amsterdam
Paramaribo
Cayenne
C. Orange

GUYANA   **SURINAM**   **FRENCH GUIANA**

Esequibo
Branco

Equator

Macapá
Ilha de Marajó
Belém (Pará)

Napo
Putumayo
Caquetá
Japurá
Amazonas (Amazon)
Santarem

Quito
ECUADOR
Riobamba
Cuenca
Guayaquil
G. de Guayaquil
Pta. Aguja

Iquitos
Benjamim Constant
Marañón
Juruá
Purus
Manicoré
Madeira
Tapajós
Xingu
Tocantins
Araguaia

São Luis
Bacabal
Teresina

Fortaleza (Ceara)
C. de São Roque
Natal
João Pessoa (Paraíba)
Recife (Pernambuco)
Maceió

Chiclayo
Trujillo
Cruzeiro do Sul
Pôrto Velho
Rio Branco
Guajará-Mirim
Madre de Dios

PERU

B R A Z I L

Parnaíba
São Francisco

Callao
Lima
Huancayo
Ayacucho
Cuzco
Juliaca
Tefé
Ucayali

Aracaju
Salvador (Bahía)

Pucallpa

L. Titicaca
Arequipa
La Paz
Cochabamba
BOLIVIA
Oruro
Sucre
Santa Cruz
Guaporé
Mamoré

Cuiabá
Brasília
Goiânia
Jataí
Montes Claros
Gov. Valadares

Mollendo
Tacna
Arica
Iquique

Uyuni
Tarija
Corumbá
Campo Grande
Uberaba
Ribeirão Prêto
Belo Horizonte
Vitória

Tropic of Capricorn
Antofagasta
Salta

Pedro Juan Caballero
PARAGUAY
Asunción
Paraná
Pres. Prudente
Bauru
Londrina
Campinas
Campos
Juiz de Fora
Niterój
RIO DE JANEIRO
SÃO PAULO
Santos

San Miguel de Tucumán
Pilcomayo

Isla San Félix (Chile)
Isla San Ambrosio (Chile)

P A C I F I C   O C E A N

Resistencia
Corrientes
Uruguay
Ponta Grossa
Curitiba
Florianópolis

Santiago del Estero
Salado
Santa Maria
Pôrto Alegre

Arch. de Juan Fernández (Chile)

ARGENTINA
Córdoba
Coquimbo
Santa Fe
Paraná
Rosario
URUGUAY
Uruaiana
Lagoa dos Patos
Pelotas

Honolulu
Yokohama 9339

Mendoza
Mercedes
Santa Rosa

Valparaíso
Santiago
San Rafael
Talca
San Luis
BUENOS AIRES
Río de la Plata
Montevideo
Tandil
Mar del Plata

C H I L E

Concepción
Bahía Blanca
Colorado
Negro
Viedma

Valdivia
Zapala

SOUTH ATLANTIC OCEAN

Puerto Montt
Isla de Chiloé
San Carlos de Bariloche
Trelew
Peninsula Valdés
Chubut

Archipiélago de los Chonos
Golfo Comodoro Rivadavia
San Jorge
G. de Penas

Montevideo — Cape Town 3649

Buenos Aires — Adelaide 8885, Melbourne 9099, Sydney 9564

Santa Cruz
I. Wellington
Rio Gallegos
Estrecho de Magallanes
Strait of Magellan
Punta Arenas
Isla Grande de Tierra del Fuego

FALKLAND ISLANDS (ISLAS MALVINAS) (U.K.)
West Falkland
Stanley
East Falkland

Punta Arenas — Cape Town 4036

Cabo de Hornos (Cape Horn)

West from Greenwich

Projection: Lambert's Equivalent Azimuthal

COPYRIGHT. GEORGE PHILIP & SON. LTD.

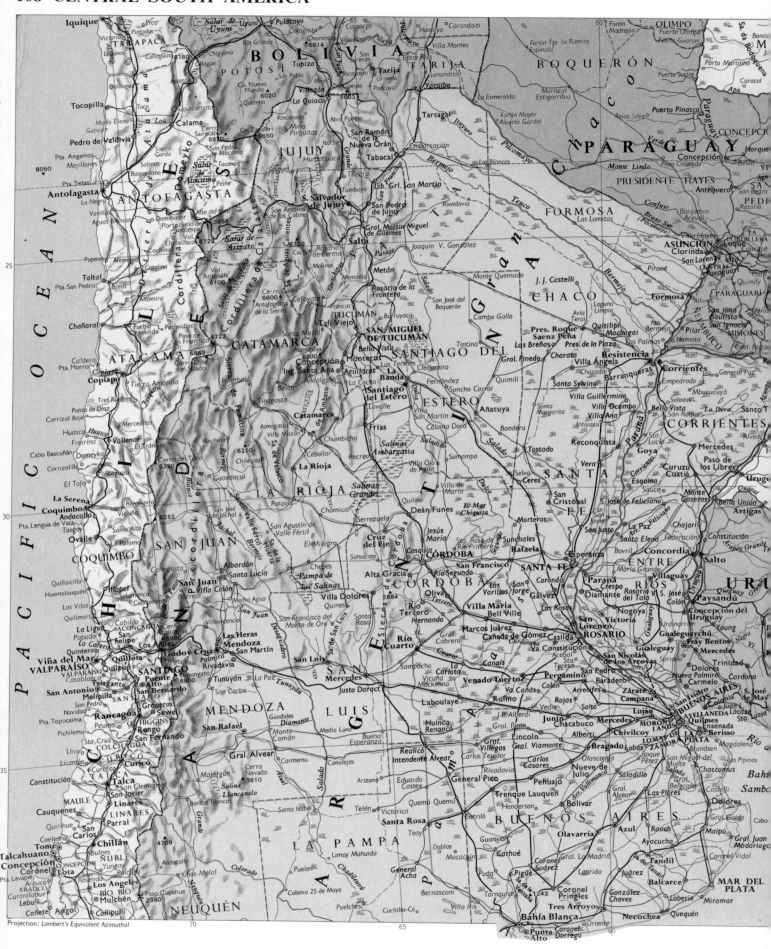

Projection: Lambert's Equivalent Azimuthal

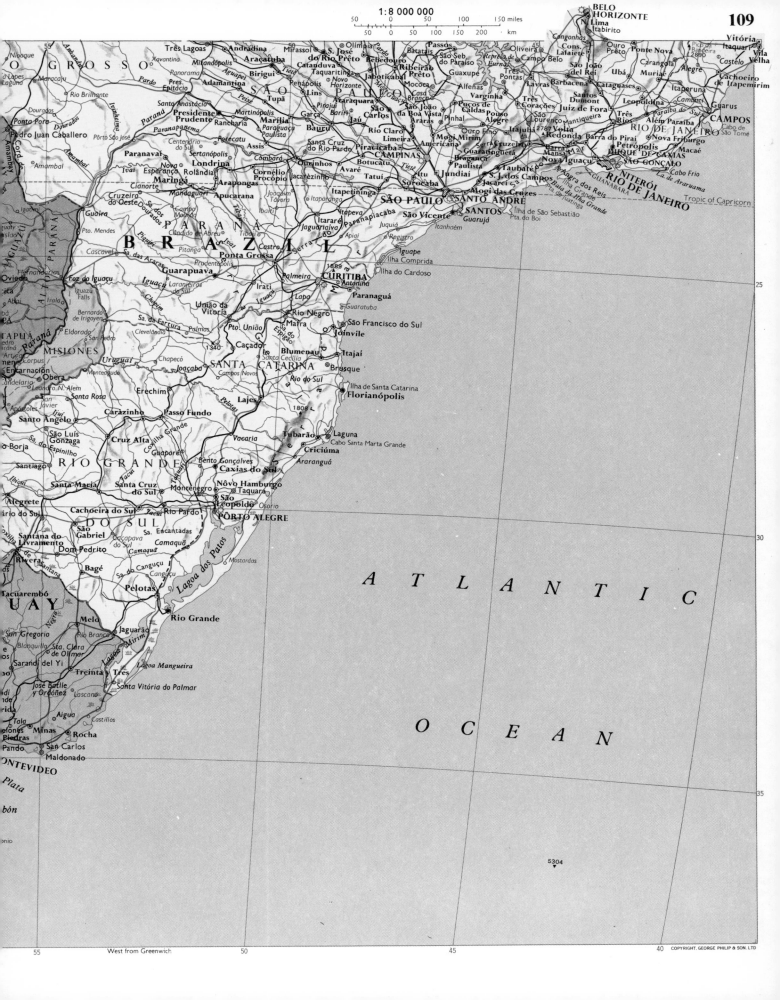

1:8 000 000

50   0   50   100   150 miles

50 0 50 100 150 200 km

BELO
HORIZONTE
Lima
Itabirito
Vitória
Iof GROSSO

MATO GROSSO

BRAZIL

PARANÁ

SÃO PAULO

SANTA CATARINA

RIO GRANDE

DO SUL

RIO DE JANEIRO

Tropic of Capricorn

SÃO PAULO

CURITIBA

Florianópolis

PÔRTO ALEGRE

MISIONES

UAY

ATLANTIC

OCEAN

5304

55   West from Greenwich   50   45   40 COPYRIGHT. GEORGE PHILIP & SON. LTD

25

30

35

1:16 000 000

100   50   0   100   200   300 miles
100   0   100   200   300   400 km

PARAGUAY

BRASIL

PARANÁ

SANTA CATARINA

RIO DE JANEIRO
SÃO PAULO
Santos

Curitiba
Ponta Grossa
Paranaguá
São Francisco do Sul
Joinvile
Blumenau
Florianópolis

RIO GRANDE DO SUL
PÔRTO ALEGRE
Pelotas
Rio Grande
Lagoa dos Patos

Tropic of Capricorn

Antofagasta

San Miguel de Tucumán
Salta
Santiago del Estero
Catamarca
La Rioja

Asunción
Villarrica
Formosa
Resistencia
Corrientes
Posadas
Encarnación

ARGENTINA

Córdoba
Santa Fe
Paraná
Rosario
San Juan
Mendoza
San Luis
Río Cuarto

URUGUAY
MONTEVIDEO
Paysandú
Salto

Valparaíso
SANTIAGO
San Antonio
Rancagua
San Fernando
Talca

BUENOS AIRES
La Plata
Avellaneda

Mar del Plata
Bahía Blanca
Necochea

Talcahuano
Concepción
Los Ángeles
Temuco
Valdivia

CHILE

Osorno
Pto. Varas
Puerto Montt
Ancud
I. de Chiloé

Neuquén

Golfo San Matías
Viedma
Península Valdés
Golfo Nuevo
Trelew
Rawson

Archipiélago de los Chonos

Golfo San Jorge
Comodoro Rivadavia

SOUTH ATLANTIC OCEAN

I. Wellington

FALKLAND ISLANDS
(ISLAS MALVINAS) (Br.)
West Falkland   Stanley
East Falkland
Weddell I.

Río Gallegos

Estrecho de Magallanes (Magellan's Str.)
Punta Arenas

Tierra del Fuego

South Georgia (Br.)

Cabo de Hornos (C. Horn)

Projection: Sanson-Flamsteed's Sinusoidal

60 West from Greenwich

Index to the Maps

The number in bold type which precedes each name in the index refers to the number of the page where that feature or place will be found.

The geographical co-ordinates which follow the place name are sometimes only approximate but are close enough for the place name to be located.

An open square □ signifies that the name refers to an administrative division of a country while a solid square ■ follows the name of a country.

Rivers have been indexed to their mouth or to their confluence.

The alphabetical order of names composed of two or more words is governed primarily by the first word and then by the second. This is an example of the rule:

> West Wyalong
> West Yorkshire
> Westbrook
> Westbury
> Westerland
> Western Australia

Names composed of a proper name (Gibraltar) and a description (Strait of) are positioned alphabetically by the proper name. All river names are followed by R. If the same word occurs in the name of a town and a geographical feature, the town name is listed first followed by the name or names of the geographical features.

Names beginning with M', Mc are all indexed as if they were spelled Mac.

If the same place name occurs two or more times in the index and all are in the same country, each is followed by the name of the administrative subdivision in which it is located. The names are placed in the alphabetical order of the subdivisions. For example:

> Stour, R., Dorset
> Stour, R., Hereford and Worcester
> Stour, R., Kent
> Stour, R., Suffolk

If the same place name occurs twice or more in the index and the places are in different countries they will be followed by the country names and the latter in alphabetical order.

> Sheffield, U.K.
> Sheffield, U.S.A.

If there is a mixture of these situations, the primary order is fixed by the alphabetical sequence of the countries and the secondary order by that of the country subdivisions. In the latter case the country names are omitted.

> Rochester, U.K.
> Rochester, Minn.   (U.S.A.) are omitted from
> Rochester, N.H.   (U.S.A.) the index
> Rochester, N.Y.   (U.S.A.)
> Rochester, Pa.   (U.S.A.)

The following is a list of abbreviations used in the index

A.S.S.R. – *Autonomous Soviet Socialist Republic*
Ala. – *Alabama*
Alas. – *Alaska*
Ang. – *Angola*
Arch. – *Archipelago*
Arg. – *Argentina*
Ariz. – *Arizona*
Ark. – *Arkansas*
B. – *Baie, Bahía, Bay, Boca, Bucht, Bugt*
B.C. – *British Columbia*
Br. – *British*
C. – *Cabo, Cap, Cape*
C.A.R. – *Central African Republic*
C. Prov. – *Cape Province*
Calif. – *California*
Chan. – *Channel*
Col. – *Colombia*
Colo. – *Colorado*
Conn. – *Connecticut*
Cord. – *Cordillera*
D.C. – *District of Columbia*
Del. – *Delaware*
Dep. – *Dependency*
Des. – *Desert*
Dist. – *District*
Dom. Rep. – *Dominican Republic*
E. – *East*
Eng. – *England*

Fd. – *Fjord*
Fed. – *Federal, Federation*
Fla. – *Florida*
Fr. – *France, French*
G. – *Golfe, Golfo, Gulf, Guba*
Ga. – *Georgia*
Gt. – *Great*
Hants. – *Hampshire*
Hd. – *Head*
Hts. – *Heights*
I.(s) – *Ile, Ilha, Insel, Isla, Island (s)*
Id. – *Idaho*
Ill. – *Illinois*
Ind. – *Indiana*
J. – *Jezero (L.)*
K. – *Kap, Kapp*
Kans. – *Kansas*
Kep. – *Kepulauan (I.)*
Kól. – *Kólpos (B.)*
Ky. – *Kentucky*
L. – *Lac, Lacul, Lago, Lagoa, Lake, Limni, Loch, Lough*
La. – *Louisana*
Ld. – *Land*
Mad. P. – *Madhya Pradesh*
Man. – *Manitoba*
Mass. – *Massachusetts*
Md. – *Maryland*
Me. – *Maine*
Mich. – *Michigan*
Minn. – *Minnesota*

Miss. – *Mississippi*
Mo. – *Missouri*
Mont. – *Montana*
Mt.(s) – *Mont, Monte, Monti, Muntii, Montaña, Mountain (s)*
Mys. – *Mysore*
N. – *North, Northern*
N.B. – *New Brunswick*
N.C. – *North Carolina*
N.D. – *North Dakota*
N.H. – *New Hampshire*
N. Ire. – *Northern Ireland*
N.J. – *New Jersey*
N. Mex. – *New Mexico*
N.S.W. – *New South Wales*
N.Y. – *New York*
N.Z. – *New Zealand*
Nat. Park – *National Park*
Nebr. – *Nebraska*
Neth. – *Netherlands*
Nev. – *Nevada*
Newf. – *Newfoundland*
Nic. – *Nicaragua*
Nig. – *Nigeria*
O.F.S. – *Orange Free State*
Okla. – *Oklahoma*
Ont. – *Ontario*
Oreg. – *Oregon*
Os. – *Ostrov (I.)*
Oz – *Ozero (L.)*
P. – *Pass, Passo, Pasul*

P.N.G. – *Papua New Guinea*
Pa. – *Pennsylvania*
Pak. – *Pakistan*
Pass. – *Passage*
Pen. – *Peninsula*
Pk. – *Peak*
Plat. – *Plateau*
Pol. – *Poluostrov*
Port. – *Portugal, Portuguese*
Prov. – *Province, Provincial*
Pt. – *Point*
Pta. – *Ponta, Punta*
Pte. – *Pointe*
Que. – *Quebec*
Queens. – *Queensland*
R. – *Rio, River*
R.S.F.S.R. – *Russian Soviet Federal Socialist Republic*
Ra.(s) – *Range(s)*
Reg. – *Region*
Rep. – *Republic*
Res. – *Reserve, Reservoir*
S. – *South*
S. Africa – *South Africa*
S.C. – *S. Carolina*
S.D. – *South Dakota*
S. Leone – *Sierra Leone*
S.S.R. – *Soviet Socialist Republic*
Sa. – *Serra, Sierra*
Sask. – *Saskatchewan*
Scot. – *Scotland*

Sd. – *Sound*
Sp. – *Spain, Spanish*
St. – *Saint*
Str. – *Strait, Stretto*
Switz. – *Switzerland*
Tanz. – *Tanzania*
Tas. – *Tasmania*
Tenn. – *Tennessee*
Terr. – *Territory*
Tex. – *Texas*
U.K. – *United Kingdom*
U.S.A. – *United States of America*
U.S.S.R. – *Union of Soviet Socialist Republics*
Ut. P. – *Uttar Pradesh*
Va. – *Virginia*
Vdkhr. – *Vodokhranilishche (Res.)*
Ven. – *Venezuela*
Vic. – *Victoria*
Vt. – *Vermont*
W. – *West*
W. Va. – *West Virginia*
Wis. – *Wisconsin*
Wyo. – *Wyoming*
Yorks. – *Yorkshire*
Yug. – *Yugoslavia*

Aachen Albany, R.

A

24 Aachen 50 47N 6 4 E
73 A'Âlâ en Nîl □ 8 50N 29 55 E
25 Aalen 48 49N 10 6 E
16 Aalsmeer 52 17N 4 43 E
16 Aalst 50 56N 4 2 E
16 Aalten 51 56N 6 35 E
25 Aarau 47 23N 8 4 E
25 Aare, R. 47 37N 8 13 E
25 Aargau □ 47 26N 8 10 E
45 Aarhus □ 56 15N 10 15 E
16 Aarschot 50 59N 4 49 E
72 Aba 5 10N 7 19 E
55 Abā Saud 17 15N 43 55 E
56 Abadan 30 22N 48 20 E
30 Abadin 43 21N 7 29W
109 Abai 25 58S 55 54W
51 Abakan 53 40N 91 10 E
32 Abanilla 38 12N 1 3W
57 Abarqu 31 10N 53 20 E
54 Abasan 31 19N 34 21 E
66 Abashiri 44 0N 144 15 E
66 Abashiri-Wan, G. 44 0N 144 30 E
50 Abay 49 38N 72 53 E
74 Abaya, L. 6 30N 37 50 E
50 Abaza 52 39N 90 6 E
54 Abba Hillēl 31 42N 34 38 E
19 Abbeville, Fr. 50 6N 1 49 E
99 Abbeville, U.S.A. 30 0N 92 7W
36 Abbiategrasso 45 23N 8 55 E
58 Abbottabad 34 10N 73 15 E
73 Abéché 13 50N 20 35 E
30 Abejar 41 48N 2 47W
45 Åbenrå 55 3N 9 25 E
72 Abeokuta 7 3N 3 19 E
13 Aberayron 52 15N 4 16W
13 Aberdare 51 43N 3 27W
84 Aberdeen, Australia 32 9S 150 56 E
14 Aberdeen, U.K. 57 9N 2 6W
102 Aberdeen, Id. 42 57N 112 50W
99 Aberdeen, Miss. 33 49N 88 13W
100 Aberdeen, S.D. 45 28N 98 29W
102 Aberdeen, Wash. 46 59N 123 50W
13 Aberdovey 52 33N 4 3W
14 Aberfeldy 56 37N 3 50W
30 Abergaria-a-Velha 40 41N 8 32W
13 Abergavenny 51 49N 3 1W
13 Aberystwyth 52 25N 4 6W
55 Abhā 18 0N 42 34 E
72 Abidjan 5 26N 3 58W
100 Abilene, Kans. 39 0N 97 16W
101 Abilene, Tex. 32 22N 99 40W
13 Abingdon 51 40N 1 17W
49 Abkhaz A.S.S.R. 43 0N 41 0 E
51 Abkit 64 10N 157 10 E
60 Abohar 30 10N 74 10 E
72 Abomey 7 10N 2 5 E
74 Abong Mbang 4 0N 13 8 E
27 Abony 47 12N 20 3 E
73 Abou Deïa 11 20N 19 20 E
14 Aboyne 57 4N 2 48W
56 Abqaiq 26 0N 49 45 E
31 Abrantes 39 24N 8 7W
30 Abraveses 40 41N 7 55 E
19 Abreschviller 48 39N 7 6 E
37 Abruzzi □ 42 15N 14 0 E
102 Absaroka Ra. 44 40N 110 0W
56 Abū al Khasib 30 25N 48 0 E
55 Abu Arish 16 53N 42 48 E
73 Abu Dis 19 12N 33 38 E
54 Abū Ghōsh 31 48N 35 6 E
73 Abu Hamed 19 32N 33 13 E
73 Abu Tig 27 4N 31 15 E
73 Abū Zabad 12 25N 29 10 E
57 Abū Zabī 24 28N 54 36 E
73 Abyad, Gebel Reg. 17 30N 28 0 E
104 Acajutla 13 36N 89 50W
104 Acámbaro 20 0N 100 40W
104 Acaponeta 22 30N 105 20W
104 Acapulco 16 51N 99 56W
111 Acará 1 57S 48 11W
104 Acatlan 18 10N 98 3W
104 Acayucan 17 59N 94 58W
36 Accéglio 44 28N 6 59 E
72 Accra 5 35N 0 6W
12 Accrington 53 46N 2 22W
64 Aceh □ 4 50N 96 0 E
39 Acerra 40 57N 14 22 E
31 Aceuchal 38 39N 6 30W
60 Achalpur 21 22N 77 32 E
26 Achenkirch 47 32N 11 45 E
26 Achensee, L. 47 26N 11 45 E
60 Acher 23 10N 72 32 E
15 Achill 53 56N 9 55W
15 Achill, I. 53 58N 10 5W
51 Achinsk 56 20N 90 20 E
39 Acireale 37 37N 15 9 E
105 Acklins I. 22 30N 74 0W
92 Acme 51 33N 113 30W
108 Aconcagua, Cerro, Mt. 32 39S 70 0W
108 Aconcagua □ 32 15S 70 30W
39 Acquaviva delle Fonti 40 53N 16 50 E
36 Acqui 44 40N 8 28 E
110 Acre □ 9 1S 71 0W
39 Acri 39 29N 16 23 E
27 Acs 47 42N 18 0 E
55 Ad Dam 20 33N 44 45 E
56 Ad Dammam 26 20N 50 5 E
56 Ad Khālis 33 40N 44 55 E
101 Ada, U.S.A. 34 50N 96 45W
40 Ada, Yug. 45 49N 20 9 E
30 Adaja, R. 41 32N 4 52W
55 Adale 2 58N 46 27 E
109 Adamantina 21 42S 51 4W
73 Adamaoua, Massif de l' 7 20N 12 20 E
36 Adamello, Mt. 46 10N 10 34 E
97 Adams, Mass. 42 38N 73 8W
100 Adams, Wis. 43 59N 89 50W
102 Adams, Mt. 46 10N 121 28W
62 Adam's Bridge 9 15N 79 40 E
62 Adam's Pk. 6 55N 80 45 E
31 Adamuz 38 2N 4 32W
56 Adana 37 0N 35 16 E
30 Adanero 40 56N 4 36W
65 Adaut 8 8S 131 7 E
36 Adda, R. 45 8N 9 53 E
73 Addis Ababa= Addis Abeba 9 2N 38 42 E
73 Addis Abeba 9 2N 38 42 E
81 Adelaide 34 52S 138 30 E
5 Adelaide I. 67 15S 68 30W
88 Adelaide Pen. 67 40N 98 0W
82 Adelaide River 13 15S 131 7 E
32 Ademuz 40 5N 1 13W
55 Aden= Al 'Adan 12 50N 45 0 E
55 Aden, G. of 13 0N 50 0 E
36 Adige, R. 45 10N 12 20 E
62 Adilabad 19 33N 78 35 E
62 Adirampattinam 10 28N 79 20 E
97 Adirondack Mts. 44 0N 74 15W
41 Adjud 46 7N 27 10 E
82 Admiralty, G. 14 20S 125 55 E
102 Admiralty Inlet 48 0N 122 40W
92 Admiralty I. 57 50N 134 30W
76 Admiralty Is. 2 0S 147 0 E
62 Adoni 15 33N 77 18 E
27 Adony 47 6N 18 52 E
20 Adour, R. 43 32N 1 32W
61 Adra, India 23 30N 86 42 E
33 Adra, Sp. 36 43N 3 3W
39 Adrano 37 40N 14 19 E
72 Adrar des Iforas, Mts. 19 40N 1 40 E
37 Ádria 45 4N 12 3 E
98 Adrian 41 55N 84 0W
62 Adur 9 8N 76 40 E
49 Adzhar A.S.S.R. 42 0N 42 0 E
43 Ægean Sea 37 0N 25 0 E
67 Aerhtai Shan, Mts. 48 0N 90 0 E
45 Ærø, I. 54 53N 10 20 E
45 Ærøsköbing 54 53N 10 20 E
57 Afghanistan ■ 33 0N 65 0 E
55 Afgoi 2 7N 44 59 E
39 Afragola 40 54N 14 15 E
71 Africa 5 0N 20 0 E
111 Afuá 0 15S 50 10W
54 Afula 32 37N 35 17 E
56 Afyon 38 20N 30 15 E
72 Agadez 16 58N 7 59 E
72 Agadir 30 28N 9 25W
61 Agapa 71 27N 89 15 E
61 Agartala 23 50N 91 23 E
41 Agăş 46 28N 26 15 E
62 Agashi 19 32N 72 47 E
65 Agats 5 34S 138 5 E
72 Agboville 5 55N 4 15W
20 Agde 43 19N 3 28 E
20 Agen 44 12N 0 38 E
45 Agger 56 47N 8 13 E
39 Agira 37 40N 14 30 E
20 Agly, R. 42 47N 3 2 E
83 Agnew 28 1S 120 30 E
20 Agout, R. 43 47N 1 41 E
60 Agra 27 17N 77 58 E
32 Agreda 41 51N 1 55W
39 Agrigento 37 19N 13 33 E
43 Agrinion 38 37N 21 27 E
39 Agrópoli 40 23N 14 59 E
111 Agua Clara 20 25S 52 45W
104 Agua Prieta 31 20N 109 32W
110 Aguadas 5 40N 75 38W
105 Aguadilla 18 27N 67 10W
91 Aguanish 50 14N 62 2W
104 Aguascalientes 22 0N 102 12W
104 Aguascalientes □ 22 0N 102 20W
30 Agueda 40 34N 8 27W
31 Aguilar 37 31N 4 40W
30 Aguilar de Campóo 42 47N 4 15W
108 Aguilares 27 26S 65 35W
33 Aguilas 37 23N 1 35W
75 Agulhas, K. 34 52S 20 0 E
54 Agur 31 42N 34 55 E
72 Ahaggar, Reg. 23 0N 6 30 E
85 Ahaura 42 20S 171 32 E
24 Ahaus 52 4N 7 1 E
24 Ahlen 51 45N 7 52 E
60 Ahmadabad 23 0N 72 40 E
62 Ahmadnagar 19 7N 74 46 E
60 Ahmadpur 29 12N 71 10 E
24 Ahrensbök 54 0N 10 34 E
104 Ahuachapán 13 54N 89 52W
56 Ahvāz 31 20N 48 40 E
47 Ahvenanmaa= Åland, I. 60 15N 20 0 E
55 Ahwar 13 31N 46 42 E
57 Aibaq 36 15N 68 5 E
66 Aichi □ 35 0N 137 15 E
39 Aidone 37 26N 14 26 E
19 Aignay-le-Duc 47 40N 4 43 E
109 Aigua 34 12S 54 45W
20 Aigueperse 46 3N 3 13 E
21 Aigues-Mortes 43 35N 4 2 E
21 Aigues-Mortes, G. d' 43 31N 4 3 E
20 Aiguillon 44 18N 0 21 E
68 Aihun 49 55N 127 30 E
59 Aijal 23 40N 92 44 E
99 Aiken 33 44N 81 50W
14 Ailsa Craig, I. 55 15N 5 7W
51 Aim 59 0N 133 55 E
111 Aimorés 19 30S 41 4W
21 Ain □ 46 5N 5 20 E
72 Aïn Beida 35 50N 7 35 E
56 Ain Dār 25 55N 49 10 E
55 Ainabo 9 0N 46 25 E
43 Aínos Óros 38 10N 20 35 E
72 Aïr 18 0N 8 0 E
14 Airdrie 55 53N 3 57W
20 Aire, Landes 43 40N 0 20W
19 Aire, Pas-de-Calais 50 37N 2 22 E
19 Aire, R., Fr. 49 19N 4 49 E
12 Aire, R., U.K. 53 44N 0 44W
20 Airvault 46 50N 0 8W
19 Aisne, R. 49 26N 2 50 E
19 Aisne □ 49 42N 3 40 E
33 Aitana, Sa. de 38 35N 0 24W
43 Aitolía kai Akarnanía □ 38 45N 21 18 E
43 Aitolikón 38 26N 21 21 E
67 Aitush 39 54N 75 40 E
41 Aiud 46 19N 23 44 E
21 Aix-en-Provence 43 32N 5 27 E
21 Aix-les-Bains 45 41N 5 53 E
20 Aix-les-Thermes 42 43N 1 51 E
43 Aíyina, I. 37 45N 23 26 E
42 Aiyínion 40 28N 22 28 E
43 Aiyion 38 15N 22 5 E
18 Aizenay 46 44N 1 38W
21 Ajaccio 41 55N 8 40 E
21 Ajaccio, G. d' 41 52N 8 40 E
83 Ajana 27 56S 114 35 E
96 Ajax 43 50N 79 1W
73 Ajdabiyah 30 54N 20 4 E
54 'Ajlun 32 18N 35 47 E
57 Ajman 25 25N 55 30 E
60 Ajmer 26 28N 74 37 E
103 Ajo 32 18N 112 54W
62 Akalkot 17 32N 76 12 E
85 Akaroa 43 49S 172 59 E
66 Akashi 34 45N 135 0 E
44 Akershus □ 60 10N 11 15 E
74 Aketi 2 38N 23 47 E
43 Akhaïa □ 38 5N 21 45 E
43 Akharnaí 38 5N 23 44 E
56 Akhisar 38 56N 27 48 E
43 Akhladhókambos 37 31N 22 35 E
73 Akhmîm 26 31N 31 47 E
90 Akimiski I. 52 50N 81 30W
66 Akita 39 45N 140 0 E
66 Akita □ 39 40N 140 30 E
72 Akjoujt 19 45N 14 15W
54 Akko 32 35N 35 4 E
50 Akkol 43 36N 70 45 E
88 Aklavik 68 25N 135 0W
66 Akō 34 45N 134 24 E
60 Akola 20 42N 77 2 E
73 Akordat 15 30N 37 40 E
60 Akot 21 10N 77 10 E
89 Akpatok I. 60 30N 68 0W
46 Akranes 64 19N 22 6W
96 Akron 41 7N 81 31W
56 Aksarka 66 31N 67 50 E
56 Aksehir 38 18N 31 30 E
51 Aksenovo Zilovskoye 53 20N 117 40 E
67 Aksu 41 4N 80 5 E
73 Aksum 14 5N 38 40 E
50 Aktogay 44 25N 76 44 E
50 Aktyubinsk 50 10N 57 3 E
72 Aku 6 40N 7 18 E
72 Akure 7 15N 5 5 E
46 Akureyri 65 40N 18 5W
59 Akyab 20 15N 92 45 E
55 Al 'Adan 12 50N 45 0 E
56 Al Amārah 31 55N 47 15 E
56 Al 'Aqabah 29 37N 35 0 E
54 Al Barah 31 55N 35 12 E
56 Al Basrah 30 30N 47 55 E
73 Al Baydā 32 30N 21 40 E
57 Al Buraimi 24 15N 55 53 E
56 Al Hadithan 34 0N 41 13 E
56 Al Hadr 35 35N 42 44 E
56 Al Hasa, Reg. 25 40N 50 0 E
56 Al Hasakah 36 35N 40 45 E
55 Al Hauta 16 5N 48 20 E
55 Al Hawra 13 49N 47 37 E
56 Al Hillah, Iraq 32 30N 44 25 E
56 Al Hillah, Saudi Arabia 23 35N 46 50 E
23 Al Hilwah 23 24N 46 48 E
56 Al Hindiyah 32 30N 44 10 E
72 Al-Hoceïma 35 15N 3 58W
56 Al Hufūf 25 25N 49 45 E
56 Al Jahrah 29 25N 47 40 E
56 Al Jalāmid 31 20N 39 45 E
55 Al Jazir 18 30N 56 31N
56 Al Jazirah, Reg. 26 10N 21 20 E
56 Al Jubail 27 0N 49 50 E
55 Al Juwara 19 0N 57 13 E
57 Al Khābūrah 23 57N 57 5 E
55 Al Khalaf 20 30N 57 56 E
73 Al Khums 32 40N 14 17 E
56 Al Kūt 32 30N 46 0 E
56 Al Kuwayt 29 20N 48 0 E
56 Al Ladhiqiyah 35 30N 35 45 E
55 Al Līth 20 9N 40 15 E
56 Al Madīnah 24 35N 39 52 E
54 Al Mafraq 32 17N 36 14 E
57 Al Manamāh 26 10N 50 30 E
73 Al Marj 32 25N 20 30 E
55 Al Masīrah 20 25N 58 50 E
55 Al Matamma 16 43N 33 22 E
56 Al Mawsil 36 15N 43 5 E
54 Al Mazra' 31 18N 35 32 E
56 Al Miqdadiyah 34 0N 45 0 E
56 Al Mubarraz 25 30N 49 40 E
57 Al Muharraq 26 15N 50 40 E
55 Al Mukha 13 18N 43 15 E
56 Al Qamishli 37 10N 41 10 E
56 Al Qatif 26 35N 50 0 E
73 Al-Qatrūn 24 56N 15 3 E
55 Al Qunfidha 19 3N 41 4 E
55 Al Ubailah 21 59N 50 57 E
73 Al 'Ugaylah 30 12N 19 10 E
57 Al Wakrah 25 10N 51 40 E
56 Al Wari 'ah 27 50N 47 30 E
36 Ala 45 46N 11 0 E
68 Ala Shan, Reg. 40 0N 104 0 E
99 Alabama, R. 31 8N 87 57W
99 Alabama □ 31 0N 87 0W
111 Alagôa Grande 7 3S 35 35W
111 Alagôas □ 9 0S 36 0W
111 Alagoinhas 12 0S 38 20W
32 Alagón 41 46N 1 12W
30 Alagón, R. 39 44N 6 53W
105 Alajuela 10 2N 84 8W
48 Alakurtti 67 0N 30 30 E
103 Alameda 35 10N 106 43W
103 Alamogordo 32 59N 106 0W
103 Alamosa 37 30N 106 0W
62 Aland 17 36N 76 35 E
47 Åland, I. 60 15N 20 0 E
31 Alandroal 38 41N 7 24W
31 Alanis 38 3N 5 43W
50 Alapayevsk 57 52N 61 42 E
30 Alar del Rey 42 38N 4 20W
30 Alaraz 40 45N 5 17W
68 Alashanchih 38 58N 105 14 E
88 Alaska □ 65 0N 150 0W
88 Alaska, G. of 58 0N 145 0W
88 Alaska Pen. 56 0N 160 0W
88 Alaska Ra. 62 50N 151 0W
38 Alatri 41 44N 13 21 E
48 Alatyr 54 45N 46 35 E
110 Alausi 2 0S 78 50W
30 Álava □ 42 48N 2 28W
81 Alawoona 34 45S 140 30 E
36 Alba 44 41N 8 1 E
30 Alba de Tormes 40 50N 5 30W
40 Albac 46 28N 23 1 E
33 Albacete 39 0N 1 50W
33 Albacete □ 38 50N 2 0W
45 Ålbæk 57 14N 10 26 E
33 Albaida 38 51N 0 31W
32 Albalate del Arzobispo 41 6N 0 31W
41 Alba-Iulia 46 4N 23 35 E
42 Albania ■ 41 0N 20 0 E
38 Albano Laziale 41 44N 12 40 E
83 Albany, Australia 35 1S 117 58 E
99 Albany, Ga. 31 40N 84 10W
97 Albany, N.Y. 42 40N 73 47W
102 Albany, Oreg. 44 41N 123 0W
90 Albany, R. 52 17N 81 31W

Albardón Amindaion

108 Albardón 31 20 s 68 30 w
32 Albarracín 40 25 N 1 26 w
32 Albarracín, Sa. de 40 30 N 1 30 w
99 Albemarle 35 27 N 80 15 w
36 Albenga 44 3 N 8 12 E
30 Alberche, R. 39 58 N 4 46 w
33 Alberique 39 7 N 0 31 w
32 Alberes, Mts. 42 28 N 2 56 w
92 Alberni 49 20 N 124 50 w
24 Albersdorf 54 8 N 9 19 E
91 Albert, Canada 45 51 N 64 38 w
19 Albert, Fr. 50 0 N 2 38 E
74 Albert, L.= Mobutu Sese Seko, L. 1 30 N 31 0 E
100 Albert Lea 43 32 N 93 20 w
74 Albert Nile, R. 3 36 N 32 2 E
105 Albert Town 18 17 N 77 33 w
92 Alberta □ 54 40 N 115 0 w
84 Alberton 38 35 s 146 40 E
21 Albertville 45 40 N 6 22 E
74 Albertville= Kalemie 5 55 s 29 9 E
57 Alberz, Reshteh-Ye-Kūkhā-Ye, Mts. 36 0 N 52 0 E
20 Albi 43 56 N 2 9 E
111 Albina 5 37 N 54 15 w
36 Albino 45 46 N 9 17 E
98 Albion 42 15 N 84 45 w
33 Alboran, I. 35 57 N 3 0 w
33 Alborea 39 17 N 1 24 w
45 Ålbôrg 57 2 N 9 54 E
33 Albox 37 23 N 2 8 w
31 Albufeira 37 5 N 8 15 w
33 Albuñol 36 48 N 3 11 w
103 Albuquerque 35 5 N 106 47 w
39 Alburno, Mt. 40 32 N 15 20 E
31 Alburquerque 39 15 N 6 59 w
84 Albury 36 3 s 146 56 E
31 Alcácer do Sol 38 22 N 8 33 w
31 Alcáçovas 38 23 N 8 9 w
32 Alcalá de Chisvert 40 19 N 0 13 E
31 Alcalá de Guadaira 37 20 N 5 50 w
31 Alcalá de los Gazules 36 29 N 5 43 w
30 Alcalá de Henares 40 28 N 3 22 w
31 Alcalá la Real 37 27 N 3 57 w
38 Alcamo 37 59 N 12 55 E
32 Alcanadre 42 24 N 2 7 w
32 Alcanadre, R. 41 37 N 0 12 w
32 Alcanar 40 33 N 0 28 E
31 Alcanede 39 25 N 8 49 w
31 Alcanena 39 27 N 8 40 w
32 Alcañíz 41 2 N 0 8 w
111 Alcântara, Brazil 2 20 s 44 30 w
31 Alcântara, Sp. 39 41 N 6 57 w
33 Alcantarilla 37 59 N 1 12 w
33 Alcaracejos 38 24 N 4 58 w
33 Alcaraz 38 40 N 2 29 w
33 Alcaraz, Sa. de 38 40 N 2 20 w
31 Alcaudete 37 35 N 4 5 w
31 Alcazar de San Juan 39 24 N 3 12 w
33 Alcira 39 9 N 0 30 w
30 Alcobaça 39 32 N 9 0 w
30 Alcobendas 40 32 N 3 38 w
32 Alcolea del Pinar 41 2 N 2 28 w
31 Alcora 40 5 N 0 14 w
31 Alcoutim 37 25 N 7 28 w
33 Alcoy 38 43 N 0 30 w
32 Alcubierre, Sa. de 41 45 N 0 22 w
32 Alcublas 39 48 N 0 43 w
32 Alcudia 39 51 N 3 9 E
32 Alcudia, B. de 39 45 N 3 14 E
31 Alcudia, Sa. de la 38 34 N 4 30 w
71 Aldabra Is. 9 22 s 46 28 E
51 Aldan, R. 63 28 N 129 35 E
13 Aldeburgh 52 9 N 1 35 E
31 Aldeia Nova 37 55 N 7 24 w
18 Alderney, I. 49 42 N 2 12 w
13 Aldershot 51 15 N 0 43 w
72 Aleg 17 3 N 13 55 w
109 Alegre 20 50 s 41 40 w
109 Alegrete 29 40 s 56 0 w
50 Aleisk 52 40 N 83 0 E
77 Alejandro Selkirk, I. 33 50 s 80 15 w
49 Aleksandrov Gai 50 15 N 48 35 E
51 Aleksandrovsk-Sakhalinskiy 50 50 N 142 20 E
51 Aleksandrovskiy Zavod 50 40 N 117 50 E
50 Aleksandrovskoye 60 35 N 77 50 E
28 Aleksandrów Kujawski 52 53 N 18 43 E
28 Aleksandrów Łódzki 51 49 N 19 17 E
40 Aleksinac 43 31 N 21 12 E
109 Além Paraíba 21 52 s 42 41 w
45 Ålen 62 49 N 11 17 E
18 Alençon 48 27 N 0 4 E
94 Alenuihaha Chan. 20 25 N 156 0 w
56 Aleppo=Ḥalab 36 10 N 37 15 E
21 Aléria 42 5 N 9 30 E
92 Alert Bay 50 30 N 127 35 w
21 Alès 44 9 N 4 5 E
36 Alessandria 44 54 N 8 37 E
76 Aleutian Is. 52 0 N 175 0 w
92 Alexander Arch. 57 0 N 135 0 w
75 Alexander Bay 28 36 s 16 33 E
99 Alexander City 32 56 N 85 57 w
5 Alexander I. 69 0 s 70 0 w
85 Alexandra 45 14 s 169 25 E
73 Alexandria=El Iskandarîya 31 0 N 30 0 E
90 Alexandria, Canada 45 19 N 74 38 w
41 Alexandria, Rumania 43 57 N 25 24 E
75 Alexandria, S. Africa 33 38 s 26 28 E
101 Alexandria, La. 31 20 N 92 30 w
100 Alexandria, Minn. 45 50 N 95 20 w
98 Alexandria, Va. 38 47 N 77 1 w
97 Alexandria Bay 44 20 N 75 52 w
42 Alexandroúpolis 40 50 N 25 24 E
32 Alfambra 40 33 N 1 5 w
32 Alfaro 42 10 N 1 50 w
41 Alfatar 43 59 N 27 13 E
24 Alfeld 52 0 N 9 49 E
109 Alfenas 21 25 s 45 57 w
37 Alfonsine 44 30 N 12 1 E
14 Alford 53 16 N 0 10 E
12 Alfreton 53 6 N 1 22 w
50 Alga 49 46 N 57 20 E
31 Algar 36 40 N 5 39 w
29 Algarve, Reg. 37 15 N 8 10 w
31 Algeciras 36 9 N 5 28 w
33 Algemesí 39 11 N 0 27 w
72 Alger 36 42 N 3 8 E
72 Algeria ■ 35 10 N 3 0 E
38 Alghero 40 34 N 8 20 E
72 Algiers=Alger 36 42 N 3 8 E
75 Algoabaai 33 50 s 25 45 E
31 Algodanales 36 54 N 3 48 w
90 Algonquin Prov. Park 45 35 N 78 35 w
33 Alhama de Almería 36 57 N 2 34 w
32 Alhama de Aragón 41 18 N 1 54 w
33 Alhama de Murcia 37 51 N 1 25 w
33 Alhambra, Sp. 38 54 N 3 4 w
103 Alhambra, U.S.A. 34 0 N 118 10 w
31 Alhaurín el Grande 36 39 N 4 41 w
32 Aliaga 40 40 N 0 42 w
42 Aliákmon, R. 40 30 N 22 36 E
40 Alibunar 45 5 N 20 57 E
33 Alicante 38 23 N 0 30 w
33 Alicante □ 38 30 N 0 37 w
101 Alice 27 47 N 98 1 w
92 Alice Arm 55 29 N 129 23 w
82 Alice Downs 17 45 s 127 56 E
80 Alice Springs 23 40 s 135 50 E
75 Alicedale 33 15 s 26 4 E
60 Aligarh 27 55 N 78 10 E
56 Aligudarz 33 25 N 49 45 E
30 Alijó 41 16 N 7 27 w
45 Alingsås 57 56 N 12 31 E
61 Alipore 22 32 N 88 24 E
61 Alipur Duar 26 30 N 89 35 E
96 Aliquippa 40 38 N 80 18 w
75 Aliwal Nord 30 45 s 26 45 E
30 Aljezur 37 18 N 8 49 w
31 Aljustrel 37 55 N 8 10 w
16 Alkmaar 52 37 N 4 45 E
103 All American Canal 32 45 N 115 0 w
61 Allahabad 25 25 N 81 58 E
93 Allan 51 53 N 106 4 w
91 Allard Lake 50 40 N 63 10 w
30 Allariz 42 11 N 7 50 w
20 Allassac 45 15 N 1 29 E
86 Allegheny Mts. 38 0 N 80 0 w
96 Allegheny, R. 40 27 N 80 0 w
20 Allègre 45 12 N 3 41 E
104 Allende 28 20 N 100 50 w
97 Allentown 40 36 N 75 30 w
26 Allentsteig 48 31 N 15 20 E
62 Alleppey 9 30 N 76 28 E
24 Aller, R. 52 57 N 9 11 E
21 Allevard 45 24 N 6 5 E
100 Alliance, Nebr. 42 10 N 102 50 w
96 Alliance, Ohio 40 53 N 81 7 w
20 Allier, R. 46 58 N 3 4 E
20 Allier □ 46 25 N 3 0 E
80 Alligator Creek 19 23 s 146 58 E
90 Alliston 44 15 N 79 55 w
14 Alloa 56 7 N 3 49 w
21 Allos 44 15 N 6 38 E
62 Alluru Kottapatnam 15 30 N 80 10 E
90 Alma, Canada 48 35 N 71 40 w
91 Alma, U.S.A. 43 25 N 84 40 w
50 Alma Ata 43 15 N 76 57 E
31 Almada 38 40 N 9 9 w
80 Almaden 17 22 s 144 40 E
31 Almadén 38 49 N 4 52 w
31 Almagro 38 50 N 3 45 w
33 Almansa 38 51 N 1 5 w
30 Almanza 42 39 N 5 3 w
30 Almanzor, P. de 40 15 N 5 18 w
33 Almanzora, R. 37 14 N 1 46 w
40 Almaş, Mt. 44 49 N 22 12 E
32 Almazán 41 30 N 2 30 w
32 Almazora 39 57 N 0 3 w
111 Almeirim, Brazil 1 30 s 52 0 w
31 Almeirim, Port. 39 12 N 8 37 w
32 Almenara 39 46 N 0 14 w
16 Almelo 52 22 N 6 42 E
32 Almenar 41 43 N 2 12 w
33 Almenara, Sa. de 37 34 N 1 32 w
31 Almendralejo 38 41 N 6 26 w
33 Almería 36 52 N 2 32 w
33 Almería, G. de 36 40 N 2 30 w
33 Almería □ 37 20 N 2 20 w
45 Älmhult 56 32 N 14 10 E
105 Almirante 9 10 N 82 30 w
43 Almirós 39 11 N 22 45 E
31 Almodóvar 37 11 N 8 2 w
31 Almodóvar del Campo 38 43 N 4 10 w
31 Almogia 36 50 N 4 32 w
61 Almora 29 38 N 79 4 E
33 Almoradi 38 7 N 0 46 w
30 Almorox 40 14 N 4 24 w
31 Almuñécar 36 43 N 3 41 w
45 Almvik 57 49 N 16 30 E
12 Alnwick 55 25 N 1 42 w
59 Alon 22 12 N 95 5 E
93 Alonsa 50 50 N 99 0 w
65 Alor, I. 8 15 s 124 30 E
63 Alor Setar 6 7 N 100 22 E
31 Alora 36 49 N 4 46 w
31 Alosno 37 33 N 7 7 w
83 Aloysius, Mt. 26 0 s 128 38 E
30 Alpedrinha 40 6 N 7 27 w
98 Alpena 45 6 N 83 24 w
21 Alpes-Maritimes □ 43 55 N 7 10 E
21 Alpes-de-Haute-Provence □ 44 8 N 6 10 E
80 Alpha 24 8 s 146 39 E
36 Alpi Apuane, Mts. 44 7 N 10 14 E
36 Alpi Atesine, Mts. 46 55 N 11 30 E
25 Alpi Lepontine, Mts. 46 22 N 8 27 E
36 Alpi Orobie, Mts. 46 7 N 10 0 E
25 Alpi Pennine, Mts. 46 0 N 7 30 E
25 Alpi Retiche, Mts. 46 45 N 10 0 E
31 Alpiarça 39 15 N 8 35 w
101 Alpine 30 35 N 103 35 w
8 Alps, Mts. 47 0 N 8 0 E
80 Alroy Downs 19 20 s 136 5 E
45 Als, I. 54 59 N 9 55 E
19 Alsace, Reg. 48 15 N 7 25 E
32 Alsasua 42 54 N 2 10 w
24 Alsfeld 50 44 N 9 19 E
12 Alston 54 48 N 2 26 w
46 Alta 69 55 N 23 12 E
108 Alta Gracia 31 40 s 64 30 w
92 Alta Lake 50 10 N 123 0 w
46 Altaelv, R. 69 57 N 23 17 E
110 Altagracia 10 45 N 71 30 w
52 Altai, Mts. 48 0 N 90 0 E
67 Altai, Mts.= Aerhtai Shan, Mts. 48 0 N 90 0 E
111 Altamira 3 0 s 52 10 w
39 Altamura 40 50 N 16 33 E
68 Altanbulag 50 19 N 106 30 E
25 Altdorf 46 52 N 8 36 E
33 Altea 38 38 N 0 2 w
24 Altenberg 50 46 N 13 47 E
24 Altenburg 50 59 N 12 28 E
26 Altenmarkt 47 43 N 14 39 E
31 Alter do Chão 39 12 N 7 40 w
19 Altkirch 47 37 N 7 15 E
25 Altmühl, R. 48 55 N 11 52 E
29 Alto-Alentejo, Reg. 38 50 N 7 40 w
111 Alto Araguaia 17 15 s 53 20 w
109 Alto Paraná □ 25 0 s 54 50 w
13 Alton, U.K. 51 8 N 0 59 w
100 Alton, U.S.A. 38 55 N 90 5 w
24 Altona 53 32 N 9 56 E
96 Altoona 40 32 N 78 24 w
25 Altstätten 47 22 N 9 33 E
101 Altus 34 30 N 99 25 w
67 Altyn Tagh, Mts. 39 0 N 89 0 E
55 Alula 11 50 N 50 45 E
65 Alusi 7 35 s 131 40 E
32 Alustante 40 36 N 1 40 w
101 Alva 36 50 N 98 50 w
30 Alvaiázere 39 49 N 8 23 w
104 Alvarado 18 40 N 95 50 w
44 Alvdalen, R. 59 23 N 13 30 E
31 Alverca 38 56 N 9 1 w
45 Alvesta 56 54 N 14 35 E
84 Alvie 38 15 s 143 30 E
31 Alvito 38 15 N 8 0 w
45 Alvsborgs □ 58 30 N 12 30 E
46 Älvsbyn 65 39 N 20 59 E
60 Alwar 27 38 N 76 34 E
62 Alwaye 10 8 N 76 24 E
49 Alyat Pristan 39 59 N 49 28 E
14 Alyth 56 38 N 3 15 w
73 Am-Timan 11 0 N 20 10 E
89 Amadjuak 64 0 N 72 50 w
89 Amadjuak L. 65 0 N 71 0 w
31 Amadora 38 45 N 9 13 w
97 Amagansett 40 58 N 72 8 w
66 Amagasaki 34 42 N 135 20 E
45 Amager, I. 55 37 N 12 37 E
66 Amakusa-Shotō, Is. 32 15 N 130 10 E
44 Åmål 59 2 N 12 40 E
62 Amalapuram 16 35 N 81 55 E
43 Amaliás 37 47 N 21 22 E
60 Amalner 21 5 N 75 5 E
109 Amambaí 20 30 s 56 0 w
109 Amambay □ 23 0 s 56 0 w
50 Amangeldy 50 10 N 65 10 E
39 Amantea 39 8 N 16 3 E
111 Amapá 2 5 N 50 50 w
111 Amapá □ 1 40 N 52 0 w
111 Amarante, Brazil 6 14 s 42 50 w
30 Amarante, Port. 41 16 N 8 5 w
60 Amaravati= Amraoti 20 55 N 77 45 E
62 Amaravati, R. 10 58 N 78 12 E
31 Amaraleja 38 12 N 7 13 w
111 Amargosa 13 2 s 39 36 w
101 Amarillo 35 14 N 101 46 w
37 Amaro, Mt. 42 5 N 14 6 E
56 Amasya 40 40 N 35 50 E
104 Amatitlán 14 29 N 90 38 w
111 Amazon= Amazonas, R. 2 0 s 53 30 w
111 Amazonas, R. 2 0 s 53 30 w
110 Amazonas □ 4 20 s 64 0 w
60 Ambala 30 23 N 76 56 E
62 Ambalangoda 6 15 N 80 5 E
62 Ambalapuzha 9 25 N 76 25 E
75 Ambanja 13 40 s 48 27 E
51 Ambarchik 69 40 N 162 20 E
108 Ambargasta, Salinas, Reg. 29 0 s 64 30 w
62 Ambarnath 19 12 N 73 22 E
62 Ambasamudram 8 43 N 77 25 E
110 Ambato 1 5 s 78 42 w
75 Ambatolampy 19 20 s 47 35 E
25 Amberg 49 25 N 11 52 E
104 Ambergris Cay 18 0 N 88 0 w
21 Ambérieu 45 57 N 5 20 E
85 Amberley 43 9 s 172 44 E
20 Ambert 45 33 N 3 44 E
12 Ambleside 54 26 N 2 58 w
65 Ambon 3 35 s 128 20 E
75 Ambositra 20 31 s 47 25 E
103 Amboy 34 33 N 115 51 w
75 Ambre, C. d' 12 40 s 49 10 E
96 Ambridge 40 36 N 80 15 w
62 Ambur 12 47 N 78 43 E
81 Amby 26 30 s 148 11 E
50 Amderma 69 45 N 61 30 E
104 Ameca 20 30 N 104 0 w
16 Ameland, I. 53 27 N 5 45 E
37 Amélia 42 34 N 12 25 E
20 Amélie-les-Bains-Palalda 42 29 N 2 41 E
51 Amen 68 45 N 180 0 E
102 American Falls 42 46 N 112 56 E
5 American Highland 73 0 s 75 0 E
85 American Samoa, I. 14 20 s 170 0 w
109 Americana 22 45 s 47 20 w
99 Americus 32 0 N 84 10 w
16 Amersfoort 52 9 N 5 23 E
83 Amery, Australia 31 9 s 117 5 E
93 Amery, Canada 56 45 N 94 0 w
100 Ames 42 0 N 93 40 w
97 Amesbury 42 50 N 70 52 w
43 Amfiklia 38 38 N 22 35 E
42 Amfípolis 40 48 N 23 52 E
43 Amfissa 38 32 N 22 22 E
43 Amflokhía 38 52 N 21 9 E
51 Amga, R. 62 38 N 134 32 E
51 Amgu 45 45 N 137 15 E
59 Amherst, Burma 16 0 N 97 40 E
91 Amherst, Canada 45 48 N 64 8 w
97 Amherst, Mass. 42 21 N 72 30 w
96 Amherst, Ohio 41 23 N 82 15 w
90 Amherstburg 42 6 N 83 6 w
37 Amiata, Mte. 42 54 N 11 40 E
19 Amiens 49 54 N 2 16 E
42 Amindaion 40 42 N 21 42 E

Amirantes, Is. Argonne, Mts.

53 Amirantes, Is. 6 0S 53 0E
12 Amlwch 53 24N 4 21W
54 'Ammān 32 0N 35 52E
25 Ammersee, L. 48 0N 11 7E
54 Ammi'ad 32 55N 35 32E
19 Amnéville 49 16N 6 9E
30 Amorebieta 43 13N 2 44W
43 Amorgós, I. 36 50N 25 59E
90 Amos 48 35N 78 5W
69 Amoy=Hsiamen 24 25N 118 4E
32 Amposta 40 43N 0 34E
91 Amqui 48 28N 67 27W
60 Amroati 20 55N 77 45E
60 Amreli 21 35N 71 17E
60 Amritsar 31 35N 74 57E
60 Amroha 28 53N 78 30E
24 Amrum, I. 54 37N 8 21E
16 Amsterdam, Neth. 52 23N 4 54E
97 Amsterdam, U.S.A. 42 58N 74 10W
3 Amsterdam, I. 37 30S 77 30E
26 Amstetten 48 7N 14 51E
50 Amu Darya, R. 43 40N 59 1E
88 Amukta Pass. 52 25N 172 0W
88 Amundsen G. 70 30N 123 0W
5 Amundsen Sea 72 0S 115 0W
51 Amur, R. 52 56N 141 10E
30 Amurrio 43 3N 3 0W
30 Amusco 42 10N 4 28W
43 Amvrakíkós Kól. 39 0N 20 55E
56 An Najaf 32 3N 44 15E
56 An Nasiriyah 31 0N 46 15E
63 An Nhon 13 53N 109 6E
56 An Nu'ayriyah 27 30N 48 30E
15 An Uaimh 53 39N 6 40W
54 Anabta 32 19N 35 7E
102 Anaconda 46 7N 113 0W
102 Anacortes 48 30N 122 40W
101 Anadarko 35 4N 98 15W
30 Anadia 40 26N 8 27W
56 Anadolu, Reg. 38 0W 39 0E
51 Anadyr 64 35N 177 20E
51 Anadyr, R. 64 55N 176 5E
38 Anagni 41 44N 13 8E
92 Anahim Lake 52 28N 125 18W
62 Anai Mudi, Mt. 10 12N 77 20E
62 Anaimalai Hills 10 20N 76 40E
62 Anakapalle 17 42N 83 6E
80 Anakie 23 32S 147 45E
64 Anambas, Kep. 3 20N 106 30E
66 Anan 33 54N 134 40E
60 Anand 22 32N 72 59E
62 Anantapur 14 39N 77 42E
58 Anantnag 33 45N 75 10E
111 Anápolis 16 15S 48 50W
57 Anar 30 55N 55 13E
56 Anatolia, Reg.= Anadolu, Reg. 38 0N 39 0E
108 Añatuya 28 20S 62 50W
18 Ancenis 47 21N 1 10W
88 Anchorage 61 10N 149 50W
30 Ancião 39 56N 8 27W
110 Ancohuma, Mt. 16 0S 68 50W
37 Ancona 43 37N 13 30E
112 Ancud 42 0S 73 50W
112 Ancud, G. de 42 0S 73 0W
108 Andacollo 13 14S 71 6W
44 Andalsnes 62 35N 7 43E
31 Andalucía, Reg. 37 35N 5 0W
99 Andalusia 31 51N 86 30W
63 Andaman Is. 12 30N 92 30E
63 Andaman Sea 13 0N 96 0E
16 Andenne 50 30N 5 5E
25 Andermatt 46 38N 8 35E
24 Andernach 50 24N 7 25E
20 Andernos 44 44N 1 6W
102 Anderson, Calif. 40 30N 122 19W
98 Anderson, Ind. 40 5N 85 40W
99 Anderson, S.C. 34 32N 82 40W
88 Anderson, R. 69 43N 128 58W
106 Andes, Mts. 20 0S 68 0W
62 Andhra Pradesh □ 15 0N 80 0E
43 Andikíthira, I. 35 52N 23 15E
43 Andíparos, I. 37 0N 25 3E
50 Andizhan 41 10N 72 0E
57 Andkhui 36 52N 65 8E
32 Andorra ■ 42 30N 1 30E
13 Andover 51 13N 1 29W
32 Andraitx 39 35N 2 25E
88 Andreanof Is. 51 0N 178 0W
28 Andrespol 51 45N 19 34E
39 Ándria 41 13N 16 17E
40 Andrijevica 42 45N 19 48E
48 Andropov 58 3N 38 52E
105 Andros, I. 24 30N 78 04
43 Ándros I. 37 50N 24 50E
105 Andros Town 24 43N 77 47W
27 Andrychów 49 51N 19 18E
31 Andújar 38 3N 4 5W
72 Anécho 6 12N 1 34E
105 Anegada I. 18 45N 64 20W
105 Anegada Pass. 18 15N 63 45W
32 Aneto, Pico de 42 37N 0 40E
68 Anganki 47 9N 123 48E
51 Angara, R. 58 6N 93 0E
51 Angarsk 52 30N 104 0E
81 Angaston 34 30S 139 8E
44 Ånge 62 31N 15 35E
104 Angel de la Guarda, I. 29 30N 113 30W
65 Angeles 15 9N 120 35E
45 Ängelholm 56 15N 12 58E
103 Angels Camp 38 8N 120 30W
46 Ångermanälven, R. 62 48N 17 56E
21 Angermünde 53 1N 14 0E
18 Angers 47 30N 0 35E
19 Angerville 48 19N 2 0E
32 Anglés 41 57N 2 38E
12 Anglesey, I. 53 17N 4 20W
20 Anglet 43 29N 1 21W
19 Anglure 48 35N 3 50E
4 Angmagssalik 65 40N 37 20W
74 Ango 4 10N 26 5E
75 Angoche 16 8S 40 0E
108 Angol 37 48S 72 43W
75 Angola ■ 12 0S 18 0E
96 Angola 42 38N 79 2W
20 Angoulême 45 39N 0 10E
20 Angoumois, Reg. 45 30N 0 25E
109 Angra dos Reis 23 0S 44 10W
50 Angren 41 1N 69 45E
105 Anguilla, I. 18 14N 63 5W
80 Angurugu 14 0S 136 25E
14 Angus, Braes of 56 51N 3 0W
45 Anholt, I. 56 42N 11 33E
69 Anhsien 31 30N 104 35E
69 Anhwei □ 33 15N 116 50E
40 Anina 45 5N 21 51E
60 Anjangaon 21 10N 77 20E
60 Anjar 23 6⅛ 70 10E
18 Anjou, Reg. 47 20N 0 15W
68 Anju 39 36N 125 40E
69 Ankang 32 38N 109 5E
56 Ankara 40 0N 32 54E
69 Anking 30 31N 117 2E
24 Anklam 53 51N 13 41E
60 Anklesvar 21 38N 73 3E
98 Ann Arbor 42 17N 83 45W
82 Anna Plains 19 17S 121 37E
72 Annaba 36 50N 7 46E
24 Annaberg-Buchholz 50 34N 12 58E
63 Annam, Reg.= Trung-Phan, Reg. 16 30N 107 30E
63 Annamitique, Chaîne, Mts. 17 0N 106 0E
14 Annan 54 59N 3 16W
14 Annan, R. 54 59N 3 16W
98 Annapolis 38 59N 76 30W
91 Annapolis Royal 44 4[illegible]N 65 32W
61 Annapurna, Mt. 28 34N 84 50E
21 Annecy 45 55N 6 8E
21 Annecy, L. d' 45 52N 6 10E
21 Annemasse 46 12N 6 16E
67 Anning 24 58N 102 30E
99 Anniston 33 45N 85 50W
21 Annonay 45 15N 4 40E
21 Annot 43 58N 6 38E
43 Ano Viánnos 35 2N 25 21E
100 Anoka 45 10N 93 26W
69 Anping 23 0N 120 6E
25 Ansbach 49 17N 10 34E
68 Anshan 41 3N 122 58E
69 Anshun 26 2N 105 57E
67 Ansi 40 21N 96 10E
32 Ansó 42 51N 0 48W
82 Anson, B. 13 20S 130 6E
97 Ansonia 41 21N 73 6W
90 Ansonville 48 46N 80 43W
14 Anstruther 56 14N 2 40W
65 Ansuda 2 11S 139 22E
68 Anta 46 18N 125 34E
56 Antakya 36 14N 36 10E
75 Antalaha 14 57S 50 20E
56 Antalya 36 52N 30 45E
56 Antalya Körfezi 36 15N 31 30E
75 Antananarivo 18 55S 47 35E
5 Antarctica 90 0S 0 0
5 Antarctic Pen. 67 0S 60 0W
30 Antela, L. de 42 7N 7 40W
108 Antequera, Paraguay 24 8S 57 7W
31 Antequera, Sp. 37 5N 4 33W
103 Anthony 32 1N 106 37W
80 Anthony Lagoon 18 0S 135 30E
21 Antibes 43 34N 7 6E
21 Antibes, C. d' 43 31N 7 7E
91 Anticosti I. 49 20N 62 40W
18 Antifer, C. d' 49 41N 0 10E
100 Antigo 45 8N 89 5W
91 Antigonish 45 38N 61 58W
104 Antigua 14 34N 90 41W
105 Antigua, I. 17 0N 61 50W
105 Antilla 20 40N 75 50W
103 Antimony 38 7N 112 0W
20 Antioche, Pertuis d' 46 5N 1 30W
110 Antioquia 6 40N 75 55W
76 Antipodes Is. 49 45S 178 40E
108 Antofagasta 23 50S 70 30W
108 Antofagasta □ 23 30S 69 0W
108 Antofalla, Mt. 25 33S 67 56W
75 Antongil, B. d' 15 30S 49 50E
109 Antonina 25 26S 48 42W
75 António Enes= Angoche 16 8S 40 0E
18 Antrain 48 28N 1 30W
15 Antrim 54 43N 6 13W
15 Antrim □ 54 55N 6 10W
75 Antsirabe 19 55S 47 2E
68 Antung 40 10N 124 18E
16 Antwerp= Antwerpen 51 13N 4 25E
16 Antwerpen 51 13N 4 25E
16 Antwerpen □ 51 15N 4 40E
62 Anuradhapura 8 22N 80 28E
16 Anvers= Antwerpen 51 13N 4 25E
88 Anvik 62 40N 160 12W
68 Anyang 36 7N 114 26E
65 Anyer-Lor 6 6S 105 56E
69 Anyi 28 50N 115 31E
50 Anzhero Sudzhensk 56 10N 83 40E
38 Ánzio 41 28N 12 37E
32 Aoiz 42 46N 1 22W
66 Aomori 40 45N 140 45E
66 Aomori □ 40 45N 140 40E
60 Aonla 28 16N 79 11E
36 Aosta 45 43N 7 20E
73 Aozou 21 49N 17 25E
65 Aparri 18 22N 121 38E
40 Apatin 45 40N 19 0E
104 Apatzingán 19 0N 102 20W
16 Apeldoorn 52 13N 5 57E
24 Apen 53 12N 7 47E
64 Apenam 8 35S 116 13E
9 Apennines, Mts.= Appennini, Mts. 41 0N 15 0E
104 Apizaco 19 26N 98 9W
24 Apolda 51 1N 11 30E
73 Apollonia= Marsa Susa 32 52N 21 59E
100 Apostle Is. 47 0N 90 30W
109 Apóstoles 27 55S 55 45W
110 Apoteri 4 2N 58 32W
86 Appalachian Mts. 38 0N 80 0W
37 Appennini, Mts. 41 0N 15 0E
36 Appenino Ligure, Mts. 44 30N 9 0E
25 Appenzell □ 47 23N 9 23E
37 Appiano 46 27N 11 27E
12 Appleby 54 35N 2 29W
98 Appleton 44 17N 88 25W
111 Approuagne 4 20N 52 0W
39 Apricena 41 47N 15 25E
21 Apt 43 53N 5 24E
109 Apucarana 23 55S 51 33W
40 Apuseni, Mts. 46 30N 22 45E
57 Aq Chah 37 0N 66 5E
56 'Aqaba 29 31N 35 0E
56 'Aqaba, Khalîj al 28 15N 33 20E
73 Aqiq 18 14N 38 12E
54 Aqraba 32 9N 35 20E
111 Aquidauana 20 30S 55 50W
55 Ar Rab' al Khālī 21 0N 51 0E
56 Ar Ramthā 32 34N 36 0E
56 Ar Raqqah 35 56N 39 1E
56 Ar Riyāḍ 24 41N 46 42E
57 Ar Ruska 23 35N 53 30E
56 Ar Ruṭbah 33 0N 40 15E
73 Arab, Bahr el, R. 9 2N 29 28E
52 Arabia, Reg. 25 0N 45 0E
70 Arabian Des. 28 0N 32 30E
111 Aracajú 10 55S 37 4W
110 Aracataca 10 38N 74 9W
111 Aracati 4 30S 37 44W
109 Araçatuba 21 10S 50 30W
31 Aracena 37 53N 6 58W
31 Aracena, Sa. de 37 48N 6 40W
111 Araçuai 16 52S 42 4W
54 'Arad 31 17N 35 12E
27 Arad 46 10N 21 20E
27 Arad □ 46 20N 21 45E
32 Aragón, R. 42 13N 1 44W
32 Aragon, Reg. 41 0N 1 0W
38 Aragona 37 24N 13 36E
111 Araguacema 8 50S 49 20W
111 Araguaia, R. 5 21S 48 41W
111 Araguari 18 38S 48 11W
56 Arāk 34 0N 49 40E
59 Arakan Coast 19 0N 94 0E
59 Arakan Yoma, Mts. 20 0N 94 30E
49 Araks, R. 40 1N 48 28E
50 Aral Sea= Aralskoye More 44 30N 66 0E
50 Aralsk 46 50N 61 20E
50 Aralskoye More 44 30N 60 0E
61 Arambagh 22 53N 87 48E
15 Aran, I. 55 0N 8 30W
15 Aran Is. 53 5N 9 42W
32 Arán, Valle de 42 45N 1 0E
30 Aranda de Duero 41 39N 3 42W
30 Aranjuez 40 1N 3 40W
101 Aransas P. 28 0N 97 9W
109 Arapongas 23 29S 51 28W
109 Araranguá 29 0S 49 30W
109 Araraquara 21 50S 48 0W
109 Araras 22 22S 47 23W
84 Ararat 37 16S 143 0E
109 Araruama, L. de 23 0S 42 20W
110 Arauca 7 0N 70 40W
108 Arauco □ 37 50S 73 15W
111 Araxá 19 35S 46 55W
110 Araya, Pen. de 10 40N 64 0W
38 Arbatax 39 57N 9 42E
56 Arbīl 36 15N 44 5E
44 Arboga 59 24N 15 52E
21 Arbois 46 55N 5 46E
14 Arbroath 56 34N 2 35W
38 Arborea 39 46N 8 34E
19 Arc 47 28N 5 34E
20 Arcachon 44 40N 1 10W
20 Arcachon, Bassin d' 44 42N 1 10W
100 Arcadia 44 13N 91 29W
102 Arcata 40 55N 124 4W
37 Arcévia 43 29N 12 58E
48 Archangel= Arkhangelsk 64 40N 41 0E
97 Archbald 41 30N 75 31W
33 Archena 38 9N 1 16W
38 Arci, Mte. 39 47N 8 44E
19 Arcis-sur-Aube 48 32N 4 10E
36 Arco 45 55N 10 54E
93 Arcola 49 40N 102 30W
32 Arcos 41 12N 2 16W
31 Arcos de los Frontera 36 45N 5 49W
62 Arcot 12 53N 79 20E
111 Arcoverde 8 25S 37 4W
89 Arctic Bay 73 2N 85 11W
4 Arctic Ocean 78 0N 160 0W
88 Arctic Red River 67 15N 134 0W
56 Ardabrīl 38 15N 48 18E
31 Ardales 36 53N 4 51W
44 Årdalstangen 61 15N 7 45E
21 Ardeche, R. 44 16N 4 39E
21 Ardèche □ 44 42N 4 16E
15 Ardee 53 51N 6 32W
16 Ardennes, Reg. 49 30N 5 10E
19 Ardennes □ 49 35N 4 40E
19 Ardentes 46 45N 1 50E
57 Ardestan 33 20N 52 25E
14 Ardgour, Reg. 56 45N 5 25W
37 Ardino 41 34N 25 9E
84 Ardlethan 34 22S 146 53E
101 Ardmore, Australia 21 39S 139 11E
101 Ardmore, U.S.A. 34 10N 97 5W
15 Ardnacrusha 52 43N 8 38W
14 Ardnamurchan Pt. 56 44N 6 14W
19 Ardres 50 50N 2 0E
14 Ardrossan 55 39N 4 50W
15 Ards □ 54 35N 5 30W
15 Ards Pen. 54 30N 5 25W
105 Arecibo 18 29N 66 42W
111 Areia Branca 5 0S 37 0W
30 Arenas 40 17N 5 6W
45 Arendal 58 28N 8 46E
32 Arenys de Mar 41 35N 2 33E
36 Arenzano 44 24N 8 40E
110 Arequipa 16 20S 71 30W
74 Arero 4 41N 38 50E
20 Arès 44 47N 1 8E
30 Arévalo 41 3N 4 43W
37 Arezzo 43 28N 11 50E
32 Arga, R. 42 18N 1 47W
31 Argamasilla de Alba 39 8N 3 5W
30 Arganda 40 19N 3 26W
20 Argelès-Gazost 43 0N 0 6W
20 Argelès-sur-Mer 42 34N 3 1E
19 Argent 47 33N 2 25E
37 Argenta 44 37N 11 50E
18 Argentan 48 45N 0 1W
37 Argentário, Mte. 42 23N 11 11E
21 Argentera, Mt. de l' 44 10N 7 18E
36 Argentera, P. 44 11N 7 17E
19 Argenteuil 48 57N 2 14E
91 Argentia 47 18N 53 58W
38 Argentiera, C. dell' 40 44N 8 8E
106 Argentine Basin, Reg. 44 0S 51 0E
112 Argentina ■ 35 0S 66 0W
112 Argentino, L. 50 10S 73 0W
20 Argenton Château 46 59N 0 27W
20 Argenton-sur-Creuse 46 36N 1 30E
18 Argentré 48 5N 0 40W
41 Arges, R. 44 10N 26 45E
73 Argo 19 28N 30 30E
43 Argolikós Kól. 37 20N 22 52E
43 Argolis □ 37 38N 22 50E
19 Argonne, Mts. 49 0N 5 20E

Argos Ayre, Pt. of

43 Árgos ... 37 40N 22 43 E
43 Argostólion ... 38 12N 20 33 E
103 Arguello, Pt. ... 34 34N 120 40W
51 Argun, R. ... 43 22N 45 55 E
82 Argyle, L. ... 16 20S 128 40 E
45 Århus ... 56 8N 10 11 E
39 Ariano Irpino ... 41 10N 15 4 E
110 Arica, Chile ... 18 32S 70 20W
110 Arica, Col. ... 1 30S 75 30W
83 Arid, C. ... 34 1S 123 10 E
66 Arida ... 33 29N 135 44 E
20 Ariège, R. ... 43 31N 1 32 E
20 Ariège □ ... 42 56N 1 30 E
105 Arima ... 10 38N 61 17W
14 Arisaig ... 56 50N 5 40W
62 Ariyalur ... 11 8N 79 8 E
32 Ariza ... 41 19N 2 3W
103 Arizona □ ... 34 20N 111 30W
110 Arjona ... 10 14N 75 22W
51 Arka ... 60 15N 142 0 E
67 Arka Tagh, Mts. ... 36 30N 90 0 E
101 Arkadelphia ... 34 5N 93 0W
43 Arkadhía □ ... 38 48N 21 3 E
14 Arkaig, L. ... 56 58N 5 10W
101 Arkansas, R. ... 33 48N 91 4W
101 Arkansas □ ... 35 0N 92 30W
101 Arkansas City ... 37 4N 97 3W
48 Arkhangelsk ... 64 40N 41 0 E
15 Arklow ... 52 48N 6 10W
24 Arkona, C. ... 54 41N 13 26 E
62 Arkonam ... 13 7N 79 43 E
20 Arlanc ... 45 25N 3 42 E
30 Arlanza, R. ... 42 6N 4 9W
30 Arlanzón, R. ... 42 3N 4 17W
26 Arlberg P. ... 49 9N 10 12 E
21 Arles ... 43 41N 4 40 E
101 Arlington ... 44 25N 97 4W
16 Arlon ... 49 42N 5 49 E
45 Arlöy ... 55 38N 13 5 E
83 Armadale ... 32 12S 116 0 E
15 Armagh ... 54 22N 6 40W
15 Armagh □ ... 54 16N 6 35W
20 Armagnac, Reg. ... 43 44N 0 10 E
19 Armançon, R. ... 47 57N 3 30 E
49 Armavir ... 45 2N 41 7 E
110 Armenia ... 4 35N 75 45W
49 Armenian S.S.R. □ 40 0N 41 10 E
40 Armeniş ... 45 13N 22 17 E
19 Armentières ... 50 40N 2 50 E
81 Armidale ... 30 30S 151 40 E
92 Armstrong, B.C. ... 50 25N 119 10W
90 Armstrong, Ont. ... 50 20N 89 0W
62 Armur ... 18 48N 78 16 E
19 Arnay-le-Duc ... 47 10N 4 27 E
32 Arnedo ... 42 12N 2 5W
16 Arnhem ... 51 58N 5 55 E
80 Arnhem, B. ... 12 20S 136 10 E
62 Arni ... 12 43N 79 19 E
36 Arno, R. ... 43 31N 10 17 E
96 Arnold ... 40 36N 79 44W
26 Arnoldstein ... 46 33N 13 43 E
90 Arnprior ... 45 23N 76 25W
24 Arnsberg ... 51 25N 8 10 E
24 Arnstadt ... 50 50N 10 56 E
31 Aroche ... 37 56N 6 57 E
30 Arosa, Ria de ... 42 28N 8 57W
41 Arpaşu de Jos ... 45 45N 24 38 E
38 Arpino ... 41 40N 13 35 E
81 Arrabury ... 26 45S 141 0 E
61 Arrah ... 25 35N 84 32 E
31 Arraiolos ... 38 44N 7 59W
14 Arran, I. ... 55 34N 5 12W
19 Arras ... 50 17N 2 46 E
20 Arreau ... 42 54N 0 22 E
20 Arrats, R. ... 44 6N 0 52 E
72 Arrecife ... 28 59N 13 40W
108 Arrecifes ... 34 5S 60 5N
18 Arrée, Mts. d' ... 48 26N 3 55W
83 Arrino ... 29 30S 115 40 E
18 Arromanches ... 49 20N 0 38W
31 Arronches ... 39 8N 7 16W
20 Arros, R. ... 43 30N 0 2W
18 Arrou ... 48 6N 1 8 E
92 Arrowhead ... 50 40N 117 55W
85 Arrowtown ... 44 57S 168 50 E
31 Arroyo de la Luz ... 39 30N 6 38W
20 Ars ... 46 13N 1 30W
41 Arsache ... 43 47N 25 45 E
68 Arshan ... 46 59N 120 0 E
37 Arsiero ... 45 49N 11 22 E
62 Arsikere ... 13 15N 76 15 E
19 Ars-sur-Moselle ... 49 5N 6 4 E
32 Artá ... 39 40N 3 20 E
43 Árta ... 39 8N 21 2 E
89 Artemovsk ... 48 35N 37 55 E
19 Artenay ... 48 5N 1 50 E
32 Artesa de Segre ... 41 54N 1 3 E
101 Artesia ... 32 55N 104 25W
80 Arthur, Pt. ... 22 7S 150 3 E
108 Artigas ... 30 20S 56 30W
19 Artois, Reg. ... 50 20N 2 30 E
56 Artvin ... 41 14N 41 44 E
65 Aru, Kep. ... 6 0S 134 30 E
74 Arua ... 3 1N 30 58 E
111 Aruanã ... 15 0S 51 10W
105 Aruba, I. ... 12 30N 70 0W
59 Arunachal
Pradesh □ ... 28 0N 95 0 E
62 Aruppukottai ... 9 31N 78 8 E
74 Arusha ... 3 20S 36 40 E
102 Arvada ... 44 43N 106 6W
68 Arvayheer ... 46 15N 102 48 E
21 Arve, R. ... 46 12N 6 8 E
60 Arvi ... 20 59N 78 16 E
91 Arvida ... 48 16N 71 14W
46 Arvidsjaur ... 65 35N 19 10 E
44 Arvika ... 59 40N 12 36 E
50 Arys ... 42 26N 68 48 E
48 Arzamas ... 55 27N 43 55 E
72 Arzew ... 35 50N 0 23W
37 Arzignano ... 45 30N 11 20 E
26 Aš ... 50 13N 12 12 E
54 As Salt ... 32 2N 35 43 E
56 As Samāwah ... 31 15N 45 15 E
56 As Sulaimānīyah ... 24 8N 47 10 E
56 As Sulamāniyah ... 35 35N 45 29 E
57 As Suwaih ... 22 10N 59 33 E
56 As Suwayda ... 32 40N 36 30 E
56 As Suwayrah ... 32 55N 45 0 E
66 Asahikawa ... 43 45N 142 30 E
61 Asansol ... 23 40N 87 1 E
91 Asbestos ... 45 47N 71 58W
97 Asbury Park ... 40 15N 74 1W
104 Ascensión, B. de la 19 50N 87 20W
71 Ascension, I. ... 8 0S 14 15W
26 Aschach ... 48 23N 14 0 E
25 Aschaffenburg ... 49 58N 9 8 E
24 Aschersleben ... 51 45N 11 28 E
37 Ascoli Piceno ... 42 51N 13 34 E
39 Áscoli Satriano ... 41 11N 15 32 E
55 Aseb ... 13 0N 42 40 E
45 Aseda ... 57 10N 15 20 E
41 Asenovgrad ... 42 1N 24 51 E
103 Ash Fork ... 35 14N 112 32W
56 Ash Shāmiyah ... 31 55N 44 35 E
56 Ash Sharma ... 28 1N 35 18 E
54 Ash Shuna ... 32 32N 35 34 E
48 Asha ... 35 10N 33 38 E
85 Ashburton ... 43 53S 171 48 E
82 Ashburton, R. ... 37 52S 145 5 E
82 Ashburton Downs ... 23 25S 117 4 E
12 Ashby-de-la-Zouch 52 45N 1 29W
54 Ashdod ... 31 39N 34 35 E
54 Ashdot Yaaqov ... 32 39N 35 35 E
99 Asheboro ... 35 43N 79 46W
99 Asheville ... 35 39N 82 30W
13 Ashford ... 51 8N 0 53 E
66 Ashikaga ... 36 28N 139 29 E
12 Ashington ... 55 12N 1 35W
50 Ashkhabad ... 38 0N 57 50 E
98 Ashland, Ky. ... 38 25N 82 40W
96 Ashland, Ohio ... 40 52N 82 20W
102 Ashland, Oreg. ... 42 10N 122 38W
97 Ashland, Pa. ... 40 45N 76 22W
100 Ashland, Wis. ... 46 40N 90 52W
97 Ashley ... 41 12N 75 55W
54 Ashquelon ... 31 42N 34 55 E
96 Ashtabula ... 41 52N 80 50W
102 Ashton ... 44 6N 111 30W
12 Ashton-under-
Lyne ... 53 30N 2 8W
1 Asia ... 45 0N 75 0 E
72 Asilah ... 35 29N 6 0W
38 Asinara, G. dell' ... 41 0N 8 30 E
38 Asinara, I. ... 41 5N 8 15 E
50 Asino ... 57 0N 86 0 E
55 Asir, Ras ... 11 55N 51 0 E
55 Asir, Reg. ... 18 40N 42 30 E
54 Asira esh
Shamaliya ... 32 16N 35 16 E
44 Askim ... 59 35N 11 10 E
57 Asmar ... 35 10N 71 27 E
73 Asmera ... 15 19N 38 55 E
45 Asnen, L. ... 56 35N 15 45 E
36 Ásola ... 45 12N 10 25 E
33 Aspe ... 38 20N 0 40W
85 Aspiring, Mt. ... 44 23S 168 46W
21 Aspres ... 44 32N 5 44 E
59 Assam □ ... 25 45N 92 30 E
16 Asse ... 50 54N 4 6 E
16 Assen ... 53 0N 6 35 E
93 Assiniboia ... 49 40N 106 0W
92 Assiniboine, Mt. ... 50 52N 115 39W
93 Assiniboine, R. ... 49 53N 97 8W
109 Assis ... 22 40S 50 20W
37 Assisi ... 43 4N 12 36 E
14 Assynt, L. ... 58 25N 5 10W
49 Astara ... 38 30N 48 50 E
36 Asti ... 44 54N 8 11 E
43 Astipálaia, I. ... 36 32N 26 22 E
30 Astorga ... 42 29N 6 8W
102 Astoria ... 46 16N 123 50W
45 Astorp ... 56 6N 12 55 E
49 Astrakhan ... 46 25N 48 5 E
30 Asturias, Reg. ... 43 15N 6 0W
108 Asunción ... 25 21S 57 30W
73 Aswân ... 24 4N 32 57 E
73 Aswân High Dam ... 24 5N 32 54 E
73 Asyût ... 27 11N 31 4 E
56 At Ta'if ... 21 5N 40 27 E
106 Atacama Des. ... 24 0S 69 20W
108 Atacama, Salar de ... 24 0S 68 20W
108 Atacama □ ... 27 30S 70 0W
72 Atakpamé ... 7 31N 1 13 E
43 Atalándi ... 38 39N 22 58 E
66 Atami ... 35 0N 139 55 E
72 Atar ... 20 30N 13 5W
51 Atara ... 63 10N 129 10 E
31 Atarfe ... 37 13N 3 40W
50 Atasu ... 48 30N 71 0 E
73 Atbara ... 17 42N 33 59 E
73 'Atbara, Nahr, R ... 17 40N 33 56 E
50 Atbasar ... 51 48N 68 20 E
100 Atchison ... 39 40N 95 0W
32 Ateca ... 41 20N 1 49W
37 Atessa ... 42 5N 14 27 E
16 Ath ... 50 38N 3 47 E
92 Athabasca ... 54 45N 113 20W
93 Athabasca, L. ... 59 10N 109 30W
93 Athabasca, R. ... 58 40N 110 50W
15 Athboy ... 53 37N 6 55W
15 Athenry ... 53 18N 8 45W
99 Athens, Ala. ... 34 49N 86 58W
99 Athens, Ga. ... 33 56N 83 24W
98 Athens, Ohio ... 39 52N 82 64W
101 Athens, Tex. ... 32 11N 95 48W
43 Athens=Athínai ... 37 58N 23 46 E
80 Atherton ... 17 17S 145 30 E
43 Athínai ... 37 58N 23 46 E
15 Athlone ... 53 26N 7 57W
62 Athni ... 16 44N 75 6 E
14 Atholl, Forest of ... 56 51N 3 50W
91 Atholville ... 48 5N 67 5W
42 Athos, Mt. ... 40 9N 24 22 E
15 Athy ... 53 0N 7 0W
51 Atka ... 60 50N 151 48 E
88 Atka I. ... 52 15N 174 30W
99 Atlanta ... 33 50N 84 24W
100 Atlantic ... 41 25N 95 0W
98 Atlantic City ... 39 25N 74 25W
1 Atlantic Ocean ... 0 0 30 0W
72 Atlas, Anti, Mts. ... 30 0N 8 0W
72 Atlas, Moyen,
Mts. ... 37 0N 5 0W
72 Atlas Saharien,
Mts. ... 34 10N 3 30 E
92 Atlin ... 59 31N 133 41W
54 Atlit ... 32 42N 34 56 E
62 Atmakur ... 14 37N 79 40 E
99 Atmore ... 31 2N 87 30W
104 Atotonilco ... 20 20N 98 40W
31 Atouguia ... 39 20N 9 20W
37 Atri ... 42 35N 14 0 E
90 Attawapiskat ... 53 0N 82 30W
90 Attawapiskat L. ... 52 20N 88 0W
90 Attawapiskat, R. ... 52 57N 82 18W
26 Attersee ... 47 55N 13 31 E
26 Attersee, L. ... 47 52N 13 33 E
19 Attigny ... 49 28N 4 35 E
43 Attikí □ ... 38 10N 23 40 E
54 Attil ... 32 23N 35 4 E
97 Attleboro ... 41 56N 71 18W
58 Attock ... 33 52N 72 20 E
88 Attu I. ... 52 55N 173 0 E
62 Attur ... 11 35N 78 30 E
45 Atvidaberg ... 58 12N 16 0 E
100 Atwood ... 39 52N 101 3W
21 Aubagne ... 43 17N 5 37 E
19 Aube, R. ... 48 34N 3 43 E
19 Aube □ ... 48 15N 4 0 E
21 Aubenas ... 44 37N 4 24 E
19 Aubigny-sur-Nère ... 47 30N 2 24 E
20 Aubrac, Mts. d' ... 44 38N 2 58 E
99 Auburn, Ala. ... 32 57N 85 30W
102 Auburn, Calif. ... 38 50N 121 10W
99 Auburn, Me. ... 44 6N 70 14W
97 Auburn, N.Y. ... 42 57N 76 39W
20 Aubusson ... 45 57N 2 11 E
20 Auch ... 43 39N 0 36 E
19 Auchel ... 50 30N 2 39 E
85 Auckland ... 36 52S 174 46 E
76 Auckland Is. ... 51 0S 166 0 E
20 Aude □ ... 44 13N 3 15 E
90 Auden ... 50 17N 87 54W
18 Auderville ... 49 43N 1 57W
18 Audierne ... 48 1N 4 34W
19 Audincourt ... 47 30N 6 50 E
24 Aue ... 50 34N 12 43 E
24 Auerbach ... 50 30N 12 25 E
18 Auffay ... 49 43N 1 7 E
81 Augathella ... 25 48S 146 35 E
25 Augsburg ... 48 22N 10 54 E
83 Augusta,
Australia ... 34 22S 115 10 E
39 Augusta, Italy ... 37 14N 15 12 E
99 Augusta, U.S.A. ... 33 29N 81 59W
99 Augusta ... 44 20N 69 46W
75 Augusto Cardoso ... 12 44S 34 50 E
28 Augustów ... 53 51N 23 0 E
83 Augustus, Mt. ... 24 20S 116 50 E
80 Augustus Downs ... 18 35S 139 55 E
18 Aulne, R. ... 48 17N 4 16W
19 Aulnoye ... 46 2N 0 22W
20 Aunis, Reg. ... 46 0N 0 50W
61 Aurangabad,
Bihar ... 24 25N 84 18 E
60 Aurangabad,
Maharashtra ... 19 50N 75 23 E
18 Auray ... 47 40N 3 0W
24 Aurich ... 53 28N 7 30 E
20 Aurillac ... 44 55N 2 26 E
100 Aurora, Colo. ... 39 44N 104 55W
98 Aurora, Ill. ... 41 42N 88 20W
96 Aurora, Ohio ... 41 21N 81 20W
47 Aust-Agde □ ... 58 55N 7 40 E
100 Austin, Minn. ... 43 37N 92 59W
102 Austin, Nev. ... 39 30N 117 1W
101 Austin, Tex. ... 30 20N 97 45W
78 Australia ■ ... 23 0S 135 0 E
84 Australian Alps,
Mts. ... 36 30S 148 8 E
84 Australian
Capital Terr. □ ... 35 15S 149 8 E
5 Australian
Dependency □ ... 73 0S 90 0 E
26 Austria ■ ... 47 0N 14 0 E
19 Authie, R. ... 50 21N 1 38 E
104 Autlán ... 19 40N 104 30W
21 Autun ... 46 58N 4 17 E
82 Auvergne ... 15 39S 130 1 E
20 Auvergne, Mts. ... 45 20N 2 45 E
20 Auvergne, Reg. ... 45 30N 3 20 E
20 Auvézère, R. ... 45 12N 0 51 E
19 Auxerre ... 47 48N 3 32 E
21 Auxonne ... 47 10N 5 20 E
20 Auzances ... 46 2N 2 30 E
20 Auzat ... 45 27N 3 19 E
19 Avallon ... 47 30N 3 53 E
91 Avalon Pen. ... 47 0N 53 20W
62 Avanigadda ... 16 0N 80 56 E
109 Avaré ... 23 5S 48 55W
42 Ávas ... 40 57N 25 56 E
111 Aveiro, Brazil ... 3 10S 55 5W
30 Aveiro, Port. ... 40 37N 8 38W
30 Aveiro □ ... 40 40N 8 35W
108 Avellaneda ... 34 50S 58 10W
39 Avellino ... 40 54N 14 46 E
44 Averøya, I. ... 63 0N 7 35 E
39 Aversa ... 40 58N 14 11 E
110 Aves, Is. de ... 12 0N 67 40W
19 Avesnes ... 50 8N 3 55 E
44 Avesta ... 60 9N 16 10 E
20 Aveyron, R. ... 44 5N 1 16 E
20 Aveyron □ ... 44 22N 2 45 E
37 Avezzano ... 42 2N 13 24 E
14 Aviemore ... 57 11N 3 50W
39 Avigliano ... 40 44N 15 41 E
21 Avignon ... 43 57N 4 50 E
30 Ávila ... 40 39N 4 43W
30 Ávila, Sa. de ... 40 40N 5 0W
30 Ávila □ ... 40 30N 5 0W
30 Avilés ... 43 35N 5 57W
84 Avoca ... 37- 5S 143 28 E
15 Avoca, R. ... 52 48N 6 10W
92 Avola, Canada ... 51 45N 119 30W
39 Avola, Italy ... 36 56N 15 7 E
39 Avola ... 36 56N 15 7 E
83 Avon, R,
Australia ... 31 40S 116 7 E
13 Avon, R., Avon ... 51 30N 2 43W
13 Avon, R., Dorset ... 50 43N 1 46W
13 Avon, R.,
Gloucester ... 51 59N 2 10W
13 Avon □ ... 51 30N 2 40W
97 Avonmore ... 45 11N 74 57W
13 Avonmouth ... 51 30N 2 42W
18 Avranches ... 48 40N 1 20W
41 Avrig ... 45 43N 24 21 E
66 Awaji-Shima, I. ... 34 30N 134 50 E
57 Awali ... 26 0N 50 30 E
74 Awash ... 9 1N 40 10 E
85 Awatere, R. ... 41 37S 174 10 E
14 Awe, L. ... 56 15N 5 15W
73 Awjilah ... 29 8N 21 7 E
86 Axel Heiberg
Ld. ... 80 0N 90 0W
20 Ax-les-Thermes ... 42 44N 1 50 E
13 Axminster ... 50 47N 3 1W
19 Ay ... 49 3N 4 0 E
66 Ayabe ... 35 20N 135 20 E
110 Ayacucho, Arg. ... 37 5S 58 20W
108 Ayacucho, Peru ... 13 0S 74 0W
50 Ayaguz ... 48 10N 80 0 E
31 Ayamonte ... 37 12N 7 24W
51 Ayan ... 56 30N 138 16 E
63 Ayer Itam ... 1 55N 103 11 E
42 Ayía Paraskevi ... 39 14N 26 16 E
42 Ayíos Evstrátios ... 39 34N 24 58 E
48 Aykin ... 62 20N 49 56 E
93 Aylesbury, Canada 50 55N 105 53W
13 Aylesbury, U.K. ... 51 48N 0 49W
88 Aylmer, L. ... 64 0N 109 0W
80 Ayr, Australia ... 19 35S 147 25 E
14 Ayr, U.K. ... 55 28N 4 37W
14 Ayr, R. ... 55 29N 4 28W
12 Ayre, Pt. of ... 54 27N 4 21W

Aytos Barat □, Java

41 Aytos 42 47N 27 16 E
56 Ayvalik 39 20N 26 46 E
54 Az Zahiriya 31 25N 34 58 E
56 Az Zahrān 26 10N 50 7 E
54 Az-Zarqā' 32 5N 36 4 E
56 Az Zilfi 26 12N 44 52 E
56 Az Zubayr 30 20N 47 50 E
31 Azambuja 39 4N 8 51W
61 Azamgarh 26 35N 83 13 E
56 Āzārbāijān □ 37 0N 44 30 E
72 Azare 11 55N 10 10 E
72 Azbine=Aïr 18 0N 8 0 E
49 Azerbaijan S.S.R. □ 40 20N 48 0 E
31 Aznalcóllar 37 32N 6 17W
54 Azor 32 2N 34 40 E
8 Azores, Is. 38 44N 29 0W
49 Azov 47 3N 39 25 E
49 Azov Sea= Azovskoye More 46 0N 36 30 E
49 Azovskoye More 46 0N 36 30 E
58 Azovy 64 55N 64 35 E
103 Aztec 36 54N 108 0W
105 Azua 18 25N 70 44W
31 Azuaga 38 16N 5 39W
31 Azuer, R. 39 8N 3 36W
105 Azuero, Pen. de 7 40N 80 30W
108 Azul 36 42S 59 43W

B

63 Ba Don 17 45N 106 26 E
30 Baamonde 43 7N 7 44W
57 Baba, Koh-i-, Mts. 34 40N 67 20 E
62 Baba Budan Hills 13 30N 75 40 E
41 Babadag 44 53N 28 48 E
110 Babahoyo 1 40S 79 30W
83 Babakin 32 11S 117 52 E
65 Babelthuap, I. 7 30N 134 36 E
80 Babinda 17 27S 146 0 E
65 Babo 2 30S 133 30 E
57 Bābol 36 40N 52 50 E
57 Babol Sar 36 45N 52 45 E
65 Babuyan Chan. 18 58N 122 0 E
69 Babuyan Is. 19 0N 122 0 E
56 Babylon, Iraq 32 40N 44 30 E
97 Babylon, U.S.A. 40 42N 73 20W
63 Bac Ninh 21 13N 106 4 E
63 Bac-Phan, Reg. 22 0N 105 0 E
63 Bac Quang 22 30N 104 48 E
111 Bacabal 5 20S 56 45W
65 Bacan, I. 1 0S 127 30 E
41 Bacău 46 35N 26 55 E
19 Baccarat 48 28N 6 42 E
25 Bacharach 50 3N 7 46 E
50 Bachelina 57 45N 67 20 E
88 Back, R. 67 15N 95 15W
40 Bačka Palanka 45 17N 19 27 E
40 Bačka Topola 45 48N 19 37 E
25 Backnang 48 57N 9 26 E
65 Bacolod 10 50N 123 0 E
27 Bacs-Kiskun □ 46 43N 19 30 E
27 Bácsalmás 46 8N 19 17 E
26 Bad Aussee 47 43N 13 45 E
24 Bad Driburg 51 44N 9 0 E
25 Bad Ems 51 22N 7 44 E
25 Bad Frankenhausen 51 21N 11 3 E
24 Bad Freienwalde 52 46N 14 2 E
24 Bad Godesberg 50 41N 7 4 E
24 Bad Hersfeld 50 52N 9 42 E
26 Bad Hofgastein 47 17N 13 6 E
25 Bad Homburg 50 17N 8 33 E
24 Bad Honnef 50 39N 7 13 E
26 Bad Ischl 47 44 13 38 E
25 Bad Kissingen 50 11N 10 5 E
25 Bad Kreuznach 49 47N 7 47 E
24 Bad Lauterberg 51 38N 10 29 E
26 Bad Leonfelden 48 31N 14 18 E
25 Bad Mergentheim 49 29N 9 47 E
25 Bad Nauheim 50 24N 8 45 E
24 Bad Oldesloe 53 56N 10 17 E
24 Bad Pyrmont 51 59N 9 5 E
24 Bad Salzuflen 52 8N 8 44 E
24 Bad Segeberg 53 58N 10 16 E
25 Bad Tölz 47 43N 11 34 E
24 Bad Wildungen 51 7N 9 10 E
62 Badagara 11 35N 75 40 E
31 Badajoz 38 50N 6 59W
31 Badajoz □ 38 40N 6 30W
57 Badakhshan □ 36 30N 71 0 E
32 Badalona 41 26N 2 15 E
57 Badalzal 29 50N 65 35 E
56 Badanah 30 58N 41 30 E
64 Badas 4 20N 114 37 E
27 Baden, Austria 48 1N 16 13 E
25 Baden, Switz. 47 28N 8 18 E
25 Baden-Baden 48 45N 8 14 E
25 Baden Württemberg □ 48 40N 9 0 E
14 Badenoch, Reg. 57 0N 4 0W
26 Badgastein 47 7N 13 9 E
57 Badghis □ 35 0N 63 0 E
37 Badia Polèsine 45 6N 11 30 E
60 Badnera 20 48N 77 44 E
62 Badulla 7 1N 81 7 E
31 Baena 37 37N 4 20W
31 Baeza 37 57N 3 25W
89 Baffin B. 72 0N 65 0W
89 Baffin I. 68 0N 77 0W
56 Bafra 41 34N 35 54W
57 Bāft 29 15N 56 38W
62 Bagalkot 16 10N 75 40W
74 Bagamoyo 6 28S 38 55 E
60 Bagasra 21 2N 70 57 E
51 Bagdarin 54 26N 113 36 E
109 Bagé 31 20S 54 15W
56 Baghdād 32 20N 44 30 E
61 Bagherhat 22 40N 89 47 E
38 Bagheira 38 5N 13 30 E
57 Baghīn 30 12N 56 45 E
57 Baghlan 36 12N 69 0 E
57 Baghlan □ 36 0N 68 30 E
37 Bagnacavallo 44 25N 11 58 E
39 Bagnara Cálabria 38 16N 15 49 E
20 Bagnères-de-Bigorre 43 5N 0 9 E
20 Bagnères-de-Luchon 42 47N 0 38 E
36 Bagni di Lucca 41 1N 10 37 E
37 Bagno di Romagna 43 50N 11 59 E
21 Bagnols-sur-Cèze 44 10N 4 36 E
91 Bagotville 48 22N 70 54W
67 Bagrash Kol, L. 42 0N 87 0 E
40 Bagrdan 44 5N 21 11 E
65 Baguio 16 26N 120 34 E
30 Bahabòn de Esgueva 41 52N 3 43W
60 Bahadurgarh 28 40N 76 57 E
105 Bahamas ■ 24 0N 74 0W
63 Bahau 2 48N 102 26 E
60 Bahawalnagar 30 0N 73 15 E
60 Bahawalpur 29 37N 71 40 E
60 Bahawalpur □ 29 5N 71 3 E
61 Baheri 28 45N 79 34 E
111 Bahia= Salvador 13 0S 38 30W
105 Bahia, Is. de la 16 45N 86 15W
111 Bahia □ 12 0N 42 0 E
108 Bahia Blanca 38 35S 62 13W
110 Bahia de Caráquez 0 40S 80 27W
112 Bahia Laura 48 10S 66 30W
110 Bahia Negra 20 5S 58 5W
73 Bahr el Ghazâl □ 7 0N 28 0 E
61 Bahraich 27 38N 81 50 E
57 Bahrain ■ 26 0N 50 35 E
111 Baião 2 50S 49 15W
41 Baicoi 45 3N 25 52 E
91 Baie Comeau 49 12N 68 10W
91 Baie T. Paul 47 28N 70 32W
56 Ba 'iji 35 0N 43 30 E
15 Baile Atha Cliath=Dublin 53 20N 6 18W
31 Bailén 38 8N 3 48W
41 Baileşti 44 1N 23 20 E
62 Bailhongal 15 55N 74 53 E
99 Bainbridge, Ga. 30 53N 84 34W
97 Bainbridge, N.Y. 42 17N 75 29W
88 Baird Mts. 67 10N 160 15W
84 Bairnsdale 37 48S 147 36 E
29 Baixo-Alentejo, Reg. 38 0N 8 40W
27 Baja 46 12N 18 59 E
104 Baja California Norte □ 30 0N 116 0W
104 Baja California Sur □ 26 0N 112 0W
81 Bajimba, Mt. 29 17S 152 6 E
61 Bajitpur 24 13N 91 0 E
80 Bajool 24 30S 150 35 E
50 Bakchar 57 0N 82 5 E
102 Baker, Calif. 36 16N 116 2W
100 Baker, Mont. 46 22N 104 12W
76 Baker I. 0 10N 176 35 E
88 Baker L. 64 0N 97 0W
102 Baker, Mt. 48 50N 121 49W
88 Baker Lake 64 20N 96 10W
90 Baker's Dozen Is. 57 30N 79 0W
103 Bakersfield 35 25N 119 0W
56 Bakhtiari □ 32 0N 49 0 E
49 Bakinskikh Komissarov 39 20N 49 15 E
27 Bakony Forest= Bakony Hegyseg, Reg. 47 10N 17 30 E
27 Bakony Hegyseg, Reg. 47 10N 17 30 E
49 Baku 40 25N 49 45 E
96 Bala 45 2N 79 38 E
54 Bal'a 32 20N 35 6 E
12 Bala, L. 52 53N 3 38W
64 Balabac I. 8 0N 117 0 E
64 Balabac Str. 7 53N 117 5 E
61 Balaghat 21 49N 80 12 E
62 Balaghat Ra. 18 50N 76 30 E
32 Balaguer 41 50N 0 50 E
81 Balaklava, Australia 34 7S 138 22 E
49 Balaklava, U.S.S.R. 44 30N 33 30 E
48 Balakovo 52 4N 47 55 E
61 Balangir 20 43N 83 35 E
60 Balapur 21 22N 76 45 E
48 Balashov 51 30N 43 10 E
61 Balasore 21 35N 87 3 E
27 Balassaguarmat 48 4N 19 15 E
27 Balaton, L. 46 50N 17 40 E
33 Balazote 38 54N 2 9W
104 Balboa 9 0N 79 30W
15 Balbriggan 53 35N 6 10W
108 Balcarce 38 0S 58 10W
41 Balchik 43 28N 28 11 E
85 Balclutha 46 15S 169 45 E
83 Bald, Hd. 35 6S 118 1 E
97 Baldwinsville 43 10N 76 19W
103 Baldy Pk. 33 55N 109 35W
32 Baleares, Is. 39 30N 3 0 E
80 Balfe's Creek 20 12S 145 55 E
64 Bali, I. 8 20S 115 0 E
56 Balikesir 39 35S 27 58 E
64 Balikpapan 1 10S 116 55 E
63 Baling 5 41N 100 55 E
69 Balintang Chan. 19 50N 122 0 E
59 Balipara 26 50N 92 45 E
111 Baliza 16 0S 52 20W
41 Balkan, Mts.= Stara Planina 43 15N 23 0 E
9 Balkan Pen. 42 0N 22 0 E
57 Balkh □ 36 30N 67 0 E
50 Balkhash 46 50N 74 50 E
50 Balkhash, Oz. 46 0N 74 50 E
14 Ballachulish 56 40N 5 10W
83 Balladonia 32 27S 123 51 E
84 Ballarat 37 33S 143 50 E
83 Ballard, L. 29 20S 120 10 E
61 Ballarpur 19 50N 79 23 E
14 Ballater 57 2N 3 2W
61 Ballia 25 46N 84 12 E
83 Ballidu 30 35S 116 45 E
81 Ballina, Australia 28 50S 153 31 E
15 Ballina, Mayo 54 7N 9 10W
15 Ballina, Tipperary 52 49N 8 27W
15 Ballinasloe 53 20N 8 12W
101 Ballinger 31 45N 99 58W
15 Ballinrobe 53 36N 9 13W
15 Ballycastle 55 12N 6 15W
15 Ballymena 54 53N 6 18W
15 Ballymena □ 54 53N 6 18W
15 Ballymoney 55 5N 6 30W
15 Ballymoney □ 55 5N 6 30W
15 Ballyshannon 54 30N 8 10W
112 Balmaceda 46 0S 71 50W
27 Balmazújváros 47 37N 21 21 E
14 Balmoral 57 3N 3 13W
75 Balovale 13 30S 23 15 E
61 Balrampur 27 30N 82 20 E
84 Balrana!d 34 38S 143 33 E
41 Bals 44 22N 24 5 E
104 Balsas, R. 17 55N 102 10W
49 Balta 48 2N 29 45 E
9 Baltic Sea 56 0N 20 0 E
28 Baltiisk 54 38N 19 55 E
15 Baltimore, Eire 51 29N 9 22W
98 Baltimore, U.S.A. 39 18N 76 37W
58 Baluchistan, Reg. 27 30N 65 0 E
57 Bam 29 7N 58 14 E
72 Bamako 12 34N 7 55W
74 Bambari 5 40N 20 35 E
80 Bambaroo 18 50S 146 10 E
25 Bamberg 49 54N 10 53 E
72 Bamenda 5 57N 10 11 E
57 Bamian □ 35 0N 67 0 E
57 Bampur 27 15N 60 21 E
63 Ban Aranyaprathet 13 41N 102 30 E
63 Ban Bua Yai 15 33N 102 26 E
63 Ban Houei Sai 20 22N 100 32 E
63 Ban Mae Sot 16 40N 98 30 E
63 Ban Nong Pling 15 40N 100 10 E
63 Ban Phai 16 4N 102 44 E
63 Ban Takua Pa 8 55N 98 25 E
57 Banadar Daryay Oman □ 25 30N 56 0 E
74 Banalia 1 32N 25 5 E
72 Banamba 13 29N 7 22W
80 Banana 24 32S 150 12 E
111 Bananal, I. de 11 30S 50 30W
73 Bânâs, Ras 23 57N 35 50 E
60 Banas, R. 25 55N 76 45 E
15 Banbridge 54 26N 6 16W
15 Banbridge □ 54 21N 6 16W
13 Banbury 52 4N 1 21W
14 Banchory 57 3N 2 30W
90 Bancroft 45 3N 77 51W
57 Band-e Charak 26 45N 54 20 E
57 Band-e Nakhīlu 26 58N 53 30 E
61 Banda 25 30N 80 26 E
64 Banda Aceh 5 35N 95 20 E
81 Banda Banda, Mt. 31 10S 152 28 E
65 Banda Sea 6 0S 130 0 E
57 Bandar Abbas 27 15N 56 15 E
63 Bandar Maharani 2 2N 102 34 E
63 Bandar Penggaram 1 50N 102 56 E
64 Bandar Seri Begawan 4 52N 115 0 E
57 Bandar-e Bushetir 28 55N 50 55 E
57 Bandar-e Lengeh 26 35N 54 58 E
56 Bandar-e Ma'shur 30 35N 49 10 E
56 Bandar-e-Pahlavi 37 30N 49 30 E
57 Bandar-e Rig 29 30N 50 45 E
57 Bandar-e Sháh 37 0N 54 10 E
56 Bandar-e Shahpur 30 30N 49 5 E
75 Bandawe 11 58S 34 5 E
109 Bandeira, Pico da 20 26S 41 47W
56 Bandirma 40 20N 28 0 E
15 Bandon 51 44N 8 45W
15 Bandon, R. 51 40N 8 35W
74 Bandundu 3 15S 17 22 E
65 Bandung 6 36S 107 48 E
33 Bañeres 38 44N 0 38W
105 Banes 20 58N 75 43W
92 Banff, Canada 51 20N 115 40W
14 Banff, U.K. 57 40N 2 32W
92 Banff Nat. Park 51 38N 116 22W
63 Bang Saphan 11 14N 99 28 E
75 Bangala Dam 21 7S 31 25 E
62 Bangalore 12 59N 77 40 E
61 Bangaon 23 0N 88 47 E
74 Bangassou 4 55N 23 55 E
73 Banghazı 32 11N 20 3 E
65 Bangil 7 36S 112 50 E
64 Bangka, I., Selatan 3 30S 105 30 E
65 Bangka, I., Utara 7 2S 112 46 E
65 Bangkalan 7 2S 112 46 E
63 Bangkok=Krung Thep 13 45N 100 31 E
59 Bangladesh ■ 24 0N 90 0 E
12 Bangor, Gwynedd 53 13N 4 9W
15 Bangor, N. Down 54 40N 5 40W
97 Bangor, Pa. 40 51N 75 13W
99 Bangor, Me. 44 48N 68 42W
65 Bangued 17 40N 120 37 E
74 Bangui 4 23N 18 35 E
74 Bangweulu, L. 11 0S 30 0 E
105 Bani 18 16N 70 22W
54 Bani Na'im 31 31N 35 10 E
73 Banınah 32 0N 20 12 E
40 Banja Luka 44 49N 17 26 E
65 Banjar 7 24S 108 30 E
64 Banjarmasin 3 20S 114 35 E
65 Banjarnegara 7 24S 109 42 E
72 Banjul 13 28N 16 40W
80 Banka Banka 18 50S 134 0 E
61 Bankipore 25 35N 85 10 E
86 Banks I. 73 30N 120 0W
85 Banks, Pen. 43 45S 173 15 E
61 Bankura 23 11N 87 18 E
15 Bann, R. 55 2N 6 35W
18 Bannalec 47 57N 3 42W
103 Banning 48 44N 91 56W
60 Bannu 33 0N 70 18S
14 Bannockburn 56 5N 3 55W
60 Bañolas 42 16N 2 44 E
30 Baños de Molgas 42 15N 7 40W
27 Banská Bystrica 48 46N 19 14 E
27 Banská Stiavnica 48 25N 18 55 E
60 Banswara 23 32N 74 24 E
65 Banten 6 5S 106 8 E
15 Bantry 51 40N 9 28W
15 Bantry, B. 51 35N 9 50W
65 Bantul 7 55S 110 19 E
60 Bantva 21 29N 70 12 E
62 Bantval 12 55N 75 0 E
41 Banya 42 33N 24 50 E
20 Banyuls 42 29N 3 8 E
62 Bapatla 15 55N 80 30 E
54 Baqa el Gharbiya 32 25N 35 2 E
40 Bar 42 8N 19 8 E
64 Barabai 2 32S 115 34 E
50 Barabinsk 55 20N 78 20 E
100 Baraboo 43 28N 89 46W
105 Baracoa 20 20N 74 30W
108 Baradero 33 52S 59 29S
105 Barahona, Dom. Rep. 18 13N 71 7W
30 Barahona, Sp. 41 17N 2 39W
59 Barail Ra. 25 15N 93 20 E
66 Barak □ 38 20N 140 0 E
59 Barakhola 25 0N 92 45 E
62 Baramati 18 11N 74 33 E
58 Baramula 34 15N 74 20 E
60 Baran 25 9N 76 40 E
92 Baranof 57 0N 135 10W
92 Baranof I. 57 0N 135 10W
48 Baranovichi 53 10N 26 0 E
27 Baranya □ 46 0N 18 15 E
65 Barat □, Java 7 0S 107 0 E

Barat □, Kalimantan — Belmonte, Port.

64 Barat, □ Kalimantan 0 0S 111 0E
64 Barat, Sumatera 1 0S 101 0E
Sumatera 1 0S 101 0E
65 Barat Daja, Kep. 7 30S 128 0E
109 Barbacena 21 15S 43 56W
110 Barbacoas 1 45N 78 0W
105 Barbados ■ 13 0N 59 30W
32 Barbastro 42 2N 0 5E
31 Barbate 36 13N 5 56W
75 Barberton, S. Africa 25 42S 31 2E
96 Barberton, U.S.A. 41 0N 81 40W
105 Barbuda, I. 17 30N 61 40W
80 Barcaldine 22 33S 145 13E
73 Barce=Al Marj 32 25N 20 40E
32 Barcelona, Sp. 41 21N 2 10E
110 Barcelona, Ven. 10 10N 64 40W
32 Barcelona □ 41 30N 2 0E
39 Barcellona Pozzo di Gotto 38 8N 15 15E
21 Barcelonnette 44 23N 6 40E
110 Barcelos 1 0S 63 0W
73 Bardaï 21 25N 17 0E
55 Bardera 2 20N 42 0S
73 Bardiyah 31 45N 25 0E
12 Bardsey I. 52 46N 4 47W
61 Bareilly 28 22N 79 27E
18 Barentin 49 33N 0 58E
4 Barents Sea 73 0N 39 0E
18 Barfleur 49 40N 1 17W
18 Barfleur, Pte. de 49 42N 1 17W
36 Barga 44 5N 10 30E
55 Bargal 11 25N 51 0E
80 Bargara 24 50S 152 25E
51 Barguzin 53 37N 109 37E
61 Barh 25 29N 85 46E
61 Barhaj 26 18N 83 44E
61 Barhi 24 15N 85 25E
60 Bari, India 26 39N 77 39E
39 Bari, Italy 41 6N 16 52E
60 Bari Doab, Reg. 30 20N 73 0E
110 Barinas 8 36N 70 15W
88 Baring, C. 70 0N 116 30W
73 Bâris 24 42N 30 31E
61 Barisal 22 30N 90 20E
64 Barisan, Bukit, Mts. 3 30S 102 15E
64 Barito, R. 4 0S 114 50E
57 Barkah 24 30N 58 0E
67 Barkha 31 0N 81 45E
80 Barkly Tableland 19 50S 138 40E
19 Bar-le-Duc 48 47N 5 10E
83 Barlee, L. 29 15S 119 30E
39 Barletta 41 20N 16 17E
84 Barmedman 34 9S 147 21E
60 Barmer 25 45N 71 20E
81 Barmera 34 15S 140 28E
12 Barmouth 52 44N 4 3W
60 Barnagar 23 7N 75 19E
12 Barnard Castle 54 33N 1 55W
50 Barnaul 53 20N 83 40E
100 Barnesville 33 6N 84 9W
13 Barnet 51 37N 0 15W
16 Barneveld 52 7N 5 36E
18 Barneville 49 23N 1 46W
12 Barnsley 53 33N 1 29W
13 Barnstaple 51 5N 4 3W
60 Baroda= Vadodara 22 20N 73 10E
73 Barqa 27 0N 20 0E
31 Barquinha 39 28N 8 25W
110 Barquisimeto 9 58N 69 13W
111 Barra 11 5S 43 10W
14 Barra, I. 57 0N 7 30W
111 Barra de Corda 5 30S 45 10W
109 Barra do Piraí 22 30S 43 50W
109 Barra Mansa 22 35S 44 12W
81 Barraba 30 21S 150 35E
61 Barrackpur 22 44N 88 30E
39 Barrafranca 37 22N 14 10E
110 Barranca 10 45S 77 50W
110 Barrancabermeja 7 0N 73 50W
110 Barrancas 8 55N 62 5W
31 Barrancos 38 10N 6 58W
108 Barranqueras 27 30S 59 0W
110 Barranquilla 11 0N 74 50W
111 Barras 1 45S 73 13W
90 Barraute 47 30N 76 50W
97 Barre 44 15N 73 30W
111 Barreiras 12 8S 45 0W
111 Barreirinhas 2 30S 42 50W
31 Barreiro 38 40N 9 6W
111 Barreiros 8 49S 35 12W
111 Barretos 20 30S 48 35W
92 Barrhead 54 10N 114 30W
90 Barrie 44 25N 79 45W
97 Barrington 41 43N 71 20W
12 Barrow, U.K. 54 8N 3 15W
88 Barrow, U.S.A. 71 16N 156 50W
82 Barrow, I. 20 45S 115 20E
15 Barrow, R. 52 46N 7 0W
80 Barrow Creek 21 30S 133 55E
30 Barruecopardo 41 4N 6 40W
30 Barruelo 42 54N 4 17W
13 Barry 51 23N 3 19W
90 Barry's Bay 45 30N 77 40W
62 Barsi 18 10N 75 50E
103 Barstow 34 58N 117 2W
19 Bar-sur-Aube 48 14N 4 40E
110 Bartica 6 25N 58 40W
101 Bartlesville 36 50N 95 58W
83 Barton Siding 30 31S 132 39E
12 Barton-upon-Humber 53 41N 0 27W
28 Bartoszyce 54 15N 20 55E
99 Bartow 27 53N 81 49W
68 Baruun Urt 46 46N 113 15E
60 Barwani 22 2N 74 57E
19 Bas Rhin □ 48 40N 7 30E
41 Basarabi 44 10N 28 26E
108 Bascuñan, C. 28 52S 71 35W
25 Basel 47 35N 7 35E
25 Basel Landschaft □ 47 26N 7 45E
39 Basento, R. 40 25N 16 40E
48 Bashkir A.S.S.R. □ 54 0N 57 0E
65 Basilan, I. 6 35N 122 0E
65 Basilan City= Lamitan 6 37N 122 0E
65 Basilan Str. 13 10S 122 0E
13 Basildon 51 34N 0 29E
39 Basilicata □ 40 30N 16 0E
13 Basingstoke 51 15N 1 5W
61 Basirhat 22 40N 88 54E
90 Baskatong Res. 46 46N 75 50W
25 Basle=Basel 47 35N 7 35E
62 Basmat 19 15N 77 12E
74 Basoka 1 16N 23 40E
14 Bass Rock 56 5N 2 40W
80 Bass, Str. 39 15S 146 30E
37 Bassano del Grappa 45 45N 11 45E
75 Bassas da India, I. 22 0S 39 0E
105 Basse Terre 16 0N 61 40W
59 Bassein, Burma 16 45N 94 30E
62 Bassein, India 19 26N 72 48E
105 Basseterre 17 17N 62 43W
100 Bassett 42 37N 99 30W
60 Bassi 30 44N 76 21E
19 Bassigny, Reg. 48 0N 5 10E
57 Bastak 27 15N 54 25E
61 Basti 26 52N 82 55E
21 Bastia 42 40N 9 30E
16 Bastogne 50 1N 5 43E
54 Bat Yam 32 2N 34 44E
74 Bata 1 57N 9 50E
65 Bataan, Pen. 14 38N 120 30E
105 Barabanó, G. de 22 30N 82 30W
51 Batagoy 67 38N 134 38E
51 Batamay 63 30N 129 15E
69 Batan Is. 20 25N 121 59E
65 Batang 6 55S 109 40E
65 Batangas 13 35N 121 10E
109 Batatais 20 54S 47 37W
96 Batavia 43 0N 78 10W
82 Batchelor 13 4S 131 1E
101 Batesville 35 48N 91 40W
13 Bath, U.K. 51 22N 2 22W
96 Bath, Me. 43 50N 69 49W
99 Bath, N.Y. 42 20N 77 17W
14 Bathgate 55 54N 3 38W
72 Bathurst=Banjul 13 28N 16 40W
84 Bathurst, Australia 33 25S 149 31E
91 Bathurst, Canada 47 37N 65 43W
88 Bathurst, C. 70 30N 128 30W
82 Bathurst, I., Australia 11 30S 130 10E
86 Bathurst I., Canada 76 30N 130 10W
88 Bathurst Inlet 67 15N 108 30W
91 Bathurst Mines 47 30N 65 47W
57 Batinah, Reg. 24 0N 57 0E
72 Batna 35 34N 6 15E
101 Baton Rouge 30 30N 91 5W
74 Batouri 4 30N 14 25E
63 Battambang 13 7N 103 12E
62 Batticaloa 7 43N 81 45E
39 Battipáglia 40 38N 15 0E
54 Battir 31 44N 35 8E
13 Battle 50 55N 0 30E
93 Battle, R. 52 45N 108 15W
98 Battle Creek 42 20N 85 10W
91 Battle Harbour 52 13N 55 42W
102 Battle Mountain 40 45N 117 0W
93 Battleford 52 45N 108 15W
27 Battonya 46 16N 21 03E
64 Batu, Kep. 0 30S 98 25E
63 Batu Gajah 4 28N 101 3E
63 Batu Pahat= Bandar Penggaram 1 50N 102 56E
49 Batumi 41 30N 41 30E
64 Baturadja 4 11S 104 15E
111 Baturité 4 28S 38 45W
65 Baubau 5 25S 123 50E
72 Bauchi 10 22N 9 48E
18 Baud 47 52N 3 1W
31 Bauer, C. 32 44N 134 4E
18 Baugé 47 31N 0 8W
80 Bauhinia Downs 24 35S 149 18E
24 Baunatal 51 19N 9 15E
109 Bauru 22 10S 49 0W
111 Baus 18 22S 52 47½
24 Bautzen 51 11N 14 25W
59 Bawdwin 23 5N 97 50E
64 Bawean, I. 5 46S 112 35E
59 Bawlake 19 11N 97 21E
98 Bay City, Mich. 43 35N 83 51W
101 Bay City, Tex. 28 59N 95 55W
97 Bay Shore 40 44N 73 15W
85 Bay View 39 25W 176 50E
105 Bayamón 18 24N 66 10W
68 Bayan 47 20N 107 55E
67 Bayan Kara Shan, Mts. 34 0N 98 0E
68 Bayan-Uul 49 6N 112 12E
50 Bayanaul 50 45N 75 45E
68 Bayantsogt 47 58N 105 1E
25 Bayerischer Wald, Reg. 49 0N 13 0E
25 Bayern □ 49 7N 11 30E
18 Bayeux 49 17N 0 42W
51 Baykal, Oz. 53 0N 108 0E
51 Baykal, L.= Baykal, Oz. 53 0N 108 0S
51 Baykir 61 50N 95 50E
50 Baykonur 47 48N 65 50E
19 Bayon 48 30N 6 20E
20 Bayonne, Fr. 43 30N 1 28E
97 Bayonne, U.S.A. 40 40N 74 5W
25 Bayreuth 49 56N 11 35E
56 Bayrūt 33 53N 35 31E
54 Bayt Aula 31 37N 35 2E
54 Bayt Jālā 31 43N 35 11E
54 Bayt Lahm 31 43N 35 12E
54 Bayt Sāhūr 31 42N 35 13E
54 Baytin 31 56N 35 14E
101 Baytown 29 42N 94 57W
33 Baza 37 30N 2 47W
75 Bazaruto, I. do 21 40S 35 28E
20 Bazas 44 27N 0 13W
93 Beach 46 57N 104 0W
13 Beachy Hd. 50 44N 0 16E
83 Beacon, Australia 30 20S 117 55E
97 Beacon, U.S.A. 41 32N 73 58W
112 Beagle, Can. 55 0S 68 30W
85 Bealey 43 2S 171 36E
90 Beardmore 49 36N 87 59W
100 Beardstown 40 0N 90 25W
20 Béarn, Reg 43 28N 0 36W
20 Béarn, R. 43 40N 0 47W
33 Beas de Segura 38 15N 2 53W
32 Beasain 43 3N 2 11W
100 Beatrice 40 20N 96 40W
21 Beaucaire 43 48N 4 39E
91 Beauceville 46 13N 70 46W
81 Beaudesert 27 59S 153 0E
64 Beaufort, Malaysia 5 30N 115 40E
84 Beaufort, Australia 37 25S 143 25E
99 Beaufort, U.S.A. 34 45N 76 40W
86 Beaufort Sea 70 30N 146 0W
75 Beaufort West 32 18S 22 36E
90 Beauharnois 45 20N 73 20W
21 Beaujolais, Reg. 46 0N 4 25E
21 Beaulieu 43 45N 7 20E
14 Beauly 57 29N 4 27W
12 Beaumaris 53 16N 4 7W
18 Beaumont, Fr. 44 45N 0 46E
101 Beaumont, U.S.A. 30 5N 94 8W
19 Beaumont-sur-Oise 49 9N 2 17E
21 Beaune 47 2N 4 50E
93 Beausejour 50 5N 96 35E
19 Beauvais 49 25N 2 8E
93 Beauval 55 9N 107 35W
20 Beauvoir 46 12N 0 30W
20 Beauvoir-sur-Mer 46 55N 2 1W
96 Beaver, Canada 40 40N 80 18W
88 Beaver, U.S.A. 66 40N 147 50W
100 Beaver Dam 43 28N 88 50W
96 Beaver Falls 40 44N 80 20W
60 Beawar 26 3N 74 18E
109 Bebedouro 21 0S 48 25W
13 Beccles 52 27N 1 33E
40 Bečej 45 36N 20 3E
30 Becerreá 42 51N 7 10W
72 Béchar 31 38N 2 18E
98 Beckley 37 50N 81 8W
24 Beckum 51 47N 8 5E
18 Bécon 47 30N 0 50W
33 Bédar 37 11N 1 59W
20 Bédarieux 43 37N 3 10E
90 Bedford, Canada 45 10N 73 0W
75 Bedford, S. Africa 32 40S 26 10E
13 Bedford, U.K. 52 8N 0 29W
96 Bedford, Pa. 40 1N 78 30W
98 Bedford, Ind. 38 50N 86 30W
13 Bedford □ 52 4N 0 28W
92 Bednesti 53 50N 123 10W
80 Bedourie 24 30S 139 30E
27 Bedzin 50 19N 19 7E
24 Beelitz 52 14N 12 58E
81 Beenleigh 27 43S 153 10E
54 Be'er Sheva 31 15N 34 48E
54 Be'erotayim 32 19N 34 59E
12 Beeston 52 55N 1 11W
24 Beetzendorf 52 42N 11 6E
101 Beeville 28 27N 97 44W
84 Bega 36 41S 149 51E
40 Bega, Canalul 45 37N 20 46E
18 Bégard 48 38N 3 18W
30 Begonte 43 10N 7 40W
61 Begu-Sarai 25 24N 86 9E
56 Behbehan 30 30N 50 15E
57 Behshahr 36 45N 53 35E
68 Beijing 39 45N 116 25E
16 Beilen 52 52N 6 27E
25 Beilngries 49 1N 11 27E
75 Beira 19 50S 34 52E
29 Beira-Alta, Reg. 41 0N 7 20W
29 Beira-Baixa, Reg. 40 0N 7 30W
29 Beira Litoral, Reg. 40 0N 7 30W
56 Beirut=Bayrut 33 53N 35 31E
54 Beit Hanun 31 32N 34 32E
54 Beit'Ur et Tahta 31 54N 35 5E
75 Beitbridge 22 12S 30 0E
54 Beituniya 31 54N 35 10E
31 Beja, Port. 38 2N 7 53W
72 Béja, Tunisia 36 10N 9 0E
31 Beja □ 37 55N 7 55W
72 Béjaïa 36 42N 5 2E
30 Béjar 40 23N 5 46W
27 Békés 46 47N 21 9E
27 Békés □ 46 45N 21 0E
27 Békéscsaba 46 40N 21 10E
63 Bekok 2 20N 103 7E
61 Bela, India 25 50N 82 0E
58 Bela, Pak. 26 12N 66 20E
40 Bela Crkva 44 55N 21 27E
40 Bela Palanka 43 13N 22 17E
64 Belawan 3 33N 98 32E
49 Belaya Tserkov 49 45N 30 10E
90 Belcher Is. 56 20N 79 20W
32 Belchite 41 18N 0 43W
48 Belebey 54 72N 54 7E
111 Belém 1 20S 48 30W
108 Belén 27 40S 67 5W
103 Belen 34 40N 106 50W
41 Belene 43 39N 25 10E
55 Belet Uen 4 30N 45 5E
15 Belfast, U.K. 54 35N 5 56W
99 Belfast, U.S.A. 44 30N 69 0W
15 Belfast, L. 54 40N 5 50W
15 Belfast □ 54 35N 5 56W
19 Belfort 47 38N 6 50E
19 Belfort, Terr. de □ 47 38N 6 52E
62 Belgaum 15 55N 74 35E
16 Belgium ■ 51 30N 5 0E
15 Belgooly 51 44N 8 30W
49 Belgorod 50 35N 36 35E
49 Belgorod-Dnestrovskiy 46 11N 30 23E
40 Belgrade= Beograd 44 50N 20 37E
64 Belitung, Pulau, I. 3 10S 107 50E
104 Belize ■ 17 0N 88 30W
104 Belize City 17 25N 88 0W
108 Bell Ville 32 40S 62 40W
92 Bella Coola 52 25N 126 40W
108 Bella Unión 30 15S 57 40W
108 Bella Vista 28 33S 59 0W
36 Bellágio 45 59N 9 15E
96 Bellaire 40 1N 80 46W
62 Bellary 15 10N 76 56E
81 Bellata 29 53S 149 46E
18 Belle I. 47 20N 3 10W
91 Belle I, Str. of 51 30N 56 30W
100 Belle Fourche 44 43N 103 52W
99 Belle Glade 26 43N 80 38W
21 Belledonne, Mts. 45 11N 6 0E
98 Bellefontaine 40 20N 83 45E
21 Bellegarde 46 4N 3 49E
21 Belleville, Fr. 46 7N 4 45E
100 Belleville, Ill. 38 30N 90 0W
96 Belleville, N.Y. 43 46N 76 10W
92 Bellevue, Can. 46 35N 84 10W
96 Bellevue, U.S.A. 40 29N 80 3W
21 Belley 45 46N 5 41E
89 Bellin 60 0N 70 0W
81 Bellingen 30 25S 152 50E
102 Bellingham 48 45N 122 27W
5 Bellingshausen Sea 66 0S 80 0W
25 Bellinzona 46 11N 9 1E
97 Bellows Falls 43 10N 72 30W
32 Bellpuig 41 37N 1 1E
37 Belluno 46 8N 12 6E
97 Belmar 40 10N 74 2W
31 Bélmez 38 17N 5 17W
84 Belmont 33 4S 151 42E
111 Belmonte, Brazil 16 0S 39 0W
30 Belmonte, Port. 40 21N 7 20W

Belmopan Bischofshofen

104 Belmopan 17 18N 88 30W
15 Belmullet 54 13N 9 58W
109 Belo Horizonte 19 55S 43 56W
51 Belogorsk 51 0N 128 20E
40 Belogradchik 43 37N 22 40E
100 Beloit 42 35N 89 0W
48 Belomorsk 64 35N 34 30E
48 Beloretsk 53 58N 58 24E
50 Belovo 54 30N 86 0E
48 Beloye, Oz. 60 10N 37 35E
48 Beloye More 66 0N 38 0E
48 Belozersk 60 0N 37 30E
39 Belpasso 37 37N 15 0E
38 Belsito 37 50N 13 47E
49 Belsty 47 48N 28 0E
81 Beltana 30 48S 138 25E
111 Belterra 2 45S 55 0W
101 Belton 31 4N 97 30W
15 Belturbet 54 6N 7 28W
39 Belvedere Marittimo 39 37N 15 52E
100 Belvidere 42 15N 88 55W
50 Belyy Os. 73 30N 71 0E
50 Belyy Yar 58 26N 84 30E
24 Belzig 52 8N 12 36E
31 Bembézar, R. 38 0N 5 20W
100 Bemidji 47 30N 94 50W
14 Ben Cruachan, Mt. 56 26N 5 8W
73 Ben Gardane 33 11N 11 11E
14 Ben Hope, Mt. 58 24N 4 36W
14 Ben Lawers, Mt. 56 33N 4 13W
81 Ben Lomond, Mt., Australia 30 1S 151 43E
14 Ben Lomond, Mt., U.K. 56 12N 4 39W
14 Ben Macdhui, Mt. 57 4N 3 40W
14 Ben More, Mt. 56 26N 6 2W
14 Ben More Assynt, Mt. 58 7N 4 51W
14 Ben Nevis, Mt. 56 48N 5 0W
14 Ben Wyvis, Mt. 57 40N 4 35W
74 Bena Dibele 4 4S 22 50E
31 Benagalbón 36 45N 4 15W
84 Benalla 36 30S 146 0E
61 Benares=Varanasi 25 22N 83 8E
30 Benavente 38 59N 8 49W
30 Benavides 42 30N 5 54W
14 Benbecula, I. 57 26N 7 20W
81 Benbonyathe Hill 30 25S 139 11E
83 Bencubbin 30 48S 117 52E
102 Bend 44 2N 121 15W
55 Bender Beila 9 30N 50 48E
83 Bendering 32 23S 118 18E
49 Bendery 46 50N 29 50E
84 Bendigo 36 40S 144 15E
54 Bene Beraq 32 5N 34 50E
26 Benešov 49 46N 14 41E
19 Bénestroff 48 54N 6 45E
39 Benevento 41 7N 14 45E
19 Benfeld 48 22N 7 34E
73 Benghazi=Banghazī 32 11N 20 3E
64 Bengkalis 1 30N 102 10E
64 Bengkulu 3 50S 102 12E
64 Bengkulu □ 3 50S 102 10E
93 Bengough 49 25N 105 10W
75 Benguela 12 37S 13 25E
74 Beni 32 11S 148 43E
73 Beni Mazar 28 32N 30 44E
72 Beni Mellal 32 21N 6 21W
73 Benī Suêf 29 5N 31 6E
32 Benicarló 40 23N 0 23E
33 Benidorm 38 33N 0 9W
72 Benin, B. of 5 0N 3 0E
72 Benin City 6 20N 5 31E
33 Benisa 38 43N 0 3E
108 Benjamin Aceval 24 58S 57 34W
110 Benjamin Constant 4 40S 70 15W
80 Benlidi 24 35S 144 50E
99 Bennettsville 34 38N 79 39W
97 Bennington 42 52N 73 12W
18 Bénodet 47 53N 4 7W
75 Benoni 26 11S 28 18E
25 Bensheim 49 40N 8 38E
103 Benson 31 59N 110 19W
65 Benteng 6 10S 120 30E
101 Benton, Ark. 34 30N 92 35W
100 Benton, Ill. 38 0N 88 55W
98 Benton Harbor 42 10N 86 28W
63 Bentong 3 31N 101 55S
72 Benue, R. 7 47N 6 45E
40 Beograd 44 50N 20 37E
66 Beppu 33 15N 131 30E
54 Ber Dagan 32 1N 34 49E
42 Berati 40 43N 19 59E
73 Berber 18 0N 34 0E
55 Berbera 10 30N 45 2E
74 Berbérati 4 15N 15 40E
33 Berberia, C. 38 39N 1 24E
36 Berceto 44 30N 10 0E
25 Berchtesgaden 47 37N 13 1E
19 Berck 50 25N 1 36E
49 Berdicher 49 57N 28 30E
50 Berdsk 54 47N 83 2E
49 Berdyansk 46 45N 36 50E
55 Bereda 11 45N 51 0E
72 Berekum 7 29N 2 34W
93 Berens River 52 25N 97 0W
27 Berettyóújfalu 47 13N 21 33E
48 Berezniki 59 24N 56 46E
50 Berezovo 64 0N 65 0E
32 Berga 42 6N 1 48E
36 Bergamo 45 42N 9 40E
30 Bergantiños 43 20N 8 40W
24 Bergedorf 53 28N 10 12E
24 Bergen, E. Germany 50 24N 13 26E
16 Bergen, Neth. 52 40N 4 42E
47 Bergen, Norway 60 23N 5 27E
16 Bergen-op-Zoom 51 30N 4 18E
20 Bergerac 44 51N 0 30E
24 Bergheim 50 57N 6 38E
24 Bergisch-Gladbach 50 59N 7 9E
19 Bergues 50 58N 2 24E
16 Bergum 53 13N 5 59E
61 Berhampore 24 2N 88 27E
62 Berhampur 19 15N 84 54E
88 Bering Sea 66 0N 170 0W
4 Bering Str. 65 0N 168 0W
16 Beringen 51 3N 5 14E
51 Beringovskiy 63 3N 179 19E
108 Berisso 34 40S 58 0W
33 Berja 36 50N 2 56W
102 Berkeley 38 0N 122 20W
5 Berkner I. 79 30S 50 0W
41 Berkovitsa 43 16N 23 8E
13 Berkshire □ 51 30N 1 20W
31 Berlanga 38 17N 5 50W
24 Berleburg 51 3N 8 22E
31 Berlenga, I. 39 25N 9 30W
24 Berlin, Germany 52 32N 13 24W
97 Berlin, U.S.A. 44 29N 71 10W
31 Bermeja, Sa. 36 45N 5 11W
32 Bermeo 43 25N 2 47W
105 Bermuda, I. 32 45N 65 0W
25 Bern 46 57N 7 28E
25 Bern □ 46 45N 7 40E
39 Bernalda 40 24N 16 44E
103 Bernalilo 35 17N 106 37W
109 Bernardo de Irigoyen 26 15S 53 40W
24 Bernau 47 53N 12 20E
18 Bernay 49 5N 0 35E
26 Berndorf 47 59N 16 1E
25 Berne=Bern 46 57N 7 28E
25 Berner Alpen, Mts. 46 27N 7 35E
83 Bernier, I. 24 50S 113 12E
25 Bernina, Piz 46 20N 9 54E
26 Beroun 49 57N 14 5E
26 Berounka, R. 50 0N 13 47E
84 Berowra 33 35S 151 12E
21 Berre 43 28N 5 11E
21 Berre, Étang de 43 27N 5 5E
72 Berrechid 33 18N 7 36W
81 Berri 34 14S 140 35E
84 Berrigan 35 38S 145 49E
19 Berry, Reg. 47 0N 2 0E
24 Bersenbrück 52 33N 7 56E
19 Bertincourt 50 5N 2 58E
74 Bertoua 4 30N 13 45E
97 Berwick 41 4N 76 17W
12 Berwick-upon-Tweed 55 47N 2 0W
12 Berwyn Mts. 52 54N 3 26W
27 Berzence 46 12N 17 11E
19 Besançon 47 9N 6 0E
21 Bessèges 44 18N 4 8E
99 Bessemer 46 27N 90 0W
18 Bessin, Reg. 49 21N 1 0W
18 Bessines-sur-Gartempe 46 6N 1 22E
54 Bet Ha 'Emeq 32 58N 35 8E
54 Bet Ha Shitta 32 31N 35 27E
54 Bet Ha'tmeq 32 58N 35 8E
54 Bet Oren 32 43N 34 59E
54 Bet Qeshet 32 41N 35 21E
54 Be't She'an 32 30N 35 30E
54 Bet Shemesh 31 45N 35 0E
54 Bet Yosef 32 34N 35 33E
30 Betanzos 43 15N 8 12W
74 Bétaré-Oya 5 40N 14 5E
32 Betera 39 35N 0 28W
75 Bethanien 26 31S 17 8E
54 Bethany=Eizariya 31 47N 35 15E
97 Bethel, Conn. 41 22N 73 25W
96 Bethel, Pa. 40 20N 80 2W
97 Bethel, Vt. 43 50N 72 37W
54 Bethlehem, Jordan=Bayt Lahm 31 43N 35 12E
75 Bethlehem, S. Africa 28 14S 28 18E
97 Bethlehem, U.S.A. 40 39N 75 24W
75 Bethulie 30 30S 25 29E
19 Béthune 50 30N 2 38E
18 Béthune, R. 49 56N 1 5E
19 Betan Bazoches 48 42N 3 15E
80 Betoota 25 40S 140 42E
61 Bettiah 26 48N 84 33E
36 Béttola 44 46N 9 35E
66 Betung 2 0S 103 10E
41 Beuca 44 14N 24 56E
21 Beuil 44 6N 7 0E
84 Beulah, Australia 35 58S 142 29E
93 Beulah, Canada 50 16N 101 2W
24 Bevensen 53 5N 10 34E
83 Beverley, Australia 32 9S 116 56E
12 Beverley, U.K. 53 52N 0 26W
92 Beverly, Canada 53 36N 113 21W
97 Beverly, U.S.A. 42 32N 70 50W
103 Beverly Hills 34 4N 118 29W
16 Beverwijk 52 28N 4 38E
25 Bex 46 15N 7 0E
72 Beyla 8 30N 8 38W
13 Bexhill 50 51N 0 29E
50 Beyneu 45 10N 55 3E
56 Beypazari 40 10N 31 48E
56 Beyşehir Gólú, L. 37 40N 31 45E
62 Bezawada=Vijayawada 16 31N 80 39E
40 Bezdan 45 28N 18 57E
54 Bezet 33 4N 35 8E
48 Bezhitsa 53 19N 34 17E
20 Béziers 43 20N 3 12E
61 Bhadrakh 21 10N 86 30E
62 Bhadravati 13 49N 76 15E
61 Bhagalpur 25 10N 87 0E
62 Bhaisa 19 10N 77 58E
60 Bhakkar 31 40N 71 5E
61 Bhakra Dam 31 30N 76 45E
59 Bhamo 24 15N 97 15E
62 Bhamragarh 19 30N 80 40E
61 Bhandara 21 5N 79 42E
61 Bhanrer Ra. 23 40N 79 45E
58 Bharūch 21 47N 73 0E
60 Bharatpur 27 15N 77 30E
60 Bhatinda 30 15N 74 57E
62 Bhatkal 13 58N 74 35E
61 Bhatpara 22 50N 88 25E
62 Bhattiprolu 16 7N 80 45E
60 Bhaun 32 55N 72 40E
62 Bhavani 11 27N 77 43E
60 Bhavnagar 21 45N 72 10E
60 Bhera 32 29N 72 57E
60 Bhilwara 25 25N 74 38E
62 Bhima, R. 17 20N 76 30E
62 Bhimavaram 16 30N 81 30E
60 Bhind 26 30N 78 46E
62 Bhiwandi 19 15N 73 0E
60 Bhiwani 28 50N 76 9E
62 Bhiwndi 19 15N 73 0E
62 Bhongir 17 30N 78 56E
60 Bhopal 23 20N 77 53E
62 Bhor 18 12N 73 53E
61 Bhubaneswar 20 15N 85 50E
60 Bhuj 23 15N 69 49E
60 Bhusaval 21 15N 69 49E
61 Bhutan ■ 27 25N 89 50E
27 Biała, R 49 46N 17 40E
28 Biała Piska 53 37N 22 5E
28 Biała Podlaska 52 4N 23 6E
28 Biała Podlaska □ 52 0N 23 0S
28 Białogard 54 2N 15 58E
28 Białystok 53 10N 23 10E
28 Białystok □ 52 50N 23 10E
39 Biancaville 37 39N 14 50E
20 Biarritz 43 29N 1 33W
25 Biasca 46 22N 18 58E
25 Biberach 48 5N 9 49E
30 Bibey, R. 42 24N 7 13W
72 Bibiani 6 30N 2 8W
91 Bic 48 20N 68 41W
39 Bîccari 41 23N 15 12E
72 Bida 9 3N 5 58E
13 Bicester 51 53N 1 9W
62 Bidar 17 55N 77 35E
99 Biddeford 43 30N 70 28E
13 Bideford 51 1N 4 13W
63 Bidor 4 6N 101 15E
75 Bié 12 22S 16 55E
75 Bié Plat. 12 0S 16 0E
102 Bieber 41 4N 121 6W
25 Biel 47 8N 7 14E
28 Bielawa 50 43N 16 37E
27 Bielé Karpaty, Mts. 49 5N 18 0E
24 Bielefeld 52 2N 8 31E
36 Biella 45 33N 8 3E
28 Bielsk Podlaski 52 47N 23 12E
27 Bielsko-Biała 49 50N 19 8E
27 Bielsko Biała 49 45N 19 10E
63 Biên Hoa 10 57N 106 49E
25 Bienne=Biel 47 8N 7 14E
31 Bienvenida 38 18N 6 12W
32 Biescas 42 37N 0 20W
39 Biferno, R. 41 40N 14 38E
90 Big Beaver House 52 59N 89 50W
101 Big Bend Nat. Park 29 15N 103 15W
88 Big Delta 64 15N 145 0W
97 Big Moose 43 49N 74 58W
98 Big Rapids 43 42N 85 27W
93 Big River 53 50N 107 0W
88 Big Salmon 61 50N 136 0W
101 Big Spring 32 10N 101 25W
99 Big Stone Gap 36 52N 82 45W
90 Big Trout L. 53 40N 90 0W
20 Biganos 44 39N 0 59W
93 Biggar, Canada 52 10N 108 0W
14 Biggar, U.K. 55 38N 3 31W
82 Bigge, I. 14 35S 125 10E
81 Biggenden 25 31S 152 4E
102 Bighorn Mts. 44 30N 107 20W
20 Bigorre, Reg. 43 5N 0 2E
102 Bigtimber 45 33N 110 0W
37 Bihać 44 49N 15 57E
61 Bihar 25 5N 85 40E
61 Bihar □ 25 0N 86 0E
27 Bihor □ 47 0N 22 10E
72 Bijagos, Arquipélago dos 11 15N 16 10W
62 Bijapur 26 2N 77 36E
40 Bijeljina 44 46N 19 17E
60 Bijnor 29 27N 78 11E
60 Bikaner 28 2N 73 18E
51 Bikin 46 50N 134 20E
76 Bikini Atoll, I. 12 0N 167 30E
60 Bilara 26 14N 73 53E
61 Bilaspur, Mad. P. 22 2N 82 15E
60 Bilaspur, Punjab 31 19N 76 50E
63 Bilauk Taungdan, Ra. 13 0N 99 0E
30 Bilbao 43 16N 2 56W
40 Bileća 42 53N 18 27E
56 Bilecik 40 5N 30 5E
51 Bilibino 68 3N 166 20E
51 Bilir 65 40N 131 20E
42 Bilishti 40 37N 20 59E
83 Billabalong 27 25S 115 49E
82 Billiluna 19 37S 127 41E
12 Billingham 54 36N 1 18W
102 Billings 45 43N 108 29W
44 Billingsfors 58 59N 12 15E
20 Billom 45 43N 3 20E
73 Bilma 18 50N 13 30E
40 Bilo Gora 45 53N 17 15E
80 Biloela 24 34S 150 31E
101 Biloxi 30 30N 89 0W
73 Biltine 14 40N 20 50E
80 Bilyana 18 5S 145 50E
65 Bima 8 22S 118 49E
60 Bina-Etawah 24 13N 78 14E
65 Binalbagan 10 12N 122 50E
64 Binatang 2 10N 111 40E
80 Binbee 20 19S 147 56E
16 Binche 50 26N 4 10E
83 Bindi Bindi 30 37S 116 22E
75 Bindura 17 18S 31 18E
81 Bingara, N.S.W. 29 40S 150 40E
81 Bingara, Queens. 28 10S 144 37E
25 Bingen 49 57N 7 53E
102 Bingham Canyon 40 31N 112 10W
97 Binghamton 42 9N 75 54W
63 Binh Dinh=An Nhon 13 55N 109 7E
63 Binh Son 15 20N 104 40E
64 Binjai 3 50N 98 30E
54 Binyamina 32 32N 34 56E
72 Binzerte 37 15N 9 50E
108 Bío Bío □ 37 35S 72 0W
37 Biograd 43 56N 15 29E
40 Biokovo 43 23N 17 0E
62 Bir 19 0N 75 54E
73 Bir Atrun 18 15N 26 40E
54 Bir Nabala 31 52N 35 12E
73 Bîr Shalatein 23 5N 35 25E
54 Bir Zeit 31 59N 35 11E
61 Biratnagar 26 18N 87 17E
93 Birch Hills 53 10N 105 10W
84 Birchip 35 52S 143 0E
79 Bird, I. 22 20S 155 20E
80 Birdsville 25 51S 139 20E
82 Birdum 15 50S 133 0E
64 Bireuen 5 14N 96 39E
109 Birigui 21 18S 50 16W
57 Birjand 32 57N 59 10E
12 Birkenhead 53 24N 3 1W
26 Birkfeld 47 21N 15 45E
41 Bîrlad 46 15N 27 38E
13 Birmingham, U.K. 52 30N 1 55W
99 Birmingham, U.S.A. 33 31N 86 50W
72 Birnin-Kebbi 12 32N 4 12E
51 Birobidzhan 48 50N 132 50E
15 Birr 53 7N 7 55W
93 Birtle 50 30N 101 5W
61 Bisalpur 28 14N 79 48E
103 Bisbee 31 30N 110 0W
20 Biscarrosse, Étang de 44 22N 1 10W
29 Biscay, B. of 45 0N 2 0W
39 Biscéglie 41 14N 16 30E
26 Bischofshofen 47 26N 13 14E

Bischofswerda Brasilia Legal

24 Bischofswerda .... 51 8N 14 11 E
19 Bischwiller .... 48 47N 7 50 E
103 Bishop 37 20N 118 26W
12 Bishop Auckland .. 54 40N 1 40W
91 Bishop's Falls 49 2N 55 24W
13 Bishop's
Stortford .... 51 52 0 11 E
72 Biskra .... 34 50N 5 52 E
28 Biskupiec .... 53 53N 20 58 E
100 Bismarck 46 49N 100 49W
76 Bismark Arch. .... 3 30S 148 30 E
72 Bissau 11 45N 15 45W
93 Bissett 46 14N 78 4W
61 Biswan .... 27 29N 81 2 E
40 Bitola .... 41 5N 21 21 E
39 Bitonto .... 41 7N 16 40 E
24 Bitterfeld .... 51 36N 12 20 E
75 Bitterfontein ...... 31 0S 18 32 E
102 Bitterroot Ra. 46 0N 114 20W
38 Bitti .... 40 29N 9 20 E
66 Biwa-Ko, L. ...... 35 15N 135 45 E
50 Biysk .... 52 40N 85 0 E
66 Bizen .... 34 44N 134 9 E
72 Bizerte=Binzerte .. 37 15N 9 50 E
45 Bjärka .... 58 16N 15 44 E
40 Bjelašnica, Mt. .... 43 11N 18 21 E
37 Bjelovar .... 45 56N 16 49 E
4 Bjørnøya, I ...... 74 25N 19 0 E
45 Bjuv .... 56 7N 12 56 E
40 Blace .... 43 18N 21 17 E
97 Black, R. 43 59N 76 4W
100 Black Hills, Mts ... 44 0N 103 50W
13 Black Mts. 51 52N 3 50W
9 Black Sea .... 43 30N 35 0 E
72 Black Volta, R. ... 8 41N 1 33W
80 Blackall .... 24 26S 145 27 E
80 Blackbull .... 18 0S 141 7 E
12 Blackburn 53 44N 2 30W
102 Blackfoot 43 13N 112 12W
84 Blackheath .... 33 39S 150 17 E
12 Blackpool 53 48N 3 3W
91 Blacks Harbour ... 45 3N 66 49W
91 Blackville 47 5N 65 58W
80 Blackwater .... 23 35S 149 0 E
15 Blackwater, R.,
Cork 51 51N 7 50W
15 Blackwater, R.,
Dungannon 54 31N 6 34W
15 Blackwater, R.,
Meath 53 39N 6 43W
101 Blackwell 36 55N 97 20W
12 Blaenau
Ffestiniog 53 0N 3 57W
20 Blagnac .... 43 38N 1 24 E
49 Blagodarnoye ..... 45 7N 43 37 E
40 Blagoevgrad ...... 42 2N 23 5 E
51 Blagoveshchensk .. 50 20N 127 30 E
93 Blaine Lake 52 51N 106 52W
80 Blair Atholl,
Australia .... 22 42S 147 31 E
14 Blair Atholl, U.K. . 56 46N 3 50W
14 Blairgowrie 56 36N 3 20W
92 Blairmore 49 40N 114 25W
41 Blaj .... 46 10N 23 57 E
19 Blamont .... 48 35N 6 50 E
72 Blanc, C.=
Ras Nouadhibou 37 15N 9 56 E
21 Blanc, Mt. .... 45 50N 6 52 E
112 Blanca, B. 39 10S 61 30W
103 Blanca Pk. 37 35N 105 29W
33 Blanco, C. .... 39 21N 2 51 E
13 Blandford 50 52N 2 10W
103 Blanding 37 35N 109 30W
32 Blanes .... 41 40N 2 48 E
19 Blangy .... 49 14N 0 17 E
26 Blanice .... 49 10N 14 5 E
109 Blanquillo 32 53S 55 37W
27 Blansko .... 49 22N 16 40 E
75 Blantyre .... 15 45S 35 0 E
15 Blarney 51 57N 8 35W
12 Blaydon 54 56N 1 47W
20 Blaye 45 8N 0 40W
84 Blayney .... 33 32S 149 14 E
24 Bleckede .... 53 18N 10 43 E
37 Bled .... 46 27N 14 7 E
26 Bleiburg .... 46 35N 14 49 E
45 Blekinge □ .... 56 15N 15 15 E
85 Blenheim .... 41 38S 174 5 E
13 Bletchley 51 59N 0 54W
72 Blida .... 36 30N 2 49 E
90 Blind River 46 15N 83 0W
65 Blitar .... 8 5S 112 11 E
97 Block I. 41 13N 71 35W
97 Block Island Sd. ... 41 10N 71 45W
75 Bloemfontein ..... 29 6S 26 14 E
18 Blois .... 47 35N 1 20 E
28 Błonie .... 52 12N 20 37 E
97 Bloomingdale 41 0N 74 20W
100 Bloomington, Ill. .. 40 25N 89 0W
98 Bloomington, Ind. . 39 10N 86 30W
97 Bloomsburg 41 0N 76 30W
26 Bludenz .... 47 10N 9 50 E
98 Blue Island 41 40N 87 41W
80 Blue Mud, B. ..... 13 30S 136 0 E
97 Blue Mts. 45 15N 119 0W
73 Blue Nile, R.=
Nîl el Azraq, R. . 10 30N 35 0 E
86 Blue Ridge, Mts ... 36 30N 80 15W
98 Bluefield 37 18N 81 14W
105 Bluefields 12 0N 83 50W
80 Bluff, Australia ... 23 40S 149 0 E
85 Bluff, N.Z. .... 46 36S 168 21 E
83 Bluff Knoll, Mt. ... 34 23S 118 20 E
98 Bluffton 40 43N 85 9W
109 Blumenau 27 0S 49 0W
12 Blyth 55 8N 1 32W
103 Blythe 33 40N 114 33W
101 Blytheville 35 56N 89 55W
72 Bo 7 55N 11 50W
110 Boa Vista 2 48N 60 30W
105 Boaco 12 29N 85 35W
74 Boali .... 4 48N 18 7 E
31 Boatman .... 27 16S 146 55 E
62 Bobbili .... 18 35N 83 30 E
90 Bobcaygeon 44 33N 78 35W
72 Bobo-Dioulasso ... 11 8N 4 13W
41 Boboc .... 45 13N 26 59 E
28 Bobr R. .... 52 4N 15 4 E
48 Bobruysk .... 53 10N 29 15 E
111 Bocaiuva 17 7S 43 49W
105 Bocas del Toro 9 15N 82 20W
30 Boceguillas 41 20N 3 39W
27 Bochnia .... 49 58N 29 27 E
24 Bocholt .... 51 50N 6 35 E
24 Bochum .... 51 28N 7 12 E
21 Bocognano .... 42 5N 9 3 E
40 Boçsa .... 45 21N 21 47 E
74 Boda .... 4 19N 17 26 E
51 Bodaybo .... 57 50N 114 0 E
83 Boddington .... 32 50S 116 30 E
46 Boden .... 65 50N 21 42 E
25 Bodensee, L. 47 35N 9 25N
62 Bodhan .... 18 40N 77 55 E
62 Bodinayakkanur ... 10 2N 77 10 E
13 Bodmin 50 28N 4 44W
13 Bodmin Moor, Reg. 50 33N 4 36W
46 Bodø .... 67 17N 14 27 E
27 Bodrog, R. .... 48 15N 21 35 E
27 Bodva, R. .... 48 19N 20 45 E
101 Bogalusa 30 50N 89 55W
84 Bogan Gate ...... 33 6S 147 44 E
80 Bogantungan ..... 23 41S 147 17 E
75 Bogenfels .... 27 25S 15 25 E
81 Boggabri .... 30 45S 150 0 E
13 Bognor Regis 50 47N 0 40W
65 Bogor .... 6 36S 106 48 E
51 Bogorodskoye .... 52 22N 140 30 E
110 Bogota 4 34N 74 0W
50 Bogotal .... 56 15N 89 50 E
61 Bogra .... 24 26N 89 22 E
51 Boguchany .... 58 40N 97 30 E
19 Bohain .... 49 59N 3 28 E
25 Böhmerwald, Mts. . 49 30N 12 40 E
65 Bohol, I. .... 9 58N 124 20 E
55 Bohotleh .... 8 20N 46 25 E
109 Boi, Pta. do 23 55S 45 15W
91 Boiestown 46 27N 66 26W
102 Boise 43 43N 116 9W
93 Boissevain 49 15N 100 0W
24 Boizenburg .... 55 16N 13 36 E
65 Bojonegoro .... 7 9S 111 52 E
72 Boké 10 56N 14 17W
47 Bokna, Fd. .... 59 12N 5 30 E
74 Bokote .... 0 12S 21 8 E
57 Bol, Kuh-e .... 30 40N 52 45 E
72 Bolama 11 30N 15 30W
18 Bolbec .... 49 30N 0 30 E
41 Boldeşti .... 45 3N 26 2 E
28 Bolesławiec ...... 51 17N 15 37 E
110 Bolívar, Arg. 36 2S 60 53W
102 Bolívar, Col. 2 0N 77 0W
110 Bolivia ■ 17 6S 64 0W
106 Bolivian Plat. 19 0S 69 0W
40 Boljevac .... 45 31N 21 58 E
21 Bollène .... 44 18N 4 45 E
44 Bollnäs .... 61 22N 16 28 E
31 Bollullos 37 19N 6 32W
45 Bolmen, L. .... 56 57N 13 45 E
37 Bologna .... 44 30N 11 20 E
19 Bologne .... 48 10N 5 8 E
48 Bologoye .... 57 55N 34 0 E
63 Boloven, Cao
Nguyen, Mts. ... 15 10N 106 30 E
61 Bolpur .... 23 40N 87 45 E
37 Bolsena, L. di ..... 42 35N 11 55 E
51 Bolshevik, Os. .... 78 30N 102 0 E
49 Bolshoi Kavkaz ... 42 50N 44 0 E
50 Bolshoy Atlym .... 62 25N 66 50 E
51 Bolshoy Shantar,
Os. .... 55 0N 137 42 E
12 Bolton 53 35N 2 26W
37 Bolzana .... 46 30N 11 20 E
111 Bom Despacho 19 46S 45 15W
111 Bom Jesus da Lapa 13 10S 43 30W
74 Boma .... 5 50S 13 4 E
84 Bomaderry .... 34 52S 150 37 E
84 Bombala .... 36 56S 149 15 E
62 Bombay .... 18 55N 72 50 E
74 Bomboma .... 2 25N 18 55 E
67 Bomda .... 29 59N 96 25 E
73 Bon, C. .... 37 1N 11 2 E
105 Bonaire, I. 12 10N 68 15W
82 Bonaparte Arch. .. 15 0S 124 30 E
91 Bonaventure 48 5N 63 32W
91 Bonavista 48 40N 53 5W
91 Bonavista B. 48 58N 53 25W
37 Bondeno .... 44 53N 11 22 E
72 Bondoukoro 9 51N 4 25W
72 Bondoukou 8 2N 2 47W
65 Bondowoso .... 7 56S 113 49 E
65 Bone, Teluk, G. ... 4 10S 120 50 E
14 Bo'ness 56 0N 3 38W
73 Bongor .... 10 35N 15 20 E
101 Bonham 33 30N 96 10W
21 Bonifacio .... 41 24N 9 10 E
38 Bonifacio,
Bouches de ..... 41 23N 9 10 E
76 Bonin Is. .... 27 0N 142 0 E
108 Bonito 21 8S 56 28W
24 Bonn .... 50 43N 7 6 E
102 Bonners Ferry 48 38N 116 21W
18 Bonneval .... 48 11N 1 24 E
21 Bonneville .... 46 5N 6 24 E
83 Bonnie Rock ..... 30 29S 118 22 E
70 Bonny, B. of ...... 4 0N 8 0 E
93 Bonnyville 54 20N 110 45W
38 Bonorva .... 40 25N 8 47 E
64 Bontang .... 0 10N 117 30 E
65 Bonthain .... 5 34S 119 56 E
16 Boom .... 51 6N 4 20 E
81 Boonah .... 28 0S 152 35 E
100 Boone 42 5N 93 46W
98 Boonville, Ind 38 3N 87 13W
100 Boonville, Mo. 38 57N 92 45W
97 Boonville, N.Y. 43 31N 75 20W
89 Boothia, G. of 70 0N 90 0W
88 Boothia Pen. 70 30N 95 0W
12 Bootle 53 28N 3 1W
74 Booué .... 0 5S 11 55 E
81 Bopeechee .... 29 35S 137 30 E
108 Boquerón 21 30S 60 0W
40 Bor .... 44 5N 22 7 E
45 Borås .... 57 42N 13 1 E
110 Borba 4 12S 59 34W
20 Bordeaux 44 50N 0 36W
83 Borden, Australia . 34 3S 118 12 E
91 Borden, Canada ... 46 18N 63 47W
14 Borders □ 55 30N 3 0W
84 Bordertown .... 36 14S 140 58 E
36 Bordighera .... 43 47N 7 40 E
16 Borger, Neth. ..... 52 54N 7 33 E
101 Borger, U.S.A. 35 40N 101 20W
36 Borgo .... 46 3N 11 27 E
36 Borgomanera ..... 45 41N 8 28 E
36 Borgosésia .... 45 43N 8 9 E
49 Borisoglebsk ...... 51 27N 42 5 E
48 Borisov .... 54 17N 28 28 E
110 Borja 4 20S 77 40W
32 Borjas Blancas .... 41 31N 0 52 E
24 Borken .... 51 3N 9 21 E
73 Borkou .... 18 15N 18 50 E
24 Borkum, I. .... 53 35N 6 41 E
44 Borlänge .... 60 28N 14 33 E
5 Borley, C. .... 66 15S 52 30 E
25 Borna .... 51 8N 12 31 E
64 Borneo, I. .... 1 0N 115 0 E
45 Bornholm, I. ...... 55 8N 14 55 E
31 Bornos 36 48N 5 42W
51 Borogontsy .... 62 42N 131 8 E
48 Borovichi .... 58 25N 35 55 E
45 Borrby .... 55 27N 14 10 E
32 Borriol 40 4N 0 4W
80 Borroloola .... 16 4S 136 17 E
60 Borsad .... 22 24N 72 56 E
48 Borsod-Abaúj-
Zemplén □ ..... 48 20N 21 0 E
20 Bort-les-Orgues ... 45 24N 2 29 E
56 Borujerd .... 33 55N 48 50 E
51 Borzya .... 50 24N 116 31 E
40 Bosanska
Gradiška .... 45 9N 17 15 E
37 Bosanska
Kostajnica ...... 45 11N 16 33 E
37 Bosanska Krupa ... 44 53N 16 10 E
37 Bosanski Novi .... 45 2N 16 22 E
55 Bosaso .... 11 13N 49 8 E
13 Boscasble 50 42N 4 42W
39 Boscotrecase ...... 40 46N 14 28 E
40 Bosna, R. .... 45 4N 18 29 E
37 Bosna i
Hercegovina □ .. 44 0N 18 0 E
41 Bosporus, Str.=
Karadeniz
Boğazi, Str. ..... 41 10N 29 10 E
74 Bossangoa .... 6 35N 17 30 E
101 Bossier City 32 28N 93 38W
12 Boston, U.K. 52 59N 0 2W
97 Boston, U.S.A. 42 20N 71 0W
60 Botad .... 22 15N 71 40 E
84 Botany B. .... 34 2S 151 6 E
41 Botevgrad .... 42 55N 23 47 E
46 Bothnia, G. .... 63 0N 21 0 E
80 Bothwell 42 37N 81 54W
75 Botletle, R. .... 20 10S 24 10 E
41 Botoroaga .... 44 8N 25 32 E
75 Botswana ■ ...... 23 0S 24 0 E
109 Botucatu 22 55S 48 30W
91 Botwood 49 6N 55 23W
72 Bou Saâda .... 35 11N 4 9 E
72 Bouaké 7 40N 5 2W
74 Bouar .... 6 0N 15 40 E
72 Bouârfa .... 32 32N 1 58 E
21 Bouches-du-Rhône 43 37N 5 2 E
82 Bougainville, C. ... 13 57S 126 4 E
72 Bougouni 11 30N 7 20W
100 Boulder 40 3N 105 10W
103 Boulder City 36 0N 114 58W
80 Boulia .... 22 52S 139 51 E
19 Bouligny .... 49 17N 5 45 E
19 Boulogne-sur-Mer . 50 42N 1 36 E
102 Bountiful 40 57N 111 58W
20 Bourbon-Lancy ... 46 37N 3 45 E
20 Bourbonnais, Reg. . 46 28N 3 0 E
45 Bourg 45 3N 0 34W
21 Bourg en Bresse .. 46 13N 5 12 E
20 Bourg Madame ... 42 29N 1 58 E
21 Bourg-de-Péage ... 45 2N 5 3 E
20 Bourges .... 47 5N 2 22 E
45 Bourget, L. du .... 45 44N 5 52 E
18 Bourgneuf 47 2N 1 58W
18 Bourgneuf, B. de .. 47 3N 2 10W
19 Bourgogne, Reg. .. 47 0N 4 30 E
21 Bourgoin-Jallieu ... 45 36N 5 17 E
81 Bourke .... 30 8S 145 55 E
90 Bourlamaque 48 5N 77 56W
13 Bournemouth 50 43N 1 53W
20 Boussac .... 46 22N 2 13 E
20 Boussens .... 43 12N 1 2 E
7 Bouvet, I. .... 55 0S 3 30 E
92 Bow Island 49 50N 111 23W
83 Bowelling .... 33 25S 116 30 E
80 Bowen .... 20 0S 148 16 E
103 Bowie 32 15N 109 30W
12 Bowland Forest ... 54 0N 2 30W
98 Bowling Green, Ky. 37 0N 86 25W
98 Bowling Green,
Ohio 41 22N 83 40W
80 Bowling Green, C. 19 19S 147 25 E
100 Bowman 46 12N 103 21W
90 Bowmanville 43 55N 78 40W
14 Bowmore 55 45N 6 18W
92 Bowness 50 55N 114 25W
84 Bowser .... 36 19S 146 23 E
93 Bowsman 52 15N 101 12W
16 Boxtel .... 51 36N 5 9 E
15 Boyle 53 58N 8 19W
15 Boyne, R. 53 40N 6 34W
70 Boyoma, Chutes .. 0 12N 25 25 E
83 Boyup Brook ..... 33 47S 116 40 E
102 Bozeman 45 40N 111 0W
74 Bozoum .... 6 25N 16 35 E
36 Bra .... 44 41N 7 50 E
16 Brabant □ .... 49 15N 5 20 E
37 Brac, I. .... 43 20N 16 40 E
37 Bracciano, L. di ... 42 6N 12 10 E
90 Bracebridge 45 5N 79 20W
44 Bräcke .... 62 42N 15 32 E
40 Brad .... 46 10N 22 50 E
39 Brádano, R. ...... 40 41N 16 20 E
96 Braddock 40 24N 79 51W
99 Bradenton 27 25N 82 35W
12 Bradford, U.K. 53 47N 1 45W
96 Bradford, U.S.A. .. 41 58N 78 41W
91 Bradore Bay 51 27N 57 18W
101 Brady 31 8N 99 25W
14 Braemar 57 2N 3 20W
30 Braga 41 35N 8 32W
30 Braga □ 41 30N 8 30W
108 Bragado 35 2S 60 27W
111 Bragança 1 0S 47 2W
30 Bragança □ 41 30N 6 45W
109 Bragança Paulista . 22 55S 46 52W
61 Brahmanbaria ..... 23 50N 91 15 E
61 Brahmani, R. ..... 21 0N 85 15 E
61 Brahmaputra, R. .. 26 30N 93 30 E
12 Braich-y-Pwll, Pt. . 52 47N 4 46W
41 Brăila .... 45 19N 27 59 E
100 Brainerd 46 20N 94 10W
13 Braintree, U.K. ... 51 53N 0 34 E
97 Braintree, U.S.A. . 42 11N 71 0W
24 Brake .... 53 19N 8 30 E
24 Brakel .... 51 43N 9 10 E
92 Bralorne 50 50N 123 15W
90 Brampton, Canada 43 42N 79 46W
96 Brampton, U.S.A. . 46 0N 97 46W
110 Branco, R. 1 30N 61 15W
45 Brande .... 55 47N 9 7 E
24 Brandenburg ...... 52 24N 12 33 E
93 Brandon 49 50N 100 0W
26 Brandýs .... 50 10N 14 40 E
28 Braniewo .... 54 25N 19 50 E
96 Brantford 43 15N 80 15W
20 Brantôme .... 45 22N 0 39 E
84 Branxholme ...... 37 52S 141 49 E
111 Brasília 15 55S 47 40W
111 Brasilia Legal 3 45S 55 40W

Brasov Bzenec

41 Braşov 45 7N 25 39 E
16 Brasschaat 51 19N 4 27 E
27 Bratislava 48 10N 17 7 E
51 Bratsk 56 10N 101 3 E
97 Brattleboro 42 53N 72 37w
41 Braţul Chilia, R. 45 25N 29 20 E
41 Braţul Sfîntu Gheorghe 45 0N 29 20 E
41 Braţul Sulina, R. 45 10N 29 20 E
26 Braunau 48 15N 13 3 E
24 Braunschweig 52 17N 10 28 E
13 Braunton 51 6N 4 9w
55 Brava 1 20N 44 8 E
103 Brawley 32 58N 115 30w
15 Bray 53 12N 6 6w
19 Bray, Reg. 49 40N 1 40 E
19 Bray-sur-Seine 48 25N 3 14 E
107 Brazil ■ 10 0s 50 0w
98 Brazil 39 30N 87 8w
106 Brazilian Highlands, Mts. 18 0s 46 30w
101 Brazol, R. 30 30N 96 20w
74 Brazzaville 4 9s 15 12 E
40 Brčko 44 54N 18 46 E
80 Breadalbane 23 48s 139 33 E
14 Breadalbane, Reg. 56 30N 4 15w
85 Bream, B. 35 56s 174 35 E
85 Bream Head 35 51s 174 36 E
65 Brebes 6 52s 109 3 E
14 Brechin 56 44N 2 40w
101 Breckenridge 32 48N 98 55w
13 Breckland, Reg. 52 30N 0 40 E
27 Breclav 48 46N 16 53 E
13 Brecon 51 57N 3 23w
13 Brecon Beacons, Mts. 51 53N 3 27w
16 Breda 51 35N 4 45 E
75 Bredasdorp 34 33s 20 2 E
84 Bredbo 35 38s 149 10 E
26 Bregenz 47 30N 9 45 E
46 Breidafjördur 65 20N 23 0w
21 Breil 43 56N 7 31 E
111 Brejo 3 41s 42 50w
24 Bremen 53 4N 8 47 E
24 Bremerhaven 53 34N 8 35 E
102 Bremerton 47 30N 122 48w
31 Brenes 37 32N 5 54w
101 Brenham 30 5N 96 27w
26 Brenner P. 47 0N 11 30 E
90 Brent, Canada 46 0N 78 30w
13 Brent, U.K. 51 33N 0 18w
13 Brentwood 51 37N 0 19w
36 Bréscia 45 33N 10 13 E
28 Breslau=Wrocław 51 5N 17 5 E
19 Bresles 49 25N 2 13 E
37 Bressanone 46 43N 11 40 E
14 Bressay, I. 60 10N 1 5w
21 Bresse, Plaine de 46 20N 5 10 E
20 Bressuire 46 51N 0 30w
18 Brest, Fr. 48 24N 4 31w
48 Brest, U.S.S.R. 52 10N 23 40 E
18 Bretagne, Reg. 48 0N 3 0w
41 Bretçu 46 7N 26 18 E
19 Breteuil 49 38N 2 18 E
20 Breton, Pertuis 46 16N 1 22w
85 Brett, C. 35 10s 174 20 E
111 Breves 1 38s 50 25w
81 Brewarrina 30 0s 146 51 E
99 Brewer 44 43N 68 50w
97 Brewster 41 23N 73 37w
99 Brewton 31 9N 87 2w
27 Brezno 48 50N 19 40 E
74 Bria 6 30N 21 58 E
21 Briançon 44 54N 6 39 E
19 Briare 47 38N 2 45 E
19 Bricon 48 5N 5 0 E
18 Bricquebec 49 29N 1 39w
13 Bridgend 51 30N 3 35w
97 Bridgeport 41 12N 73 12w
98 Bridgeton 39 29N 75 10w
83 Bridgetown, Australia 33 58s 116 7 E
105 Bridgetown, Barbados 13 0N 59 30w
91 Bridgetown, Canada 44 55N 65 12w
84 Bridgewater, Australia 36 36s 143 59 E
91 Bridgewater, Canada 44 25N 64 31w
13 Bridgnorth 52 33N 2 25w
13 Bridgwater 51 7N 3 0w
12 Bridlington 54 4N 0 10w
13 Bridport 50 43N 2 45w
19 Brie, Plaine de la 48 35N 3 10 E
19 Brie-Comte Robert 48 40N 2 35 E
19 Brienon 48 0N 3 35 E
25 Brienzersee, L. 46 44N 7 53 E
25 Brig 46 18N 7 59 E
12 Brigg 53 33N 0 30w
102 Brigham City 41 30N 112 1w
81 Brighton, Australia 35 1s 138 30 E
90 Brighton, Canada 44 3N 77 44w
13 Brighton, U.K. 50 50N 0 9w
18 Brignogan-Plages 48 40N 4 20w
21 Brignoles 43 25N 6 5 E
39 Bríndisi 40 39N 17 55 E
20 Brioude 45 18N 3 23 E
81 Brisbane 27 25s 152 54 E
37 Brisighella 44 13N 11 46 E
13 Bristol, U.K. 51 26N 2 35w
97 Bristol, Conn. 41 44N 72 37w
97 Bristol, Mass. 41 40N 71 15w
97 Bristol, Pa. 40 7N 74 52w
88 Bristol B. 58 0N 159 0w
13 Bristol Chan. 51 18N 3 30w
101 Bristow 35 5N 96 28w
5 British Antarctic Terr. 66 0s 45 0w
92 British Columbia □ 55 0N 125 15w
11 British Is. 55 0N 4 0w
75 Britstown 30 37s 23 30 E
99 Britt 45 46N 80 35w
100 Britton 45 50N 97 47w
20 Brive-la-Gaillarde 45 10N 1 32 E
30 Briviesca 42 32N 3 19w
80 Brixton 23 32s 144 52 E
27 Brno 49 10N 16 35 E
60 Broach 21 47N 73 0 E
83 Broad Arrow 30 23s 121 15 E
14 Broad Law, Mt. 55 30N 3 22w
84 Broadford 37 14s 145 4 E
12 Broads, The 52 30N 1 15 E
93 Brock 51 27N 108 42w
96 Brockport 43 12N 77 56w
97 Brockton 42 8N 71 2w
90 Brockville 44 37N 75 38w
89 Brodeur Pen. 72 0N 88 0w
14 Brodick 55 34N 5 9w
28 Brodnica 53 15N 19 25 E
100 Broken Bow 41 25N 99 35w
84 Broken Hill 31 58s 141 29 E
13 Bromley 51 20N 0 5 E
45 Bromölla 56 5N 14 25 E
45 Brönderslev 57 17N 9 55 E
39 Bronte 37 48N 14 49 E
80 Bronte Pk. 42 8s 146 30 E
100 Brookfield 39 50N 92 50w
101 Brookhaven 31 40N 90 25w
100 Brookings 44 19N 96 48w
88 Brooks Ra. 68 40N 147 0w
83 Brookton 32 22N 116 57 E
14 Broom, L. 57 55N 5 15w
82 Broome 18 0s 122 15w
83 Broomehill 33 40s 117 36 E
14 Brora 58 0N 3 50w
45 Brösarp 55 44N 14 8 E
15 Brosna, R. 53 8N 8 0w
40 Broşteni 47 14N 25 43 E
89 Broughton I. 67 35N 63 50w
14 Broughty Ferry 56 29N 2 50w
13 Brown Willy, Mt. 50 35N 4 34w
101 Brownfield 33 10N 102 15w
102 Browning 48 35N 113 10w
93 Brownlee 50 43N 105 59N
101 Brownsville 25 54N 97 30w
101 Brownwood 31 45N 99 0w
19 Bruay 50 29N 2 33 E
82 Bruce, Mt. 22 31s 118 6 E
90 Bruce Mines 46 20N 83 45w
96 Bruce Pen. 45 0N 81 15w
83 Bruce Rock 31 51s 118 2 E
25 Bruchsal 49 9N 8 39 E
26 Bruck 47 24N 15 16 E
13 Brue, R. 51 10N 2 50w
25 Brugg 47 29N 8 11 E
16 Brugge 51 13N 3 13 E
92 Brule 53 15N 117 38w
111 Brumado 14 13s 41 40w
19 Brumath 48 43N 7 40 E
64 Brunei ■ 4 52N 115 0 E
80 Brunette Downs 18 38s 135 57 E
44 Brunflo 63 4N 14 50 E
37 Brunico 46 48N 11 56 E
44 Brunkeberg 59 25N 8 30 E
85 Brunner 42 27s 171 20 E
93 Bruno 52 20N 105 30w
24 Brunsbüttelkoog 53 52N 9 13 E
16 Brunssum 50 57N 5 59 E
24 Brunswick, W. Germany= Braunschweig 52 17N 10 28 E
99 Brunswick, Ga. 31 10N 81 30w
99 Brunswick, Me. 43 53N 69 50w
96 Brunswick, Ohio 41 15N 81 50w
112 Brunswick, Pen. 53 30s 71 30w
83 Brunswick Junction 33 15s 115 50 E
40 Brusartsi 43 40N 23 5 E
109 Brusque 27 5s 49 0w
16 Brussel 50 51N 4 21 E
84 Bruthen 37 43s 147 48 E
16 Bruxelles= Brussel 50 51N 4 21 E
19 Bruyères 48 10N 6 40 E
28 Brwinow 52 9N 20 40 E
98 Bryan, Ohio 41 30N 84 30w
101 Bryan, Tex. 30 40N 96 27w
48 Bryansk 53 13N 34 25 E
47 Bryne 58 45N 5 36 E
40 Brzava, R. 45 21N 20 45 E
27 Brzeg 50 52N 17 30 E
28 Brzeg Din 51 16N 16 41 E
56 Bucak 37 28N 30 36 E
110 Bucaramanga 7 0N 73 0w
14 Buchan, Reg. 57 32N 2 8w
14 Buchan Ness, Pt. 57 29N 1 48w
93 Buchanan, Canada 51 40N 102 45w
72 Buchanan, Liberia 5 57N 10 2w
91 Buchans 49 0N 57 2w
24 Buchholz 53 19N 9 51 E
24 Bückeburg 52 16N 9 2 E
103 Buckeye 33 28N 112 40w
98 Buckhannon 39 2N 80 10w
14 Buckie 57 40N 2 58w
13 Buckingham, U.K. 52 0N 0 59w
90 Buckingham, U.S.A. 45 37N 75 24w
62 Buckingham Canal 14 0N 80 5 E
13 Buckinghamshire □ 51 50N 0 55w
91 Buctouche 46 30N 64 45w
41 Bucureşti 44 27N 26 10 E
98 Bucyrus 40 48N 83 0w
27 Budafok 47 26N 19 2 E
59 Budalin 22 20N 95 10 E
27 Budapest 47 29N 19 5 E
60 Budaun 28 5N 79 10 E
13 Bude 50 49N 4 33w
41 Budeşti 44 13N 26 30 E
61 Budge Budge 22 30N 88 25 E
37 Búdrio 44 31N 11 31 E
40 Budva 42 17N 18 50 E
110 Buenaventura 29 15s 69 40w
32 Buendia, Pantano de 40 25N 2 43w
108 Buenos Aires 34 30s 58 20w
112 Buenos Aires, L. 46 35s 72 30w
108 Buenos Aires □ 34 30 58 20w
93 Buffalo, Canada 50 49N 110 42w
96 Buffalo, U.S.A. 42 55N 78 50w
93 Buffalo Narrows 55 52N 108 28w
28 Bug, R. 51 20N 23 40 E
110 Buga 4 0N 77 0w
40 Bugojno 44 2N 17 25 E
48 Bugulma 54 38N 52 40 E
68 Bugun Shara, Mts. 48 30N 102 0 E
48 Buturuslan 53 39N 52 26 E
48 Bui 58 23N 41 27 E
13 Builth Wells 52 10N 3 26w
30 Buitrago 41 0N 3 38w
31 Bujalance 37 54N 4 23w
40 Bujanovac 42 27N 21 46 E
32 Bujaraloz 41 29N 0 10w
74 Bujumbura 3 16s 29 18 E
51 Bukachacha 52 55N 116 50 E
74 Bukavu 2 20s 28 52 E
74 Bukene 4 15s 32 48 E
50 Bukhara 39 50N 64 10 E
63 Bukit Mertajam 5 22N 100 28 E
64 Bukittinggi 0 20s 100 20 E
62 Bukkapatnam 14 14N 77 46 E
74 Bukoba 1 20s 31 49 E
67 Bulak 45 2N 82 5 E
60 Bulandshahr 28 28N 77 58 E
75 Bulawayo 20 7s 28 32 E
41 Bulgaria ■ 42 35N 25 30 E
55 Bulhar 10 25N 44 30 E
83 Bullabulling 31 0s 120 55 E
31 Bullaque, R. 39 20N 4 13w
82 Bullara 22 30s 114 2 E
83 Bullaring 32 28s 117 40 E
33 Bullas 38 2N 1 40w
80 Bullock Creek 17 40s 144 30 E
85 Bulls 40 10s 175 24 E
19 Bully-les-Mines 50 27N 2 44 E
55 Bulo Burti 3 50N 45 33 E
60 Bulsar 20 40N 72 58 E
51 Bulun 70 37N 127 30 E
74 Bumba 2 13N 22 30 E
41 Bumbeşti Jiu 45 10N 23 22 E
59 Bumhpa Bum, Mt. 26 40N 97 20 E
83 Bunbury 33 20s 115 35 E
15 Buncrana 55 8N 7 28w
81 Bundaberg 24 54s 152 22 E
60 Bundi 25 30N 75 35 E
80 Bundooma 24 54s 134 16 E
12 Bure, R. 52 38N 1 38 E
24 Burg 54 25N 11 10 E
41 Burgas 42 33N 27 29 E
41 Burgaski Zaliv, B. 42 30N 27 39 E
25 Burgdorf, Switz. 47 3N 7 37 E
24 Burgdorf, W. Germany 52 27N 10 0 E
27 Burgenland □ 47 20N 16 20 E
91 Burgeo 47 36N 57 34w
75 Burgersdorp 31 0s 26 20 E
30 Burgo de Osma 41 35N 3 4w
30 Burgos 42 21N 3 41w
30 Burgos □ 42 21N 3 41w
24 Burgstädt 50 55N 12 49 E
24 Burgsteinfurt 52 9N 7 23 E
31 Burguillos del Cerro 38 23N 6 35w
60 Burhanpur 21 18N 76 20 E
65 Burias, I. 13 5N 122 55 E
105 Burica, Pta 8 3N 82 51w
54 Burin 32 11N 35 15 E
63 Buriram 15 0N 103 0 E
80 Burketown 17 45s 139 33 E
72 Burkina Faso ■ 12 0N 0 30w
90 Burks Falls 45 37N 79 10w
102 Burley 42 37N 113 55w
96 Burlington, Canada 43 25N 79 45w
100 Burlington, Colo. 39 21N 102 18w
100 Burlington, Iowa 40 50N 91 5w
100 Burlington, Kans. 38 15N 95 47w
99 Burlington, N.C. 36 7N 79 27w
97 Burlington, N.J. 40 5N 74 50w
102 Burlington, Wash. 48 29N 122 19w
50 Burlyu-Tyube 46 30N 79 10 E
59 Burma ■ 21 0N 96 30 E
83 Burngup 33 0s 118 35 E
80 Burnie 41 4s 145 56 E
12 Burnley 53 47N 2 15w
102 Burns 43 40N 119 4w
92 Burns Lake 54 20N 125 45w
96 Burnt River 44 40N 78 42 E
93 Burntwood, L. 55 35N 99 40w
54 Burqa 32 18N 35 11 E
81 Burra 33 40s 138 55 E
84 Burrendong Res. 32 45s 149 10 E
32 Burriana 39 50N 0 4w
13 Burry Port 51 41N 4 17w
56 Bursa 40 15N 29 5 E
12 Burton-on-Trent 52 48N 1 39w
65 Buru, I. 3 30s 126 30 E
74 Burundi ■ 3 15s 30 0 E
64 Burung 0 21N 108 25 E
72 Burutu 5 20N 5 29 E
12 Bury 53 36N 2 19w
13 Bury St. Edmunds 52 15N 0 42 E
51 Buryat A.S.S.R. □ 53 0N 110 0 E
44 Buskerud □ 60 20N 9 0 E
40 Busovača 44 6N 17 53 E
19 Bussang 47 50N 6 50 E
83 Busselton 33 42s 115 15 E
16 Bussum 52 16N 5 10 E
30 Busto, C. 43 34N 6 28w
36 Busto Arsizio 45 38N 8 50 E
74 Busu-Djanoa 1 50N 21 5 E
65 Busuanga, I. 12 10N 120 0 E
24 Büsum 54 7N 8 50 E
74 Buta 2 50N 24 53 E
74 Butare 2 31s 29 52 E
14 Bute, I. 55 48N 5 2w
74 Butembo 0 9N 29 18 E
39 Butera 37 10N 14 10 E
74 Butiaba 1 50N 31 20 E
96 Butler 40 52N 79 52w
14 Butt of Lewis, Pt. 58 30N 6 20w
102 Butte, Mont. 46 0N 112 31w
100 Butte, Neb. 42 56N 98 54w
63 Butterworth 5 24N 100 23 E
65 Butuan 8 52N 125 36 E
65 Butung, I. 5 0s 122 45 E
49 Buturlinovka 50 50N 40 35 E
24 Butzbach 50 24N 8 40 E
61 Buxar 25 34N 83 58 E
12 Buxton 53 16N 1 54w
51 Buyaga 59 50N 127 0 E
68 Buyr Nuur, L. 47 50N 117 35 E
41 Buzău 45 10N 26 50 E
41 Buzău, R. 45 10N 27 20 E
66 Buzen 33 35N 131 5 E
37 Buzet 45 24N 13 58 E
48 Buzuluk 52 48N 52 12 E
97 Buzzards Bay 41 45N 70 38w
41 Byala, Bulgaria 42 53N 27 55 E
41 Byala, Bulgaria 43 28N 25 44 E
41 Byala Slatina 43 26N 23 55 E
28 Bydgoszcz 53 10N 18 0 E
28 Bydgoszcz □ 53 16N 18 0 E
48 Byelorussian S.S.R. □ 53 30N 27 0 E
103 Bylas 33 11N 110 9w
45 Bylderup 54 58N 9 8 E
89 Bylot I. 73 0N 78 0w
75 Byrd Ld. 79 30s 125 0w
5 Byrd Sub-Glacial Basin 82 0s 120 0w
81 Byrock 30 40s 146 27 E
81 Byron Bay 28 30s 153 30 E
46 Byske 64 59N 21 17 E
51 Byrranga, Gory 75 0N 100 0 E
27 Bystrzyca Kłodzka 50 19N 16 39 E
27 Bytom 50 25N 19 0 E
28 Bytów 54 10N 17 30 E
27 Bzenec 48 58N 17 18 E

C

Chao Phraya, R. Circle

63 Chao Phraya, R. . . 13 32N 100 36 E
69 Chaoan . . . . 23 45N 117 11 E
69 Chaochow . . . . 23 45N 116 32 E
69 Chaohwa . . . . 32 16N 105 41 E
67 Chaotung . . . . 27 30N 103 40 E
68 Chaoyang . . . . 41 46N 120 16 E
104 Chapata, L. 20 10N 103 20W
50 Chapayevo . . . . 50 25N 51 10 E
48 Chapayevsk . . . . 53 0N 49 40 E
109 Chapecó . . . . 27 14 S 52 41W
99 Chapel Hill 35 53N 79 3W
90 Chapleau 47 45N 83 30W
61 Chapra . . . . 25 48N 84 50 E
110 Charagua . . . . 19 45 S 63 10W
110 Charambira, Pta. . . 4 20N 77 30W
110 Charaña . . . . 17 30 S 69 35W
108 Charata . . . . 27 13 S 61 14W
67 Charchan . . . . 38 4N 85 16 E
67 Charchan, R. . . . . . 39 0N 86 0 E
13 Chard, U.K. 50 52N 2 59W
93 Chard, U.S.A. 55 55N 111 10W
50 Chardara . . . . 41 16N 67 59 E
50 Chardzhou . . . . 39 0N 63 20 E
20 Charente □ 45 50N 0 36W
20 Charente, R. 45 57N 1 5W
20 Charente-Maritime □ 45 50N 0 35W
73 Chari, R. . . . . 12 58N 14 31 E
57 Charikar . . . . 35 0N 69 10 E
67 Charkhlikh . . . . 39 16N 88 17 E
16 Charleroi . . . . 50 24N 4 27 E
98 Charles, C. 37 10N 75 52W
100 Charles City 43 2N 92 41W
101 Charleston, Mass. . 34 2N 90 3W
99 Charleston, S.C. . . . 32 47N 79 56W
98 Charleston, W. Va. . 38 24N 81 36W
105 Charlestown, Nevis 17 8N 62 37W
97 Charlestown, U.S.A. 38 29N 85 40W
81 Charleville, Australia . . . . 26 24 S 146 15 E
15 Charleville, Eire= Rath Luire 52 21N 8 40W
19 Charleville-Mézières . . . . 49 44N 4 40 E
99 Charlotte 35 16N 80 46W
105 Charlotte Amalie . . 18 22N 64 56W
98 Charlottesville 38 1N 78 30W
91 Charlottetown 46 19N 63 3W
84 Charlton . . . . 36 16 S 143 24 E
100 Charlton 40 59N 93 20W
90 Charlton I. 52 0N 79 20W
91 Charny 46 43N 71 15W
21 Charolles . . . . 46 27N 4 16 E
20 Charroux . . . . 46 9N 0 25 E
80 Charters Towers . . 20 5 S 146 13 E
18 Chartres . . . . 48 29N 1 30 E
108 Chascomús . . . . 35 30 S 58 0W
41 Chatal Balkan= Udvoy, Mts. . . . . 42 50N 26 50 E
88 Chatanika 65 7N 147 31W
20 Château Chinon . . . 47 4N 3 56 E
18 Château-du-Loir . . 47 40N 0 25 E
18 Château Gontier . . 47 50N 0 42W
19 Château Porcien . . 49 31N 4 13 E
18 Château Renault . . 47 36N 0 56 E
19 Château Thierry . . . 49 3N 3 20 E
18 Château-la-Vallière 47 30N 0 20 E
18 Châteaubourg 48 7N 1 25W
18 Châteaubriant 47 43N 1 23W
18 Châteaudun . . . . . . 48 3N 1 20 E
18 Châteaulin 48 11N 4 8W
20 Châteaumeillant . . . 46 35N 2 12 E
20 Châteaunuef-sur-Charente 45 36N 0 3W
19 Châteauneuf-sur-Loire . . . . 47 52N 2 13 E
20 Châteauroux . . . . . . 46 50N 1 40 E
20 Châtelaillon Plage . 46 5N 1 5W
20 Châtelguyon . . . . . . 45 55N 3 4 E
20 Châtellerault . . . . . . 46 50N 0 30 E
13 Chatham, U.K. . . . . 51 22N 0 32 E
91 Chatham, N.B. 47 2N 65 28W
96 Chatham, Ont. 42 23N 82 15W
98 Chatham, Alas. . . . 57 30N 135 0W
97 Chatham, N.Y. 42 21N 73 32W
76 Chatham Is. . . . . . . 44 0 S 176 40W
92 Chatham Str. 57 0N 134 40W
20 Châtillon-en-Bazois . . . . 47 3N 3 39 E
21 Châtillon-en-Diois . 44 41N 5 29 E
20 Châtillon-sur-Indre 46 48N 1 10 E
19 Châtillon-sur-Seine 47 50N 4 33 E
20 Châtillon-sur-Sèvre 46 56N 0 45W
99 Chattahoochee 30 43N 84 51W
99 Chattanooga 35 2N 85 17W
19 Chaulnes . . . . 49 48N 2 47 E
19 Chaumont . . . . 48 7N 5 8 E
19 Chauny . . . . 49 37N 3 12 E
21 Chaussin . . . . 46 59N 5 22 E
20 Chauvigny . . . . 46 34N 0 39 E
111 Chaves, Brazil . . . . 0 15 S 49 55W
30 Chaves, Port. 41 45N 7 32W
26 Cheb . . . . 50 9N 12 20 E
48 Cheboksary . . . . 56 8N 47 30 E
98 Cheboygan 45 38N 84 29W
68 Chefoo=Yentai . . . 37 30N 121 21 E
51 Chegdomyn . . . . 51 7N 132 52 E
102 Chehallis 46 44N 122 59W
69 Cheju . . . . 33 28N 126 30 E
69 Cheju Do, I. . . . . . . 33 29N 126 34 E
69 Chekiang □ . . . . 29 30N 120 0 E
112 Chelforó . . . . 39 0 S 66 40W
50 Chelkar . . . . 47 40N 59 32 E
50 Chelkar Tengiz Solonchak . . . . . . 48 0N 62 30 E
19 Chelles . . . . 48 52N 2 33 E
28 Chełm . . . . 51 8N 23 30 E
28 Chełm □ . . . . 51 20N 23 20 E
28 Chełmno . . . . 53 20N 18 30 E
13 Chelmsford . . . . 51 44N 0 29 E
28 Chełmno . . . . 53 20N 18 30 E
84 Chelsea . . . . 38 5 S 145 8 E
13 Cheltenham 51 55N 2 5W
50 Chelyabinsk . . . . . . 55 10N 61 35 E
92 Chemainus 48 54N 123 41W
75 Chemba . . . . 17 11 S 34 53 E
48 Chemikovsk 54 58N 56 0W
18 Chemillé 47 14N 0 45W
63 Chemor . . . . 4 44N 101 6 E
102 Chemult 43 14N 121 54W
60 Chenab, R. . . . . 29 23N 71 2 E
69 Chengchow . . . . 34 47N 113 46 E
67 Chengkiang . . . . 24 58N 102 59 E
68 Chengteh . . . . 41 0N 117 55 E
68 Chengting . . . . 38 8N 114 37 E
67 Chengtu . . . . 30 45N 104 0 E
68 Chengyang . . . . 36 20N 120 16 E
69 Chenhsien . . . . 25 45N 112 37 E
69 Chenning . . . . 25 57N 105 51 E
68 Chentung . . . . 46 2N 123 1 E
69 Chenyuan . . . . 27 0N 108 20 E
41 Chepelare . . . . 41 44N 24 40 E
105 Chepo 9 10N 79 6W
13 Chepstow 51 39N 2 41W
100 Chequamegon B. . . 46 40N 90 30W
19 Cher □ . . . . 47 10N 2 30 E
18 Cherbourg 49 39N 1 40W
72 Cherchell . . . . 36 35N 21 63 E
48 Cherdyn . . . . 60 20N 56 20 E
51 Cheremkhovo . . . . . 53 32N 102 40 E
50 Cherepanovo . . . . . 54 15N 83 30 E
49 Cherkassy . . . . 49 30N 32 0 E
41 Cherni, Mt. . . . . 42 35N 23 28 E
48 Chernigov . . . . 51 28N 31 20 E
49 Chernovtsy . . . . 48 0N 26 0 E
51 Chernoye . . . . 70 30N 89 10 E
100 Cherokee 42 40N 95 30W
48 Cheropovets . . . . . . 59 5N 37 55 E
112 Cherquenco . . . . . . 38 35 S 72 0W
51 Cherskogo Khrebet . . . . 65 0N 143 0 E
41 Cherven-Bryag . . . . 43 17N 24 7 E
13 Cherwell, R. 51 44N 1 15W
98 Chesapeake B. 38 0N 76 12W
12 Cheshire □ 53 14N 2 30W
33 Cheste 39 30N 0 41W
12 Chester, U.K. 53 12N 2 53W
98 Chester, Pa. 39 54N 75 20W
99 Chester, S.C. 34 44N 81 13W
12 Chesterfield 53 14N 1 26W
88 Chesterfield Inlet . . 63 30N 91 0W
76 Chesterfield Is. . . . . 19 52 S 158 15 E
104 Chetumal 18 30N 88 20W
104 Chetumal, B. de . . . 18 40N 88 10W
20 Chevanceaux 45 18N 0 14W
12 Cheviot, The, Mt. . 55 28N 2 8W
12 Cheviot Hills 55 20N 2 30W
74 Chew Bahir, L. . . . 4 40N 30 50 E
102 Chewelah 48 25N 117 56W
100 Cheyenne 41 9N 104 49W
100 Cheyenne, R. 44 40N 101 15W
60 Chhindwara . . . . . . 22 2N 78 59 E
63 Chi, R. . . . . 15 13N 104 45 E
69 Chiai . . . . 23 29N 120 25 E
75 Chianje . . . . 15 35 S 13 40 E
104 Chiapas □ 17 0N 92 45W
39 Chiaramonte Gulfi 37 1N 14 41 E
36 Chiari . . . . 45 31N 9 55 E
36 Chiávari . . . . 44 20N 9 20 E
36 Chiavenna . . . . 46 18N 9 23 E
66 Chiba . . . . 35 30N 140 7 E
66 Chiba □ . . . . 35 30N 140 20 E
75 Chibemba . . . . 15 48 S 14 8 E
90 Chibougamau 49 56N 74 24W
98 Chicago 41 45N 87 40W
98 Chicago Heights . . 41 29N 87 37W
92 Chichagof I. 58 0N 136 0W
13 Chichester 50 50N 0 47W
104 Chichén Itzá 20 40N 88 34W
66 Chichibu . . . . 36 5N 139 10 E
68 Chichirin . . . . 50 35N 123 45 E
101 Chickasha 35 0N 98 0W
31 Chiclana de la Frontera 36 26N 6 9W
110 Chiclayo . . . . 6 42 S 79 50W
102 Chico 39 45N 121 54W
112 Chico, R. . . . . 43 50 S 66 25W
97 Chicopee 42 6N 72 37W
91 Chicoutimi 48 28N 71 5W
62 Chidambaram . . . . . 11 20N 79 45 E
89 Chidley, C. 60 30N 64 15W
25 Chiemsee, L. . . . . . 47 53N 12 27 E
74 Chiengi . . . . 8 38 S 29 10 E
63 Chiengmai . . . . 18 55N 98 55 E
37 Chienti, R. . . . . 43 18N 13 45 E
36 Chieri . . . . 45 0N 7 50 E
19 Chiers, R. . . . . 49 39N 5 0 E
37 Chieti . . . . 42 22N 14 10 E
68 Chihfeng . . . . 42 10N 118 56 E
69 Chihing . . . . 25 2N 113 45 E
69 Chihkiang . . . . 27 21N 109 45 E
68 Chihli, G. of= Po Hai, G. . . . . . 38 30N 119 0 E
69 Chihsien . . . . 35 29N 114 1 E
104 Chihuahua 28 40N 106 3W
104 Chihuahua □ 28 40N 106 3W
50 Chiilí . . . . 44 10N 66 55 E
62 Chik Ballapur . . . . . 13 25N 77 45 E
62 Chikmagalur . . . . . . 13 15N 75 45 E
62 Chikodi . . . . 16 26N 74 38 E
58 Chilas . . . . 35 25N 74 5 E
81 Childers . . . . 25 15 S 152 17 E
101 Childress 34 30N 100 50W
107 Chile ■ . . . . 35 0 S 71 15W
110 Chilete . . . . 7 10 S 78 50W
75 Chililabombwe . . . . 12 18 S 27 43 E
61 Chilka L. . . . . 19 40N 85 25 E
108 Chillán . . . . 36 40 S 72 10W
100 Chillicothe, Mo. . . . 39 45N 93 30W
98 Chillicothe, Ohio. . 39 53N 82 58W
92 Chilliwack 49 10N 122 0W
112 Chiloé, I. de . . . . . . 42 50 S 73 45W
104 Chilpancingo 17 30N 99 40W
84 Chiltern . . . . 36 10 S 146 36 E
13 Chiltern Hills 51 44N 0 42W
69 Chilung . . . . 25 3N 121 45 E
75 Chilwa, L. . . . . 15 15 S 35 40 E
67 Chimai . . . . 34 0N 101 39 E
110 Chimborazo, Mt. . . 1 20 S 78 55W
110 Chimbote . . . . 9 0 S 78 35W
50 Chimkent . . . . 42 40N 69 25 E
59 Chin □ . . . . 22 0N 93 0 E
67 China ■ . . . . 35 0N 100 0 E
105 Chinandega 12 30N 87 0W
110 Chincha Alta . . . . . 13 20 S 76 0W
81 Chinchilla . . . . 26 45 S 150 38 E
33 Chinchilla de Monte Aragón . . 38 53N 1 40W
68 Chinchow . . . . 41 10N 121 2 E
75 Chinde . . . . 18 45 S 36 30 E
59 Chindwin, R. . . . . . 21 26N 95 15 E
69 Ching Ho, R. . . . . . 34 20N 109 0 E
62 Chingleput . . . . 12 42N 79 58 E
75 Chingola . . . . 12 31 S 27 53 E
75 Chingole . . . . 13 4 S 34 17 E
68 Chinhae . . . . 35 9N 128 58 E
60 Chiniot . . . . 31 45N 73 0 E
68 Chinju . . . . 35 12N 128 2 E
69 Chinkiang . . . . 32 2N 119 29 E
103 Chino Valley 34 54N 112 28W
18 Chinon . . . . 47 10N 0 15 E
93 Chinook, Canada . . 51 28N 110 59W
102 Chinook, U.S.A. . . 48 35N 109 19W
61 Chinsura . . . . 22 53N 88 27 E
62 Chintamani . . . . 13 26N 78 3 E
68 Chinwangtao . . . . . . 40 0N 119 31 E
37 Chióggia . . . . 45 13N 12 15 E
92 Chip Lake 53 35N 115 35W
75 Chipata . . . . 13 38 S 32 28 E
31 Chipiona 36 44N 6 26W
62 Chiplun . . . . 17 31N 73 34 E
96 Chippawa 43 5N 79 10W
13 Chippenham 51 27N 2 7W
100 Chippewa, R. 44 25N 92 10W
100 Chippewa Falls 44 56N 91 24W
104 Chiquimula 14 51N 89 37W
110 Chiquinquira 5 37N 73 50W
62 Chirala . . . . 15 50N 80 20 E
60 Chirawa . . . . 28 14N 75 42 E
62 Chirayinkil . . . . 8 41N 76 49 E
50 Chirchik . . . . 81 58N 69 15 E
88 Chirikof I. 55 50N 155 35W
105 Chiriquí, G. de 8 0N 82 10W
105 Chiriquí, L. de 9 10N 82 0W
105 Chiriqui, Mt. 8 55N 82 35W
75 Chiromo . . . . 16 30 S 35 7 E
41 Chirpan . . . . 42 10N 25 19 E
75 Chisamba . . . . 14 55 S 28 20 E
60 Christian Mandi . . . 29 50N 72 55 E
51 Chita . . . . 52 0N 113 25 E
62 Chitapur . . . . 17 10N 76 50 E
75 Chitembo . . . . 13 30 S 16 50 E
60 Chitorgarh . . . . 24 52N 74 43 E
62 Chitradurga . . . . 14 15N 76 28 E
105 Chitré 7 59N 80 27W
59 Chittagong . . . . 22 19N 91 55 E
61 Chittagong □ . . . . . 24 5N 91 25 E
62 Chittoor . . . . 13 15N 79 5 E
62 Chittur . . . . 10 40N 76 45 E
33 Chiva 39 27N 0 41W
36 Chivasso . . . . 45 10N 7 52 E
108 Chivilcoy . . . . 35 0 S 60 0W
26 Chlumec . . . . 50 9N 15 29 E
28 Chodziez . . . . 52 58N 17 0 E
62 Chodavaram . . . . . . 17 40N 82 50 E
112 Choele Choel . . . . . 39 11 S 65 40W
19 Choisy . . . . 48 45N 2 24 E
28 Choinice . . . . 53 42N 17 40 E
20 Cholet 47 4N 0 52W
105 Choluteca 13 20N 87 14W
75 Choma . . . . 16 48 S 26 59 E
60 Chomu . . . . 27 15N 75 40 E
26 Chomutov . . . . 50 28N 13 23 E
63 Chon Buri . . . . 13 21N 101 1 E
68 Chonan . . . . 36 56N 127 3 E
110 Chone . . . . 0 40 S 80 0W
68 Chongjin . . . . 41 51N 129 58 E
68 Chŏngju, N. Korea 39 41N 125 13 E
68 Chŏngju, S. Korea . 36 39N 127 27 E
68 Chŏnju . . . . 35 50N 127 4 E
112 Chonos, Arch. de los . . . . 45 0 S 75 0W
60 Chopda . . . . 21 20N 75 15 E
12 Chorley 53 39N 2 39W
27 Chorzow . . . . 50 18N 19 0 E
66 Chóshi . . . . 35 45N 140 45 E
28 Choszczno . . . . 53 7N 15 25 E
102 Choteau 47 50N 112 10W
68 Choybalsan . . . . 48 3N 114 28 E
85 Christchurch, N.Z. . 43 33 S 172 47W
13 Christchurch, U.K. 50 44N 1 47W
75 Christiana . . . . 27 52 S 25 8 E
82 Christmas Creek . . 18 29 S 125 23 E
77 Christmas I. 1 58N 157 27W
26 Chrudim . . . . 49 58N 15 43 E
27 Chrzanów . . . . 50 10N 19 21 E
50 Chu . . . . 43 36N 73 42 E
69 Chu Kiang, R. . . . . 24 50N 113 37 E
69 Chuanchow . . . . 24 57N 118 31 E
69 Chuanhsien . . . . 25 50N 111 12 E
66 Chūbu □ . . . . 36 45N 137 0 E
112 Chubut, R. . . . . 43 20 S 65 5W
68 Chucheng . . . . 36 0N 119 16 E
69 Chuchow . . . . 27 56N 113 3 E
48 Chudskoye, Oz. . . . 58 13N 27 30 E
88 Chugiak 61 25N 149 30W
66 Chūgoku □ . . . . 35 0N 133 0 E
66 Chūgoku-Sanchi, Mts. . . . . 35 0N 133 0 E
69 Chuhsien . . . . 30 51N 107 1 E
63 Chukai . . . . 4 13N 103 25 E
51 Chukotskiy Khrebet 68 0N 175 0 E
51 Chukotskoye More 68 0N 175 0W
103 Chula Vista 33 44N 117 8W
69 Chumatien . . . . 33 0N 114 4 E
51 Chumikan . . . . 54 40N 135 10 E
63 Chumphon . . . . 10 35N 99 14 E
68 Chuncho E9n . . . . . 37 58N 127 44 E
69 Chunghsien . . . . 30 17N 108 4 E
69 Chungking . . . . 29 30N 106 30 E
67 Chungtien . . . . 28 0N 99 30 E
68 Chungwei . . . . 37 35N 105 10 E
60 Chunian . . . . 31 10N 74 0 E
74 Chunya . . . . 8 30 S 33 27 E
25 Chur . . . . 46 52N 9 32 E
93 Churchill 58 45N 94 5W
93 Churchill, R., Man. 58 47N 94 12W
91 Churchill, R., Newf. 53 30N 60 10W
92 Churchill Pk. 58 10N 125 10W
60 Churu . . . . 28 20N 75 0 E
69 Chusan, I. . . . . 30 0N 122 20 E
48 Chuvash A.S.S.R. □ . . . . . 53 30N 48 0 E
48 Chuvovoy . . . . 58 15N 57 40 E
65 Cianjur . . . . 6 81 S 107 7 E
109 Cianorte . . . . 23 37 S 52 37W
65 Cibatu . . . . 7 8 S 107 59 E
98 Cicero 41 48N 87 48W
28 Ciechanów . . . . 52 52N 20 38 E
28 Ciechańow □ . . . . . 53 0N 20 0 E
105 Ciego de Avila 21 50N 78 50W
110 Ciénaga 11 0N 74 10W
105 Cienfuegos 22 10N 80 30W
26 Cieplice Slaskie Zdrój . . . . 50 50N 15 40 E
20 Cierp . . . . 42 55N 0 40 E
27 Cieszyn . . . . 49 45N 18 35 E
33 Cieza 38 17N 1 23W
32 Cifuentes 40 47N 2 37W
31 Cijara, Pantano, Res. 39 18N 4 52W
65 Cilacap . . . . 7 43 S 109 0 E
101 Cimarron, R. 36 10N 96 17W
65 Cimahi . . . . 6 53 S 107 33 E
36 Cimone, Mte. . . . . . 44 12N 10 42 E
41 Cîmpina . . . . 45 10N 25 45 E
41 Cîmpulung . . . . 45 17N 25 3 E
32 Cinca, R. . . . . 41 26N 0 21 E
98 Cincinnati 39 10N 84 26W
37 Cíngoli . . . . 43 23N 13 10 E
21 Cinto, Mt. . . . . 42 24N 8 54 E
38 Circéo, Mte. . . . . . . 41 14N 13 3 E
88 Circle 47 26N 105 35W

Coonana Dalkeith

83 Coonana 31 0s 123 0E
62 Coondapoor 13 42N 74 40E
81 Coongoola 27 43s 145 47E
62 Coonoor 11 10N 76 45E
99 Cooper 39 57N 75 7w
81 Cooper Creek, R., L. 28 0s 139 0E
81 Coorong, The 35 50s 139 20E
83 Coorow 29 50s 115 59E
81 Cooroy 26 22s 152 54E
102 Coos Bay 43 26N 124 7w
84 Cootamundra 34 36s 148 1E
15 Cootehill 54 5N 7 5w
33 Cope, C. 37 26N 1 28w
45 Copenhagen= København 55 41N 12 34E
39 Copertino 40 17N 18 2w
108 Copiapó 27 15s 70 20E
37 Copparo 44 52N 11 49E
88 Copper Center 62 10N 145 25w
90 Copper Cliff 46 30N 81 4w
92 Copper Mountain 49 20N 120 30w
88 Coppermine 68 0N 116 0w
41 Copşa Mică 46 6N 24 15E
12 Coquet, R. 55 22N 1 37w
74 Coquilhatville= Mbandaka 0 1N 18 18E
108 Coquimbo 30 0s 71 20w
108 Coquimbo □ 30 0s 71 0w
41 Corabia 43 48N 24 30E
110 Coracora 15 5s 73 45w
89 Coral Harbour 64 0N 83 0w
90 Coral Rapids 50 20N 81 40w
76 Coral Sea 15 0s 150 0E
96 Coraopolis 40 30N 80 10w
39 Corato 41 12N 16 22E
19 Corbeil-Essonnes 48 36N 2 25E
20 Corbières, Mts. 42 55N 2 35E
98 Corbin 37 0N 84 3w
31 Corbones, R. 37 36N 5 39w
13 Corby 52 29N 0 41w
33 Corcoles, R. 39 12N 2 40w
103 Corcoran 36 6N 119 35w
30 Corcubión 42 56N 9 12w
99 Cordele 31 55N 83 49w
108 Córdoba, Arg. 31 20s 64 10w
108 Córdoba, Arg. □ 31 22s 64 15w
104 Córdoba, Mexico 26 20N 103 20w
31 Córdoba, Sp. 37 50N 4 50w
108 Córdoba □, Arg. 31 22s 64 15w
31 Córdoba □, Sp. 38 5N 5 0w
65 Cordon 16 42N 121 32E
88 Cordova 60 36N 145 45w
80 Corfield 21 40s 143 21E
42 Corfu, I.= Kérkira, I. 39 38N 19 50E
30 Corgo 42 56N 7 25w
30 Coria 40 0N 6 33w
39 Corigliano Cálabro 39 36N 16 31E
43 Corinth, Greece= Kórinthos 37 56N 22 55E
99 Corinth, U.S.A. 34 54N 88 30w
43 Corinth Canal 37 48N 23 0E
111 Corinto, Brazil 18 20s 44 30w
105 Corinto, Nic. 12 30N 87 10w
15 Cork 51 54N 8 30w
15 Cork □ 51 54N 8 30w
38 Corleone 37 48N 13 16E
56 Çorlu 41 11N 27 49E
93 Cormorant 54 5N 100 45w
105 Corn Is. 12 0N 83 0w
109 Cornélio Procópio 23 7s 50 40w
91 Corner Brook 49 0N 58 0w
102 Corning, Calif. 39 56N 122 9w
96 Corning, N.Y. 42 10N 77 3w
90 Cornwall 45 5N 74 45w
13 Cornwall □ 50 26N 4 40w
110 Coro 11 30N 69 45w
111 Coroatá 4 20s 44 0w
110 Corocoro 17 15s 69 19w
85 Coromandel 36 45s 175 31E
62 Coromandel Coast Reg. 12 30N 81 0E
103 Corona 33 49N 117 36w
103 Coronado 32 45N 117 9w
105 Coronado, B. de 9 0N 83 40w
88 Coronation G. 68 0N 114 0w
108 Coronda 31 58s 60 56w
108 Coronel 37 0s 73 10w
108 Coronel Bogado 27 11s 56 18w
108 Coronel Dorrego 38 40s 61 10w
108 Coronel Oviedo 25 24s 56 30w
108 Coronel Pringles 38 0s 61 30w
108 Coronel Suárez 37 30s 62 0w
109 Corpus 27 10s 55 30w
101 Corpus Christi 27 50N 97 28w
30 Corral de Almaguer 39 45N 3 10w
36 Corréggio 44 46N 10 47E
20 Corrèze □ 45 20N 1 50E
15 Corrib, L. 53 25N 9 10w
108 Corrientes 27 30s 58 45w
108 Corrientes □ 28 0s 57 0w
105 Corrientes, C., Cuba 21 43N 84 30w
110 Corrientes, C., Col. 5 30N 77 34w
83 Corrigin 32 18s 117 45E
96 Corry 41 55N 79 39w
21 Corse, C. 43 1N 9 25E
21 Corse, I. 42 0N 9 0E
21 Corsica, I.= Corse, I. 42 0N 9 0E
101 Corsicana 32 5N 96 30w
21 Corte 42 19N 9 11E
31 Cortegana 37 52N 6 49w
103 Cortez 37 24N 108 35w
37 Cortina d'Ampezzo 46 32N 12 9E
97 Cortland 42 35N 76 11w
37 Cortona 43 16N 12 0E
31 Coruche 38 57N 8 30w
56 Çorum 40 30N 35 5E
110 Corumbá 19 0s 57 30w
102 Corvallis 44 36N 123 15w
104 Cosamalopan 18 23N 95 50w
39 Cosenza 39 17N 16 14E
41 Coşereni 44 38N 26 35E
96 Coshocton 40 17N 81 51w
19 Cosne-sur-Loire 47 24N 2 54E
108 Cosquín 31 15s 64 30w
36 Cossato 45 34N 8 10E
33 Costa Blanca, Reg. 38 25N 0 10w
32 Costa Brava, Reg. 41 30N 3 0E
31 Costa del Sol, Reg. 36 30N 4 30w
32 Costa Dorada, Reg. 40 45N 1 15E
105 Costa Rica ■ 10 0N 84 0w
41 Costeşti 44 40N 24 53E
38 Cost Smeralda 41 5N 9 35E
25 Coswig 51 52N 12 31E
65 Cotabato 7 8N 124 13E
21 Côte d'Azur, Reg. 43 25N 6 50E
19 Côte d'Or □ 47 30N 4 50E
21 Côte d'Or, Reg. 47 10N 4 50E
18 Cotentin, Reg. 49 30N 1 30w
19 Côtes de Meuse, Reg. 49 15N 5 22E
18 Côtes-du-Nord □ 48 28N 2 50w
72 Cotonou 6 20N 2 25E
110 Cotopaxi, Mt. 0 30s 78 30w
13 Cotswold Hills 51 42N 2 10w
102 Cottage Grove 43 48N 123 2w
24 Cottbus 51 44N 14 20E
24 Cottbus □ 51 43N 13 30E
103 Cottonwood 34 48N 112 1w
31 Couço 38 59N 8 17w
102 Coulee City 47 44N 119 12w
19 Coulommiers 48 50N 3 3E
21 Coulon, R. 43 51N 5 0E
88 Council, Alas. 64 55N 163 45w
102 Council, Id. 44 45N 116 30w
100 Council Bluffs 41 20N 95 50w
21 Couronne, C. 43 19N 5 3E
18 Courseulles 49 20N 0 29w
21 Cours 46 7N 4 19E
92 Courtenay 49 45N 125 0w
18 Courville 48 28N 1 15E
18 Coutances 49 3N 1 28w
20 Coutras 45 3N 0 8w
30 Covilhã 40 17N 7 31w
99 Covington, Ga. 33 36N 83 50w
98 Covington, Ky. 39 5N 84 30w
93 Cowan 52 5N 100 45w
83 Cowan, L. 31 45s 121 45E
84 Cowangie 35 12s 141 26E
90 Cowansville 45 14N 72 46w
14 Cowdenbeath 56 7N 3 20w
81 Cowell 33 38s 136 40E
13 Cowes 50 45N 1 18w
84 Cowra 33 49s 148 42E
111 Coxim 18 30s 54 55w
59 Cox's Bazar 21 25N 92 3E
104 Cozumel, I. de 20 30N 86 40w
75 Cradock 32 8s 25 36E
102 Craig 40 32N 107 44w
15 Craigavon □ 54 27N 6 26w
41 Craiova 44 21N 23 48E
74 Crampel 7 8N 19 8E
93 Cranberry Portage 54 36N 101 22w
80 Cranbrook, Tas. 42 0s 148 5E
83 Cranbrook, W. Australia 34 20s 117 35E
92 Cranbrook Canada 49 30N 115 55w
97 Cranston 41 47N 71 27w
43 Crasna 46 32N 27 51E
111 Crateús 5 10s 40 50w
111 Crato, Brazil 7 10s 39 25w
31 Crato, Port. 39 16N 7 39w
21 Crau, Reg. 43 32N 4 40E
98 Crawfordsville 40 2N 86 51w
13 Crawley 51 7N 0 10w
19 Crécy 48 50N 2 53E
93 Cree L. 57 30N 107 0w
19 Creil 49 15N 2 34E
36 Crema 45 21N 9 40E
36 Cremona 45 8N 10 2E
19 Crépy 49 37N 3 32E
19 Crépy-en-Valois 49 14N 2 54E
37 Cres, I. 44 58N 14 25E
102 Crescent City 41 45N 124 12w
108 Crespo 32 2s 60 20w
90 Cressman 47 40N 72 55w
21 Crest 44 44N 5 2E
92 Creston, Canada 49 10N 116 40w
100 Creston, U.S.A. 41 0N 94 20w
99 Crestview 30 45N 86 35w
43 Crete=Kriti, I. 35 10N 25 0E
43 Crete, Sea of 26 0N 25 0E
32 Creus, C. 42 20N 3 19E
20 Creuse □ 46 0N 2 0E
20 Creuse, R. 47 0N 0 34E
37 Crevalcore 44 41N 11 10E
33 Crevillente 38 12N 0 48w
12 Crewe 53 6N 2 28w
109 Criciúma 28 40s 49 23w
14 Crieff 56 22N 3 50w
37 Crikvenica 45 11N 14 40E
49 Crimea= Krymskaya, Reg. 45 0N 34 0E
24 Crimmitschau 50 48N 12 23E
14 Crinan 56 4N 5 30w
104 Cristóbal 9 10N 80 0w
101 Crockett 31 20N 95 30w
21 Croisette, C. 43 13N 5 20E
82 Croker, I. 11 12s 132 32E
14 Cromarty 57 40N 4 2w
12 Cromer 52 56N 1 18E
85 Cromwell 45 3s 169 14E
84 Cronulla 34 3s 151 8E
105 Crooked I. 22 50N 74 10w
100 Crookston 47 50N 96 40w
12 Cross Fell, Mt. 54 44N 2 29w
15 Crosshaven 51 48N 8 19w
97 Croton-on-Hudson 41 19N 73 55w
39 Crotone 39 5N 17 6E
102 Crow Agency 45 40N 107 30w
15 Crow Hd. 51 34N 10 9w
101 Crowley 30 15N 92 20w
97 Crown Point 41 24N 87 23w
92 Crowsnest P. 49 40N 114 40w
80 Croydon, Australia 18 15s 142 14E
13 Croydon, U.K. 51 18N 0 5w
18 Crozon 48 15N 4 30w
109 Cruz Alta 28 40s 53 32w
108 Cruz del Eje 30 45s 64 50w
109 Cruzeiro 22 50s 45 0w
109 Cruzeiro do Oeste 23 46s 53 4w
110 Cruzeiro do Sul 7 35s 72 35w
81 Crystal Brook 33 21s 138 13E
101 Crystal City 38 15N 90 23w
27 Csongrád 46 43N 20 12E
27 Csongrád □ 46 32N 20 15E
27 Csurgo 46 16N 17 9E
75 Cuamba 14 45s 36 22E
75 Cuando, R. 14 0s 19 30E
31 Cuba 38 10N 7 54w
105 Cuba ■ 22 0N 79 0w
83 Cuballing 32 50s 117 15E
110 Cucui 1 10N 66 50w
110 Cúcuta 7 54N 72 31w
62 Cuddalore 11 46N 79 45E
62 Cuddapah 14 30N 78 47E
30 Cudillero 43 33N 6 9w
83 Cue 27 20s 117 55E
30 Cuéllar 41 23N 4 21E
32 Cuenca, Sp. 40 5N 2 10w
110 Cuenca, Ecuador 2 50s 79 9w
32 Cuenca, Sp. □ 40 0N 2 0w
32 Cuenca, Sa. de 39 55N 1 50w
104 Cuernavaca 18 50N 99 20w
101 Cuero 29 5N 97 17w
111 Cuiabá 15 30s 56 0w
14 Cuillin Hills 57 14N 6 15w
21 Cuiseaux 46 30N 5 22E
104 Cuitzeo, L. 19 55N 101 5w
20 Culan 46 34N 2 20E
84 Culcairn 35 41s 147 3E
30 Culebra, Sa. de la 41 55N 6 20w
104 Culiacán 24 50N 107 40w
33 Cúllar de Baza 37 35N 2 34w
14 Cullen 57 45N 2 50w
82 Cullen, Pt. 11 50s 141 47E
33 Cullera 39 9N 0 17w
14 Culloden Moor 57 29N 4 7w
21 Culoz 45 47N 5 46E
85 Culverden 42 47s 172 49E
110 Cumaná 10 30N 64 5w
92 Cumberland, Canada 49 40N 125 0w
98 Cumberland, U.S.A. 39 40N 78 43w
89 Cumberland Pen. 67 0N 65 0w
86 Cumberland Plat. 36 0N 84 30w
89 Cumberland Sd. 65 30N 66 0w
31 Cumbres Mayores 38 4N 6 39w
12 Cumbria □ 54 44N 2 55w
12 Cumbrian, Mts. 54 30N 3 0w
31 Cummins 34 16s 135 44E
83 Cunderdin 31 39s 117 15E
75 Cunene, R. 17 20s 11 50E
36 Cúneo 44 23N 7 32E
81 Cunnamulla 28 4s 145 41E
93 Cupar, Canada 51 0N 104 10w
14 Cupar, U.K. 56 20N 3 0w
110 Cupica, G. de 6 25N 77 30w
40 Ćuprija 34 57N 21 26E
105 Curaçao 12 10N 69 0w
19 Cure, R. 47 40N 3 41E
110 Curiapo 8 33N 61 5w
108 Curicó 34 55s 71 20w
108 Curicó □ 34 50s 71 15w
109 Curitiba 25 20s 49 10w
111 Currais Novos 6 13s 36 30w
111 Curralinho 1 35s 49 30w
80 Currawilla 25 10s 141 20E
102 Currie 40 16N 114 45w
80 Curtis, I. 23 40s 151 15E
111 Curuçá 0 35s 47 50w
111 Cururupu 1 50s 44 50w
108 Curuzú Cuatiá 29 50s 58 5w
111 Curvelo 18 45s 44 27w
84 Curya 35 53s 142 54E
101 Cushing 31 43N 94 50w
36 Cusna, Mte. 44 17N 10 23E
20 Cusset 46 8N 3 28E
100 Custer 43 45N 103 38w
102 Cut Bank 48 40N 112 15w
39 Cutro 39 1N 16 58E
61 Cuttack 20 25N 85 57E
83 Cuvier, C. 23 14s 113 22E
24 Cuxhaven 53 51N 8 41E
96 Cuyahoga Falls 41 8N 81 30w
110 Cuzco, Mt. 20 0s 66 50w
110 Cuzco 13 32s 72 0w
80 Cygnet 43 8s 147 1E
56 Cyprus ■ 35 0N 33 0E
73 Cyrenaica=Barqa Reg. 27 0N 20 0E
73 Cyrene=Shahhat 32 39N 21 18E
27 Czechoslovakia ■ 49 0N 17 0E
27 Czechowice Dziedzice 49 54N 18 59E
27 Czeladz 50 16N 19 2E
28 Czempiń 52 9N 16 33E
27 Czerwionka 50 7N 18 37E
27 Częstochowa 50 49N 19 7E
28 Czestichowa □ 50 50N 19 0E
28 Człuchów 53 41N 17 22E

D

63 Da, R. 16 0N 107 0E
63 Da Lat 12 3N 108 32E
63 Da Nang 16 10N 108 7E
72 Dabakala 8 15N 4 20w
60 Dabhoi 22 10N 73 20E
28 Dąbie 53 27N 14 45E
72 Dabola 10 50N 11 5w
27 Dabrowa Gornieza 50 15N 19 10E
27 Dabrowa Tarnówska 50 10N 21 0E
61 Dacca 23 43N 90 26E
61 Dacca □ 24 0N 90 0E
25 Dachau 48 16N 11 27E
110 Dadanawa 3 0N 59 30w
60 Dadau 26 45N 67 45E
49 Dagesta A.S.S.R. □ 42 30N 47 0E
65 Dagupan 16 3N 120 33E
72 Dahomey ■= Benin ■ 8 0N 2 0E
31 Daimiel 39 5N 3 35w
15 Daingean 53 18N 7 15w
68 Dairen=Talien 39 0N 121 31E
73 Dairût 27 34N 30 43E
83 Dairy Creek 25 12s 115 48E
66 Daisetsu-Zan, Mt. 43 30N 142 57E
80 Dajarra 21 42s 139 30E
72 Dakar 14 34N 17 29w
72 Dakhla 23 50N 15 53w
49 Dakhovskaya 44 13N 40 13E
60 Dakor 22 45N 73 11E
40 Dakovica 42 22N 20 26E
40 Dakovo 45 19N 18 24E
68 Dalai Nor, L. 49 0N 117 50E
44 Dalälven, R. 60 38N 17 27E
68 Dalandzadgad 43 35N 104 30E
58 Dalbandin 28 53N 64 25E
14 Dalbeattie 54 56N 3 49w
81 Dalby 27 11s 151 16E
101 Dalhart 36 4N 102 31w
91 Dalhousie 48 0N 66 26w
54 Daliyat el Karmel 32 41N 35 3E
40 Dalj 45 29N 18 59E
14 Dalkeith 55 54N 3 4w

Dallas Dinara Planina, Mts.

101 Dallas 32 47N 96 48W
57 Dalmā, I. 24 30N 52 20E
37 Dalmacija, Reg. 43 0N 17 0E
14 Dalmellington 55 20N 4 25W
51 Dalnerechensk 45 50N 133 40E
72 Daloa 6 53N 6 27W
90 Dalton, Canada 60 10N 137 0N
97 Dalton, Mass. 42 28N 73 11W
99 Dalton, Neb. 41 27N 103 0W
61 Daltonganj 24 3N 84 4E
82 Daly, R. 13 20S 130 19E
80 Daly Waters 16 15S 133 22E
60 Daman 20 25N 72 57E
60 Daman, Dadra & Nagar Haveli □ 20 25N 72 58E
73 Damanhûr 31 2N 30 28E
75 Damaraland, Reg. 22 33S 17 6E
56 Damascus= Dimashq 33 30N 36 18E
57 Damāvand 35 45N 52 10E
57 Damāvand, Qolleh-ye, Mt. 35 56N 52 8E
41 Dâmboviţa, R. 44 40N 26 0E
57 Dāmaghan 36 10N 54 17E
73 Damietta= Dumyât 31 24N 31 48E
54 Damiya 32 6N 35 34E
24 Damme 52 32N 8 12E
61 Damodar, R. 23 17N 87 35E
61 Damoh 23 50N 79 28E
82 Dampier 20 39S 116 45E
65 Dampier, Selat 0 40S 130 40E
54 Dan 33 13N 35 39E
72 Danané 7 16N 8 9W
97 Danbury 41 23N 73 29W
84 Dandenong 37 52S 145 12E
77 Danger Is. 10 53S 165 49W
91 Daniel's Harbour 50 13N 57 35W
48 Danilov 58 16N 40 13E
40 Danilovgrad 42 38N 19 9E
24 Dannenberg 53 7N 11 4E
85 Dannevirke 40 12S 176 8E
96 Dannsville 42 32N 77 41W
9 Danube, R.= Donau, R. 45 20N 29 40E
97 Danvers 42 34N 70 55E
98 Danville, Ill. 40 10N 87 45W
98 Danville, Ky. 37 40N 84 45W
97 Danville, Vt. 44 24N 72 12W
99 Danville, Va. 36 40N 79 20W
28 Danzig= Gdánsk 54 22N 18 40E
84 Dapto 34 30S 150 47E
54 Dar'a 32 37N 36 6E
74 Dar-es-Salaam 6 50S 39 12E
57 Dārāb 28 50N 54 30E
58 Darband 34 30N 72 50E
61 Darbhanga 26 15N 86 3E
92 D'Arcy 50 35N 122 30W
56 Dardanelles= Cannakale Boğazi, Str. 40 0N 26 20E
36 Darfo 45 43N 10 11E
73 Dârfûr □ 15 35N 25 0E
73 Dârfûr, Reg. 12 35N 25 0E
58 Dargai 34 25N 71 45E
50 Dargan Ata 40 40N 62 20E
85 Dargaville 35 57S 173 52E
68 Darhan 49 27N 105 57E
110 Darién, G. del 9 0N 77 0W
61 Darjeeling 27 3N 88 18E
91 Dark Cove 49 54N 54 5W
83 Darkan 33 19S 116 37E
84 Darling, R. 34 4S 141 54E
81 Darling Downs 27 30S 150 30E
83 Darling Ra. 32 0S 116 30E
12 Darlington 54 33N 1 33W
28 Darłowo 54 26N 16 23E
41 Dármănesti 46 21N 26 33E
25 Darmstadt 49 51N 8 40E
88 Darnley, B. 69 30N 124 30W
32 Daroca 41 9N 1 25W
80 Darr 24 34S 144 52E
25 Darsser Ort, C. 44 27N 12 30E
13 Dart, R. 50 34N 3 56W
84 Dartmoor 37 56S 141 19E
13 Dartmoor, Reg. 50 36N 4 0W
80 Dartmouth, Australia 23 30S 144 40E
91 Dartmouth Canada 44 40N 63 30W
13 Dartmouth, U.K. 50 21N 3 35W
32 Dartuch, C. 39 55N 3 49E
40 Daruvar 45 36N 17 13E
50 Darvaza 40 12N 58 24E
60 Darwha 20 15N 77 45E
82 Darwin 12 20S 130 50E
82 Darwin River 12 49S 130 58E
56 Daryācheh-ye Reza'iyeh, L. 37 30N 45 30E
60 Daryapur 23 19N 71 50E
57 Das 35 5N 75 4E
73 Dashen, Ras, Mt. 13 10N 38 26E
68 Dashinchilen 47 50N 103 60E
58 Dasht, R. 25 10N 61 40E
57 Dasht-e Kavir, Des. 34 30N 55 0E
57 Dasht-e Lút, Des. 31 30N 58 0E
60 Daska 32 20N 74 21E
60 Datia 25 39N 78 27E
60 Dattapur 20 45N 78 15E
60 Daud Khel 32 53N 71 34E
48 Daugavpils 55 53N 26 32E
57 Daulat Yar 34 33N 65 46E
93 Dauphin 51 15N 100 5W
21 Daupniné, Reg. 45 15N 5 25E
62 Davangere 14 25N 75 50E
65 Davao 7 0N 125 40E
65 Davao G. 6 30N 125 48E
100 Davenport, Iowa 41 30N 90 40W
102 Davenport, Wash. 47 40N 118 5W
13 Daventry 52 16N 1 10W
105 David 8 30N 82 30W
88 Davis, Alas. 51 52N 176 39W
102 Davis, Calif. 38 39N 121 45W
91 Davis Inlet 55 50N 60 45W
5 Davis Sea 66 0S 92 0E
89 Davis Str. 68 0N 58 0W
25 Davos 46 48N 9 50E
88 Dawson 64 4N 139 25W
92 Dawson Creek 55 46N 120 14W
112 Dawson, I. 53 50S 70 50W
20 Dax 43 43N 1 3W
54 Dayr al-Ghusūn 32 21N 35 5E
56 Dayr az Zawr 35 20N 40 9E
54 Dayral Balah 31 25N 34 21E
98 Dayton, Ohio 39 45N 84 10W
102 Dayton, Wash. 46 20N 118 0W
99 Daytona Beach 29 14N 81 0W
83 D'Entrecasteaux, Pt. 34 50S 116 0E
75 De Aar 30 39S 24 0E
82 De Grey 20 30S 120 0E
82 De Grey, R. 20 12S 119 11E
100 De Kalb 41 55N 88 45W
99 De Land 29 1N 81 19W
101 De Ridder 30 48N 93 15W
100 De Soto 38 8N 90 34W
54 Dead Sea= Miyet, Bahr el 31 30N 35 30E
100 Deadwood 44 25N 103 43W
83 Deakin 30 46S 129 0E
13 Deal 51 13N 1 25E
13 Dean, Forest of 51 50N 2 35W
108 Deán Funes 30 20S 64 20W
88 Dease Arm, B. 66 45N 120 6W
92 Dease Lake 58 40N 130 5W
103 Death Valley 36 0N 116 40W
103 Death Valley Nat. Mon. 36 30N 117 0W
103 Death Valley Junction .15N 11630W
18 Deauville 49 23N 0 2E
40 Debar 41 21N 20 37E
27 Dębica 50 2N 21 25E
28 Dęblin 51 34N 21 50E
28 Dębno 52 45N 14 40E
73 Debre Markos 10 20N 37 40E
73 Debre Tabor 11 50N 38 5E
27 Debrecen 47 33N 21 42E
40 Dečani 42 30N 29 10E
99 Decatur, Ala. 34 35N 87 0W
99 Decatur, Ga. 33 47N 84 17W
100 Decatur, Ill. 39 50N 89 0W
98 Decatur, Ind. 40 52N 85 28W
20 Decazeville 44 34N 2 15E
62 Deccan, Reg. 14 0N 77 0E
26 Děčín 50 47N 14 12E
20 Decize 46 50N 3 28E
100 Decorah 43 20N 91 50W
97 Dedham 42 14N 71 10W
14 Dee, R. Scot. 57 4N 3 7W
12 Dee, R., Wales 53 15N 3 7W
80 Deep Well 24 25S 134 5E
81 Deepwater 29 25S 151 51E
91 Deer Lake 49 11N 57 27W
102 Deer Lodge 46 25N 112 40W
60 Deesa 24 18N 72 10E
98 Defiance 41 20N 84 20W
54 Deganya 32 43N 35 34E
31 Degebe, R. 38 21N 7 37W
55 Degeh Bur 8 14N 43 35E
44 Degerfors 64 16N 19 46E
25 Deggendorf 48 49N 12 59E
62 Degloor 18 34N 77 33E
57 Deh Bīd 30 39N 53 11E
62 Dehiwala 6 50N 79 57E
60 Dehra Dun 30 20N 78 4E
61 Dehri 24 50N 84 15E
54 Deir Dibwan 31 55N 35 15E
44 Deje 59 35N 13 29E
103 Del Norte 37 47N 106 27W
101 Del Rio 29 15N 100 50W
70 Delagoa B. 25 50S 32 45E
103 Delano 35 48N 119 13W
98 Delaware 40 20N 83 0W
98 Delaware □ 39 0N 75 40W
98 Delaware, R. 41 50N 75 15W
25 Delémont 47 22N 7 20E
96 Delevan 42 27N 78 28W
16 Delft 52 1N 4 22E
62 Delft I. 9 30N 79 40E
16 Delfzijl 53 20N 6 55E
74 Delgado, C. 10 45S 40 40E
73 Delgo 20 6N 30 40E
60 Delhi 28 38N 77 17E
104 Delicias 28 10N 105 30W
24 Delitzsch 51 32N 12 22E
19 Delle 47 30N 7 2E
97 Delmar 42 37N 73 47W
24 Delmenhorst 53 3N 8 37E
111 Delmiro Gonveia 9 24S 38 6W
37 Delnice 45 23N 14 50E
51 Delong, Os. 76 30N 153 0E
80 Deloraine 41 30S 146 40E
43 Delphi 38 28N 22 30E
98 Delphos 40 51N 84 17W
99 Delray Beach 26 27N 80 4W
103 Delta 38 44N 108 5W
81 Delungra 29 40S 150 45E
42 Delvinë 39 59N 20 4E
30 Demanda, Sa. de 42 15N 3 0W
103 Deming 48 49N 122 13W
24 Demmin 53 54N 13 2E
92 Demmit 55 26N 119 54W
99 Demopolis 32 31N 87 50W
64 Dempo, Mt. 4 2S 103 9E
16 Den Helder 52 54N 4 45E
19 Denain 50 20N 3 23E
50 Denau 38 16N 67 54E
12 Denbigh 53 11N 3 25W
64 Dendang 3 5S 107 54E
16 Dendermonde 51 2N 4 7E
83 Denham 25 55S 113 32E
93 Denholm 52 40N 108 0W
84 Deniliquin 35 32S 144 58E
101 Denison 33 45N 96 33W
56 Denizli 37 46N 29 6E
83 Denmark 34 57S 117 21E
45 Denmark ■ 56 0N 10 0E
4 Denmark Str. 67 0N 25 0W
64 Denpasar 8 39S 115 13E
101 Denton 33 13N 97 8W
100 Denver 39 43N 105 1W
60 Deoband 29 41N 77 41E
61 Deoghar 24 30N 86 59E
61 Deoha, R. 27 0N 79 90E
60 Deolali 19 56N 73 50E
61 Deoria 26 30N 83 47E
58 Deosai Mts. 35 10N 75 20E
96 Depew 42 55N 78 43W
83 Depot Springs 27 55S 120 3E
51 Deputatskiy 69 18N 139 54E
60 Dera Ghazi Khan 30 3N 70 38E
60 Dera Ismail Khan □ 31 50N 70 54E
49 Derbent 42 3N 48 18E
82 Derby, Australia 17 18S 123 38E
12 Derby, U.K. 52 55N 1 29W
97 Derby, U.S.A. 41 19N 73 5N
12 Derby □ 52 55N 1 29W
27 Derecske 47 21N 21 34E
15 Derg, L. 53 0N 8 20W
73 Derna 32 40N 22 35E
84 Derrinallum 37 57S 143 13E
84 Derriwong 33 6S 147 21E
15 Derryveagh Mts. 55 0N 8 40W
73 Derudub 17 31N 36 7E
43 Dervéni 38 8N 22 25E
12 Derwent R. Cumbria 54 42N 3 22W
12 Derwent, R. Derby 53 26N 1 44W
12 Derwent, R. Yorks 54 13N 0 35W
12 Derwentwater, L. 53 34N 3 9W
100 Des Moines 41 35N 93 37W
100 Des Moines, R. 41 15N 93 0W
112 Deseado, R. 40 0S 69 0W
36 Desenzano del Garda 45 28N 10 32E
103 Desert Center 33 45N 115 27W
48 Desna, R. 52 0N 33 15E
112 Desolación, I. 53 0S 74 10W
24 Dessau 51 50N 12 14E
19 Dèsvres 50 40N 1 50E
40 Deta 45 24N 21 13E
24 Detmold 51 56N 8 52E
98 Detroit 42 20N 83 3W
100 Detroit Lakes 46 49N 95 57W
16 Deurne, Belgium 51 13N 4 28E
16 Deurne, Neth. 51 28N 5 47E
24 Deutsche, B. 54 30N 7 30E
26 Deutschlandsberg 46 49N 15 13E
20 Deux-Sèvres □ 46 30N 0 20W
40 Deva 45 53N 22 55E
62 Devakottai 9 57N 78 49E
27 Dévaványa 47 2N 20 58E
16 Deventer 52 15N 6 10E
14 Deveron, R. 57 22N 3 0W
60 Devgad Baria 22 42N 73 54E
100 Devils Lake 48 7N 98 59W
13 Devizes 51 22N 1 59W
41 Devnya 43 13N 27 33E
92 Devon 53 22N 113 44W
13 Devon □ 50 45N 3 50W
86 Devon I. 75 0N 87 0W
80 Devonport, Australia 41 11S 146 21E
85 Devonport, N.Z. 36 49S 174 48E
13 Devonport, U.K. 50 22N 4 10W
60 Dewas 22 57N 76 4E
12 Dewsbury 53 42N 1 37W
57 Deyhūk 33 17N 57 30E
57 Deyyer 27 50N 51 55E
56 Dezfūl 32 23N 48 24E
56 Dezh Shāhpūr 35 31N 46 10E
56 Dhahaban 21 58N 39 3E
56 Dhahran= Az Zahrān 26 10N 50 7E
55 Dhamar 14 46N 44 23E
60 Dhampur 29 19N 78 31E
61 Dhamtari 20 42N 81 33E
61 Dhanbad 23 47N 86 26E
60 Dhar 22 36N 75 18E
60 Dharangaon 21 1N 75 16E
62 Dharapuram 10 44N 77 32E
62 Dharmapuri 12 8N 78 10E
62 Dharmavaram 14 25N 77 44E
60 Dharmsala 32 13N 76 19E
62 Dharwar 15 28N 75 1E
61 Dhaulagiri, Mt. 28 42N 83 31E
61 Dhenkanal 20 45N 85 35E
43 Dhenoúsa, I. 37 8N 25 48E
43 Dhesfina 38 25N 22 31E
42 Dhidhimotikhon 41 21N 26 30E
43 Dhimitsána 37 37N 22 3E
43 Dhodhekánisos, Is. 36 35N 27 10E
60 Dholka 22 44N 72 27E
60 Dholpur 26 42N 77 54E
62 Dhond 18 26N 74 40E
60 Dhrangadhra 23 0N 71 30E
60 Dhrol 22 34N 70 25E
61 Dhubri 26 1N 89 59E
55 Dhula 15 5N 48 5E
60 Dhulia 20 54N 74 47E
108 Diamante 32 5S 60 35W
111 Diamantina 18 5S 43 40W
80 Diamantina, R. 26 45S 139 10E
111 Diamantino 14 25S 56 27W
60 Dibai 28 13N 78 15E
74 Dibaya Lubue 4 12S 19 54E
57 Dibba 25 45N 56 16E
55 Dibi 4 12N 41 58E
59 Dibrugarh 27 29N 94 55E
100 Dickinson 46 53N 102 47W
97 Dickson City 41 27N 75 37W
92 Didsbury 51 40N 114 8W
60 Didwana 27 24N 74 34E
21 Die 44 45N 5 22E
93 Diefenbaker L. 51 0N 106 55W
3 Diego Garcia, I. 7 20S 72 25E
112 Diego Ramirez, Is. 56 30S 68 44W
75 Diégo-Suarez 12 16S 49 17E
63 Dien Bien Phu 21 23N 103 1E
24 Diepholz 52 35N 8 21E
18 Dieppe 49 56N 1 5E
16 Differdange 49 32N 5 32E
91 Digby 44 41N 65 50W
59 Dighinala 23 15N 92 5E
21 Digne 44 6N 6 14E
20 Digoin 46 29N 3 59E
59 Dihang, R. 27 30N 96 30E
56 Dijlah, Nahr 30 90N 47 50E
19 Dijon 47 19N 5 1E
50 Dikson 73 30N 80 35E
73 Dikwa 12 2N 13 56E
63 Di Linh, Cao Nguyen 11 35N 108 4E
65 Dili 8 33S 125 35E
24 Dillenburg 50 44N 8 17E
102 Dillon, Mont. 45 13N 112 38W
99 Dillon, S.C. 34 25N 79 22W
56 Dimashq 33 30N 36 18E
72 Dimbokro 6 39N 4 42W
84 Dimboola 36 27S 142 2E
41 Dîmbovnic, R. 44 28N 25 18E
41 Dimitrovgrad, Bulgaria 42 3N 25 36E
48 Dimitrovgrad, U.S.S.R. 54 25N 49 33E
40 Dimitrovgrad, Yug. 43 1N 22 47E
40 Dimovo 43 43N 22 50E
65 Dinagat, I. 10 10N 125 35E
61 Dinajpur 35 38N 88 38E
18 Dinan 48 27N 2 2W
16 Dinant 50 16N 4 55E
61 Dinapore 25 38N 85 5E
56 Dinar 38 4N 30 10E
57 Dinar, Kuh-e, Mt. 30 48N 51 40E
37 Dinara Planina, Mts. 43 50N 16 35E

Dinard Eagle Pass

18 Dinard 48 38N 2 4W
9 Dinaric Alps, Mts. 43 50N 16 35W
62 Dindigul 10 21N 77 58E
15 Dingle 52 8N 10 15W
15 Dingle, B. 52 5N 10 15W
80 Dingo 23 39S 149 20E
72 Dinguiraye 11 18N 10 43W
14 Dingwall 57 35N 4 29W
102 Dinosaur Nat. Mon. 40 32N 108 58W
103 Dinuba 36 32N 119 23W
27 Diósgyör 48 7N 20 43E
72 Diourbel 14 40N 16 15W
65 Dipolog 8 36N 123 20E
55 Dire Dawa 9 37N 41 52E
105 Diriamba 11 53N 86 15W
83 Dirk Hartog, I. 25 48S 113 0E
81 Dirranbandi 28 35S 148 14E
102 Disappointment.C. 46 18N 124 3W
82 Disappointment, L. 23 30S 122 50E
88 Discovery 63 0N 115 0W
84 Discovery, B. 38 12S 141 7E
4 Disko, I. 69 50N 53 30W
13 Diss 52 23N 1 6E
58 Disteghil Sar, Mt. 36 22N 75 12E
111 Districto Federal □ 15 45S 47 45W
104 Distrito Federal □ 19 15N 99 10W
60 Diu 20 43N 70 69E
18 Dives 49 18N 0 8W
18 Dives, R. 48 55N 0 5W
49 Divnoye 45 55N 43 27E
100 Dixon 41 50N 89 29W
92 Dixon Entrance 54 25N 132 30W
56 Diyarbakir 37 55N 40 14E
74 Djambala 2 33S 14 45E
64 Djangeru 2 20S 116 29E
72 Djelfa 34 30N 3 20E
74 Djema 6 3N 25 19E
73 Djerba, I. de 33 56N 11 0E
72 Djerid, Chott el, Reg. 35 50N 8 30E
55 Djibouti 11 36N 43 9E
72 Djidjelli 36 52N 5 50E
74 Djolu 0 37N 22 21E
72 Djougou 9 42N 1 40E
73 Djourab, Erg du 16 40N 18 50E
74 Djugu 1 55N 30 30E
46 Djúpivogur 64 40N 14 10W
44 Djursholm 59 24N 18 5E
45 Djursland, Reg. 56 27N 10 40E
49 Dnepr, R. 46 30N 32 18E
49 Dneprodzerzhinsk 48 30N 34 37E
49 Dnepropetrovsk 48 30N 35 0E
49 Dnestr, R. 46 18N 30 17E
49 Dnieper, R.= Dnepr, R. 46 30N 32 18E
49 Dniester, R.= Dnestr, R. 46 18N 30 17E
73 Doba 8 39N 16 51E
24 Döbeln 51 7N 13 7E
65 Dobo 5 46S 134 13E
40 Doboj 44 44N 18 6E
40 Dobra 45 54N 22 36E
41 Dobruja, Reg. 44 30N 28 30E
44 Döda Fallet. 63 4N 16 35E
62 Dodballapur 13 18N 77 32E
101 Dodge City 37 45N 100 1W
74 Dodoma 6 11S 35 45E
93 Dodsland 51 48N 108 49W
16 Doetinchem 51 58N 6 17E
41 Doftana 45 17N 25 45E
92 Dog Creek 51 35N 122 18W
57 Doha 25 15N 51 36E
60 Dohad 22 50N 74 15E
59 Dohazari 22 10N 92 5E
63 Doi Luang, Ra. 18 20N 101 30E
40 Dojransko, J. 41 11N 22 44E
18 Dol 48 34N 1 47W
91 Dolbeau 48 53N 72 14W
21 Dôle 47 6N 5 30E
12 Dolgellau 52 44N 3 53W
38 Dolianova 39 23N 9 11E
74 Dolisie 4 12S 12 41E
41 Dolni Dŭbnik 43 24N 24 26E
37 Dolo, Italy 45 25N 12 5E
55 Dolo, Somali Rep. 4 13N 42 8E
37 Dolomiti, Mts. 46 25N 11 50E
110 Dolores, Arg. 36 19S 57 40W
108 Dolores, Uruguay 33 33S 58 13W
112 Dolphin, C. 51 15S 58 58W
88 Dolphin & Union Str. 69 5N 114 45W
109 Dom Pedrito 31 0S 54 40W
50 Dombarovskiy 50 46N 59 39E
44 Dombås 62 5N 9 8E
19 Dombasle 48 38N 6 21E
21 Dombes, Reg. 46 0N 5 3E
108 Domeyko, Cord. 24 30S 69 0W
18 Domfront 48 37N 0 4W
105 Dominica, I. 15 30N 61 20W
105 Dominica Pass 15 10N 61 20W
105 Dominican Rep. ■ 19 0N 70 40W
36 Domodossola 46 7N 8 17E
19 Dompaire 48 13N 6 13E
12 Don, R., Eng. 53 39N 0 59W
14 Don, R., Scot. 57 10N 2 4W
49 Don, R., U.S.S.R. 47 4N 39 18E
31 Don Benito 38 57N 5 52W
15 Donaghadee 54 39N 5 33W
8 Donald 36 22S 143 0E
92 Donalda 52 35N 112 34W
25 Donauwörth 48 43N 10 46E
26 Donawitz 47 22N 15 4E
12 Doncaster 53 32N 1 7W
62 Dondra Hd. 5 55N 80 35E
15 Donegal 54 39N 8 7W
15 Donegal □ 54 50N 0 8W
15 Donegal, B. 54 30N 8 30W
49 Donetsk 48 0N 37 48E
63 Dong Hoi 17 18N 106 36E
83 Dongara 29 15S 114 56E
61 Dongargarh 21 11N 80 45E
18 Donges 47 18N 2 4W
73 Dongola 19 9N 30 22E
40 Donji Vakuf 44 8N 17 25E
91 Donnacona 46 40N 71 47W
85 Donnelly's Crossing 35 43S 173 33E
83 Donnybrook 33 35S 115 48E
96 Donora 40 11N 79 52W
80 Donor's Hills 18 42S 140 33E
83 Doodlakine 31 35S 117 28E
14 Doon, R. 55 26N 4 38W
54 Dor 32 37N 34 55E
13 Dorchester 50 43N 2 26W
89 Dorchester, C. 65 29N 77 30W
20 Dordogne □ 45 10N 0 45E
20 Dordogne, R. 45 2N 0 35W
16 Dordrecht 51 49N 107 45W
93 Dore Lake 54 56N 107 45W
90 Dorion 45 23N 74 3W
37 Dornberg 45 45N 13 50E
26 Dornbirn 47 25N 9 44E
14 Dornie 57 17N 5 30W
14 Dornoch 57 52N 4 2W
14 Dornoch Firth 57 52N 4 2W
67 Döröö Nuur, L. 47 40N 93 30E
83 Dorre, I. 25 9S 113 7E
81 Dorrigo 30 21S 152 43E
13 Dorset □ 50 47N 2 20W
24 Dorsten 51 39N 6 58E
24 Dortmund 51 31N 7 28E
112 Dos Bahias, C. 44 55S 65 32W
31 Dos Hermanas 37 17N 5 55W
57 Doshi 35 37N 68 41E
72 Dosso 13 3N 3 12E
92 Dot 50 12N 121 25W
99 Dothan 31 13N 85 24W
19 Douai 50 22N 3 4E
72 Douala 4 3N 9 42E
18 Douarnenez 48 6N 4 20W
26 Doubrava, R. 49 40N 15 30E
19 Doubs □ 47 10N 6 25E
85 Doubtless, B. 34 55S 173 27E
90 Doucet 48 15N 76 35W
12 Douglas, U.K. 54 9N 4 25W
103 Douglas, Ariz 31 21N 109 33W
99 Douglas, Ga. 31 31N 82 51W
100 Douglas, Wyo. 42 45N 105 24W
43 Doukáton, Ákra, Pt. 38 34N 20 30E
19 Doulevant 48 22N 4 53E
19 Doullens 50 9N 2 21E
14 Dounreay 58 40N 3 28W
111 Dourada, Sa. 13 10S 48 45W
30 Douro, R. 41 8N 8 40W
29 Douro Litoral, Reg. 41 5N 8 20W
20 Douze, R. 43 54N 0 30W
12 Dove, R. 54 20N 0 55W
80 Dover, Australia 43 19S 147 1E
13 Dover, U.K. 51 8N 1 19E
98 Dover, Del. 39 10N 75 32W
97 Dover, N.H. 43 12N 70 56W
97 Dover, N.J. 40 53N 74 34W
97 Dover Plains 41 44N 73 35W
13 Dovey, R. 52 32N 4 0W
44 Dovrefjell, Mts. 62 6N 9 25E
98 Dowagiac 41 59N 86 6W
57 Dowlātābad 28 18N 56 40E
15 Down □ 54 24N 5 55W
13 Downham Market 52 36N 0 23E
15 Downpatrick 54 20N 5 43W
97 Doylestown 40 19N 75 8W
21 Drac, R. 45 13N 5 41E
41 Drăgăneşti Olt. 44 10N 24 32E
41 Drăgănesti Vlaşca 44 6N 25 36E
41 Drăgăşani 44 40N 24 16E
40 Dragina 44 30N 19 25E
40 Dragocvet 44 0N 21 15E
21 Draguignan 43 32N 6 28E
5 Drake Pass. 58 0S 70 0W
75 Drakensberg, Mts. 27 0S 30 0E
42 Dráma 41 9N 24 8E
42 Dráma □ 41 9N 24 8E
44 Drammen 59 44N 10 15E
26 Drau, R.= Drava R. 45 33N 18 55E
37 Drava, R. 45 33N 18 55E
19 Draveil 48 41N 2 25E
92 Drayton Valley 53 13N 114 59W
16 Drenthe □ 52 45N 6 30E
24 Dresden 51 3N 13 44E
24 Dresden □ 51 10N 14 0E
18 Dreux 48 44N 1 22E
12 Driffield 54 0N 0 27W
40 Drin, R. 41 60N 19 32E
42 Drin-i-zi 41 37N 20 28E
37 Drniš 43 51N 16 10E
15 Drogheda 53 43N 6 21W
49 Drogobych 49 20N 23 30E
13 Droitwich 52 16N 2 9W
21 Drôme □ 44 35N 5 10E
21 Drôme, R. 44 46N 4 46E
84 Dromedary, C. 36 17S 150 10E
80 Dronfield 53 19S 1 27W
20 Dronne, R. 45 2N 0 9W
5 Dronning Maud Ld. 75 0S 10 0E
26 Drosendorf 48 52N 15 37E
84 Drouin 38 8S 145 51E
92 Drumheller 51 28N 112 42W
90 Drummondville 45 53N 72 30W
51 Druzhina 68 11N 14S 19E
28 Drwęca R. 53 0N 18 42E
41 Dryanovo 42 59N 25 28E
93 Dryden 49 47N 92 50W
82 Drysdale, R. 13 59S 126 51E
96 Du Bois 41 7N 78 46W
100 Du Quoin 38 0N 89 10W
80 Duaringa 23 42S 149 42E
56 Dubā 27 10N 35 40E
88 Dubawnt L. 63 0N 102 0W
57 Dubayy 25 18N 55 18E
84 Dubbo 32 15S 148 36E
15 Dublin, Eire 53 20N 6 15W
99 Dublin, U.S.A. 32 32N 82 54W
15 Dublin □ 53 20N 6 15W
102 Dubois 44 10N 112 14W
49 Dubovka 49 5N 44 50E
61 Dubrajpur 23 48N 87 23E
72 Dubreka 9 48N 13 31W
40 Dubrovnik 42 38N 18 7E
51 Dubrovskoye 47 28N 42 40E
100 Dubuque 42 30N 90 41W
102 Duchesne 40 10N 110 24W
80 Duchess 21 22S 139 52E
77 Ducie I. 24 47S 124 50W
93 Duck Lake 52 47N 106 13W
93 Duck Mt. Prov. Park 51 36N 100 55W
24 Duderstadt 51 31N 10 16E
51 Dudinka 69 25N 86 15E
13 Dudley 52 30N 2 5W
62 Dudna, R. 19 17N 76 54E
30 Dueñas 41 52N 4 33W
30 Duero, R. 41 37N 4 25W
14 Dufftown 57 26N 3 9W
37 Dugi Otok, I. 44 0N 15 0E
37 Dugo Selo 45 51N 16 18E
24 Duisburg 51 27N 6 42E
57 Dukhan 25 25N 50 50E
72 Duku 10 43N 10 43E
105 Dulce, G. 8 40N 83 20W
41 Dulgopol 43 3N 27 22E
24 Dülmen 51 49N 7 18E
41 Dulovo 43 48N 27 9E
80 Dululu 23 48S 150 15E
100 Duluth 46 48N 92 10W
61 Dum-Dum 22 39N 88 26E
59 Dum Duma 27 40N 95 40E
64 Dumai 1 35N 101 20E
101 Dumas 35 50N 101 58W
14 Dumbarton 55 58N 4 35W
83 Dumbleyung 33 17S 117 42E
41 Dumbrăveni 46 14N 24 34E
14 Dumfries 55 4N 3 37W
14 Dumfries-Galloway □ 55 12N 3 30W
84 Dumosa 35 52S 143 6E
73 Dumyât 31 25N 31 48E
15 Dun Laoghaire 53 17N 6 9W
27 Dunaföldvár 46 50N 18 57E
41 Dunarea= Donau, R. 45 20N 29 40E
27 Dunaújváros 47 0N 18 57E
40 Dunav 45 0N 20 21E
40 Dunavtsi 42 57N 22 53E
85 Dunback 42 23S 170 36E
14 Dunbar 56 0N 2 32W
93 Dunblane, Canada 51 11N 106 52W
14 Dunblane, U.K. 56 10N 3 58W
92 Duncan, Canada 48 45N 123 40W
101 Duncan, U.S.A. 34 25N 98 0W
63 Duncan Pass. 11 0N 92 30E
105 Duncan Town 22 20N 75 80W
96 Dundalk, Canada 44 10N 80 24W
15 Dundalk, U.K. 53 55N 6 45W
90 Dundas 43 17N 79 59W
83 Dundas, L. 32 35S 121 50E
82 Dundas, Str. 11 15S 131 35E
75 Dundee, S. Africa 28 11S 30 15E
14 Dundee, U.K. 56 29N 3 0W
15 Dundrum 54 17N 5 50W
15 Dundrum, B. 54 12N 5 40W
60 Dundwara 27 48N 79 9E
85 Dunedin 45 50S 170 33E
14 Dunfermline 56 5N 3 28W
15 Dungannon 54 30N 6 47W
15 Dungannon □ 54 30N 6 47W
60 Dungarpur 23 52N 73 45E
15 Dungarvan 52 6N 7 40W
67 Dunbure Shan, Mts. 35 0N 90 0E
13 Dungeness, Pt. 50 54N 0 59E
74 Dungu 3 42N 28 32E
84 Dunkeld, Australia 37 40S 142 22E
14 Dunkeld, U.K. 56 34N 3 36W
19 Dunkerque 51 2N 2 20E
13 Dunkery Beacon 51 15N 3 37W
96 Dunkirk 42 30N 79 18W
72 Dunkwa 6 0N 1 47W
80 Dunmara 16 42S 133 25E
97 Dunmore 41 27N 75 38W
15 Dunmore Hd. 53 37N 8 44W
99 Dunn 35 18N 78 36W
14 Dunnet Hd. 58 38N 3 22W
96 Dunnville 42 57N 79 37W
14 Dunoon 55 57N 4 56W
14 Duns 55 47N 2 20W
102 Dunsmuir 41 0N 122 10W
13 Dunstable 51 53N 0 31W
109 Duque de Caxias 22 45S 43 19W
96 Duquesne 40 22N 79 55W
85 D'Urville, I. 40 50S 173 55E
54 Dūrā 31 30N 35 2E
82 Durack, R. 15 33S 127 52E
21 Durance, R. 43 55N 4 44E
104 Durango, Mexico 24 3N 104 39W
30 Durango, Sp. 43 13N 2 40W
103 Durango, U.S.A. 37 10N 107 50W
104 Durango □ 25 0N 105 0W
83 Duranillin 33 30S 116 45E
101 Durant 34 0N 96 25W
30 Duratón, R. 41 37N 4 7W
108 Durazno 33 25S 56 38W
75 Durban 29 49S 31 1E
31 Durcal 37 0N 3 34W
40 Durdevac 46 2N 17 3E
24 Düren 50 48N 6 30E
61 Durg 21 15N 81 22E
90 Durham, Canada 44 10N 80 48W
12 Durham, U.K. 54 47N 1 34W
99 Durham, U.S.A. 36 0N 78 55W
12 Durham □ 54 42N 1 45W
40 Durmitor, Mt. 43 18N 19 0E
42 Durrësi 41 19N 19 28E
18 Durtal 47 40N 0 18W
97 Duryea 41 20N 75 45W
55 Dushak 37 20N 60 10E
50 Dushanbe 38 40N 68 50E
85 Dusky, Sd. 45 47S 166 29E
24 Düsseldorf 51 15N 6 46E
88 Dutch Harbor 53 54N 166 35W
56 Duzce 40 50N 31 10E
41 Dve Mogili 43 47N 25 55E
48 Drinskaya Guba 65 0N 39 45E
26 Dvur Králové 50 27N 15 50E
60 Dwarka 22 18N 69 8E
83 Dwellingup 32 38S 115 58E
5 Dyer Plat. 70 0S 65 0W
101 Dyersburg 36 2N 89 20W
13 Dyfed □ 52 0N 4 30W
48 Dzerzhinsk 56 15N 43 15E
50 Dzhalal Abad 41 0N 73 0E
51 Dzhalinda 53 50N 124 0E
50 Dzhambul 43 10N 71 0E
49 Dzhankoi 45 40N 34 30E
51 Dzhardzhan 68 43N 124 2E
51 Dzhelinde 70 0N 114 20E
50 Dzhezkazgan 47 10N 67 40E
50 Dzhizak 40 20N 68 0E
51 Dzhugdzur Khrebet, Ra. 57 30N 138 0E
28 Działdowo 53 15N 20 15E
27 Dzierżoniow 50 45N 16 39E
67 Dzungaria, Reg. 44 10N 88 0E
67 Dzungarian Gate= Dzungarskiye Vorota 45 25N 82 25E
67 Dzungarskiye Vorota 45 25N 82 25E
68 Dzuunbulag 46 58N 115 30E
68 Dzuunmod 47 45N 106 58E

E

88 Eagle 64 44N 141 29W
101 Eagle Pass 28 45N 100 35W

Erechim Finale nell' Emília

109 Erechim 27 35s 52 15w
56 Ereğli 41 15n 31 30e
30 Eresma, R. 41 26n 4 45w
24 Erfurt 50 58n 11 2e
24 Erfurt □ 51 10n 10 30e
56 Ergani 38 26n 39 49e
49 Ergeni
Vozvyshennost' 47 0n 44 0e
68 Erhlien 43 42n 112 2e
30 Eria, R. 42 3n 5 44w
14 Eriboll, L. 58 28n 4 41w
38 Érice 38 4n 12 34e
96 Erie 42 10n 80 7w
98 Erie, L. 42 30n 82 0w
96 Erie Canal 43 15n 78 0w
55 Erigavo 10 35n 47 35e
93 Eriksdale 50 52n 98 5w
92 Erith 53 25n 116 46w
73 Eritrea □ 14 0n 41 0e
25 Erlangen 49 35n 11 0e
80 Erldunda 25 14s 133 12e
16 Ermelo 52 35n 5 35e
43 Ermióni 37 23n 23 15e
62 Ernakulam 9 59n 76 19e
15 Erne, L. 54 14n 7 30w
15 Erne, R. 54 30n 8 16w
62 Erode 11 24n 77 45e
62 Erramala Hills 15 30n 78 15e
19 Erstein 48 25n 7 38e
24 Erzgebirge Mts. 50 25n 13 0e
56 Erzurum 39 57n 41 15e
73 Es Sider 30 50n 18 21e
45 Esbjerg 55 29n 8 29e
30 Escalona 40 9n 4 29w
98 Escanaba 45 44n 87 5w
16 Esch 49 32n 6 0e
24 Eschwege 51 10n 10 3e
103 Escondido 33 9n 117 4w
104 Escuintla 14 20n 90 48w
32 Esera, R. 42 6n 0 15e
57 Esfahan 32 40n 51 38e
57 Esfahan □ 33 0n 53 0e
30 Esgueva, R. 41 40n 4 43w
73 Esh Shimâliya □ 20 0n 31 0e
54 Eshta'ol 31 47n 35 0e
12 Esk, R., Eng. 54 29n 0 37w
14 Esk, R., Scot. 54 58n 3 2w
14 Esk, North, R. 56 54n 2 38w
14 Esk, South, R. 56 40n 2 40w
44 Eskilstuna 59 22n 16 32e
93 Eskimo Point 61 10n 94 15w
56 Eskisehir 39 50n 30 35e
30 Esla, Pantano
del, L. 41 45n 5 50w
30 Esla, R. 41 29n 6 3w
45 Eslöv 55 50n 13 20e
110 Esmeraldas 1 0n 79 40w
20 Espalion 44 32n 2 47e
90 Espanola 46 15n 81 46w
50 Espe 44 0n 74 5e
31 Espejo 37 40n 4 34w
83 Esperance 33 51s 121 53e
83 Esperance, B. 33 48s 121 55e
108 Esperanza 31 29s 61 3w
31 Espichel, C. 38 22n 9 16w
110 Espinal 4 9n 74 53w
111 Espinhaço, Sa. do 17 30s 43 30w
30 Espinho 41 1n 8 38w
104 Espíritu Santo,
B. del 19 15n 79 40w
111 Espírito Santo □ 19 30s 40 30w
32 Espluga de
Francolí 41 24n 1 7e
33 Espuña, Sa. 37 51n 1 35w
112 Esquel 42 40s 71 20w
108 Esquina 30 0s 59 30w
72 Essaouira 31 32n 9 42w
16 Essen, Belgium 51 28n 4 28e
24 Essen,
W. Germany 51 28n 6 59e
13 Essex □ 51 48n 0 30e
25 Esslingen 48 43n 9 19e
19 Essonne □ 48 30n 2 20e
30 Estaca, Pta de la 43 46n 7 42w
32 Estadilla 42 4n 0 16e
112 Estados,
I. de los 54 40s 64 30w
111 Estância, Brazil 11 15s 37 30w
103 Estancia, U.S.A. 34 50n 106 1w
37 Este 45 12n 11 40e
30 Esteban 43 33n 6 5w
105 Estelí 13 9n 86 22w
32 Estella 42 40n 2 0w
31 Estepa 37 17n 4 52w
31 Estepona 36 24n 5 7w
93 Esterhazy 50 37n 102 5w
19 Esternay 48 44n 3 33e
93 Estevan 49 10n 103 0w
100 Estheville 43 25n 94 50w
48 Estonian S.S.R. □ 48 30n 25 30e
31 Estoril 38 42n 9 23w
30 Estrêla, Sa. da 40 10n 7 45w
31 Estrella, Mt. 38 25n 3 35w
29 Estremadura, Reg. 39 0n 9 0w
31 Estremoz 38 51n 7 39w
111 Estrondo, Sa. de 7 20s 48 0w
27 Esztergom 47 47n 18 44e
18 Étables 48 38n 2 51w
60 Etah 27 35n 78 40e
19 Étain 49 13n 5 38e
19 Étampes 48 26n 2 10e
21 Étang 46 52n 4 10e
19 Étaples 50 30n 1 39e
60 Etawah 26 48n 79 6e
82 Ethel Creek 22 55s 120 11e
93 Ethelbert 51 32n 100 25w
55 Ethiopia ■ 8 0n 40 0e
70 Ethiopian
Highlands, Mts. 10 0n 37 0e
14 Etive, L. 56 30n 5 12w
39 Etna, Mt. 37 45n 15 0e
75 Etoshapan 18 40s 16 30e
18 Étretat 49 42n 0 12e
25 Ettlingen 48 58n 8 25e
14 Ettrick, R. 55 31n 2 55w
104 Etzatlán 20 48n 104 5w
18 Eu 50 3n 1 26e
96 Euclid 41 32n 81 31w
84 Eucumbene, L. 36 2s 148 40e
99 Eufaula 31 55n 85 11w
102 Eugene 44 0n 123 8w
101 Eunice 30 35n 92 28w
16 Eupen 50 37n 6 3e
56 Euphrates, R.=
Furat, Nahr al 33 30n 43 0e
18 Eure, R. 49 18n 1 12e
18 Eure □ 49 6n 1 0e
102 Eureka, Calif. 40 50n 124 0w
102 Eureka, Nev. 39 32n 116 2w
102 Eureka, Utah 40 0n 112 0w
84 Euroa 36 44s 145 35e
75 Europa, Île 22 20s 40 22e
30 Europa, Picos de 43 10n 5 0w
31 Europa, Pta. de 36 3n 5 21w
10 Europe 50 0n 20 0e
16 Europoort 51 57n 4 10e
24 Euskirchen 50 40n 6 45e
24 Eutin 54 7n 10 38e
81 Evans Head 29 7s 153 27e
97 Evans Mills 44 6n 75 48w
98 Evanston, Ill. 42 0n 87 40w
102 Evanston, Wyo. 41 10n 111 0w
98 Evansville 38 0n 87 35w
20 Evaux 46 12n 2 29e
100 Eveleth 47 35n 92 40w
54 Even Yehuda 32 16n 34 53e
61 Everest, Mt. 28 5n 86 58e
102 Everett 48 0n 122 10w
99 Everglades
Nat. Park 25 50n 80 40w
13 Evesham 52 6n 1 57w
21 Evian 46 24n 6 35w
31 Évora □ 38 33n 7 50w
18 Évreux 49 0n 1 8e
43 Evritanía □ 39 5n 21 30e
54 Evron 32 59n 35 6e
18 Évron 48 23n 1 58w
42 Évros □ 41 10n 26 0e
43 Evvoia □ 38 40n 23 40e
14 Ewe, L. 57 49n 5 38w
100 Excellsior Springs 39 20n 94 10w
13 Exe, R. 50 37n 3 25w
13 Exeter, U.K. 50 43n 3 31w
97 Exeter, U.S.A. 42 59n 70 57w
13 Exmoor, Reg. 51 10n 3 55w
82 Exmouth,
Australia 22 6s 114 0e
13 Exmouth, U.K. 50 37n 3 24w
82 Exmouth, G. 22 15s 114 15e
31 Extremadura, Reg. 39 30n 6 5w
105 Exuma Sd. 24 30n 76 20w
74 Eyasi, L. 3 30s 35 0e
14 Eye Pen. 58 20n 0 51e
14 Eyemouth 55 53n 2 5w
20 Eymoutiers 45 45n 1 45e
81 Eyre, L. 28 30s 136 45e
81 Eyre, Pen. 33 30s 137 17e

F

103 Fabens 31 30n 106 8w
45 Fåborg 55 6n 10 15e
37 Fabriano 43 20n 12 52e
110 Facatativa 4 49n 74 22w
20 Fracture 44 39n 0 58w
72 Fada N'Gourma 12 10n 0 30e
27 Fadd 46 28n 18 49e
37 Faenza 44 17n 11 53e
30 Fafe 41 27n 8 11w
41 Fagaraş 45 48n 24 58e
41 Făgăraş, Mt. 45 40n 24 40e
44 Fagernes 61 0n 9 16e
44 Fagersta 61 1n 15 46e
112 Fagnano, L. 54 30s 68 0w
57 Fahraj 29 0n 59 0e
69 Fahsien 21 19n 110 33e
57 Fahud 22 18n 56 28e
103 Fairbank 31 44n 110 12w
88 Fairbanks 64 59n 147 40w
100 Fairbury 40 5n 97 5w
84 Fairfield,
Australia 37 45s 175 17e
99 Fairfield, Ala. 33 30n 87 0w
102 Fairfield, Calif. 38 14n 122 1w
97 Fairfield, Conn. 41 8n 73 16w
100 Fairfield, Ill. 38 20n 88 20w
100 Fairfield, Iowa 41 0n 91 58w
101 Fairfield, Tex. 31 40n 96 0w
85 Fairlie 44 5s 170 49e
100 Fairmont, Minn. 43 37n 94 30w
98 Fairmont, W. Va. 39 29n 80 10w
96 Fairport 43 8n 77 29w
80 Fairview,
Australia 15 31s 144 17e
92 Fairview, Canada 56 5n 118 25w
88 Fairweather, Mt. 58 55n 137 45w
57 Faizabad,
Afghanistan 37 7n 70 33e
61 Faizabad, India 26 45n 82 10e
60 Faizpur 21 14n 75 49e
105 Fajardo 18 20n 65 39w
12 Fakenham 52 50n 0 51e
65 Fakfak 3 0s 132 15e
45 Fakse, B. 55 11n 12 15e
68 Faku 42 31n 123 26e
18 Falaise 48 54n 0 12w
42 Falakrón Óros,
Mt. 41 15n 23 58e
59 Falam 23 0n 93 45e
37 Falconara
Marittima 43 37n 13 23e
101 Falfurrias 27 8n 98 8e
45 Falkenberg 56 54n 12 30e
24 Falkensee 52 35n 13 6e
24 Falkenstein 50 27n 12 24e
14 Falkirk 56 0n 3 47w
112 Falkland, Sd. 52 0s 60 0w
112 Falkland Is. □ 51 30s 59 0w
45 Falköping 58 12n 13 33e
97 Fall River 41 45n 71 5w
102 Fallon 39 31n 118 51w
100 Falls City 40 0n 95 40w
105 Falmouth, Jamaica 18 30n 77 40w
13 Falmouth, U.K. 50 9n 5 5w
97 Falmouth, U.S.A 38 40n 84 20w
32 Falset 41 7n 0 50e
105 Falso, C. 17 45n 71 40w
45 Falster, I. 54 48n 11 58e
45 Falsterbo 55 23n 12 50e
44 Falun 60 37n 15 37e
56 Famagusta 35 8n 33 55e
69 Fangcheng 31 2n 118 13e
77 Fanning I. 3 51n 159 22w
37 Fano 43 50n 13 0e
45 Fanø, I. 55 25n 8 25e
92 Fanshaw 57 11n 133 30w
74 Faradje 3 50n 29 45e
72 Faranah 10 2n 10 45w
57 Farar 32 30n 62 17e
57 Farar □ 32 25n 62 10e
55 Farasán, Jazá'ir, I. 16 45n 41 55e
13 Fareham 50 52n 1 11w
85 Farewell, C. 39 36s 143 55e
100 Fargo 47 0n 97 0w
100 Faribault 44 15n 93 19w
60 Faridkot 30 44n 74 45e
61 Faridpur,
Bangladesh 23 36n 89 53e
61 Faridpur, India 18 14n 79 34e
81 Farina 30 3s 138 15e
103 Farmington,
N. Mex. 36 45n 108 28w
102 Farmington, Utah 41 0n 111 58w
13 Farnborough 51 17n 0 46w
12 Farne Is. 55 38n 1 37w
97 Farnham 45 20n 72 55w
111 Faro, Brazil 2 0s 56 45w
31 Faro, Port. 37 2n 7 55w
31 Faro □ 37 12n 8 10w
8 Faroe Is. 62 0n 7 0w
83 Farquhar, C. 23 38s 113 36e
57 Farráshband 28 57n 52 5e
96 Farrell 41 13n 80 29w
81 Farrell Flat 33 48s 138 48e
61 Farrukhabad 27 30n 79 32e
57 Fars □ 29 30n 55 0e
47 Farsund 58 5n 6 55e
4 Farvel, R. 59 48n 43 55w
57 Faryab □ 36 0n 65 0e
39 Fasano 40 50n 17 20e
15 Fastnet Rock 51 22n 9 27w
61 Fatehgarh 27 25n 79 35e
60 Fatehpur,
Rajasthan 28 0n 75 4e
61 Fatehpur,
Ut.P. 27 8n 81 7e
31 Fátima 39 37n 8 39w
69 Fatshan 23 0n 113 4e
19 Faucilles, Mts. 48 5n 5 50e
100 Faulkton 45 4n 99 8w
19 Faulquemont 49 3n 6 36e
83 Faure, I. 25 52s 113 50e
41 Faurei 45 6n 27 19e
75 Fauresmith 29 44s 25 17e
46 Fauske 67 17n 15 25e
38 Favara 37 19n 13 39e
21 Favone 41 47n 9 26e
46 Faxaflói, B. 64 29n 23 0w
101 Fayetteville, Ark. 36 0n 94 5w
99 Fayetteville, N.C. 35 0n 78 58w
32 Fayón 41 15n 0 20e
60 Fazilka 30 27n 74 2e
72 F'Dérik 22 40n 12 45e
15 Feale, R. 52 26n 9 28w
99 Fear, C. 33 45n 78 0w
85 Featherston 41 6s 175 20e
18 Fécamp 49 45n 0 22e
24 Fehmarn, I. 54 26n 11 10e
85 Feilding 40 13s 175 35e
111 Feira de
Santana 12 15s 38 57w
27 Fejér □ 47 9n 18 30e
33 Felanitx 39 27n 3 7e
26 Feldbach 46 57n 15 52e
26 Feldkirch 47 15n 9 37e
26 Feldkirchen 46 44n 14 6e
104 Felipe
Carillo Puerto 19 38n 88 3w
13 Felixstowe 51 58n 1 22w
37 Feltre 46 1n 11 55e
68 Fen Ho, R. 35 36n 110 42e
69 Fencheng 28 2n 115 46e
68 Fengcheng,
Heilungkiang 45 41n 128 54e
68 Fengcheng,
Liaoning 40 28n 124 4e
69 Fenghsien 33 56n 106 41e
69 Fengkieh 31 0n 109 33e
68 Fengtai 39 57n 116 21e
69 Fengyuan 24 10n 120 45e
12 Fens, Reg. 52 45n 0 2e
68 Fenyang 37 19n 111 46e
49 Feodosiya 45 2n 35 28e
19 Fère Champenoise 48 45n 4 0e
19 Fère-en-
Tardenois 49 10n 3 30e
38 Ferentino 41 42n 13 14e
50 Fergana 40 23n 71 46e
90 Fergus 43 43n 80 24w
100 Fergus Falls 46 25n 96 0w
40 Feričanci 45 32n 18 0e
26 Ferlach 46 32n 14 18e
90 Ferland 50 19n 88 27w
15 Fermanagh □ 54 21n 7 40w
37 Fermo 43 10n 13 42e
30 Fermoselle 41 19n 6 27w
15 Fermoy 52 4n 8 18w
111 Fernando de
Noronha, Is. 4 0s 33 10w
92 Fernie 49 30n 115 5w
80 Fernlees 23 51s 148 7e
62 Feroke 11 9n 75 46e
60 Ferozepore 30 55n 74 40e
42 Férrai 40 53n 26 10e
37 Ferrara 44 50n 11 36e
38 Ferrato, C. 39 18n 9 39e
31 Ferreira do
Alentejo 38 4n 8 6w
20 Ferret, C. 44 38n 1 15w
72 Fès 34 0n 5 0w
41 Feteşti 44 22n 27 51e
14 Fetlar, I. 60 36n 0 52w
21 Feurs 45 45n 4 13e
73 Fezzan 27 0n 15 0e
75 Fianarantsoa 21 26s 47 5e
25 Fichtelgebirge, Mts. 50 10n 12 0e
75 Ficksburg 28 51s 27 53e
36 Fidenza 44 51n 10 3e
14 Fife □ 56 13n 3 2w
20 Figeac 44 37n 2 2e
30 Figueira Castelo
Rodrigo 40 54n 6 58w
30 Figueira da
Foz 40 7n 8 54w
30 Figueiro dos
Vinhos 39 55n 8 16w
32 Figueras 42 18n 2 58e
72 Figuig 32 5n 1 11w
42 Fieri 40 43n 19 33e
85 Fiji ■ 17 20s 179 0e
33 Filabres,
Sa. de los 37 13n 2 20w
5 Filchner Ice Shelf 78 0s 60 0w
12 Filey 54 13n 0 10w
41 Filiaşi 44 32n 23 31e
44 Filipstad 59 43n 14 9e
44 Fillefjell, Mts. 61 8n 8 10e
103 Fillmore 34 23n 118 58w
36 Finale Lígure 44 10n 8 21e
37 Finale nell
'Emília 44 50n 11 18e

Fulda Giong, Teluk B.

24 Fulda 50 32N 9 41 E
24 Fulda, R. 51 25N 9 39 E
103 Fullerton 33 52N 117 58W
100 Fulton, Mo. 38 50N 91 55W
97 Fulton, N.Y. 43 20N 76 22W
19 Fumay 50 0N 4 40 E
20 Fumel 44 30N 0 58 E
66 Funabashi 35 45N 140 0 E
76 Funafuti, I. 8 30S 179 0 E
72 Funchal 32 45N 16 55W
110 Fundación 10 31N 74 11W
30 Fundão 40 8N 7 30W
91 Fundy, B. of 45 0N 66 0W
72 Funtua 11 31N 7 17 E
56 Furat, Nahr al, R. 33 30N 43 0 E
109 Furnas, Représa de, L. 20 45S 46 0W
12 Furness 54 14N 3 8W
26 Fürstenfeld 47 3N 16 3 E
25 Furstenfeldbruck 48 10N 11 15 E
24 Furstenwalde 52 20N 14 3 E
25 Fürth 49 29N 11 0 E
89 Fury & Hecla Str. 69 40N 81 0W
110 Fusagasugá 4 21N 74 22W
68 Fushan 37 30N 121 5 E
68 Fushun 42 0N 123 59 E
68 Fusin 42 12N 121 33 E
25 Füssen 47 12N 121 33 E
69 Futing 27 15N 120 10 E
69 Futsing 25 46N 119 29 E
76 Futuna, I. 14 25S 178 20 E
69 Fuyang 30 5N 119 56 E
68 Fuyu 45 10N 124 50 E
12 Fylde, R. 53 47N 2 56W
45 Fyn, I. 55 20N 10 30 E
14 Fyne, L. 56 0N 5 20W
45 Fyns □ 55 15N 10 30 E

G

72 Gabès 33 53N 10 2 E
73 Gabès, G. de 34 0N 10 30 E
74 Gabon ■ 0 10S 10 0 E
75 Gaborone 24 37S 25 57 E
97 Gabriels 44 26N 74 12W
41 Gabrovo 42 52N 25 27 E
57 Gach-Sārān 30 15N 50 45 E
40 Gacko 43 10N 18 33 E
62 Gadag 15 30N 75 45 E
60 Gadarwara 22 50N 78 50 E
33 Gádor, Sa. de 36 57N 2 45W
99 Gadsden, Ala. 34 1N 86 0W
103 Gadsden, Ariz. 32 35N 114 47W
62 Gadwal 16 10N 77 50 E
41 Găesti 44 48N 25 14 E
38 Gaeta 41 12N 13 35 E
38 Gaeta, G. di 41 0N 13 25 E
99 Gaffney 35 10N 81 31W
72 Gafsa 34 24N 8 51 E
91 Gagetown 45 46N 66 29W
72 Gagnoa 6 4N 5 55W
91 Gagnon 51 50N 68 5W
20 Gah 43 12N 0 27W
61 Gahmar 25 27N 83 55 E
61 Gaibandha 25 20N 89 36 E
26 Gail, R. 46 36N 13 53 E
20 Gaillac 43 54N 1 54 E
18 Gaillon 49 10N 1 20 E
96 Gaines 41 45N 77 35W
99 Gainesville, Fla. 29 38N 82 20W
99 Gainesville, Ga. 34 17N 83 47W
101 Gainesville, Tex. 33 40N 97 10W
12 Gainsborough 53 23N 0 46W
81 Gairdner, L. 32 0S 136 0 E
14 Gairloch, L. 57 43N 5 45W
75 Galangue 13 48S 16 3 E
77 Galápagos, Is. 0 0N 89 0W
14 Galashiels 55 37N 2 50W
41 Galaţi 45 27N 28 2 E
39 Galatina 40 10N 18 10 E
39 Galátone 40 8N 18 3 E
99 Galax 36 42N 80 57W
43 Galaxídhion 38 22N 22 23 E
83 Galena 27 50S 114 41 E
33 Galera 37 45N 2 33W
100 Galesburg 40 57N 90 23W
48 Galich 58 23N 42 18 E
30 Galicia, Reg. 42 43N 8 0W
54 Galilee= Hagalil, Reg. 32 53N 35 18 E
54 Galilee, Sea of= Kinneret, Yam 32 49N 35 36 E
36 Gallarte 45 40N 8 48 E
99 Gallatin 36 24N 86 27W
62 Galle 6 5N 80 10 E
32 Gállego, R. 41 39N 0 51W
112 Gallegos, R. 51 35S 69 0W
110 Gallinas, Pta. 12 28N 71 40W
39 Gallipoli 40 8N 18 0 E
98 Gallipolis 38 50N 82 10W
46 Gällivare 67 7N 20 32 E
32 Gallocanta, L. de 40 58N 1 30W
14 Galloway, Reg. 55 0N 4 25W
14 Galloway, Mull of 54 38N 4 50W
103 Gallup 35 30N 108 54W
96 Galt= Cambridge 43 21N 80 19W
26 Galtür 46 58N 10 11 E
30 Galve de Sorbe 41 13N 3 10W
101 Galveston 29 15N 94 48W
101 Galveston B. 29 30N 94 50W
108 Gálvez 32 0S 61 20W
15 Galway 53 16N 9 4W
15 Galway, B. 53 10N 9 20W
15 Galway □ 53 16N 9 3W
66 Gamagori 34 50N 137 14 E
72 Gambaga 10 30N 0 28W
72 Gambia ■ 13 20N 15 45W
72 Gambia, R. 13 28N 16 34W
82 Gambier, C. 11 56S 130 57 E
104 Gamboa 9 8N 79 42W
103 Gamerco 35 33N 108 56W
20 Gan 0 10S 71 10 E
54 Gan Shamu'el 32 28N 34 56 E
54 Gan Yavne 31 48N 34 42 E
90 Gananoque 44 20N 76 10W
61 Gandak, R. 25 32N 85 5 E
91 Gander 49 1N 54 33W
32 Gandesa 41 3N 0 26 E
72 Gandi 12 55N 5 49 E
33 Gandía 38 58N 0 9W
61 Ganga, Mouths of the 21 30N 90 0 E
61 Ganga, R. 23 22N 90 32 E
60 Ganganagar 29 56N 73 56 E
60 Gangapur 26 32N 76 37 E
62 Gangavati 15 30N 76 36 E
59 Gangaw 22 5N 94 15 E
61 Ganges, R.= Ganga, R. 23 22N 90 32 E
61 Gangtok 27 20N 88 40 E
60 Ganj 27 45N 78 47 E
20 Gannat 46 7N 3 11 E
27 Ganserdorf 48 20N 16 43 E
72 Gao 18 0N 1 0 E
72 Gaoual 11 45N 13 25W
21 Gap 44 33N 6 5 E
111 Garanhuns 8 50S 36 30W
102 Garberville 40 11N 123 50W
109 Garça 22 14S 49 37W
21 Gard □ 44 2N 4 10 E
36 Garda, L. di 45 40N 10 40 E
24 Gardelegen 52 32N 11 21 E
101 Garden City 38 0N 100 45W
57 Gardez 33 31N 68 59 E
102 Gardiner 45 3N 110 53W
97 Gardner 42 35N 72 0W
55 Gardo 9 18N 49 20 E
102 Garfield 47 3N 117 8W
43 Gargaliánoi 37 4N 21 38 E
39 Gargano, Testa del, Pt. 41 49N 16 12 E
38 Garigliano, R. 41 13N 13 45 E
102 Garland 41 47N 112 10W
50 Garm 39 0N 70 20 E
25 Garmisch-Partenkirchen 47 30N 11 5 E
57 Garmsār 35 20N 52 25 E
61 Garo Hills 25 30N 90 30 E
55 Garoe 8 35N 48 40 E
20 Garonne, R. 45 2N 0 36W
20 Garrigues, Reg. 43 40N 3 30 E
102 Garrison 46 37N 112 56W
100 Garrison Res. 47 30N 102 0W
88 Garry, L. 65 40N 100 0W
90 Garson 50 5N 96 50W
20 Gartempe, R. 46 48N 0 50 E
67 Gartok 31 59N 80 30 E
24 Gartz 54 17N 13 21 E
65 Garut 7 14S 107 53 E
31 Garvão 37 42N 8 21W
85 Garvie, Mts. 45 27S 169 59 E
98 Gary 41 35N 87 20W
110 Garzón 2 10N 75 40W
17 Gascogne, G. de 44 0N 2 0W
20 Gascogne, Reg. 43 45N 0 20 E
83 Gascoyne, R. 24 52S 113 37 E
83 Gascoyne Junction 25 3S 115 12 E
72 Gashaka 7 20N 11 29 E
91 Gaspé 48 52N 64 30W
91 Gaspé, C. 48 48N 64 7W
91 Gaspé Pass. 49 10N 64 0W
91 Gaspé Pen. 48 45N 65 40W
91 Gaspesian Prov. Park 49 0N 66 45W
99 Gastonia 35 17N 81 10W
43 Gastoúni 37 51N 21 15 E
42 Gastoúri 39 34N 19 54 E
112 Gastre 42 10S 69 15W
33 Gata, C. de 36 41N 2 13W
30 Gata, Sa. de 40 20N 6 20W
40 Gătaia 45 26N 21 30 E
14 Gatehouse of Fleet 54 53N 4 10W
12 Gateshead 54 57N 1 37W
19 Gatinais, Reg. 48 5N 2 40 E
20 Gâtine, Hauteurs de 46 40N 0 50W
97 Gatineau 45 28N 75 40W
90 Gatineau Nat. Park 45 30N 75 52W
75 Gatooma 18 21S 29 55 E
104 Gatun 9 16N 79 55W
104 Gatun L. 9 7N 79 56W
31 Gaucín 36 31N 5 19W
61 Gauhati 26 5N 91 55 E
5 Gaussberg, Mt. 66 45S 89 0 E
32 Gavá 41 18N 2 0 E
20 Gavarnie 42 44N 0 3W
57 Gavater 25 10N 61 23 E
43 Gávdhos, I. 34 50N 24 6 E
31 Gavião 39 28N 7 50W
44 Gavle 60 41N 17 13 E
44 Gävleborgs □ 61 20N 16 15 E
36 Gavorrano 42 55N 10 55 E
18 Gavray 49 55N 1 20W
60 Gawilgarh Hills 21 15N 76 45 E
81 Gawler 34 30S 138 42 E
61 Gaya 24 47N 85 4 E
81 Gayndah 25 35S 151 39 E
54 Gaza 31 30N 34 28 E
54 Gaza Strip 31 29N 34 25 E
56 Gaziantep 37 6N 37 23 E
28 Gdańsk 54 22N 18 40 E
28 Gdansk □ 54 10N 18 30 E
28 Gdynia 54 35N 18 33 E
73 Gebeit Mine 21 3N 36 29 E
73 Gedaref 14 2N 35 28 E
54 Gedera 31 49N 34 46 E
20 Gèdre 42 47N 0 2 E
45 Gedser 54 35N 11 55 E
84 Geelong 38 2S 144 20 E
83 Geelvink, Chan. 28 30S 114 10 E
16 Geeraadsbergen 50 45N 3 53 E
24 Geesthacht 53 25N 10 20 E
73 Geili 16 1N 32 37 E
44 Geilo 60 32N 8 14 E
25 Geislingen 47 55N 8 37 E
74 Geita 2 48S 32 12 E
39 Gela 37 3N 14 15 E
39 Gela, G. di 37 0N 14 8 E
16 Gelderland □ 52 5N 6 10 E
16 Geldrop 51 25N 5 32 E
16 Geleen 50 57N 5 49 E
56 Gelibolu 40 28N 26 43 E
25 Gelnhausen 50 12N 9 12 E
24 Gelsenkirchen 51 30N 7 5 E
24 Gelting 54 43N 9 53 E
63 Gemas 2 37N 102 36 E
16 Gembloux 50 34N 4 43 E
74 Gemena 3 20N 19 40 E
37 Gemona del Fruiuli 46 16N 13 7 E
25 Gemünden 50 3N 9 43 E
20 Gençay 46 23N 0 23 E
108 General Acha 37 20S 64 38W
108 General Alvear 36 0S 60 0W
108 General Artigas 26 52S 56 16W
108 General Juan Madariaga 37 0S 57 0W
108 General Martin Miguel de Güemes 24 50S 65 0W
108 General Pico 35 45S 63 50W
108 General Pinedo 27 15S 61 30W
112 General Roca 30 0S 67 40W
41 General Toshevo 43 42N 28 6 E
108 General Viamonte 35 1S 61 3W
108 General Villegas 35 0S 63 0W
96 Genesee, R. 43 16N 77 36W
25 Geneva= Genève, Switz. 46 12N 6 9 E
96 Geneva, U.S.A. 42 53N 77 0W
25 Geneva, L.= Léman, L. 46 26N 6 30 E
25 Genève 46 12N 6 9 E
31 Genil, R. 37 42N 5 19W
21 Génissiat, Barrage de 46 1N 5 48 E
16 Genk 50 58N 5 32 E
38 Gennargentu, Mt. del 39 59N 9 19 E
36 Genova 44 24N 8 56 E
36 Génova, G. di 44 0N 9 0 E
16 Gent 51 2N 3 37 E
24 Genthin 52 24N 12 10 E
83 Geographe, B. 33 30S 115 15 E
83 Geographe, Chan. 24 30S 113 0 E
75 George 33 58S 22 29 E
97 George, L. 43 30N 73 30W
89 George R.=Port Nouveau-Quebec 58 30N 65 50W
80 George Town Australia 41 5S 148 55 E
63 George Town, W. Malaysia 5 25N 100 19 E
80 Georgetown, Australia 18 17S 143 33 E
90 Georgetown, Ont. 43 40N 80 0W
91 Georgetown, P.E.I. 46 13N 62 24W
72 Georgetown, Gambia 13 30N 14 47W
110 Georgetown, Guyana 6 50N 58 12W
99 Georgetown, U.S.A. 33 22N 79 15W
99 Georgia □ 32 0N 82 0W
92 Georgia Str. 49 20N 124 0W
90 Georgian B. 45 15N 81 0W
49 Georgian S.S.R. □ 41 0N 45 0 E
49 Georgiu-Dezh 51 3N 39 20 E
49 Georgiyevsk 44 12N 43 28 E
24 Gera 50 53N 12 5 E
24 Gera □ 50 45N 11 30 E
83 Geraldton, Australia 28 48S 114 32 E
90 Geraldton, Canada 49 44N 86 59W
19 Gérardmer 48 3N 6 50 E
88 Gerdine, Mt. 61 32N 152 50W
56 Gerede 40 45N 32 10 E
33 Gérgal 37 7N 2 31W
25 Gerlafingen 47 10N 7 34 E
55 Gerlogubi 6 53N 45 3 E
92 Germansen Landing 55 43N 124 40W
75 Germiston 26 15S 28 5 E
66 Gero 35 48N 137 14 E
27 Gerlachovka, Mt. 49 11N 20 7 E
32 Gerona 41 58N 2 46 E
32 Gerona □ 42 11N 2 30 E
20 Gers □ 43 35N 0 38 E
20 Gers, R. 44 9N 0 39 E
24 Geseke 51 38N 8 29 E
30 Getafe 40 18N 3 44W
20 Gevaudan, Reg. 44 40N 3 40 E
40 Gevgelija 41 9N 22 30 E
21 Gex 46 21N 6 3 E
102 Geyser 47 17N 110 30W
46 Geysir 64 19N 20 18W
54 Gezer 31 52N 34 55 E
61 Ghaghara, R. 25 45N 84 40 E
72 Ghana ■ 6 0N 1 0W
72 Ghardaïa 32 31N 3 37 E
56 Ghat 24 59N 10 19 E
61 Ghatal 22 40N 87 46 E
62 Ghatprabha, R. 16 21N 75 51 E
73 Ghazal, Bahr el, R. 9 31N 30 25 E
72 Ghazaouet 35 8N 1 50W
60 Ghaziabad 28 42N 77 35 E
61 Ghazipur 25 38N 83 35 E
57 Ghazni 33 30N 68 17 E
57 Ghazni □ 33 0N 68 0 E
36 Ghedi 45 24N 10 16 E
41 Gheorghe Gheorghiu-Dej 46 17N 26 47 E
21 Ghisonaccia 42 1N 9 26 E
57 Ghor □ 34 0N 64 20 E
90 Ghost River 51 25N 83 20W
72 Ghudāmes 30 11N 9 29 E
57 Ghuriān 34 17N 61 25 E
15 Giant's Causeway 55 15N 6 30W
36 Giaveno 45 3N 7 20 E
105 Gibara 21 0N 76 20W
38 Gibellina 37 48N 13 0 E
75 Gibeon 25 7S 17 45 E
31 Gibraléon 37 23N 6 58W
31 Gibraltar ■ 36 7N 5 22W
31 Gibraltar, Str. of 35 55N 5 40W
82 Gibson, Des. 24 0S 126 0 E
19 Gien 47 40N 2 36 E
24 Giessen 50 34N 8 40 E
24 Gifhorn 52 29N 10 32 E
66 Gifu 35 30N 136 45 E
66 Gifu □ 36 0N 137 0 E
104 Giganta, Sa. de la 25 30N 111 30W
14 Gigha, I. 55 42N 5 45W
36 Giglio, I. 42 20N 10 52 E
20 Gignac 43 39N 3 32 E
30 Gijón 43 32N 5 42W
103 Gila, R. 32 43N 114 33W
103 Gila Bend 32 57N 112 43W
56 Gilan □ 37 0N 49 0 E
76 Gilbert Is. 1 0N 176 0 E
93 Gilbert Plains 51 9N 100 28W
80 Gilbert River 18 9S 142 50 E
83 Gilgai 31 15S 119 56 E
84 Gilgandra 31 42S 148 39 E
58 Gilgit 35 50N 74 15 E
93 Gillam 56 20N 94 40W
80 Gilliat 20 40S 141 28 E
13 Gillingham 51 23N 0 34 E
90 Gilmour 44 48N 77 37W
103 Gilroy 37 10N 121 37W
80 Gindie 23 45S 148 10 E
83 Gingin 31 22S 115 37 E
54 Ginnosar 32 51N 35 32 E
39 Ginosa 40 35N 16 45 E
39 Gióia, G. di 38 30N 15 50 E
39 Gióia del Colle 40 49N 16 55 E
39 Gióia Táuro 38 26N 15 53 E
43 Gióna, Mt. 38 38N 22 14 E
65 Giong, Teluk, B. 4 50N 118 20 E

H

Hallandsås Mt. Hindukush, Mts.

45 Hallandsås Mt. 56 23N 13 0 E
16 Halle, Belgium 50 44N 4 13W
24 Halle, E. Germany 51 29N 12 0 E
24 Halle □ 51 28N 11 58 E
44 Hällefors 59 46N 14 30 E
26 Hallein 47 40N 13 5 E
81 Hallett 33 25 S 138 55 E
5 Halley Bay 76 30 S 27 0W
44 Hallingdalselv, R. 60 24N 9 35 E
46 Hällnäs 64 18N 19 40 E
82 Halls Creek 18 20 S 128 0 E
44 Hallsberg 59 5N 15 7 E
44 Hallstahammar 59 38N 16 15 E
26 Hallstatt 47 33N 13 38 E
97 Hallstead 41 56N 75 45W
65 Halmahera, I. 0 40N 128 0 E
45 Halmstad 56 37N 12 56 E
73 Halq el Oued 36 53N 10 10 E
24 Haltern 51 44N 7 10 E
56 Hamā 35 5N 36 40 E
66 Hamada 34 50N 132 10 E
56 Hamadān 34 52N 48 32 E
56 Hamadān □ 35 0N 48 40 E
66 Hamamatsu 34 45N 137 45 E
44 Hamar 60 48N 11 7 E
24 Hamburg, Germany 53 32N 9 59 E
96 Hamburg, U.S.A. 40 37N 95 38W
97 Hamden 41 21N 72 56W
47 Häme □ 61 30N 24 30 E
47 Hämeenlinna 61 3N 24 26 E
83 Hamelin Pool 26 22 S 114 20 E
24 Hameln 52 7N 9 24 E
82 Hamersley Ra. 22 0 S 117 45 E
68 Hamhung 40 0N 127 30 E
67 Hami 42 54N 93 28 E
84 Hamilton, Aus. 37 37 S 142 0 E
105 Hamilton, Bermuda 32 15N 64 45W
96 Hamilton, Canada 43 20N 79 50W
85 Hamilton, N.Z. 37 47 S 175 19 E
14 Hamilton, U.K. 55 47N 4 2W
102 Hamilton, Mont. 46 20N 114 6W
98 Hamilton, Ohio 39 20N 84 35W
80 Hamilton Hotel 22 45 S 140 40 E
97 Hamilton Mt. 43 25N 74 22W
93 Hamiota 50 11N 100 38W
99 Hamlet 34 56N 79 40W
24 Hamm 51 40N 7 58 E
44 Hammarö, I. 59 20N 13 30 E
46 Hammerfest 70 33N 23 50 E
98 Hammond, Ind. 41 40N 87 30W
101 Hammond, La. 30 30N 90 28W
85 Hampden 45 18 S 170 50 E
13 Hampshire □ 51 3N 1 20W
98 Hampton 37 4N 76 8W
56 Hamra 24 2N 38 55 E
44 Hamrånge 60 59N 17 5 E
69 Han Kiang, R. 30 32N 114 22 E
69 Hanchung 33 10N 107 2 E
100 Hancock 47 10N 88 35W
55 Handa, Japan 34 53N 137 0 E
66 Handa, Somalia 10 37N 51 2 E
74 Handeni 5 25 S 38 2 E
27 Handlová 48 45N 18 35 E
54 Hanegev, Reg. 30 50N 35 0 E
92 Haney 49 12N 122 40W
103 Hanford 36 25N 119 45W
69 Hangchow 30 12N 120 1 E
69 Hangchow Wan, G. 30 30N 121 30 E
47 Hangö 59 59N 22 57 E
68 Hanh 51 32N 100 35 E
54 Hanita 33 5N 35 10 E
69 Hankow 30 32N 114 20 E
68 Hanku 39 16N 117 50 E
85 Hanmer 42 32 S 172 50 E
92 Hanna 51 40N 112 0W
100 Hannibal 39 42N 91 22W
24 Hannover 52 23N 9 43 E
45 Hanö, B. 55 45N 14 60 E
45 Hanö, I. 56 0N 14 50 E
63 Hanoi 21 5N 150 40 E
90 Hanover, Canada 44 9N 81 2W
97 Hanover, N.H. 43 43N 72 17W
98 Hanover, Pa. 39 46N 76 59W
112 Hanover, I. 50 58 S 74 40W
60 Hansi 29 10N 75 57 E
68 Hantan 36 42N 114 30 E
69 Hanyang 30 30N 114 19 E
46 Haparanda 65 52N 24 8 E
91 Happy Valley 155 53N 60 10W
60 Hapur 28 45N 77 45 E
68 Har-Ayrag 45 50N 109 30 E
67 Har Us Nuur, L. 48 0N 92 0 E
54 Har Yehuda, Reg. 31 40N 35 0 E
56 Harad 24 15N 49 0 E
55 Haradera 4 33N 47 38 E
75 Harare 17 50 S 31 2 E
68 Harbin 45 46N 126 51 E
91 Harbour Breton 47 29N 55 50W
91 Harbour Deep 50 25N 56 30W
91 Harbour Grace 47 40N 53 22W
24 Harburg 53 27N 9 58 E
60 Harda 22 27N 77 5 E
47 Hardanger Fd. 60 15N 6 0 E
75 Hardap Dam 24 28 S 17 48 E
16 Harderwijk 52 21N 5 36 E
75 Harding 30 22 S 29 55 E
60 Hardwar 29 58N 78 16 E
112 Hardy, Pen. 55 30 S 68 20W
55 Harer 9 20N 42 8 E
18 Harfleur 49 30N 0 10 E
55 Hargeisa 9 30N 44 2 E
62 Harihar 14 32N 75 44 E
62 Haripad 9 14N 76 28 E
12 Harlech 52 52N 4 7W
102 Harlem 48 29N 108 39W
16 Harlingen, Neth. 53 11N 5 25 E
101 Harlingen, U.S.A. 26 30N 97 50W
13 Harlow 51 47N 0 9 E
102 Harlowton 46 30N 109 54W
102 Harney L. 43 0N 119 0W
102 Harney Basin 43 30N 119 0W
100 Harney Pk. 43 52N 103 33W
44 Härnösand 62 38N 18 5 E
30 Haro 42 35N 2 55W
62 Harpanahalli 14 47N 75 59 E
99 Harriman 36 0N 84 35W
91 Harrington Harbour 50 31N 59 30W
14 Harris, I. 57 50N 6 55W
98 Harrisburg, Ill. 37 42N 88 30W
97 Harrison, N.Y. 40 58N 73 43W
101 Harrison, Ohio 36 10N 93 4W
96 Harrisburg, Pa. 40 18N 76 52W
88 Harrison B. 70 25N 151 0W
98 Harrisonburg 38 28N 78 52W
100 Harrisonville 38 45N 93 45W
90 Harriston 43 57N 80 53W
12 Harrogate 53 59N 1 32W
13 Harrow 51 35N 0 15W
97 Hartford 41 47N 72 41W
91 Hartland 46 20N 67 32W
13 Hartland Pt. 51 2N 4 32W
12 Hartlepool 54 42N 1 11W
75 Hartley 18 10 S 30 7 E
92 Hartley Bay 46 4N 80 45W
93 Hartney 49 30N 100 35W
99 Hartsville 34 23N 80 2W
60 Harunabad 29 35N 73 2 E
83 Harvey, Australia 33 4 S 115 48 E
98 Harvey, U.S.A. 41 40N 87 40W
13 Harwich 51 56N 1 18 E
60 Haryana 29 0N 76 10 E
24 Harz, Mts. 51 40N 10 40 E
13 Haslemere 51 5N 0 41W
20 Hasparren 43 24N 1 18W
62 Hassan 13 0N 76 5 E
16 Hasselt 50 56N 5 21 E
72 Hassi Messaoud 31 15N 6 35 E
72 Hassi R'Mel 32 35N 3 24 E
45 Hässleholm 56 9N 13 46 E
85 Hastings, N.Z. 39 39 S 176 52 E
13 Hastings, U.K. 50 51N 0 36 E
98 Hastings, Mich. 42 40N 85 20 E
100 Hastings, Neb. 40 34N 98 22W
103 Hatch 32 45N 107 8W
40 Hateg 45 36N 22 55 E
67 Hatgal 50 40N 100 0 E
60 Hathras 27 36N 78 6 E
61 Hatia I. 22 50N 91 20 E
99 Hatteras, C. 35 10N 75 30W
101 Hattiesburg 31 20N 89 20W
27 Hatvan 47 40N 19 45 E
47 Haugesund 59 23N 5 13 E
41 Haunţii Sebeşului, Mt. 45 30N 23 30 E
55 Haura 13 50N 47 35 E
85 Hauraki, G. 36 35 S 175 5 E
26 Hausruck, Mts. 48 6N 13 30 E
19 Haut-Rhin □ 48 0N 7 15 E
21 Haute-Corse □ 42 30N 9 20 E
20 Haute-Garonne □ 43 28N 1 30 E
20 Haute-Loire □ 45 5N 3 50 E
19 Haute-Marne □ 48 10N 5 20 E
91 Hauterive 49 10N 68 25W
19 Hautmont 50 15N 3 55 E
19 Haute-Saône □ 47 45N 6 10 E
21 Haute-Savoie □ 46 0N 6 20 E
20 Haute-Vienne □ 45 50N 1 10 E
21 Hautes-Alpes □ 44 40N 6 30 E
20 Hautes-Pyrénées □ 43 0N 0 10 E
13 Havant 50 51N 0 59W
90 Havelock 44 26N 77 53W
85 Havelock North 39 42 S 176 53 E
13 Haverfordwest 51 48N 4 59W
97 Haverhill 42 50N 71 2W
62 Haveri 14 53N 75 24 E
13 Havering 51 33N 0 20 E
97 Haverstraw 41 12N 73 58W
26 Havlickuv Brod 49 36N 15 33 E
102 Havre 48 40N 109 34W
91 Havre St. Pierre 50 18N 63 33W
56 Havza 41 0N 35 35 E
94 Hawaii □ 20 0N 155 0W
94 Hawaii, I. 20 0N 155 0W
85 Hawea, L. 44 28 S 169 19 E
85 Hawera 39 35 S 174 19 E
14 Hawick 55 25N 2 48W
90 Hawk Junction 48 5N 84 35W
85 Hawke, B. 39 25 S 177 20 E
81 Hawker 31 59 S 138 22 E
85 Hawke's Bay □ 39 45 S 176 35 E
91 Hawke's Harbour 53 2N 55 50W
91 Hawkesbury, Nova Scotia 45 40N 61 10W
90 Hawkesbury, Ont. 45 35N 74 40W
102 Hawthorne 38 37N 118 47W
84 Hay, Australia 34 30 S 144 51 E
13 Hay, U.K. 52 4N 3 9W
92 Hay River 60 50N 115 50W
19 Hayange 49 20N 6 2 E
103 Hayden 40 30N 107 22W
80 Haydon 18 0 S 141 30 E
88 Hayes, Mt. 63 37N 146 43W
93 Hayes, R. 57 3N 92 9W
13 Hayling I. 50 40N 1 0W
100 Hays 38 55N 99 25W
13 Haywards Heath 51 0N 0 5W
57 Hazārān, Kūh-e, Mt. 29 35N 57 20 E
98 Hazard 37 18N 83 10W
61 Hazaribagh 23 58N 85 26 E
19 Hazebrouck 50 42N 2 31 E
92 Hazelton 55 20N 127 42W
97 Hazleton 40 58N 76 0W
54 Hazor 33 2N 35 2 E
57 Hazrat Imam 37 15N 68 50 E
102 Healdsburg 38 33N 122 51W
12 Heanor 53 1N 1 20W
3 Heard I. 53 0 S 74 0 E
90 Hearst 49 40N 83 41W
91 Heart's Content 47 54N 53 27W
91 Heath Steele 48 30N 66 20W
81 Hebel 28 59 S 147 48 E
91 Hebertville 47 0N 71 30W
14 Hebrides, Inner, Is. 57 20N 6 40W
14 Hebrides, Outer, Is. 57 50N 7 25W
89 Hebron, Canada 58 10N 62 50W
54 Hebron, Jordan 31 32N 35 6 E
92 Hecate Str. 53 10N 130 30W
44 Hedemora 60 18N 15 58 E
44 Hedmark □ 61 45N 11 0 E
16 Heemstede 52 19N 4 37 E
16 Heerde 52 24N 6 2 E
16 Heerenveen 52 57N 5 55 E
16 Heerlen 50 55N 6 0 E
24 Heide 54 10N 9 7 E
25 Heidelberg 49 23N 8 41 E
25 Heidenheim 48 40N 10 10 E
75 Heilbron 27 16 S 27 59 E
25 Heilbronn 49 8N 9 13 E
24 Heiligenstadt 51 22N 10 9 E
68 Heilungkiang □ 47 30N 129 0 E
47 Heinola 61 13N 26 10 E
93 Heinsburg 53 50N 110 30W
59 Heinze Is. 14 25N 97 45 E
46 Hekla, Mt. 63 56N 19 35W
101 Helena, Ark. 34 30N 90 35W
102 Helena, Mont. 46 40N 112 0W
14 Helensburgh 56 0N 4 44W
85 Helensville 36 41 S 174 29 E
54 Helez 31 36N 34 39 E
45 Helgasjön, L. 57 0N 14 54 E
24 Heligoland, I. 54 10N 7 51 E
75 Hell-Ville 13 25 S 48 16 E
16 Hellendoorn 52 24N 6 27 E
33 Hellín 38 31N 1 40W
57 Helmand, Hāmun 31 0N 61 0 E
57 Helmand □ 31 0N 64 0 E
57 Helmand, R. 31 12N 61 34 E
16 Helmond 51 29N 5 41 E
14 Helmsdale 58 7N 3 40W
24 Helmstedt 52 16N 11 0 E
45 Helsingborg 56 3N 12 42 E
47 Helsingfors= Helsinki 60 15N 25 3 E
45 Helsingør 56 2N 12 35 E
47 Helsinki 60 15N 25 3 E
13 Helston 50 7N 5 17W
12 Helvellyn, Mt. 54 31N 3 1W
73 Helwân 29 50N 31 20 E
13 Hemel Hempstead 51 45N 0 28W
32 Henares, R. 40 24N 3 30W
20 Hendaye 43 23N 1 47W
98 Henderson, Ky. 37 50N 87 38W
99 Henderson, N.C. 36 18N 78 23W
101 Henderson, Tex. 32 5N 94 49W
99 Hendersonville 35 21N 82 28W
81 Hendon 28 5 S 151 50 E
16 Hengelo 52 15N 6 48 E
69 Hengyang 26 57N 112 28 E
19 Hénin Beaumont 50 25N 2 58 E
18 Hennebont 47 49N 3 19W
24 Henningsdorf 52 38N 13 13 E
90 Henrietta Maria, C. 55 10N 82 30W
74 Henrique de Carvalho 9 39 S 20 24 E
101 Henryetta 35 2N 96 0W
84 Henty 35 30N 147 0 E
59 Henzada 17 38N 95 35 E
102 Heppner 45 27N 119 34W
57 Herat 34 20N 62 7 E
57 Herat □ 34 20N 62 7 E
20 Hérault □ 43 34N 3 15 E
20 Hérault, R. 43 17N 3 26 E
93 Herbert 50 30N 107 10W
80 Herbert Downs 23 0 S 139 11 E
40 Hercegnavi 42 30N 18 33 E
13 Hereford, U.K. 52 4N 2 42W
101 Hereford, U.S.A. 34 50N 102 28W
13 Hereford and Worcester □ 52 14N 1 42W
16 Herentals 51 12N 4 51 E
24 Herford 52 7N 8 40 E
19 Héricourt 47 32N 6 55 E
25 Herisau 47 22N 9 17 E
97 Herkimer 43 0N 74 59W
18 Herm, I. 49 30N 2 28W
26 Hermagor-Pressegger See, L. 46 38N 13 23 E
84 Hermidale 31 30 S 146 42 E
102 Hermiston 45 50N 119 16W
85 Hermitage 43 44 S 170 5 E
112 Hermite, I. 55 50 S 68 0W
56 Hermon, Mt.= Sheikh, Jabal ash 33 20N 26 0 E
104 Hermosillo 29 10N 111 0W
27 Hernad R. 47 56N 21 8 E
109 Hernandarias 25 20 S 54 50W
108 Hernando 32 28 S 64 50W
24 Herne 51 33N 7 12 E
13 Herne Bay 51 22N 1 8 E
45 Herning 56 8N 9 0 E
90 Heron Bay 48 40N 85 25W
56 Herowabad 37 37N 48 32 E
30 Herrera de Pisuerga 42 35N 4 20W
31 Herrera del Duque 39 10N 5 3W
101 Herrin 37 50N 89 0W
45 Herrljunga 58 5N 13 5 E
16 Herstal 50 40N 5 38 E
13 Hertford 51 47N 0 4W
13 Hertford □ 51 51N 0 5W
30 Hervás 40 16N 5 52W
77 Hervey Is. 19 30 S 159 0W
24 Herzberg 51 38N 10 20 E
54 Herzliyya 32 10N 34 50 E
26 Herzogenburg 48 17N 15 41 E
24 Hessen □ 50 57N 9 20 E
24 Hettstedt 51 39N 11 30 E
18 Heve, C. de la 49 30N 0 5 E
27 Heves □ 47 50N 20 0 E
89 Hewett, C. 70 30N 68 0W
12 Hexham 54 58N 2 7W
12 Heysham 54 5N 2 53W
84 Heywood 38 8 S 141 37 E
100 Hibbing 47 30N 93 0W
99 Hickory 35 46N 81 17W
97 Hicksville 40 46N 73 30W
66 Hida Sammyaku, Mts. 36 0N 137 10 E
104 Hidalgo □ 20 30N 99 10W
104 Hidalgo del Parral 26 10N 104 50W
26 Hieflau 47 36N 14 46 E
72 Hierro, I. 27 57N 17 56W
69 Hifung 22 59N 115 17 E
66 Higashiósaka 34 39N 135 35 E
83 Higginsville 31 42 S 121 38 E
99 High Point 35 57N 79 58W
92 High Prairie 55 30N 116 30W
92 High River 50 30N 113 50W
13 High Wycombe 51 37N 0 45W
70 High Veld 26 30 S 30 0 E
14 Highland □ 57 30N 4 50W
98 Highland Park, Ill. 42 10N 87 50W
98 Highland Park, Mich. 42 25N 83 6W
32 Hijar 41 10N 0 27W
56 Hijāz, Reg. 26 0N 37 30 E
66 Hikari 33 58N 131 56 E
66 Hikone 35 15N 136 10 E
85 Hikurangi 37 54 S 178 5 E
24 Hildersheim 52 9N 9 55 E
16 Hillegom 52 18N 4 35 E
45 Hillerød 55 56N 12 19 E
13 Hillingdon 51 33N 0 29W
100 Hillsboro, Kan. 38 28N 97 10W
102 Hillsboro, Oreg. 45 31N 123 0W
101 Hillsboro, Tex. 32 0N 97 10W
90 Hillsport 49 27N 85 34W
84 Hillston 33 30 S 145 31 E
94 Hilo 19 44N 155 5W
16 Hilversum 52 14N 5 10 E
60 Himachal Pradesh □ 31 30N 77 0 E
52 Himalaya, Mts. 29 0N 84 0 E
66 Himeji 34 50N 134 40 E
66 Himi 36 50N 137 0 E
45 Himmerland, Reg. 56 50N 9 38 E
56 Hims=Homs 34 40N 36 45 E
80 Hinchinbrook, I. 18 20 S 146 15 E
13 Hinckley 52 33N 1 21W
60 Hindaun 26 44N 77 5 E
84 Hindmarsh, L. 35 50 S 141 55 E
57 Hindukush, Mts. 36 0N 71 0 E

Jaguariaíva Kalmar

109 Jaguariaíva 24 10s 49 50w
105 Jaguey 22 35n 81 7w
84 Jagungal, Mt. 36 12s 148 28w
57 Jahrom 28 30n 53 31 e
60 Jaipur 26 54n 72 52 e
60 Jaisalmer 26 55n 70 55 e
40 Jajce 44 19n 17 17 e
61 Jajpur 20 53n 86 22 e
65 Jakarta 6 9s 106 49 e
46 Jakobstad 63 40n 22 43 e
57 Jalalabad 34 30n 70 29 e
60 Jalapur Jattan 32 38n 74 19 e
104 Jalapa, Guatemala 14 45n 89 59w
104 Jalapa, Mexico 19 30n 96 50w
60 Jalgaon 21 0n 75 42 e
104 Jalisco □ 20 0n 104 0w
60 Jalna 19 48n 75 57 e
32 Jalón, R. 41 47n 1 4w
61 Jalpaiguri 26 32n 88 46 e
105 Jamaica ■ 18 10n 77 30w
61 Jamalpur, Bangladesh 24 52n 90 2 e
61 Jamalpur, India 25 18n 86 28 e
64 Jambi 1 38s 103 30 e
64 Jambi □ 1 30s 103 30 e
60 Jambusar 22 3n 72 51 e
90 James B. 53 30n 80 30w
100 James, R. 44 50n 98 0w
81 Jamestown, Australia 33 10s 138 32 e
100 Jamestown, N.D. 47 0n 98 30w
96 Jamestown, N.Y. 42 5n 79 18w
62 Jamkhandi 16 30n 75 15 e
62 Jammalamadugu 14 51n 78 25 e
45 Jammer, B. 57 15n 9 20 e
60 Jammu 32 46n 75 57 e
58 Jammu and Kashmir □ 34 25n 77 0w
60 Jamnagar 22 30n 70 0 e
60 Jamner 20 45n 75 45 e
60 Jampur 29 39n 70 32 e
61 Jamshedpur 22 44n 86 20 e
44 Jämtlands □ 62 40n 13 50 e
4 Jan Mayen, I. 71 0n 11 0w
58 Jand 33 30n 72 0 e
31 Janda, L. de 36 15n 5 51w
81 Jandowae 26 45s 151 7 e
100 Janesville 42 39n 89 1w
62 Jangaon 17 44n 79 5 e
111 Januária 15 25s 44 25w
18 Janzé 47 55n 1 28w
60 Jaora 23 40n 75 10 e
66 Japan ■ 36 0n 136 0 e
65 Japara 6 30s 110 40 e
110 Japurá, R. 3 8s 64 46w
31 Jaraicejo 39 40n 5 49 e
30 Jaraiz 40 4n 5 45w
103 Jarales 34 44n 106 51w
30 Jarama, R. 40 2n 3 39w
112 Jaramillo 47 10s 67 7w
60 Jaranwala 31 15n 73 20 e
33 Jardin, R. 39 12n 1 60w
105 Jardines de la Reina, Is. 20 50n 78 50w
68 Jargalant 47 2n 115 1 e
19 Jargeau 47 50n 2 7 e
20 Jarnac 45 40n 0 11w
19 Jarny 49 9n 5 53 e
28 Jarocin 51 59n 17 29 e
26 Jaroměř 50 22n 15 52 e
27 Jarosław 50 2n 22 42 e
77 Jarvis I. 0 15s 159 55w
40 Jaša Tomić 45 26n 20 50 e
63 Jasin 2 20n 102 26 e
57 Jāsk 25 38n 57 45 e
27 Jasło 49 45n 21 30 e
112 Jason Is, 51 0s 61 0w
92 Jasper, Canada 52 55n 118 0w
99 Jasper, U.S.A. 30 31n 82 58w
92 Jasper Nat. Park 52 53n 118 3w
92 Jasper Place 53 33n 113 25w
27 Jastrzebie Zdroj 49 57n 18 35 e
27 Jászárokszállás 47 39n 20 1 e
27 Jászberény 47 30n 19 55 e
27 Jászladány 47 23n 20 18 e
111 Jataí 17 50s 51 45w
65 Jatibarang 6 28s 108 18 e
65 Jatinegara 6 13s 106 52 e
33 Játiva 39 0n 0 32w
111 Jatobal 4 35s 49 33w
54 Jatt 32 24n 35 2 e
109 Jaú 22 10s 48 30w
61 Jaunpur 25 46n 82 44 e
65 Java, I. 7 0s 110 0 e
64 Java Sea 4 35s 107 15 e
64 Java Trench 10 0s 110 0 e
33 Jávea 38 48n 0 10 e
62 Javla 17 18n 75 9 e
28 Jawor 51 4n 16 11 e
27 Jaworzno 50 13n 19 22 e
65 Jaya, Puncak, Mt. 4 0s 137 20 e
65 Jayapura 2 28s 140 38 e
65 Jayawijaya, Pengunungan 4 50s 139 0 e
93 Jaydot 49 15n 110 15w
88 Jean Marie River 62 0n 121 0w
96 Jeannette 40 20n 79 36w
57 Jebāl Bārez, Kūh-e 29 0n 58 0 e
72 Jebba, Morocco 35 11n 4 43w
72 Jebba, Nigeria 9 9n 4 48 e
40 Jebel 40 35n 21 15 e
73 Jebel, Bahr el, R. 9 40n 30 30 e
14 Jedburgh 55 28n 2 33w
27 Jędrzejów 50 35n 20 15 e
102 Jefferson, Mt. 38 51n 117 0w
100 Jefferson City 38 34n 92 10w
98 Jeffersonville 38 20n 85 42w
72 Jega 12 15n 4 23 e
26 Jelenia Góra 50 50n 15 45 e
48 Jelgava 56 41n 22 49 e
65 Jember 8 11s 113 41 e
16 Jemeppe 50 37n 5 30 e
24 Jena 50 56n 11 33 e
26 Jenbach 47 24n 11 47 e
54 Jenīn 32 28n 35 18 e
98 Jenkins 37 13n 82 41w
101 Jennings 30 10n 92 45w
111 Jequié 13 51s 40 5w
111 Jequtinhonha 16 30s 41 0w
72 Jerada 34 40n 2 10w
63 Jerantut 3 56n 102 22 e
105 Jérémie 18 40n 74 10w
104 Jerez de Gacia Salinas 22 39n 103 0w
31 Jerez de la Frontera 36 41n 6 7w
31 Jerez de los Caballeros 38 20n 6 45w
80 Jericho, Australia 23 38s 146 6 e
54 Jericho, Jordan = El Ariha 31 52n 35 27 e
84 Jerilderie 35 20s 145 41 e
103 Jerome 34 50n 112 0w
18 Jersey, I. 49 13n 2 7w
97 Jersey City 40 41n 74 8w
96 Jersey Shore 41 17n 77 18w
100 Jerseyville 39 5n 90 20w
54 Jerusalem 31 47n 35 10 e
37 Jesenice 50 6n 13 28 e
64 Jesselton = Kota Kinabalu 6 0n 116 12 e
24 Jessnitz 51 42n 12 19 e
61 Jessore 23 10n 89 10 e
108 Jesús María 30 59s 64 5w
60 Jetpur 21 45n 70 10 e
62 Jeypore 18 50n 82 38 e
58 Jhal Jhao 26 20n 65 35 e
60 Jhansi 25 30n 78 36 e
61 Jharia 23 45n 86 18 e
61 Jharsuguda 21 51n 84 1 e
60 Jhelum 33 0n 73 45 e
60 Jhelum, R. 31 12n 72 8 e
60 Jhunjhunu 28 10n 75 20 e
26 Jičín 50 25n 15 20 e
56 Jiddah 21 29n 39 16 e
54 Jifna 31 58n 35 13 e
69 Jihchao 35 18n 119 28 e
26 Jihlava 49 28n 15 35 e
26 Jihočeský □ 49 8n 14 35 e
27 Jihomoravsky □ 49 5n 16 30 e
55 Jijiga 9 20n 42 50 e
33 Jijona 38 34n 0 30w
32 Jiloca, R. 41 21n 1 39w
73 Jima 7 40n 36 55 e
40 Jimbolia 45 47n 20 57 e
31 Jimena de la Frontera 36 27n 5 24w
104 Jiménez 27 10n 105 0w
26 Jindřichuv Hradec 49 10n 15 2 e
74 Jinja 0 25n 33 12 e
68 Jinné 51 32n 121 25 e
105 Jinotega 13 6n 85 59w
105 Jinotepe 11 50n 86 10w
100 Jipijapa 1 0s 80 40w
56 Jisr ash Shughur 35 49n 36 18 e
83 Jitarning 32 48s 117 57 e
41 Jiu, R. 43 47n 23 48 e
109 Joaçaba 27 5s 51 31w
111 João Pessoa 7 10s 34 52w
109 Joaquim Távora 23 30s 49 58w
31 Jodar 37 50n 3 21w
60 Jodhpur 26 23n 73 2 e
5 Joerg Plat. 75 0s 70 0w
19 Joeuf 49 12n 6 1 e
91 Joggins 45 42n 64 27w
75 Johannesburg 26 10s 28 8 e
14 John O'Groats 58 39n 3 3w
97 Johnson City, N.Y. 42 9n 67 0w
99 Johnson City, Tenn. 36 18n 82 21w
92 Johnson's Crossing 60 33n 133 27w
77 Johnston I. 17 10n 169 8 e
63 Johore, R. 1 39n 103 57 e
97 Johnstown, N.Y. 43 1n 74 20w
96 Johnstown, Pa. 40 19n 78 53w
63 Johor Baharu 1 45n 103 47 e
63 Johore □ 2 5n 103 20 e
19 Joigny 48 0n 3 20 e
109 Joinvile 26 15s 48 55 e
19 Joinville 48 27n 5 10 e
46 Jokkmokk 66 35n 19 50 e
98 Joliet 41 30n 88 0w
90 Joliette 46 3n 73 24w
65 Jolo, I. 6 0n 121 0 e
65 Jombang 7 32s 112 12 e
90 Jones, C. 54 33n 79 35w
101 Jonesboro 35 50n 90 45w
45 Jönköping 57 45n 14 10 e
45 Jönköpings □ 57 30n 14 30 e
45 Jonsered 57 45n 12 10 e
20 Jonzac 45 27n 0 28w
101 Joplin 37 0n 94 25w
56 Jordan ■ 31 0n 36 0 e
54 Jordan, R. 31 46n 35 33 e
59 Jorhat 26 45n 94 20 e
46 Jörn 65 5n 20 12 e
72 Jos 9 53n 8 51 e
109 José Batlle y Ordóñez 33 20s 55 10w
112 José de San Martín 44 4s 70 26w
82 Joseph Bonaparte, G. 14 0s 29 0 e
18 Josselin 47 57n 2 33w
44 Jotunheimen, Mts. 61 30n 9 0 e
56 Jounieh 33 59n 35 30 e
57 Jouzjan □ 22 40n 81 10w
28 Jozefow 52 9n 21 12 e
92 Juan de Fuca Str. 48 15n 124 0w
107 Juan Fernández, Arch. de 33 50s 80 0w
108 Juan Lacaze 34 26s 57 25w
108 Juárez 37 40s 59 43w
109 Juatinga, Pta. de 23 17s 44 30w
111 Juàzeiro 9 30s 40 30w
111 Juazeiro do Norte 7 10s 39 18w
73 Jûbâ 4 57n 31 35 e
56 Jubaila 24 55n 46 25 e
72 Juby, C. 28 0n 12 59w
32 Júcar, R. 39 40n 2 18w
104 Juchitán 16 27n 95 5w
54 Judaea = Har Yehuda, Reg. 31 35n 34 57 e
26 Judenburg 47 12n 14 38 e
97 Judith, Pt. 41 20n 71 30w
24 Juist, I. 53 40n 7 0 e
109 Juiz de Fora 21 43s 43 19w
108 Jujuy □ 23 20s 65 40w
110 Juli 16 10s 69 25w
80 Julia Creek 20 40s 141 55 e
110 Juliaca 15 25s 70 10w
110 Julianatop, Mt. 3 40n 56 30w
4 Julianehåb 60 43n 46 0w
37 Julijske Alpe, Mts. 46 15n 14 1 e
60 Jullundur 31 20n 75 40 e
105 Jumento Cays 23 40n 75 40 e
16 Jumet 50 27n 4 25 e
33 Jumilla 38 28n 1 19w
60 Junagadh 21 30n 70 30 e
100 Junction City, Kans. 39 4n 96 55w
102 Junction City, Oreg. 44 20n 123 12w
80 Jundah 24 46s 143 2 e
109 Jundiaí 23 10s 47 0w
92 Juneau 58 26n 134 30w
84 Junee 34 49s 147 32w
25 Jungfrau, Mt. 46 32n 7 58 e
108 Junín 34 33s 60 57w
112 Junin de los Andes 39 45s 71 0w
96 Juniata, R. 40 24n 77 1w
109 Juquiá 24 19s 47 38w
14 Jura, I. 56 0n 5 50w
17 Jura, Mts. 46 45n 6 30 e
21 Jura □ 46 47n 5 45 e
110 Jurado 7 7n 77 46w
41 Jurilovca 44 46n 28 52w
57 Jurm 36 50n 70 45 e
110 Juruá, R. 2 37s 65 44w
111 Juruti 2 9s 56 4w
19 Jussey 47 50n 5 55 e
108 Justo Daract 33 52s 65 12w
24 Jüterbog 51 59n 13 6 e
105 Juticalpa 14 40n 85 50w
19 Juvisy 48 43n 2 23 e
67 Jyekundo 33 0n 96 50 e
45 Jylland, Reg. 56 25n 9 30 e
46 Jyväskylä 62 12n 25 47 e

K

58 K2, Mt. 36 0n 77 0 e
75 Kaap Plato 28 30s 24 0 e
75 Kaapstad = Cape Town 33 55s 18 22 e
65 Kabaena, I. 5 15s 122 0 e
74 Kabale 9 38n 11 37w
74 Kabalo 6 0s 27 0 e
74 Kabambare 4 41s 27 39 e
74 Kabarega Falls 2 15s 31 38 e
72 Kabba 7 57n 6 3 e
74 Kabinda 6 23s 24 38 e
74 Kabongo 7 22s 25 33 e
80 Kabra 23 25s 150 25 e
57 Kabul 34 28n 69 18 e
57 Kabul □ 34 0n 68 30 e
75 Kabwe 14 30s 28 29 e
40 Kacanik 42 13n 21 12 e
59 Kachin □ 26 0n 97 0 e
50 Kachiry 53 10n 75 50 e
62 Kadayanallur 9 3n 77 22 e
60 Kadi 23 18n 72 23 e
81 Kadina 34 0s 137 43 e
49 Kadiyerka 48 35n 38 30 e
72 Kaduna 10 30n 7 21 e
72 Kaesŏng 37 58n 126 35 e
73 Kafia Kingi 9 20n 24 25 e
43 Kafirévs, Ákra 38 9n 24 8 e
54 Kafr Kanna 32 45n 35 20 e
54 Kafr Ra'i 32 23n 35 9 e
75 Kafue, R. 15 56s 28 55 e
50 Kagan 39 43n 64 33 e
66 Kagawa □ 34 15n 134 0 e
66 Kagoshima 31 36n 130 40 e
66 Kagoshima □ 30 0n 130 0 e
65 Kai, Kep. 5 35s 132 45 e
85 Kaiapoi 42 24s 172 40 e
69 Kaifeng 34 50n 114 27 e
85 Kaikohe 35 25s 173 49 e
85 Kaikoura 42 25s 173 43 e
94 Kailua 21 24n 157 44w
61 Kaimganj 27 33n 79 24 e
61 Kaimur Hills 24 30n 82 0 e
72 Kainji Dam 10 1n 4 40 e
85 Kaipara, Harbour 36 25s 174 14 e
68 Kaiping 40 28n 122 10 e
60 Kairana 29 33n 77 15 e
72 Kairouan 35 45n 10 5 e
25 Kaiserslautern 49 30n 7 43 e
85 Kaitaia 35 8s 173 17 e
85 Kaitangata 46 17s 169 51 e
60 Kaithal 29 48n 76 26 e
68 Kaiyuan 42 33n 124 4 e
46 Kajaani 64 17n 27 46 e
63 Kajang 2 59n 101 48 e
66 Kake 34 6n 132 19 e
66 Kakegawa 34 45n 138 1 e
49 Kakhovka 46 46n 34 28 e
62 Kakinada 16 50n 82 11 e
66 Kakogawa 34 46n 134 51 e
60 Kalabagh 33 0n 71 28 e
65 Kalabahi 8 13s 124 31 e
49 Kalach 50 22n 41 0 e
59 Kaladan, R. 20 9n 92 57 e
75 Kalahari, Des. 24 0s 22 0 e
62 Kalahasti 13 45n 79 44 e
51 Kalakan 55 15n 116 45 e
42 Kalamariá 40 33n 22 55 e
43 Kalamata 37 3n 22 10 e
98 Kalamazoo 42 20n 85 35w
62 Kalamb 18 3n 74 48 e
83 Kalamunda 32 0s 116 0 e
56 Kalan 39 7n 39 32 e
83 Kalannie 30 22s 117 5 e
27 Kalárovo 47 54n 18 0 e
60 Kalat 29 8n 66 31 e
57 Kalat-i-Ghilzai 32 15n 66 58 e
43 Kalávrita 38 3n 22 8 e
74 Kalemie 5 55s 29 9 e
59 Kalewa 22 41n 95 32 e
83 Kalgoorlie 30 40s 121 22 e
41 Kaliakra, C. 43 21n 28 30 e
65 Kalibo 11 43n 122 22 e
64 Kalimantan □ 0 0 115 0 e
43 Kálimnos, I. 37 0n 27 0 e
61 Kalimpong 27 4n 88 35 e
48 Kalinin 56 55n 35 55 e
48 Kaliningrad 54 44n 20 32 e
41 Kalipetrovo 44 5n 27 14 e
102 Kalispell 48 10n 114 22 e
28 Kalisz 53 17n 15 55 e
60 Kalka 30 56n 76 57 e
62 Kallakurichi 11 44n 79 1 e
45 Kållandsö, I. 58 40n 13 5 e
45 Källby 58 30n 13 0 e
54 Kallia 31 46n 35 30 e
62 Kallidaikurichi 8 38n 77 31 e
43 Kallithéa 37 55n 23 41 e
43 Kallonís, Kól. 39 10n 26 10 e
45 Kalmar 56 40n 16 20 e

Knud Rasmussen Ld. Kurya

4 Knud Rasmussen Ld. 80 0N 55 0W
27 Knurów 50 13N 18 38 E
89 Koartac 61 5N 69 36W
65 Koba 6 37S 134 37 E
66 Kobe 34 45N 135 10 E
45 København 55 41N 12 34 E
25 Koblenz 50 21N 7 36 E
28 Kobyłka 52 21N 21 10 E
40 Kočane 41 53N 22 27 E
40 Kočani 41 55N 22 25 E
37 Kočevje 45 39N 14 50 E
66 Kōchi 33 30N 133 35 E
66 Kōchi □ 33 40N 133 30 E
62 Kodaikanal 10 13N 77 32 E
62 Koddiyar B. 8 33N 81 15 E
88 Kodiak 57 48N 152 23W
88 Kodiak I. 57 30N 152 45 E
60 Kodinar 20 46N 70 46 E
73 Kodok 9 53N 32 7 E
26 Köflach 47 4N 15 4 E
72 Koforidua 6 3N 0 17W
66 Kōfu 35 40N 138 30 E
45 Køge 55 27N 12 11 E
45 Køge, B. 55 30N 12 20 E
58 Kohat 33 40N 71 29 E
59 Kohima 25 35N 94 10 E
5 Kohler Ra. 77 0S 110 0W
83 Kojonup 33 48S 117 10W
50 Kokand 40 30N 70 57 E
92 Kokanee Glacier Prov. Park 49 47N 117 10W
50 Kokchetav 53 20N 69 10 E
54 Kokhav Mikha'el 31 37N 34 40 E
67 Kokiu 23 22N 103 6 E
46 Kokkola 63 50N 23 8 E
63 Koko Kyunzu, Is. 14 10N 93 30 E
67 Koko Nor, L. 37 0N 100 0 E
98 Kokomo 40 30N 86 6W
89 Koksoak, R. 58 30N 68 10W
75 Kokstad 30 32S 29 29 E
51 Kokuora 61 30N 145 0 E
48 Kola 68 45N 33 8 E
68 Kolan 38 43N 111 32 E
62 Kolar 13 12N 78 15 E
62 Kolar Gold Fields 12 58N 78 16 E
41 Kolarovgrad 43 27N 26 42 E
40 Kolašin 42 50N 19 31 E
45 Kolding 55 30N 9 29 E
65 Kolepom, I. 8 0S 138 30 E
48 Kolguyev 69 20N 48 30 E
62 Kolhapur 16 43N 74 15 E
26 Kolín 50 2N 15 9 E
62 Kollegal 12 9N 77 9 E
62 Kolleru L. 16 40N 81 10 E
24 Köln 50 56N 9 58 E
28 Koło 52 14N 18 40 E
28 Kołobrzeg 54 10N 15 35 E
48 Kołomna 55 8N 38 45 E
49 Kolomyya 48 31N 25 2 E
59 Kolosib 24 15N 92 45 E
50 Kolpashevo 58 20N 83 5 E
48 Kolskiy Pol. 67 30N 38 0 E
48 Kolskiy Zaliv 69 23N 34 0 E
74 Kolwezi 10 40S 25 25 E
51 Kolyma, R. 64 40N 153 0 E
27 Komárno 47 49N 18 5 E
27 Komarom 47 43N 18 7 E
27 Komarom □ 47 35N 18 20 E
66 Komatsu 36 25N 136 30 E
48 Komi A.S.S.R. 64 0N 55 0 E
27 Komló 46 15N 18 16 E
66 Komoro 36 19N 138 26 E
42 Komotini 41 9N 25 26 E
40 Komovi, Mt. 42 40N 19 40 E
63 Kompong Cham 11 54N 105 30 E
63 Kompong Som 10 38N 103 30 E
51 Komsomolets, Os. 80 30N 95 0 E
51 Komsomolsk 50 30N 137 0 E
51 Kondakovo 69 20N 151 30 E
83 Kondinin 32 34S 118 8 E
72 Koudougou 12 10N 2 20W
51 Kondratyevo 57 30N 98 30 E
5 Kong Haakon VII Hav, Sea 65 0S 20 0 E
68 Kongju 36 30N 127 0 E
59 Konglu 27 13N 97 57 E
69 Kongmoon 22 35N 113 1 E
74 Kongolo 5 22S 27 0 E
44 Kongsberg 59 39N 9 39 E
48 Königsberg= Kaliningrad 54 42N 20 32 E
28 Konin 52 12N 18 15 E
28 Konin □ 52 15N 18 20 E
40 Konjic 43 42N 17 58 E
48 Konosha 61 0N 40 5 E
49 Konotop 51 12N 33 7 E
28 Końskie 51 15N 20 23 E
28 Konstantynów Łódźki 51 45N 19 20 E
25 Konstanz 47 39N 9 10 E
72 Kontagora 10 23N 5 27 E
56 Konya 37 52N 32 35 E
83 Kookynie 29 17S 121 22 E
82 Kooline 22 57S 116 20 E
83 Koolyanobbing 30 48S 119 46 E
81 Koonibba 31 58S 133 27 E
83 Koorda 30 48S 117 35 E
92 Kootenay Nat. Park 51 0N 116 0W
84 Koo-wee-rup 38 13S 145 28 E
40 Kopaonik, Mts. 43 10N 21 0 E
62 Kopargaon 19 51N 74 28 E
47 Kopervik 59 17N 5 17 E
50 Kopeysk 55 7N 61 37 E
44 Köping 59 31N 16 3 E
62 Koppal 15 23N 76 5 E
44 Kopparbergs □ 61 20N 14 15 E
37 Koprivnica 46 12N 16 45 E
40 Korab, Mt. 41 44N 20 40 E
24 Korbach 51 17N 8 50 E
42 Korça 40 37N 20 50 E
42 Korça □ 40 40N 20 50 E
37 Korčula, I. 42 57N 17 0 E
56 Kordestān □ 36 0N 47 0 E
73 Kordofân □ 13 0N 29 0 E
68 Korea B. 39 0N 124 0 E
62 Koregaon 17 40N 74 10 E
72 Korhogo 9 29N 5 28 E
43 Korinthiakós Kól. 38 16N 22 30 E
43 Korinthía □ 37 50N 22 35 E
43 Korinthos 37 26N 22 55 E
66 Kōriyama 37 24N 140 23 E
67 Korla 41 45N 86 4 E
37 Kornat, I. 43 50N 15 20 E
85 Koro Sea 17 30S 179 45W
84 Koroit 38 18S 142 24 E
43 Koróni 36 48N 21 57 E
28 Koronowo 53 19N 17 55 E
27 Körös, R. 46 30N 142 42 E
51 Korsakov 46 30N 142 42 E
45 Korsør 55 20N 11 9 E
28 Korsze 54 11N 21 9 E
16 Kortrijk 50 50N 3 17 E
84 Korumburra 38 26S 145 50 E
51 Koryakskiy Khrebet, Mts. 61 0N 171 0 E
43 Kos, I. 36 50N 27 15 E
28 Koscierzyna 54 8N 17 59 E
101 Kosciusko 33 3N 89 34W
92 Kosciusko I. 56 0N 133 40W
84 Kosciusko, Mt. 36 27S 148 16 E
62 Kosgi 16 58N 77 43 E
60 Kosi 27 48N 77 29 E
27 Košice 48 42N 21 15 E
40 Kosjerić 44 0N 19 55 E
48 Koslan 63 28N 48 52 E
40 Kosovska-Mitrovica 42 54N 20 52 E
37 Kostajnica 45 17N 16 30 E
41 Kostenets 42 15N 23 52 E
73 Kôstî 13 8N 32 43 E
48 Kostroma 57 50N 41 58 E
28 Kostrzyn 52 24N 17 14 E
28 Koszalin 54 12N 16 8 E
28 Koszalin □ 54 10N 16 10 E
27 Köszeg 47 23N 16 33 E
60 Kot Adu 30 30N 71 0 E
60 Kot Moman 32 13N 73 0 E
60 Kota 25 14N 75 49 E
63 Kota Baharu 6 7N 102 14 E
64 Kota Kinabalu 6 0N 116 12 E
63 Kota Tinggi 1 44N 103 53 E
64 Kotabaru 3 20S 116 20 E
64 Kotabumi 4 49S 104 46 E
64 Kotawaringin 2 28S 111 27 E
48 Kotelnich 58 20N 48 10 E
62 Kothagudam 17 30N 80 40 E
62 Kothapet 19 21N 79 28 E
24 Köthen 51 44N 11 59 E
47 Kotka 60 28N 26 55 E
48 Kotlas 61 15N 47 0 E
88 Kotlik 63 2N 163 33W
40 Kotor 42 25N 18 47 E
40 Kotoriba 46 37N 16 48 E
60 Kotri 25 22N 68 22 E
43 Kótronas 36 38N 22 29 E
26 Kotschach Mauthern 46 40N 13 0 E
62 Kottayam 9 35N 76 33 E
62 Kottur 10 34N 76 56 E
88 Kotzebue 66 53N 162 39W
43 Koufonísi, I. 34 56N 26 8 E
74 Koula-Moutou 1 15S 12 25 E
80 Koumala 21 38S 149 15 E
50 Kounradskiy 47 20N 75 0 E
111 Kourou 5 9N 52 39W
72 Kouroussa 10 45N 9 45W
40 Kovačica 45 5N 20 38 E
48 Kovdor 67 34N 30 22 E
48 Kovel 51 10N 25 0 E
62 Kovilpatti 9 10N 77 50 E
48 Kovrov 56 25N 41 25 E
62 Kovur, Andhra Pradesh 17 3N 81 39 E
62 Kovur, Andhra Pradesh 14 30N 80 1 E
69 Kowloon 22 20N 114 15 E
69 Koyiu 23 2N 112 28 E
88 Koyukuk, R. 64 56N 157 30W
42 Kozáni 40 19N 21 47 E
42 Kozáni □ 40 20N 21 45 E
40 Kozara, Mts. 45 0N 17 0 E
40 Kozarac 44 58N 16 48 E
62 Kozhikode= Calicut 11 15N 75 43 E
48 Kozhva 65 10N 57 0 E
28 Kozmin 51 48N 17 27 E
28 Kozuchów 51 45N 15 35 E
72 Kpandu 7 2N 0 18 E
63 Kra, Isthmus of= Kra, Kho Khot 10 15N 99 30 E
63 Kra, Kho Khot 10 15N 99 30 E
63 Kra Buri 10 22N 98 46 E
40 Kragujevac 44 2N 20 56 E
27 Kracków 50 4N 19 57 E
27 Krakow □ 50 5N 20 0 E
65 Kraksaan 7 43S 113 23 E
40 Kraljevo 43 44N 20 41 E
26 Kralupy 50 13N 14 20 E
49 Kramatorsk 48 50N 37 30 E
44 Kramfors 62 55N 17 48 E
37 Kranj 46 16N 14 22 E
37 Krapina 46 10N 15 52 E
27 Krapkowice 50 29N 17 55 E
48 Krasavino 60 58N 46 26 E
51 Kraskino 42 45N 130 58 E
26 Kraslice 50 19N 12 31 E
27 Krasnik 50 55N 22 5 E
49 Krasnodar 45 5N 38 50 E
48 Krasnokamsk 58 0N 56 0 E
50 Krasnoselkupsk 65 20N 82 10 E
50 Krasnoturinsk 59 39N 60 1 E
48 Krasnoufimsk 56 30N 57 37 E
50 Krasnouralsk 58 0N 60 0 E
50 Krasnovodsk 40 0N 52 52 E
48 Krasnovishersk 60 23N 56 59 E
51 Krasnoyarsk 56 8N 93 0 E
28 Krasnystaw 50 57N 23 5 E
49 Krasnyy Yar 46 43N 48 23 E
24 Krefeld 51 20N 6 22 E
43 Kremaston, L. 38 52N 21 30 E
49 Kremenchug 49 5N 33 25 E
49 Kremenchugskoye, Vdkhr. 49 20N 32 30 E
40 Kremenica 40 55N 21 25 E
26 Krems 48 25N 15 36 E
26 Kremsmünster 48 3N 14 8 E
41 Krichem 46 16N 24 28 E
62 Krishna, R. 15 43N 80 55 E
62 Krishnagiri 12 32N 78 16 E
61 Krishnanagar 23 24N 88 33 E
47 Kristiansand 58 5N 7 50 E
45 Kristianstad 56 5N 14 7 E
45 Kristianstads □ 56 0N 14 0 E
44 Kristiansund 63 10N 7 45 E
44 Kristinehamn 59 18N 14 13 E
46 Kristinestad 62 18N 21 25 E
43 Kriti, I. 35 15N 25 0 E
43 Kritsá 35 10N 25 41 E
40 Kriva Palanka 42 11N 22 19 E
49 Krivoy Rog 47 51N 33 20 E
40 Križevci 46 3N 16 32 E
37 Krk, I. 45 5N 14 56 E
37 Krka, R. 45 50N 15 30 E
26 Krkonoše, Mts. 50 50N 15 30 E
27 Krnov 50 5N 17 40 E
28 Krobia 51 47N 16 59 E
26 Kročehlavy 50 8N 14 9 E
27 Kroměříz 49 18N 17 21 E
45 Kronobergs □ 56 45N 14 30 E
48 Kronshtadt 60 5N 29 35 E
75 Kroonstad 27 43S 27 19 E
51 Kropotkin 58 50N 115 10 E
28 Krośniewice 52 15N 19 11 E
27 Krosno 49 35N 21 56 E
27 Krosno □ 49 30N 21 40 E
28 Krosno Odrz 52 3N 15 7 E
28 Krotoszyn 51 42N 17 23 E
26 Krsko 45 57N 15 30 E
75 Krugersdorp 26 5S 27 46 E
41 Krumovgrad 41 29N 25 38 E
63 Krung Thep 13 45N 100 35 E
27 Krupinica, R. 48 5N 18 53 E
40 Kruševac 43 35N 21 28 E
44 Krylbo 60 7N 16 15 E
49 Krymskaya 44 57N 37 50 E
28 Krzyz 52 52N 16 0 E
72 Ksar El Boukhari 35 5N 2 52 E
72 Ksar-el-Kebir 35 0N 6 0W
64 Kuala 2 46N 105 47 E
63 Kuala Dungun 4 46N 103 25 E
63 Kuala Kangsar 4 49N 100 57 E
63 Kuala Kubu Baharu 3 35N 101 38 E
63 Kuala Lipis 4 22N 102 5 E
63 Kuala Lumpur 3 9N 101 41 E
63 Kuala Pilah 2 45N 102 14 E
63 Kuala Selangor 3 20N 101 15 E
63 Kuala Terengganu 5 20N 103 8 E
64 Kualakapuas 2 55S 114 20 E
64 Kualakurun 1 10S 113 50 E
64 Kualapembuang 3 14S 112 38 E
64 Kualasimpang 4 16N 98 4 E
63 Kuantan 3 49N 103 20 E
49 Kuba 41 21N 48 22 E
58 Kubak 27 10N 63 10 E
49 Kuban, R. 45 20N 37 30 E
66 Kubokawa 33 12N 133 8 E
67 Kucha 41 50N 82 30 E
60 Kuchaman 27 13N 74 47 E
26 Kuchenspitze, Mt. 47 3N 10 14 E
64 Kuching 1 33N 110 25 E
66 Kuchinotsu 32 36N 130 11 E
64 Kudat 7 0N 116 42 E
65 Kudus 6 48N 110 51 E
73 Kufra, El Wâhât et 24 17N 23 15 E
26 Kufstein 47 35N 12 11 E
26 Kuhnsdorf 46 37N 14 38 E
57 Kūhpāyeh 32 44N 52 20 E
83 Kukerin 33 13S 118 0 E
42 Kukësi □ 42 15N 20 15 E
40 Kula, Bulgaria 43 52N 22 36 E
40 Kula, Yug. 45 37N 19 32 E
61 Kula Kangri, Mt. 28 14N 90 47 E
63 Kulai 1 44N 103 35 E
62 Kulasekharapattanam 8 20N 78 0 E
80 Kulgera 25 50S 133 18 E
83 Kulin 32 40S 118 2 E
83 Kulja 30 35S 117 31 E
50 Kulsary 46 59N 54 1 E
61 Kulti 23 43N 86 50 E
50 Kulunda 52 45N 79 15 E
50 Kulyab 37 55N 69 50 E
67 Kum Darya, R. 41 0N 89 0 E
50 Kum Tekei 43 10N 79 30 E
64 Kumai 2 52S 111 45 E
66 Kumamoto 32 45N 130 45 E
66 Kumamoto □ 32 30N 130 40 E
40 Kumanovo 42 9N 21 42 E
85 Kumara 42 37S 171 12 E
83 Kumari 32 45S 121 30 E
72 Kumasi 6 41N 1 38 E
72 Kumba 4 36N 9 24 E
62 Kumbakonam 10 58N 79 25 E
81 Kumbarilla 27 15S 150 55 E
66 Kumagaya 36 9N 139 22 E
48 Kumertau 52 46N 55 47 E
44 Kumla 59 8N 15 10 E
25 Kummerower See 53 49N 12 52 E
72 Kumo 10 1N 11 12 E
59 Kumon Bum, Mts. 26 0N 97 15 E
62 Kumta 14 29N 74 32 E
57 Kunar □ 35 15N 71 0 E
60 Kunch 26 0N 79 10 E
83 Kundip 33 42S 120 10 E
60 Kundla 21 21N 71 25 E
57 Kunduz 36 50N 68 50 E
57 Kunduz □ 36 50N 68 50 E
45 Kungälv 57 54N 12 0 E
68 Kungchuling 43 31N 124 58 E
67 Kungho 36 28N 100 45 E
50 Kungrad 43 6N 58 54 E
45 Kungsbacka 57 30N 12 7 E
44 Kungsör 59 25N 16 5 E
27 Kunhegyes 47 22N 20 36 E
69 Kunhsien 32 30N 111 17 E
65 Kuningan 6 59S 108 29 E
59 Kunlong 23 20N 98 50 E
52 Kunlun Shan, Mts. 36 0N 82 0 E
67 Kunming 25 11N 102 37 E
62 Kunnamkulam 10 38N 76 7 E
68 Kunsan 35 59N 126 35 E
82 Kununurra 15 40S 128 39 E
80 Kunwarara 22 25S 150 7 E
46 Kuopio 62 53N 27 35 E
46 Kuopio □ 63 25N 27 10 E
65 Kupang 10 19S 123 39 E
92 Kupreanof I. 56 50N 133 30W
40 Kupres 44 1N 17 15 E
49 Kura, R. 39 24N 49 24 E
62 Kurandvad 16 45N 74 39 E
66 Kurashiki 34 40N 133 50 E
66 Kurayoshi 35 26N 133 50 E
62 Kurduvadi 18 8N 75 29 E
41 Kŭrdzhali 41 38N 25 21 E
66 Kure 34 14N 132 32 E
50 Kurgaldzhino 50 35N 70 20 E
50 Kurgan 55 30N 65 0 E
62 Kurichchi 11 36N 77 35 E
51 Kurilskiye Os. 45 0N 150 0 E
66 Kurino 31 57N 130 43 E
62 Kurla 19 5N 72 52 E
62 Kurnool 15 45N 78 0 E
85 Kurow 44 4S 170 29 E
84 Kurri Kurri 32 50S 151 28 E
61 Kurseong 26 56N 88 18 E
48 Kursk 51 42N 36 11 E
40 Kuršumlija 43 9N 21 19 E
66 Kurume 33 15N 130 30 E
62 Kurunegala 7 30N 80 18 E
51 Kurya 61 15N 108 10 E

Kushan Landi Kotal

68 Kushan 39 58N 123 30E
66 Kushikino 31 44N 130 16E
66 Kushima 31 29N 131 14E
66 Kushimoto 33 28N 135 47E
66 Kushiro 43 0N 144 30E
57 Kushk 34 55N 62 30E
50 Kushka 35 20N 62 18E
61 Kushtia 23 55N 89 5E
88 Kuskokwim, R. 60 17N 162 27W
88 Kuskokwim B. 59 45N 162 25W
50 Kustanai 53 20N 63 45E
56 Kutahya 39 25N 29 59E
49 Kutaisi 42 19N 42 40E
64 Kutaraja=Banda Aceh 5 35N 95 20E
60 Kutch, G. of. 22 50N 69 15E
60 Kutch, Rann of, Reg. 24 0N 70 0N
40 Kutina 45 29N 16 48E
60 Kutiyana 21 36N 70 2E
26 Kutná Hora 49 57N 15 16E
28 Kutno 52 15N 19 23E
80 Kuttabul 21 5S 148 48E
73 Kutum 14 20N 24 10E
56 Kuwait ■ 29 30N 47 30E
66 Kuwana 35 0N 136 43E
68 Kuyang 41 8N 110 1E
48 Kuybyshev, Kuyb. Obl. 53 12N 50 9E
48 Kuybyshev, Tatar A.S.S.R. 54 57N 49 5E
50 Kuybyshev, Novosibirsk Obl. 55 27N 78 19E
48 Kuybyshevskoye Vdkhr. 55 2N 49 30E
51 Kuyumba 61 10N 97 10E
48 Kuyto, Oz. 64 40N 31 0E
62 Kuzhithura 8 18N 77 11E
48 Kuznetsk 53 12N 46 40E
48 Kuzomen 66 22N 36 50E
37 Kvarner, G. 44 50N 14 10E
37 Kvarneric 44 43N 14 37E
111 Kwakoegron 5 25N 55 25W
75 Kwando, R. 16 48S 22 45E
69 Kwangan 30 35N 106 40E
69 Kwangchow 23 10N 113 10E
69 Kwangchow Wan, G. 21 0N 111 0E
68 Kwangju 35 10N 126 45E
67 Kwangnan 24 10N 105 0E
69 Kwangsi-Chuang Aut.Dist. □ 23 30N 108 55E
69 Kwangtseh 27 30N 117 25E
69 Kwangtung □ 23 35N 114 0E
69 Kwangyuan 32 30N 105 49E
67 Kwanhsien 30 59N 103 40E
67 Kwantung 25 12N 101 37E
65 Kwatisore 3 7S 139 59E
69 Kwei Kiang, R. 23 30N 110 30E
69 Kweichih 30 40N 117 30E
69 Kweichow= Fengkieh 31 0N 109 33E
69 Kweichow □ 26 40N 107 0E
69 Kweihsien 22 59N 109 44E
69 Kweiki 28 10N 117 8E
69 Kweilin 25 16N 110 15E
69 Kweiping 23 12N 110 0E
69 Kweiting 26 0N 113 35E
69 Kweiyang 25 30N 106 35E
88 Kwiguk Island 62 45N 164 28W
83 Kwinana 32 15S 115 47E
28 Kwisa, R. 51 35N 15 25E
69 Kwo Ho, R. 33 20N 116 50E
65 Kwoka, Mt. 0 31S 132 27E
51 Kyakhta 50 30N 106 25E
81 Kyancutta 33 8S 135 34E
59 Kyaukpadaung 20 52N 95 8E
59 Kyaukpyu 19 28N 93 30E
59 Kyaukse 21 36N 96 10E
75 Kyle Dam 20 14S 31 0E
80 Kynuna 21 35S 141 55E
74 Kyoga, L. 1 35N 33 0E
81 Kyogle 28 40S 153 0E
68 Kyongju 35 59N 129 26E
59 Kyonpyaw 17 12N 95 10E
66 Kyōto 35 0N 135 45E
66 Kyōto □ 35 15N 135 30E
56 Kyrínia 35 20N 33 19E
51 Kystatyam 67 15N 123 0E
51 Kytal Ktakh 65 30N 123 40E
59 Kyunhla 23 25N 95 15E
66 Kyūshū, I. 32 30N 131 0E
66 Kyūshū □ 32 30N 131 0E
40 Kyustendil 42 25N 22 41E
51 Kyusyur 70 30N 127 0E
51 Kyzyl 51 50N 94 30E
50 Kzyl Orda 44 50N 65 10E

L

32 La Alcarria 40 31N 2 45W
32 La Almarcha 39 41N 2 24W
32 La Almunia de Doña Godino 41 29N 1 23W
110 La Asunción 11 2N 63 53W
108 La Banda 27 45S 64 10W
30 La Bañeza 42 17N 5 54W
104 La Barca 20 20N 102 40W
19 La Bassée 50 31N 2 49E
20 La Bastide-Puylaurent 44 35N 3 55E
18 La Baule 47 18N 2 23E
32 La Bisbal 41 58N 3 2E
110 La Blanquilla, I. 11 51N 64 37W
104 La Boca 9 0N 79 30E
19 La Bresse 48 0N 6 53E
30 La Bureba 42 36N 3 24W
108 La Calera 32 50S 71 10W
31 La Campiña 37 45N 4 45W
19 La Capelle 49 59N 3 50E
108 La Carlota 33 30S 63 20W
31 La Carolina 38 17N 3 38W
105 La Ceiba, Honduras 15 40N 86 50W
110 La Ceiba, Ven. 9 30N 71 0W
19 La Chapelle-d'Angillon 47 21N 2 25E
18 La Chapelle Glain 47 38N 1 11W
20 La Charité-sur-Loire 47 10N 3 0E
20 La Châtre 46 35N 1 59E
25 La Chaux-de-Fonds 47 7N 6 50E
21 La Ciotat 43 12N 5 36E
30 La Coruña 43 20N 8 25W
30 La Coruña □ 43 10N 8 30W
100 La Crosse 43 48N 91 13W
110 La Dorada 5 30N 74 40W
30 La Estrada 42 43N 8 27W
98 La Fayette 40 22N 86 52W
19 La Fere 49 40N 3 20E
19 La Ferté 48 57N 3 6E
18 La Ferté-Bernard 48 10N 0 40E
18 La Ferté-Mace 48 35N 0 21W
18 La Flèche 47 42N 0 5W
99 La Folette 36 23N 84 9W
30 La Fregeneda 40 58N 6 54W
30 La Fuente de S. Esteban 40 49N 6 15W
33 La Gineta 39 8N 2 1W
21 La Grand' Comb 44 13N 4 2E
102 La Grande 45 15N 118 0W
21 La Grande-Motte 48 35N 1 4E
99 La Grange 33 4N 85 0W
110 La Guaira 10 36N 66 56W
30 La Guardia 41 56N 8 52W
20 La Guerche-sur-l'Aubois 46 58N 2 56E
105 La Mabana 23 8N 82 22W
18 La Haye du Puits 49 17N 1 33W
32 La Junquera 42 25N 2 53E
101 La Junta 38 0N 103 30W
108 La Ligua 32 30S 71 16W
31 La Linea de la Concepción 36 15N 5 23W
93 La Loche 56 29N 109 27W
30 La Lora 42 45N 4 0W
16 La Louvière 50 27N 4 10E
20 La Machine 46 54N 3 27E
38 La Maddalena 41 13N 9 25E
91 La Malbaie 47 40N 70 10W
33 La Mancha 39 10N 2 54W
30 La Mariña 43 30N 7 40W
88 La Martre, L. 63 0N 118 0W
103 La Mesa 32 48N 117 5W
32 La Muela 41 36N 1 7W
21 La Mure 44 55N 5 48E
21 La Napoule 43 31N 6 56E
110 La Orchila, I. 12 30N 67 0W
110 La Oroya 11 32S 75 54W
20 La Pacaudière 46 10N 3 50E
31 La Palma 37 21N 6 38W
105 La Palma 8 15N 78 0W
72 La Palma, I. 28 40N 17 52W
108 La Pampa □ 37 0S 66 0W
110 La Paragua 6 50N 63 20W
108 La Paz, Arg. 30 50S 59 45W
110 La Paz, Bolivia 16 20S 68 10W
104 La Paz, Mexico 24 10N 110 20W
110 La Pedrera 1 18S 69 43W
66 La Perouse, Str. 45 40N 142 0E
104 La Piedad 20 20N 102 1W
102 La Pine 40 53N 80 45W
108 La Plata 35 0S 57 55W
30 La Pola de Gordón 42 51N 5 41W
98 La Porte 41 40N 86 40W
31 La Puebla de Cazalla 37 14N 5 19W
30 La Puebla de Montalbán 39 52N 4 22W
33 La Puerta 38 22N 2 45W
108 La Quiaca 22 5S 65 35W
90 La Reine 48 50N 79 30W
20 La Réole 44 35N 0 1W
108 La Rioja, Arg. 29 20S 67 0W
32 La Rioja, Sp. 42 20N 2 20W
108 La Rioja □ 29 20S 67 0W
21 La Roche 46 4N 6 19E
18 La Roche Bernard 47 32N 2 18W
20 La Roche-sur-Yon 46 40N 1 25W
20 La Rochefoucauld 45 44N 0 24E
20 La Rochelle 46 10N 1 9W
33 La Roda 39 13N 2 15W
105 La Romana 18 27N 68 57W
33 La Sagra, Mt. 38 0N 2 35W
100 La Salle 41 20N 89 5W
30 La Sanabria 42 0N 6 30W
90 La Sarre 48 45N 79 15W
32 La Selva 42 0N 2 45E
108 La Serena, Chile 29 55S 71 10W
31 La Serena, Sp. 38 45N 5 40W
21 La Seyne-sur-Mer 43 7N 5 52E
39 La Sila, Mt. 39 15N 16 35E
31 La Solana 38 59N 3 14W
20 La Souterraine 46 15N 1 30E
36 La Spézia 44 8N 9 50E
18 La Suze 47 54N 0 2E
110 La Tagua 0 3N 74 40W
20 La Teste 44 34N 1 9W
110 La Tortuga, I. 10 56N 65 20W
21 La-Tour-du-Pin 45 34N 5 27E
20 La Tranche 46 20N 1 26W
90 La Tuque 47 30N 72 50W
112 La Unión, Chile 40 10S 73 0W
104 La Union, Salvador 13 20N 87 50W
33 La Unión, Sp. 37 38N 0 53W
110 La Urbana 7 8N 66 56W
105 La Vega 19 20N 70 30W
110 La Vela 11 30N 69 30W
90 La Verendrye Prov. Park 47 15N 77 10W
110 La Victoria 10 14N 67 20W
72 Labé 11 24N 12 16W
63 Labis 2 22N 103 2E
20 Labouheyre 44 13N 0 55W
108 Laboulaye 34 10S 63 30W
86 Labrador, Reg. 53 20N 61 0W
91 Labrador City 52 42N 67 0W
20 Labrède 44 41N 0 32W
65 Labuha 0 30S 127 30E
65 Labuhan 6 26S 105 50E
92 Lac la Biche 54 45N 111 50W
93 Lac Seul 50 28N 92 0W
20 Lacanau 44 59N 1 5W
20 Lacanau, Étang de 44 58N 1 7W
20 Lacaune, Mts. de 43 43N 2 50E
53 Laccadive Is. 10 0N 72 30E
90 Lachine 45 30N 73 40W
84 Lachlan, R. 34 21S 143 57E
90 Lachute 45 39N 74 21W
96 Lackawanna 42 49N 78 50W
92 Lacombe 52 30N 113 50W
38 Laconi 39 54N 9 4E
97 Laconia 43 32N 71 30W
20 Lacq 43 25N 0 35W
58 Ladakh Ra. 34 0N 78 0E
43 Ládhon, R. 37 40N 21 50E
57 Lādiz 28 55N 61 15E
60 Ladnun 27 38N 74 25E
48 Ladozhskoye, Oz. 61 15N 30 30E
75 Lady Grey 30 43S 27 13E
92 Ladysmith, Canada 49 0N 124 0W
75 Ladysmith, S. Africa 28 32S 29 46E
76 Lae 6 40S 147 2E
45 Laesø, I. 57 15N 10 53E
101 Lafayette 30 18N 92 0W
72 Lafia 8 30N 8 34E
90 Laforest 47 4N 81 12W
45 Lagan, R. 56 33N 12 56E
30 Lage, Sp. 43 13N 9 0W
24 Lage, W. Germany 52 0N 8 47E
44 Lågen, R. 61 8N 10 25E
57 Laghman □ 34 20N 70 0E
72 Laghouat 33 50N 2 59E
31 Lagōa 37 8N 8 27W
30 Lagoaça 41 11N 6 44W
39 Lagónegro 40 8N 15 45E
65 Lagonoy G. 13 50N 123 50E
72 Lagos, Nigeria 6 25N 3 27E
31 Lagos, Port. 37 5N 8 41W
104 Lagos de Moreno 21 21N 101 55W
82 Lagrange 14 13S 125 46E
32 Laguardia 42 33N 2 35W
20 Laguépie 44 8N 1 57E
109 Laguna 28 30S 48 50E
103 Laguna Beach 33 31N 117 52W
68 Laha 48 9N 124 30E
65 Lahad Datu 5 0N 118 30E
94 Lahaina 20 52N 156 41W
64 Lahat 3 45S 103 30E
56 Lahijan 37 12N 50 1E
60 Lahore 31 32N 74 22E
60 Lahore □ 31 55N 74 5E
25 Lahr 48 20N 7 52E
68 Laichow Wan, G. 37 30N 119 30E
81 Laidley 27 39S 152 20E
18 L'Aigle 48 45N 0 38E
56 Laila 22 10N 46 40E
69 Laipin 23 42N 109 16E
24 Lairg 58 1N 4 24W
64 Lais 3 35S 102 0E
68 Laiyang 36 58N 120 41E
109 Lajes 27 48S 50 20W
40 Lajkovac 44 27N 20 14E
27 Lajosmizse 47 3N 19 32E
101 Lake Charles 31 10N 93 10W
99 Lake City, Fla. 30 10N 82 40W
99 Lake City, S.C. 33 51N 79 44W
97 Lake George 43 25N 73 36W
83 Lake Grace 33 7S 118 28E
89 Lake Harbour 62 30N 69 50W
103 Lake Havasu City 34 25N 114 20W
83 Lake King 33 5S 119 45E
103 Lake Mead Nat. Rec. Area 36 20N 114 30W
80 Lake Nash 20 57S 138 0E
90 Lake Superior Prov. Park 47 45N 85 0W
90 Lake Traverse 45 56N 78 4W
99 Lake Worth 26 36N 80 3W
90 Lakefield 44 25N 78 16W
99 Lakeland 28 0N 82 0W
102 Lakeport 39 1N 122 56W
84 Lakes Entrance 37 50S 148 0E
102 Lakeview 34 12N 109 59W
97 Lakewood, N.J. 40 5N 74 13W
96 Lakewood, Ohio 41 28N 81 50W
61 Lakhimpur 27 14N 94 7E
60 Lakki 32 38N 70 50E
43 Lakonía □ 36 55N 22 30E
43 Lakonikós Kól. 36 40N 22 40E
46 Lakselv 70 2N 24 56E
61 Lakshmi Kantapur 22 5N 88 20E
59 Lala Ghat 24 30N 92 40E
60 Lala Musa 32 40N 73 57E
68 Lalin 45 14N 126 52E
20 Lalinde 44 50N 0 44E
61 Lalitapur 27 42N 85 12E
60 Lalitpur 24 42N 78 28E
59 Lamaing 15 25N 97 53E
26 Lambach 48 6N 13 51E
18 Lamballe 48 29N 2 31W
74 Lambaréné 0 20S 10 12E
63 Lambi Kyun, I. 10 50N 98 20E
43 Lámbia 37 52N 21 53E
72 Lame 10 27N 9 12E
30 Lamego 41 5N 7 52W
81 Lameroo 35 19S 140 33E
101 Lamesa 32 45N 101 57W
43 Lamía 38 55N 22 41E
65 Lamitan 6 40N 122 10E
14 Lammermuir Hills 55 50N 24 0W
65 Lamon B. 14 30N 122 20E
63 Lampang 18 18N 99 31E
18 Lampaul 48 28N 5 7W
73 Lampedusa, I. 35 36N 12 40E
13 Lampeter 52 6N 4 6W
93 Lampman 49 25N 102 50W
26 Lamprechtshavsen 48 0N 12 58E
64 Lampung □ 5 30S 105 0E
74 Lamu 2 10S 40 55E
14 Lanark 55 40N 3 48W
12 Lancashire □ 53 40N 2 30W
91 Lancaster, Canada 45 17N 66 10W
12 Lancaster, U.K. 54 3N 2 48W
103 Lancaster, Calif. 34 47N 118 8W
98 Lancaster, Ky. 37 40N 84 40W
96 Lancaster, N.Y. 42 53N 78 43W
97 Lancaster, Pa. 40 4N 76 19W
99 Lancaster, S.C. 34 45N 80 47W
89 Lancaster Sd. 74 0N 84 0W
69 Lanchi 29 11N 119 30E
68 Lanchow 36 4N 103 44E
37 Lanciano 42 15N 14 22E
25 Landau 49 12N 8 7E
26 Landeck 47 9N 10 34E
102 Lander 42 50N 108 49W
18 Landerneau 48 28N 4 17W
20 Landes □ 43 57N 0 48W
20 Landes, Reg. 44 0N 1 5W
58 Landi Kotal 34 7N 71 6E

Louis Trichardt Maiduguri

75 Louis Trichardt ... 23 0s 25 55 E
91 Louisbourg 45 55N 60 0w
90 Louiseville 46 20N 73 0w
76 Louisiade Arch. ... 11 10s 153 0 E
101 Louisiana □ 30 50N 92 0w
98 Louisville, Ky. 38 15N 85 45w
101 Louisville, Miss. ... 33 7N 89 3w
20 Loulay 46 3N 0 30w
31 Loulé 37 9N 8 0w
26 Louny .... 50 20N 13 48 E
100 Loup City .... 41 19N 98 57 E
20 Lourdes 43 6N 0 3w
75 Lourenço Marques= Maputo .... 25 58s 32 32 E
31 Lourinha 39 14N 9 17w
30 Lousã 40 7N 8 14w
81 Louth, Australia .. 30 30s 145 8 E
15 Louth, Eire 53 47N 6 33w
12 Louth, U.K. 53 23N 0 0
15 Louth □ 53 55N 6 30w
43 Loutra-Aidhipsoú . 38 54N 23 2 E
18 Louviers .... 49 12N 1 10 E
93 Love 53 29N 104 9w
41 Lovech .... 43 8N 24 43 E
100 Loveland 40 27N 105 4w
102 Lovelock 40 17N 118 25w
30 Lovios .... 41 55 E 8 4w
47 Lovisa .... 60 28N 26 12 E
26 Lovosice .... 50 30N 14 2 E
37 Lovran .... 45 18N 14 15 E
40 Lovrin .... 45 58N 20 48 E
97 Lowell 42 38N 71 19w
85 Lower Hutt ...... 41 10s 174 55 E
13 Lowestoft .... 52 29N 1 44 E
28 Łowicz .... 52 6N 19 55 E
97 Lowville 43 48N 75 30w
81 Loxton .... 34 28s 140 31 E
76 Loyalty Is .... 21 0s 167 30 E
69 Loyang .... 34 41N 112 28 E
69 Loyung .... 24 25N 109 25 E
20 Lozère □ .... 44 35N 3 30 E
40 Loznica .... 44 32N 19 14 E
68 Lu-ta .... 39 0N 121 31 E
74 Lualaba, R. ...... 0 26N 25 20 E
74 Luanda .... 8 58s 13 9 E
63 Luang Prabang ... 19 45N 102 10 E
75 Luangwa, R. ..... 15 40N 30 25 E
75 Luanshya .... 13 3s 28 28 E
30 Luarca 43 32N 6 32w
28 Lubań .... 51 5N 15 15 E
65 Lubang Is. .... 13 50N 120 12 E
28 Lubartów .... 51 28N 22 42 E
54 Lubban .... 32 9N 35 14 E
24 Lübben .... 51 56N 13 54 E
101 Lubbock 33 40N 102 0w
24 Lübeck .... 53 52N 10 41 E
74 Lubefu .... 4 47s 24 27 E
28 Lubin .... 51 24N 16 11 E
28 Lublin .... 51 12N 22 38 E
28 Lublin □ .... 51 5N 22 30 E
27 Lubliniec .... 50 43N 18 45 E
56 Lubnān, Mts. ..... 34 0N 36 0 E
28 Lubon .... 52 21N 16 51 E
28 Lubsko .... 51 45N 14 57 E
64 Lubuklinggau ..... 3 15s 102 55 E
64 Lubuksikaping .... 0 10N 100 15 E
75 Lubumbashi ...... 11 32s 27 28 E
74 Lubutu .... 0 45s 26 30 E
88 Lucania, Mt. 60 48N 141 25w
36 Lucca .... 43 50N 10 30 E
14 Luce B. 54 45N 4 48w
65 Lucena, Philippines 13 56N 121 37 E
31 Lucena, Sp. 37 27N 4 31w
32 Lucena del Cid 40 9N 0 17w
27 Lučenec .... 48 18N 19 42 E
39 Lucera .... 41 30N 15 20 E
33 Luchena, R. 37 44N 1 50w
24 Lüchow .... 52 58N 11 8 E
69 Luchow .... 29 2N 105 10 E
24 Luckenwalde ..... 52 5N 13 11 E
61 Lucknow .... 26 50N 81 0 E
20 Luçon 46 28N 1 10w
37 Ludbreg .... 46 15N 16 38 E
24 Lüdenscheid ...... 51 13N 7 37 E
75 Lüderitz .... 26 41s 15 8 E
60 Ludhiana .... 30 57N 75 56 E
98 Ludington 43 58N 86 27w
13 Ludlow 52 23N 2 42w
41 Ludus .... 46 29N 24 5 E
44 Ludvika .... 60 8N 15 14 E
25 Ludwigsburg ...... 48 53N 9 11 E
25 Ludwigshafen ..... 49 27N 8 27 E
24 Ludwigslust ...... 53 19N 11 28 E
101 Lufkin 31 25N 94 40w
48 Luga .... 58 40N 29 55 E
25 Lugano .... 46 0N 8 57 E
25 Lugano, L. di ..... 46 0N 9 0 E
49 Lugansk= Voroshilovgrad .. 48 35N 39 29 E
55 Lugh Ganana ..... 3 48N 42 40 E
30 Lugo, Sp. 43 2N 7 35w
37 Lugo, It. .... 44 25N 11 53 E
30 Lugo □ 43 0N 7 30w
40 Lugoj .... 45 42N 21 57 E
30 Lugones 43 26N 5 50w
50 Lugovoy .... 43 0N 72 20 E
36 Luino .... 46 0N 8 24 E
111 Luis Correia 3 0s 41 35w
108 Luján 34 45s 59 5w
69 Lukang .... 24 0N 120 19 E
61 Lukhisarai .... 27 11N 86 5 E
41 Lukovit .... 43 13N 24 11 E
28 Łuków .... 51 56N 22 23 E
75 Lukulu .... 14 35s 23 25 E
46 Luleå .... 65 35N 22 10 E
74 Lulonga, R. .... 0 43N 18 23 E
74 Lulua, R. .... 5 2s 21 7 E
74 Luluabourg= Kananga .... 5 55s 22 18 E
99 Lumberton 34 37N 78 59w
85 Lumsden .... 45 44s 168 27 E
68 Lun .... 47 55N 105 1 E
60 Lunavada .... 23 8N 73 37 E
45 Lund .... 55 41N 13 12 E
75 Lundazi .... 12 20s 33 7 E
13 Lundy, I. 51 10N 4 41w
12 Lune, R. 54 2N 2 50w
24 Lüneburg .... 53 15N 10 23 E
24 Lüneburger Heide, Reg. .... 53 0N 10 0 E
21 Lunel .... 43 39N 7 31 E
24 Lunen .... 51 36N 7 31 E
91 Lunenburg 44 22N 64 18w
19 Lunéville .... 48 36N 6 30 E
68 Lunghwa .... 41 15N 117 51 E
68 Lungkiang .... 47 22N 123 4 E
68 Lungkow .... 37 40N 120 25 E
59 Lungleh .... 22 55N 92 45 E
68 Lungsi .... 35 0N 104 35 E
60 Luni, R. .... 24 40N 71 15 E
74 Luofu .... 0 1s 29 15 E
41 Lupeni .... 45 21N 23 13 E
108 Luque 37 35N 4 16w
19 Lure .... 47 40N 6 30 E
15 Lurgan 54 28N 6 20w
75 Lusaka .... 15 28s 28 16 E
42 Lushnja .... 40 55N 19 41 E
74 Lushoto .... 4 47s 38 20 E
68 Lushun .... 38 48N 121 16 E
75 Luso .... 11 47s 19 52 E
20 Lussac-les-Châteaux .... 46 24N 0 43 E
13 Luton 51 53N 0 24w
64 Lutong .... 4 30N 114 0 E
48 Lutsk .... 50 50N 25 15 E
5 Lütsow Holnbukta, B. .... 69 0s 38 0 E
16 Luxembourg ...... 49 37N 6 9 E
16 Luxembourg ■ .... 50 0N 6 0 E
16 Luxembourg □ .... 49 58N 5 30 E
19 Luxeuil-les-Bains .. 47 49N 6 24 E
73 Luxor=El Uqsur .. 25 41N 32 38 E
20 Luy, R. 43 39N 1 8w
48 Luza .... 60 39N 47 10 E
25 Luzern .... 47 3N 8 18 E
25 Luzern □ .... 47 2N 7 55 E
111 Luziania 16 20s 48 0w
65 Luzon, I. .... 16 0N 121 0 E
20 Luzy .... 46 47N 3 58 E
49 Lvov .... 49 40N 24 0 E
68 Lwanhsien .... 39 45N 118 45 E
28 Lwówek Śl .... 51 7N 15 38 E
51 Lyakhovskiye Os. . 73 40N 141 0 E
60 Lyallpur .... 31 30N 73 5 E
41 Lyaskovets .... 43 6N 25 44 E
14 Lybster 58 18N 3 16w
45 Lyckeby .... 56 12N 15 37 E
46 Lycksele .... 64 38N 18 40 E
54 Lydda=Lod ...... 31 57N 34 54 E
75 Lydenburg .... 25 10s 30 29 E
85 Lyell .... 41 48s 172 4 E
85 Lyell, Ra. .... 41 38s 172 20 E
13 Lyme Regis 50 44N 2 57w
13 Lymington 50 46N 1 32w
98 Lynchburg 37 23N 79 10w
84 Lyndhurst, N.S.W. . 33 41N 149 2 E
80 Lyndhurst, Queens. 18 56s 144 30 E
97 Lyndonville 44 32N 72 1w
97 Lynn 42 28N 70 57w
93 Lynn Lake 56 51N 101 3w
13 Lynton 51 14N 3 50w
21 Lyon .... 45 46N 4 50 E
21 Lyonnais, Reg. .... 45 45N 4 15 E
83 Lyons, R. 25 2N 115 9w
97 Lyons Falls 43 37N 75 22w
26 Lysá .... 50 11N 14 51 E
45 Lysekil .... 58 17N 11 26 E
48 Lysra .... 57 7N 57 47 E
12 Lytham St. Annes 53 45N 2 58w
85 Lyttelton .... 43 35s 172 44 E
41 Lyubimets .... 41 50N 26 5 E

M

54 Ma'ad .... 32 37N 35 36 E
69 Maanshan .... 31 40N 118 30 E
16 Maas, R. .... 51 49N 5 1 E
16 Maastricht .... 50 50N 5 40 E
12 Mablethorpe ...... 53 21N 0 14 E
109 Macaé 20 20s 41 55w
101 McAllen 26 12N 98 15w
101 McAlester 34 57N 95 40w
111 Macapá 0 5N 51 10w
80 McArthur, R. ..... 15 54s 136 40 E
111 Macau 5 0s 36 40w
69 Macau ■ .... 22 16N 113 35 E
92 McBride 53 20N 120 10w
102 McCammon 42 41N 112 11w
12 Macclesfield 53 16N 2 9w
93 McClintock 57 45N 94 15w
88 M'Clintock Chan. . 71 0N 103 0w
101 McComb 31 20N 90 30w
100 McCook 40 15N 100 35w
3 McDonald I. ...... 54 0s 73 0 E
82 Macdonnell, Ras. .. 23 40s 133 0 E
81 McDouall Peak ... 29 51s 134 55 E
88 Macdougall, L. 66 20N 98 30w
14 Macduff 57 40N 2 30w
90 Mace 48 55N 80 0w
30 Maceda 42 16N 7 39w
30 Macedo de Cavaleiros 41 31N 6 57w
111 Maceió 9 40s 35 41w
72 Macenta 8 35N 9 20w
37 Macerata .... 43 19N 13 28 E
102 McGill 35 27N 114 50w
15 Macgillycuddy's Reeks, Mts. 52 2N 9 45w
108 Machagai 26 56s 60 2w
74 Machakos .... 1 30s 37 15 E
110 Machala 3 10s 79 50w
51 Machefna .... 61 20N 172 20 E
30 Machichaco, C. ... 43 28N 2 47w
110 Machiques 10 4N 72 34w
13 Machynlleth 52 36N 3 51w
72 Macias Nguema Biyoga, I. ...... 3 30N 8 40 E
81 Macintyre, R. ..... 28 38s 150 47 E
30 Macizo Galaico ... 42 30N 7 30w
80 Mackay, Australia . 21 36s 148 39 E
102 Mackay, U.S.A. ... 43 58N 113 37w
82 Mackay, L. .... 22 40s 128 35 E
96 McKees Rocks 40 27N 80 3w
96 McKeesport 40 21N 79 50w
92 Mackenzie 55 20N 123 5w
88 Mackenzie, Reg. .. 61 30N 144 30w
88 Mackenzie, R. ... 69 15N 134 8w
110 Mackenzie City ... 6 0N 58 10w
88 Mackenzie Mts. ... 64 0N 130 0w
80 McKinlay .... 21 16s 141 17 E
88 McKinley, Mt. 63 10N 151 0w
4 McKinley Sea 84 0N 10 0w
101 McKinney 33 10N 96 40w
93 Macklin 52 20N 109 56w
81 Macksville .... 30 40s 152 56 E
81 Maclean .... 29 26s 153 16 E
75 Maclear .... 31 2s 28 23 E
81 Macleay, R. ...... 30 52s 153 1 E
92 McLennan 55 42N 116 50w
83 McLeod, L. ...... 24 9s 113 47 E
92 McLure 50 55N 120 20w
86 M'Clure Str. 74 40N 117 30w
102 McMinnville, Oreg. 45 16N 123 11w
99 McMinnville, Tenn. 35 43N 85 45w
93 McMurray 56 45N 111 27w
103 McNary 34 4N 109 53w
100 Macomb 40 25N 90 40w
38 Macomer .... 40 16N 8 48 E
21 Mâcon .... 46 19N 4 50 E
99 Macon 32 50N 83 37w
100 McPherson 38 25N 97 40w
76 Macquarie Is. ..... 54 36s 158 55 E
84 Macquarie, R. .... 30 7s 147 24 E
5 Mac Robertson Coast .... 68 30s 63 0 E
15 Macroom 51 54N 8 57w
56 Madā'in Sālih .... 26 51N 37 58 E
75 Madagascar ■ .... 20 0s 47 0 E
73 Madama .... 22 0N 14 0 E
62 Madanapalle ..... 13 33N 78 34 E
76 Madane .... 5 0s 145 46 E
61 Madaripur .... 23 2N 90 15 E
59 Madauk .... 17 56N 96 52 E
96 Madawaska 45 30N 77 55w
59 Madaya .... 22 20N 96 10 E
38 Maddalena, I. ..... 41 15N 9 23 E
39 Maddaloni .... 41 4N 14 23 E
104 Madden L. 9 20N 79 37w
72 Madeira, I. 32 50N 17 0w
110 Madeira, R. 3 22s 58 45w
103 Madera 37 0N 120 1w
61 Madhupur .... 24 18N 86 37 E
60 Madhya Pradesh □ 21 50N 81 0 E
55 Madinat al Shaab .... 12 50N 45 0 E
74 Madingou .... 4 10s 13 33 E
98 Madison, Ind. 38 42N 85 20w
100 Madison, S.D. 44 0N 97 8w
100 Madison, Wis. 43 5N 89 25w
98 Madisonville 37 42N 86 30w
65 Madiun .... 7 38s 111 32 E
62 Madras, India ..... 13 8N 80 19 E
102 Madras, U.S.A. ... 44 40N 121 10w
104 Madre, Laguna ... 25 0N 97 30w
110 Madre de Dios, R. 10 59s 66 8w
112 Madre de Dios, I. 50 20s 75 10w
104 Madre del Sur, Sa. 17 30N 100 0w
104 Madre Occidental, Sa. 27 0N 107 0w
104 Madre Oriental, Sa. 25 0N 100 0w
30 Madrid 40 25N 3 45w
30 Madrid □ 40 30N 3 45w
31 Madridejos 39 28N 3 33w
31 Madrona, Sa. 38 27N 4 16w
31 Madroñera 39 26N 5 42w
65 Madura, I. .... 7 0N 113 20 E
65 Madura, Selat .... 7 30s 113 20 E
83 Madura Motel .... 31 55s 127 0 E
62 Madurai .... 9 55N 78 10 E
62 Madurantakam ... 12 30N 79 50 E
66 Maebashi .... 36 23N 139 4 E
41 Măeruş .... 45 53N 25 31 E
13 Maesteg 51 36N 3 40w
105 Maestra, Sa. 20 15N 77 0w
32 Maestrazgo, Mts. de 40 30N 0 25w
75 Maevatanana ..... 16 56s 46 49 E
93 Mafeking, Canada . 52 40N 101 10w
75 Mafeking, S.Africa 25 50s 25 38 E
74 Mafia I. .... 7 45s 39 50 E
109 Mafra 36 10N 50 0w
51 Magadan .... 59 30N 151 0 E
74 Magadi .... 1 54s 36 19 E
112 Magallanes, Estrecho de, Str. 52 30s 75 0w
110 Magangue 9 14N 74 45w
91 Magdalen Is. 47 30N 61 40w
104 Magdalena, Mexico 30 50N 112 0w
103 Magdalena, U.S.A. 34 10N 107 20w
112 Magdalena, I., Chile 44 42s 73 10w
104 Magdalena, I., Mexico 24 40N 112 15w
24 Magdeburg ...... 52 8N 11 36 E
24 Magdeburg □ .... 52 20N 11 40 E
54 Magdi'el .... 32 10N 34 54 E
15 Magee, I. 54 48N 5 44w
65 Magelang .... 7 29s 110 13 E
36 Maggiorasca, Mt. .. 44 33N 9 29 E
36 Maggiore, L. ...... 46 0N 8 35 E
54 Maghar .... 32 54N 35 24 E
15 Magherafelt 54 45N 6 36w
15 Magherafelt □ 54 45N 6 36w
37 Magione .... 43 10N 12 12 E
39 Máglie .... 40 8N 18 17 E
43 Magnisía □ ...... 39 24N 22 46 E
50 Magnitogorsk ..... 53 20N 59 0 E
101 Magnolia 33 18N 93 12w
91 Magog 45 18N 72 9w
92 Magrath 49 25N 112 50w
33 Magro, R. 39 11N 0 25w
111 Maguarinho, C. ... 0 15s 48 30w
59 Magwe .... 20 10N 95 0 E
56 Mahābād .... 36 50N 45 45 E
61 Mahabharat Lekh, Mts. .... 28 30N 82 0 E
62 Mahad .... 18 6N 73 29 E
55 Mahaddei Uen .... 3 0N 45 32 E
60 Mahadeo Hills .... 22 20N 78 30 E
75 Mahalapye .... 23 1s 26 51 E
57 Mahallāt .... 33 55N 50 30 E
61 Mahanadi, R. ..... 20 0N 86 25 E
61 Mahananda, R. ... 24 29N 88 18 E
97 Mahanoy City 40 48N 76 10w
60 Maharashtra □ ... 19 30N 75 30 E
62 Mahboobabad .... 17 42N 80 2 E
62 Mahbubnagar ..... 16 45N 77 59 E
73 Mahdia .... 35 28N 11 0 E
62 Mahé .... 11 42N 75 34 E
85 Maheno .... 45 10s 170 50 E
85 Mahia Pen. .... 39 9s 177 55 E
61 Mahoba .... 25 15N 79 55 E
32 Mahón .... 39 50N 4 18 E
91 Mahone Bay 44 27N 64 23w
60 Mahuva .... 25 7N 71 46 E
74 Mai-Ndombe, L. .. 2 0s 18 0 E
13 Maidenhead 51 31N 0 42w
93 Maidstone, Canada 53 5N 109 20w
13 Maidstone, U.K. .. 51 16N 0 31 E
73 Maiduguri .... 12 0N 13 20 E

Martapura, Sumatera | Metropolis

64 Martapura, Sumatera 4 19s 104 22 E
73 Marte 12 23N 13 46 E
33 Martes, Sa. 39 20N 1 0W
81 Marthaguy Creek 30 16s 147 35 E
97 Marha's Vineyard 41 25N 70 35W
25 Martigny 46 6N 7 3 E
21 Martigues 43 24N 5 4 E
27 Martin 49 6N 18 48 E
32 Martín, R. 41 18N 0 19W
7 Martin Vaz, I. 20 30s 28 15W
39 Martina Franca 40 42N 17 20 E
105 Martinique, I. 14 40N 61 0W
105 Martinique Pass. 15 15N 61 0W
109 Martinópolis 22 11s 51 12W
96 Martins Ferry 40 5N 80 46W
26 Martinsberg 48 22N 15 9 E
98 Martinsburg 39 30N 77 57W
98 Martinsville, Ind. 39 29N 86 23W
99 Martinsville, Va. 36 41N 79 52W
85 Marton 40 4s 175 23 E
31 Martos 37 44N 3 58W
66 Marugame 34 15N 133 55 E
84 Marulan 34 43s 150 3 E
20 Marvejols 44 33N 3 19 E
60 Marwar 25 43N 73 45 E
50 Mary 37 40N 61 50 E
80 Mary Kathleen 20 35s 139 48 E
89 Mary River 70 30N 78 0W
81 Maryborough, Queens. 25 31s 152 37 E
84 Maryborough, Vic. 37 0s 143 44 E
98 Maryland □ 39 10N 76 40W
12 Maryport 54 43N 3 30W
91 Marystown 47 10N 55 10W
103 Marysvale 38 25N 112 17W
102 Marysville 39 14N 121 40W
99 Maryville 35 50N 84 0W
73 Marzūq 25 53N 14 10 E
72 Mascara 35 26N 0 6 E
57 Mashhad 36 20N 59 35 E
32 Masnou 41 28N 2 20 E
92 Masset 54 0N 132 0W
57 Masqat 23 37N 58 36 E
56 Mastura 23 7N 38 52 E
62 Masulipatnam 16 12N 81 12 E
74 Masaka 0 21s 31 45 E
65 Masamba 2 30s 120 15 E
68 Masan 35 11N 128 32 E
33 Masanasa 39 25N 0 25W
57 Masandam, Ras. 26 30N 56 30 E
74 Masasi 10 45s 38 52 E
105 Masaya 12 0N 86 7W
65 Masbate 12 20N 123 30 E
65 Masbate, I. 12 20N 123 30 E
75 Maseru 29 18s 27 30 E
90 Mashkode 47 2N 84 7W
74 Masindi 1 40N 41 43 E
56 Masjed Soleyman 31 55N 49 25 E
15 Mask, L. 53 36N 9 24W
100 Mason City 48 0N 119 0W
36 Massa 44 2N 10 7 E
36 Massa Maríttima 43 3N 10 52 E
97 Massachusetts □ 42 25N 72 0W
97 Massachusetts B. 42 30N 70 0W
39 Massafra 40 35N 17 8 E
36 Massarossa 43 53N 10 17 E
73 Massawa=Mitsiwa 15 35N 39 25 E
97 Massena 44 52N 74 55W
20 Massiac 45 15N 3 11 E
20 Massif Central Reg. 45 30N 2 21 E
96 Massillon 40 47N 81 30W
85 Masterton 40 56s 175 39 E
43 Mástikho, Ákra 38 10N 26 2 E
66 Masuda 34 40N 131 51 E
65 Mataboor 1 41s 138 3 E
31 Matachel, R. 38 50N 6 17W
90 Matachewan 47 50N 80 55W
66 Matad 47 12N 115 29 E
74 Matadi 5 52s 13 31 E
105 Matagalpa 13 10N 85 40W
90 Matagami 49 45N 77 34W
62 Matale 7 30N 80 44 E
104 Matamoros 18 2N 98 17W
91 Matane 48 50N 67 33W
88 Matanuska 61 38N 149 0W
105 Matanzas 23 0N 81 40W
62 Matara 5 58N 80 30 E
64 Mataram 8 41s 116 10 E
82 Mataranka 14 55s 133 4 E
32 Mataró 41 32N 2 29 E
32 Matarraña, R. 41 14N 0 22 E
85 Mataura 46 11s 168 51 E
104 Matehuala 23 40N 100 50W
37 Matélica 43 15N 13 0 E
39 Matera 40 40N 16 37 E
27 Mátészalka 47 58N 22 20 E
60 Mathura 27 30W 77 48 E
28 Matkinia Grn 52 42N 22 2 E
12 Matlock 53 8N 1 32W
72 Matmata 33 30N 9 59 E
111 Mato Grosso □ 14 0s 54 0W
70 Matopo 20 36s 28 20 E
30 Matosinhos 41 11N 8 42W
57 Matrah 23 37N 58 30 E
73 Matrûh 31 19N 27 9 E
69 Matsu, I. 26 9N 119 56 E
66 Matsue 35 25N 133 10 E
66 Matsumoto 36 15N 138 0 E
66 Matsusaka 34 34N 136 32 E
66 Matsuyama 33 45N 132 45 E
62 Mattancheri 9 50N 76 15 E
90 Mattawa 46 20N 78 45W
25 Matterhorn, Mt. 45 58N 7 39 E
105 Matthew Town 20 57N 73 40W
100 Mattoon 39 30N 88 20W
64 Matua 2 58s 110 52 E
110 Maturín 9 45N 63 11W
60 Mau Ranipur 25 16N 79 8 E
19 Maubeuge 50 17W 3 57 E
20 Maubourguet 43 29N 0 1 E
110 Maués 3 20s 57 45W
94 Maui, I. 20 45N 156 20 E
59 Maulamyaing 16 30N 97 40 E
108 Maule □ 36 5s 72 30W
65 Maumere 8 38s 122 13 E
75 Maun 20 0s 23 26 E
94 Mauna Loa, Mt. 19 50N 155 28 E
61 Maunath Bhanjan 25 56N 83 33 E
59 Maungmagan Is. 41 0s 97 48 E
21 Maures, Mts. 43 15N 6 15 E
21 Maurienne 45 15N 6 20 E
72 Mauritania ■ 20 50N 10 0W
71 Mauritius 20 0s 57 0 E
21 Maurienne, Reg. 45 15N 6 20 E
20 Maurs 44 43N 2 12 E
26 Mauterndorf 47 9N 13 40 E
62 Mavelikara 9 14N 76 32 E
54 Mavqi'im 31 38N 34 32 E
59 Mawkmai 20 14N 97 50 E
59 Mawlaik 23 40N 94 26 E
80 Maxwelton 39 51s 174 49 E
105 May Pen 17 58N 77 15W
32 Maya 43 12N 1 29W
104 Maya Mts. 16 30N 89 0W
105 Mayaguana I. 21 30N 72 44W
105 Mayagüez 18 12N 67 9W
83 Mayanup 33 58s 116 25 E
80 Maydena 42 45s 146 39 E
25 Mayen 50 18N 7 10 E
18 Mayenne 48 20N 0 38W
18 Mayenne □ 48 10N 0 40W
18 Mayenne, R. 47 30N 0 33W
92 Mayerthorpe 53 57N 115 15W
99 Mayfield 36 45N 88 40W
49 Maykop 44 35N 40 25 E
97 Maynard 42 30N 71 33W
90 Maynooth, Canada 45 14N 77 56W
15 Maynooth, Eire 53 22N 6 38W
88 Mayo 63 38N 135 57W
15 Mayo □ 43 47N 9 7W
30 Mayorga 42 10N 5 16W
98 Maysville 38 43N 84 16W
74 Mayumba 3 25s 10 39 E
62 Mayuram 11 3N 79 42 E
51 Mayya 61 44N 130 18 E
75 Mazabuka 15 52s 27 44 E
111 Mazagão 0 20s 51 50W
92 Mazama 49 43N 120 8W
20 Mazamet 43 30N 2 20 E
57 Mazan Deran □ 36 30N 53 30 E
38 Mazara del Vallo 37 40N 12 34 E
57 Mazar-i-Sharif 36 41N 67 0 E
112 Mazarredo 47 10s 66 50W
33 Mazarrón 37 38N 1 19W
33 Mazarrón, G. de 37 27N 1 19W
104 Mazatenango 14 35N 91 30W
104 Mazatlán 23 10N 106 30W
39 Mazzarino 37 19N 14 12 E
75 Mbabane 26 18s 31 6 E
74 M'Baiki 3 53N 18 1 E
74 Mbala 8 46s 31 17 E
74 Mbale 1 8N 34 12 E
74 Mbandaka 0 1s 18 18 E
74 Mbarara 0 35s 30 25 E
74 Mbeya 8 54s 33 29 E
74 Mbuji-Mayi 6 9s 23 40 E
74 Mbulu 3 45s 35 30 E
75 Mchinji 13 47s 32 58 E
103 Mead, L. 36 10N 114 10W
83 Meadow 26 35s 114 30 E
93 Meadow Lake 54 10N 108 10W
93 Meadow Lake Prov. Park 52 25N 109 0W
96 Meadville 41 39N 80 9W
90 Meaford 44 40N 80 36W
15 Meath □ 53 32N 6 40W
20 Meaulne 46 36N 2 28 E
19 Meaux 48 58N 2 50 E
56 Mecca=Makkah 21 30N 39 54 E
96 Mechanicsburg 40 12N 77 0W
97 Mechanicville 42 54N 73 41W
16 Mechelen 51 2N 4 29 E
24 Mecklenburger, B. 54 20N 11 40 E
82 Meda P.O. 17 20s 123 59 E
62 Medak 18 1N 78 15 E
64 Medan 3 40N 98 38 E
112 Medanosa, Pta. 48 0s 66 0W
72 Médéa 36 12N 2 50 E
110 Medellín 6 15N 75 35W
72 Médenine 33 21N 10 30 E
72 Mederdra 17 0N 15 38W
102 Medford 42 20N 122 52W
41 Medgidia 44 15N 28 19 E
41 Mediaş 46 9N 24 22 E
37 Medicina 44 29N 11 38 E
102 Medicine Bow 41 56N 106 11W
102 Medinine Bow Ra. 41 10N 106 25W
93 Medicine Hat 50 0N 110 45W
96 Medina 43 15N 78 27W
30 Medina de Rioseco 41 53N 5 3W
30 Medina del Campo 41 18N 4 55W
31 Medina-Sidonia 36 28N 5 57W
32 Medinaceli 41 12N 2 30W
34 Mediterranean Sea 35 0N 15 0 E
20 Médoc, Reg. 45 10N 0 56W
49 Medveditsa, R. 49 0N 43 58 E
51 Medvezhi Oshova 71 0N 161 0 E
48 Medvezhyegorsk 63 0N 34 25 E
13 Medway, R. 51 27N 0 44 E
83 Meeberrie 26 57s 116 0 E
83 Meekatharra 26 32s 118 29 E
24 Meerane 50 51N 12 30 E
60 Meerut 29 1N 77 50 E
74 Mega 3 57N 38 30 E
43 Megalópolis 37 25N 22 7 E
91 Mégantic 45 36N 70 56W
43 Mégara 37 58N 23 22 E
21 Mégève 45 51N 6 37 E
61 Meghalaya □ 25 50N 91 0 E
61 Meghna, R. 22 50N 90 50 E
54 Megiddo 32 36N 15 11 E
40 Mehadia 44 56N 22 23 E
60 Mehsana 23 39N 72 26 E
20 Mehun-sur-Yèvre 47 10N 2 13 E
68 Meihokow 42 37N 125 46 E
69 Meihsien 24 20N 116 0 E
59 Meiktila 21 0N 96 0 E
24 Meiningen 50 32N 10 25 E
30 Meira, Sa. de 43 15N 7 15W
25 Meiringen 46 43N 8 12 E
24 Meissen 51 10N 13 29 E
24 Meissner, Mt. 51 12N 9 50 E
20 Méjean, Causse 44 15N 3 30 E
73 Mekele 13 33N 39 30 E
72 Meknès 33 57N 5 33W
63 Mekong, R. 10 33N 105 24 E
63 Melaka 2 15N 102 15 E
63 Melaka □ 2 17N 102 18 E
64 Melalap 5 10N 116 5 E
43 Mélambes 35 8N 24 40 E
76 Melanesia, Arch. 4 0s 155 0 E
62 Melapalaiyam 8 39N 77 44 E
84 Melbourne 37 40s 145 0 E
104 Melchor Múzquiz 27 50N 101 40W
37 Méldola 44 7N 12 3 E
24 Meldorf 54 5N 9 5 E
36 Melegnano 45 21N 9 20 E
48 Melekess= Dimitrovgrad 54 25N 49 33 E
39 Melfi 41 0N 15 40 E
93 Melfort 52 50N 105 40W
30 Melgar de Fernamental 42 27N 4 17W
43 Meligalá 37 15N 21 59 E
72 Melilla 35 21N 2 57W
54 Melilot 31 22N 34 37 E
108 Melipilla 33 42s 71 15W
93 Melita 49 15N 101 5W
49 Melitopol 46 50N 35 22 E
26 Melk 48 13N 15 20 E
20 Melle 46 14N 0 10W
45 Mellerud 58 41N 12 28 E
26 Mělník 50 22N 14 23 E
109 Melo 32 20s 54 10W
14 Melrose 55 35N 2 44W
12 Melton Mowbray 52 46N 0 52W
19 Melun 48 32N 2 39 E
62 Melur 10 2N 78 23 E
93 Melville 32 2s 115 48 E
82 Melville, I., Australia 11 30s 131 0 E
86 Melville, I., Canada 75 30N 111 0W
91 Melville, L. 53 45N 59 40W
89 Melville Pen. 68 0N 84 0W
48 Memel=Klaipeda 55 43N 21 10 E
25 Memmingen 47 59N 10 12 E
101 Memphis 35 7N 90 0W
97 Memphremagog L. 45 8N 72 17W
12 Menai Str. 53 7N 4 20W
100 Menasha 44 13N 88 27W
64 Menate 0 12s 112 47 E
69 Mencheng 33 27N 116 45 E
20 Mende 44 31N 3 30 E
13 Mendip Hills 51 17N 2 40W
102 Mendocino 39 26N 123 50W
103 Mendota 36 46N 120 24W
108 Mendoza 32 50s 68 52W
108 Mendoza □ 33 0s 69 0W
110 Mene de Mauroa 10 45N 70 50W
110 Mene Grande 9 49N 70 56W
56 Menemen 38 36N 27 4 E
16 Menen 50 47N 3 7 E
38 Menfi 37 36N 12 57 E
64 Menggala 4 20s 105 15 E
31 Mengíbar 37 58N 3 48W
67 Mengtz 23 20N 103 20 E
84 Menindee 32 20N 142 25 E
100 Menominee 45 9N 87 39W
100 Menomonie 44 50N 91 54W
32 Menorca, I. 40 0N 4 0 E
64 Mentawai, Kep. 2 0s 99 0 E
21 Menton 43 50N 7 29 E
73 Menzel Temime 36 46N 11 0 E
48 Menzelinsk 55 43N 53 8 E
83 Menzies 29 40s 120 58 E
54 Me'ona 33 1N 35 15 E
16 Meppel 52 42N 6 12 E
24 Mepper 52 41N 7 20 E
32 Mequinenza 41 22N 0 17 E
43 Merabéllou, Kól. 35 10N 25 50 E
65 Merak 5 55s 106 1 E
37 Merano 46 40N 11 10 E
65 Merauke 8 29s 120 24 E
55 Merca 1 48N 44 50 E
32 Mercadal 39 59N 4 5 E
37 Mercato Saraceno 43 57N 12 11 E
103 Merced 37 25N 120 30W
108 Mercedes, Buenos Aires 34 40s 59 30W
108 Mercedes, Corrientes 29 10s 58 5W
108 Mercedes, San Luis 33 40s 65 30W
108 Mercedes, Uruguay 33 12s 58 0W
85 Mercer 37 16s 175 5 E
89 Mercy, C. 65 0N 62 30W
13 Mere 51 5N 2 16W
112 Meredith, C. 52 15s 60 40W
41 Merei 45 7N 26 43 E
19 Méréville 48 20N 2 5 E
63 Mergui 12 30N 98 35 E
63 Mergui Arch.= Myeik Kyunzu 11 30N 97 30 E
104 Mérida, Mexico 20 50N 89 40W
31 Mérida, Sp. 38 55N 6 25W
110 Mérida, Ven. 8 36N 71 8W
97 Meriden 41 33N 72 47W
102 Meridian, Id. 43 41N 116 20W
101 Meridian, Miss. 32 20N 88 42W
111 Meriruma 1 15N 54 50W
16 Merksem 51 16N 4 25 E
19 Merlebach 49 5N 6 52 E
73 Merowe 18 29N 31 46 E
83 Merredin 31 28s 118 18 E
100 Merrill 45 11N 89 41W
97 Merrimack, R. 42 49N 70 49W
92 Merritt 50 10N 120 45W
83 Merroe 27 53s 117 50 E
74 Mersa Fatma 14 57N 40 17 E
13 Mersea I. 51 48N 0 55 E
24 Merseburg 51 20N 12 0 E
12 Mersey, R. 53 25N 3 0W
12 Merseyside □ 53 25W 2 55W
56 Mersin 36 51N 34 36 E
63 Mersing 2 25N 103 50 E
13 Merthyr Tydfil 51 45N 3 23W
31 Mértola 37 40N 7 40 E
101 Mertzon 31 17N 100 48W
19 Méru 49 13N 2 8 E
74 Meru 0 3N 37 40 E
19 Méry 48 30N 3 52 E
25 Merzig 49 26N 6 37 E
103 Mesa 33 20N 111 56W
39 Mesagne 40 33N 17 49 E
43 Mesaras, Kól. 35 6N 24 47 E
57 Meshed=Mashhad 36 20N 59 35 E
103 Mesilla 32 20N 107 0W
18 Meslay-du-Maine 47 58N 0 33W
43 Mesolóngion 38 27N 21 28 E
56 Mesopotamia, Reg.=Al Jazirah, Reg. 33 30N 44 0 E
39 Messina, It. 38 10N 15 32 E
75 Messina, S.Africa 22 20s 30 12 E
39 Messina, Str. di 38 5N 15 35 E
43 Messíni 37 4N 22 1 E
43 Messinía □ 37 10N 22 0 E
43 Messiniakós Kól. 36 45N 22 5 E
37 Mestre 45 30N 12 13 E
110 Meta, R. 6 12N 67 28W
90 Metagama 47 0N 81 55W
108 Metán 25 30s 65 0W
85 Methven 43 38s 171 40 E
41 Metkovets 43 37N 23 10 E
40 Metković 43 6N 17 39 E
92 Metlakatia 55 8N 131 35W
37 Metlika 45 40N 15 20 E
101 Metropolis 37 10N 88 47W

Moza Nasser, L.=Naser, Buheiret en

54 Moza 31 48N 35 8E
75 Mozambique ■ 19 0s 35 0E
70 Mozambique Chan. 20 0s 39 0E
48 Mozyr 52 0N 29 15E
74 Mpanda 6 23s 31 40E
75 Mpika 11 51s 31 25E
28 Mrągowo 53 57N 21 18E
73 Msaken 35 49N 10 33E
75 Msoro 13 35s 31 50E
74 Mtwara 10 20s 40 20E
111 Muaná 1 25s 49 15W
63 Muang Chiang Rai 19 52N 99 50E
63 Muang Lamphun 18 40N 98 53E
63 Muang Phichit 16 29N 100 21E
63 Muar=Bandar Maharani 2 3N 102 34E
64 Muarabungo 1 40s 101 10E
64 Muarakaman 0 2s 116 45E
64 Muaratembesi 1 42s 103 2E
64 Muaratewe 0 50s 115 0E
56 Mubairik 23 22N 39 8E
74 Mubende 0 33N 31 22E
73 Mubi 10 18N 13 16E
25 Mücheln 51 18N 11 49E
14 Muck, I. 56 50N 6 15W
111 Mucuri 18 0s 40 0W
75 Mufulira 12 32s 28 15W
30 Mugardos 43 27N 8 15W
31 Muge 39 3N 8 40W
30 Mugia 43 3N 9 17W
73 Muhammad Qol 20 53N 37 9E
25 Mühldorf 48 14N 12 23E
24 Mühlhausen 51 12N 10 29E
15 Muine Bheag 52 42N 6 59W
30 Muiños 41 58N 7 59W
55 Mukalla 14 33N 49 2E
68 Mukden=Shenyang 41 48N 123 27E
55 Mukeiras 13 59N 45 52E
83 Mukinbudin 30 55s 118 5E
64 Mukomuko 2 20s 101 10E
60 Muktsar 30 30N 74 30E
33 Mula 38 3N 1 33W
105 Mulatas, Arch. de las 6 51N 78 31W
108 Mulchén 37 45s 72 20W
24 Mulde, R. 51 10N 12 48E
91 Mulgrave 45 38N 61 31W
31 Mulhacén, Mt. 37 4N 3 20W
24 Mülheim 51 26N 6 53W
19 Mulhouse 47 40N 7 20E
14 Mull of Galloway, Pt. 54 40N 4 55W
14 Mull of Kintyre, Pt. 55 20N 5 45W
14 Mull, I. 56 27N 6 0W
84 Mullengudgery 31 43s 147 29E
15 Mullet, Pen. 54 10N 10 2W
83 Mullewa 28 29s 115 30E
15 Mullingar 53 31N 7 20W
81 Mullumbimby 28 30s 153 30E
60 Multan □ 30 29N 72 29E
60 Multan 30 15N 71 30E
84 Mulwala 35 59s 146 0E
63 Mun, R. 15 19N 105 31E
65 Muna, I. 5 0s 122 30E
25 Munchberg 50 11N 11 48E
24 Muncheberg 52 30N 14 9E
25 München 48 8N 11 33E
98 Muncie 40 10N 85 20W
62 Mundakayam 9 30N 76 32E
24 Münden 51 25N 9 42E
82 Mundiwindi 23 47s 120 9E
33 Mundo, R. 38 30N 2 15W
111 Mundo Novo 11 50s 40 29W
60 Mundra 22 54N 69 26E
83 Mundrabilla 31 52s 127 51E
33 Munera 39 2N 2 29W
81 Mungallala 26 25s 147 34E
80 Mungana 17 8s 144 27E
81 Mungindi 28 58s 149 1E
75 Munhango 12 9s 18 36E
25 Munich=München 48 8N 11 33E
45 Munkedal 58 28N 11 40E
44 Munkfars 59 50N 13 30E
112 Muñoz Gamero, Pen. 52 30s 73 5E
19 Munster 48 2N 7 8E
15 Munster □ 52 20N 8 40W
24 Münster, Niedersachsen 52 59N 10 5E
24 Münster, Nordrhein-Westfalen 51 58N 7 37E
83 Muntadgin 31 48s 118 30E
64 Muntok 2 5s 105 10E
46 Muonio, R. 67 48N 23 25E
26 Mur, R. 46 18N 16 53E
37 Mura, R. 46 18N 16 53E
112 Murallón, Mt. 49 55s 73 30W
74 Murangá 0 45s 37 9E
48 Murashi 59 30N 49 0E
20 Murat 45 7N 2 53E
26 Murau 47 6N 14 10E
38 Muravera 39 25N 9 35E
30 Murça 41 24N 7 28W
84 Murchison, Australia 36 39s 145 14E
85 Murchison, N.Z. 41 49s 172 21E
83 Murchison, R. 26 1s 117 6E
33 Murcia 38 2N 1 10W
33 Murcia □ 37 50N 1 30W
33 Murcia, Reg. 38 35N 1 50W
41 Mureş 46 45N 24 40E
41 Mureşul, R. 46 15N 20 13E
20 Muret 43 30N 1 20E
99 Murfreesboro 35 50N 86 21W
50 Murgab 38 10N 73 59E
81 Murgon 26 15s 151 54E
109 Muriaé 21 8s 42 23W
24 Müritzsee 53 25N 12 40E
48 Murmansk 68 57N 33 10E
32 Muro 39 45N 3 3E
48 Murom 55 35N 42 3E
66 Muroran 42 25N 141 0E
30 Muros 42 45N 9 5W
39 Muro Lucano 40 45N 15 30E
101 Murphysboro 37 50N 89 20W
99 Murray, Ky. 36 40N 88 20W
102 Murray, Utah 40 41N 111 58W
81 Murray, R. 35 22s 139 22E
81 Murray Bridge 35 6s 139 14E
84 Murrayville 35 16s 141 11E
58 Murree 33 56N 73 28E
83 Murrin Murrin 28 50s 121 45E
84 Murrumbidgee, R. 34 43s 143 12E
84 Murrurundi 31 42s 150 51E
61 Murshidabad 24 11N 88 19E
60 Murtazapur 20 40N 77 25E
84 Murtoa 36 35s 142 28E
30 Murtosa 40 44N 8 40W
85 Murupara 38 30s 178 40E
61 Murwara 23 46N 80 28E
81 Murwillumbah 28 18s 153 27E
26 Mürzzuschlag 47 36N 15 41E
41 Musala, Mt. 41 13N 23 27E
57 Muscat=Masqat 23 37N 58 36E
100 Muscatine 41 25N 91 5W
74 Mushie 2 56s 17 4E
98 Muskegon 43 15N 86 17W
98 Muskegon Heights 43 12N 86 17W
101 Muskogee 35 50N 95 25W
73 Musmar 18 6N 35 40E
74 Musoma 1 30s 33 48E
14 Musselburgh 55 57N 3 3W
20 Mussidan 45 2N 0 22E
38 Mussomeli 37 35N 13 43E
112 Musters, L. 45 20s 69 25W
84 Muswellbrook 32 16s 150 56E
73 Mût 25 28N 28 58E
68 Mutankiang 44 35N 129 30E
80 Muttaburra 22 38s 144 29E
91 Mutton Bay 50 50N 59 2W
62 Muvatupusha 9 53N 76 35E
51 Muya 56 27N 115 39E
58 Muzaffarabad 34 25N 73 30E
60 Muzaffargarh 30 5N 71 14E
60 Muzaffarnagar 29 26N 77 40E
61 Muzaffarpur 26 7N 85 32E
50 Muzhi 65 25N 64 40E
18 Muzillac 47 35N 2 30W
67 Muztagh, Mt. 36 30N 87 22E
74 Mvadhi Ousye 1 13N 13 12E
74 Mwanza, Tanzania 2 30s 32 58E
74 Mwanza, Zaire 7 55s 26 43E
74 Mweka 4 50s 21 40E
74 Mweru, L. 9 0s 28 45E
63 My Tho 10 29N 106 23E
59 Myanaung 18 25N 95 10E
59 Myaungmya 16 30N 95 0E
59 Myingyan 21 30N 95 30E
59 Myitkyina 25 30N 97 26E
27 Myjava 48 41N 17 37E
61 Mymensingh=Nasirabad 24 42N 90 30E
102 Myrtle Creek 43 0N 123 19W
102 Myrtle Point 43 0N 124 4W
28 Myślibórz 52 55N 14 50E
27 Mystowice 50 15N 19 12E
62 Mysore 12 17N 76 41E
27 Myszkow 50 45N 19 22E
46 Mývatn, L. 65 36N 17 0W
26 Mže, R. 49 46N 13 24E

N

54 Na'an 31 53N 34 52E
47 Naantali 60 27N 21 57E
15 Naas 53 12N 6 40W
61 Nabadwip 23 34N 88 20E
73 Nabenl 36 30N 10 51E
60 Nabha 30 26N 76 14E
54 Nabi Rubin 31 56N 34 44E
54 Nābulus 32 14N 35 15E
74 Nachingwea 10 49s 38 49E
27 Náchod 50 25N 16 8E
44 Nacka 59 17N 18 12E
81 Nackara 32 48s 139 12E
101 Nacogdoches 31 33N 95 30W
104 Nacozari 30 30N 109 50W
60 Nadiad 22 41N 72 56E
57 Nadūshan 32 2N 53 35E
48 Nadvoitsy 63 52N 34 15E
50 Nadym 63 35N 72 42E
45 Næstved 55 13N 11 44E
72 Nafada 11 8N 11 20E
65 Naga 13 38N 123 15E
59 Nagaland □ 26 0N 95 0E
66 Nagano 36 40N 138 10E
66 Nagano □ 36 15N 138 0E
66 Nagaoka 32 27N 138 51E
62 Nagappattinam 10 46N 79 51E
66 Nagasaki 32 47N 129 50E
66 Nagasaki □ 32 50N 129 40E
66 Nagato 36 15N 138 16E
60 Nagaur 27 15N 73 45E
62 Nagercoil 8 12N 77 33E
60 Nagina 29 30N 78 30E
51 Nagornyy 55 58N 124 57E
66 Nagoya 35 10N 136 50E
60 Nagpur 21 8N 79 10E
27 Nagykanizsa 46 28N 17 0E
27 Nagykörös 47 2N 19 48E
69 Naha 26 12N 127 40E
88 Nahannai Butte 61 5N 123 30W
54 Nahariyya 33 1N 35 5E
56 Nahavand 34 10N 48 30E
54 Nahf 32 56N 35 18E
112 Nahuel Huapi, L. 41 0s 71 32W
93 Naicam 52 30N 104 30W
25 Naila 50 19N 11 43E
91 Nain 56 34N 61 40W
18 Naintré 46 46N 0 29E
14 Nairn 57 35N 3 54W
74 Nairobi 1 17s 36 48E
74 Naivasha 0 40s 36 30E
57 Najafābād 32 40N 51 15E
56 Najd, Reg. 26 30N 42 0E
30 Najerilla, R. 42 15N 2 45W
60 Najibabad 29 40N 78 20E
66 Nakamura 33 0N 133 0E
56 Nakhi Mubarak 24 10N 38 10E
49 Nakhichevan 39 14N 45 30E
51 Nakhodka 43 10N 132 45E
63 Nakhon Phanom 17 23N 104 43E
63 Nakhon Ratchasima 14 59N 102 12E
63 Nakhon Sawan 15 35N 100 12E
63 Nakhon Si Thammarat 8 29N 100 0E
90 Nakina 50 10N 86 40W
60 Nakodar 31 8N 75 31E
45 Nakskov 54 50N 11 8E
74 Nakuru 0 15s 35 5E
92 Nakusp 50 20N 117 45W
58 Nal, R. 26 2N 65 19E
68 Nalayh 47 43N 107 22E
49 Nalchik 43 30N 43 33E
62 Nalgonda 17 6N 79 15E
62 Nallamalai Hills 15 30N 78 50E
30 Nalon, R. 43 32N 6 4W
73 Nālūt 31 54N 11 0E
63 Nam Dinh 20 25N 106 5E
63 Nam-Phan, Reg. 10 30N 106 0E
63 Nam Tha 20 58N 101 30E
63 Nam Tok 14 21N 99 0E
67 Nam Tso, L. 30 40N 90 30E
62 Namakkal 11 13N 78 13E
75 Namaland, Reg. 29 43s 19 5E
50 Namangan 41 30N 71 30E
75 Namapa 13 43s 39 50E
65 Namber 1 2s 134 57E
81 Nambour 26 38s 152 49E
81 Nambucca Heads 30 40s 152 48E
67 Namcha Barwa, Mt. 29 30N 95 10E
75 Namib Des.=Namibwoestyn 22 30s 15 0W
75 Namibia ■ 22 0s 18 9E
75 Namibwoestyn 22 30s 15 0W
65 Namlea 3 10s 127 5E
102 Nampa 43 40N 116 40W
75 Nampula 15 6s 39 7E
65 Namrole 3 46s 126 46E
46 Namsen, R. 64 27N 11 28E
46 Namsos 64 29N 11 30E
59 Namtu 23 5N 97 28E
16 Namur 50 27N 4 52E
16 Namur □ 50 17N 5 0E
75 Namutoni 18 49s 16 55E
75 Namwala 15 44s 26 30E
28 Namysłów 51 6N 17 42E
69 Namyung 25 15N 114 5E
67 Nan Shan, Mts. 38 0N 98 0E
92 Nanaimo 49 10N 124 0W
81 Nanango 26 40s 152 0E
66 Nanao 37 0N 137 0E
69 Nanchang 28 34N 115 48E
69 Nancheng 27 30N 116 28E
69 Nancheng=Hanchung 33 10N 107 2E
69 Nanchung 30 47N 105 59E
19 Nancy 48 42N 6 12E
61 Nanda Devi, Mt. 30 30N 80 30E
62 Nander 19 10N 77 20E
85 Nandi 17 25s 176 50E
62 Nandikotkur 15 52N 78 18E
60 Nandura 20 52N 76 25E
60 Nandurbar 21 20N 74 15E
62 Nandyal 15 30N 78 30E
58 Nanga Parbat, Mt. 35 10N 74 35E
57 Nangarhar □ 34 15N 70 30E
19 Nangis 48 33N 3 0E
62 Nanjangud 12 6N 76 43E
60 Nankana Sahib 31 27N 73 38E
69 Nankang 25 42N 114 35E
69 Nanking 32 10N 118 50E
66 Nankoku 33 39N 133 44E
83 Nannine 26 51s 118 18E
69 Nanning 22 51N 108 18E
83 Nannup 33 59s 115 45E
61 Nanpara 27 52N 81 33E
69 Nanping 26 45N 118 5E
66 Nansei-Shotō, Is. 29 0N 129 0E
83 Nanson 28 34s 114 46E
20 Nant 44 1N 3 18E
69 Nantan 25 0N 107 35E
18 Nantes 47 12N 1 33W
19 Nanteuil-le-Haudouin 49 9N 2 48E
20 Nantiat 46 1N 1 11E
97 Nanticoke 41 12N 76 1W
92 Nanton 50 20N 113 50W
69 Nantou 23 57N 120 35E
21 Nantua 46 10N 5 35E
86 Nantucket I. 41 16N 70 3W
69 Nantung 32 0N 120 50E
111 Nanuque 17 50s 40 21W
69 Nanyang 33 2N 112 35E
68 Nanyuan 39 48N 116 23E
74 Nanyuki 0 2N 37 4E
33 Nao, C. de la 38 44N 0 14E
66 Naoetsu 37 12N 138 10E
61 Naogaon 24 52N 88 52E
42 Náousa 40 42N 22 9E
102 Napa 38 18N 122 17W
90 Napanee 44 15N 77 0W
85 Napier 39 30s 176 56E
82 Napier Broome, B. 14 0s 127 0E
82 Napier Downs 16 20s 124 30E
110 Napo, R. 3 20s 72 40W
100 Napoleon 46 32N 99 49W
39 Nápoli 40 50N 14 5E
66 Nara 34 40N 135 49E
66 Nara □ 34 30N 136 0E
60 Nara, R. 24 7N 69 7E
84 Naracoorte 36 50s 140 44E
62 Narasapur 16 26N 81 50E
62 Narasaraopet 16 14N 80 4E
63 Narathiwat 6 40N 101 55E
61 Narayanganj 23 31N 90 33E
62 Narayanpet 16 45N 77 30E
20 Narbonne 43 11N 3 0E
30 Narcea, R. 43 28N 6 6W
39 Nardo 40 10N 18 0E
83 Narembeen 32 4s 118 24E
83 Naretha 31 0s 124 50E
28 Narew 52 55N 23 30E
28 Narew, R. 52 26N 20 42E
60 Narmada, R. 21 35N 72 35E
60 Narnaul 28 5N 76 11E
37 Narni 42 30N 12 30E
38 Naro 37 18N 13 48E
60 Narowal 32 6N 74 52E
81 Narrabri 30 19s 149 46E
81 Narran, R. 29 45s 147 20E
84 Narrandera 34 42s 146 31E
83 Narrogin 32 58s 117 14E
84 Narromine 32 12s 148 12E
66 Naruto 35 36N 140 25E
46 Narvik 68 28N 17 26E
60 Narwana 29 39N 76 6E
31 Naryilco 28 37s 141 53E
50 Narym 59 0N 81 58E
50 Narymskoye 49 10N 84 15E
50 Naryn 41 30N 76 10E
72 Nasarawa 8 32N 7 41E
73 Naser, Buheiret en 23 0N 32 30E
102 Nashua, Mont. 48 10N 106 25W
97 Nashua, N.H. 42 50N 71 25W
99 Nashville 36 12N 86 46W
40 Nasice 45 32N 18 4W
60 Nasik 20 2N 73 50E
60 Nasirabad, Bangladesh 26 15N 74 45E
60 Nasirabad, India 26 15N 74 45E
61 Nasirabad, Pak. 28 25N 68 25E
105 Nassau 25 0N 77 30W
112 Nassau, B. 55 20s 68 0W
73 Nasser, L.=Naser, Buheiret en 23 0N 32 30E

Nässjö Nipigon

45 Nässjö 57 38N 14 45 E
90 Nastapoka Is. 57 0N 77 0W
59 Nat Kyizio 14 55N 98 0 E
110 Natagaima 3 37N 75 6W
111 Natal, Brazil 5 47S 35 13W
64 Natal, Indonesia 0 35N 99 0 E
75 Natal □ 28 30S 30 30 E
91 Natashquan 50 14N 61 46W
91 Natashquan, R. 50 6N 61 49W
101 Natchez 31 35N 91 25W
101 Natchitoches 31 47N 93 4W
60 Nathdwara 24 55N 73 50 E
97 Natick 42 16N 71 19W
84 Natimuk 36 35S 141 59 E
72 Natitingou 10 20N 1 26 E
103 National City 32 45N 117 7W
111 Natividade 11 43S 47 47W
74 Natron, L. 2 20S 36 0 E
64 Natuna Besar, Kep. 4 0N 108 0 E
64 Natuna Selatan, Kep. 3 0N 109 55 E
20 Naucelle 44 13N 2 20 E
26 Nauders 46 54N 10 30 E
24 Nauen 52 36N 12 52 E
97 Naugatuck 41 28N 73 4W
24 Naumburg 51 10N 11 48 E
76 Naurn Is. 0 25N 166 0 E
58 Naushahra 33 9N 74 15 E
30 Nava del Rey 41 22N 5 6W
31 Navahermosa 39 41N 4 28W
103 Navajo Res. 36 55N 107 30W
30 Navalcarnero 40 17N 4 5W
30 Navalmoral de la Mata 39 52N 5 16W
15 Navan=An Uaimh 53 39N 6 40W
112 Navarino, I. 55 0S 67 30W
32 Navarra □ 42 40N 1 40W
20 Navarre, Reg. 43 15N 1 20 E
105 Navassa, I. 18 30N 75 0W
30 Navia 43 24N 6 42W
30 Navia, R. 43 32N 6 43W
30 Navia de Suarna 42 58N 6 59W
50 Navoi 40 9N 65 22 E
104 Navojoa 27 0N 109 30W
48 Navolok 62 33N 39 57 E
43 Návpaktos 38 23N 21 42 E
43 Navplion 37 33N 22 50 E
60 Navsari 20 57N 72 59 E
61 Nawabganj, Bangladesh 24 35N 81 14 E
61 Nawabganj, Ut.P. 28 32N 79 40 E
61 Nawabganj, Ut.P. 26 56N 81 14 E
60 Nawabshah 26 15N 68 25 E
61 Nawada 24 50N 85 25 E
60 Nawalgarh 27 50N 75 15 E
43 Náxos, I. 37 5N 25 30 E
57 Nāy Band 27 20N 52 40 E
51 Nayakhan 62 10N 159 0 E
104 Nayarit □ 22 0N 105 0W
111 Nazaré, Brazil 13 0S 39 0W
31 Nazaré, Port. 39 36N 9 4W
54 Nazareth, Israel 32 42N 35 17 E
97 Nazareth, U.S.A. 40 44N 75 19W
59 Nazir Hat 22 35N 91 55 E
74 N'Délé 8 25N 20 36 E
74 Ndendé 2 29S 10 46 E
73 Ndjamena 12 4N 15 8 E
75 Ndola 13 0S 28 34 E
15 Neagh, L. 54 35N 6 25W
43 Neápolis, Kozan 40 20N 21 24 E
43 Neápolis, Kriti 35 15N 25 36 E
43 Neápolis, Lakonia 36 27N 23 8 E
88 Near Is. 53 0N 172 0W
13 Neath 51 39N 3 49W
80 Nebo 39 27N 90 47W
100 Nebraska □ 41 30N 100 0W
100 Nebraska City 40 40N 95 52W
25 Neckar, R. 49 31N 8 26 E
108 Necochea 38 30S 58 50W
103 Needles 34 50N 114 35W
108 Ñeembucú □ 27 0S 58 0W
60 Neemuch 24 30N 74 50 E
100 Neenah 44 10N 88 30W
93 Neepawa 50 20N 99 30W
72 Nefta 33 53N 7 58 E
49 Neftyannyye Kamni 40 20N 50 55 E
12 Nefyn 52 57N 4 31W
62 Negapatam= Nagappattinam 10 46N 79 38 E
98 Negaunee 46 30N 87 36W
63 Negeri Sembilan □ 2 50N 102 10 E
41 Negoiu, Mt. 45 48N 24 32 E
62 Negombo 7 12N 79 50 E
40 Negotin 44 16N 22 37 E
65 Negra Pt. 18 40N 120 50 E
110 Negra, Pta. 6 6S 81 10W
30 Negreira 42 54N 8 45W
112 Negro, R., Arg. 41 2S 62 47W
110 Negro, R., Brazil 3 10S 59 58W
65 Negros, I. 10 0N 123 0 E
41 Negru Vodă 43 47N 28 21 E
57 Nehbandān 31 35N 60 5 E
25 Neheim 51 27N 7 58 E
41 Nehoiașu 45 24N 26 20 E
69 Neikiang 29 35N 105 10 E
30 Neira de Jusá 42 53N 7 14W
28 Neisse, R. 52 4N 14 47 E
110 Neiva 2 56N 75 18W
73 Nekemte 9 4N 36 30 E
30 Nelas 40 32N 7 52W
51 Nelkan 57 50N 136 15 E
62 Nellikuppam 11 46N 79 43 E
62 Nellore 14 27N 79 59 E
51 Nelma 47 30N 139 0 E
92 Nelson, Canada 49 30N 117 20W
85 Nelson, N.Z. 41 18S 173 16 E
12 Nelson, U.K. 53 50N 2 14W
85 Nelson □ 42 11S 172 15 E
112 Nelson, Estrecho 51 30S 75 0W
93 Nelson, R. 55 30N 96 50W
92 Nelson Forks 59 30N 124 0W
75 Nelspruit 25 29S 30 59 E
72 Néma 16 40N 7 15W
19 Nemours 48 16N 2 40 E
66 Nemuro 43 20N 145 35 E
66 Nemuro-Kaikyō, Str. 43 30N 145 30 E
51 Nemuy 55 40N 135 55 E
15 Nenagh 52 52N 8 11W
88 Nenana 63 34N 149 7W
12 Nene, R. 52 48N 0 13 E
42 Néon Petritsi 41 16N 23 15 E
101 Neosho 35 59N 95 10W
61 Nepal ■ 28 0N 84 30 E
102 Nephi 39 43N 111 52W
97 Neptune City 40 13N 74 4W
40 Néra, R. 42 26N 12 24 E
20 Nérac 44 19N 0 20 E
51 Nerchinsk 52 0N 116 39 E
51 Nerchinskiyzavod 51 10N 119 30 E
40 Neretva, R. 43 1N 17 27 E
40 Neretvanski, Kanal 43 7N 17 10 E
31 Nerja 36 43N 3 55W
33 Nerpio 38 11N 2 16W
31 Nerva 37 42N 6 30W
54 Nes Ziyyona 31 56N 34 48W
54 Nesher 32 45N 35 3 E
44 Neslandvatn 58 57N 9 10 E
19 Nesle 49 45N 2 53 E
14 Ness, L. 57 15N 4 30W
42 Néstos, R. 41 20N 24 35 E
47 Nesttun 60 19N 5 21 E
54 Netanya 32 20N 34 51 E
16 Netherlands ■ 52 0N 5 30 E
61 Netrakona 24 53N 90 47 E
19 Nettancourt 48 51N 4 57 E
89 Nettilling L. 66 30N 71 0W
25 Neu-Isenburg 50 3N 8 42 E
25 Neu-Ulm 48 23N 10 2 E
24 Neubrandenburg 53 33N 13 17 E
24 Neubrandenburg □ 53 30N 13 20 E
25 Neuchâtel 47 0N 6 55 E
25 Neuchâtel □ 47 0N 6 55 E
25 Neuchâtel, L. de 46 53N 6 50 E
19 Neufchâteau 48 21N 5 40 E
18 Neufchâtel 49 43N 1 30 E
19 Neufchâtel -sur-Aisne 49 26N 4 0 E
18 Neuillé-Pont-Pierre 47 33N 0 33 E
25 Neumarkt 49 16N 11 28 E
24 Neumünster 54 4N 9 58 E
26 Neunkirchen, Austria 47 43N 16 4 E
25 Neunkirchen, Germany 49 23N 7 6 E
112 Neuquén 38 0S 68 0 E
108 Neuquén □ 38 0S 69 50W
24 Neuruppin 52 56N 12 48 E
27 Neusiedler See, L. 47 50N 16 47 E
24 Neuss 51 12N 6 39 E
25 Neustadt, Bayern 49 42N 12 10 E
25 Neustadt, Bayern 50 23N 11 0 E
24 Neustadt, Potsdam 52 50N 12 27 E
24 Neustadt, Rheinland-Pfalz 49 21N 8 10 E
24 Neustrelitz 53 22N 13 4 E
20 Neuvic 45 23N 2 16 E
20 Neuville 45 52N 4 51 E
19 Neuville-aux-Bois 48 4N 2 3 E
20 Neuvy-St.-Sépulchre 46 35N 1 48 E
24 Neuwied 50 26N 7 29 E
101 Nevada 37 20N 94 40W
102 Nevada □ 39 20N 117 0W
31 Nevada, Sa. 37 3N 3 15W
110 Nevada de Sta. Marta, Sa. 10 55N 73 50W
51 Nevanka 56 45N 98 55 E
20 Nevers 47 0N 3 9 E
84 Nevertire 31 50S 147 44 E
105 Nevis, I. 17 0N 62 30W
98 New Albany 38 20N 85 50W
110 New Amsterdam 6 15N 57 30W
97 New Bedford 41 40N 70 52W
99 New Bern 35 8N 77 3W
101 New Braunfels 29 43N 98 9W
85 New Brighton, N.Z. 43 29S 172 43 E
96 New Brigthton, U.S.A. 40 44N 80 19W
97 New Britain 41 41N 72 47W
76 New Britain, I. 6 0S 151 0 E
97 New Brunswick 40 30N 74 28W
91 New Brunswick □ 46 50N 66 30W
76 New Caledonia, I. 21 0S 165 0 E
98 New Castle, Ind. 39 55N 85 23W
96 New Castle, Pa. 41 0N 80 20W
97 New City 41 8N 74 0W
60 New Delhi 28 37N 77 13 E
92 New Denver 50 0N 117 25W
13 New Forest, Reg. 50 53N 1 40W
91 New Glasgow 45 35N 62 36W
76 New Guinea, I. 4 0S 146 0 E
97 New Hampshire □ 43 40N 71 40W
97 New Haven 41 20N 72 54W
101 New Iberia 30 2N 91 54W
76 New Ireland, I. 3 0S 151 30 E
98 New Jersey □ 39 50N 74 10W
96 New Kensington 40 36N 79 43W
90 New Liskeard 47 31N 79 41W
97 New London 41 23N 72 8W
103 New Mexico □ 34 30N 106 0W
83 New Norcia 30 58S 116 13 E
80 New Norfolk 42 46S 147 2 E
101 New Orleans 30 0N 90 5W
96 New Philadelphia 40 29N 81 25W
85 New Plymouth 39 4S 174 5 E
105 New Providence I. 25 0N 77 30W
13 New Radnor 52 15N 3 10W
97 New Rochelle 40 55N 73 46W
13 New Romney 50 59N 0 57 E
79 New South Wales □ 33 0S 146 0 E
100 New Ulm 44 15N 94 30W
91 New Waterford 46 13N 60 4W
92 New Westminster 49 10N 122 52W
97 New York 40 45N 74 0W
97 New York □ 42 40N 76 0W
12 Newark, U.K. 53 6N 0 48W
97 Newark, N.J. 40 41N 74 12W
96 Newark, N.Y. 43 2N 77 10W
96 Newark, Ohio 40 5N 82 30W
99 Newberry 46 20N 85 32W
97 Newburgh 41 30N 74 1W
13 Newbury 51 24N 1 19W
97 Newburyport 42 48N 70 50W
84 Newcastle, Australia 32 52S 151 49 E
91 Newcastle, Canada 47 1N 65 38W
15 Newcastle, Eire 52 27N 9 3W
75 Newcastle, S.Africa 27 45S 29 58 E
15 Newcastle, N. Ireland 54 13N 5 54W
12 Newcastle, Tyne and Tees 54 59N 1 37W
13 Newcastle Emlyn 52 2N 4 29W
80 Newcastle Waters 17 30S 133 28 E
12 Newcastle-under-Lyme 53 2N 2 15W
96 Newcomerstown 40 16N 81 36W
83 Newdegate 33 17N 118 58 E
54 Newe Etan 32 30N 35 32 E
54 Newe Sha'anan 32 47N 34 59 E
54 Newe Zohar 31 9N 35 21 E
88 Newenham, C. 58 37N 162 12W
91 Newfoundland □ 48 28N 56 0W
91 Newfoundland, I. 48 30N 56 0W
13 Newhaven 50 47N 0 4 E
82 Newman, Mt. 23 20S 119 34 E
15 Newmarket, Eire 52 13N 9 0W
13 Newmarket, U.K. 52 15N 0 23 E
97 Newmarket, U.S.A. 43 4N 70 56W
99 Newnan 33 22N 84 48W
13 Newport, Gwent 51 35N 3 0W
13 Newport, I. of Wight 50 42N 1 18W
101 Newport, Ark. 35 38N 91 15W
98 Newport, Ky. 39 5N 84 23W
97 Newport, N.H. 43 23N 72 8W
102 Newport, Oreg. 44 41N 124 2W
97 Newport, Rhode I. 41 30N 71 19W
103 Newport Beach 33 40N 117 58W
98 Newport News 37 2N 76 54W
13 Newquay 50 24N 5 6W
15 Newry 54 10N 6 20W
15 Newry & Mourne □ 54 10W 6 20W
100 Newton, Iowa 41 40N 93 3W
101 Newton, Kans. 38 2N 97 30W
97 Newton, N.J. 41 3N 74 46W
13 Newton Abbot 50 32N 3 37W
96 Newton Falls 41 11N 80 59W
14 Newton Stewart 54 57N 4 30W
14 Newtonmore 57 4N 4 7W
84 Newtown, Australia 54 37N 5 40W
13 Newtown, U.K. 52 31N 3 19W
15 Newtownabbey □ 54 40N 5 55W
15 Newtownards 54 37N 5 40W
48 Neya 58 21N 43 49 E
57 Neyshābūr 36 10N 58 20 E
62 Neyyattinkara 8 26N 77 5 E
49 Nezhin 51 5N 31 55 E
75 Ngami Depression 20 30S 22 46 E
65 Nganjuk 7 32S 111 55 E
73 Ngaoundéré 7 15N 13 35 E
85 Ngapara 44 57S 170 46 E
65 Ngawi 7 24S 111 26 E
67 Ngoring Nor, L. 34 50N 98 0 E
72 Nguru 12 56N 10 29 E
63 Nha Trang 12 16N 109 10 E
84 Nhill 36 18S 141 40 E
96 Niagara Falls, Canada 43 7N 79 5W
96 Niagara Falls, U.S.A. 43 5N 79 0W
64 Niah 3 58S 113 46 E
72 Niamey 13 27N 2 6 E
74 Niangara 3 50N 27 50 E
64 Nias, I. 1 0N 97 40 E
36 Nibbiano 44 54N 9 20 E
105 Nicaragua ■ 11 40N 85 30W
39 Nicastro 39 0N 16 18 E
21 Nice 43 42N 7 14 E
66 Nichinan 31 28N 131 26 E
82 Nicholson Ra. 27 12S 116 40 E
53 Nicobar Is. 9 0N 93 0 E
92 Nicola 50 8N 120 40W
90 Nicolet 46 17N 72 35W
56 Nicosia=Levkosia, Cyprus 35 10N 33 25 E
39 Nicosia, Italy 37 45N 14 22 E
39 Nicótera 38 33N 15 57 E
105 Nicoya, G. de 10 0N 85 0W
105 Nicoya, Pen. de 9 45N 85 40W
27 Nida, R. 50 18N 20 52 E
12 Nidd, R. 54 1N 1 12W
28 Nidzica 53 25N 20 28 E
24 Niebüll 54 45N 8 49 E
19 Niederbronn 48 57N 7 39 E
26 Niederösterreich □ 48 25N 15 40 E
24 Niedersachsen □ 52 45N 9 0 E
26 Niedere Tauern, Mts 47 18N 14 E
24 Nienburg 52 38N 9 15 E
24 Niesky 51 18N 14 48 E
111 Nieuw Amsterdam 5 53N 55 5W
111 Nieuw Nickerie 6 0N 57 10W
30 Nieves 42 7N 7 26W
19 Nièvre □ 47 10N 5 40 E
56 Niğde 37 59N 34 42 E
72 Niger ■ 13 30N 10 0 E
72 Niger, R. 5 33N 6 33 E
72 Nigeria ■ 8 30N 8 0 E
85 Nightcaps 45 57S 168 14 E
66 Niigata 37 58N 139 0 E
66 Niigata □ 37 15N 138 45 E
66 Niihama 33 55N 133 10 E
94 Niihau, I. 21 55N 160 10W
66 Niimi 34 59N 133 28 E
16 Nijkerk 52 13N 5 30 E
16 Nijmegen 51 50N 5 52 E
65 Nikiniki 9 40S 124 30 E
49 Nikolayev 46 58N 32 7 E
49 Nikolayevsk 50 10N 45 35 E
51 Nikolayevskna-Am 53 40N 140 50 E
41 Nikopol, Bulgaria 43 43N 24 54 E
49 Nikopol, U.S.S.R. 47 35N 34 25 E
40 Nikšić 42 50N 18 57 E
73 Nîl, Nahr en, R. 30 10N 31 6 E
73 Nîl el Abyad, R. 15 40N 32 30 E
73 Nîl el Azraq, R. 11 40N 32 30 E
73 Nîl el Azraq □ 12 30N 34 30 E
103 Niland 33 16N 115 30W
73 Nile, R.= Nîl, Nahren, R. 30 10N 31 6 E
96 Niles 41 8N 80 40W
62 Nilgiri Hills 11 30N 76 30 E
60 Nimbahera 24 37N 74 45 E
21 Nîmes 43 50N 4 23 E
42 Nimfaíon, Akra, G. 40 5N 24 20 E
84 Nimmitabel 36 29S 149 15 E
51 Nimneryskiy 58 0N 125 10 E
74 Nimule 3 32N 32 3 E
31 Nindigully 28 21S 148 49 E
84 Ninety Mile Beach, The 38 30S 147 10 E
56 Nineveh 36 25N 43 10 E
69 Ningming 22 10N 107 59 E
69 Ningpo 29 50N 121 30 E
68 Ningsia Hui □ 37 45N 106 0 E
69 Ningteh 26 45N 120 0 E
68 Ningwu 39 2N 112 15 E
63 Ninh Binh 20 15N 105 55 E
16 Ninove 50 51N 4 2 E
109 Nioaque 21 5S 55 50W
100 Niobrara, R. 42 45N 98 0W
72 Nioro 13 40N 15 50W
20 Niort 46 19N 0 29W
62 Nipani 16 20N 74 25 E
93 Nipawin 53 20N 104 0W
93 Nipawin Prov. Park 54 0N 104 40W
90 Nipigon 49 0N 88 17W

Nipigon, L. Oakville, Man.

90 Nipigon, L. 49 40N 88 30W
111 Niquelandia 14 27S 48 27W
62 Nira, R. 17 58N 7 8E
66 Nirasaki 35 42N 138 27E
62 Nirmal 19 3N 78 20E
40 Niš 43 19N 21 58E
31 Nisa 39 30N 2 41W
55 Nisab 14 25N 46 29E
40 Nišava, R. 43 22N 21 46E
39 Niscemi 37 8N 14 21E
66 Nishinomiya 34 45N 135 20E
43 Nísiros, I. 36 35N 27 12E
45 Nissan, R. 43 22N 21 46E
45 Nissum, Fd. 56 20N 8 11E
109 Niterói 22 52S 43 0W
14 Nith, R. 55 0N 3 35W
27 Nitra 48 19N 18 4E
27 Nitra, R. 47 46N 18 10E
16 Nivelles 50 35N 4 20E
19 Nivernais, Reg. 47 0N 3 40E
62 Nizamabad 18 45N 78 7E
59 Nizamghat 28 20N 95 45E
51 Nizhne Kolymsk 68 40N 160 55E
50 Nizhne-Vartovskoye 60 56N 76 38E
51 Nizhneangarsk 56 0N 109 30E
51 Nizhneudinsk 55 0N 99 20E
50 Nizhniy Tagil 57 45N 60 0E
56 Nizip 37 1N 37 46E
27 Nizké Tatry, Mts. 48 55N 20 0E
54 Nizzanim 31 42N 34 37E
74 Njombe 9 0S 34 35E
72 Nkambe 6 35N 10 40E
72 Nkawkaw 6 36N 0 49W
74 Nkhata Bay 11 33S 34 16E
75 Nkhota Kota 12 55S 34 15E
72 Nkongsamba 4 55N 9 55E
88 Noatak 67 34N 162 59W
66 Nobeoka 32 36N 131 41E
30 Noblejas 39 58N 3 26W
39 Nocera Inferiore 40 45N 14 37E
39 Noci 40 47N 17 7E
66 Noda 47 30N 142 5E
104 Nogales, Mexico 31 36N 94 29W
103 Nogales, U.S.A. 31 33N 110 59W
66 Nōgata 33 48N 130 54E
18 Nogent-le-Rotrou 48 20N 0 50E
19 Nogent-sur-Seine 48 30N 3 30E
83 Noggerup 33 32S 116 5E
51 Noginsk 55 50N 38 25E
108 Nogoya 32 24S 59 50W
27 Nograd □ 48 0N 19 30E
30 Nogueira de Ramuin 42 21N 7 43W
32 Noguera Pallaresa, R. 42 15N 0 54E
32 Noguera Ribagorzana, R. 41 40N 0 43E
60 Nohar 29 11N 74 49E
63 Noi, R. 17 5N 105 2E
18 Noire, Mts., Finistere 48 11N 3 40W
20 Noire, Mts., Tarn 43 26N 2 12W
20 Noirétable 45 48N 3 46E
20 Noirmoutier 47 0N 2 15W
20 Noirmoutier, Î. de 46 58N 2 10W
58 Nok Kundi 28 50N 62 45E
51 Nokhhuysk 60 0N 117 45E
39 Nola 40 54N 14 29E
21 Nolay 46 58N 4 35E
36 Noli, C. di 44 12N 8 26E
88 Nome 64 30N 165 30W
18 Nonancourt 48 47N 1 11E
18 Nonant-le-Pin 48 42N 0 12E
80 Nonda 20 40S 142 28E
63 Nong Khae 14 29N 100 53E
63 Nong Khai 17 50N 102 46E
20 Nontron 45 31N 0 40E
82 Noonamah 12 38S 131 4E
81 Noondoo 28 35S 148 30E
16 Noord Beveland, I. 51 45N 3 50E
16 Noord Brabant □ 51 40N 5 0E
16 Noord Holland □ 52 30N 4 45E
16 Noordoost-Polder 52 45N 5 45E
16 Noordwijk 52 14N 4 26E
92 Nootka I. 49 40N 126 50W
44 Nora 59 32N 15 2E
90 Noranda 48 20N 79 0E
44 Norberg 60 4N 15 56E
37 Nórcia 42 50N 13 5E
19 Nord □ 50 15N 3 30E
24 Nord-Friesische, Is. 54 50N 8 20E
24 Nord-Ostsee Kanal 54 5N 9 15E
24 Nord-Süd Kanal 53 0N 10 32E
4 Nordaustlandet 79 55N 23 0E
45 Nordborg 55 5N 9 50E
24 Norddeich 53 37N 7 10E
92 Nordegg 52 29N 116 5W
24 Norden 53 35N 7 12E
24 Nordenham 53 29N 8 28E
24 Norderney 53 42N 7 9E
24 Norderney, I. 53 42N 7 15E
24 Nordhausen 51 29N 10 47E
24 Nordhorn 52 27N 7 4E
46 Nordkapp, Norway 71 11N 25 48E
4 Nordkapp, Svalbard 80 31N 20 0E
46 Nordland □ 65 40N 13 0E
25 Nördlingen 48 50N 10 30E
24 Nordrhein Westfalen □ 51 45N 7 30E
24 Nordstrand, I. 54 27N 8 50E
51 Nordvik 73 40N 110 57E
45 Nordyllands □ 57 0N 10 0E
15 Nore, R. 52 25N 6 58W
100 Norfolk, Nebr. 42 3N 97 25W
98 Norfolk, Va. 36 52N 76 15W
12 Norfolk □ 52 39N 1 0E
76 Norfolk I. 28 58S 168 3E
51 Norilsk 69 20N 88 0E
100 Normal 40 30N 89 0W
101 Norman 35 12N 97 30W
88 Norman Wells 65 40N 126 45W
18 Normandie, Reg. 48 45N 0 10E
18 Normandie, Collines de 48 55N 0 45W
90 Normandin 48 49N 72 31W
80 Normanton 17 40S 141 10E
83 Nornalup 35 0S 116 49E
112 Norquinco 41 51S 70 55W
45 Norrahammar 57 43N 14 7E
46 Norrbotten □ 66 45N 23 0E
45 Nørresundby 57 5N 9 52E
97 Norristown 40 9N 75 15W
45 Norrköping 58 37N 16 11E
44 Norrtälje 59 46N 18 42E
83 Norseman 32 8S 121 43E
45 Norsholm 58 31N 15 59E
51 Norsk 52 30N 130 0E
111 Norte, C. do 1 40N 49 55W
85 North, C. 34 23S 173 4E
85 North I. 38 0S 176 0E
97 North Adams 42 42N 73 6W
1 North America 45 0N 100 0W
63 North Andaman, I. 13 15N 92 40E
6 North Atlantic Ocean 30 0N 50 0W
93 North Battleford 52 50N 108 10W
90 North Bay 46 20N 79 30W
90 North Belcher Is. 56 30N 79 0W
92 North Bend, Canada 49 50N 121 35W
102 North Bend, Oreg. 43 28N 124 7W
96 North Bend, Pa. 41 20N 77 42W
14 North Berwick 56 4N 2 44W
99 North Carolina □ 35 30N 80 0W
14 North Channel 55 0N 5 30W
98 North Chicago 42 19N 87 50W
100 North Dakota □ 47 30N 100 0W
83 North Dandalup 32 31S 115 58E
15 North Down □ 54 40N 5 45W
13 North Downs 51 17N 0 30W
9 North European Plain 55 0N 25 0E
13 North Foreland, Pt. 51 22N 1 28E
92 North Kamloops 50 40N 120 25W
68 North Korea ■ 40 0N 127 0E
59 North Lakhimpur 27 15N 94 10E
14 North Minch 58 5N 5 55W
100 North Platte 41 10N 100 50W
4 North Pole 90 0N 0 0E
14 North Ronaldsay, I. 59 20N 2 30W
93 North Saskatchewan, R. 53 15N 105 6W
8 North Sea 56 0N 4 0E
91 North Sydney 46 12N 60 21W
97 North Syracuse 43 8N 76 8W
96 North Tonawanda 43 5N 78 50W
101 North Truchas Pk. 36 0N 105 30W
12 North Tyne, R. 54 59N 2 8W
14 North Uist, I. 57 40N 7 15W
92 North Vancouver 49 25N 123 20W
105 North Village 32 15N 64 45W
12 North Walsham 52 49N 1 22E
82 North West, C. 21 45S 114 9E
14 North West Highlands, Mts. 57 35N 5 2W
88 North West Territories □ 65 0N 100 0W
12 North York Moors 54 25N 0 50W
12 North Yorkshire □ 54 10N 1 25W
12 Northallerton 54 20N 1 26W
83 Northam 31 35S 116 42E
83 Northampton, Australia 28 21S 114 33E
13 Northampton, U.K. 52 14N 0 54W
97 Northampton, Mass. 42 22N 72 39W
97 Northampton, Pa. 40 38N 75 24W
13 Northampton □ 52 16N 0 55W
80 Northampton Downs 24 35S 145 48E
83 Northcliffe 34 36S 116 7E
24 Northeim 51 42N 10 0E
15 Northern Ireland ■ 54 45N 7 0W
78 Northern Territory □ 16 0S 133 0E
100 Northfield 44 37N 93 10W
97 Northport 45 8N 85 39W
12 Northumberland □ 55 12N 2 0W
80 Northumberland, Is. 21 45S 150 20E
91 Northumberland Str. 46 20N 64 0W
12 Northwich 53 16N 2 30W
88 Norton Sd. 64 0N 165 0W
24 Nortorf 54 14N 10 47E
97 Norwalk, Conn. 41 7N 73 27W
96 Norwalk, Ohio 41 15N 82 37W
46 Norway ■ 67 0N 11 0E
93 Norway House 53 55N 98 50W
5 Norwegian Dependency 75 0S 15 0E
4 Norwegian Sea 66 0N 1 0E
12 Norwich, U.K. 52 38N 1 17E
97 Norwich, Conn. 41 33N 72 5W
97 Norwich, N.Y. 42 32N 75 30W
97 Norwood 42 10N 71 10W
50 Nosok 70 10N 82 20E
57 Nosratabad 29 55N 60 0E
14 Noss Hd. 58 29N 3 4W
75 Nossob, R. 26 55S 20 37E
28 Noteć R. 52 44N 15 26E
43 Notios Evvoïkos, Kól. 38 20N 24 0E
92 Notikewin 57 15N 117 5W
39 Noto 36 52N 15 4E
44 Notodden, Reg. 59 35N 9 17E
91 Notre Dame B. 49 45N 55 30W
89 Notre Dame de Koartac=Koartac 60 55N 69 40W
89 Notre Dame d'Ivugivik=Ivugivik 62 20N 78 0W
96 Nottawasaga B. 44 40N 80 30W
12 Nottingham 52 57N 1 10W
12 Nottinghamshire □ 53 10N 1 0W
72 Nouadhibou 21 0N 17 0W
72 Nouakchott 18 20N 15 50W
76 Noumea 22 17S 166 30E
75 Nouport 31 10S 24 57E
90 Nouveau Comptoir 53 2N 78 55W
19 Nouzonville 49 48N 4 44E
27 Nová Bana 48 28N 18 39E
26 Nová Bystrice 49 2N 15 8E
111 Nova Cruz 6 28S 35 25W
109 Nova Esperança 23 8S 52 13W
109 Nova Friburgo 22 10S 42 30W
111 Nova Granada 20 29S 49 19W
40 Nova Gradiška 45 17N 17 28E
109 Nova Iguaçu 22 45S 43 28W
75 Nova Lisboa=Huambo 12 42S 15 54E
26 Nova Paka 50 29N 15 30E
91 Nova Scotia □ 45 10N 63 0W
75 Nova Sofola 20 7S 34 48E
111 Nova Venecia 18 45S 40 24E
41 Nova Zagora 42 32N 25 59E
41 Novaci 45 10N 23 42E
36 Novara 45 27N 8 36E
48 Novaya Ladoga 60 7N 32 16E
50 Novaya Lyalya 58 50N 60 35E
51 Novaya Sibir, Os. 75 10N 150 0E
50 Novaya Zemlya, I. 75 0N 56 0E
27 Nové Mesto 49 33N 16 7E
27 Nové Zámky 47 59N 18 11E
33 Novelda 38 24N 0 45W
36 Novellara 44 50N 10 43E
48 Novgorod 58 30N 31 25E
40 Novi Bečej 45 36N 20 10E
40 Novi Kneževac 46 4N 20 8E
41 Novi Krichim 42 22N 24 31E
36 Novi Lígure 44 45N 8 47E
41 Novi Pazar, Bulgaria 43 25N 27 15E
40 Novi Pazar, Yug. 43 12N 20 28E
40 Novi-Sad 45 18N 19 52E
37 Novi Vinodolski 45 10N 14 48E
109 Nôvo Hamburgo 29 37S 51 7W
109 Nôvo Horizonte 21 28S 49 13W
74 Novo Redondo 11 10S 13 48E
49 Novocherkassk 47 27N 40 5E
50 Novokazalinsk 45 40N 61 40E
48 Novokiybyshevsk 53 7N 49 58E
50 Novo-kuznetsk 54 0N 87 10E
48 Novomoskovsk 54 5N 38 15E
49 Novorossiyk 44 43N 37 52E
49 Novoshakhtinsk 47 39N 39 58E
50 Novosibirsk 55 0N 83 5E
51 Novosibirskiye Os. 75 0N 140 0E
48 Novotroitsk 51 10N 58 15E
49 Novouzensk 50 32N 48 17E
40 Novska 45 19N 17 0E
26 Novy Bydžov 50 14N 15 29E
28 Nŏvy Dwór 52 26N 20 44E
27 Nový Jičín 49 15N 18 0E
57 Now Shahr 36 40N 51 40E
84 Nowa Nowa 37 44S 148 3E
28 Nowa Sól 51 48N 15 44E
28 Nowe Warpno 53 42N 14 18E
59 Nowgong 26 20N 92 50E
28 Nowogrod 53 14N 21 53E
84 Nowra 34 53S 150 35E
27 Nowy Sącz 49 40N 20 41E
30 Noya 42 48N 8 53W
18 Noyant 47 30N 0 6E
19 Noyers 47 40N 4 0E
19 Noyon 49 34N 3 0E
18 Nozay 47 34N 1 38W
75 Nsanje 16 55S 35 12E
72 Nsawam 5 50N 0 24W
75 Nuanetsi 21 22S 30 45E
70 Nubian Des. 21 30N 33 30E
73 Nûbîya, Es Sahrâ en 21 30N 33 30E
108 Ñuble □ 37 0S 72 0W
108 Nueva Palmira 33 52S 58 20W
104 Nueva Rosita 28 0N 101 20W
108 Nueve de Julio 35 30S 60 50W
105 Nuevitas 21 30N 77 20W
112 Nuevo, G. 43 0S 64 30W
104 Nuevo Laredo 27 30N 99 40W
104 Nuevo León □ 25 0N 100 0W
85 Nuhaka 39 3S 177 45E
19 Nuits 47 10N 4 56E
21 Nuits St. Georges 47 10N 4 56E
73 Nukheila 19 1N 26 21E
50 Nukus 42 20N 59 40E
88 Nulato 64 43N 158 6W
32 Nules 39 51N 0 9W
82 Nullagine 21 53S 120 6E
83 Nullarbor 31 26S 130 55E
83 Nullarbor Plain 31 20S 128 0E
66 Numata 36 38N 139 3E
66 Numazu 35 7N 138 51E
44 Numedal 60 6N 9 6E
84 Numurkah 36 0S 145 26E
13 Nuneaton 52 32N 1 29W
88 Nunivak I. 60 0N 166 0W
68 Nunkiang 49 11N 125 12E
16 Nunspeet 52 21N 5 45E
38 Núoro 40 20N 9 20E
25 Nürnberg 49 26N 11 5E
64 Nusa Tenggara Barat 8 50S 117 30E
65 Nusa Tenggara Timur □ 9 30S 122 0E
58 Nushki 29 35N 65 59E
89 Nutak 57 30N 61 59W
62 Nuwara Eliya 6 58N 80 55E
75 Nuweveldberge 32 10S 21 45E
62 Nuzvid 16 47N 80 51E
83 Nyabing 33 30S 118 7E
97 Nyack 41 5N 73 57W
74 Nyahanga 2 20S 33 37E
73 Nyâlâ 12 2N 24 58E
75 Nyasa, L. 12 0S 34 30E
45 Nyborg 55 18N 10 47E
45 Nybro 56 44N 15 55E
50 Nyda 66 40N 73 10E
67 Nyenchen, Ra. 30 30N 95 0E
74 Nyeri 0 23S 36 56E
27 Nyirbátor 47 49N 22 9E
27 Nyíregyháza 48 0N 21 47E
46 Nykarleby 63 32N 22 31E
45 Nykøbing 54 56N 11 52E
45 Nykøbing Mors 56 49N 8 51E
45 Nyköping 58 45N 17 0E
75 Nylstroom 24 42S 28 22E
26 Nymburk 50 10N 15 1E
44 Nynäshamn 58 54N 17 57E
84 Nyngan 31 30S 147 8E
25 Nyon 46 23N 6 14E
21 Nyons 44 22N 5 10E
84 Nyora 38 20S 145 41E
27 Nysa 50 40N 17 22E
28 Nysa, R. 52 4N 14 46E
51 Nyurba 63 17N 118 20E
74 Nzega 4 10S 33 12E
72 Nzérékoré 7 49N 8 48W

O

100 Oahe Dam 44 28N 100 25W
100 Oahe Res. 45 30N 100 15W
94 Oahu, I. 21 30N 158 0W
102 Oak Creek 40 15N 106 59W
98 Oak Park 41 55N 87 45W
99 Oak Ridge 36 1N 84 5W
101 Oakdale 30 50N 92 28W
12 Oakengates 52 42N 2 29W
102 Oakesdale 47 11N 117 9W
81 Oakey 27 25S 151 43E
12 Oakham 52 40N 0 43W
103 Oakland 37 50N 122 18W
84 Oakleigh 37 54S 145 6E
96 Oakmont 40 31N 79 50W
82 Oakover, R. 20 43S 120 33E
102 Oakridge 43 47N 122 31W
93 Oakville, Man. 49 56N 97 58W

Oakville, Ont. Osborne

96 Oakville, Ont. 43 27N 79 41W
85 Oamaru 45 6S 170 58E
41 Oancea 45 4N 28 7E
104 Oaxaca □ 17 0N 97 0W
50 Ob, R. 62 40N 66 0E
90 Oba 49 4N 84 7W
14 Oban 56 25N 5 30W
92 Obed 53 30N 117 10W
109 Obera 27 21S 55 2W
25 Oberammergau 47 35N 11 3E
26 Oberdrauburg 46 44N 12 58E
24 Oberhausen 51 28N 6 50E
96 Oberlin 41 15N 82 10W
26 Oberösterreich □ 48 10N 14 0E
25 Oberpfälzer Wald 49 30N 12 25E
25 Oberstdorf 47 25N 10 16E
31 Obidos 1 50S 55 30W
66 Obihiro 42 55N 143 10E
24 Öbisfelde 52 27N 10 57E
51 Obluchye 49 10N 130 50E
28 Oborniki 52 39N 16 59E
37 Obrovac 44 11N 15 41E
50 Obskaya Guba 70 0N 73 0E
72 Obuasi 6 17N 1 40W
41 Obzor 42 50N 27 52E
99 Ocala 29 11N 82 5W
110 Ocaña, Col. 8 15N 73 20W
110 Ocaña, Sp. 39 55N 3 30W
110 Occidental, Cord. 5 0N 76 0W
98 Ocean City 39 18N 74 34W
92 Ocean Falls 52 25N 127 40W
76 Ocean I. 0 45S 169 50E
102 Oceanlake 45 0N 124 0W
103 Oceanside 33 13N 117 26W
14 Ochil Hills 56 14N 3 40W
44 Ockelbo 60 54N 16 45E
100 Oconto 44 52N 87 53W
104 Ocatlán 20 21N 102 42W
18 Octeville 49 38N 1 40W
110 Ocumare del Tuy 10 7N 66 46W
65 Ocussi 9 20S 124 30E
66 Ōda 5 50N 1 5W
46 Odáðahraun 65 5N 17 0W
45 Ödåkra 56 9N 12 45E
66 Odawara 35 20N 139 6E
47 Odda 60 3N 6 35E
45 Odder 55 58N 10 10E
55 Oddur 4 0N 43 35E
56 Ödemiş 38 15N 28 0E
45 Odense 55 22N 10 23E
25 Odenwald, Mts. 49 18N 9 0E
28 Oder=Odra R. 53 0N 14 12E
49 Odessa 46 30N 30 45E
101 Odessa 31 51N 102 23W
31 Odiel, R. 37 30N 6 55W
72 Odienné 9 30N 7 34W
41 Odorhei 46 21N 25 21E
28 Odra, R., Poland 53 33N 14 38E
30 Odra, R., Sp. 42 30N 4 15W
40 Odžaci 45 30N 19 17E
75 Odzi 18 58S 32 23E
111 Oeiras 7 0S 42 8W
24 Oelsnitz 50 24N 12 11E
100 Oelwein 42 39N 91 55W
82 Oenpelli 12 20S 133 4E
39 Ofanto, R. 41 8N 15 50E
72 Offa 8 13N 4 42E
15 Offaly □ 53 20N 7 30W
25 Offenbach 50 6N 8 46E
25 Offenburg 48 27N 7 56E
90 Ogahalla 50 6N 85 51W
66 Ōgaki 35 25N 136 35E
100 Ogallala 50 6N 85 51W
72 Ogbomosho 8 1N 3 29E
102 Ogden 41 13N 112 1W
97 Ogdensburg 44 40N 75 27W
36 Oglio, R. 45 15N 10 15E
80 Ogmore 22 37S 149 35E
90 Ogoki 51 35N 86 0W
74 Ogooué, R. 1 0S 10 0E
37 Ogulin 45 16N 15 16E
112 O'Higgins, L. 49 0S 72 40W
108 O'Higgins □ 34 15S 71 1W
85 Ohakune 39 24S 175 24E
101 Ohio, R. 38 0N 86 0W
98 Ohio □ 40 20N 83 0W
25 Ohre, R. 50 10N 12 30E
40 Ohrid 41 8N 20 52E
40 Ohrid, L.=
Ohridsko, J. 41 8N 20 52E
40 Ohridsko, J. 41 8N 20 52E
111 Oiapoque 3 50N 51 50W
96 Oil City 41 26N 79 40W
19 Oise, R. 49 53N 3 50E
19 Oise □ 49 28N 2 30E
66 Ōita 33 15N 131 36E
108 Ojos del Salado,
Cerro, Mt. 27 0S 68 40W
75 Okahandja 22 0S 16 59E
102 Okanagan 48 24N 119 24W
60 Okara 30 50N 73 25E
85 Okarito 43 15S 170 9E
75 Okavango, R. 17 40S 19 30E
75 Okavango Swamps 19 30S 23 0E
66 Okaya 36 0N 138 10E
66 Okayama 34 40N 133 54E
66 Okayama □ 35 0N 133 50E
66 Okazaki 34 36N 137 0E
99 Okeechobee, L. 21 0N 80 50W
99 Okefenokee
Swamp 30 50N 82 15W
13 Okehampton 50 44N 4 1W
72 Okene 7 32N 6 11E
25 Oker, R. 52 7N 10 34E
51 Okha 53 40N 143 0E
43 Ókhi Óros 38 5N 24 25E
51 Okhotsk 59 20N 143 10E
51 Okhotsk, Sea of 55 0N 145 0E
51 Okhotskiy
Perevoz 61 52N 135 35E
51 Oknotsko
kolymskoy 63 0N 157 0E
66 Oki-Shotō 36 15N 133 15E
75 Okiep 29 39S 17 53E
69 Okinawa, I. 26 40N 128 0E
69 Okinawa-guntō, Is. 26 0N 127 30E
101 Oklahoma □ 35 20N 97 30W
101 Oklahoma City 35 25N 97 30W
101 Okmulgee 35 38N 96 0W
72 Okrika 4 47N 7 4E
51 Oktyabriskoy
Revolyutsii Os. 79 30N 97 0E
48 Oktyabrski 53 11N 48 40E
85 Okura 43 55S 168 55E
66 Okushiri-Tō, I. 42 15N 139 30E
45 Öland, I. 56 45N 16 50E
81 Olary 32 17S 140 19E
100 Olathe 38 50N 94 50W
108 Olavarría 36 55S 60 20W
27 Olawa 50 57N 17 20E
38 Ólbia 40 55N 9 30E
38 Ólbia, G. di 40 55N 9 35E
96 Olcott 43 20N 78 43W
88 Old Crow 67 35N 139 50W
90 Old Factory 52 36N 78 43W
97 Old Forge 41 22N 75 44W
99 Old Town 45 0N 68 50W
15 Oldcastle 53 46N 7 10W
24 Oldenburg 53 10N 8 10E
24 Oldenburg 54 16N 10 53E
16 Oldenzaal 52 19N 6 53E
92 Olds 51 50N 114 10W
96 Olean 42 8N 78 25W
28 Olecko 54 3N 22 30E
51 Olekminsk 60 40N 120 30E
48 Olenegorsk 68 9N 33 15E
51 Olenek 68 20N 112 30E
20 Oléron, Î. d' 45 55N 1 15W
28 Oleśnica 51 13N 17 22E
51 Olga 43 50N 135 0E
83 Olga, Mt. 25 20S 130 40E
31 Olhão 37 3N 7 48W
75 Olifants, R. 24 10S 32 40S
109 Olímpia 20 44S 48 54W
108 Olimpo □ 20 30S 58 45W
32 Olite 42 29N 1 40W
33 Oliva 38 58N 0 15W
108 Oliva 32 0S 63 38W
30 Oliva, Pta. del 43 37N 5 28W
31 Oliva de la
Frontera 38 17N 6 54W
32 Olivares 39 46N 2 20W
109 Oliveira 20 50S 44 50W
30 Oliveira de
Azemeis 40 49N 8 29W
31 Olivenza 38 41N 7 9W
92 Oliver 49 20N 119 30W
27 Olkusz 50 18N 19 33E
30 Olmedo 41 20N 4 43W
98 Olney 38 40N 88 0W
45 Olofström 56 17N 14 32E
27 Olomouc 49 38N 17 12E
32 Olot 42 11N 2 30E
40 Olovo 44 8N 18 35E
51 Olovyannaya 50 50N 115 10E
24 Olpe 51 2N 7 50E
28 Olsztyn 53 48N 20 29E
28 Olsztyn □ 54 0N 21 0E
41 Olt, R. 43 50N 24 40E
25 Olten 47 21N 7 53E
41 Oltenita 44 7N 26 42E
32 Oluego 41 47N 2 0W
31 Olvera 36 55N 5 18W
102 Olympia 47 0N 122 58W
102 Olympic Mts. 48 0N 124 0W
102 Olympic Nat. Park 47 35N 123 30W
102 Olympus Mt. 47 52N 123 40W
42 Olympus, Mt.=
Óros Ólimbos 40 6N 22 23E
97 Olyphant 41 27N 75 36W
15 Omagh 54 36N 7 20W
15 Omagh □ 54 35N 7 20W
100 Omaha 41 15N 96 0W
102 Omak 48 25N 119 24W
55 Oman ■ 23 0N 58 0E
57 Oman, G. of 24 30N 58 30E
75 Omaruru 21 26S 16 0E
110 Omate 16 45S 71 0W
65 Ombai, Selat,
Str. 8 30S 124 50E
36 Ombrone, R. 42 48N 11 15E
73 Omdurmân 15 40N 32 28E
36 Omegna 45 52N 8 23E
54 Omez 32 22N 35 0E
37 Omiš 43 28N 16 40E
66 Ōmiya 35 54N 139 38E
74 Omo, R. 8 48N 37 14E
50 Omsk 55 0N 73 38E
41 Omul, Mt. 45 27N 25 29E
28 Omulew, R. 53 5N 21 32E
66 Ōmura 33 8N 130 0E
41 Omurtag 43 8N 26 26E
66 Ōmuta 33 0N 130 26E
30 Oña 42 43N 3 25W
32 Onda 39 55N 0 17W
75 Ondangua 17 57S 16 4E
30 Ondárroa 43 19N 2 25W
72 Ondo 7 4N 4 47E
68 Ondörhaan 47 22N 110 31E
48 Onega 64 0N 38 10E
48 Onega, R. 63 0N 39 0E
85 Onehunga 36 55N 174 30E
97 Oneida 43 5N 75 40W
97 Oneida L. 43 12N 76 0W
100 O'Neill 42 30N 98 38W
97 Oneonta 42 26N 75 5W
48 Onezhskaya Guba 64 30N 37 0E
48 Onezhskoye, Oz 62 0N 35 30E
85 Ongarue 38 42S 175 19E
83 Ongerup 33 58S 118 29E
62 Ongole 15 33N 80 2E
72 Onitsha 6 6N 6 42E
66 Onoda 34 2N 131 10E
30 Ons, Is. 42 23N 8 55W
82 Onslow 21 40S 115 0E
16 Onstwedde 52 2N 7 4E
66 Ontake-San, Mt. 35 50N 137 15E
103 Ontario 34 2N 117 40W
96 Ontario, L. 43 40N 78 0W
90 Ontario □ 52 0N 88 10W
33 Onteniente 38 50N 0 35W
81 Oodnadatta 27 33S 135 30E
83 Ooldea 30 27S 131 50E
80 Oorindi 20 40S 141 1E
16 Oostende 51 15N 2 50E
16 Oosterhout 51 38N 4 51E
16 Oosterschelde, R. 51 30N 4 0E
62 Ootacamund 11 30N 76 44E
51 Opala, U.S.S.R. 52 15N 156 15E
74 Opala, Zaïre 0 37S 24 21E
37 Opatija 45 21N 14 17E
27 Opava 49 57N 17 58E
101 Opelousas 30 35N 92 0W
88 Ophir 63 10N 156 31W
28 Opoczno 51 22N 20 18E
27 Opole 50 42N 17 58E
27 Opole □ 50 40N 17 56E
85 Opotiki 38 1S 177 19E
99 Opp 31 19E 86 13W
39 Oppido Mamertina 38 16N 15 59E
44 Oppland □ 61 15N 9 30E
93 Optic Lake 54 46N 101 13W
85 Opua 35 19S 174 9E
85 Opunake 39 26S 173 52E
40 Opuzen 43 1N 17 34E
19 Or, Côtes d' 47 10N 4 50E
54 Or Yehuda 32 2N 34 50E
37 Ora 46 20N 11 19E
27 Oradea 47 2N 21 58E
46 Öraefajökull, Mt. 64 2N 16 15W
61 Orai 25 58N 79 30E
72 Oran 35 37N 0 39W
84 Orange,
Australia 33 15S 149 7E
21 Orange, Fr. 44 8N 4 47E
101 Orange, U.S.A. 30 0N 93 40W
75 Orange=Oranje, R. 28 30S 18 0E
111 Orange, C. 4 20N 51 30W
75 Orange Free
State □ 28 30S 27 0E
104 Orange Walk 17 15N 88 47W
99 Orangeburg 33 27N 80 53W
90 Orangeville 43 55N 80 5W
24 Oranienburg 52 45N 13 15E
75 Oranje, R. 28 41S 16 28E
75 Oranje-Vrystaat □ 28 30S 27 0E
75 Oranjemund 28 32S 16 29E
75 Orapa 24 13S 25 25E
40 Orašje 45 1N 18 42E
41 Orăştie 45 50N 23 10E
40 Oravita 45 6N 21 43E
20 Orb, R. 43 15N 3 18E
25 Orbe 46 43N 6 32E
37 Orbetello 42 26N 11 11E
84 Orbost 37 40S 148 29E
44 Örbynus 60 15N 17 43E
33 Orce 37 44N 2 28W
33 Orce, R. 37 44N 2 28W
19 Orchies 50 28N 3 14E
14 Orchy, Bridge of 56 30N 4 46W
82 Ord, Mt. 17 20S 125 34E
82 Ord, R. 15 30S 128 21E
14 Ord of Caithness 58 35N 3 37W
82 Ord River 17 23S 128 51E
30 Ordenes 43 5N 8 29W
56 Ordu 40 55N 37 53E
30 Orduña 42 58N 2 58W
31 Orduña, Mt. 37 20N 3 30W
49 Ordzhonlkidze 43 0N 44 35E
40 Orebic 43 0N 17 11E
44 Örebro 59 20N 15 18E
44 Örebro □ 59 27N 15 0E
102 Oregon □ 44 0N 120 0W
102 Oregon City 45 28N 122 35W
48 Orekhovo-Zuyevo 55 50N 38 55E
48 Orel 52 59N 36 5E
31 Orellana,
Pantano de, L. 39 5N 5 10W
31 Orellana La Vieja 39 1N 5 32W
102 Orem 40 27N 111 45W
48 Orenburg 51 45N 55 6E
30 Orense 42 19N 7 55W
30 Orense □ 42 15N 7 30W
85 Orepuki 46 19S 167 46E
42 Orestiás 41 30N 26 33E
45 Øresund 55 45N 12 45E
13 Orford Ness, C. 52 6N 1 31E
21 Orgon 43 47N 5 3E
39 Ória 40 30E 17 38E
90 Orient Bay 49 20N 88 10W
110 Oriental, Cord. 5 0N 74 0W
19 Origny 49 50N 3 30E
33 Orihuela 38 7N 0 55W
96 Orillia 44 40N 79 24W
110 Orinoco, R. 8 37N 62 15W
93 Orion 49 28N 110 49W
61 Orissa □ 21 0N 85 0E
38 Oristano 39 54N 8 35E
38 Oristano, G. di 39 50N 8 22E
104 Orizaba 18 50N 97 10W
33 Orjiva 36 53N 3 24W
44 Orkanger 63 18N 9 52E
45 Orkelljunga 56 17N 13 17E
45 Örken 51 6N 6 34E
27 Orkery 47 9N 19 26E
14 Orkney □ 59 0N 3 0W
102 Orland 39 46N 120 10W
99 Orlando 28 30N 81 25W
19 Orléanais, Reg. 48 0N 2 0E
19 Orléans, Fr. 47 54N 1 52E
97 Orleans, U.S.A. 44 49N 72 10W
91 Orleans, I. d' 46 54N 70 58W
72 Orléansville=El
Asnam 36 10N 1 20E
27 Orlické hory 50 15N 16 30E
51 Orlik 52 30N 99 55E
27 Orlov 49 17N 20 51E
58 Ormara 25 16N 64 33E
38 Ormea 44 9N 7 54E
65 Ormoc 11 0N 124 37E
85 Ormond 38 33S 177 56E
37 Ormož 46 25N 16 10E
12 Ormskirk 53 35N 2 54W
19 Ornans 47 7N 6 10E
18 Orne, R. 49 18N 0 14E
18 Orne □ 48 40N 0 0E
44 Örnsköldsvik 63 17N 18 40E
110 Orocué 4 48N 71 20W
30 Orol 43 34N 7 39W
91 Oromocto 45 54N 66 37W
54 Oron 30 55N 35 1E
30 Oropesa 39 57N 5 10W
111 Orós 6 15S 38 55W
42 Óros Ólimbos,
Mt. 40 6N 22 23E
43 Óros Óthris,
Mt. 39 4N 22 42E
38 Orosei, G. di 40 15N 9 40E
27 Orosháza 46 32N 20 42E
102 Oroville 39 40N 121 30W
81 Orroroo 32 44S 138 37E
96 Orrville 40 50N 81 46W
44 Orsa 61 7N 14 37E
48 Orsha 54 30N 30 25E
48 Orsk 51 20N 58 34E
40 Orşova 44 41N 22 25E
36 Orta, L. d' 45 48N 8 21E
39 Orta Nova 41 20N 15 40E
30 Ortegal, C. 43 43N 7 52W
20 Orthez 43 29N 0 48W
30 Ortigueira 43 40N 7 50W
36 Ortles, Mt. 46 31N 10 33E
37 Ortona 42 21N 14 24E
110 Oruro 18 0S 67 19W
18 Orvault 47 17N 1 38E
37 Orvieto 42 43N 12 8E
13 Orwell, R. 51 57N 1 17E
41 Oryakhovo 43 40N 23 57E
36 Orzinuovi 45 24N 9 55E
28 Orzyc, R. 52 47N 21 13E
28 Orzysz 53 50N 21 58E
105 Osa, Pen. de 8 0N 84 0W
100 Osage, R. 38 35N 91 57W
66 Ōsaka 34 40N 135 30E
66 Ōsaka □ 34 40N 135 30E
100 Osborne 39 30N 98 45W

Phatthalung Port Cartier

63 Phatthalung 7 39N 100 6E
99 Phenix City 32 30N 85 0W
63 Phetchaburi 16 25N 101 8E
63 Phichai 17 22N 100 10E
98 Philadelphia 40 0N 75 10W
42 Philippi 41 0N 24 19E
8 Philippine Trench= Mindanao Trench 8 0N 128 0E
65 Philippines ■ 12 0N 123 0E
84 Phillip, I. 38 30S 145 12E
97 Phillipsburg 40 43N 75 12W
81 Phillott 27 53S 145 50E
102 Philomath 44 28N 123 21W
63 Phitsanulok 16 50N 100 12E
63 Phnom Penh 11 33N 104 55E
103 Phoenix 33 30N 112 10W
77 Phoenix Is. 3 30S 172 0W
97 Phoenixville 40 12N 75 29W
63 Phra Nakhon Si Ayutthaya 14 25N 100 30E
63 Phu Doan 21 40N 105 10E
63 Phu Loi, Mt. 20 14N 103 14E
63 Phu Ly 20 35N 105 50E
63 Phu Quoc, I. 10 15N 104 0E
63 Phuket 8 0N 98 28E
60 Phul 30 19N 75 14E
36 Piacenza 45 2N 9 42E
81 Pialba 25 20S 152 45E
81 Pian Creek 30 2S 148 12E
21 Piana 42 14N 8 38E
31 Pias 38 1N 7 29W
28 Piaseczno 52 5N 21 2E
28 Piastów 52 12N 20 48E
41 Piatra 43 51N 25 9E
111 Piaui □ 7 0S 43 0W
37 Piave, R. 45 32N 12 44E
39 Piazza Armerina 37 21N 14 20E
19 Picardie, Plaine de 50 0N 2 0E
19 Picardie, Reg. 50 0N 2 15E
101 Picayune 30 40N 89 40W
12 Pickering 54 15N 0 46W
90 Pickle Crow 51 30N 90 0W
8 Pico, I. 38 28N 28 20W
112 Pico Truncado 46 40S 68 10W
30 Picos Anceres, Sa. de 42 51N 6 52W
19 Picquigny 49 56N 2 10E
84 Picton, Australia 34 12S 150 34E
90 Picton, Canada 44 1N 77 9W
85 Picton, N.Z. 41 18S 174 3E
91 Pictou 45 41N 62 42W
92 Picture Butte 49 55N 112 45W
112 Picún Leufú 39 30S 69 5W
62 Pidurutalagala, Mt. 7 10N 80 50E
31 Piedrabuena 39 0N 4 10W
103 Piedras Blancas Pt. 35 45N 121 18W
104 Piedras Negras 28 35N 100 35W
36 Piermonte □ 45 0N 7 30E
97 Piercefield 44 13N 74 35W
42 Piería □ 40 13N 22 25E
100 Pierre 44 23N 100 20W
19 Pierrefonds 49 20N 3 0E
27 Piešťany 48 35N 17 50E
75 Piet Retief 27 1S 30 50E
39 Pietraperzia 37 26N 14 8E
75 Pietermaritzburg 29 35S 30 25E
75 Pietersburg 23 54S 29 25E
36 Pietrasanta 43 57N 10 12E
90 Pigeon River 48 1N 89 42W
108 Pigüé 37 36S 62 25W
75 Piketberg 32 55S 18 40E
98 Pikeville 37 30N 82 30W
28 Piła 53 10N 16 48E
28 Piła □ 53 0N 17 0E
108 Pilar 26 50S 58 10W
111 Pilar 14 30S 49 45W
28 Pilawa 51 58N 21 31E
108 Pilcomayo, R. 25 21S 57 42W
61 Pilibhit 28 40N 78 50E
28 Pilica, R. 51 52N 21 17E
42 Pilion, Mt. 39 27N 23 7E
60 Pilkhawa 28 43N 77 42E
28 Pillau=Baltiisk 54 38N 19 55E
43 Pilos 36 55N 21 42E
103 Pima 32 54N 109 50W
81 Pimba 31 18S 136 46E
63 Pinang □ 5 25N 100 15E
105 Pinar del Rio 22 26N 83 40W
93 Pinawa 50 15N 95 50W
92 Pincher Creek 49 30N 113 35W
60 Pind Dadan Khan 32 55N 73 47E
83 Pindar 28 30S 115 47E
72 Pindiga 9 58N 10 53E
42 Pindos Óros 40 0N 21 0E
42 Pindus Mts.= Pindos Óros 40 0N 21 0E
91 Pine, C. 46 37N 53 30W
101 Pine Bluff 34 10N 92 0W
82 Pine Creek 13 49S 131 49E
93 Pine Falls 50 51N 96 11W
92 Pine Point 60 50N 114 40W
48 Pinega, R. 64 8N 41 54E
80 Pinehill 23 38S 146 57E
36 Pinerolo 44 47N 7 21E
37 Pineto 42 36N 14 4E
75 Pinetown 29 48S 30 54E
101 Pineville 31 22N 92 30W
19 Piney 48 22N 4 21E
63 Ping, R. 15 42N 100 9E
83 Pingaring 32 40S 118 32E
83 Pingelly 32 29S 116 59E
69 Pingkiang 28 45N 113 30E
68 Pingliang 35 32N 106 50E
69 Pingsiang 22 2N 106 55E
69 Pingtingshan 33 43N 113 28E
69 Pingtung 22 38N 120 30E
68 Pingyao 37 12N 112 10E
109 Pinhal 22 10S 46 46W
30 Pinhel 40 18N 7 0W
68 Pinhsien 35 10N 108 10E
83 Pinjarra 32 37S 115 52E
84 Pinnaroo 35 13S 140 56E
105 Pinos, I. de 21 40N 82 40W
103 Pinos, Pt. 36 50N 121 57W
31 Pinos Puente 37 15N 3 45W
65 Pinrang 3 46S 119 34E
48 Pinsk 52 10N 26 8E
93 Pinto Butte, Mt. 49 22N 107 25W
83 Pintumba 31 50S 132 18E
69 Pinyang 23 12N 108 35E
48 Pinyug 60 5N 48 0E
103 Pioche 38 0N 114 35N
36 Piombino 42 54N 10 30E
28 Pionki 51 29N 21 28E
28 Piotrków Trybunalski 51 23N 19 43E
28 Piotrków Trybunalski □ 51 20N 19 30E
60 Pipar 26 25N 73 31E
60 Pipariya 22 45N 78 23E
100 Pipestone 44 0N 96 20W
91 Pipmuacan Res. 49 40N 70 25W
82 Pippingarra 20 27S 118 42E
98 Piqua 40 10N 84 10W
109 Piracicaba 22 45S 47 30W
111 Piracuruca 3 50S 41 50W
43 Piraeus= Piraiévs 37 57N 23 42E
43 Piraiévs 37 57N 23 42E
43 Piraiévs □ 37 0N 23 30E
109 Pirajui 21 59S 49 29W
37 Piran 45 31N 13 33E
108 Pirané 25 44S 59 7W
41 Pirdop 42 40N 24 10E
43 Pirgos, Ilia 37 40N 21 27E
43 Pírgos, Messinia 36 50N 22 16E
18 Piriac-sur-Mer 47 23N 2 31W
108 Piribebuy 25 29S 57 3W
111 Piripiri 4 15S 41 46W
25 Pirmasens 49 12N 7 30E
24 Pirna 50 57N 13 57E
61 Pirojpur 22 35N 90 1E
40 Pirot 43 9N 22 39E
65 Piru 3 3S 128 12E
36 Pisa 43 43N 10 23E
110 Pisagua 19 40S 70 15W
110 Pisco 13 50S 76 5W
41 Piscu 45 30N 27 43E
26 Pisek 49 19N 14 10E
39 Pisticci 40 24N 16 33E
36 Pistóia 43 57N 10 53E
30 Pisuerga, R. 41 33N 4 52W
28 Pisz 53 38N 21 49E
109 Pitanga 24 46S 51 44W
77 Pitcairn I. 25 5S 130 5W
46 Pitea 65 20N 21 25E
41 Piteşti 44 52N 24 54E
62 Pithapuram 17 10N 82 15E
83 Pithara 30 20S 116 35E
42 Píthion 41 24N 26 40E
19 Pithiviers 48 10N 2 13E
14 Pitlochry 56 43N 3 43W
102 Pittsburg, Calif. 38 1N 121 50W
101 Pittsburg, Kans. 37 21N 94 43W
96 Pittsburgh, Pa. 40 25N 79 55W
101 Pittsburgh, Tex. 32 59N 94 58W
97 Pittsfield 42 28N 73 17W
97 Pittston 41 19N 75 50W
81 Pittsworth 27 41S 151 37E
110 Piura 5 5S 80 45W
91 Placentia 47 20N 54 0W
102 Placerville 38 47N 120 51W
105 Placetas 22 15N 79 44W
97 Plainfield 40 37N 74 28W
101 Plainview 34 10N 101 40W
101 Plaquemine 30 20N 91 15W
30 Plasencia 40 3N 6 8W
37 Plaški 45 4N 15 22E
91 Plaster Rock 46 53N 67 22W
108 Plata, R. de la 34 45S 57 30W
110 Plato 9 47N 74 47W
100 Platte, R. 41 4N 95 53W
100 Platteville 40 18N 104 47W
25 Plattling 48 46N 12 53E
97 Plattsburgh 44 41N 73 30W
100 Plattsmouth 41 0N 96 0W
24 Plauen 50 29N 12 9E
40 Plavnica 42 10N 19 20E
98 Pleasantville 39 25N 74 30W
18 Plélan-le-Grand 48 0N 2 7W
18 Pléneuf-val-André 48 37N 2 32W
85 Plenty, B. of 37 45S 177 0E
48 Plesetsk 62 40N 40 10E
91 Plessisville 46 14N 71 46W
28 Pleszew 51 53N 17 47E
41 Pleven 43 26N 24 37E
40 Ploče 43 4N 17 26E
28 Płock 52 32N 19 40E
18 Ploëmeur 47 44N 3 26W
18 Ploërmel 47 55N 2 26W
41 Ploieşti 44 57N 26 5E
24 Plön 54 8N 10 22E
28 Płonsk 52 37N 20 21E
28 Płoty 53 48N 15 18E
18 Plouaret 48 37N 3 28W
26 Ploucnice 50 47N 14 13E
18 Ploudalmézeau 48 34N 4 41W
41 Plovdiv 42 8N 24 44E
75 Plumtree 20 27S 27 55E
18 Pluvigner 47 46N 3 1W
105 Plymouth, Montserrat 16 42N 62 13W
13 Plymouth, U.K. 50 23N 4 9W
98 Plymouth, Ind. 41 20N 86 19W
97 Plymouth, N.H. 43 44N 71 41W
97 Plymouth, Pa. 41 17N 76 0W
26 Plzeň 49 45N 13 22E
28 Pniewy 52 31N 16 16E
37 Po, Foci del 44 52N 12 30E
36 Po, R. 44 57N 12 4E
68 Po Hai, G. 38 40N 119 0E
51 Pobedino 49 51N 142 49E
30 Pobladura de Valle 42 6N 5 44W
102 Pocatello 42 50N 112 25W
26 Pochlarn 48 12N 15 12E
109 Poços de Caldas 21 50S 46 45W
26 Poděbrady 50 9N 15 8E
51 Podkamenndya Tunguska 61 50N 90 26E
26 Podmokly 50 48N 14 10E
48 Podolsk 55 30N 37 30E
48 Podporozny 60 55N 34 2E
40 Podravska Slatina 45 42N 17 45E
24 Poel, I. 54 0N 11 25E
37 Poggibonsi 43 27N 11 8E
42 Pogradeci 40 57N 20 48E
68 Pohang 36 8N 129 23E
37 Pohorje, Mt. 46 30N 15 7E
40 Poiana Ruscăi Mt. 45 45N 22 25E
90 Point Edward 43 10N 82 30W
97 Point Pleasant 38 50N 82 7W
97 Pointe Claire 45 26N 73 49W
74 Pointe-Noire 4 48S 12 0E
105 Pointe-à-Pitre 16 10N 61 30W
19 Poissy 48 55N 2 0E
20 Poitou, Plaines du 46 30N 0 1W
20 Poitou, Reg. 46 25N 0 15W
19 Poix 49 47N 2 0E
19 Poix Terron 49 38N 4 38E
28 Pojezierze Mazurski, Reg. 53 40N 21 0E
81 Pokataroo 29 30S 148 34E
74 Poko 3 7N 26 52E
68 Pokotu 48 46N 121 54E
51 Pokrovsk 61 29N 129 6E
30 Pola de Lena 43 10N 5 49W
30 Pola de Siero 43 24N 5 39W
103 Polacca 35 52N 110 25W
28 Poland ■ 52 0N 20 0E
5 Polar Sub-Glacial Basin 85 0S 100 0E
13 Polden Hills 51 7N 2 50W
27 Polgar 47 54N 21 6E
68 Poli 8 34N 12 54E
43 Políaigos, I. 36 45N 24 38E
39 Policastro, G. di 39 55N 15 35E
28 Police 53 33N 14 33E
39 Polignano a Mare 41 0N 17 12E
21 Poligny 46 50N 5 42E
43 Polikhnitos 39 4N 26 10E
65 Polillo Is. 14 56N 122 0E
39 Polístena 38 25N 16 4E
62 Pollachi 10 35N 77 0E
32 Pollensa 39 54N 3 2E
50 Polnovat 63 50N 66 5E
48 Polotsk 55 30N 28 50E
41 Polski Trumbosh 43 20N 25 38E
41 Polsko Kosovo 43 23N 25 38E
102 Polson 47 45N 114 12W
49 Poltava 49 35N 34 35E
62 Polur 12 32N 79 11E
48 Polyarny 69 8N 33 20E
111 Pombal, Brazil 6 55S 37 50W
30 Pombal, Port. 39 55N 8 40W
103 Pomona 34 2N 117 49W
41 Pomorie 42 26N 27 41E
99 Pompano 26 12N 80 6W
76 Ponape, I. 6 55N 158 10E
101 Ponca City 36 40N 97 5W
105 Ponce 18 1N 66 37W
89 Pond Inlet 72 30N 75 0W
62 Pondicherry 11 59N 79 50E
30 Ponferrada 42 32N 6 35W
62 Ponnani 10 45N 75 59E
59 Ponnyadaung, Mts. 22 0N 94 10E
48 Ponoi 67 0N 41 0E
92 Ponoka 52 35N 113 40W
65 Ponorogo 7 52S 111 29E
20 Pons 45 35N 0 34W
18 Pont-Audemer 49 21N 0 30E
91 Pont Lafrance 47 40N 64 58W
21 Pont St. Esprit 44 16N 4 40E
18 Pont-l'Abbé 47 52N 4 15W
18 Pont-l'Evêque 49 18N 0 11E
109 Ponta Grossa 25 0S 50 10W
19 Pont-à-Mousson 45 54N 6 1E
109 Ponta Pora 22 20S 55 35W
21 Pontarlier 46 54N 6 20E
18 Pontaubault 48 40N 1 20W
101 Pontchartrain, L. 30 12N 90 0W
18 Pontchâteau 47 26N 2 8W
31 Ponte de Sor 39 17N 7 57W
21 Ponte Leccia 42 28N 9 13E
109 Ponte Nova 20 25S 42 54W
38 Pontecorvo 41 28N 13 40E
36 Pontedera 43 40N 10 37E
12 Pontefract 53 42N 1 19W
93 Ponteix 49 46N 107 29W
30 Pontevedra 42 26N 8 40W
30 Pontevedra, Ria de 42 22N 8 45W
30 Pontevedra □ 42 25N 8 39W
100 Pontiac, Ill. 40 50N 88 40W
98 Pontiac, Mich. 42 40N 83 20W
63 Pontian Kechil 1 29N 103 23E
64 Pontianak 0 3S 109 15E
56 Pontine Mts.= Karadeniz Dağlari, Mts. 41 30N 35 0E
18 Pontivy 48 5N 3 0W
19 Pontoise 49 3N 2 5E
18 Pontorson 48 34N 1 30W
36 Pontrémoli 44 22N 9 52E
13 Pontypool 51 42N 3 1W
13 Pontypridd 51 36N 3 21S
38 Ponziane, Is. 40 55N 13 0E
81 Poochera 32 43S 134 51E
13 Poole 50 42N 2 2W
62 Poona=Pune 18 29N 73 57E
62 Poonamelle 13 3N 80 10E
110 Poopó, L. 18 30S 67 35W
83 Popanyinning 32 40S 117 2E
110 Popayán 2 27N 76 36W
16 Poperinge 50 51N 2 42E
51 Popigay 71 55N 110 47E
101 Poplar Bluff 36 45N 90 22W
104 Popocatepetl, Mt. 19 10N 98 40W
37 Popovača 45 30N 16 41E
41 Popovo 43 21N 26 18E
27 Poprád 49 3N 20 18E
60 Porbandar 21 44N 69 43E
31 Porcuna 37 52N 4 11W
88 Porcupine, R. 66 35N 145 15W
37 Pordenone 45 58N 12 40E
41 Pordim 43 23N 24 51E
37 Poreč 45 14N 13 36E
109 Porecatu 22 43S 51 24W
21 Poretta 42 35N 9 28E
47 Pori 61 29N 21 48E
46 Porjus 66 57N 19 50E
47 Porkkala 59 59N 24 26E
110 Porlamar 10 57N 63 51W
30 Prma, R. 42 29N 5 28W
18 Pornic 47 7N 2 5W
51 Poronaysk 49 20N 143 0E
43 Póros 37 30N 23 30E
21 Porquerolles, Î. de 43 0N 6 13E
36 Porretta, P. 44 9N 10 59E
44 Porsgrunn 59 10N 9 40E
81 Port Adelaide 34 46S 138 30E
92 Port Alberni 49 15N 124 50W
60 Port Albert Victor 21 0N 71 30E
91 Port Alfred 48 18N 70 53W
92 Port Alice 50 25N 127 25W
96 Port Allegany 41 49N 78 17W
102 Port Angeles 48 0N 123 30W
90 Port Arthur, Canada= Thunder Bay 48 25N 89 10W
68 Port Arthur, China= Lushun 38 48N 121 16E
101 Port Arthur, U.S.A. 30 0N 94 0W
Thunder Bav 48 25N 89 10W
81 Port Augusta 32 30S 137 50E
91 Port aux Basques 47 32N 59 8W
32 Port Bou 42 25N 3 9E
81 Port Broughton 33 37S 137 56E
91 Port Cartier 50 10N 66 50W

Port Chalmers Pulaski, N.Y.

85 Port Chalmers 45 49 S 170 30 E
97 Port Chester 41 0 N 73 41 W
90 Port Colborne 42 50 N 79 10 W
92 Port Coquitlam 49 20 N 122 45 W
96 Port Credit 43 34 N 79 35 W
78 Port Darwin 12 18 S 130 55 E
105 Port de Paix 19 50 N 72 50 W
63 Port Dickson 2 30 N 101 49 E
80 Port Douglas 16 30 S 145 30 E
92 Port Edward 54 14 N 130 18 W
90 Port Elgin 44 25 N 81 25 W
75 Port Elizabeth 33 58 S 25 40 E
14 Port Ellen 55 39 N 6 12 W
12 Port Erin 54 5 N 4 45 W
72 Port Étienne= Nouadhibou 21 0 N 17 0 W
84 Port Fairy 38 22 S 142 12 E
74 Port-Gentil 0 47 S 8 40 E
14 Port Glasgow 55 57 N 4 40 W
72 Port Harcourt 4 43 N 7 5 E
92 Port Hardy 50 41 N 127 30 W
89 Port Harrison= Inoucdouac 58 25 N 78 15 W
82 Port Hedland 20 25 S 118 35 E
97 Port Henry 44 0 N 73 30 W
91 Port Hood 46 0 N 61 32 W
90 Port Hope 44 0 N 78 20 W
96 Port Huron 43 0 N 82 28 W
97 Port Jervis 41 22 N 74 42 W
84 Port Kembla 34 29 S 150 56 E
63 Port Klang 3 0 N 101 21 E
20 Port La Nouvelle 43 1 N 3 3 E
15 Port Laoise 53 2 N 7 20 W
101 Port Lavaca 28 38 N 96 38 W
81 Port Lincoln 34 42 S 135 52 E
72 Port-Lyautey= Kenitra 34 15 N 6 40 W
81 Port Macquarie 31 25 S 152 54 E
91 Port Maitland 44 0 N 66 2 W
92 Port Mellon 49 32 N 123 31 W
91 Port Menier 49 51 N 64 15 W
76 Port Moresby 9 24 S 147 8 E
93 Port Nelson 57 5 N 92 56 W
75 Port Nolloth 29 17 S 16 52 E
89 Port Nouveau-Quebec 58 30 N 65 50 W
105 Port of Spain 10 40 N 61 20 W
102 Port Orchard 47 31 N 122 47 W
90 Port Perry 44 6 N 78 56 W
81 Port Pirie 33 10 S 137 58 E
88 Port Radium 66 10 N 117 40 W
73 Port Said= Bûr Saîd 31 16 N 32 18 E
75 Port St. Johns= Umzimvubu 31 38 S 29 33 E
21 Port-St.-Louis 43 23 N 4 50 E
91 Port St. Servain 51 21 N 58 0 W
75 Port Shepstone 30 44 S 30 28 E
92 Port Simpson 54 30 N 130 20 W
90 Port Stanley 42 40 N 81 10 W
73 Port Sudan= Bûr Sûdân 19 32 N 37 9 E
13 Port Talbot 51 35 N 3 48 W
102 Port Townsend 48 0 N 122 50 W
20 Port-Vendres 42 32 N 3 8 E
48 Port Vladimir 69 25 N 33 6 E
81 Port Wakefield 34 12 S 138 10 E
63 Port Weld 4 50 N 100 38 E
15 Portadown 54 27 N 6 26 W
100 Portage 43 31 N 89 25 W
93 Portage la Prairie 49 58 N 98 18 W
31 Portalegre 39 19 N 7 25 W
31 Portalégre □ 39 15 N 7 40 W
101 Portales 34 12 N 103 25 W
15 Portarlington 53 10 N 7 10 W
105 Port-au-Prince 18 40 N 72 20 W
21 Port-de-Bouc 43 24 N 4 59 E
18 Port-en-Bessin 49 20 N 0 45 W
103 Porterville 36 5 N 119 0 W
20 Portet 43 31 N 1 25 E
13 Porthcawl 51 28 N 3 42 W
31 Portimão 37 8 N 8 32 W
84 Portland, Australia 33 13 S 149 59 E
97 Portland, Conn. 41 34 N 72 39 W
99 Portland, Me. 43 40 N 70 15 W
102 Portland, Oreg. 45 35 N 122 30 W
13 Portland Bill 50 31 N 2 27 W
13 Portland I. 50 32 N 2 25 W
89 Portland Promontory 59 0 N 78 0 W
12 Portmadoc 52 51 N 4 8 W
91 Portneuf 46 43 N 71 55 W
21 Porto, Fr. 42 16 N 8 38 E
30 Porto, Port. 41 8 N 8 40 W
30 Porto □ 41 8 N 8 20 W
21 Porto, G. de 42 17 N 8 34 E
109 Pôrto Alegre 30 5 S 51 3 W
75 Porto Amélia= Pemba 12 58 S 40 30 E
111 Pôrto de Móz 1 41 S 52 22 W
38 Porto Empédocle 37 18 N 13 30 E
111 Porto Franco 9 45 S 47 0 W
111 Porto Grande 0 42 N 51 24 W
108 Pôrto Murtinho 21 45 S 57 55 W
111 Porto Nacional 10 40 S 48 30 W
72 Porto-Novo 6 23 N 2 42 E
37 Porto Recanati 43 26 N 13 40 E
37 Porto San Giórgio 43 11 N 13 49 E
111 Porto Seguro 16 20 S 39 0 W
37 Porto Tolle 44 57 N 12 20 E
38 Porto Torres 40 50 N 8 23 E
109 Porto União 26 10 S 51 0 W
21 Porto-Vecchio 41 35 N 9 16 E
110 Porto Velho 8 46 S 63 54 W
36 Portoferráio 42 50 N 10 20 E
37 Portogruaro 45 57 N 12 50 E
102 Portola 39 49 N 120 28 W
37 Portomaggiore 44 41 N 11 47 E
36 Portovénere 44 2 N 9 50 E
110 Portoviejo 1 0 S 80 20 W
14 Portpatrick 54 50 N 5 7 W
14 Portree 57 25 N 6 11 W
15 Portrush 55 13 N 6 40 W
13 Portsmouth, U.K. 50 48 N 1 6 W
97 Portsmouth, N.H. 43 5 N 70 45 W
98 Portsmouth, Ohio 38 45 N 83 0 W
97 Portsmouth, R.I. 41 35 N 71 44 W
98 Portsmouth, Va. 36 50 N 76 50 W
14 Portsoy 57 41 N 2 41 W
46 Porttipahta, I. 68 5 N 26 40 E
30 Portugalete 43 19 N 3 4 W
29 Portugal ■ 40 0 N 7 0 W
72 Portuguese Guinea ■= Guinea Bissau ■ 12 0 N 15 0 W
15 Portumna 53 5 N 8 12 W
112 Porvenir 53 10 S 70 30 W
47 Provoo 60 27 N 25 50 E
109 Posadas, Arg. 27 30 S 56 0 W
31 Posadas, Sp. 37 47 N 5 11 W
69 Poseh 23 50 N 106 0 E
65 Poso 1 20 S 120 55 E
111 Posse 14 4 S 46 18 W
24 Pössneck 50 42 N 11 34 E
90 Poste de la Baleine 55 20 N 77 40 W
72 Poste Maurice Cortier 22 14 N 1 2 E
37 Postojna 45 46 N 14 12 E
75 Potchefstroom 26 41 S 27 7 E
39 Potenza 40 40 N 15 50 E
37 Potenza, R. 43 25 N 13 40 E
37 Potenza Picena 43 22 N 13 37 E
30 Potes 43 15 N 4 42 W
75 Potgietersrus 24 10 S 29 3 E
49 Poti 42 10 N 41 38 E
72 Potiskum 11 39 N 11 2 E
98 Potomac, R. 38 0 N 76 20 W
110 Potosí 19 38 S 65 50 W
108 Potosí □ 20 30 S 67 0 W
65 Potatan 10 56 N 122 38 E
68 Potow 38 8 N 116 31 E
24 Potsdam, E. Germany 52 23 N 13 4 E
97 Potsdam, U.S.A. 44 40 N 74 59 W
24 Potsdam □ 52 40 N 13 30 E
97 Pottersville 42 38 N 84 45 W
97 Pottsdown 40 17 N 75 40 W
97 Pottsville 40 39 N 76 12 W
92 Pouce Coupe 55 40 N 120 10 W
97 Poughkeepsie 41 40 N 73 57 W
19 Pouilly 47 18 N 2 57 E
109 Pouso Alegre 11 55 S 57 0 W
85 Poverty B. 38 43 S 178 0 E
30 Póvoa de Varzim 41 25 N 8 46 W
48 Povenets 62 48 N 35 0 E
90 Powassan 46 5 N 79 25 W
100 Powder, R. 46 44 N 105 26 W
102 Powder River 43 5 N 107 0 W
102 Powell 44 45 N 108 45 W
103 Powell, L. 37 25 N 110 45 W
92 Powell River 49 48 N 125 20 W
13 Powys □ 52 20 N 3 30 W
69 Poyang 28 59 N 116 40 E
69 Poyang Hu, L. 29 10 N 116 10 E
51 Poyarkovo 49 38 N 128 45 E
30 Poza de la Sal 42 35 N 3 31 W
40 Požarevac 44 35 N 21 18 E
40 Požega 45 21 N 17 41 E
28 Poznań 52 25 N 17 0 E
28 Poznań □ 52 30 N 18 0 E
33 Pozo Alcón 37 42 N 2 56 W
110 Pozo Almonte 20 10 S 69 50 W
31 Pozoblanco 38 23 N 4 51 W
39 Pozzallo 36 44 N 15 40 E
39 Pozzuoli 40 49 N 14 7 E
40 Praca 43 47 N 18 43 E
63 Prachin Buri 14 0 N 101 25 E
20 Prades 42 38 N 2 23 E
111 Prado 17 20 S 39 20 W
37 Pragerska 46 27 N 15 42 E
26 Prague=Praha 50 5 N 14 22 E
26 Praha 50 5 N 14 22 E
20 Prahecq 46 19 N 0 26 W
41 Prahova, R. 44 43 N 26 27 E
40 Prahovo 44 18 N 22 39 E
41 Praid 46 32 N 25 10 E
111 Prainha 1 45 S 53 30 W
80 Prairie 20 50 S 144 35 E
102 Prairie City 45 27 N 118 44 W
100 Prairie du Chien 43 1 N 91 9 W
100 Prairies, Coteau des 44 0 N 97 0 W
64 Praja 8 39 S 116 37 E
111 Prata 19 25 S 49 0 W
37 Prato 43 53 N 11 5 E
37 Prátola Peligna 42 7 N 13 51 E
101 Pratt 37 40 N 98 45 W
30 Pravia 43 30 N 6 12 W
108 Precordillera 30 0 S 69 1 W
37 Predáppio 44 7 N 11 58 E
40 Predejane 42 51 N 22 9 E
93 Preeceville 52 0 N 102 50 W
92 Premier 56 4 N 130 1 W
40 Prenj, Mt. 43 33 N 17 53 E
24 Prenzlau 53 19 N 13 51 E
40 Prepansko, J. 40 45 N 21 0 E
63 Preparis North Chan. 15 12 N 93 40 E
63 Preparis South Chan. 14 36 N 93 40 E
27 Prerov 49 28 N 17 27 E
90 Prescott, Canada 44 45 N 75 30 W
103 Prescott, U.S.A. 34 35 N 112 30 W
40 Preševo 42 19 N 21 39 E
108 Presidencia Roque Saenz Peña 26 50 S 60 30 W
108 Presidente de la Plaza 27 0 S 60 0 W
109 Presidente Epitácio 21 46 S 52 6 W
108 Presidente Hayes □ 24 0 S 59 0 W
109 Presidente Prudente 15 45 S 54 0 W
41 Preslav 43 10 N 26 52 E
27 Prešov 49 0 N 21 15 E
99 Presque Isle 46 40 N 68 0 W
72 Prestea 5 22 N 2 7 W
13 Presteign 52 17 N 3 0 W
96 Preston, Canada 43 25 N 80 20 W
12 Preston, U.K. 53 46 N 2 42 W
14 Prestonpans 55 58 N 3 0 W
14 Prestwick 55 30 N 4 38 W
75 Pretoria 25 44 S 28 12 E
43 Préveza 38 57 N 20 47 E
88 Pribilov Is. 56 0 N 170 0 W
26 Příbram 49 41 N 14 2 E
102 Price 39 40 N 110 48 W
32 Priego 40 38 N 2 21 W
31 Priego de Córdoba 37 27 N 4 12 W
75 Prieska 29 40 S 22 42 E
27 Prievidza 48 46 N 18 36 E
40 Prijedor 44 58 N 16 41 E
49 Prikaspiyskaya Nizmennost 47 30 N 50 0 E
49 Prikumsk 44 30 N 44 10 E
40 Prilep 41 21 N 21 37 E
49 Priluki 50 30 N 32 15 E
93 Prince Albert 53 15 N 105 50 W
93 Prince Albert Nat. Park 54 0 N 106 25 W
88 Prince Albert Pen. 72 0 N 116 0 W
88 Prince Albert Sd. 70 25 N 115 0 W
89 Prince Charles I. 68 0 N 76 0 W
3 Prince Edward Is. 45 15 S 39 0 E
91 Prince Edward I. □ 44 2 N 77 20 W
92 Prince George 53 50 N 122 50 W
86 Prince of Wales, C. 53 50 N 131 30 W
80 Prince of Wales, I., Australia 10 35 S 142 0 E
88 Prince of Wales I., Canada 73 0 N 99 0 W
92 Prince of Wales I., U.S.A. 53 30 N 131 30 W
92 Prince Rupert 54 20 N 130 20 W
80 Princess Charlotte, B. 14 15 S 144 0 E
5 Princesse Astrid Kyst 71 0 S 10 0 E
5 Princesse Ragnhild Kyst 71 0 S 30 0 E
92 Princeton, Canada 49 27 N 120 30 W
98 Princeton, Ind. 38 20 N 87 35 W
98 Princeton, Ky. 37 6 N 87 55 W
97 Princeton, N.J. 40 18 N 74 40 W
98 Princeton, W.Va. 37 21 N 81 8 W
71 Principé, I. 1 37 N 7 25 E
30 Prior, C. 43 34 N 8 17 W
48 Priozersk 61 2 N 30 4 E
48 Pripyat, R. 51 20 N 30 20 E
40 Priština 42 40 N 21 13 E
99 Pritchard 30 47 N 88 5 W
24 Pritzwalk 53 10 N 12 11 E
38 Priverno 41 29 N 13 10 E
40 Prizren 42 13 N 20 45 E
38 Prizzi 37 44 N 13 24 E
65 Probolinggo 7 46 S 113 13 E
62 Proddatur 14 45 N 78 30 E
104 Progreso 21 20 N 89 40 W
42 Prokletije, Mt. 42 30 N 19 45 E
50 Prokopyevsk 54 0 N 87 3 E
40 Prokuplje 43 16 N 21 36 E
59 Prome 18 45 N 95 30 E
111 Propriá 10 13 S 36 51 W
21 Propriano 41 41 N 8 52 E
80 Proserpine 20 21 S 148 36 E
102 Prosser 46 11 N 119 52 W
27 Prostějov 49 30 N 17 9 E
41 Provadiya 43 12 N 27 30 E
21 Provence, Reg. 43 40 N 5 45 E
97 Providence 41 41 N 71 15 W
90 Providence Bay 45 41 N 82 15 W
105 Providencia, I. de 13 25 N 81 26 W
51 Provideniya 64 23 N 173 18 W
92 Provincial Cannery 51 33 N 127 36 W
19 Provins 48 33 N 3 15 E
102 Provo 40 16 N 111 37 W
93 Provost 52 25 N 110 20 W
40 Prozor 43 50 N 17 34 E
109 Prudentópolis 25 12 S 50 57 W
80 Prudhoe, I. 21 23 S 149 45 E
88 Prudhoe Bay 70 10 N 148 0 W
93 Prudhomme 52 22 N 105 47 W
27 Prudnik 50 20 N 17 38 E
28 Pruszez Gdańska 54 17 N 19 40 E
28 Pruszków 52 9 N 20 49 E
49 Prut, R. 45 28 N 28 12 E
5 Prydz B. 69 0 S 74 0 E
28 Przasnysz 53 2 N 20 45 E
27 Przemysl 49 50 N 22 45 E
27 Przemysl □ 50 0 N 22 0 E
50 Przhevalsk 42 30 N 78 20 E
43 Psará, I. 38 37 N 25 38 E
48 Pskov 57 50 N 28 25 E
27 Pszczyna 49 59 N 18 58 E
42 Ptolemaís 40 30 N 21 43 E
110 Pucallpa 8 25 S 74 30 W
69 Puchi 29 42 N 113 54 E
41 Pucioasia 45 4 N 25 26 E
62 Pudukkottai 10 28 N 78 47 E
104 Puebla 19 0 N 98 10 W
104 Puebla □ 18 30 N 98 0 W
31 Puebla de Guzman 37 33 N 7 15 W
30 Puebla de Sanabria 42 4 N 6 38 W
100 Pueblo 38 20 N 104 40 W
108 Puente Alto 33 32 S 70 35 W
31 Puente Genil 37 22 N 4 47 W
32 Puente la Reina 42 40 N 1 49 W
30 Puenteareas 42 10 N 8 28 W
30 Puentedeume 43 24 N 8 10 W
67 Puerh 23 11 N 100 56 E
105 Puerto Armuelles 8 20 N 83 10 W
110 Puerto Asís 0 30 N 76 30 W
110 Puerto Ayacucho 5 40 N 67 35 W
104 Puerto Barrios 15 40 N 88 40 W
110 Puerto Berrío 6 30 N 74 30 W
110 Puerto Bolívar 3 10 S 79 55 W
110 Puerto Cabello 10 28 N 68 1 W
105 Puerto Cabezas 14 0 N 83 30 W
110 Puerto Carreño 6 12 N 67 22 W
105 Puerto Cortes 15 51 N 88 0 W
104 Puerto Cortés 8 20 N 82 20 W
112 Puerto Coyle 50 54 S 69 15 W
110 Puerto Cumarebo 11 29 N 69 21 W
31 Puerto de Santa María 36 35 N 6 15 W
72 Puerto del Rosario 28 30 N 13 52 W
112 Puerto Deseado 47 45 S 66 0 W
110 Puerto Páez 6 13 N 67 28 W
110 Puerto Leguizamo 0 12 S 74 46 W
112 Puerto Lobos 42 0 S 65 3 W
33 Puerto Lumbreras 37 34 N 1 48 W
112 Puerto Madryn 42 48 S 65 4 W
33 Puerto Mazarrón 37 34 N 1 15 W
112 Puerto Montt 41 28 S 72 57 W
112 Puerto Natales 51 45 S 72 25 W
105 Puerto Padre 21 13 N 76 35 W
108 Puerto Pinasco 22 30 S 57 50 W
112 Puerto Pirámides 42 35 S 64 20 W
110 Puerto Piritu 10 5 N 65 0 W
105 Puerto Plata 19 40 N 70 45 W
65 Puerto Princesa 9 55 N 118 50 E
112 Puerto Quellón 43 7 S 73 37 W
31 Puerto Real 36 33 N 6 12 W
105 Puerto Rico, I. 18 15 N 66 45 W
112 Puerto Saavedra 38 47 S 73 24 W
110 Puerto Suárez 18 58 S 57 52 W
112 Puerto Varas 41 19 S 72 59 W
31 Puertollano 38 43 N 4 7 W
112 Pueyrredón, L. 47 20 S 72 0 W
48 Pugachev 52 0 N 48 55 E
102 Puget Sd. 47 15 N 123 30 W
39 Puglia □ 41 0 N 16 30 E
40 Pui 45 30 N 23 4 E
32 Puig Mayor, Mt. 39 49 N 2 47 E
32 Puigcerda 42 24 N 1 50 E
19 Puisaye, Collines de la 47 35 N 3 30 E
85 Pukaki, L. 44 5 S 170 1 E
93 Pukatawagan 55 45 N 101 20 W
85 Pukekohe 37 12 S 174 55 E
37 Pula 39 0 N 9 0 E
108 Pulacayo 20 25 S 66 41 W
68 Pulantien 39 25 N 122 0 E
97 Pulaski, N.Y. 43 32 N 76 9 W

Pulaski, Tenn. Reading, U.K.

99 Pulaski, Tenn. 35 10N 87 0W
98 Pulaski, Va. 37 4N 80 49W
28 Puławy 51 23N 21 59E
62 Pulicat L. 13 40N 80 15E
62 Puliyangudi 9 11N 77 24E
102 Pullman 46 49N 117 10W
64 Puloraja 4 55N 95 24E
28 Pułtusk 52 43N 21 6E
67 Puluntohai 47 2N 87 29E
61 Punakha 27 42N 89 52E
62 Punalur 9 0N 76 56E
58 Punch 33 48N 74 4E
58 Pune 18 29N 73 57E
60 Punjab □ 31 0N 76 0E
110 Puno 15 55S 70 3W
108 Punta Alta 38 53S 62 4W
112 Punta Arenas 53 0S 71 0W
112 Punta Delgada 42 43S 63 38W
104 Punta Gorda 16 10N 88 45W
81 Puntabie 32 12S 134 5E
105 Puntarenas 10 0N 84 50W
110 Punto Fijo 11 42N 70 13W
110 Purace, Mt. 2 21N 76 23W
13 Purbeck, I. of 50 40N 2 5W
33 Purchena Tetica 37 21N 2 21W
61 Puri 19 50N 85 58E
62 Purli 18 50N 76 35E
60 Purna, R. 21 5N 76 0E
61 Purnea 25 45N 87 31E
63 Pursat 12 34N 103 50E
61 Purulia 23 17N 86 33E
110 Purus, R. 3 42S 61 28W
41 Pŭrvomay 42 8N 25 17E
65 Purwakarta 6 35S 107 29E
65 Purwodadi, Jawa 7 7S 110 55E
65 Purwodadi, Jawa 7 51S 110 0E
65 Purwokerto 7 25S 109 14E
65 Purworedjo 7 43S 110 2E
68 Pusan 35 5N 129 0E
51 Pushchino 54 20N 158 10E
49 Pushkino 51 16N 47 9E
27 Püspökladány 47 19N 21 6E
59 Putao 27 28N 97 30E
85 Putaruru 38 3S 175 47E
68 Putehachi 48 4N 122 45E
69 Putien 22 28N 119 0E
39 Putignano 40 50N 17 5E
41 Putna, R. 45 35N 27 30E
97 Putnam 41 55N 71 55W
24 Puttgarden 54 28N 11 15E
62 Puttur 12 46N 75 12E
110 Putumayo, R. 3 7S 67 58E
20 Puy de Dôme, Mt. 45 46N 2 57E
20 Puy de Sancy, Mt. 45 32N 2 41E
20 Puy l'Evêque 44 31N 1 9E
102 Puyallup 47 10N 122 22W
20 Puy-de-Dôme □ 45 47N 3 0E
20 Puyoô 43 33N 0 56W
49 Pyatigorsk 44 2N 43 0E
59 Pyinmana 19 45N 96 20E
68 Pyŏngyang 39 0N 125 30E
17 Pyrenees, Mts. 42 45N 0 20E
20 Pyrénées-Atlantiques □ 43 15N 0 45W
20 Pyrénées-Orientales □ 42 35N 2 25E
28 Pyrzyce 53 10N 14 55E
59 Pyu 18 30N 96 35E

Q

54 Qabatiya 32 25N 35 16E
57 Qadam 32 55N 66 45E
56 Qadhima 22 20N 39 13E
60 Qadian 31 51N 74 19E
56 Qal'at al Mu'azzam 27 43N 37 27E
56 Qal'at Sālih 31 31N 47 16E
56 Qal'at Sura 26 10N 38 40E
57 Qala-i-Kirta 32 15N 63 0E
57 Qala Nau 35 0N 63 5E
54 Qalqīlya 32 12N 34 58E
73 Qâra 29 38N 26 30E
57 Qasr-e Qand 26 15N 60 45E
73 Qasr Farâfra 27 0N 28 1E
55 Qasr Hamam 21 5N 46 5E
57 Qatar ■ 25 30N 51 15E
73 Qattara, Munkhafed el 29 30N 27 30E
56 Qazvin 36 15N 50 0E
73 Qena 26 10N 32 43E
54 Qesari 32 30N 34 53E
57 Qeshm 26 55N 56 10E
57 Qeshm, I. 26 50N 56 0E
57 Qeys, Jazireh-ye 26 32N 53 56E
54 Qezi'ot 30 52N 34 28E
58 Qila Safed 29 0N 61 30E
54 Qiryat Bialik 32 50N 35 5E
54 Qiryat 'Eqron 31 52N 34 49E
54 Qiryat Gat 31 36N 35 47E
54 Qiryat Hayyim 32 49N 35 4E
54 Qiryat Mal'akhi 31 44N 34 45E
54 Qiryat Shemona 33 13N 35 35E
54 Qiryat Tiv'om 32 43N 35 8E
54 Qiryat Yam 32 51N 35 4E
55 Qīzân 16 57N 42 3E
57 Qom 34 40N 51 4E
97 Quabbin Res. 42 22N 72 18W
24 Quackenbrück 52 40N 7 59E
83 Quairading 32 0S 117 21E
97 Quakerstown 40 27N 75 20W
83 Qualeup 33 48S 116 48E
63 Quang Ngai 15 13N 108 58E
63 Quang Tri 16 45N 107 13E
63 Quang Yen 21 3N 106 52E
13 Quantock Hills 51 8N 3 10W
108 Quaraí 30 15S 56 20W
38 Quartu Sant'Elena 39 15N 9 10E
57 Qūchān 37 10N 58 27E
75 Que Que 18 58S 29 48E
84 Queanbeyan 35 17S 149 14E
91 Québec 46 52N 71 13W
91 Québec □ 50 0N 70 0W
24 Quedlinburg 51 47N 11 9E
5 Queen Alexandra Ra. 85 0S 170 0E
92 Queen Charlotte 53 28N 132 2W
92 Queen Charlotte Is. 53 10N 132 0W
92 Queen Charlotte Str. 51 0N 128 0W
86 Queen Elizabeth Is. 75 0N 95 0W
5 Queen Mary Coast 70 0S 95 0E
88 Queen Maud G. 68 15N 102 0W
5 Queen Maud Ra. 86 0S 160 0W
79 Queensland □ 15 0S 142 0E
80 Queenstown, Australia 42 4S 145 35E
85 Queenstown, N.Z. 45 1S 168 40E
75 Queenstown, S.Africa 31 52S 26 52E
111 Queimadas 11 0S 39 38W
74 Quela 9 10S 16 56E
75 Quelimane 17 53S 36 58E
69 Quemoy, I. = Kinmen, I. 24 25N 118 25E
108 Quenquên 38 30S 58 30W
104 Querètaro 20 40N 100 23W
104 Querètaro □ 20 30N 100 30W
33 Quesada 37 51N 3 4W
92 Quesnel 53 5N 122 30W
18 Questembert 47 40N 2 28W
90 Quetico 48 45N 90 55W
90 Quetico Prov. Park 48 15N 91 45W
60 Quetta 30 15N 66 55E
60 Quetta □ 30 15N 68 30E
104 Quezaltenango 14 40N 91 30W
65 Quezon City 14 38N 121 0E
63 Qui Nhon 13 40N 109 13E
110 Quibdo 5 42N 76 40W
18 Quiberon 47 29N 3 9W
108 Quiindy 25 58S 57 16W
112 Quilân, C. 43 15S 74 30W
75 Quilengues 14 12S 15 12E
20 Quillan 42 53N 2 10E
108 Quillota 32 54S 71 16W
108 Quilmes 34 50S 58 0W
62 Quilon 8 50N 76 38E
81 Quilpie 26 35S 144 11E
108 Quilpué 33 3S 71 27W
18 Quimper 48 0N 4 9W
18 Quimperlé 47 53N 3 33W
97 Quincy, Mass. 42 14N 71 0W
99 Quincy, Fla. 30 34N 84 34W
100 Quincy, Ill. 39 55N 91 20W
104 Quintana Roo □ 19 0E 88 0W
32 Quintanar de la Orden 39 36N 3 5W
33 Quintanar del Rey 39 21N 1 56W
108 Quintero 32 45S 71 30W
32 Quinto 41 25N 0 32W
30 Quiroga 42 28N 7 18W
21 Quissac 43 55N 4 0E
108 Quitilipi 26 50S 60 13W
110 Quito 0 15S 78 35W
111 Quixadá 4 55S 39 0W
54 Qumran 31 43N 35 27N
82 Quoin, I. 14 54S 129 32E
81 Quorn 32 25S 138 0E
67 Qurug-Tagh, Mts. 41 30N 90 0E
73 Qûs 25 55N 32 50E
73 Quseir 26 7N 34 16E
42 Qytet Stalin 40 47N 19 57E

R

26 Raab 47 42N 17 38E
54 Ra'anana 32 12N 34 52E
46 Raane 64 40N 24 28E
14 Raasay, I. 57 25N 6 4W
37 Rab, I. 44 45N 14 45E
27 Raba, R. 50 9N 20 30E
65 Raba 8 36S 118 55E
30 Rabaçal, R. 41 30N 7 12W
20 Rabastens 43 50N 1 43E
72 Rabat 34 2N 6 48W
76 Rabaul 4 24S 152 18E
56 Rabigh 22 50N 39 5E
27 Rabka 49 37N 19 59E
38 Racalmuto 37 25N 13 41E
40 Răcăşdia 44 59N 21 36E
91 Race, C. 46 40N 53 18W
27 Racibórz 50 7N 18 18E
98 Racine 42 41N 87 51W
26 Radbuza, R. 49 46N 13 24E
24 Radeburg 51 6N 13 45E
98 Radford 37 8N 80 32W
27 Radlin 50 3N 18 29E
28 Radom 51 23N 21 12E
28 Radom □ 51 20N 21 0E
40 Radomir 42 37N 23 4E
28 Radomka R. 51 43N 21 26E
28 Radomsko 51 5N 19 28E
37 Radovljica 46 22N 14 12E
26 Radstadt 47 24N 13 28E
13 Radstock 51 17N 2 25W
40 Raduša 42 7N 21 15E
93 Radville 49 30N 104 15W
92 Rae 62 45N 115 50W
61 Rae Bareli 26 18N 81 20E
89 Rae Isthmus 66 40N 87 30W
85 Raetihi 39 25S 175 17E
108 Rafaela 31 10S 61 30W
38 Raffadali 37 23N 13 29E
56 Rafhā 29 35N 43 35E
57 Rafsanjān 30 30N 56 5E
73 Râgâ 8 28N 25 41E
80 Raglan, Australia 23 42S 150 49E
85 Raglan, N.Z. 37 55S 174 55E
39 Ragusa 36 56N 14 42E
73 Rahad el Bardi 11 20N 23 40E
60 Rahimyar Khan 28 30N 70 25E
62 Raichur 16 10N 77 20E
61 Raiganj 25 37N 88 10E
61 Raigarh 21 56N 83 25E
60 Raikot 30 38N 75 36E
80 Railton 41 25S 146 28E
102 Rainier, Mt. 46 50N 121 50W
93 Rainy River 48 50N 94 30W
61 Raipur 21 17N 81 45E
90 Raith 48 50N 90 0W
62 Rajahmundry 17 1N 81 48E
62 Rajapalaiyam 9 25N 77 35E
60 Rajasthan □ 26 45N 73 30E
60 Rajasthan Can. 30 31N 71 0E
61 Rajbari 23 47N 89 41E
60 Rajgarh, Mad. P. 24 2N 76 45E
60 Rajgarh, Rajasthan 28 40N 75 25E
37 Rajhenburg 46 1N 15 29E
60 Rajkot 22 15N 70 56E
61 Rajmahal Hills 24 30N 87 30E
61 Rajnandgaon 21 5N 81 5E
60 Rajpipla 21 50N 73 30E
60 Rajpura 30 32N 76 32E
61 Rajshahi 24 22N 88 39E
61 Rajshahi □ 25 0N 89 0E
85 Rakaia 43 45S 172 1E
85 Rakaia, R. 43 54S 172 12E
27 Rákospalota 47 30N 19 5E
26 Rakovník 50 6N 13 42E
41 Rakovski 42 21N 24 57E
93 Raleigh, Australia 30 27S 153 2E
99 Raleigh, Canada 49 30N 92 5W
40 Ralja 44 33N 20 34E
54 Rám Alláh 31 55N 35 10E
84 Ram Head 37 47S 149 30E
54 Rama 32 56N 35 21E
39 Ramacca 37 24N 14 40E
62 Ramachandrapuram 16 50N 82 4E
62 Ramanathapuram 9 25N 78 55E
54 Ramat Gan 32 4N 34 48E
54 Ramat Ha Sharon 32 7N 34 50E
54 Ramat Ha Shofet 32 36N 35 5E
19 Rambervillers 48 20N 6 38E
19 Rambouillet 48 40N 1 48E
59 Rambre Kyun, I. 19 0N 94 0E
62 Ramdurg 15 58N 75 22E
65 Ramelau, Mt. 8 55S 126 22E
56 Rāmhormoz 31 15N 49 35E
54 Ramla 31 55N 34 52E
60 Ramnaga 32 47N 75 18E
103 Ramona 33 1N 116 56W
88 Rampart 65 30N 150 10W
60 Rampur 23 25N 73 53E
60 Rampura 24 30N 75 27E
61 Rampurhat 24 10N 87 50E
90 Ramsey, Canada 47 25N 82 20W
12 Ramsey, U.K. 54 20N 4 21W
13 Ramsgate 51 20N 1 25E
61 Ranaghat 23 15N 88 35E
108 Rancagua 34 10S 70 50W
18 Rance, R. 48 31N 1 59W
109 Rancharia 22 15S 50 55W
102 Ranchester 44 57N 107 12W
61 Ranchi 23 19N 85 27E
112 Ranco, L. 40 15S 72 25W
41 Rancu 44 32N 24 15E
39 Rándazzo 37 53N 14 56E
45 Randers 56 29N 10 1E
45 Randers, Fd. 56 37N 10 20E
97 Randolph 43 55N 72 39W
44 Randsfjorden 60 25N 10 24E
46 Råneå 65 53N 22 18E
85 Rangaunu, B. 34 51S 173 15E
85 Rangitaiki, R. 37 54S 176 53E
85 Rangitata, R. 44 11S 171 30E
65 Rangkasbitung 6 22S 106 16E
59 Rangoon 16 45N 96 20E
61 Rangpur 25 42N 89 22E
62 Ranibennur 14 35N 75 30E
62 Ranipet 12 56N 79 23E
88 Rankin Inlet 62 30N 93 0W
84 Rankins Springs 33 49S 146 14E
14 Rannoch, L. 56 41N 4 20W
63 Ranong 9 56N 98 40E
64 Rantauprapat 2 15N 99 50E
65 Rantemario, Mt. 3 15S 119 57E
54 Rantis 32 4N 35 3E
98 Rantoul 40 18N 88 10W
77 Rapa Iti, Is. 27 35S 144 20W
36 Rapallo 44 21N 9 12E
65 Rapang 3 45S 119 55E
100 Rapid City 44 0N 103 0W
97 Raquette, R. 45 0N 74 42W
77 Rarotonga, I. 21 30S 160 0W
112 Rasa, Pte. 40 55S 63 20N
57 Ras al Khaima 25 50N 56 5E
73 Ra's Al-Unuf 30 25N 18 15E
56 Ra's al Tannūrah 26 40N 50 10E
73 Rashad 11 55N 31 0E
73 Rashîd 31 21N 30 22E
56 Rasht 37 20N 49 40E
62 Rasipuram 11 30N 78 25E
40 Raška 43 19N 20 39E
61 Rasra 25 50N 83 50E
25 Rastatt 48 50N 8 12E
63 Rat Buri 13 30N 99 54E
88 Rat Is. 51 50N 178 15E
60 Ratangarh 28 5N 74 35E
61 Rath 25 36N 79 37E
15 Rath Luirc 52 21N 8 40W
15 Rathdrum, Eire 52 57N 6 13W
102 Rathdrum, U.S.A 47 50N 116 58W
24 Rathenow 52 38N 12 23E
15 Rathkeale 52 32N 8 57W
15 Rathlin, I. 55 18N 6 14W
26 Ratikon, Ra. 47 3N 9 50E
60 Ratlam 23 20N 75 0E
62 Ratnagiri 16 57N 73 18E
62 Ratnapura 6 40N 80 20E
101 Raton 37 0N 104 30W
26 Ratten 47 28N 15 44E
14 Rattray Hd. 57 38N 1 50W
24 Ratzeburg 53 41N 10 46E
63 Raub 3 47N 101 52E
108 Rauch 36 45S 59 5W
85 Raukumara, Ra. 38 5S 177 55E
47 Rauma 61 10N 21 30E
61 Raurkela 22 14N 84 50E
38 Ravanusa 37 16N 13 58E
57 Rāvar 31 20N 56 51E
37 Ravenna, Italy 44 28N 12 15E
96 Ravenna, U.S.A. 41 11N 81 15W
25 Ravensburg 47 48N 9 38E
80 Ravenshoe 17 37S 145 29E
83 Ravensthorpe 33 35S 120 2E
60 Raver 21 15N 76 5E
44 Ravfoss 60 44N 10 37E
28 Rawa Mazowiecka 51 46N 20 12E
58 Rawalpindi 33 38N 73 8E
58 Rawalpindi □ 33 38N 73 8E
63 Rawang 3 19N 101 35E
90 Rawdon 46 3N 73 40W
85 Rawene 35 25S 173 32E
28 Rawicz 51 36N 16 52E
28 Rawka R. 52 9N 20 8E
83 Rawlinna 30 58S 125 28E
102 Rawlins 41 50N 107 20W
112 Rawson 43 15S 65 0W
91 Ray, C. 47 33N 59 15W
62 Rayachoti 14 4N 78 50E
62 Rayadrug 14 40N 76 50E
51 Raychikhinsk 49 46N 129 25E
92 Raymond, Canada 49 30N 112 35W
102 Raymond, U.S.A. 46 45N 123 48W
101 Raymondville 26 30N 97 50W
93 Raymore 50 25N 104 31W
101 Rayne 30 16N 92 16W
18 Raz, Pte. du 48 2N 4 47W
40 Ražana 44 6N 19 55E
40 Ražanj 43 40N 21 31E
41 Razdelna 43 13N 27 41E
41 Razelm, L. 44 50N 29 0E
41 Razgrad 43 33N 26 34E
41 Razlog 41 53N 23 28E
20 Ré, I. de 46 12N 1 30W
13 Reading, U.K. 51 27N 0 57W

Ronse St. George's Chan.

16 Ronse 50 45N 3 35 E
75 Roodepoort-Maraisburg 26 11 S 27 54 E
60 Roorkee 29 52N 77 59 E
16 Roosendaal 51 32N 4 29 E
103 Roosevelt Res. 33 46N 111 0W
80 Roper, R. 14 43 S 135 27 E
20 Roquefort 44 2N 0 20W
32 Roquetas 40 50N 0 30 E
110 Roraima □ 2 0N 61 30W
110 Roraima, Mt. 5 10N 60 40W
44 Røros 62 35N 11 23 E
31 Rosal de la Frontera 37 59N 7 13W
108 Rosario, Arg. 33 0 S 60 50W
111 Rosário, Brazil 3 0 S 44 15W
104 Rosario, Mexico 23 0 S 105 52W
108 Rosario, Urug. 34 20 S 57 20W
108 Rosario de la Frontera 25 50 S 65 0W
108 Rosario del Tala 32 20 S 59 10W
109 Rosário do Sul 30 15 S 54 55W
32 Rosas 42 19N 3 10 E
18 Roscoff 48 44N 4 0W
15 Roscommon 53 38N 8 11W
15 Roscommon □ 53 40N 8 15W
15 Roscrea 52 57N 7 47W
91 Rose Blanche 47 38N 58 45W
92 Rose Harbour 52 15N 131 10W
93 Rose Valley 52 19N 103 49W
105 Roseau 48 56N 96 0W
101 Rosenberg 29 30N 95 48W
102 Rosebud 31 5N 97 0W
102 Roseburg 43 10N 123 10W
84 Rosedale 38 11 S 146 48 E
19 Rosendaël 51 3N 2 24 E
25 Rosenheim 47 51N 12 9 E
37 Roseto degli Abruzzi 42 40N 14 2 E
93 Rosetown 57 33N 108 0 E
73 Rosetta = Rashid 31 21N 30 22 E
102 Roseville 38 46N 121 41W
81 Rosewood 35 38 S 147 52 E
54 Rosh Ha'Ayin 32 5N 34 47 E
54 Rosh Pinna 32 58N 35 32 E
45 Roshage, C. 57 7N 8 35 E
19 Rosières 48 36N 6 20 E
36 Rosignano 43 23N 10 28 E
110 Rosignol 6 15N 57 30W
45 Roskilde 55 38N 12 3 E
45 Roskilde □ 55 35N 12 5 E
45 Roskilde, Fd. 55 50N 12 2 E
48 Roslavl 53 57N 32 55 E
85 Ross, N.Z. 42 53 S 170 49 E
13 Ross, U.K. 51 55N 2 34W
15 Ross □ 70 0 S 170 5W
5 Ross Ice Shelf 80 0 S 180 0W
5 Ross Sea 74 0 S 178 0 E
39 Rossano Cálabro 39 36N 16 39 E
92 Rossland 49 6N 117 50W
15 Rosslare 52 17N 6 23W
25 Rosslau 57 52N 12 15 E
72 Rosso 16 30N 15 49W
49 Rossosh 50 15N 39 20 E
93 Rosthern 52 40N 106 20W
24 Rostock 54 4N 12 9 E
24 Rostock □ 54 10N 12 30 E
49 Rostov 47 15N 39 45 E
101 Roswell 33 26N 104 32W
14 Rosyth 56 2N 3 26W
31 Rota 36 37N 6 20W
24 Rotenburg 53 6N 9 24 E
25 Rothenburg ob der Tauber 49 21N 10 11 E
13 Rother, R. 50 59N 0 40W
12 Rotherham 53 26N 1 21W
14 Rothes 57 31N 3 12W
14 Rothesay 55 50N 5 3W
65 Roti, I. 10 50 S 123 0 E
84 Roto 33 0 S 145 30 E
85 Rotorua 38 9 S 176 16 E
85 Rotorua, L. 38 5 S 176 18 E
26 Rottenmann 47 31N 14 22 E
16 Rotterdam 51 55N 4 30 E
83 Rottnest, I. 32 0 S 115 27 E
25 Rottweil 48 9N 8 38 E
76 Rotuma, I. 12 25 S 177 5 E
19 Roubaix 50 40N 3 10 E
26 Roudnice 50 25N 14 15 E
18 Rouen 49 27N 1 4 E
20 Rouergue, Reg. 44 20N 2 20 E
81 Round, Mt. 30 26 S 152 16 E
102 Roundup 46 25N 108 35W
14 Rousay, I. 59 10N 3 2W
97 Rouses Point 44 58N 73 22W
20 Roussillon, Reg. 45 24N 4 49 E
90 Rouyn 48 20N 79 0W
46 Rovaniemi 66 29N 25 41 E
36 Rovereto 45 53N 11 3 E
37 Rovigo 45 4N 11 48 E
41 Rovinari 44 55N 23 11 E
37 Rovinj 45 18N 13 40 E
49 Rovno 50 40N 26 10 E
65 Roxas 11 36N 122 49 E
85 Roxburgh 45 33 S 169 19 E
45 Roxen, L. 58 30N 15 41 E
82 Roy Hill 22 37 S 119 58 E
32 Roya, Peña 40 25N 0 40W
98 Royal Oak 42 30N 83 5W
100 Royale, I. 48 0N 89 0W
20 Royan 45 37N 1 2W
19 Roye 47 40N 6 31 E
27 Rǒžnava 48 37N 20 35 E
48 Rtishchevo 52 35N 43 50 E
30 Rúa 42 24N 7 6W
85 Ruapehu, Mt. 39 18 S 175 35 E
110 Rubio 7 43N 72 22W
50 Rubtsovsk 51 30N 80 50 E
88 Ruby 38 27 S 145 55 E
27 Ruda Slaska 50 16N 18 50 E
81 Rudall 33 43 S 136 17 E
24 Rüdersdorf 52 28N 13 48 E
45 Rudkøbing 54 56N 10 41 E
48 Rudnichny 59 38N 52 26 E
51 Rudnogorsk 57 15N 103 42 E
50 Rudnyy 52 57N 63 7 E
74 Rudolf, L. = Turkana, L. 4 10N 36 10 E
24 Rudolstädt 50 44N 11 20 E
19 Rue 50 15N 1 40 E
73 Rufa'a 14 44N 33 32 E
20 Ruffec 46 2N 0 42 E
74 Rufiji, R. 8 0 S 39 20 E
108 Rufino 34 20 S 62 50W
72 Rufisque 14 43N 17 17W
13 Rugby, U.K. 52 23N 1 16W
100 Rugby, U.S.A. 48 21N 100 0W
24 Rügen, I. 54 22N 13 25 E
55 Ruhāma 31 31N 34 43 E
24 Ruhla 50 53N 10 21 E
24 Ruhr, R. 51 27N 6 44 E
74 Ruki, R. 0 5N 18 17 E
74 Rukwa, L. 7 50 S 32 10 E
82 Rum Jungle 13 0 S 130 59 E
40 Ruma 45 8N 19 50 E
41 Rumania ■ 46 0N 25 0 E
80 Rumbalara 25 20 S 134 29 E
97 Rumford 44 30N 70 30W
21 Rumilly 45 53N 5 56 E
66 Rumoi 43 56N 141 39W
97 Rumson 40 22N 74 0W
85 Runanga 42 25 S 171 15 E
12 Runcorn 53 20N 2 44W
74 Rungwa 6 55 S 33 32 E
60 Rupar 31 2N 76 38 E
64 Rupat, I. 1 45N 101 40 E
90 Rupert House = Fort Rupert 51 30N 78 40W
75 Rusape 18 35 S 32 8 E
41 Ruse 43 48N 25 59 E
13 Rushden 52 17N 0 37W
98 Rushville 39 38N 85 22W
84 Rushworth 36 32 S 145 1 E
111 Russas 4 56 S 37 58W
93 Russell, Canada 50 50N 101 20W
100 Russell, Kans. 38 56N 98 55W
97 Russell, N.Y. 44 26N 75 11W
99 Russellville, Ala. 34 30N 87 44W
101 Russellville, Ark. 35 15N 93 0W
50 Russkaya Polyana 53 47N 73 53 E
75 Rustenburg 25 41 S 27 14 E
101 Ruston 32 30N 92 40W
31 Rute 37 19N 4 29W
65 Ruteng 8 26 S 120 30 E
102 Ruth 39 15N 115 1W
84 Rutherglen, Australia 36 5 S 146 29 E
14 Rutherglen, U.K. 55 50N 4 11W
39 Rutigliano 41 1N 17 0 E
97 Rutland 43 38N 73 0W
74 Rutshuru 1 13 S 29 25 E
39 Ruvo di Púglia 41 7N 16 27 E
74 Ruvuma, R. 10 29 S 40 28 E
74 Ruwenzori, Mts. 0 30N 29 55 E
27 Ruzomberok 49 3N 19 17 E
74 Rwanda ■ 2 0 S 30 0 E
14 Ryan, L. 55 0N 5 2W
48 Ryazan 54 38N 39 44 E
48 Ryazhsk 53 40N 40 7 E
50 Rybache 46 40N 81 20 E
48 Rybachiy Pol. 69 43N 32 0 E
48 Rybinsk = Andropov 58 3N 38 52 E
48 Rybinskoye, Vdkhr. 58 30N 38 25 E
27 Rybnik 50 6N 18 32 E
13 Ryde 50 44N 1 9W
27 Rydułtowy 50 4N 18 23 E
13 Rye 50 57N 0 46 E
12 Rye, R. 54 12N 0 53W
28 Rypin 53 3N 19 32 E
69 Ryūkyū, Is. 26 0N 128 0 E
27 Rzeszów 50 5N 21 58 E
27 Rzeszów □ 50 0N 22 0 E
28 Rzepin 52 20N 14 49 E
48 Rzhev 56 15N 34 18 E

S

54 Sa'ad 31 28N 34 33 E
57 Sa'ādatābād 30 10N 53 5 E
24 Saale, R. 51 57N 11 55 E
24 Saaler Bodden 54 20N 12 25 E
24 Saalfeld 50 39N 11 21 E
26 Saalfelden 47 26N 12 51 E
25 Saanen 46 29N 7 15 E
25 Saarbrücken 49 15N 6 58 E
25 Saarburg 49 36N 6 32 E
48 Saaremaa, I. 58 30N 22 30 E
25 Saarland □ 49 20N 0 75 E
25 Saarlouis 49 19N 6 45 E
105 Saba, I. 17 30N 63 10W
40 Šabac 44 48N 19 42 E
32 Sabadell 41 28N 2 7 E
64 Sabah □ 6 0N 117 0 E
56 Sabalan, Kuhha-ye 38 15N 47 49 E
110 Sabanalargo 10 38N 74 55W
64 Sabang 5 50N 95 15 E
111 Sabará 19 55 S 43 55W
60 Sabarmati, R. 22 25N 73 20 E
55 Sabastiya 32 17N 35 12 E
38 Sabáudia 41 17N 13 2 E
73 Sabhah 27 9N 14 29 E
60 Sabi, R. 36 48N 140 4 E
33 Sabinal, Pta. del 36 43N 2 44W
104 Sabinas 27 50N 101 10W
104 Sabinas Hidalgo 26 40N 100 10W
101 Sabine, R. 30 0N 93 45W
18 Sablé 47 50N 0 21W
87 Sable, C., Canada 43 29N 65 38W
91 Sable, C., U.S.A. 25 5N 81 0W
91 Sable I. 44 0N 60 0W
20 Sables-d'Olonne, Les 46 30N 1 45W
30 Sabôr, R. 41 10N 7 7W
30 Sabugal 40 20N 7 5W
57 Sabzevār 36 15N 57 40 E
57 Sabzvāran 28 45N 57 50 E
32 Sacedón 40 29N 2 41W
97 Sackets Harbor 43 57N 76 7W
25 Säckingen 47 34N 7 56 E
99 Saco 43 29N 70 28W
102 Sacramento 38 39N 121 30 E
102 Sacramento, R. 38 3N 121 56W
103 Sacramento Mts. 32 30N 105 30W
31 Sacratif, C. 36 42N 3 28W
30 Sada 43 22N 8 15W
32 Sádaba 42 19N 1 12W
62 Sadasivpet 17 38N 77 50 E
73 Sadd el Aali 24 5N 32 54 E
66 Sado, I. 38 15N 138 30 E
31 Sado, R. 38 29N 8 55W
60 Sadri 24 28N 74 30 E
45 Sæby 57 20N 10 32 E
32 Saelices 39 55N 2 49W
56 Safaniya 28 5N 48 42 E
57 Safed Koh 34 15N 64 0 E
44 Säffle 59 8N 12 55 E
103 Safford 32 54N 109 52W
13 Saffron Walden 52 5N 0 15 E
72 Safi 32 20N 9 17W
65 Saga, Indonesia 2 40 S 132 55 E
66 Saga, Japan 33 15N 130 18 E
66 Saga □ 33 15N 130 20 E
59 Sagaing 22 0N 96 0 E
60 Sagar 23 50N 78 50 E
62 Sagara 14 14N 75 6 E
67 Sagil 50 15N 91 15 E
98 Saginaw 43 26N 83 55W
98 Saginaw B. 43 50N 83 40W
89 Saglouc 62 30N 74 15W
21 Sagone 42 7N 8 42 E
21 Sagone, G. de 42 4N 8 40 E
31 Sagres 37 0N 8 58W
105 Sagua la Grande 22 50N 80 10W
103 Saguache 38 10N 106 4W
91 Saguenay, R. 48 10N 69 45W
32 Sagunto 39 42N 0 18W
30 Sahagun 42 18N 5 2W
72 Sahara 23 0N 5 0W
60 Saharanpur 29 58N 77 33 E
60 Sahaswan 28 5N 78 45 E
61 Sahibganj 25 12N 87 55 E
60 Sahiwal 30 45N 73 8 E
27 Sahy 48 4N 18 55 E
27 Saïda 34 50N 0 11 E
57 Sa'idābād 29 30N 55 45 E
62 Saidapet 13 0N 80 15 E
58 Saidu 34 50N 72 15 E
57 Saighan 35 10N 67 55 E
20 Saignes 45 20N 2 31 E
63 Saigon = Phan Bho Ho Chi Minh 10 58N 106 40 E
55 Saihut 15 12N 51 10 E
66 Saijō 34 0N 133 5 E
66 Saiki 32 35N 131 50 E
14 St. Abbs Hd. 55 55N 2 10W
26 St. Aegyd 47 52N 15 33 E
20 St. Affrique 43 57N 2 53 E
18 St. Aignan 47 16N 1 22 E
13 St. Albans, U.K. 51 46N 0 21W
97 St. Albans, U.S.A. 44 49N 73 5W
13 St. Albans Hd. 50 34N 2 3W
19 St. Amand 50 25N 3 6 E
20 St. Amand-Mont-Rond 46 43N 2 30 E
19 St. Amarin 47 54N 7 0 E
21 St. Amour 46 26N 5 21 E
26 St. Andra 46 46N 14 50 E
20 St. André-de-Cubzac 44 59N 0 26W
21 St. André-les-Alpes 43 58N 6 30 E
14 St. Andrews 56 20N 2 48W
84 St. Arnaud 36 32 S 143 16 E
12 St. Asaph 53 15N 3 27W
20 St. Astier 45 8N 0 31 E
18 St. Aubin de Cormier 48 15N 1 26W
91 St. Augustin 51 19N 58 48W
99 St. Augustine 29 52N 81 20W
13 St. Austell 50 20N 4 48W
19 St. Avold 49 7N 6 40 E
105 St. Barthelémy, I. 17 50N 62 50W
12 St. Bees Hd. 54 30N 3 38 E
20 St. Benoit-du-Sault 46 26N 1 24 E
93 St. Boniface 49 50N 97 10W
21 St. Bonnet 44 40N 6 5 E
18 St. Brice en Coglès 48 25N 1 22W
13 St. Bride's B. 51 48N 5 15W
18 St. Brieuc 48 30N 2 46W
18 St. Cast 48 37N 2 18W
96 St. Catherines 43 10N 79 15W
13 St. Catherine's Pt. 50 34N 1 18W
20 St. Céré 44 51N 1 54 E
21 St. Chamond 45 28N 4 31 E
100 St. Charles 38 46N 90 30W
20 St. Chély-d'Apcher 44 48N 3 17 E
20 St. Chinian 43 25N 2 56 E
105 St. Christopher, I. 17 20N 62 40W
20 St. Ciers sur Gironde 45 17N 0 37W
97 St. Clair 40 42N 76 12W
90 St. Clair, L. 42 30N 82 45W
20 St. Claud 45 54N 0 28 E
93 St. Claude, Canada 49 40N 98 22W
21 St. Claude, Fr. 46 22N 5 52 E
100 St. Cloud 45 30N 94 11W
91 St. Cœur de Marie 48 39N 71 43W
83 St. Cricq, C. 25 17 S 113 6 E
20 St. Cyprien 42 37N 3 0 E
21 St. Cyr 43 11N 5 43 E
13 St. Davids 51 54N 5 16W
13 St. David's Hd. 51 54N 5 16W
105 St. David's I. 32 22N 64 39W
19 St. Denis 48 56N 2 22 E
18 St. Denis d'Orques 48 2N 0 17W
19 St. Dié 48 17N 6 56 E
19 St. Dizier 48 40N 5 0 E
21 St.-Egrève 45 14N 5 41 E
88 St. Elias, Mt. 60 20N 141 59W
20 St. Eloy 46 10N 2 51 E
20 St. Émilion 44 53N 0 9W
21 St. Étienne 45 27N 4 22 E
21 St. Étienne de Tinée 44 16N 6 56 E
90 St. Félicien 48 40N 72 25W
91 St. Fintan's 48 10N 58 50W
21 St. Florent 42 41N 9 18 E
20 St. Florent-sur-Cher 46 59N 2 15 E
19 St. Florentin 48 0N 3 45 E
20 St. Flour 45 2N 3 6 E
21 St. Fons 45 42N 4 52 E
20 St. Foy-la Grande 44 50N 0 13 E
75 St. Francis, C. 34 14 S 24 49 E
97 St. Francis, L. 45 10N 74 20W
90 St. Gabriel de Brandon 46 17N 73 24W
25 St. Gallen 47 25N 9 23 E
25 St. Gallen □ 47 10N 9 8 E
20 St. Gaudens 43 6N 0 44 E
20 St. Gaultier 46 39N 1 26 E
81 St. George, Australia 28 1 S 148 41 E
105 St. George, Bermuda 32 24N 64 42W
91 St. George, Canada 45 11N 66 57W
103 St. George, U.S.A. 37 10N 113 35W
99 St. George, C. 29 36N 85 2W
84 St. George Hd. 35 11 S 150 45 E
93 St. George West 50 33N 96 7W
16 St. Georges, Belgium 50 37N 4 20 E
90 St. Georges, Canada 46 42N 72 35W
111 St. George's, Fr. Guiana 4 0N 52 0W
105 St. Georges, Grenada 12 5N 61 43W
91 St. George's B. 48 20N 59 0W
11 St. George's Chan. 52 0N 6 0W

São João do Araguaia Seyðisfjörður

111 São João do Araguaia 5 23s 48 46w
111 São João do Piaui 8 10s 42 15w
109 São Leopoldo 29 50s 51 10w
109 São Lourenço 16 30s 55 5w
111 São Luís 2 39s 44 15w
109 São Luís Gonzaga 28 25s 55 0w
111 São Marcos, B. de 2 0s 44 0w
111 São Mateus 18 44s 39 50w
8 São Miguel, I. 37 33n 25 27w
109 São Paulo 23 40s 56 50w
109 São Paulo □ 22 0s 49 0w
30 São Pedro do Sul 40 46n 8 4w
111 São Roque, C. de 5 30s 35 10w
74 São Salvador do Congo 6 18s 14 16e
109 São Sebastião, I. de 23 50s 45 18w
109 São Sebastião do Paraíso 20 54s 46 59w
71 São Tomé, I. 0 10n 7 0e
109 São Vicente 23 57s 46 23w
31 São Vicente, C. de 37 0n 9 0w
21 Saône, R. 45 44n 4 50e
21 Saône-et-Loire □ 46 25n 4 50e
72 Sapele 5 50n 5 40e
110 Saposoa 6 55s 76 30w
66 Sapporo 43 0n 141 15e
39 Sapri 40 5n 15 37e
61 Sapt Kosi, R. 26 30n 86 55e
101 Sapulpa 36 0n 96 40w
56 Saqqez 36 15n 46 20e
32 Saragossa 41 39n 0 53w
40 Sarajevo 43 52n 18 26e
97 Saranac Lake 44 20n 74 10w
42 Saranda 39 59n 19 55e
109 Sarandí del Yi 33 21s 55 58w
108 Sarandí Grande 33 20s 55 50w
65 Sarangani B. 6 0n 125 13e
48 Saransk 54 10n 45 10e
48 Sarapul 56 28n 53 48e
99 Sarasota 27 10n 82 30w
97 Saratoga Springs 43 5n 73 47w
48 Saratov 51 30n 46 2e
64 Sarawak □ 2 0s 113 0e
57 Sarbāz 26 38n 61 19e
57 Sarbisheh 32 30n 59 40e
27 Sârbogârd 46 55n 18 40e
61 Sarda, R. 27 22n 81 23e
60 Sardarshahr 28 30n 74 29e
38 Sardegna, I. 39 57n 9 0e
60 Sardhana 29 9n 77 39e
38 Sardinia, I.= Sardegna, I. 39 57n 9 0e
6 Sargasso Sea 27 0n 67 0w
60 Sargodha 32 10n 72 40e
73 Sarh 9 5n 18 23e
57 Sarī 36 30n 53 11e
56 Sarikamiş 40 22n 42 35e
64 Sarikei 2 8n 111 30e
80 Sarina 21 22s 149 13e
32 Sariñena 41 47n 0 10w
68 Sariwon 38 31n 125 44e
13 Sark, I. 49 25n 2 20w
27 Sarkeḍ 46 47n 21 17e
20 Sarlat-la-Canéda 44 54n 1 13e
112 Sarmiento 45 35s 69 5w
37 Sarnano 43 2n 13 17e
96 Sarnia 43 0n 82 30w
39 Sarno 40 48n 14 35e
48 Sarny 51 17n 26 40e
43 Saronikós Kól. 37 45n 23 45e
36 Saronno 45 38n 9 2e
27 Sárospatak 58 18n 21 33e
44 Sarpsborg 59 16n 11 12e
30 Sarracín 42 15n 3 45w
19 Sarralbe 48 55n 7 1e
19 Sarrebourg 48 43n 7 3e
19 Sarreguemines 49 1n 7 4e
30 Sarriá 42 41n 7 49w
32 Sarrión 40 9n 0 49w
21 Sartène 41 38n 9 0e
18 Sarthe □ 47 58n 0 10e
18 Sarthe, R. 47 30n 0 32w
50 Sartynya 63 30n 62 50e
57 Sarur 23 17n 58 4e
50 Sary Tash 39 45n 73 40e
50 Saryshagan 46 12n 73 48e
18 Sarzeau 47 31n 2 48w
36 Sarzana 44 7n 9 57e
55 Sasabeneh 7 59n 44 43e
61 Sasaram 24 57n 84 5e
40 Sasca Montanǎ 44 41n 21 45e
66 Sasebo 33 15n 129 50e
93 Saskatchewan □ 53 40n 103 30w
93 Saskatchewan, R. 53 12n 99 16w
93 Saskatoon 52 10n 106 45w
51 Saskylakh 71 55n 114 1e
48 Sasovo 54 25n 41 55e
72 Sassandra 5 0n 6 8w
72 Sassandra, R. 4 58n 6 5w
38 Sássari 40 44n 8 33e
24 Sassnitz 54 29n 13 39e
36 Sassuolo 44 31n 10 47e
62 Satara 17 44n 73 58e
48 Satka 55 3n 59 1e
61 Satkhira 22 43n 89 8e
60 Satmala Hills 20 15n 74 40e
61 Satna 24 35n 80 50e
27 Sátoraljaújhely 48 25n 21 41e
60 Satpura Ra. 21 40n 75 0e
63 Sattahip 12 41n 100 54e
62 Sattenapalle 16 25n 80 6e
27 Satu Mare 47 48n 22 53e
27 Satu-Mare □ 47 45n 23 0e
47 Sauda 59 38n 6 21e
46 Sauðarkrókur 65 45n 19 40w
55 Saudi Arabia ■ 26 0n 44 0e
24 Sauerland, Mts. 51 0n 8 0e
20 Saujon 45 41n 0 55w
19 Sauldre, R. 47 16n 1 30e
19 Saulieu 47 17n 4 14e
90 Sault Ste. Marie, Canada 46 30n 84 20w
98 Saulte Ste. Marie, U.S.A. 46 27n 84 22w
18 Saumur 47 15n 0 5w
46 Saurbaer 64 24n 21 35w
40 Sava, R. 44 50n 20 26e
85 Savaii, I. 13 35s 172 25w
72 Savalou 7 57n 2 4e
100 Savanna 42 5n 90 10w
99 Savannah 32 4n 81 4w
99 Savannah, R. 32 2n 80 53w
63 Savannakhet 16 30n 104 49e
90 Savant Lake 50 20n 90 40w
62 Savantvadi 15 55n 73 54e
62 Savanur 14 59n 75 28e
60 Savda 21 9n 75 56e
72 Savé 8 2n 2 17e
20 Save, R. 43 47n 1 17e
56 Sáveh 35 2n 50 20e
72 Savelugu 9 38n 0 54w
18 Savenay 47 20n 1 55w
19 Saverne 48 39n 7 20e
36 Savigliano 44 39n 7 40e
30 Saviñao 42 35n 7 38w
21 Savoie □ 45 26n 6 35e
21 Savoie, Reg. 45 30n 5 20e
36 Savona 44 19n 8 29e
45 Sävsjö 57 20n 14 40e
45 Sävsjöström 57 1n 15 25e
65 Sawai 3 0s 129 5e
63 Sawankhalok 17 19n 99 54e
103 Sawatch Mts. 38 30n 106 30w
73 Sawknah 29 4n 15 47e
75 Sawmills 19 30s 28 2e
65 Sawu Sea 9 30s 121 50e
91 Sayabec 38 35n 67 41w
56 Sayda 33 35n 35 25e
68 Saynshand 44 55n 110 11e
97 Sayre 42 0n 76 30w
97 Sayville 40 45n 73 7w
26 Sazava 49 50n 15 0e
58 Sazin 35 35n 73 30e
12 Sca Fell, Mt 54 27n 3 14w
18 Scaër 48 2n 3 42e
36 Scandiano 44 36n 10 40e
14 Scapa Flow 58 52n 3 0w
12 Scarborough 54 17n 0 24w
25 Schaal See 53 40n 10 57e
25 Schaffhausen 47 42n 8 36e
26 Schärding 48 27n 13 27e
26 Scharnitz 47 23n 11 15e
91 Schefferville 54 50n 66 40w
26 Scheibbs 48 1n 15 9e
16 Schelde, R. 51 22n 4 15e
97 Schenectady 42 50n 73 58w
16 Scheveningen 52 6n 4 18e
16 Schiedam 51 55n 4 25e
25 Schifferstadt 49 22n 8 23e
19 Schiltigheim 48 35n 7 45e
37 Schío 45 42n 11 21e
26 Schladming 47 23n 13 41e
24 Schleswig 54 32n 9 34e
24 Schleswig-Holstein □ 54 10n 9 40e
24 Schmalkalden 50 43n 10 28e
24 Schmölin 50 54n 12 22e
24 Schneeberg 47 53n 15 55e
24 Schönebeck 52 2n 11 42e
65 Schouten, Kep. 1 0s 136 0e
25 Schramberg 48 12n 8 24e
90 Schreiber 48 45n 87 20w
26 Schruns 47 5n 9 56e
90 Schumacher 48 30n 81 16w
102 Schurz 38 59n 118 57w
97 Schuykill Haven 40 37n 76 11w
25 Schwabach 49 19n 11 3e
25 Schwäbisch Gmünd 48 49n 9 48e
25 Schwabisch Hall 49 7n 9 45e
25 Schwäbische Alb, Mts. 48 30n 9 30e
68 Schwangcheng 45 27n 126 27e
68 Schwangyashan 46 35n 131 15e
26 Schwarzach R. 50 30n 11 30e
24 Schwarzenberg 50 31n 12 49e
25 Schwarzwald 48 0n 8 0e
26 Schwaz 47 20n 11 44e
25 Schweinfurt 50 3n 10 12e
25 Schwenningen 48 3n 8 32e
24 Schwerin 53 37n 11 22e
24 Schwerin □ 53 35n 11 20e
24 Schweriner See, L. 53 45n 11 26e
25 Schwetzingen 49 22n 8 35e
25 Schwyz 47 2n 8 39e
25 Schwyz □ 47 2n 8 39e
38 Sciacca 37 30n 13 3e
39 Scicli 36 48n 14 41e
55 Scillave 6 22n 44 32e
13 Scilly Is. 49 55n 6 15w
28 Scinawa 51 25n 16 26e
100 Scobey 48 47n 105 30w
84 Scone, Australia 32 0s 150 52e
14 Scone, U.K. 56 25n 3 26w
4 Scoresbysund 70 20n 23 0w
5 Scotia Sea 56 5s 56 0w
14 Scotland ■ 57 0n 4 0w
5 Scott, C. 71 30s 168 0e
100 Scott City 38 30n 100 52w
100 Scottsbluff 41 55n 103 35w
80 Scottsdale 41 9s 147 31e
97 Scranton 41 22n 75 41w
12 Scunthorpe 53 35n 0 38w
84 Sea Lake 35 28s 142 55e
90 Seaforth 43 35n 81 25w
93 Seal, R. 59 4n 94 48w
103 Searchlight 35 31n 111 57w
101 Searcy 35 15n 91 45w
102 Seattle 47 41n 122 15w
104 Sebastián Vizcaíno, B. 28 0n 114 0w
102 Sebastopol 38 16n 122 56w
41 Sebeş 45 58n 23 34e
99 Sebring 27 36n 81 47w
40 Sečanj 45 25n 20 47e
19 Seclin 50 33n 3 2e
85 Secretary, I. 45 15s 166 56e
62 Secunderabad 17 28n 78 30e
100 Sedalia 38 40n 93 18w
19 Sedan 49 43n 4 57e
85 Seddon 41 40s 174 7e
85 Seddonville 41 33e 172 1e
54 Sede Ya'aqov 32 43n 35 7e
92 Sedgewick 52 48n 111 41w
54 Sedom 31 5n 35 20e
102 Sedro Woolley 48 30n 122 15w
26 Seefeld 51 53n 13 17e
75 Seeheim 26 32s 17 52e
18 Sées 48 38n 0 10e
24 Seesen 51 35n 10 10e
63 Segamat 2 30n 102 50e
32 Segorbe 39 50n 0 30w
72 Ségou 13 30n 6 10w
30 Segovia 40 57n 4 10w
30 Segovia □ 40 55n 4 10w
18 Segré 47 40n 0 52w
72 Séguéla 7 57n 6 40w
101 Seguin 29 34n 97 58w
33 Segura, R. 38 6n 0 54w
33 Segura, Sa. de 38 5n 2 45w
57 Sehkonj, Kuh-e 30 0n 57 30e
60 Sehore 23 10n 77 5e
41 Şeica Mare 46 1n 24 7e
21 Seille, R. 49 7n 6 11e
46 Seinäjoki 62 47n 22 50e
18 Seine, B. de la 49 30n 0 30w
18 Seine, R. 49 26n 0 26e
19 Seine-et-Marne □ 48 45n 3 0e
18 Seine-Maritime □ 49 40n 1 0e
72 Sekondi-Takoradi 5 2n 1 48w
63 Selangor □ 3 20n 101 30e
64 Selatan □, Kalimantan 3 0s 115 0e
65 Selatan □, Sulawesi 3 0s 120 0e
64 Selatan □, Sumatera 3 0s 105 0e
25 Selb 50 9n 12 9e
12 Selby 53 47n 1 5w
88 Seldovia 59 27n 151 43w
75 Selebi-Pikwe 22 0s 27 45e
68 Selenge 49 25n 103 59e
19 Sélestat 48 10n 7 26e
72 Sélibaby 15 20n 12 15w
93 Selkirk, Canada 50 10n 97 20w
14 Selkirk, U.K. 55 33n 2 50w
92 Selkirk Mts. 51 0n 117 10w
99 Selma, Ala. 32 30n 87 0w
103 Selma, Calif. 36 39n 119 30w
19 Seltz 48 48n 8 4w
75 Selukwe 19 40s 30 0e
65 Semarang 7 0s 110 26e
65 Semeru, Mt. 8 4s 113 3e
102 Seminoe Res. 42 0n 107 0w
101 Seminole, Okla. 35 15n 96 45w
101 Seminole, Tex. 32 41n 102 38w
50 Semiozernoye 52 35n 64 0e
50 Semipalatinsk 50 30n 80 10e
26 Semmering P. 47 41n 15 45e
57 Semnān 35 55n 53 25e
57 Semnān □ 36 0n 54 0e
65 Semporna 4 30n 118 33e
110 Sena Madureira 9 5s 68 45w
111 Senador Pompeu 5 40s 39 20w
63 Senai 1 38s 103 38e
75 Senanga 16 2s 23 14e
66 Sendai, Kagoshima 31 50n 130 20e
66 Sendai, Miyagi 38 15n 141 0e
102 Seneca 44 10n 119 2w
96 Seneca L. 42 40n 76 58w
72 Senegal ■ 14 30n 14 30w
72 Senegal, R. 16 30n 15 30w
70 Senegambia, Reg. 14 0n 14 0w
25 Senftenberg 51 30n 13 51e
111 Senhor-do Bonfim 10 30s 40 10w
37 Senigállia 43 42n 13 12e
37 Senj 45 0n 14 58e
73 Sennâr 13 30n 33 35e
90 Senneterre 48 25n 77 15w
19 Sens 48 11n 3 15e
40 Senta 45 55n 20 3e
65 Sentolo 7 55s 110 13e
32 Seo de Urgel 42 22n 1 23e
60 Seohara 29 15n 78 33e
61 Seonath, R. 21 44n 82 27e
61 Seoni 22 5n 79 30e
68 Seoul=Soul 37 20n 126 15e
91 Separation Pt. 53 40n 57 16w
63 Sepone 16 45n 106 13e
91 Sept Iles 50 13n 66 22w
41 Septemvri 42 13n 24 6e
102 Sequim 48 3n 123 9w
103 Sequoia Nat. Park 36 20n 118 30w
16 Seraing 50 35n 5 32e
65 Seram, I. 3 10s 129 0e
65 Seram Sea 3 0s 130 0e
61 Serampore 22 44n 88 30e
65 Serang 6 8s 106 10e
48 Serdobsk 52 28n 44 10e
36 Seregno 45 40n 9 12e
63 Seremban 2 43n 101 53e
75 Serenje 13 11s 30 52e
111 Sergipe □ 10 30s 37 30w
64 Seria 4 37n 114 30e
64 Serian 1 10n 110 40e
19 Sérifontaine 49 20n 1 45e
43 Sérifos, I. 37 9n 24 30e
37 Sérmide 45 0n 11 17e
50 Serov 59 40n 60 20e
75 Serowe 22 25s 26 43e
75 Serpa Pinto 14 48s 17 52e
83 Serpentine 32 22s 115 59e
38 Serpeddi, Pta. 39 19n 9 28e
33 Serpis, R. 38 45n 0 21w
48 Serpukhov 54 55n 37 28e
42 Sérrai 41 5n 23 32e
42 Sérrai □ 41 5n 23 37e
38 Serramanna 39 26n 8 56e
111 Serrinha 11 39e 39 0w
111 Sertania 8 5s 37 20w
75 Serule 21 57s 27 11e
42 Sérvia 40 9n 21 58e
31 Sesimbra 38 28n 9 20w
30 Sestao 43 18n 3 0w
36 Sesto S. Giovanni 45 32n 9 14e
36 Sestri Levante 44 17n 9 22e
20 Sète 43 25n 3 42e
111 Sete Lagôas 19 27s 44 16w
72 Sétif 36 9n 5 26e
66 Seto 35 14n 137 6e
66 Setonaikai 34 10n 133 10e
72 Settat 33 0n 7 40w
74 Setté Cama 2 32s 9 57e
36 Séttimo Tor 45 9n 7 46e
12 Settle 54 5n 2 18w
31 Setúbal 38 30n 8 58w
31 Setúbal □ 38 25n 8 35w
31 Setúbal, B. de 38 40n 8 56w
64 Seulimeum 5 27n 95 15e
49 Sevastopol 44 35n 33 30e
20 Sévérac-le-Château 44 20n 3 5e
90 Severn, R., Canada 56 2n 87 36w
13 Severn, R., U.K. 51 25n 3 0w
51 Severnaya Zemlya, I. 79 0n 100 0e
48 Severnyye Uvaly, Reg. 58 0n 48 0e
26 Severoceský □ 50 35n 14 15e
48 Severodvinsk 64 27n 39 58e
27 Severomoravsky □ 49 38n 17 40e
31 Sevilla 37 23n 6 0w
31 Sevilla □ 37 0n 6 0w
41 Sevlievo 43 1n 25 6e
18 Sèvre Nantaise, R. 47 12n 1 30w
20 Sèvre Niortaise, R. 46 20n 1 12w
88 Seward 60 0n 149 40w
88 Seward Pen. 65 0n 164 0w
108 Sewell 34 10s 70 45w
53 Seychelles, Is. 5 0s 56 0e
46 Seyðisfjörður 65 16n 14 0w

Swords Te Puke

15 Swords 53 27N 6 15w
84 Sydney, Australia 33 53s 151 10E
91 Sydney, Canada 46 7N 60 7w
91 Sydney Mines 46 18N 60 15w
4 Sydprøven 60 30N 45 35w
25 Syke 52 55N 8 50E
48 Syktyvkar 61 45N 50 40E
99 Sylacauga 33 10N 86 15w
59 Sylhet 24 43N 91 55E
24 Sylt, I. 54 50N 8 20E
92 Sylvan Lake 52 20N 114 10w
50 Sym 60 20N 87 50E
50 Syr Darya, R. 46 3N 61 0E
97 Syracuse 38 0N 101 40w
56 Syria ■ 35 0N 38 0E
51 Syul'dzhyukyor 63 25N 113 40E
48 Syzran 53 12N 48 30E
27 Szabolcs-Szatmar □ 48 2N 21 45E
27 Szarvas 46 50N 20 38E
28 Szczecin 53 27N 14 27E
28 Szczecin □ 53 27N 14 32E
28 Szczecinek 53 43N 16 41E
28 Szczythna 53 33N 21 0E
69 Szechwan □ 30 15N 103 15E
27 Szeged 46 16N 20 10E
27 Szeghalom 47 1N 21 10E
27 Székesfehérvár 47 15N 18 25E
27 Szekszárd 46 22N 18 42E
67 Szemao 22 50N 101 0E
69 Szengen 24 50N 108 0E
27 Szentendre 47 39N 19 4E
27 Szentes 46 39N 20 21E
68 Szeping 43 10N 124 18E
27 Szolnok 47 10N 20 15E
27 Szolnok □ 47 15N 20 30E
27 Szombathely 47 14N 16 38E
28 Szprotawa 51 33N 15 35E

T

68 Ta Hingan Ling, Mts. 48 0N 120 0E
67 Ta Liang Shan, Mts. 28 0N 103 0E
108 Tabacal 23 15s 64 15w
14 Tabasco □ 17 45N 93 30w
92 Taber 49 48N 111 5w
33 Tabernas 37 4N 2 26w
33 Tabernes de Valldigna 39 5N 0 13w
65 Tablas, I. 12 20N 122 10E
75 Table Mt. 34 0s 18 22E
82 Tableland 17 16s 126 51E
80 Tabletop, Mt. 23 30s 147 0E
26 Tábor 49 25N 14 39E
74 Tabora 5 2s 32 57E
72 Tabou 4 30N 7 20w
56 Tabriz 38 7N 56 20E
56 Tabuk 28 30N 36 25E
44 Täby 59 29N 18 4E
110 Tachira 8 7N 72 21w
65 Tacloban 11 1N 125 0E
110 Tacna 18 0s 70 20w
102 Tacoma 47 15N 122 30w
109 Tacuarembó 31 45s 56 0w
72 Tademait, Plateau du 28 30N 2 30E
55 Tadjoura 11 50N 44 55E
85 Tadmor, N.Z. 41 27s 172 45E
56 Tadmor, Syria 34 30N 37 55E
91 Tadoussac 48 11N 69 42w
62 Tadpatri 14 55N 78 1E
50 Tadzhik S.S.R. □ 35 30N 70 0E
68 Taegu 35 50N 128 25E
68 Taejon 35 30N 127 22E
32 Tafalla 42 30N 1 41w
75 Tafelbaai 33 35s 18 25E
13 Taff, R. 51 27N 3 9w
108 Tafi Viejo 26 43s 67 17w
57 Taftan, Kūh-e, Mt. 28 36N 61 6E
49 Taganrog 47 12N 38 50E
65 Tagbilaran 9 42N 124 3E
36 Tággia 43 52N 7 50E
37 Tagliacozzo 42 4N 13 13E
111 Taguatinga 12 26s 45 40w
85 Tahakopa 46 30s 169 23E
67 Tahcheng 46 50N 83 1E
77 Tahiti, I. 17 45s 149 30w
102 Tahoe, L. 39 6N 120 0w
72 Tahoua 14 57N 5 16E
69 Tahsien 31 12N 108 13E
73 Tahta 26 44N 31 32E
69 Tai Hu 31 10N 120 0E
69 Taichow 32 30N 119 50E
69 Taichung 24 10N 120 35E
68 Taihan Shan, Mts. 36 0N 114 0E
85 Taihape 39 41s 175 48E
69 Taiho 26 50N 114 54E
68 Taiku 37 46N 112 28E
68 Tailai 46 28N 123 18E
81 Tailem Bend 35 12s 139 29E
25 Tailfingen 48 15N 9 1E
56 Taima 27 35N 38 45E
14 Tain 57 49N 4 4w
69 Tainan 23 0N 120 15E
43 Taínaron, Ákra 36 22N 22 27E
69 Taipei 25 2N 121 30E
63 Taiping 4 50N 100 43E
112 Taitao, Pen. de 46 30s 75 0w
69 Taitung 22 43N 121 4E
69 Taiwan ■ 23 30N 121 0E
43 Táiyeto Óros, Mts. 37 0N 22 23E
54 Taiyiba, Israel 32 36N 35 27E
54 Taiyiba, Jordan 31 55N 35 17E
68 Taiyuan 38 0N 112 30E
55 Ta'izz 13 38N 44 4E
30 Tajuña, R. 40 7N 3 35w
73 Tājūra 32 51N 13 27E
63 Tak 17 0N 99 10E
66 Takachiho 32 42N 131 18E
66 Takada 37 7N 138 15E
85 Takaka 40 51s 172 50E
66 Takamatsu 34 20N 134 5E
66 Takaoka 36 40N 137 0E
85 Takapuna 36 47s 174 47E
66 Takasaki 36 20N 139 0E
66 Takatsuki 34 40N 135 37E
74 Takaungu 3 38s 39 52E
66 Takayama 36 10N 137 5E
66 Takefu 35 50N 136 10E
63 Takeo 11 3N 104 50E
57 Takhar □ 36 30N 69 30E
67 Takla Makan, Reg. 39 40N 85 0E
109 Tala 34 21s 55 46w
108 Talagante 33 40s 70 50w
110 Talara 4 30s 81 10w
65 Talaud, Kep. 4 30N 127 10E
30 Talavera de la Reina 39 55N 4 46w
108 Talca 35 20s 71 46w
108 Talca □ 35 20s 71 46w
108 Talcahuano 36 40s 73 10w
50 Taldy Kurgan 45 10N 78 45E
54 Talfit 32 5N 35 17E
69 Tali, Shensi 34 48N 109 48E
67 Tali, Yunnan 25 50N 100 0E
65 Taliabu, I. 1 45s 125 0E
68 Talien 38 53N 121 35E
62 Talikoti 16 29N 76 17E
64 Taliwang 8 50s 116 55E
88 Talkeetna 62 20N 149 50w
99 Talladega 33 28N 86 2w
99 Tallahassee 30 25N 84 15w
84 Tallangatta 36 10s 147 14E
48 Tallinn 59 29N 24 58E
101 Tallulah 32 25N 91 12w
54 Talluza 32 17N 35 18E
41 Talmaciu 45 38N 24 19E
108 Taltal 25 23s 70 40w
81 Talwood 28 27s 149 20E
72 Tamale 9 22N 0 50w
66 Tamano 34 35N 133 59E
72 Tamanrasset 22 56N 5 30E
97 Tamaqua 40 46N 75 58w
13 Tamar, R. 50 22N 4 10w
66 Tamashima 34 27N 133 18E
75 Tamatave 18 10s 49 25E
104 Tamaulipas □ 24 0N 99 0w
72 Tambacounda 13 55N 13 45w
83 Tambellup 34 4s 117 37E
80 Tambo 24 54s 146 14E
64 Tambora, I. 8 14s 117 55E
48 Tambov 52 45N 41 20E
30 Tambre, R. 42 49N 8 53w
72 Tamchaket 17 25N 10 40w
30 Tamega, R. 41 5N 8 21w
104 Tamiahua, Laguna de 21 30N 97 30w
62 Tamil Nadu □ 11 0N 77 0E
68 Taming 36 20N 115 10E
61 Tamluk 22 18N 87 58E
54 Tammun 32 18N 35 23E
99 Tampa 27 57N 82 30w
47 Tampere 61 30N 23 50E
104 Tampico 22 20N 97 50w
63 Tampin 2 28N 102 13E
55 Tamra 32 51N 35 12E
68 Tamsagbulag 47 15N 117 5E
26 Tamsweg 47 7N 13 49E
31 Tamuja, R. 39 33N 6 8w
81 Tamworth, Australia 31 0s 150 58E
13 Tamworth, U.K. 52 38N 1 2w
46 Tana 70 23N 28 13E
73 Tana, L. 12 0N 37 20E
74 Tana, R. 2 32s 40 31E
66 Tanabe 33 44N 135 22E
88 Tanacross 63 40N 143 30w
64 Tanahgrogot 1 55s 116 15E
65 Tanahmeroh 6 0s 140 7E
82 Tanami, Des. 23 15s 132 20E
88 Tanana 65 10N 152 15w
88 Tanana, R. 64 25N 145 30w
75 Tananarive = Antananarivo 18 55s 47 31E
18 Tancarville 46 50N 0 55w
60 Tanda, Ut.P. 28 57N 78 56E
61 Tanda, Ut.P. 26 33N 82 35E
41 Tandarei 44 39N 27 40E
108 Tandil 37 15s 59 6w
60 Tandlianwala 31 3N 73 9E
60 Tando Adam 25 45N 48 40E
60 Tando Mohommad Khan 25 8N 68 32E
62 Tandur 19 11N 79 30E
85 Taneatua 38 4s 177 1E
66 Tane-ga-Shima, I. 30 30N 131 0E
59 Tanen Tong Dan, Mts. 19 40N 99 0E
72 Tanezrouft 23 9N 0 11E
74 Tanga 5 5s 39 2E
61 Tangail 24 15N 90 0E
74 Tanganyika, L. 6 40s 30 0E
72 Tanger 35 50N 5 49w
65 Tangerang 6 12s 106 39E
24 Tangermünde 52 32N 11 57E
67 Tanghla Shan, Mts. 33 10N 90 0E
69 Tangshan, Anhwei 34 23N 116 34E
68 Tangshan, Hopei 39 40N 118 10E
69 Tangtu 31 37N 118 39E
69 Tangyang 30 50N 111 45E
65 Tanimbar, Kep. 7 30s 131 30E
63 Tanjong Malim 3 44N 101 27E
62 Tanjore = Thanjavur 10 48N 79 12E
64 Tanjung 2 10s 115 25E
64 Tanjungbalai 2 55N 99 44E
64 Tanjungkarang 5 25s 105 16E
64 Tanjungpandan 2 45s 107 39E
64 Tanjungredeb 2 12N 117 35E
64 Tanjungselor 2 55N 117 25E
90 Tannin 49 40N 91 0E
45 Tannis, B. 57 40N 10 10E
73 Tanta 30 45N 30 57E
62 Tanuku 16 45N 81 44E
81 Tanunda 34 30s 139 0E
62 Tanur 11 1N 75 46E
20 Tanus 44 8N 2 19E
74 Tanzania ■ 6 40s 34 0E
68 Taonan 45 30N 122 20E
69 Taoyuan 25 0N 121 4E
69 Tapa Shan, Mts. 31 45N 109 30E
104 Tapachula 14 54N 92 17w
64 Tapaktuan 3 30N 97 10E
85 Tapanui 45 56N 169 18E
30 Tapia 43 34N 6 56w
27 Tápiószele 47 45N 19 55E
60 Tapti, R. 21 5N 72 40E
85 Tapuaenuka, Mt. 41 55s 173 50E
109 Taquara 29 36s 50 46w
109 Taquaritinga 21 24s 48 30w
50 Tara 56 55N 74 30E
50 Tara, R. 56 42N 74 36E
51 Tarabagatay, Khrebet, Mts. 47 30N 84 0E
56 Tarābulus, Lebanon 34 31N 33 52E
73 Tarābulus, Libya 32 49N 13 7E
84 Tarago 35 6s 149 39E
64 Tarakan 3 20N 117 35E
85 Taranaki □ 39 5s 174 51E
30 Tarancón 40 1N 3 1w
60 Taranga Hill 24 0N 72 40E
39 Táranto 40 30N 17 11E
39 Táranto, G. di 40 0N 17 15E
110 Tarapaca 2 56s 69 46w
108 Tarapaca □ 20 45s 69 30w
110 Tarapoto 6 30s 76 20w
21 Tarare 45 55N 4 26E
20 Tarascon 42 50N 1 37E
85 Tarawera 39 2s 176 36E
85 Tarawera, L. 38 13s 176 27E
32 Tarazona 41 55N 1 43w
33 Tarazona de la Mancha 39 16N 1 55w
14 Tarbat Ness 57 52N 3 48w
58 Tarbela Dam 34 0N 72 52E
14 Tarbert 57 54N 6 49w
20 Tarbes 43 15N 0 3E
37 Tarcento 46 12N 13 12E
20 Tardets 43 7N 0 53w
84 Taree 31 50s 152 30E
21 Tarentaise, Reg. 45 30N 6 35E
31 Tarifa 36 1N 5 36w
108 Tarija 21 30s 64 40w
108 Tarija □ 21 30s 63 30w
67 Tarim, R. 41 5N 86 40E
49 Tarkhankut, Mys. 45 25N 32 30E
50 Tarko Sale 64 55N 77 50E
72 Tarkwa 5 20N 2 0w
65 Tarlac 15 30N 120 25E
80 Tarlton Downs 22 40s 136 45E
20 Tarn, R. 44 5N 1 6E
20 Tarn □ 43 50N 2 8E
27 Tarna, R. 47 31N 19 59E
45 Tarnby 55 37N 12 36E
20 Tarn-et-Garonne □ 44 8N 1 20E
27 Tarnobrzeg 50 35N 21 41E
28 Tarnobrzeg □ 50 40N 22 0E
27 Tarnów 50 3N 21 0E
27 Tarnow □ 50 0N 21 0E
27 Tarnowskie Góry 50 27N 18 54E
57 Tārom 28 11N 55 42E
37 Tarquínia 42 15N 11 45E
32 Tarragona 41 5N 1 17E
32 Tarragona □ 41 0N 1 0E
32 Tarrasa 41 26N 2 1E
32 Tárrega 41 39N 1 9E
97 Tarrytown 41 5N 73 52w
73 Tarso Emissi 21 27N 18 36E
56 Tarsus 36 58N 34 55E
108 Tartagal 22 30s 63 50w
20 Tartas 43 50N 0 48w
48 Tartu 58 25N 26 58E
56 Tartūs 34 55N 35 55E
64 Tarutung 2 0N 99 0E
37 Tarvisio 46 31N 13 35E
73 Tasāwah 26 0N 13 37E
90 Tashereau 48 40N 78 40w
62 Tasgaon 17 2N 74 39E
50 Tashauz 42 0N 59 20E
67 Tashigong 33 0N 79 30E
50 Tashkent 41 20N 69 10E
67 Tashkurgan 37 51N 74 57E
57 Tashkurghan 36 45N 67 40E
50 Tashtagol 52 47N 87 53E
65 Tasikmalaya 7 18s 108 12E
45 Tåsinge, I. 55 0N 10 36E
51 Taskan 63 5N 150 5E
85 Tasman, B. 40 59s 173 25E
85 Tasman Glacier 43 45s 170 20E
76 Tasman Sea 42 30s 168 0E
80 Tasmania, I. 49 0s 146 30E
27 Tata 47 37N 18 19E
27 Tatabánya 47 32N 18 25E
48 Tatar A.S.S.R. □ 55 30N 51 30E
50 Tatarsk 55 50N 75 20E
66 Tateyama 35 0N 139 50E
69 Tatien 25 45N 118 0E
27 Tatry, Mts. 49 20N 20 0E
67 Tatsaitan 37 55N 95 0E
109 Tatui 23 25s 48 0w
68 Tatung 40 10N 113 10E
68 Tatungkow 39 55N 124 10E
109 Taubaté 23 5s 45 30w
85 Taumarunui 38 53s 175 15E
110 Taumaturgo 9 0s 73 50w
59 Taungdwingyi 20 1N 95 40E
59 Taunggyi 20 50N 97 0E
59 Taungup Taunggya 18 20N 93 40E
13 Taunton, U.K. 51 1N 3 7w
97 Taunton, U.S.A. 41 54N 71 6w
25 Taunus, Mts. 50 15N 8 20E
85 Taupo 38 41s 176 7E
85 Taupo, L. 38 46s 175 55E
85 Tauranga 37 35s 176 11E
39 Taurianova 38 22N 16 1E
56 Taurus Mts. = Toros Daglari 37 0N 35 0E
32 Tauste 41 58N 1 18w
69 Tava Wan, G. 22 40N 114 40E
88 Tavani 62 10N 93 30w
50 Tavda 58 7N 65 8w
50 Tavda, R. 57 47N 67 16E
19 Taverny 49 2N 2 13E
74 Taveta 3 31N 37 37E
85 Taveuni, I. 16 51s 179 58w
21 Tavignano, R. 42 14N 9 20E
31 Tavira 37 8N 7 40w
13 Tavistock 50 33N 4 9w
30 Távora, R. 41 0N 7 30w
59 Tavoy 14 7N 98 18E
13 Taw, R. 51 4N 4 11w
60 Tawa, R. 22 48N 77 48E
65 Tawitawi, I. 5 2N 120 0E
14 Tay, Firth of 56 25N 3 8w
14 Tay, L. 56 30N 4 10w
14 Tay, R. 56 37N 3 58w
63 Tay Ninh 11 20N 106 5E
110 Tayabamba 8 15s 77 10E
101 Taylor 30 30N 97 30w
103 Taylor, Mt. 35 16N 107 50w
100 Taylorville 39 32N 29 20w
51 Taymyr Pol. 75 0N 100 0E
14 Tayport 56 27N 2 52w
51 Tayshet 55 58N 97 25E
14 Tayside □ 56 30N 3 35w
65 Taytay 10 45N 119 30E
69 Tayu 25 38N 114 9E
67 Tayulehsze 29 15N 98 1E
72 Taza 34 10N 4 0w
50 Tazovskiy 67 28N 78 42E
49 Tbilisi 41 50N 44 50E
73 Tchad ■ 12 30N 17 15E
73 Tchad, L. 13 30N 14 30E
74 Tchibanga 2 45s 11 12E
28 Tczew 54 8N 18 50E
85 Te Anau, L. 45 15s 167 45E
85 Te Aroha 37 32s 175 44E
85 Te Awamutu 38 1s 175 20E
85 Te Horo 40 48s 175 6E
85 Te Kuiti 38 20s 175 11E
85 Te Puke 37 46s 176 22E

Tobarão Utiel

109 Tubarão 28 30s 49 0w
54 Tubas 32 20N 35 22 E
56 Tubayq, Jabal at 29 40N 37 30 E
25 Tübingen 48 31N 9 4 E
73 Tubruq 32 7N 23 55 E
77 Tubuai Is. 23 20s 151 0w
110 Tucacas 10 48N 68 19w
28 Tuchola 53 33N 17 52 E
83 Tuckanarra 27 8s 118 1 E
105 Tucker's Town 32 19N 64 43w
103 Tucson 32 14N 110 59w
108 Tucumán □ 26 48s 66 2w
101 Tucumcari 35 12N 103 45w
110 Tucupita 9 4N 62 0w
111 Tucuruí 3 45s 49 48w
32 Tudela 42 4N 1 39w
30 Tudela de Duero 41 37N 4 39w
65 Tuguegarao 17 35N 121 42 E
51 Tugur 53 50N 136 45 E
69 Tuhshan 25 40N 107 30 E
88 Tuktoyaktuk 69 15N 133 0w
48 Tula 54 13N 37 32 E
67 Tulan 37 24N 98 1 E
103 Tulare 36 15N 119 26w
103 Tularosa 33 4N 106 1w
75 Tulbagh 33 16s 19 6 E
110 Tulcán 0 48N 77 43w
41 Tulcea 45 13N 28 46 E
75 Tuléar 23 21s 43 40 E
75 Tuli 1 24s 122 26 E
54 Tūlkarm 32 19N 35 10 E
99 Tullahoma 35 23N 86 12w
15 Tullamore 53 17N 7 30w
20 Tulle 45 16N 1 47 E
26 Tulln 48 20N 16 4 E
15 Tullow 52 48N 6 45w
80 Tully 17 30s 141 0 E
73 Tulymaythah 32 40N 20 55 E
41 Tulovo 42 33N 25 32 E
101 Tulsa 36 10N 96 0w
110 Tulua 4 6N 76 11w
51 Tulun 54 40N 100 10 E
65 Tulungagung 8 5s 111 54 E
105 Tuma, R. 13 6N 84 35w
110 Tumaco 1 50N 78 45w
110 Tumatumari 5 20N 58 55w
44 Tumba 59 12N 17 48 E
74 Tumba, L. 0 50s 18 0 E
110 Tumbes 3 30s 80 20w
81 Tumby Bay 34 21s 136 8 E
68 Tumen 42 46N 129 59 E
110 Tumeremo 7 18N 61 30w
62 Tumkur 13 18N 77 12w
14 Tummel, L. 56 43N 3 55w
58 Tump 26 7N 62 16 E
63 Tumpat 6 11N 102 10 E
111 Tumucumaque
South 2 0N 55 0w
84 Tumut 35 16s 148 13 E
13 Tunbridge Wells 51 7N 0 16 E
74 Tunduru 11 0s 37 25 E
62 Tungabhadra Dam 15 21N 76 23 E
69 Tungcheng 31 0N 117 3 E
68 Tungchow 39 58N 116 50 E
69 Tungchuan 35 4N 109 2 E
69 Tungfanghsien 18 50N 108 33 E
68 Tunghwa 41 46N 126 0 E
68 Tungkiang 47 40N 132 30 E
69 Tungkwanshan 31 0N 117 45 E
68 Tungliao 43 42N 122 11 E
69 Tunglu 29 50N 119 35 E
68 Tungping 35 50N 116 20 E
69 Tungshan 29 36N 144 28 E
69 Tungshan, I. 23 40N 117 31 E
92 Tungsten 61 52N 128 1w
69 Tungtai 32 55N 120 15 E
69 Tungting Hu, L. 28 30N 112 30 E
69 Tungtze 27 59N 106 56 E
68 Tunhwa 43 27N 128 16 E
67 Tunhwang 40 5N 94 46 E
62 Tuni 17 22N 82 43 E
72 Tunis 36 50N 10 11 E
72 Tunisia ■ 33 30N 9 0 E
110 Tunja 5 40N 73 25 E
108 Tunuyán 33 55s 69 0w
51 Tuoy-khaya 62 30N 111 0w
109 Tupã 21 57s 50 28w
99 Tupelo 34 15N 88 42w
51 Tupik 54 26N 119 57 E
108 Tupiza 21 30s 65 40w
97 Tupper Lake 44 18N 74 30w
108 Tupungato, Mt. 33 15s 69 50w
110 Túquerres 1 5N 77 37w
54 Tur 31 47N 35 14 E
61 Tura 25 30N 90 16 E
56 Turayf 31 45N 38 30 E
110 Turbaco 10 20N 75 25w
40 Turbe 44 15N 17 35 E
110 Turbo 8 6N 76 43 E
41 Turda 46 35N 23 48 E
28 Turek 52 3N 18 30 E
67 Turfah 43 6N 89 24 E
67 Turfan Depression 43 0N 88 0 E
41 Tŭrgovishte 43 17N 26 38 E
11 United Kingdom ■ 55 0N 3 0w
56 Turgutlu 38 30N 27 48 E
56 Turhal 40 24N 36 19 E
32 Turia, R. 39 27N 0 19w
111 Turiaçu 1 40s 45 28w
36 Turin=Torino 45 3N 7 40 E
74 Turkana, L. 4 10N 36 10 E
50 Turkestan 43 10N 68 10 E
27 Túrkeve 47 6N 20 44 E
56 Turkey ■ 39 0N 36 0 E
82 Turkey Creek P.O. 17 2s 128 12 E
50 Turkmen S.S.R. 39 0N 59 0 E
105 Turks Is. 21 20N 71 20w
47 Turku 60 27N 22 14 E
103 Turlock 37 30N 122 55w
104 Turneffe Is. 17 20N 87 50w
16 Turnhout 51 19N 4 57w
26 Türnitz 47 55N 15 29 E
26 Turnov 50 34N 15 10 E
41 Tûrnovo 43 5N 25 41 E
41 Turnu Măgurele 43 46N 24 56 E
40 Turnu-Severin 44 39N 22 41 E
14 Turriff 57 32N 2 58w
93 Turtle 48 52N 92 40w
93 Turtleford 53 30N 108 50w
56 Turūbah 28 20N 43 15 E
47 Turun ja Pori □ 61 0N 22 30 E
27 Turzovka 49 25N 18 41 E
99 Tuscaloosa 33 13N 87 31w
96 Tuscarora Mt. 40 10N 77 45w
99 Tuskegee 32 26N 85 42w
96 Tussey Mt. 40 25N 78 7w
62 Tuticorin 8 50N 78 12 E
111 Tutoja 2 45s 42 20w
41 Tutrakan 44 2N 26 40 E
25 Tuttlingen 47 59N 8 50 E
65 Tutuala 8 25s 127 15 E
77 Tutuila, I. 14 19s 170 50w
51 Turukhansk 65 55N 88 5 E
51 Tava, A.S.S.R. 52 0N 95 0 E
76 Tuvalu ■ 8 0s 176 0 E
56 Tuwaiq, Jabal 23 0N 46 0 E
104 Tuxpan 20 50N 97 30w
104 Tuxtla Gutiérrez 16 50N 93 10w
30 Tuy 42 3N 8 39w
63 Tuy Hoa 13 5N 109 17 E
63 Tuyen Hoa 17 55N 106 3 E
69 Tuyun 26 5N 107 20 E
56 Tuz Gölü 38 45N 33 30 E
56 Tuz Khurmātu 34 50N 44 45 E
40 Tuzla 44 34N 18 41 E
45 Tvedestrand 58 38N 8 58 E
41 Tvŭrditsa 42 42N 25 53 E
12 Tweed, R. 55 46N 2 0w
92 Tweedsmuir Prov.
Park 52 55N 126 5w
102 Twin Falls 42 30N 114 30w
98 Two Rivers 44 10N 87 31w
27 Tychy 50 9N 18 59 E
101 Tyler 32 20N 95 15w
26 Týn nad Vltavou 49 13N 14 26 E
51 Tyndinskiy 55 10N 124 43 E
12 Tyne, R. 55 1N 1 26w
12 Tyne & Wear □ 54 55N 1 35w
12 Tynemouth 55 1N 1 27w
44 Tynset 62 27N 10 47 E
56 Tyre =Sur 33 19N 35 16 E
96 Tyrone 40 39N 78 10w
84 Tyrendarra 38 12s 141 50 E
44 Tyrifjorden 60 2N 10 3 E
38 Tyrrhenian Sea 40 0N 12 30 E
50 Tyumen 57 0N 65 18 E
13 Tywi, R. 51 46N 4 22w
75 Tzaneen 23 47s 30 9 E
69 Tzeki 27 40N 117 5 E
69 Tzekung 29 25N 104 30 E
69 Tzekwei 31 0N 110 46 E
68 Tzepo 36 28N 117 58 E
68 Tzeyang 32 47N 108 58 E
42 Tzoumérka, Mt. 39 30N 21 26 E

U

55 Uarsciek 2 28N 45 55 E
110 Uaupés 0 8s 67 5w
109 Ubá 21 0s 43 0w
111 Ubaitaba 14 18s 39 20w
21 Ubaye, R. 44 28N 6 18 E
66 Ube 34 6N 131 20 E
31 Ubeda 38 3N 3 23w
111 Uberaba 19 50s 48 0w
111 Uberlândia 19 0s 48 20w
63 Ubon Ratchathani 15 15N 104 50 E
31 Ubrique 36 41N 5 27w
74 Ubundu 0 22s 25 30 E
110 Ucayali, R. 4 30s 73 30w
93 Uchi Lake 51 10N 92 40w
66 Uchiura-Wan, G. 42 25N 140 40 E
92 Ucluelet 48 57N 125 32w
60 Udaipur 24 36N 73 44 E
32 Utiel 39 37N 1 11w
62 Udamalpet 10 35N 77 15 E
37 Udbina 44 31N 15 47 E
45 Uddevalla 58 21N 11 55 E
46 Uddjaur, L. 65 55N 17 50 E
62 Udgir 18 25N 77 5 E
60 Udhampur 33 0N 75 5 E
72 Udi 6 23N 7 21 E
37 Údine 46 5N 13 10 E
62 Udipi 13 25N 74 42 E
48 Udmurt A.S.S.R. □ 57 30N 52 30 E
63 Udon Thani 17 29N 102 46 E
41 Udvoy, Mts. 42 50N 26 50 E
24 Ueckermünde 53 45N 14 1 E
66 Ueda 36 30N 138 10 E
51 Uelen 66 10N 170 0w
24 Uelzen 53 0N 10 33 E
74 Uere, R. 3 42N 25 24 E
48 Ufa 54 45N 55 55 E
74 Uganda ■ 2 0N 32 0 E
88 Ugashik Lakes 57 0N 157 0w
21 Ugine 45 45N 6 25 E
51 Uglegorsk 49 10N 142 5 E
41 Ugŭrchin 43 6N 24 26 E
27 Uherské Hradiště 49 4N 17 30 E
27 Uhersky Brod 49 1N 17 40 E
26 Uhlava, R. 49 45N 13 20 E
96 Uhrichsville 40 23N 81 22w
75 Uitenhage 33 40s 25 28 E
27 Újfehértó 47 49N 21 41 E
60 Ujhani 28 0N 79 6 E
60 Ujjain 23 9N 75 43 E
27 Ujpest 47 33N 19 6 E
65 Ujung Pandang 5 10s 119 0 E
51 Uka 57 50N 162 0 E
74 Ukerewe I. 2 0s 33 0 E
59 Ukhrul 25 10N 94 25 E
48 Ukhta 63 55N 54 0 E
102 Ukiah 39 10N 123 9w
49 Ukrainian S.S.R. □ 48 0N 35 0 E
68 Ulaanbaatar 48 0N 107 0 E
68 Ulan Bator
=Ulaanbaatar 48 0N 107 0 E
51 Ulan Ude 52 0N 107 30 E
68 Ulanhot 46 5N 122 1 E
40 Ulcinj 41 58N 19 10 E
62 Ulhasnagar 19 15N 73 10 E
40 Uljma 45 2N 21 10 E
30 Ulla, R. 42 39N 8 44w
84 Ulladulla 35 21s 150 29 E
14 Ullapool 57 54N 5 10w
32 Ulldecona 40 36N 0 20 E
12 Ullswater, L. 54 35N 2 52w
25 Ulm 48 23N 10 0 E
41 Ulmeni 45 4N 46 40 E
45 Ulricehamn 57 46N 13 26 E
44 Ulsberg 62 45N 10 3 E
15 Ulster □ 54 45N 6 30w
12 Ulverston 54 13N 3 7w
80 Ulverstone 41 11s 146 11 E
48 Ulyanovsk 54 25N 48 25 E
49 Uman 48 40N 30 12 E
4 Umanak 70 40N 52 0w
62 Umarkhed 19 37N 77 38 E
37 Umbertide 43 18N 12 20 E
37 Umbria □ 42 53N 12 30 E
46 Umeå 63 45N 20 20 E
57 Umm al Qaiwain 25 30N 55 35 E
54 Umm el Fahm 32 31N 35 9 E
73 Umm Keddada 13 36N 26 42 E
56 Umm Lajj 25 0N 37 23 E
57 Umm Said 25 0N 51 40 E
88 Umnak I. 53 0N 168 0w
75 Umniati, R. 17 30s 29 23 E
60 Umrer 20 51N 79 18 E
60 Umreth 22 41N 73 4 E
75 Umtali 18 58s 32 38 E
75 Umtata 31 36s 28 49 E
75 Umvuma 19 16s 30 30 E
75 Umzimvubu 31 38s 29 33 E
60 Una 20 46N 71 8 E
37 Unac, R. 44 30N 16 9 E
97 Unadilla 42 20N 75 17w
88 Unalakleet 63 53N 160 50w
88 Unalaska I. 54 0N 164 30w
103 Uncompahgre Pk. 38 5N 107 32w
84 Underbool 35 10s 141 51 E
84 Ungarie 33 38s 146 56 E
89 Ungava B. 59 30N 67 0w
89 Ungava Pen. 60 0N 75 0w
111 União 4 50s 37 50w
109 União da Vitoria 26 5s 51 0w
88 Unimak I. 54 30N 164 30w
99 Union 34 49N 81 39w
97 Union City, N.J. 40 47N 74 5w
101 Union City,
Tenn. 36 35N 89 0w
102 Union Gap 46 38N 120 29w
53 Union of Soviet
Socialist
Republics ■ 60 0N 60 0 E
98 Uniontown 39 54N 79 45w
57 United Arab
Emirates ■ 24 0N 54 30 E
94 United States
of America ■ 37 0N 96 0w
93 Unity 52 30N 109 5w
60 Unjha 23 46N 72 24 E
61 Unnao 26 35N 80 30 E
14 Unst, I. 60 50N 0 55w
25 Unterwalden □ 46 50N 8 15 E
56 Ünye 41 5N 37 15 E
66 Uozu 36 48N 137 24 E
110 Upata 8 1N 62 24w
4 Upernavik 72 45N 56 0w
75 Upington 28 25s 21 15 E
60 Upleta 21 46N 70 16 E
85 Upolu, I. 13 58s 172 0w
85 Upper Hutt 41 8s 175 5 E
91 Upper
Musquodoboit 45 10N 62 58w
72 Upper Volta=
Burkina Faso ■ 12 0N 0 30w
44 Uppsala 59 53N 17 42 E
44 Uppsala □ 60 0N 17 30 E
56 Ur 30 55N 46 25 E
110 Uracará 2 20s 57 50w
84 Ural, Mt. 33 21s 146 12 E
48 Ural Mts. =
Uralskie Gory 60 0N 59 0 E
50 Ural, R. 47 0N 51 48 E
81 Uralla 30 37s 151 29 E
50 Uralsk 51 20N 51 20 E
48 Uralskie Gory 60 0N 59 0 E
80 Urandangi 21 32s 138 14 E
93 Uranium City 59 28N 108 40w
62 Uravakonda 14 57N 77 12 E
66 Urawa 35 50N 139 40 E
50 Uray 60 5N 65 15 E
100 Urbana, Ill. 40 7N 88 12w
98 Urbana, Ohio 40 9N 83 44w
37 Urbino 43 43N 12 38 E
30 Urbión, Picos de 42 1N 2 52w
20 Urdos 42 51N 0 35w
12 Ure, R. 54 1N 1 12w
50 Urengoy 66 0N 78 0 E
56 Urfa 37 12N 38 50 E
26 Urfahr 48 19N 14 17 E
50 Urgench 41 40N 60 30 E
25 Uri □ 46 43N 8 35 E
110 Uribia 11 43N 72 16w
54 Urim 31 18N 34 32 E
41 Urlati 44 59N 26 15 E
56 Urmia, L. =
Daryâcheh-ye
Reza'iyeh 37 30N 45 30 E
40 Uroševac 42 23N 21 10 E
28 Ursus 52 12N 20 53
111 Uruaca 14 35s 49 16w
104 Uruapán 19 30N 102 0w
111 Uruçui 7 20s 44 28w
108 Uruguay ■ 32 30s 55 30w
108 Uruguay, R. 34 12s 58 18w
108 Uruguaiana 29 50s 57 0w
67 Urungu, R. 46 30N 88 50 E
57 Uruzgan □ 33 30N 66 0 E
41 Urziceni 44 46N 26 42 E
48 Usa, R. 65 57N 56 55 E
56 Uşak 38 43N 29 28 E
24 Usedom, I. 53 50N 13 55 E
56 Usfan 21 58N 39 27 E
50 Ush-Tobe 45 16N 78 0 E
112 Ushuaia 54 50s 68 23w
51 Ushuman 52 47N 126 32 E
13 Usk, R. 51 36N 2 58w
56 Üsküdar 41 0N 29 5 E
48 Usman 52 5N 39 48 E
51 Usolye Sibirskoye 52 40N 103 40 E
50 Uspenskiy 48 50N 72 55 E
20 Ussel 45 32N 2 18 E
51 Ussuriysk 43 40N 131 50 E
51 Ust-Ilga 55 5N 104 55 E
51 Ust-Ilimsk 58 3N 102 39 E
50 Ust Ishim 57 45N 71 10 E
51 Ust-Kamchatsk 56 10N 162 0 E
50 Ust Kamenogorsk 50 0N 82 20 E
51 Ust-Kut 56 50N 105 10 E
51 Ust Kuyga 70 1N 135 36 E
51 Ust Maya 60 30N 134 20 E
51 Ust Olenck 73 0N 120 10 E
50 Ust Post 70 0N 84 10 E
48 Ust Tsilma 65 25N 52 0 E
51 Ust-Tungir 55 25N 120 15 E
48 Ust Usa 66 0N 56 30 E
44 Ustaoset 60 30N 8 2 E
51 Ustchaun 68 47N 170 30 E
27 Ustí na Orlici 49 58N 16 38 E
26 Ustí nad Labem 50 41N 14 3 E
38 Ustica, I. 38 42N 13 10 E
51 Ustye 55 30N 97 30 E
104 Usulután 13 25N 88 28w
102 Utah □ 39 30N 111 30w
65 Utara □, Sulawesi 1 0N 120 3 E
64 Utara □, Sumatera 2 0N 99 0 E
24 Ütersen 53 40N 9 40 E
63 Uthai Thani 15 22N 100 3 E
56 Uthmaniya 25 5N 49 6 E
97 Utica 43 5N 75 18w

Wallal Willimantic

81 Wallal 26 32S 146 7E
82 Wallal Downs 19 47S 120 40E
81 Wallaroo 33 56S 137 39E
12 Wallasey 3 26S 3 2W
84 Wallerawang 33 25S 150 4E
80 Wallahallow 17 50S 135 50E
97 Wallingford 43 27N 72 58W
76 Wallis Arch. 13 20S 176 20E
102 Wallowa 45 40N 117 35W
12 Wallsend 54 59N 1 30W
81 Wallumbilla 26 33S 149 9E
12 Walney, I 54 5N 3 15W
84 Walpeup 35 10S 142 2E
13 Walsall 52 36N 1 59W
101 Walsenburg 37 42N 104 45W
24 Walsrode 52 51N 9 37E
62 Waltair 17 44N 83 23E
24 Waltershausen 50 53N 10 33E
90 Waltham, Canada 45 57N 76 57W
97 Waltham, U.S.A. 42 22N 71 12W
75 Walvisbaai 23 0S 14 28E
75 Walvis Bay = Walvisbaai 23 0S 14 28E
74 Wamba 2 10N 27 57E
31 Wanaaring 29 38S 144 0E
85 Wanaka, L. 44 33S 169 7E
65 Wanapiri 4 30S 135 50E
97 Wanaque 41 3N 74 17W
81 Wanbi 34 46S 140 17E
62 Wandiwash 12 30N 79 30E
81 Wandoan 26 5S 149 55E
85 Wanganui 39 35S 175 3E
84 Wangaratta 36 21S 146 19E
81 Wangary 34 33S 135 29E
68 Wangtu 38 42N 115 4E
69 Wanhsien 30 45N 108 20E
75 Wankie 18 18S 26 30E
93 Wanless 54 11N 101 21W
69 Wanning 18 45N 110 28E
69 Wantsai 28 1N 114 5E
69 Wanyang Shan, Mts. 26 30N 113 30E
69 Wanyuan 32 3N 108 16E
102 Wapato 46 30N 120 25W
55 Warandab 7 20N 44 2E
62 Warangal 17 58N 79 45E
85 Ward 41 49S 174 11E
57 Wardak □ 34 15N 68 0E
60 Wardha 20 45N 78 39E
97 Ware 42 16N 72 15W
24 Waren 53 30N 12 41E
24 Warendorf 51 57N 8 0E
81 Warialda 29 29S 150 33E
65 Warkopi 1 12S 134 9E
85 Warkworth 36 24S 174 41E
13 Warley 52 30N 2 0W
93 Warman 52 25N 106 30W
75 Warmbad, S.W. Africa 28 25S 18 42E
75 Warmbad, S.W. Africa 19 14S 13 51E
84 Warncoort 38 30S 143 45E
102 Warner Ra. 41 30S 120 20W
99 Warner Robins 32 41N 83 36W
24 Warnemünde 54 9N 12 5E
83 Waroona 32 50S 115 55E
60 Warora 20 14N 79 1E
84 Warracknabeal 36 9S 142 26E
84 Warragul 38 10S 145 58E
81 Warrego, R. 30 24S 145 21E
84 Warren, Australia 31 42S 147 51E
96 Warren, Ohio 41 18N 80 52W
96 Warren, Pa. 41 52N 79 10W
101 Warren 33 35N 92 3W
15 Warrenpoint 54 7N 6 15W
100 Warrensburg 38 45N 93 45W
75 Warrenton, S. Africa 28 9S 24 47E
102 Warrenton, U.S.A. 46 11N 123 59W
72 Warri 5 30N 5 41E
12 Warrington, U.K. 53 25N 2 38W
99 Warrington, U.S.A. 30 22N 87 16W
84 Warrnambool 38 25S 142 30E
58 Warsak Dam 34 10N 71 25E
98 Warsaw 41 14N 85 50W
28 Warszawa 52 13N 21 0E
28 Warszawa □ 52 35N 21 0E
28 Warta, R. 52 35N 14 39E
13 Warwick □ 52 20N 1 30W
81 Warwick, Australia 28 10S 152 1E
13 Warwick, U.K. 52 17N 1 36W
97 Warwick, U.S.A. 41 43N 71 25W
92 Wasa 49 45N 115 50W
86 Wasatch Mts. 40 30N 111 15W
103 Wasco, Calif. 35 37N 119 16W
102 Wasco, Oreg. 45 45N 120 46W
100 Waseca 44 3N 93 31W
12 Wash, The 52 58N 0 20W
96 Washago 44 46N 79 21W
102 Washington □ 47 45N 120 30W
98 Washington, D.C. 38 52N 77 0W
98 Washington, Ind. 38 40N 87 8W
100 Washington, Iowa 41 20N 91 45W
100 Washington, Mo. 38 33N 91 1W
97 Washington, N.J. 40 45N 74 59W
99 Washington, N.C. 35 35N 77 1W
98 Washington, Ohio 39 34N 83 26W
96 Washington, Pa. 40 10N 80 20W
77 Washington I. 4 43N 160 24W
97 Washington, Mt. 44 15N 71 18W
16 Wassenaar 52 8N 4 24E
24 Wasserkuppe, Mt. 50 30N 9 56E
90 Waswanipi 49 30N 77 0W
65 Watangpone 4 29S 120 25E
97 Waterbury 41 32N 73 0W
15 Waterford 52 16N 7 8W
15 Waterford □ 51 10N 7 40W
16 Waterloo, Belgium 50 43N 4 25E
100 Waterloo, Iowa 42 27N 92 20W
96 Waterloo, N.Y. 42 54N 76 53W
97 Watertown, N.Y. 43 58N 75 57W
100 Watertown, S.D. 44 57N 97 5W
100 Watertown, Wis. 43 15N 88 45W
99 Waterville 44 35N 69 40W
97 Watervliet 42 46N 73 43W
65 Wates 7 53S 110 6E
13 Watford 51 38N 0 23W
83 Watheroo 30 15S 116 0W
105 Watling, I. 24 0N 74 30W
93 Watrous 51 40N 105 25W
74 Watsa 3 4N 29 30E
83 Watson 30 19S 131 41E
92 Watson Lake 60 12N 129 0W
103 Watsonville 37 58N 121 49W
25 Wattwil 47 18N 9 6E
84 Waubra 37 21S 143 39E
84 Wauchope 31 28S 152 45E
93 Waugh 49 40N 95 20W
98 Waukegan 42 22N 87 54W
100 Waukesha 43 0N 88 15W
100 Waupun 43 38N 88 44W
100 Wausau 44 57N 89 40W
98 Wauwatosa 43 6N 87 59W
82 Wave Hill 17 32N 131 0E
13 Waveney, R. 52 28N 1 45E
85 Waverley 39 46S 174 37E
100 Waverly 42 40N 92 30W
16 Wavre 50 43N 4 38E
73 Wâw 7 45N 28 1E
101 Waxahachie 32 22N 96 53W
80 Wayatinah 42 19S 146 27E
99 Waycross 31 12N 82 25W
98 Waynesboro, Pa. 39 46N 77 32W
98 Waynesboro, Va. 38 4N 78 57W
99 Waynesville 35 31N 83 0W
57 Wazirabad, Afghanistan 36 44N 66 47E
60 Wazirabad, Pak. 32 30N 74 8E
13 Weald, The 51 7N 0 9E
12 Wear, R. 54 55N 1 22W
101 Weatherford 32 45N 97 48W
97 Webster 42 4N 71 54W
100 Webster City 42 30N 93 50W
100 Webster Green 38 38N 90 20W
65 Weda 0 30N 127 50E
112 Weddell I. 51 50S 61 0W
5 Weddell Sea 72 30S 40 0W
84 Wedderburn 36 20S 143 33E
91 Wedgeport 43 44N 65 59W
81 Wee Waa 30 11S 149 26E
102 Weed 41 29N 122 22W
16 Weert 51 15N 5 43E
28 Wegliniec 51 18N 15 10E
69 Wei Ho, R. 35 45N 114 30E
24 Weida 50 47N 12 3E
68 Weifang 36 47N 119 10E
68 Weihai 37 30N 122 10E
25 Weilheim 47 50N 11 9E
24 Weimar 51 0N 11 20E
69 Weinan 34 30N 109 35E
25 Weingarten 47 49N 9 39E
25 Weinheim 47 50N 11 9E
80 Weipa 12 24S 141 50E
93 Weir River 57 0N 94 10W
96 Weirton 40 22N 80 35W
102 Weiser 44 10N 117 0W
25 Weissenburg 49 2N 10 58E
24 Weissenfels 51 11N 11 58E
24 Weisswasser 51 30N 14 36E
26 Wêitra 48 41N 14 54E
26 Weiz 47 13N 15 39E
28 Wejherow 54 35N 18 12E
93 Wekusko 54 45N 99 45W
31 Welbourn Hill 27 21S 134 6E
98 Welch 37 29N 81 36W
25 Welden 48 27N 10 40E
75 Welkom 28 0S 26 50E
96 Welland 43 0N 79 10W
12 Welland, R. 52 53N 0 2E
80 Wellesley, Is. 17 20S 139 30E
13 Wellingborough 52 18N 0 41W
84 Wellington, Australia 32 30S 149 0E
90 Wellington, Canada 43 57N 77 20W
85 Wellington, N.Z. 41 19S 174 46E
12 Wellington, U.K. 52 42N 2 31W
101 Wellington, U.S.A. 37 15N 97 25W
85 Wellington □ 40 8S 175 36E
112 Wellington, I. 49 30S 75 0W
12 Wells, Norfolk 52 57N 0 51E
13 Wells, Somerset 51 12N 2 39W
102 Wells, U.S.A. 41 8N 115 0W
83 Wells, L. 26 44S 123 15W
97 Wells River 44 9N 72 4W
96 Wellsburg 40 15N 80 36W
28 Wełna, R. 42 9N 77 53W
26 Wels 48 9N 14 1E
84 Welshpool, Australia 38 42S 146 26E
13 Welshpool, U.K. 52 40N 3 9W
12 Wem 52 52N 2 45W
102 Wenatchee 47 30N 120 17W
69 Wenchang 19 38N 110 42E
72 Wenchi 7 46N 2 8W
69 Wenchow 28 0N 120 35E
102 Wendell 42 50N 114 51W
69 Wensiang 34 35N 110 40E
12 Wensleydale 54 20N 2 0W
67 Wensu 41 15N 80 14E
68 Wenteng 25 15S 23 16E
84 Wentworth 34 2S 141 54E
75 Wepener 29 42S 27 3E
75 Werda 25 15S 23 16E
24 Werdau 50 45N 12 20E
24 Werder 52 23N 12 56E
24 Werdohl 51 15N 7 47E
25 Werne 51 38N 7 38E
24 Wernigerode 51 49N 0 45E
84 Werribee 37 54S 144 40E
84 Werris Creek 31 8S 150 38E
25 Wertheim 49 44N 9 32E
24 Wesel 51 39N 6 34E
24 Weser, R. 53 32N 8 34E
91 Wesleyville 49 8N 53 36W
80 Wessel, Is. 11 10S 136 45E
98 West Bend 43 25N 88 10W
61 West Bengal □ 25 0N 90 0E
13 West Bromwich 52 32N 2 1W
100 West Des Moines 41 30N 93 45W
112 West Falkland, I. 51 30S 60 0W
100 West Frankfort 37 56N 89 0W
24 West Germany ■ 51 0N 9 0E
13 West Glamorgan □ 51 40N 3 55W
97 West Hartford 41 45N 72 45W
97 West Haven 41 18N 72 57W
101 West Helena 34 30N 90 40W
101 West Memphis 35 5N 90 3W
13 West Midlands □ 52 30N 2 0W
101 West Monroe 32 32N 92 7W
99 West Palm Beach 26 44N 80 3W
97 West Pittston 41 19N 75 49W
105 West Pt. 18 14N 78 30W
101 West Point, Miss. 33 36N 88 38W
98 West Point, Va. 37 35N 76 47W
13 West Sussex □ 50 55N 0 30W
98 West Virginia □ 39 0N 18 0W
84 West Wyalong 33 56S 147 10E
12 West Yorkshire □ 53 45N 1 40W
99 Westbrook 43 41N 70 21W
80 Westbury 41 30S 146 51E
24 Westerland 54 51N 8 20E
78 Western Australia □ 25 0S 118 0E
62 Western Ghats, Mts. 15 30N 74 30E
14 Western Isles □ 57 30N 7 10W
63 Western Malaysia □ 4 0N 10 2E
85 Western Samoa ■ 14 0S 172 0W
16 Westerschelde, R. 51 25N 4 0E
24 Westerstede 51 15N 7 55E
24 Westerwald, Mts. 50 39N 8 0E
97 Westfield 42 9N 72 49W
85 Westland □ 43 33S 169 59E
92 Westlock 54 20N 113 55W
15 Westmeath □ 53 30N 7 30W
98 Westminster 39 34S 77 1W
103 Westmorland 33 2N 115 42W
64 Weston, Malaysia 5 10N 115 35E
98 Weston, U.S.A. 39 3N 80 29W
13 Weston-super-Mare 51 20N 2 59W
15 Westport, Eire 53 44N 9 31W
85 Westport, N.Z. 41 46S 171 37E
14 Westray, I. 59 18N 3 0W
92 Westview 49 50N 124 31W
102 Westwood 40 26N 121 0W
65 Wetar, I. 7 30S 126 30E
92 Wetaskiwin 52 55N 113 24W
97 Wethersfield 41 43N 72 40W
16 Wetteren 51 0N 3 53E
24 Wetzlar 50 33N 8 30E
101 Wewaka 35 10N 96 35W
15 Wexford 52 20N 6 28W
15 Wexford □ 52 20N 6 40W
93 Weyburn 49 40N 103 50W
26 Weyer 47 51N 14 40E
13 Weymouth, U.K. 50 36N 2 28W
97 Weymouth, U.S.A. 42 13N 70 53W
85 Whakatane 37 57S 177 1E
89 Whale, R. 57 40N 67 0W
93 Whale Cove 62 10N 93 0W
14 Whalsay, I. 60 22N 1 0W
85 Whangamomona 39 8S 174 44E
85 Whangarei 35 43S 174 21E
85 Whangaroa, Harbour 35 4S 173 46E
12 Wharfe, R. 53 51N 1 7W
100 Wheatland 42 4N 105 58W
103 Wheeler Pk. 38 57N 114 15W
96 Wheeling 40 2N 80 41W
12 Whernside, Mt. 54 14N 2 24W
96 Whitby, Canada 43 50N 78 50W
12 Whitby, U.K. 54 29N 0 37W
98 White, R., Ind. 38 25N 87 44W
101 White, R., Ark. 33 53N 91 3W
81 White Cliffs 30 50S 143 10E
13 White Horse, Vale of 51 37N 1 30W
97 White Mts. 44 15N 71 15W
73 White Nile, R. = Nîl el Abyad 9 30N 31 40E
97 White Plains 41 2N 73 44E
90 White River 48 35N 85 20W
97 White River Junc. 43 28N 72 20W
48 White Sea= Beloye More 66 30N 38 0E
102 White Sulphur Springs 46 35N 111 0W
85 Whitecliffs 43 26S 171 55E
97 Whitefield 44 23N 71 37W
102 Whitefish 48 25N 114 22W
97 Whitehall, N.Y. 43 32N 73 28W
102 Whitehall, Wis. 44 20N 91 19W
12 Whitehaven 54 33N 3 35W
92 Whitehorse 60 45N 135 10W
93 Whiteshell Prov. Park 50 0N 95 25W
80 Whitewood 21 28S 143 30E
93 Whitewood 50 20N 102 20W
14 Whithorn 54 55N 4 25W
85 Whitianga 36 47S 175 41E
97 Whitman 42 4N 70 55W
103 Whitney, Mt. 36 35N 118 14W
97 Whitney Point 42 19N 75 59W
13 Whitstable 51 21N 1 2E
80 Whitsunday, I. 20 15S 149 4E
88 Whittier 60 46N 148 48W
91 Whittle, C. 50 11N 60 8W
81 Whyalla 33 2S 137 30E
90 Wiarton 44 50N 81 10W
161 Wichita 37 40N 97 29W
101 Wichita Falls 33 57N 98 30W
14 Wick 58 26N 3 5W
103 Wickenburg 33 58N 112 45W
83 Wickepin 32 50S 117 30E
96 Wickliffe 41 46N 81 29W
15 Wicklow 53 0N 6 2W
15 Wicklow □ 52 59N 6 25W
15 Wicklow Mts. 53 0N 6 30W
83 Widgiemooltha 31 30S 121 34E
12 Widnes 53 22N 2 44W
28 Wiecbork 53 22N 17 30E
25 Wiedenbrück 51 50N 8 18E
28 Wielbark 53 24N 20 55E
28 Wieluń 51 15N 18 40E
27 Wien 48 12N 16 22E
27 Wiener Neustadt 47 49N 16 16E
28 Wieprz, R. 51 34N 21 49E
16 Wierden 52 22N 6 35E
25 Wiesbaden 50 7N 8 17E
12 Wigan 53 33N 2 38W
14 Wigtown 54 52N 4 27W
14 Wigtown B. 54 46N 4 15W
84 Wilcannia 31 30S 143 26E
24 Wildeshausen 52 54N 8 25E
26 Wildon 46 52N 15 31E
98 Wildwood 39 5N 74 46W
26 Wilhelmsburg, Austria 48 6N 15 36E
24 Wilhelmsburg, W. Germany 53 28N 10 1E
24 Wilhelshaven 53 30N 8 9E
97 Wilkes-Barre 41 15N 75 52W
15 Wilkes Ld. 69 0S 120 0E
5 Wilkes Sub-Glacial Basin 68 0S 140 0E
93 Wilkie 52 27N 108 42W
96 Wilkinsburg 40 26N 79 50W
96 Willard 41 3N 82 44W
103 Willcox 32 13N 109 53W
105 Willemstad 12 5N 69 0W
82 Willeroo 15 14S 131 37E
81 William Creek 28 58S 136 22E
83 Williams, Australia 33 0S 117 0E
103 Williams, U.S.A. 35 16N 112 11W
92 Williams Lake 52 20N 122 10W
98 Williamsburg 37 17N 76 44W
98 Williamson 37 46N 82 17W
96 Williamsport 41 18N 77 1W
84 Williamstown, Australia 37 46S 144 58E
97 Williamstown, U.S.A. 42 41N 73 12W
97 Willimantic 41 45N 72 12W

Williston Yoweragabbie

100 Williston 48 10N 103 35W
102 Willits 39 28N 123 17W
100 Willmar 45 5N 95 0W
96 Willoughby 41 38N 81 26W
84 Willow Tree 31 40S 150 45E
75 Willowmore 33 15S 23 30E
80 Willows, Australia 23 45S 147 25E
102 Willows, U.S.A. 39 30N 122 10W
98 Wilmette 42 6N 87 44W
98 Wilmington, Del. 39 45N 75 32W
99 Wilmington, N.C. 34 14N 77 54W
98 Wilmington, Ohio 39 29N 83 46W
99 Wilson 35 44N 77 54W
103 Wilson, Mt. 37 55N 105 3W
84 Wilson's Promontory 39 5S 146 28E
13 Wilton 51 5N 1 52W
13 Wiltshire □ 51 20N 2 0W
83 Wiluna 26 40S 120 25E
19 Wimereux 50 45N 1 37E
13 Winchester, U.K. 51 4N 1 19W
97 Winchester, Conn. 41 53N 73 9W
98 Winchester, Ind. 40 10N 84 56W
98 Winchester, Ky. 38 0N 84 8W
98 Winchester, Va. 39 14N 78 8W
12 Windermere, L. 54 20N 2 57W
75 Windhoek 22 35S 17 4E
26 Windischgarsten 47 42N 14 21E
80 Windorah 25 24S 142 36E
13 Windrush, R. 51 42N 1 25W
84 Windsor, Australia 33 34S 150 44E
91 Windsor, Nova Scotia 44 59N 64 5W
90 Windsor, Ont. 42 25N 83 0W
13 Windsor, U.K. 51 28N 0 36W
105 Windward Is. 13 0N 63 0W
92 Winfield, Canada 52 58N 114 26W
101 Winfield, U.S.A. 37 15N 97 0W
84 Wingen 31 50S 150 58E
90 Wingham 43 55N 81 25W
90 Winisk, R. 55 17N 85 5W
93 Winkler 49 15N 98 0W
26 Winklern 46 52N 12 53E
72 Winneba 5 25N 0 36W
102 Winnemucca 41 0N 117 45W
93 Winnepegosis, L. 52 40N 100 0W
98 Winnetka 42 8N 87 46W
101 Winnfield 31 57N 92 38W
82 Winning 23 9S 114 32E
93 Winnipeg 49 50N 97 15W
93 Winnipeg, L. 52 30N 98 0W
93 Winnipegosis 52 40N 100 0W
97 Winnipesaukee, L. 43 35N 71 20W
100 Winona 44 2N 91 45W
97 Winooski 44 31N 73 11W
97 Winooski, R. 44 30N 73 15W
16 Winschoten 53 9N 7 3E
103 Winslow 35 2N 110 41W
97 Winsted 41 55N 73 4W
99 Winston-Salem 36 7N 80 15W
99 Winter Haven 28 0N 81 42W
99 Winter Park 28 34N 81 19W
25 Winterthur 47 30N 8 44E
80 Winton 22 21S 143 0E
85 Winton 46 8S 168 20E
19 Wintzenheim 48 4N 7 17E
81 Wirrulla 32 24S 134 31E
12 Wisbech 52 39N 0 10E
100 Wisconsin □ 44 30N 90 0W
100 Wisconsin Rapids 44 25N 89 50W
14 Wishaw 55 46N 3 55W
28 Wisła, R. 54 22N 18 55E
27 Wisłoka, R. 50 27N 21 23E
24 Wismar 53 53N 11 23E
19 Wissant 50 52N 1 40E
19 Wissembourg 49 2N 7 57E
75 Witbank 25 51S 29 14E
12 Witham, R. 52 56N 0 4E
12 Withernsea 53 43N 0 2W
13 Witney 51 47N 1 29W
75 Witsand 34 24S 20 50E
24 Witten 51 26N 7 19E
24 Wittenberg 51 51N 12 39E
24 Wittenberge 53 0N 11 44E
24 Wittenburg 53 30N 11 4E
82 Wittenoom 22 15S 118 20E
24 Wittengen 52 43N 10 43E
24 Wittow, I. 54 37N 13 21E
24 Wittstock 53 10N 12 30E
25 Witzenhausen 51 20N 9 50E
28 Wkra R. 52 27N 20 44E
65 Wlingi 8 5S 112 25E
28 Włocławek 52 39 19 2E
28 Wrocław 51 10N 17 0E
97 Woburn 42 31N 71 7W
84 Wodonga 36 5S 146 50E
27 Wodzistaw Śl. 50 1N 18 26E
65 Wokam, I. 5 45S 134 28E
90 Wolfe I. 44 7N 76 27E
24 Wolfenbüttel 52 10N 10 33E
26 Wolfsberg 46 50N 14 52E
24 Wolfsburg 52 27N 10 49E
24 Wolgast 54 3N 13 46E
112 Wollaston, Is. 55 40S 67 30W
93 Wollaston L. 58 20N 103 30W
88 Wollaston Pen. 69 30N 113 0W
84 Wollongong 34 25S 150 54E
28 Wołomin 51 21N 16 39E
93 Wolseley 50 25N 103 15W
86 Wolstenholme, C. 62 50N 78 0W
13 Wolverhampton 52 35N 2 6W
80 Wonarah P.O. 19 55S 136 20E
81 Wondai 26 20S 151 49E
83 Wongan Hills 30 53S 116 42E
68 Wŏnju 37 30N 127 59E
68 Wŏnsan 39 20N 127 25E
84 Wonthaggi 38 29S 145 31E
92 Wood Buffalo Nat. Park 59 30N 113 0W
83 Woodanilling 33 31S 117 24E
84 Woodend 37 20N 144 33E
102 Woodland 38 40N 121 50W
93 Woodridge 49 20N 96 20W
83 Woodroffe, Mt. 26 20S 131 45E
93 Woods, L. of the 49 30N 94 30W
80 Woodstock, Australia 19 22S 142 45E
91 Woodstock, N.B. 46 11N 67 37W
90 Woodstock, Ont 43 10N 80 45W
13 Woodstock, U.K. 51 51N 1 20W
96 Woodstock, Vt. 43 37N 72 31W
100 Woodstock, Ill. 42 17N 88 30W
97 Woodsville 44 10N 72 0W
85 Woodville 40 20S 175 53E
101 Woodward 36 24N 99 28W
83 Woolgangie 31 12S 120 35E
81 Woolgoolga 30 7S 153 12E
81 Woombye 26 40S 152 55E
84 Woomelang 35 37S 142 40E
81 Woomera 31 9S 136 56E
84 Woonona 34 32S 150 49E
97 Woonsocket 42 0N 71 30W
100 Woonsockett 44 5N 98 15W
83 Wooramel 25 45S 114 40E
83 Wooramel, R. 25 47S 114 10E
83 Wooroloo 31 45S 116 25E
96 Wooster 40 38N 81 55W
75 Worcester, S. Africa 33 39S 19 27E
13 Worcester, U.K. 52 12N 2 12W
97 Worcester, U.S.A. 42 14N 71 49W
26 Wörgl 47 29N 12 3E
12 Workington 54 39N 3 34W
12 Worksop 53 19N 1 9W
102 Worland 44 0N 107 59W
25 Worms 49 37N 8 21E
83 Worsley 33 15S 116 2E
26 Wörther See, L. 46 37N 14 19E
13 Worthing 50 49N 0 21W
100 Worthington 43 35N 95 30W
65 Wosi 0 15S 128 0E
92 Wrangell 56 30N 132 25W
88 Wrangell Mts. 61 40N 143 30W
14 Wrath, C. 58 38N 5 0W
12 Wrekin, The, Mt. 52 41N 2 35W
12 Wrexham 53 5N 3 0W
92 Wright, Canada 51 45N 121 30W
65 Wright, Philippines 11 42N 125 2E
88 Wrigley 63 0N 123 30W
28 Wrocław 51 5N 17 5E
28 Wrocław □ 51 0N 17 0E
28 Września 52 21N 17 36E
83 Wubin 30 8S 116 30E
68 Wuchang, Heilungkiang 44 51N 127 10E
69 Wuchang, Hupei 30 34N 114 25E
69 Wuchow 23 26N 111 19E
68 Wuchung 38 4N 106 12E
69 Wuhan 30 32N 114 22E
69 Wuhu 31 21N 118 30E
72 Wukari 7 57N 9 42E
59 Wuntho 23 55N 95 45E
24 Wuppertal 51 15N 7 8E
83 Wurarga 28 15S 116 12E
25 Würzburg 49 46N 9 55E
24 Wurzen 51 21N 12 45E
69 Wusih 31 30N 120 30E
69 Wusu 44 10N 84 55E
68 Wutai Shan 39 4N 113 35E
67 Wutunghliao 29 25N 104 0E
67 Wuwei 38 0N 102 30E
69 Wuyi Shan, Mts. 26 40N 116 30E
68 Wuying 48 10N 129 20E
68 Wuyuan 41 45N 108 30E
83 Wyalkatchem 31 8S 117 22E
98 Wyandotte 42 14N 83 13W
81 Wyandra 27 12S 145 56E
84 Wycheproot 36 0N 143 17E
13 Wye, R. 51 37N 2 39W
13 Wymondham 52 34N 1 7E
82 Wyndham 15 33S 128 3E
81 Wynnum 27 29S 152 58E
81 Wynyard, Australia 40 59S 145 45E
93 Wynyard, Canada 51 45N 104 10W
Canada 51 45N 104 10W
102 Wyoming □ 42 48N 109 0W
84 Wyong 33 14S 151 24E
28 Wyrzysk 53 10N 17 17E
28 Wyszków 52 36N 21 25E
98 Wytheville 37 0N 81 3W

X

42 Xánthi 41 10N 24 58E
42 Xánthi □ 41 10N 24 58E
98 Xenia 39 42N 83 57W
63 Xieng Khouang 19 17N 103 25E
43 Xilókastron 38 4N 22 43E
75 Xinavane 25 2S 32 47E
111 Xingu, R. 1 30S 51 53W
43 Xiniás, L. 39 2N 22 12E
111 Xique-Xique 10 40S 42 40W

Y

80 Yaamba 23 8S 150 22E
67 Yaan 30 0N 102 59E
41 Yablanitsa 43 2N 24 5E
51 Yablonovy Khrebet 53 0N 114 0E
54 Ya'Bud 32 27N 35 10E
108 Yacuiba 22 0S 63 25W
62 Yadgir 16 45N 77 5E
54 Yagur 32 45N 35 4E
69 Yaicheng 18 14N 109 7E
102 Yakima 46 42N 120 30W
68 Yakoshih 49 13N 120 35E
66 Yaku-Shima, I. 30 20N 130 30E
51 Yakut A.S.S.R. □ 66 0N 125 0E
88 Yakutat 59 50N 139 44W
51 Yakutsk 62 5N 129 40E
80 Yalboroo 20 50S 148 30E
83 Yalgoo 23 16S 116 39E
104 Yalkubul, Pta. 21 32N 88 37W
84 Yallourn 38 10S 146 18E
49 Yalta 44 30N 34 10E
68 Yalu, R. 47 30N 123 30E
67 Yalung Kiang, R. 32 0N 100 0E
50 Yalutorovsk 56 30N 65 40E
66 Yamagata 37 55N 140 20E
66 Yamagata □ 38 30N 140 0E
66 Yamaguchi 34 10N 131 32E
66 Yamaguchi □ 34 20N 131 40E
50 Yamal Pol. 71 0N 70 0E
56 Yamama 24 5N 47 30E
66 Yamanashi □ 35 40N 138 40E
84 Yamba 29 30S 153 22E
41 Yambol 42 30N 26 36E
65 Yamdena, I. 7 45S 131 20E
59 Yamethin 20 26N 96 9E
82 Yampi, Sd. 15 15S 123 30E
69 Yamhsien 21 45N 108 31E
41 Yamrukohal, Mt. 42 44N 24 52E
54 Yamun 32 29N 35 14E
61 Yamuna, R. 27 0N 78 30E
66 Yanai 33 58N 132 7E
62 Yanam 16 47N 82 15E
48 Yanaul 56 25N 55 0E
83 Yandanooka 29 18S 115 29E
59 Yandoon 17 2N 95 39E
74 Yangambi 0 47N 24 20E
69 Yangchow 32 25N 119 25E
68 Yangchuan 38 0N 113 29E
50 Yangi-Yer 40 17N 68 48E
69 Yangtze Kiang, R. 31 40N 122 0E
100 Yankton 42 55N 97 25W
81 Yanna 26 58S 146 0E
69 Yanping 22 25N 112 0E
41 Yantra, R. 43 35N 25 37E
69 Yao Shan, Mts. 24 0N 110 0E
74 Yaoundé 3 50N 1 35E
65 Yap Is. 9 30N 138 10E
65 Yapen, I. 1 50S 136 0E
65 Yapen, Teluk, G. 1 30S 136 0E
80 Yaraka 24 53S 144 3E
48 Yaransk 57 13N 47 56E
13 Yare, R. 52 40N 1 45E
48 Yarensk 61 10N 49 8E
67 Yarkand= Soche 38 24N 77 20E
58 Yarkhun, R. 36 30N 72 45E
91 Yarmouth 43 53N 65 45W
48 Yaroslavl 57 35N 39 55E
83 Yarra Yarra Lakes 29 12S 115 45E
82 Yarraloola 21 34S 115 52E
81 Yarraman 26 46S 152 1E
50 Yar-Sale 66 50N 70 50E
51 Yartsevo 60 20N 90 0E
110 Yarumal 6 58N 75 24W
85 Yasawa Is. 17 0S 177 23E
63 Yasothon 15 50N 104 10E
84 Yass 34 50S 149 0E
54 Yas'ur 32 54N 35 10E
88 Yathkyed, L. 63 0N 98 0W
66 Yatsushiro 32 30N 130 40E
54 Ya'tah 31 27N 35 6E
60 Yaval 21 10N 75 42E
54 Yavne 31 52N 34 45E
66 Yawatehama 33 27N 132 24E
57 Yazd 31 55N 54 27E
57 Yazdan 33 30N 60 50E
101 Yazoo City 32 48N 90 28W
26 Ybbs 48 12N 15 4E
59 Ye 15 15N 97 51E
83 Yealering 32 35S 117 30E
59 Yebyu 14 15N 98 13E
33 Yecla 38 35N 1 5W
68 Yehsien 37 12N 119 58E
51 Yelanskoye 61 25N 128 0E
81 Yelarbon 28 33S 150 49E
48 Yelets 52 40N 38 30E
14 Yell, I. 46 42N 2 20W
62 Yellamanchilli 38 0N 117 20E
62 Yellandu 17 36N 80 20E
83 Yellowdine 31 18S 119 39E
92 Yellowhead P. 53 0N 118 30W
92 Yellowknife 62 30N 114 10W
88 Yellowknife, R. 63 30N 113 30W
102 Yellowstone Nat. Park 44 35N 110 0W
102 Yellowtail Res. 45 6N 108 8W
80 Yelvertoft 20 13S 138 53E
55 Yemen ■ 15 0N 44 0E
59 Yenangyaung 20 30N 95 0E
69 Yencheng 36 44N 110 2E
51 Yeniseysk 58 39N 92 4E
50 Yenisey, R. 68 0N 86 30E
50 Yeniseyskiy Zaliv 72 20N 81 0E
68 Yenki 43 12N 129 30E
68 Yentai 37 30N 121 22E
51 Yenyuka 58 20N 121 30E
13 Yeo, R. 51 1N 2 46W
60 Yeola 20 0N 74 30E
60 Yeotmal 20 20N 78 15E
13 Yeovil 50 57N 2 38W
80 Yeppoon 23 5S 150 47E
49 Yerevan 40 10N 44 20E
51 Yermakovo 52 35N 126 20E
51 Yerofey Pavlovich 54 0N 122 0E
54 Yeroham 30 59N 34 55E
49 Yershov 51 15N 48 27E
13 Yes Tor 50 41N 3 59E
20 Yeu, Î.d' 46 42N 2 20W
69 Yeungchun 22 15N 111 40E
69 Yeungkong 21 55N 112 0E
49 Yeysk Stavo 46 40N 38 12E
108 Yhatí 25 45S 56 35W
109 Yhú 25 0S 56 0W
42 Yiannitsa 40 46N 22 24E
57 Yibal 22 10N 56 8E
69 Yilan 24 47N 121 44E
68 Yin Shan, Mts. 41 0N 111 0E
68 Yinchwan 38 30N 106 20E
69 Yingcheng 31 0N 113 44E
68 Yingkow 40 38N 122 30E
69 Yingtan 28 12N 117 0E
42 Yioura, I. 39 23N 24 10E
74 Yirga Alem 6 34N 38 29E
43 Yíthion 36 46N 22 34E
68 Yitu 36 40N 118 24E
69 Yiyang 28 45N 112 16E
54 Yizre'el 32 34N 35 19E
46 Ylivieska 64 4N 24 28E
101 Yoakum 29 20N 97 10W
65 Yogyakarta 7 49S 110 22E
66 Yokkaichi 35 0N 136 30E
66 Yokohama 35 30N 139 32E
66 Yokosuka 35 20N 139 40E
66 Yonago 35 25N 133 19E
68 Yŏngchŏn 35 55N 138 55E
97 Yonkers 40 57N 73 51W
19 Yonne □ 47 50N 3 40E
19 Yonne, R. 48 23N 2 58E
54 Yoqne'am 32 39N 35 7E
83 York, Australia 31 52S 116 47E
12 York, U.K. 53 38N 1 7W
100 York, Nebr. 40 55N 97 35W
98 York, Pa. 39 57N 76 43W
80 York, C. 75 55N 66 25W
82 York, Sd. 14 30S 125 0E
93 York Factory 57 0N 92 30W
12 York Wolds 54 0N 0 30W
81 Yorke, Pen. 34 40S 137 35E
93 Yorkton 51 11N 102 28W
83 Yornup 34 2S 116 10E
103 Yosemite Nat. Park 31 50N 119 30W
48 Yoshkar Ola 56 49N 47 10E
69 Yŏsu 34 47N 127 45E
54 Yotvata 29 53N 35 2E
15 Youghal 51 58N 7 51W
84 Young 34 19S 148 18E
108 Young 32 44S 57 36W
81 Younghusband, Pen. 34 45S 139 15E
96 Youngstown 43 16N 79 2W
83 Yoweragabbie 28 10S 117 30E